Teaching English in Middle and Secondary Schools

Second Edition

RHODA J. MAXWELL

MARY JORDAN MEISER

Merrill,
an imprint of Prentice Hall
Upper Saddle River, New Jersey   Columbus, Ohio

Library of Congress Cataloging-in-Publication Data

Maxwell, Rhoda J.
    Teaching English in middle and secondary schools / Rhoda J. Maxwell,
Mary Jordan Meiser.—2nd ed.
      p.   cm.
    Includes bibliographical references and index.
    ISBN 0-13-461666-9
    1. English language—Study and teaching (Secondary)—United States.
2. Language arts (Secondary)—United States.   I. Meiser, Mary Jordan. II. Title.
LB1631.M393 1997   96-14799
428′.0071′273—dc20   CIP

Cover art/photo: Karen Guzak
Editor: Bradley J. Potthoff
Production Editor: Christine M. Harrington
Design Coordinator: Jill E. Bonar
Text Designer: STELLARViSIONs
Cover Designer: Brian Deep
Production Manager: Deidra M. Schwartz
Electronic Text Management: Marilyn Wilson Phelps, Matthew Williams, Karen L. Bretz,
    Tracey Ward
Director of Marketing: Kevin Flanagan
Advertising/Marketing Coordinator: Julie Shough

This book was set in Galliard by Prentice Hall and was printed and bound by Quebecor Printing/
Book Press. The cover was printed by Phoenix Color Corp.

© 1997 by Prentice-Hall, Inc.
Simon & Schuster/A Viacom Company
Upper Saddle River, New Jersey 07458

Earlier edition © 1993 by Macmillan Publishing Company.

Printed in the United States of America

10 9 8 7 6 5 4 3

ISBN: 0-13-461666-9

Prentice-Hall International (UK) Limited, *London*
Prentice-Hall of Australia Pty. Limited, *Sydney*
Prentice-Hall of Canada, Inc., *Toronto*
Prentice-Hall Hispanoamericana, S. A., *Mexico*
Prentice-Hall of India Private Limited, *New Delhi*
Prentice-Hall of Japan, Inc., *Tokyo*
Simon & Schuster Asia Pte. Ltd., *Singapore*
Editora Prentice-Hall do Brasil, Ltda., *Rio de Janeiro*

Preface

Teaching is a difficult task; no one instructor or text can offer all of the answers to the complex questions facing teachers as they take over the responsibility of a classroom. Teaching can seem like a balancing act as teachers try to incorporate all the facets of teaching English, as well as planning for students who seem to have little in common with each other or with the teacher's own experiences. This book is not a panacea; rather, we offer a comprehensive view of teaching that takes into account the great variety of backgrounds, abilities, and interests of secondary students, so that novice teachers and their students have viable opportunities for success.

In developing this book we used a holistic, integrated approach to teaching the English language arts, including group activities throughout to provide listening and speaking opportunities in literature, composition, and language. We do not stress one curricular component of English over another, but we do emphasize the relatedness of all the parts: literature and reading; composing and writing; speaking and sharing; listening and responding; acting and creating; constructing language and meaning. Although we separate the strands of English teaching, we do so only to explore each area in some depth. Recognizing the importance of an integrated approach, we make connections among the strands in each chapter. For example, although oral language is a separate chapter, it also appears in chapters on literature, composition, and improving writing skills. Also, because our society continues to debate issues of basic skills, we devote a chapter to grammar and relate it to material in other chapters. We believe that teachers who understand the nature of language learning and the acquisition of skills can successfully integrate grammar throughout the curriculum. This type of integration appears in every chapter.

Research studies form the basis of teaching. We stress the practical application of theoretical ideas, basing our teaching suggestions on research and effective classroom practice. For this reason, we draw upon the experiences of middle and senior high school teachers, as well as college methods teachers nationwide. To achieve a balance between theory and practice, teachers must understand *why* they select certain activities and materials, not only *which ones* they select. Furthermore, we believe that the habit of reflecting on our decisions and the success or failure of their application is critical to professional growth and effective teaching. We thus ask readers to reflect on the nature of the English language arts and themselves as they read this text. We also ask readers to examine their assumptions and beliefs about teaching in light of the diverse learners in secondary classrooms, realizing that their own experiences may differ from those of their students. If teaching means helping students learn, then we cannot teach without first considering the experiences, personalities, and interests of our students. Such connections between teaching and learning guided the writing of this book.

ORGANIZATION OF THE TEXT

In Chapter 1 we provide a foundation for all the English language arts, the professional base of knowledge on which teachers build curriculum and instruction. We explore briefly the nature of the language arts as processes of making meaning and the holistic nature of learning. The real journey of discovery occurs throughout the text as readers find their individual way. Chapter 2 focuses on the students we teach, whom we believe to be the core of curriculum and instruction, not the subject matter. With students firmly in mind, we turn to curriculum and instruction in Chapter 3. We have noticed that not all contemporary methods texts include much information on curriculum, even though novice teachers are expected to understand it, deliver it, and develop it. Although terms like *scope and sequence, tracking,* and *inclusion* may appear "old hat" to experienced teachers, they are questions in the minds of novice teachers. We find, too, that novice teachers need more information on planning for classroom instruction, so we devote Chapter 4 to this important area. Learning to construct lessons and units from a student-centered, process-oriented perspective involves more than good intentions. We provide readers with examples of units and lessons developed by preservice teachers much like themselves. In the final chapter on becoming a teacher we ask readers to reflect on what they have learned, not only about teaching English language arts, but also about themselves.

Because of the pluralistic nature of our society, we devote sections in both the language and literature chapters to help prepare new teachers for the realities of their future classrooms. Another reality facing them is appropriate assessment, and we focus on this subject in a separate chapter and in individual chapters on literature, oral language, and composition. Chapter 12, "The Nature of Language," and Chapter 13, "Varieties of American English," cover language acquisition theory and practical ways of implementing theory into practice. In Chapter 7, "Teaching Literature," and Chapter 8, "Selecting Literature," we include literature by and about minorities and women and provide a wide range of resources for experienced and novice teachers. Also included are nonfiction selections, both contemporary and historical.

The organization of this book is somewhat flexible. The order in which the chapters are taught can vary depending on the structure of the methods course and wishes of the instructor. We suggest that Chapters 1 and 2 remain the introduction and foundation of the course; Chapters 3 and 4, on the other hand, could be used later, although they are designed to provide students with a context for considering each of the language arts. Chapters on oral language, literature, composition, and language could be used in any order desired. The book is designed to adapt to an individual instructor's syllabus.

ACKNOWLEDGMENTS

We could not have written this book without the help of our students: those in secondary schools who unwittingly were a major part of our learning process; our undergraduate students who help us to understand the fears and uncertainties of becoming a teacher; our graduate students who, as experienced teachers, keep us aware of the realities of the classroom. All of these students are *our* teachers, and we are grateful for the opportunities to learn from them.

In particular, we thank our friends who read our drafts with care and patience, offering suggestions, guidance, and encouragement: Laura Apfelbeck, John Fortier, Donna Hitchens, Craig Hitchens, Nik Lightfoot, and Becky Olien. We also wish to thank Mark Heike, Bay Port High School, Green Bay, WI; Marie Leonard, South Middle School, Eau Claire, WI; and Stan Nesbit, North High School, Eau Claire, WI. Without the voices of their students, this text would be far less rich.

Finally, we would like to thank the following reviewers for their helpful comments and suggestions: John H. Bushman, University of Kansas; Brenda H. Cox, University of North Carolina, Greensboro; and Richard J. Zbaracki, Iowa State University.

Contents

CHAPTER 1

The English Language Arts   *1*

Creating a Learning Environment   1
  A Professional Knowledge Base | Addressing the Questions

Characterizing the English Language Arts   3
  Interactive Processes | An Integrated Curriculum |
  Purposeful Communication | Cognitive Processes |
  A Developmental Phenomenon

Language Arts in the 1990s: A Holistic Experiences   5

Assessment in the Whole Language Classroom   9

Discussion Questions   14

References   14

CHAPTER 2

The Students We Teach   *15*

The Joy of Learning   15

Adolescents' Traits   16
  Middle School Students | High School Students

Life in the Classroom   19

Students at Risk   20
  Varying Sources of Alienation

The Forgotten "Ordinary" Students   23

Teaching All Students   24

Learning Styles   24
  Realities of Students' Lives

How Teachers Can Help   27

Discussion Questions   29

References   30

CHAPTER 3
*Understanding Curriculum
and Instruction*   *31*

Centering Curriculum on Learners and Learning   31
Definitions   32
Who Does the Defining?   34
Curricular Controversy   35
  A Curricular Controversy: Back to the Basics
Curriculum: A Joint Endeavor   38
Components of a Curriculum Guide   38
  Curricular Goals | A Theory of Instruction
From Goals to Learner Outcomes   41
  Developing Learner Outcomes | Learner Outcomes and Controversy
The Role of Textbooks   45
  Textbook Selection Criteria | Selecting English Language
  Arts Textbooks | Being a Good Scavenger
Evaluating Software   53
Online Services for the Classroom   54
Two Curriculum Terms: Scope and Sequence   55
A Spiral Curriculum   56
Another Curricular Term: Tracking   61
  The Dangers of Tracking | Why Tracking Persists | The Power
  of Expectations | Why Tracking Is Unnecessary
The "Feel Good" Curriculum   63
The Integrated Curriculum   65
  Speaking, Listening, Reading, and Writing | The Language
  Arts and Other Disciplines | Student Needs and Interests |
  A K–12 Perspective | Needed Dialogue
Discussion Questions   73
References   74

CHAPTER 4
Individual Planning   *75*

Variables Within Our Grasp   76
Playing the Variables Game   77
Some Activities for Chaotic Days   79

Seeing Students as the Heart of the Curriculum   80
    "Unteachables" | Special Needs

"Regular" Kids   82

Planning for Classroom Instruction   83

Classroom Climate   84
    Do It Yourself

Principles of Planning   86
    The Earliest Planning | Instructional Units | Planning for Reality

Suggested Activities   94

Discussion Questions   94

References   95

CHAPTER 5
Oral Language: The Neglected Language Arts

96

Some Basic Principles   96

Teacher Talk, Student Talk   97

Talk and Cultural Differences   98

Listening: Not the Same as Hearing   99
    Major Curricular Goals and Classroom Barriers |
    Listening as Process

Listening and Cooperating in Group Work   101

Effective Group Work   103
    Forming Groups | Training Groups

Speaking: More Than Just Talk   106
    Major Curricular Goals

Improving Discussion Questions   108

Using Students as Teachers   109
    Across Grade Levels | Peer Tutoring | Small-Group Work

Classroom Strategies for Fostering Authentic
    Discussion   110
    Personal Response, Small Group, Large Group |
    The Fishbowl | Creative Controversy

Teach Each Other   112

Reader Response   114

Talking About Literature   115

Oral Language Activities for Adolescents   117

Informal Classroom Drama   124
Evaluating Oral Language Activities   126
References   134

CHAPTER 6
Teaching Composition   137

Background of Teaching Composition   137
Research on Writing   137
Writing Process   139
Stages in the Writing Process   140
  Discovery Stage | Drafting Stage | Revising Stage |
  Editing Stage | Teacher Help | The Writing Process
  in Action | Publishing Student Writing
Writing for a Variety of Purposes   152
Levels of Writing   153
Types of Writing Assignments   155
Journal Writing   157
  Personal Response Journals | Project Journals | Language
  Journals | Writer's Journal | Learning Logs
Writing Short Stories   160
  Round Robin Stories | Developing Characters |
  Story Strips | Personal Narratives
Writing Poetry   163
Writing Reports and Research Papers   169
  The I–Search Paper | Difficulties With Research Papers
Collaborative Writing   173
Composition and the World of Work   174
Additional Writing Assignments   176
  Checkbook Characterizations | Personals | Mystery Packets |
  Classroom Climate
References   183

CHAPTER 7
Teaching Literature   184

Reading Literature   184
Background of Literature Study   184

Reader Response Theory   186

Implementing the Response Theory   187
  Using Factual Information | Writing Responses | Using Responses

Comprehension   192

Formal Analyses   193

Prereading Activities   194

Reading Activities   196
  Small-Group Work | Writing Assignments Given to Students

Teaching Short Stories   200
  Short Story Activities

Teaching Poetry   202

Activities for Teaching Poetry   204

Poetry Resources   206

Whole Language   207

Teaching Language in Literature Study   208
  Metaphor Focus (Andrea Kramer)

Vocabulary Study in Reading   209

Sharing Books   211

References   219

CHAPTER 8
Selecting Literature   *221*

Objectives for Teaching Literature   221

Canonical Literature   223
  Making Choices

Organizing Literature Study   225

Organizing Around a Theme   226

Reading Levels   229

Young Adult Literature   229

World Literature   231
  Thematic Approach | Studying One Culture |
  Resources for World Literature

Literature by Women   234

Minority Literature   235
  Native American Literature | Hispanic Literature | African American
  Literature | Asian American Literature | Readers and Literature

Recommended Books by or About Minorities   239

Putting It All Together   241
  Selections for a Unit on Family Relationships | Selections for
  Coming of Age or Developing a Sense of Self | Selections
  for Heroes or Courage | Selections for a Unit Focusing
  on Women and Women Writers

Media in the English Classroom   244
  Movies | Television | Videos

Censorship   246
  Strategies for Action

References   259

CHAPTER 9
Improving Writing Skills: Usage, Syntax, Mechanics   *261*

A Framework for Improving Writing Skills   261

The Teacher's Role   262
  Modeling | Self-Editing | Self-Help | The Normality of Errors |
  Skills As Purposeful | The Responsible Student

Activities to Improve Usage   266
  Understanding Usage | Manipulations: Language Activities |
  Investigating Basic Language Relationships | Daily
  Oral Language | Working from Student Drafts |
  Mini-Lessons | Keeping Logs or Analysis Charts |
  Error Analysis | Atwell's System | Grammar
  Grams | Publishing | Summing Up

Understanding and Improving Syntax   272
  Revising Sentences: Harder Than It Looks | Improving Sentences |
  Modeling | Manipulating for Meaning | Sentence Combining
  and "Decombining" | Coordinating and Subordinating Sentences |
  Coordinating Sentences | Subordinating Sentences | Major
  Sentence Errors: Run-ons, Comma Splices, and Fragments |
  If They Know Sentences, Why the Errors?

Punctuation   283
  Keeping Punctuation in Perspective | Examining the Marks
  and the Confusion | Working With Punctuation

Capitalization   287

Spelling   288
  Spelling Without Panic and Despair | Spelling and the Average
  Error-Maker | Improving Spelling 290 | Staying Calm
  and Answering Questions

References   291

CHAPTER 10
Understanding Grammar   *293*

What Is Grammar?   294
    Students Can't Put a Sentence Together | Students Don't Know a Noun From a Verb | Students Can't Speak or Write Without Making Mistakes

Studying Grammar for Its Own Sake   296
    Why Grammar Units Persist

What Teachers Need to Know About Grammar   298

Traditional Grammar   298
    Traditional Grammar in the Classroom

Structural Grammar   301
    Structural Grammar in the Classroom

Transformational Grammar   303
    Transformational Grammar in the Classroom

Why the Direct Teaching of Grammar Fails   305
    The Nature of Kids | Improving Student Skills | Making Useful Distinctions

Demystifying Grammar   306

Understanding Student Errors   307
    Novice Writers | Expecting Too Much | Smart Errors

Trial and Error   308

Sources of Errors   309

Error Analysis   310

Taking on Error   311
    Errors: For Editing Only | Errors and the World at Large

Suggested Activities   312

References   313

CHAPTER 11
Evaluating English Language Arts   *315*

Authentic Assessment   315

Planning for Evaluation   316

Purposes of Evaluation   317

Assessment   317

Evaluating Literature   318

Constructing Tests   321

Evaluating Writing   322

Evaluation by Levels   322
     Level 1 | Level 2 | Level 3

Methods of Evaluation   325
     Impression Grading | Holistic Grading | Analytical Scales |
     Some Final Points to Remember | Checkpoint Scales

Self-Evaluation   330

Evaluation of Oral Language   331

Evaluation of Units   332
     Evaluating Oral Activities | Portfolio Evaluation |
     Evaluating Portfolios

Teachers' Experiences   337
     Parents and Evaluation

The Future of Assessment   338

References   340

CHAPTER 12
The Nature of Language   *342*

The Importance of Language Study   342

Language Characteristics   342
     Commonalities Among Languages and Learning | Language Variation

Competence Versus Performance   344

What Native Speakers Can Do   345
     Recognition of Grammatical Sentences | Recognizing Relations
     Within Sentences | Recognizing Relationships Among Sentences |
     Recognizing Ambiguities | Creating Novel Sentences

Acquiring Our Native Language   348

Theories of Language Acquisition   348
     Imitation | Reinforcement | Creativity | What's the Right Theory?

Oral and Written Language Acquisition: Implications
     for Teaching   352

Learning About Language: Activities for Adolescents   353
     Origins and Relationships | Discovering Relationships | Searching
     for Meaning | Word Magic | The Symbolic Nature of Language

Using Young Adult Literature to Teach
     Language Concepts   365
     Noticing Language | A Matter of Style | American Dialects |
     A Window on History | Language as Manipulation

Word and Sentence Games   368
   Chanting and Cheering | Tripping Up the Tongue |
   Puns and Conundrums | Ready to Buy | Mad Libs |
   Found Poems | Telegraphic Messages | Adolescents and
   Language Activities

Suggested Activities   375

References   376

CHAPTER 13
Varieties of American English   *378*

Understanding Linguistic Diversity   378

Diversity in the Schools   379

Writing and Dialects   380

The Supportive Classroom   380

Dialect and Identity   380

Dialects of American English   381
   Black English | Understanding Black English

Native American Languages   383
   Bridging the Difference

Hispanic English   384

Students With Limited English Proficiency   386
   The Importance of Bilingualism

Academic English   388

The School Environment   391
   Whole Language for Bilingual Learners | Building the Oral Base |
   Concepts and Context | Culture and Reinforcement |
   Acquiring Oral Language | Acquiring Written Language

Strategies for Teaching Writing   394

Understanding Students' Errors   395

Recognizing and Working With "Smart Errors"   395

Teacher Strategies   399
   Monitoring Classroom Language | Keeping Language Meaningful |
   Structuring the Supportive Classroom

Teaching Activities for ESL   403

References   404

CHAPTER 14
Developing Thematic Units   *406*

Interactive Teaching   406

Organizing Around a Theme   407

Beginning to Plan   407
Teaching and Learning in Groups | Including Writing Activities

Components of a Unit   409
Planning a Unit | Developing Writing Activities for More Than
One Novel | A Literature Unit With a Variety of Literature

Comprehensive Thematic Units   424
Another Unit on Heroes

Interdisciplinary Units   432

References   441

CHAPTER 15
Becoming a Teacher   *443*

Why Are You Here?   443

As a Teacher, I Want To . . .   444

Schoolhouse Memories   445

No Fairy Godmother Needed   449
Realism | Openness | Positive Expectations | Responsiveness |
Flexibility | Sense of Humor | Evenhandedness | Intellectual
Curiosity | Drawing Conclusions

Realities for the Beginning Teacher   452

Personal Dilemmas   453

Thoughts, Support, and Advice from the Vets   454

References   457

Index   *459*

The English Language Arts

A PHILOSOPHY: SHAPING WHAT WE DO AND WHY WE DO IT

One must learn by doing the thing;
For though you think you know it
You have no certainty, until you try.

Sophocles

CREATING A LEARNING ENVIRONMENT

Although they are uniquely satisfying, teaching and learning are indeed hard work. For the teacher, the creation of the learning environment—the struggle to structure inquiry in ways that capture young learners—is a primary concern. For students, maintaining commitment to the discipline of learning is the struggle. No matter how well we teach, learning does belong to our students. As English language arts teachers, we can structure, facilitate, and nurture learning, but we can neither impose nor control it. Nonetheless, the English language arts classroom can and should be a powerful catalyst to learning, a place where the intellectual joy of learning and mastery is evident even to the most reluctant learner.

How we view and subsequently structure our classroom and our teaching affects the learning and outlook of every student entrusted to us. A teacher who believes that English is a subject to be taught, mastered, and tested will structure learning differently from one who believes English is a process through which students seek to understand themselves and others. For example, a teacher who believes English is a collection of basic skills or a body of knowledge to be transmitted creates a different learning environment from one who believes students acquire basic skills through sustained, authentic experiences in oral and written language. Similarly, a teacher who tells students about literature, rather than asking them to respond to it, demonstrates

1

one view of teaching English. By contrast, a teacher who believes students must connect with literature through their own experiences before they move on to more abstract and universal considerations has quite a different view.

Where do such diverse views of teaching come from? In some cases they come from tradition and teaching as one has been taught; in others, the views come from courses and programs that have integrated new learning in the English language arts and related fields of study. A contemporary view of teaching English draws upon a rich tradition but at the same time reflects current research and effective classroom practice. In the past decade, we have benefited from extensive research conducted in elementary, secondary, and college classrooms; we have learned the value of ethnographic and experimental designs, and we have gained a multidimensional picture of how students learn. Sometimes this research has shown us that our methods and materials were poorly matched with how students learn or how the language arts function as processes. At other times, research validated time-honored approaches and materials. In all cases, we were learning more about the processes of teaching and learning in the English language arts, adding substantially to our knowledge.

A Professional Knowledge Base

The base of knowledge in our field continues to grow, mainly because teachers continue to ask questions about teaching and learning in English language arts:

- What do we know about listening and speaking? About reading and literature, About writing? About language?
- What environment stimulates and nurtures the processes of oral and written language?
- Which strategies help us teach each of these areas more effectively and help students learn more easily? How can we integrate the language arts most efficiently and effectively?
- What do we know about how students learn? What new knowledge about human language and learning processes will affect our teaching methods?
- How do we account for diversity? What role does culture play? What role does gender play? What strategies will help us bridge differences and create a single learning community?
- How does socioeconomic status affect learning? What do we need to know about the effects of poverty on learning? What is our role in breaking a cycle of poverty and hopelessness? How can we be more effective, even in adverse conditions?
- What do we know about students as developing adolescents? How does this knowledge affect our lessons and activities?
- How do we appropriately measure student learning? Should there be a single set of standards for all students? How might students themselves be a more integral part of the assessment process? How can we meet legitimate parental and community demands for accountability? How can we best use assessment to further student learning and improve our teaching?

These are important questions, not only for ourselves as professional teachers in the English language arts but also as part of a learning community that includes other teachers, administrators, and parents/caregivers.

Addressing the Questions

Throughout this text, we address these questions, providing answers to some and speculating about others. Although we have based our text on current research and effective classroom practice, we cannot hope to have all the answers. Consequently, this text should not be viewed as a "cookbook" full of recipes for teaching. We do provide many activities that classroom teachers have developed and found successful; however, they are just that, examples. Teachers grow into knowledge, into highly individual approaches for planning and implementing lessons. Further, teachers are as diverse as their students; what works well for one may be a disaster for another. For this reason, we often hear comments to the effect that there is no one way, no absolutely "right" way, to teach. Although there is a grain of truth in this, there is also danger. Even allowing for a variety of teaching methods, there is *a* right way: being congruent with the ways in which adolescents learn and the ways in which the language arts themselves function. As English language arts teachers, we cannot ignore knowledge of these basic human processes. We will begin, then, with a brief explanation of the language arts from this perspective.

CHARACTERIZING THE ENGLISH LANGUAGE ARTS

Interactive Processes

When we speak of the language arts as interactive processes, we characterize them from two perspectives: the process by which they interact with one another and the process by which we interact with them to construct meaning. Listening, speaking, reading, and writing interact with and influence one another, each contributing to a growing competency in each area. For this reason, our classrooms need to be places where students engage in all the language arts, actively and consistently. Further, students need to understand and value the language arts as a means by which they construct meaning. In this sense, *interactive* means an active process by which we both bring and extract meaning in an oral or written text. Classrooms where students can make sense of themselves and their world undoubtedly have teachers who believe students construct, rather than are given, meaning.

An Integrated Curriculum

Because the language arts influence and strengthen one another, students need lessons where teachers have consciously balanced listening, speaking, reading, and writing activities. In developing units and lessons, teachers may emphasize one area, but students should be actively engaged in all of them. In a literature unit, for example, reading would be a primary activity. In a balanced, integrated curriculum, students would also be involved in varied, purposeful activities in which they write, speak, and listen. Integrating the language arts fosters student development in each area; it also makes learning more interesting. Students soon tire of a curriculum that puts them through four weeks of reading literature, followed by two weeks of writing essays, followed by one week of giving speeches.

Purposeful Communication

Whether we listen, speak, read, or write, we are engaged in communication. We are concerned with expressing ourselves or understanding others; sometimes, we are concerned with understanding only ourselves, an especially valuable aspect of the language arts, self-discovery. But in every communicative act, we have purpose and audience and context. If we want students to "stay the course," we need to keep this principle prominent in our units and lessons. Through it, we acknowledge that motivation comes from purposefulness, from students who have something to say and want to say it. A useful question as we plan lessons might be: Who ever talks to a dead phone?

Cognitive Processes

When we use language, we are engaged in an ongoing cognitive process. Because the language arts have traditionally been viewed as a subject, something to be taught, we have sometimes forgotten that they are first and foremost active processes. Speaking and listening have been more readily perceived in this way than have reading and writing. However, the emphasis on reader response theory and writing processes has reminded us that all the language arts depend on cognitive processes. What does this mean in the classroom? First, that students need structures and opportunities that provide for and stimulate active participation. Second, that students need time and experience to achieve competency or proficiency in each of the language arts. Third, that our lessons must acknowledge that language processes occur holistically. That is, we don't master one skill and then move on to another. When we speak, listen, read, or write, we use various skills all at the same time, reaching competency or proficiency in different skills at different times. As teachers, our choice of methods and materials is altered by the knowledge that sustained experience is critical to student learning. Our tolerance for error is expanded with the knowledge that cognitive overload can and does occur, that the complexity of a task may cause a student to falter badly, and that even our best students will have lapses in performance.

A Developmental Phenomenon

When we listen, speak, read, or write, we are limited by maturation—physically, cognitively, and linguistically. Some tasks are too difficult for us at the time at which they are introduced; some are too easy. Within a classroom, despite similarity of chronological age, students vary in maturation and thus in their ability to complete certain assignments. They may also vary considerably across the language arts, performing well in one area but not another. Similarly, students may vary considerably from task to task even within one area; in writing, for example, they may appear to get "worse" rather than better. From the perspective of development, however, students are demonstrating very normal behavior. This perspective tempers our judgments of competency and proficiency and reminds us that our lessons must address varying levels of development all within one classroom.

LANGUAGE ARTS IN THE 1990s: A HOLISTIC EXPERIENCE

In the last 15 years, we have seen a paradigm shift in our understanding of teaching and learning: from behaviorist to holistic. The differences in these models are striking, and they are most easily seen in graphic form. In her latest text, *Literacy Not Labels,* Kathleen Strickland provides a good overview (see Table 1–1).

Although the term *holistic education* (also referred to as *whole language*) may be new, the philosophy is not, dating back to the seventeenth century, when educator John Amos Comenius believed that education should be rooted in students' real lives—and be pleasurable (Strickland and Strickland 9). John Dewey held similar views. He wrote that the reason we have trouble remembering what we learned in school is that we learn things in isolation. Dewey believed we learn because of a present need or curiosity, and that unless goals are set by students themselves, little learning occurs. In traditional schools, goals were set by the teacher, and Dewey sought to change this situation. He was, then, the forerunner of the student-centered classroom.

The static form of instruction (e.g., assign, study, recite) that was used in schools at that time seemed illogical to Dewey. He believed learning was a dynamic concept, occurring when one wanted to solve a problem. In the lab schools Dewey developed, students designed curriculum together and shared activities. Following the guidelines of the scientific method, students would think of problems or projects, set up plans, and test them out for satisfactory completion of the project.

Previously, learning had been imposed on students, and learning meant memorizing textbooks. Students had only a passive role in school and in the lessons that were to prepare them for some remote future. Dewey, however, wanted a close relationship between actual experience and education. Unfortunately, experience education has been equated with an "anything goes" approach, but this is a misrepresentation of Dewey's model. He wanted students to have more control and responsibility over their own education, a stark contrast to decisions about their learning made solely by administrators and teachers. Curricula had been developed with only one goal: to prepare students for a later life. Dewey, however, believed that a major factor in becoming a mature, responsible adult is accepting responsibility for one's own actions. And this notion had been totally ignored in the schools.

With Dewey, learning through experience became the basis for a new educational system. Although Dewey believed all genuine education came through experience, he did not mean that all experience was equally educational. Each experience had to be

TABLE 1–1
Models of teaching and learning.

Traditional	Element	Contemporary
Behavioral Psychology Bloom's Taxonomy	Research Base	Cognitive and developmental psychology. Linguistics and anthropology.
Teacher dispenses knowledge (e.g., lectures, handouts). Teacher has "the answer."	Teacher Role	The teacher helps students build knowledge through facilitating, demonstrating, and sharing. Students, not the teacher, are the center of teaching and learning.
Students are relatively passive (e.g., expect to be told what to do, look for "right" answers).	Student Role	Students are actively engaged and involved in open-ended response and critical thinking. Teachers encourage risk-taking and exploration.
Curriculum is prescribed, emphasizing a single body of knowledge and facts to be taught and mastered. Little attention is given to variations in student development or ability. Learning is not contextualized. Textbooks are the basis of curriculum.	Curriculum	Emphases are on meaning-making and processes of learning. Teachers act on knowledge that students must connect new concepts with previous learning and that learning must be contextualized.
Skills are viewed and taught in a part-to-whole sequence (e.g., lists, exercises, and drills).	Methodology	In addition to independent work, teachers use a variety of cooperative activities. Pairs, small groups, and large groups are formed for varying purposes and specific instructional goals.
Students work mostly alone. Whole class recitation is common. Groups are often homogeneous.	Instructional Groups	Desk arrangement varies according to group work; tables and learning stations may be used. Students talk, conferencing with teacher and peers. Various types of learning materials, not just textbooks, are available and used.
Desks are arranged in rows. Few or no provisions for conferencing (i.e., small tables, flexible seating) are evident. Textbook series form the majority of instructional materials. Teacher leads discussion or recitation; students respond when called on.	Classroom Climate	Students are part of a community of learning; they are held responsible for their own behavior and often share in the development of classroom rules.
Behaviorist techniques, such as reward and punishment, are common. Emphasis is on teacher control; the quiet class is valued.	Classroom Management	Teachers are "kid watchers," interested in both process and product. Portfolios may be used to provide a view of development over time. Evaluation is not just a series of numbers in a grade book.
Teacher grades products (e.g., tests, essays) designed to show what students don't know, rather than what they are in the process of learning. Students have little or no choice in products to be evaluated and often don't understand evaluation criteria.	Evaluation Methods	Students are involved in setting goals for themselves, developing evaluation criteria, and choosing products for formal evaluation.

Source: Kathleen Strickland, 1995, 18–19.

connected with further experience rather than a haphazard series of hands-on activities. Teachers were an important part of the process because students had to be taught the significance of what they saw, heard, and touched. Guidance from teachers remained an important aspect of the classroom. Dewey's progressive education was not a planless improvisation but a developed philosophy.

Many effective educators since have followed both Comenius' and Dewey's beliefs, but the American school tradition has largely been based on a behaviorist model. In the traditional English language arts classroom, students were given "learning." Teachers fed them the pertinent facts from a canon of prescribed good books and held recitation rather than discussions. Teachers believed good writing arose from knowing analytic grammar and doing countless exercises in labeling parts of speech or searching out usage or mechanics errors. Moreover, most students were handed topics rather than encouraged to discover their own. Further, they were expected to practice with sentences or paragraphs before being allowed to develop a complete essay. Memorization and the regurgitation of information fed to students in lectures or textbooks was the accepted and appropriate method of evaluation. Student interests were not much considered in curriculum planning, and students working together on a task or product was tantamount to cheating. The good classroom was the quiet classroom, students in neat rows, and the teacher firmly in control.

This model persisted until the 1980s, when research into human development and the nature of learning forced educators to reexamine teaching and curriculum, especially in English language arts. From cognitive psychology and psycholinguistics, we learned how the brain processes information and how people learn most effectively. We learned connections between thought and language. From developmental psychology, we learned more about the significant cognitive differences that occur as we mature. And from anthropology and sociology, we learned how community and social factors influence our learning. Teachers entered into research, studying their classrooms with techniques developed by ethnographic researchers, and learning firsthand from what students do and don't do. Composition researchers used case studies and empirical research to learn how we really go about the messy business of composing—often starkly opposite to what textbooks had proclaimed and instructed. The result is an educational philosophy called *holistic* or *whole language*—and an English language arts classroom quite unlike those most of us were used to.

No simple definition exists for this philosophy, and the term itself refers to a philosophy, not a methodology. In other words, there is no program to follow. Instead, the holistic philosophy is a set of beliefs about how students learn most effectively. These beliefs guide our choice of materials, activities, and assessment procedures. They also suggest how classroom climate will evolve and how learning will be nurtured. Mostly, they turn us away from a teacher-centered classroom and toward a student-centered one.

A holistic philosophy includes the following major tenets:

- The student is an active participant within a community of learners.
- The teacher structures and facilitates learning, but does not "hand it out."

- Language is best learned through authentic communication and meaningful contexts, not through exercises about it.
- Language occurs holistically, not in small parts to be put together like Legos or building blocks.
- Oral and written language are integrated, positively influencing one another.
- Students, not subject matter, are the heart of a classroom.
- The teacher recognizes and respects the individual abilities and unique needs of students.
- Classroom environment fosters risk taking, where errors are linked to growth.
- Students learn through constructing meaning from the world around them.
- Students work both cooperatively and independently.

The research, interest, and subsequent emphasis on holistic language arose first in elementary schools, where some of its advocates became strong national voices. Not surprisingly, there was a backlash against the movement when voices became too strident and some teachers believed their time-honored methods were under attack. Thus, it is important to note some of the myths that have grown up around this philosophy:

Myth 1: Students run the class and do what they please.
Student-centered does not translate into student-run. Teachers are responsible for structuring and maintaining a learning environment; they ultimately determine the course of study, the range of materials available to students, and methods of assessment. Student choice in a range of materials and tasks does not translate into "do what they please."

Myth 2: Classrooms have no structure.
As just noted, holistic classrooms do indeed have structure. Students may work independently, in pairs or groups, in conferences with the teacher, or in whole-class discussions. But in all cases, the teacher has structured the work to achieve specific curricular and learner goals.

Myth 3: All work, regardless of quality, is acceptable.
This myth has no doubt arisen out of writing classrooms where some levels of writing are not graded and were never intended to be graded. Quality, in any case, is a relative term. What is acceptable for very capable students is different from what is acceptable for less talented students or for students with disabilities. Because students have the opportunity and the expectation of revision, their work is likely to be acceptable—after a great deal of rethinking and revising.

Myth 4: Students are not evaluated.
Nothing could be further from the truth, but the evaluation is different and more varied than the traditional pencil-and-paper test. For example, teachers watch students, observing their progress. Many also use portfolios to evaluate growth over time and

to involve students in their own learning and evaluation. Students probably do more and different kinds of projects and assignments in a holistic English language arts classroom than in a traditional one, and thus, end up with evaluations that are both fairer and more accurate. Teachers report student progress in traditional ways, according to the district's requirements.

Myth 5: This is an easy way to teach.
The teacher's work in structuring and maintaining the classroom is not easy. There are no handy kits or packaged units; there are no ready-made tests to administer and grade. Teachers must read extensively, find appropriate materials for units and lessons, translate materials into oral and written language activities for class use, and create opportunities for individual or shared projects and assignments. In a student-centered class, teachers understand diversity and unique talents, academic levels and needs. And they must devise appropriate assessment measures reflecting that diversity. Consequently, they must be aware of each student's skill level, searching for patterns and determining what must be taught next.

ASSESSMENT IN THE WHOLE LANGUAGE CLASSROOM

In the 1990s, standards of performance and assessment have been a national as well as a state and local debate. Parents and the community at large have a legitimate right to know that students are achieving the educational goals set by the state and local districts. As teachers, we have an obligation to ensure that students are achieving, to the best of their ability, the outcomes we have set for them. Consequently, we must have the means to evaluate our students' progress. There is no debate about the need for assessment, only about the methods. Those methods very much reflect a philosophy of teaching and learning; thus, we can expect to see a contrast between traditional and contemporary assessments, especially in holistic classrooms.

In their text devoted to portfolios as a major assessment tool, Carol Porter and Janell Cleland explore the contrast between the two types of assessment:

Porter and Cleland analyzed the match between what they said they believed about learning and what they valued when assessing their students. This is a critical factor. If, for example, you believe that process is as important as product, then you must evaluate process, not just product. In composition that would mean looking at students' strategies for generating, revising, and editing text—not just a final draft. And a final draft would be the product of multiple drafts, all of which are viewed as important steps in developing that final product. Student reflection and judgment about their drafts become an essential component of assessment: How did I get started? How did I keep myself going? What did I do when I got bogged down or frustrated? What is the hardest part for me? What have I learned to do better in this piece? What do I still have to work on? In a more traditional classroom, students wouldn't be asking these questions—questions that provide them with self-knowledge and strategies for the next writing task. If a teacher believes in a holistic approach,

TABLE 1–2

Models of assessment.

Traditional	Nontraditional
Teacher and students focus on skill performance.	Teacher and students focus on processes of learning.
Students acquire objective knowledge that the teacher uses as a basis for testing.	Students thoughtfully judge their own work; sharing in the setting of goals and subsequent evaluation of how well they met them.
Achievement matters most; the grade tells the story.	Development matters most. Learning is not a matter of grades nor do grades necessarily reflect authentic learning.
Learning is the teacher's responsibility.	Learning is the responsibility of both student and teacher.
Teacher uses assessment to determine grades.	Students and teacher use assessment to guide learning.

however, students will be answering questions about the process of developing a text, and thus, sharing in their own assessment.

We will discuss assessment in detail in Chapter 11 and in the chapters that focus on each of the language arts. We mention assessment here only to acknowledge the connection between what we believe as teachers—our philosophy of teaching and learning—and how we assess student learning.

CASE 1–1

Exploring an Instructional Unit

In this chapter, we've asked you to explore the English language arts themselves: What are they? How do they translate into a philosophy of teaching and learning? We then asked you to consider a holistic philosophy of teaching and learning in which teachers place students at the center of learning. And now, we would like you to explore your own understanding of these ideas through a unit on friendship developed for 10th graders by Amy Gilbride.

So that you might determine what Amy believes about teaching and learning, we have removed Amy's narrative "voice" and her many reflections about materials, methods, and students. The "proof is in the pudding" as the old saying goes, so from her decisions and choices alone, Amy's philosophy of teaching and learning should be fairly clear.

In her introduction, Amy tells us: "I believe that all people, especially high school students, are influenced by and concerned about their friendships. Friendship is a strong force in our lives; often we are sad when we don't have friends or become frustrated because of the friends we do have." With Amy's rationale for this unit to guide you, explore her philosophy of teaching and learning: What does Amy believe and how do you know?

FRIENDSHIP
GRADE LEVEL: HIGH SCHOOL/GRADE 10
WEEK ONE
Day 1

Introduction of Unit

Activity: Large-group discussion of friendship.

Teacher Activity: Present unit project and evaluation criteria. Students will each "tell" about their best friend in whatever mode of presentation they wish: writing (essay, poem, song); art (collage, drawing); or music. With teacher approval, "anything goes." The project is worth 50 points, with the following evaluation criteria:

• Project proposal submitted on due date (5 points)
• Reflective essay describing project (thought processes, creative inspiration, etc.) evaluated on organization, depth of thought, and completeness (20 points)
• Project creativity and engagement with theme; neatness (25 points)

Project proposal due on Day 5 in Week One. Presentations due on Days 4 and 5 in Week Two.

Student Activity: 10-minute journal write. List the characteristics of your best friend. Why is this person your best friend? [Note: journal writes are expressive writing, neither evaluated nor turned in.]

Student Activity: Make a friendship bracelet for your best friend (Teacher provides craft material, but choice of colors and design belong to students).

Day 2

Student Activity: If needed, time to complete friendship bracelet.

Activity: Large-group discussion/response to journal write about best friends.

Student Activity: Small-group discussion and presentation of friendship bracelet (explain choice of colors, specific design, etc.).

Teacher Activity: Read poem "Around the Corner" by Charles Hanson Towne (theme of taking friends for granted). Ask students to reflect on theme.

Student Activity: Pairs share experiences of taking friends for granted or being taken for granted themselves.

Day 3

Teacher Activity: Read short story "Celia Behind Me" by Isabel Huggan (themes of dynamics of peer pressure and "in" versus "out" groups).

Activity: Large-group discussion on themes.

Teacher Activity: Mini-lesson on language, expressiveness.

Student Activity: Volunteer to read poem "Agnes Snaggletooth" by X. J. Kennedy (themes of popularity and alienation). In pairs, discuss feelings expressed by poem's narrator. Assignment: Write poem to or about an "Agnes Snaggletooth" in their lives.

Day 4

Activity: Listen to "You've Got a Friend" by James Taylor (theme of strong friendship and support offered by friends).

Student Activity: Small-group sharing of "Agnes Snaggletooth" poems. Large-group sharing of poems by volunteers.

Activity: Read Associated Press article about students who shaved their heads to support classmate going through leukemia treatment (theme linked to Taylor's song).

Student Activity: Journal write: How far would you go for a friend? How far is too far to go even for friendship? Have you ever done anything to help out a friend? How did this make you feel? How did it make your friend feel?

Reminder: Project proposal due tomorrow. Presentations of project due on Days 4 and 5 of Week Two.

Day 5

Activity: Large-group discussion of journal write. A student volunteer reads poem "Two Friends" by Nikki Giovanni. Another student volunteers for second reading. Teacher provides drawing supplies and asks students to visualize characters in the poem and to draw them. Discuss poem and drawings (hung in room).

WEEK TWO

Day 1

Teacher Activity: Return project proposals. Read article/interview "Mr. Misenheimer's Garden" by Charles Kuralt (aged man whose garden lives on after his death; theme of unlikely friendships).

Activity: Large-group discussion of poem.

Student Activity: Write down "take home" journal prompts: What constitutes "friend" to you? (for example, how long do you have to know a person? What are the characteristics of someone you could never be friends with? Why? Can friendships change? Are there different kinds of friendships?)

Day 2

Activity: Brief large-group discussion of ideas in Kuralt's article.

Student Activity: Pairs share journal responses.

Activity: In a large group, a volunteer reads "The Chinese Checker Players" by Richard Brautigan (theme of age in friendships). Discuss theme.

Teacher Reminder: Presentations coming up.

Day 3

Activity: Listen to song "Circle of Friends" by Edie Brickell. Large- group discussion of song's theme (separation of one friend from group).

Student Activity: Journal write on own "circle" of friends. Prompt students to think about who is in their group and why.

Day 4

Student Activity: Presentation of projects. Students are expected to explain why they chose their format (poem, song, drawing, etc.) and to "tell" about their friend through the project.

Day 5

Student Activity: Presentation of projects.

Activity: Large-group discussion on student insights gained through unit and on their enjoyment (or not) of unit.

QUESTIONS ABOUT AMY'S UNIT

1. Before you respond to the following questions, jot down your answers to the two questions you were asked before you read Amy's unit: What is Amy's philosophy of teaching and learning? How do you know?
2. Use the following questions to help you refine or revise your statement of Amy's philosophy.
   a. Does Amy believe in a student-centered classroom? How do you know? In the unit presented here, what is Amy's role as teacher? Does it mesh with her concept of what students can and should be doing? Provide specific examples to support your response.
   b. Would Amy's unit allow and encourage students with diverse abilities and talents to participate? How well do you think students with limited English proficiency would do in this unit? How do you know? How well do you think students from varying cultural, economic, and social backgrounds would do in this unit? How do you know?
   c. Does Amy believe in a classroom where the language arts (listening, speaking, reading, and writing) are integrated in activities and tasks? What difference does integration make in terms of student learning?
   d. Does Amy view students as "receivers" or "constructors" of knowledge? How do you know? How does this view relate to her philosophy?
   e. What is the relationship between process and product in Amy's unit? Are they both valued?

f. What skills do you think Amy wants her students to develop through this unit? Are these skills contextualized, that is, taught or developed through meaningful activities and tasks?

g. How does Amy's assessment plan mesh with her philosophy?

DISCUSSION QUESTIONS

1. Just like you, Amy is "in process," a preservice teacher still working out her ideas. She has many good ideas, but she is open to discussion and welcomes feedback from peers. With a partner or small group, discuss additional activities, materials, or tasks that might be added to Amy's unit. Also consider the age group and determine if every activity is appropriate for 15-year-olds. What changes might you make? Articulate the underlying philosophy of teaching and learning that guides your choices.

2. James Moffett and Betty Jane Wagner, two prominent English educators, note:

    Too often, teachers do not know why they are doing what they do, and an alarming number admit that they don't believe in what they are doing. (3)

    This is a serious charge, and one that Moffett and Wagner would never make without substantial data. Discuss the implications of what they say.

    a. Why would teachers admit they don't believe in what they are doing?

    b. What does this situation suggest about the role of research and continuing education for teachers of the English language arts?

    c. Do you believe that the shift to a more student-centered model would make any difference in the teachers' attitudes?

3. Make a two-column list of what you *do* and *do not* believe about teaching and learning.

REFERENCES

Gilbride, Amy. "Friendship." English 406/606. Spring 1995. Eau Claire: University of Wisconsin.

Moffett, James, and Wagner, Betty Jane. *Student-Centered Language Arts K–13: A Handbook for Teachers.* Boston: Houghton Mifflin, 1976.

Porter, Carol, and Cleland, Janell. *The Portfolio as a Learning Strategy.* Portsmouth: Heinemann, 1995.

Strickland, Kathleen. *Literacy, Not Labels.* Portsmouth: Boynton/Cook, 1995.

Strickland, Kathleen, and Strickland, James. *Uncovering the Curriculum.* Portsmouth: Boynton/Cook, 1993.

2

The Students We Teach

Perhaps most important, interdisciplinary, inquiry-centered learning often includes something which has been ignored in a great many recent reform reports: the joy of learning. By "joy" I do not mean the "fun of easy gratification and quick laughs," but the genuine joy of mastery, the pleasure of gaining control. The same intellectual joy can be found in the mastery of language and learning.

Stephen Judy [Tchudi] (30)

The Joy of Learning

Stephen Judy [Tchudi]'s observation that most recent educational reform reports ignore the "joy of learning" reflects a national loss. In the 1990s, U.S. citizens appear to be less resilient, less optimistic, and less intellectually curious. It is no surprise then, that students in U.S. schools fail to grasp what Judy [Tchudi], a prominent English educator, believes is the heart of teaching—the intellectual joy of learning. Given the complexity of educating young people, the multiple roles and expectations placed on schools and teachers, and the difficult lives of many students, it is understandable that joy in learning is infrequent in many schools. Sara Lawrence Lightfoot, professor of education at Harvard University, believes that "When you're worried about discipline, or preoccupied with completing a prescribed curriculum in a particular amount of time, you lose the sense of joy and possibility—the sense of play" (157). Like Judy [Tchudi], Lightfoot is concerned about the nature of learning and of teaching.

Many new teachers go into the classroom with unrealistic expectations. They go into teaching because they love the subject and like young people, but that is often not enough to create in their students the sense of joy they are looking for. The student described in Box 2–1 has come up against some harsh realities.

Box 2–1

REALITIES OF A CLASSROOM

The second week of August, Chris was excited to receive a job offer to teach 10th-grade English at a suburban school of approximately 1,500 students. Although he realized he would not have much time to prepare for his new teaching assignment, he felt fairly confident because his student teaching had been a positive experience. He had worked with a supportive teacher in a small high school of 400 students teaching juniors and seniors American and British literature. For the first weeks of school, Chris prepared lessons using literature selections that he had particularly liked from his college literature class and ones he taught during student teaching. He spent hours designing discussion questions and related information he thought would interest students, but Chris became increasingly frustrated and discouraged because most of his students did not seem interested, would not pay attention, and did not become involved in the discussion. He thought about the pleasure he had experienced when he was a high school student and studied similar literature, and asked himself, "What was wrong with these students? Why weren't they interested?"

Chris has realized that his classrooms are not full of the kind of students he and most of his college friends were in their high school years. For Chris, the joy of teaching and learning does not seem to be present his classes. Rather than blame students for his frustration, however, Chris needs to look at the reality of his students' lives and remind himself of the nature of adolescents and their worlds.

ADOLESCENTS' TRAITS

Students of middle school age are different developmentally and socially from high school students. The language arts involve basic processes that are similar across age levels. For example, a 12-year-old and an 18-year-old both use the writing process in writing. However, maturation differences are critical in performance and product. An eighth grader and a junior may complete the same writing assignment, but the results will be different. We cannot expect the same level of knowledge, skill, or performance from a middle school student that we might from one in high school. Nor could we expect the same attention and concentration levels. Young adolescents are quite different from their high school counterparts; therefore, creating activities for this age group is not just a matter of making lessons less sophisticated.

Middle School Students

Early adolescence is generally considered to occur between the ages of 10 and 14. Because this period is a time of profound developmental changes, students at this age require a different educational experience that acknowledges the significant physical, cognitive, and social changes they are undergoing as they mature. These changes, of course, continue into senior high school, and maturation varies with individual students.

To help students cope with these changes, educators developed the middle school concept, the recognition that young adolescents require an environment that matches their attributes more closely than junior high schools do. Junior high schools are patterned after high schools, with separate classes throughout the day and little or no integration of classes or teaching staff. Although middle schools do vary, they are all based on the philosophy that students at early adolescence need a wealth of experiences so they can develop in a wide variety of ways. Integrated activities, small-group work, and a hands-on approach to learning are all ways of accommodating their diverse needs and acknowledging that they are not quite as grown up or independent as high schoolers.

The National Association of Secondary School Principals (NASSP) published a statement in 1983 describing students "in the middle," noting that, "We know that at no other period in the life cycle does such variance exist in the rate of individual development" (n.p.). These differences are apparent in students' intellectual, emotional, social and physical development. According to NASSP, these changes may lead middle schoolers to be

- Impulsive in actions and impatient with restrictions
- Preoccupied with popularity and self-conscious about appearance
- Deeply influenced by mass media and responsive to advertising
- Plagued by mood swings and subject to forgetfulness and boredom
- Assertive in independence and moved by competitive situations
- Charged with energy, confused by self-doubt, and fearful of failure
- Embarrassed by social situations and veneered with "wisecracks"

Considering these characteristics, middle schools organize their curriculum and activities to emphasize emotional and social needs and to develop a positive self-esteem during these critical years. Instead of individual classes with little or no interaction with other students, middle school students need group work to help them develop social skills, choices of activities to help them explore their many interests, and units of study that help them take responsibility for their own learning.

We asked our English education students to reflect on their memories of middle school. Their journal entries enforce educators' perceptions of what life is like for these young people.

> At ages 12 and 13, fitting in with my peers was most important to me. I started to wear makeup and I remember spending hours on my hair and never being satisfied with it. I started to go shopping a lot, any opportunity I had, in order to use my saved money to buy *cool* clothes. What I remember most about this age was being very self-conscious and always worried about my appearance and what others thought of me. (Brenda Meyer)

> I was unpopular because I was smart and a book worm. I made a pact with myself that I would work to become popular. My favorite movie was *Grease* and I wanted to turn out like Olivia Newton-John (heaven forbid). I worked hard at not paying atten-

tion in class and not reading anymore and acting stupid so that everyone would think I was not smart anymore. I became the class clown. (Mary Beth Koehler)

Mary Mercer Krogness, an eighth-grade teacher, observes that

body and soul, from eighth-grade boys and girls, young adults are emerging. These mysterious young people vacillate between behaving like toddlers who are going through the terrible twos and acting like young adults who scrutinize their parents' and teachers' behaviors and debate what's equitable and inequitable with these authority figures. (47)

Not surprisingly, early adolescents may feel misunderstood and misjudged by their parents and teachers. Further, many believe adults do not listen to them or consider their ideas seriously. These young people may face an unfair bias. Store clerks, for example, often ask them to leave, people frown at them, and many adults expect that they will be noisy and rude. Even though they appear to be "little kids," they are not. They know things, have experiences to draw on, and deserve credit for having worthwhile ideas. It is critical that teachers not trivialize their words and try to understand that adolescent emotions run high and are even volatile.

Working with young adolescents can be difficult for teachers, but also extremely rewarding. Middle school students may challenge authority, but they rely on their teachers for guidance and support. Despite individual differences, they have in common an overwhelming sense of fairness. They expect people to be fair with them and react strongly when they believe they have been treated unfairly. To work well with these students, teachers need to explain their reasons for and expectations of behavior and social interactions. They must be willing to listen to students and to provide a supportive environment and opportunities for choice within structure.

Linda Rief, a middle school teacher, loves to work with young teenagers, but warns that teaching at this level requires patience and humor (90). She adds that it is important to support teenagers in their search for self-discovery and self-making: "We must laugh with them, respect them, and help them find out what's good about their lives" (91).

High School Students

Socially, students in late adolescence have the same need for peer interaction as do younger middle schoolers. Although high schoolers may be able to sit still longer, they still require a classroom in which they interact with classmates. They want, desperately, to belong to a group and sort themselves out based on mutual characteristics. To develop a sense of belonging as a protection against the world, students label themselves (as jocks, druggies, preppies, brains, or shop rats, for example).

Physical growth in this age group is uneven and fairly rapid; teenagers develop a growing self-consciousness about their bodies, which may take different forms—from flaunting to camouflaging. Psychological changes continue, but not all students go through crises, nor do all feel alienated or rebellious. For some, growing up is very difficult, for others less traumatic. Some of our English education students recall how they felt in high school:

At 15 and 16, music became the center of my life. I still thought about sex, too. I began getting serious about the piano and I began to play the guitar. My close friends and I spent Friday and Saturday evenings listening to or playing music; we had no social life, nor did we desire one. (Jason Hedrington)

When I was 15 and 16, all I could think about was driving a car and going to school dances with the "right" boy. Athletics was very important to me and so was school. Friends and peer pressure were my only worry. As a 17-year-old, I was very concerned about my boyfriend and how moving to college would affect our relationship. I was scared to death of losing him. I was so in love. (Aimee Peterson)

As I went through high school, I always struggled with the acceptance thing. I never stopped yearning for friends and significant relationships. By the time I graduated, I had begun to find some. (Brian Quade)

Our understanding of the intellectual changes that adolescents undergo has been dominated by a Piagetian view of developmental stages: adolescents moving from concrete observable experience to abstract, speculative thought. However, this view is theoretical and not necessarily a reality. Some students, even as juniors and seniors in high school, struggle with abstract thinking. In late adolescence, students are more able to entertain diverse points of view, a widening from the self-centered stance of childhood and early adolescence. Cognitive awareness is heightened during the high school years. Nonetheless, some students will experience more reading comprehension problems, and the amount that they read decreases as they investigate more diverse worlds—worlds that usually include working outside of school.

Society expects high school students to act like adults, forgetting that these young people have not had time to reach full maturity. They must, however, make critical decisions that will affect them for the rest of their lives. To make these decisions wisely and bridge the difficult transition to adulthood, they need teachers who listen and respond to them in sensitive and caring ways.

BOX 2–2

ADAPTING LESSON PLANS FOR DIFFERENT LEVELS

Suppose that you are preparing to teach a unit on advertising. How would you plan an activity for middle school students? For high school students? What specifically would be different in the way you would introduce and teach a unit for each level? The level of difficulty of the material would be different, of course, but what else?

LIFE IN THE CLASSROOM

No matter how orderly the school or good the "control," tension exists between students and teachers—just as it exists in any situation where interaction is an hourly activity. The students are in same-age groups, reinforcing both the best and worst of young adolescents. Teachers work with over 100 students each day, and all teachers, no matter how experienced and talented, will experience bad days and encounter students who confound, puzzle, and trouble them.

Some students consistently please us and others, just as consistently challenge and frustrate us. No matter how good our efforts, we will lose some along the way, some dramatically and tragically to death or prison; others will simply fade into oblivion as soon as the law permits them to leave school. Apathy and alienation are real and take varying forms.

Some students do absolutely nothing and bother no one. They do not open books or bring writing materials to class. No amount of teacher effort can encourage them to participate. Other students can be physically threatening and verbally abusive, despite the fact that a teacher has done nothing to provoke such a response. You will experience these students in both inner city schools and in rural or suburban areas. Why? Because in many schools and classrooms, students have not been part of the teaching and learning process: teachers have centered instruction around themselves rather than around their students. Further, until recently, school curricula have focused on college-bound students. The tightly controlled classroom and curriculum appear to some students to be artificial, irrelevant, and exceedingly boring. Sitting in rows while one or two students recite what the teacher already knows or filling in worksheets or end-of-chapter questions sends at-risk students into their own world, into the role of the outsider.

Box 2–3

DEVELOPING MOTIVATION AND INTEREST

What activities could you use to determine students' interest in a unit of study you are planning? No matter how carefully you choose the material and plan the activities, you must generate student interest and enthusiasm. Choose a unit theme, such as adventure, conflict, or heroes, and develop activities for an entire unit. These activities should relate to the theme but do not have to be tied to any particular literature selections.

STUDENTS AT RISK

Although all adolescents can feel like outsiders at times, most grow out of it. Those who do not are labeled "at risk" by the school system. Lloyd Tindall, in a study of at-risk students, identified the following factors that contribute to at-risk students:

- Family trauma, such as divorce and abuse
- Low parental expectations and apathy
- Alcohol and drug abuse
- Poverty
- Minority status
- Lack of basic academic skills (6)

Student characteristics that may contribute to increased risk range from a desire to be left alone to being combative if they believe they are being controlled by teachers or administrators. At-risk students typically do not often participate in whole-class activities and do little, if any, homework. They will not have books or class-related materials with them when they do show up, and their attendance rate is poor. Many at-risk students are underachievers and are relegated to remedial or learning disabled classes because of it, even though they have ability.

Tracking such students into homogeneous classes creates assumptions about their learning abilities. Lower-track students are often taught through the use of skill sheets, creating a boring and superficial curriculum. Pamela Adams, a high school teacher, describes two problems with this type of instruction. One is the assumption that if students can't read well they can't think well either. The other problem is that these students do not have the opportunity to practice critical thinking or learn the type of knowledge valued in our society (424). Rather than dummy-down the curriculum, Adams suggests changing teaching methods to increase student interest and engagement. For instance, she makes a convincing case that *Romeo and Juliet* is an appropriate literature selection for classes with lower-ability students if it is taught with students' interests and knowledge in mind. These students have relevant experiences that help them to relate to what happens to Romeo and Juliet. Teachers need to allow students to share their experiences and to listen to others, thus increasing their knowledge.

Varying Sources of Alienation

"Typical" at-risk students are not the only students who experience alienation in our schools. Racial and ethnic background, gender, and disabilities also contribute to some students' sense of alienation. Being a minority student, even if one has been born and raised in the United States, can cause some students to feel alienated. Immigrant students may face even more prejudice, especially if economic times are hard and communities believe that immigrants are taking away jobs. Because different cultures have specific ways of "knowing and doing," schools serve best those who have been practicing those ways since childhood. Because they may be outside of the mainstream culture, minority students sometimes find little in the curriculum that is familiar and consequently give up.

Only recently has gender been recognized as a source of alienation in the schools. Harvard psychologist Carol Gilligan and her associates found in long-term studies of gender differences in school settings that female students often lose confidence as they move through middle school, becoming less sure of their intellectual abilities. As a result, they may participate less and not challenge male students or teachers. Teachers, too, have recognized that they may unwittingly favor male students by calling on them more often and allowing them to take center stage. Teachers tend to help females more than males by supplying answers and hints. Female teachers are also more likely to tell males to figure something out on their own. The result can be that males learn to find answers independently, whereas females look to authority figures for answers. These are not deliberate actions, but they nonetheless create gender inequity. Mary Jett-Simpson and Susan Masland, university educators, remind us that "with gender inequity a prevalent part of our society, teachers have a special role to play in being able to help their students identify where it exists in the classroom and school environment" (107). Too, they need to closely examine their own behavior so they do not unwittingly continue the status quo.

Students with learning disabilities, such as dyslexia or other perceptual or neurological problems, may have a hard time with reading and writing, the heart of language arts classrooms. These students may have serious problems, but they *are* capable of learning and can often participate fully in a "regular" classroom. As James and Kathleen Strickland point out, labeling such students allows schools to provide a less stimulating, less challenging curriculum, and worse, to expect a lot less of them. Further, once a label is attached, it sticks, and all other reasons for educational failure may be ignored. For this reason, it is vital that, for every activity and unit, teachers provide materials with varying levels of difficulty so that everyone in the classroom can find appropriate material.

Other students may be alienated because they have sought their identity through gangs, drugs, or sex. Teens with babies have become a national problem, one that some schools try to address through better sex education, counseling, and day care so that young mothers can complete high school.

Gifted adolescents may also suffer alienation, appearing bizarre or challenging to teachers and simply "weird" to classmates. Their interests and talents may leave them bored with classroom materials and routines. Often teachers long for a class of gifted students. The reality of such classes, however, is often surprising. Some gifted students are "gifted" because they have been teacher pleasers, not because they have exceptional academic talent. Others may have an inflated sense of their own worth and, thus, are critical of teachers and peers. Students may also expect high grades and rewards for everything they do. And many students are under intense pressure from family and themselves to perform. For these students, performance can be nothing less than excellent, leading some educators to refer to a "cult of excellence" surrounding gifted students. Robert Johnson, a Colorado high school teacher, notes that gifted students "have been taught by teachers and culture that by creating anything less than perfection at the first attempt, they have shown themselves to be ordinary—the worst adjective of all" (37). He also observes that his students believe "excellence has come to mean never trying anything scary in case [their] grades should suffer" (38). Their GPA is the magic number on which they and others pin further education, scholarships, and entrance to prestigious post-secondary institutions. Accordingly, competition with peers may be far stronger than cooperation.

Gifted students need to be challenged but not isolated from classroom activities. To do so is to focus solely on content or academic matters and ignore the social aspects of learning. In the past, gifted students were too often pulled out of the classroom to engage in activities unrelated to what their classmates were doing, or teachers would sent gifted students to the library not knowing how else to keep them busy. Probably even more than other students, gifted students need to learn how to get along with and respect others. Teachers can help build these skills by giving material and activities that are related to the regular students' classroom work to gifted students when they finish their class assignments.

THE FORGOTTEN "ORDINARY" STUDENTS

Because schools have so many levels of tracked and labeled kids, it is easy to ignore the vast middle, the "average" kids. For the most part, they do not cause any trouble; they do their homework, participate in class, and get along with teachers and peers. Therefore, it is even more important that we remember they need individual attention, praise, and reinforcement. Within that "average" group are students at both ends of the academic spectrum—some talented, some struggling. And ordinary kids can get into extraordinary trouble. A case in point: At a small suburban Midwest high school, students labeled as "basically good kids" vandalized their high school with eggs, paint, oil, and lawn-killing chemicals. They also flung a deer carcass onto a teacher's car. The superintendent had this to say: "It's unfortunate that this happened because many of these kids have not been discipline problems. That's what makes this more difficult. Some of these kids have been fairly good students" (*Leader Telegram* 10A). At least 15 students were suspended and banished from graduation, and several were issued tickets for property damage and disorderly conduct.

Mary Mercer Krogness reminds us:

> Good students get attention for being good. Not-so-good students get attention for their misdeeds. And the rest of the students, the large group in the middle and lower middle, may get little attention at all. These are the young people who neither wow their teachers with brilliance nor inundate them with problems; they just come in every day and settle down to work. In the average classroom, these quiet students— especially those who have learning problems and don't meet school requirements, such as achieving certain levels of proficiency on standardized tests or passing proficiency tests—can easily get lost. Because they usually don't make noise, they don't get acknowledgment or support, and without these they can lose momentum and interest. Next thing you know, they have quietly fallen through the cracks. (281)

But among the "average" are also the apathetic and mediocre, the unspecial and unmotivated.

In 1992, *The English Journal* devoted its symposium section to "Being Unspecial." In the introduction to this section, editor Ben Nelms states:

> I have always wondered when parents of so-called average students would realize how their children were being neglected and initiate lawsuits for equity. (44)

Nelms' remark was prompted by Sharon Thomas's symposium article in which Thomas concludes that "the number of needlessly mediocre students could be considerably lessened if average students were given the same attention we have provided special education" (46). Thomas, a high school English teacher in Washington state, makes a strong case for eliminating the educational waste that occurs when reluctant or unmotivated learners are left alone, pointing out that the kids themselves don't mind:

> In fact, they like it that way because it means they don't have to work very hard. These students have learned that no real consequences spring from lack of effort in high school. (45)

These students, says Thomas, "prompt leaders in business and industry to complain about education in the United States" as they continue their "slipshod ways in the work world" (45). Most secondary teachers would agree that kids understand early on that if they don't want to go to college, they'll not be held accountable for demanding academic performance and, thus, the self-fulfilling prophecy.

TEACHING ALL STUDENTS

Teachers are responsible for teaching, to the best of their ability, every student in their classroom. Through inclusion, more students with special needs (such as emotional disturbances, mental and physical disabilities, and limited language proficiency) are in a regular classroom, at least for part of a class period. Resource teachers may be present in the class and meet with regular classroom teachers outside of class to help them work with special needs students. Inclusion has many benefits for all students because they learn to work and socialize with others of varying capabilities. Such knowledge helps to dispel fears about differences among us, a major source of prejudice. Another difference among us, and one we teachers need to recognize, is learning styles.

LEARNING STYLES

Whether we are ordinary, gifted, or disabled, we all have a learning style that is a "biologically and developmentally imposed set of personal characteristics that make the same teaching method effective for some and ineffective for others" (Dunn, Beaudry, and Klavas 50). Learning styles affect how we respond to an environment, how we remember information, and how we learn. A wealth of research has accumulated on various learning styles, methods for determining individual styles, and the effects of optimal styles for individuals (51). Research studies show that in environments where instruction is compatible with one's learning style, students learn more and retain that learning longer (51–52). Characteristics of learning style include a response to noise levels, illumination, temperature, and seating arrangement. Some people learn better in the morning, others at night. Some learn best by listening, others by reading, note-taking, seeing, manipulating, or some combination (50). Students who cannot sit still, for example, might be responding to a strong learning style that requires movement or interaction. Because of the large number of students in their class, it is not feasible for teachers to identify each one's learning style. It is important, though, to be aware that every class has a mixture of styles that may or may not be the same as the teacher's. Teachers tend to use the style that works best for them. When possible, teachers should identify their own style by taking a reliable identification instrument. They can then deliberately use other methods when presenting material and creating learning environments. It is vital that teachers vary their methods and presentations to accommodate more students more of the time.

Box 2–4

PLANNING FOR LEARNING STYLES

How could you arrange a classroom to accommodate a variety of learning styles? How would this arrangement allow you to reach a broader spectrum of students? Plan activities to introduce a novel, for example, *To Kill a Mockingbird,* so that you address several learning styles.

Realities of Students' Lives

Most educators are painfully aware of the conditions that many of our students experience. Gene Tucker explains that while we can't change the harsh realities, we can create viable environments in schools.

> Violence of all kinds is a fact of life in many homes and neighborhoods. An increasing percentage of our youth live in unstable homes, most with single mothers earning marginal incomes or on welfare. Transience rates are exceptionally high with some schools experiencing turnover approaching 100% in any given year. Large numbers of children come to school with limited primary language development and very poor social skills. In many instances, alienation and despair about the prospects for a better future generate attitudes that denigrate traditional values. (1)

Tucker explains that rather than being overwhelmed by the enormity of the problem, teachers can make a difference in children's lives. "Teachers who have effectively adapted to today's students while maintaining high standards and expectations for all" create classrooms "where pupils are actively engaged with challenging content and positive learning outcomes are evident" (2).

Our classrooms must reflect an awareness of the nature of our students' lives and the content we teach. Teachers and students must interact if they are to create the most effective learning and teaching conditions. How teachers structure their classroom is critically important and dependent on many factors—from resources to personalities, personal knowledge to school policy. Although many factors influence teachers' decisions about how and what to teach, one of the major ones must be the nature of the students. Age, gender, race, ethnicity, socioeconomic status, and language proficiency all contribute to individual differences. Students' lives and experiences greatly influence their ability to learn in both positive and negative ways.

We cannot ignore the conditions of students' lives. We must be aware of deaths, separations, or serious illness in students' families. We must not ignore the student whose girlfriend just dropped him, the student who failed an important exam, the student who works nights or who gets up at 4:00 AM to do farm work, or one who has major responsibility for younger siblings. In every class, some students are struggling with difficulty, responsibility, uncertainty, or pain. Given this reality, teachers must be both understanding and flexible. A head on the desk or turned toward a window does not necessarily indicate disrespect or lack of interest, but could be evidence of a larger, more compelling concern.

Increasingly, students' lives have become more troubled, reflecting a society with a widening gap between the "have" and "have nots," a society of uncertain values, questionable ethics, and periodic violence. We need, then, to be aware of a student whose parent or sibling is in jail, whose brother has been injured or killed in a gang fight, whose alcoholic parent is abusive, whose household is overcrowded, whose home revolves in a cycle of poverty. For such students just getting to school is a major accomplishment. Keeping this perspective is not easy, but it is important that our students' experiences influence our teaching and expectations. We cannot, for example, expect students who have neither the physical space nor emotional support to complete homework assignments.

We cannot continue to teach students as if they had no life outside of the classroom. In reality, their lives can be frightening, exhausting, and overwhelming. Candy Carter, a high school teacher, argues that "students often come to school with so much unfinished business from home that it takes a real master to bring art and life together" (27). She adds that few students today, regardless of socioeconomic class, have not "been confronted with opportunities to use drugs or drink to excess" (26). Parents may lack interest altogether. Our idealism as teachers may be sorely tried by circumstances beyond our control.

Teachers cannot solve students' problems, but we can make our classrooms places where they can find temporary refuge and provide them with understanding, empathy, and patience. Through responding to literature, writing in journals, listening, and talking with peers, students may find answers to their questions and make sense of their lives.

We can say one thing with certainty. Every teacher will have a wide range of students—from the bookworm to the defiant, from students who absorb everything placed in front of them to those whose silence says, "I dare you to teach me." Their varying attitudes reflect our world at large, one which Alvin Toffler described in *Future Shock* as "the shattering stress and disorientation that we induce in individuals by subjecting them to too much change in too short time" (2). Our world is a complex kaleidoscope of changing values and attitudes. In addition to personal problems in families and relationships, students grapple with societal problems: drugs and alcohol, racism, war, overpopulation, ecological disasters, urban decay, unemployment, inflation, and sexual diseases that confront them either through personal experience or through the media. If students in past decades lived in fear of nuclear annihilation, ours live in an equally frightening world.

HOW TEACHERS CAN HELP

Twenty years ago Dwight Burton and his colleagues asked students what they needed. They responded that "they needed some hope, some feeling that mankind will not merely survive but that it deserves to survive" (17). Sobering words, words as likely to arise from the students of the 1990s.

What do these realities mean for our classrooms? Mainly that we provide both personal integrity, a modeling if you will, and opportunities for students to explore their beliefs and values. Through literature, classroom drama, and writing, students can safely explore themselves and their world, find people to admire, and see beyond the limits of their present situation. Students also need a classroom environment that encourages and respects the range of human emotions. In his important study of American schools, John Goodlad tells us:

> Data . . . suggest to me a picture of rather well-intentioned teachers going about their business somewhat detached from and not quite connecting with the "other lives" of their students. What their students see as primary concerns in their daily lives, teachers view as dissonance in conducting school and classroom business.   (80)

Goodlad goes on to note that "classes at all levels tend not to be marked with exuberance, joy, laughter, abrasiveness, praise, but by emotional neutrality" (112) and "whether we looked at how teachers related to students or how students related to teachers, the overwhelming impression was one of affective neutrality—a relationship neither abrasive nor joyous (111). Knowing how deeply felt the emotions of adolescents are, we are astounded by the affective desert presented here. What is more, we can think of no worse environment for students or ourselves. To prevent it, we need to seriously examine students' needs and interests as we choose materials and plan lessons. And even though, as teachers, we are the ones who structure learning, we have to remember that we do not own it.

No matter how well we teach, learning ultimately belongs to the student. Janet Emig explained in a talk that "Learning doesn't always follow teaching, but leads a marvelously independent life of its own." As English language arts teachers, we can structure, facilitate, and nurture learning, but we can neither impose nor control it. "Marvelously independent," we believe, captures the essence of learning, for it suggests our students follow diverse, individual paths of learning, measuring time and demonstrating growth uniquely, and finally, coming to know in their own ways. This view of diversity reminds us that we ourselves have learned in different ways, in different times, and in different places. Our own learning has not been limited to the classroom; therefore, we must value and draw on our students' experiences as we plan for teaching. Moreover, we cannot separate teaching and learning; as teachers we learn, and our students, in many respects, become our teachers.

In the final chapter of this book, "Becoming a Teacher," we will use the voices of real high school students to again describe the importance of seeing our students as teachers. Some veteran English teachers share their thoughts as well. One of them, Eileen Simons, tells us to trust our students and ourselves to explore our subject areas together:

No teacher's guide taught me the connection between Shakespeare's play *The Tempest* and Ray Bradbury's *Fahrenheit 451*. But a high school sophomore saw that Prospero and Beatty were both into "mind control." A junior English literature student spotted the similarity between King Arthur's court and modern society: Gang members are controlled by a code as rigid as that of any medieval knight. (73)

Simons is right. Students are wonderful teachers, smart and insightful, if only we share with them the journey of learning and emphasize the importance of their responses. And they are much more fun than a teacher's guide.

Exploring an Instructional Unit

Joy Hoffmann teaches at a residential treatment facility for children with emotionally disturbances or behavior disorders. Her materials and resources are extremely limited, a fact that has her "constantly fighting the budget and scrounging around for the stuff from which learning experiences are made." Some of her students are extremely bright and would benefit from higher-order thinking strategies.

Joy developed a unit based on heroic values because her students have few positive role models and even fewer heroes; they need people to look up to and emulate. She further explains that her students have "value systems that are antisocial, dangerous, and/or fragmented, but they seldom know how to develop more workable practices and beliefs." Although what follows is an abbreviated version of the unit Joy developed, we can explore what she planned in light of her specialized student group.

HEROIC VALUES

Joy chose the following materials listed in chronological order to use in a six-week unit on heroic values:

Materials List:

1. Newspaper or other nonfiction articles about people that students would consider heroic.
2. Speeches by John F. Kennedy and Martin Luther King, Jr.
3. One or two short stories or poems.
4. *Beowulf*
5. *Hamlet*
6. *Beloved* by Toni Morrison

Activity: Begin the unit by playing rap tapes and other popular songs. Ask students why these songs are popular, easy to remember, and fun to sing. What do these songs have in common? The students practice writing their own lyrics after discussion of rhythm, diction, and structure in class. Or they may develop their own unusual style.

The unit also develops the idea of audience, word choice, style, and imagery. The students do some oral reading of *Beowulf* with emphasis on rhythm. Include pantomiming and discussion on diction and style. The final assignment is for students to create a narrative that would be attractive to an audience with little education or literary background.

QUESTIONS ABOUT JOY'S UNIT

1. How has Joy considered the variety of learning styles of her students?
2. Discuss how appropriate you think her literature selections are for her students.
3. Where has Joy focused on student interests? In what other ways might she use student interest as the basis for activities?
4. What are Joy's objectives? Based on this unit, what do you think is her philosophy of teaching and learning?
5. What activities from Joy's unit could you use in a heterogeneous classroom?

DISCUSSION QUESTIONS

1. Thinking back to Chris, the first-year teacher described in Box 2-1, what assumptions did he make about his students? How could he have better prepared himself for the beginning of school? What do you recommend he do now?

2. Many new teachers get caught up in subject-matter content without considering who that content is for. Think back to your own high school experience. How would you characterize the students? What might account for these characteristics? In particular, try to recall groups of students who were labeled as troublemakers. If you had these students in your classroom today, what activities would you use to reach them?

3. Talk with as many experienced teachers as possible to learn their views on the variety of students they teach. How do they adjust content to fit the students' needs? Observe classrooms, concentrating on the students' behavior, not the teacher. Keep a log of your observations. How do you know if assumptions you make about the students are right?

4. Design an opening day activity that will help you be a more successful teacher throughout the year. Share the activity with peers and discuss which activities would be the most helpful. What goals are the most beneficial for all students?

5. Survey college students who are non-English majors to learn their views of the characteristics of "good" English teachers and classes. Then survey the students in an English education class. What are the similarities and differences? Discuss the implications for future teachers.

6. What are some ways you could get to know your students better at the beginning of the school year? What are the most important things to tell them? Usually the first day of class is spent handing out a list of rules, textbooks, course expectations, and what a teacher will not accept or allow. Reflect on your own first-day experiences and those of classes you have observed. What could Chris in Box 2-1 have done? What might you do? Why?

REFERENCES

Adams, Pamela E. "Teaching *Romeo and Juliet* in the Nontracked English Classroom." *Journal of Reading* 38.6 Mar. 1995: 424–31.

Burton, Dwight, et al. *Teaching English Today.* Boston: Houghton Mifflin, 1975.

Carter, Candy. Are teenagers different? *What Is English?* Ed. Peter Elbow. New York: Modern Language Association and Urbana: National Council of Teachers of English, 1990.

Dunn, Rita, Beaudry, Jeffrey S., and Klavas, Angela. "Survey of Research on Learning Styles." *Educational Leadership* Mar. 1989: 50–58.

Emig, Janet. "Exploring Theories of Learning for Teaching Writing." Conference on Teaching Composition to Undergraduates. Clearwater Beach, FL, 5 Jan. 1992.

Gilligan, Carol, Lyons, Nona, and Hanmer, Randy, eds. *Making Connections: The Relational Worlds of Adolescent Girls at Emma Willard School.* Cambridge: Harvard UP, 1990.

Goodlad, John. *A Place Called School.* New York: McGraw-Hill, 1984.

Hoffmann, Joy. "Heroic Values." Unpublished manuscript. Eau Claire: University of Wisconsin.

Jett-Simpson, Mary, and Masland, Susan. "Girls Are Not Dodo Birds! Reading Against the Grain: Gender Bias in Children's Books." *Language Arts* Feb. 1993: 104-08.

Johnson, Robert. "Challenging the Cult of Excellence." *English Journal* Oct. 1992: 37–40.

Judy [Tchudi], Stephen. "Invisible Thinking and the Hypertext." *English Journal* Jan. 1988: 22–30.

Krogness, Mary Mercer. *Just Teach Me, Mrs. K.: Talking, Reading, and Writing With Resistant Adolescent Learners.* Portsmouth: Heinemann, 1995.

Leader-Telegram "Vandals Barred From Graduation." 28 May 1995, 10A.

Lightfoot, Sara. Interview. *Conversations With Bill Moyers.* Public Affairs TV. WNET/NIV and UTTW/Chicago, 1988.

Nelms, Ben F. "Being Unspecial. Introduction to Symposium." *The English Journal* Oct. 1992: 44.

National Association of Secondary School Principals. *On the Threshold of Adolescence.* Reston: Author, 1983.

Rief, Linda. *Seeking Diversity.* Portsmouth: Heinemann, 1992.

Simons, Eileen. "A Quarter of a Century and Not Finished Yet." *English Journal* Feb. 1995: 73.

Strickland, Kathleen, and Strickland, James. *Uncovering the Curriculum.* Portsmouth: Boynton/Cook, 1993.

Thomas, Sharon. "The Forgotten Half." *The English Journal* Oct. 1992: 45–46.

Tindall, Lloyd W. "Retaining At-Risk Students: The Role of Career and Vocational Education." Washington: U.S. Department of Education, ERIC 303-683 Report.

Toffler, Alvin. *Future Shock.* New York: Random House, 1970.

Tucker, Gene. "Teaching Today's Students." *UCLA Graduate School of Education Quarterly* Fall 1993: 1–2.

Understanding Curriculum and Instruction

I know that as a person who is planning lessons right at the moment [preparing for a teaching internship] how frightening it is. One worries about how to fill the time, which activities work best, and one's own competence with subject matter.

Nik Lightfoot, Senior English Major

This chapter will help you absorb, explore, and apply the concepts of curriculum and instruction. In this process, you will also be able to apply your knowledge of English language arts principles and the diverse student body you are likely to teach.

CENTERING CURRICULUM ON LEARNERS AND LEARNING

Sometimes, teachers think in terms of "What can I teach?" rather than "How can my students best learn?" The English language arts curriculum should arise out of the latter perspective. We can help our students best learn by providing them with experiences that will help them to grow both intellectually and imaginatively, individually and socially, cognitively and emotionally. Curriculum and instruction should acknowledge and prepare for the inevitable changes that our students will undergo as they mature.

Knowing, for example, that the capabilities and needs of a 12-year-old are different from those of a 15-year-old is useless information unless we act on it. Intervening in the lives of students demands that we do act on the best knowledge our profession has to offer. Once teachers and administrators focus on the learner, other questions follow:

- How can students become self-motivated learners?
- How can students become independent learners?

- How will students acquire competency in basic skills?
- How can students move from competence to proficiency?
- How will students learn to express themselves with confidence and authority in both oral and written language?

Questions guide not only development but also evaluation of the established curriculum:

- Is there a *consistent* theory of instruction?
- Where did it come from (i.e., from research or observation)?
- Does the curriculum reflect current research?
- Are course goals, objectives, and materials congruent with current research and effective classroom practice?
- Does the curriculum reflect state standards?
- Does the curriculum reflect the expressed needs and concerns of the community?
- Does the curriculum connect with the "outside world," providing a link to everyday needs, problems, and interests?
- Does the curriculum indicate a concern for lifelong literacy?
- Does the curriculum address a multicultural, pluralistic society?
- Does the curriculum provide for development as students move through a K–12 sequence?
- How are students assessed?
- Are the language arts integrated and balanced?
- Does the curriculum provide for the rapid growth of adolescents and acknowledge individual differences?

Some districts maintain a cycle of curriculum review and revision; others do not, undertaking it only when new state requirements and standards demand it. Whatever the situation, well-informed teachers should be at the center of curriculum development and revision. If a district has an English language arts curriculum that runs counter to well-established research and classroom practice, teachers need to initiate discussion with their administrators to make necessary changes. Ultimately, teachers must follow through with curricular review and revision. To ensure that students receive a consistent and coherent program in English language arts, the review should be district-wide. That is, the review should address grades K–12 and involve teachers from each curricular level. Special education, bilingual education, and other special needs teachers should also be part of the review team.

DEFINITIONS

Curriculum and *instruction* are common words in education; but their familiarity may mask surprisingly diverse ideas about their meaning. As a result, some confusion or controversy may arise during discussions about curriculum and instruction. Broadly defined, *curriculum* refers to "what" is taught, the content. A curriculum guide generally contains a set of topics, goals, and objectives (student outcomes); it may also contain specific materials, methods, stated or implied, and evaluation procedures. *Instruction* refers to "how," the methods and strategies by which teachers deliver the curriculum to students. These definitions are not as straightforward as they seem, largely because people have different notions of what a curriculum is and how it should be organized. For example, some teachers believe the English language arts curriculum should focus on basic skills; others believe it should center on literature; and still others believe it should concentrate on the developing (i.e., maturing) student. Although these areas are not mutually exclusive, choosing to focus the curriculum on one of them makes a definite statement about what students in that district will be doing.

CASE 3–1

A Defensible Curriculum?

Examine the following excerpt from a 1994 curriculum guide for eighth-grade English and decide what this school district believes is central to student learning. Consider this unit to be representative of the district's curriculum for secondary composition and language. As you examine this unit, keep in mind the English language arts principles discussed in Chapter 1. Also keep in mind the diversity of students discussed in Chapter 2. What is your opinion of (a) the curricular content, (b) expectations and learner outcomes, (c) suggested activities and methodology, and (d) evaluation? Is this a defensible curriculum?

UNIT OF STUDY FOR SECONDARY COMPOSITION AND LANGUAGE

Grammar: Complements, predicate adjective, predicate noun, predicate pronoun, direct object, and indirect object

Time: 2 weeks

Expectations: The student will be able to:

1. Recognize the sublinking verb-complement pattern and identify predicate adjective, predicate noun, and predicate pronoun.
2. Recognize the direct object pattern and indirect object pattern.
3. Diagram sentences that include the above patterns.

Suggested Activities:

1. Write an original sentence and identify the verb and its complements and the verb and its indirect object or direct object.

2. Locate sentences from written material and identify which pattern they show.
3. Write original sentences with complements, then exchange papers and diagram.

Resources:

Basic text
Sentences put on board
READ magazine
Exercises to supplement text

Evaluation:

1. Students respond orally in class.
2. Teacher grades daily work.
3. Check tests.

WHO DOES THE DEFINING?

In some schools, curriculum occurs by default: Whatever is in the textbook becomes the curriculum, both the content to be taught and the general order or sequence to be followed. In this case, textbook editors and authors, not the district, have determined the curriculum. This raises another question: Just who does determine the curriculum? In some districts, school boards are thought to have this right, determining "what" will be taught but not "how," a matter reserved for professional teachers. In other districts, administrative positions are designated for "curriculum development and supervision," which means that either administrators alone or administrators working collaboratively with teachers, determine the district's curriculum. In some states, curriculum is mandated by the state itself, which means that every district has a common curriculum—a common set of topics, goals, objectives, and outcomes. A state-mandated curriculum may also specify the textbook series, materials, and methods to be used in each of its districts, as well as which tests are to be administered statewide. The logic here is apparent: If every district has the same curriculum, then every district can have the same test to check how well students have negotiated that curriculum.

Ideally, assessment *is* linked to curriculum, but the subject of assessment opens up another set of curricular problems. If a state or district mandates certain tests, no matter how inappropriate the test, teachers feel pressured to teach to it. Quite understandably, they want to ensure that their students' test performances are adequate. However, the cost of that one-time performance is high, reducing the English language arts curriculum to an opscan sheet, little circles that fail to describe important aspects of reading, writing, speaking, and listening.

Assessment is important. Teachers need to know how their students are progressing, and districts need to know which areas or programs need more attention. Assessment can be very controversial, however, as evidenced by fierce debates on every educational level and in state legislatures. Because appropriate assessment can be quite costly, especially in disciplines in which machine-scored tests may be inappropriate, the English language arts curriculum may not enjoy an assessment program congruent with its stated goals and desired learner outcomes. Assessment findings need to be clarified, placed in context, and not allowed to drive curriculum in ways antithetical to effective classroom practice.

CURRICULAR CONTROVERSY

Educators and the general public have personal definitions of curriculum. They believe they know just what should be taught in any given discipline, and equally important, just what a student should know or be able to do upon completion of that course of study. These definitions often arise out of a specific ethnic and cultural background, social class, religious views, educational achievements, and a host of other experiences. Moreover, school districts may define curriculum not only in terms of the various disciplines within it but also in terms of the community itself, its beliefs and values. A community whose members believe strongly in parental rights in matters of sex education would probably reflect this belief in its curriculum, or in this case, the lack of school curriculum in sex education. It can even be a bit more complicated than this. For example, a letter to the editor in a local paper, entitled "Mandated Sex Ed" and signed by "A Mother," stated that "SB 324 [Senate Bill], the mandated sex ed bill, is a blatant attempt to keep parents and local schools from teaching what they want." The author went on to praise a program called *Sex Respect*, take issue with Planned Parenthood of Wisconsin and the ACLU for challenging the program, and ends her letter with this: "I'm hearing much about dysfunctional families these days. How do I know my kids aren't being taught by teachers from dysfunctional homes?" This type of parental interest in curriculum is not unusual, especially when issues involving sex education, racial and ethnic diversity, or basic skills are involved.

A Curricular Controversy: Back to the Basics

The Back to Basics movement, which emerged in the 1970s, provides an example of how community interest and debate may enter into seemingly academic concerns. Back to Basics is an educational reform movement that addresses core curricular areas such as English and mathematics. Believing that language and writing skills show serious deterioration, proponents of Back to Basics advocate a return to a curriculum centered in grammar (sentence structure, usage, mechanics, and spelling). Through drills, exercises, and rote learning techniques, students should master the parts of speech and learn syntax by parsing and diagramming sentences. Students should then demonstrate their mastery through a series of competency tests. Why are people so insistent that this content and instructional method is the answer? They recall their own English classes from the 1950s and earlier when this content and method were the accepted practice. They believe, therefore, that their own writing competency is the direct result of this practice.

In the mid-1970s, Watergate, Vietnam, and a faltering economy created a dismal worldview and suspicion of just about every type of bureaucratic structure, including the schools. Stephen Judy [Tchudi], a noted English educator, suggests that the public became concerned that teachers were ignoring grammar and correctness and were focusing only on creativity (26). Further, parents and others noted that the traditional courses in English appeared to have vanished altogether, replaced by units with strange names (e.g., Death, Man and His Car). English curricula had shifted to a loosely structured collection of topical units in many schools, but this did not necessarily mean traditional literature was abandoned. And students were rewarded for more individualism and creativity, reflecting a growing interest in curriculum focused on affective goals rather than solely on cognition or basic skills. However, Back to Basics advocates believed that the English curriculum was chaotic, and that competency had been thrown out or devalued. When SAT verbal scores declined, people were further convinced that students were graduating without literacy skills.

Back to Basic advocates held a somewhat simplistic, perhaps even romantic, notion of the past, schooling in general, and their own English classes. In so doing, they ignored variables that directly affect learning. Prior to the 1960s, young people generally read and wrote more often, watched far less television, and lived in a somewhat more stable society, one less prone to drug and alcohol abuse, shattered families, and devastating economic problems. These factors must be considered when questioning student achievement and school effectiveness. Additionally, in the 1970s, postsecondary education opened its doors more widely, providing opportunities for students who lacked traditional college preparation. The increase in remedial English classes fed the public's perception that secondary schools were not doing their job. Similarly, young people entering the work force appeared to be less competent in communication skills. A great many people were alarmed. They saw a return to grammar and mastery learning as a solution, and Back to Basics became a national force. However, as Stephen Judy points out, Back to the Basics advocates, believing they had discovered the "deplorable" state of literacy, were merely part of a legacy that has existed as long as English has been taught. Judy notes, "*Every* generation seems convinced that it is in the midst of a decline in literacy, that standards have fallen, that the schools have been allowed to abolish all concern for the English language" (35).

Addressing Back to Basics, James Moffett attacked the double misnomer of the movement's title, noting that English curriculum, no matter what else it was doing, never left the drills and rules approach to grammar and writing. He contends that if this method worked, it would have done so decades ago, and a decline in literacy skills cannot be separated from societal changes. Moffett defined the *basics* in the English curriculum as speaking, listening, reading, and writing. These, not some mechanistic parts-to-whole approach to literacy, are, said Moffett, the "real basics" (96).

In *The Unschooled Mind,* Harvard psychologist Howard Gardner argues that "by focusing on basic skills, schools risk suppressing the positive aspects of children's minds—adventurousness, flexibility, creativity—as well as their natural enthusiasm for learning" (cited in Gursky 41). Gardner is not unaware of the controversy in his argument:

> To declare oneself against the institution of the three Rs in the school is like being against motherhood or the flag . . . Beyond question, students ought to be literate and ought to revel in their literacy. Yet the essential emptiness of this goal is drama-tized by the fact that young children in the United States are becoming literate in the *literal* sense; that is, they are mastering the rules of reading and writing, even as they are learning their addition and multiplication tables. What is missing are not the decoding skills, but two other facets: the capacity to read for understanding and the desire to read at all. (cited in Gursky 41)

Because Gardner's work usually attracts national attention, fueling conversations and debate among academics and the general public alike, his assertions about the gap between teaching and genuine understanding will undoubtedly contribute to the ongoing controversy over Back to Basics.

The English Coalition Conference of the National Council of Teachers of English (NCTE) argues:

> Public concern about basic knowledge and the basic skills in education is valid . . . [but] the basic elements of knowledge and skill are only part of the essentials of edu-cation. In an era dominated by cries for going "back to the basics," for "minimal com-petencies," and for "survival skills," society should reject simplistic solutions and declare a commitment to the essentials of education. (n.p.)

The Council warns against "three easy tendencies" in curriculum and instruction: limiting *essentials* to the three Rs in an increasingly complex society; defining *essentials* by what can be measured; and reducing *essentials* to a few skills "when it is obvious that people use a combination of skills, knowledge and feelings to come to terms with their world" (English Coalition Conference, n.p.).

Although the NCTE, along with 24 other professional organizations, called for a balanced education in 1978, the issue remains a critical one in the 1990s. Faced with curricular controversy and a movement as persistent as Back to the Basics, teachers need a strong response. For this reason, curriculum and instruction need to be coher-ent and related directly to how students learn.

BOX 3–1

A SECOND LOOK: A DEFENSIBLE CURRICULUM?

Return to the eighth-grade grammar unit. Given what you have just read about basic skills and the curricular controversy surrounding them, you know that this unit might be very acceptable (in fact, desirable) to some educators, parents, and community members. Suppose that this unit is being proposed for use not only as part of your district's eighth-grade curriculum but also as a representative unit for the entire middle school or junior high curriculum in composition and language. How would you respond to this proposal? What knowledge must you have to respond with confidence?

CURRICULUM: A JOINT ENDEAVOR

Few curricular areas are as visible as the English language arts. Parents and members of the community will ask questions about topics or materials that have been added or dropped, about instructional methods, and about student achievement. They have a right to these questions, both in terms of their children's education and the considerable tax base they provide in maintaining that education. Districts that have a well-defined written curriculum, based on a consistent K–12 philosophy, will no doubt be better equipped to deal the challenges.

A district's curriculum reflects not only the policies and standards of the community but also those of the state. Although some states mandate curriculum, most do not. Curriculum is generally developed at district level, with guidance, recommendations, and requirements from the state department of public instruction. John D. McNeil speaks to the importance of local curriculum development:

> Effective schools have a strong sense of community, commonly held goals, and high expectations for students and staff performance. Successful schools are characterized by staff interactions involving aspects of teaching, whereby administrators and teachers work together in planning, designing, creating and preparing materials. . . . (Foreword)

In brief, curriculum and instruction that arise out of a collaborative effort stand the best chance of success. Whatever the origin of the curriculum, however, the primary responsibility for it ultimately rests with the teachers who will deliver it.

COMPONENTS OF A CURRICULUM GUIDE

Any English language arts guide should describe the assumptions on which it is based. NCTE's English Coalition Conference noted these for English language arts curricula at both elementary and secondary levels:

1. The language arts (reading, writing, speaking, and listening) are inextricably linked to thinking.

2. Reading, writing, speaking, and listening are social and interactive.
3. Learning is a process of actively constructing meaning from experience, including encounters with many kinds of print and nonprint texts.
4. Others—parents, teachers, and peers—help learners construct meanings through serving as supportive models, providing frames and materials for inquiry, helping create and modify hypotheses, and confirming the worth of the venture.
5. All students possess a rich fund of prior knowledge, based on unique linguistic, cultural, socioeconomic, and experiential backgrounds.
6. Acknowledging and appreciating diversity is necessary to a democratic society.

In addition to a set of basic assumptions, a curriculum guide should reflect the district's aims or purpose relative to the English language arts. The English Coalition Conference centered its aims on empowerment:

1. As lifelong learners with a command of language and a sense of fulfillment and pleasure from the language arts
2. As active inquirers, problem solvers who can use the language arts to gain insight into self and others, who can reflect on their own and others' lives
3. As productive citizens who can use language to communicate with others and take charge of their own lives
4. As theorizers about their own language and learning, who can read, write, and reflect on texts from multiple perspectives

"Active inquirers" do not emerge from pages of exercises or from silent, noncollaborative classrooms; "theorizers" do not emerge from didactic methods and convergent thinking. Similarly, "lifelong learners" do not develop when ineffective and boring exercises replace actual language experience in reading, writing, speaking, and listening. These aims, then, guide teachers in choosing materials and methods in their classrooms.

Finally, the curriculum should reflect the best knowledge we have about how students grow and change from childhood to young adulthood, how they acquire and process language, and how they acquire and enhance literacy skills. The curriculum should also reflect the reality of individual differences in learning style and rate, as well as the impact of social, cultural, and gender differences.

CASE 3–2

What's Assumed Here?

Examine the following excerpt from a district's curriculum guide for a ninth-grade course entitled "Introduction to Literature and Composition." What assumptions about the English language arts appear to be underlying this unit? What assumptions about ninth graders seem apparent here? How do you think

the "average" ninth grader will respond? a gifted ninth grader? a ninth grader
with learning difficulties? a ninth grader disengaged from school in general and
English in particular?

UNIT OF STUDY ON MYTH/EPIC

Time: 2 weeks

Expectations: The student will be able to:

1. Read, understand, and enjoy myths and epics.
2. Identify and examine mythological characters and values of different cultures
   in Greece and Rome.
3. Understand and identify the values of morals displayed in myths and epics.
4. Develop an awareness of American myths, including Native American myths,
   myths of other ethnic groups, and folk legends.

Suggested Activities:

1. Read myths/epics in the text.
2. Discuss selections in class.
3. In the IMC (Instructional Media Center), research one of the early Greek or
   Roman authors and prepare an oral report.
4. Write a myth based on an old moral or belief but use modern situations and
   characters.
5. Write a library paper on mythology using card catalog, reference books, and
   encyclopedias.

Resources:

Textbook
IMC material (library, video, computers, etc.)
The *Iliad* by Homer
Mythology and fantasy; classical Greek myths, Arthurian legends, Native Ameri-
can legends and myths, and *Field of Dreams*

Evaluation Methods:

1. Discussion and observation
2. Research paper

3. Quizzes
4. Take test on material in this unit.
5. Modern myth

Curricular Goals

At the program level, goals are usually broadly stated. For example, Wisconsin's *Guide to Curriculum Planning in the English Language Arts* lists this one for composition:

> The goals of the writing program are to promote and enhance student proficiency in writing through a commitment to
>
> - a consistent K–12 philosophy for the teaching of writing.
> - a realistic view of the developing student, of growth as cumulative.
> - a regard for current research on writing and language learning.
> - a view of writing as one of the related language arts skills, to be integrated with speaking, listening and reading experiences.
> - a process that is holistic rather an accumulation of skills. (123)

Although the goal is indeed broad, it clearly delineates the underlying theoretical and philosophical base of the composition program. The teaching of writing will be developmentally appropriate (i.e., congruent with the linguistic, cognitive, and social abilities of students at a given age or level), process rather than product oriented (i.e., students understand and work through all phases of composing), holistic rather than mechanistic (i.e., skills are taught primarily through student writing, not exercises), and consciously integrated with speaking, listening, and reading activities.

A Theory of Instruction

Inherent in curricular goals is a *theory of instruction,* which Jerome Bruner, an expert in cognition and language, defines as a consistent and coherent statement about what and how students need to learn (40–42). From this statement, teachers know the appropriate materials, methods, and environment needed to achieve the goal—to promote or enhance student proficiency in writing.

FROM GOALS TO LEARNER OUTCOMES

Learner outcomes, also referred to as *objectives,* are usually stated in terms of what students are expected to know or accomplish as a result of instruction. For example, a learner outcome for writing might state that the student will be able to formulate a clear controlling idea; one in literature might state that the student will demonstrate an understanding of figurative language. In most districts, teachers have considerable freedom to develop instructional activities that help students achieve these outcomes. This is where individual creativity comes in, a necessary and wonderful part of teaching. The district, however, expects teachers to adhere to the theoretical and philosophical base either stated or implied in its curriculum. If, for example, grammar is to be taught contextually, within the writing process, teachers who teach mainly through textbook exercises violate district expectations.

Learner outcomes are the link between the curriculum and appropriate assessment instruments and procedures; therefore, clarity in stating them will make evaluation much easier. As with most aspects of curriculum, however, problems can arise. Some language arts goals (e.g., literary appreciation) are difficult to assess, which can lead districts either to discard the goal or to use inappropriate assessment. Similarly, other language arts goals (e.g., basic writing skills) are more easily and cheaply assessed through machine-scored measures, which are at best an indirect and incomplete measure of student competency. For this reason, discussions of appropriate assessment should be part of curriculum development and revision.

BOX 3–2

EVALUATING LEARNER OUTCOMES

Let's revisit the learner outcomes ("Expectations") in the ninth-grade Myth/Epic unit of study shown in Case 3–2.

The student will be able to:

1. *Read, understand, and enjoy myths and epics.* What does this outcome mean? How would you know whether students achieved it?
2. *Identify and examine mythological characters and values of different cultures in Greece and Rome.* This outcome seems quite straightforward, but is it? Does it go far enough? If you were teaching a unit on myth/epic, what learner outcomes, if any, would you add to "character" and "values"?
3. *Understand and identify the values or morals that myths and epics display.* Again, this outcome appears fairly clear, but as a teacher new to the district, how would you interpret it? Once you have interpreted it, what would you do to ensure your ninth graders could achieve it? What materials and methods might you use?
4. *Develop an awareness of American myths, including Native American myths, myths of other ethnic groups, and folk legends.* How would you rewrite this outcome (into one or more)? What guided your thinking and revision?

Developing Learner Outcomes

A learner outcome may be cognitive (knowledge), affective (attitude, personal values), skills-based (performance), or a combination of these. These outcomes are not mutually exclusive, but some district curricula or staff may stress one over another. As you have seen with the eighth-grade grammar unit, some districts believe in a basic skills approach to composition and language. And in the ninth-grade myth/epic unit, you found an emphasis on cognitive skills (e.g., with emphasis on words such as *identify, examine, understand,* and *become aware*). Some of the outcomes in the grammar unit are so concrete that they dictate a single text exercise as the only way to achieve them (e.g., diagram a sentence). In contrast, some of the outcomes in the myth/epic unit may have struck you as too abstract to be useful (e.g., "develop an awareness of"). Developing appropriate and useful learner outcomes is difficult but absolutely necessary. You seldom will write out learner outcomes, but you must know what your students are doing and why. As a result of your lesson or unit, students have gained some knowledge. Whether students have a deeper knowledge of a literary theme or an increased ability to find and correct a usage error in a rough draft, learner outcomes are important for student growth and development in the English language arts.

BOX 3–3

REVISING THE MYTH/EPIC UNIT

You've had a chance to think about the Myth/Epic unit described in Case 3–2 from various perspectives, including its stated "expectations." Now we would like you to take that section of the ninth-grade English curriculum and rework it.

You're Hired

Suppose that you are the new English teacher. Your principal has provided you with district curriculum for "Introduction to Literature and Composition," the 9th- and 10th-grade courses you will teach. The school doesn't have money for additional books, but you do have a small budget for film or video rental. Most of your students are not particularly good readers nor are they interested in classic literature. As a matter of fact, most of them plan to enter the local workforce right after high school. Nonetheless, the district wants to maintain the myth/epic unit and believes that students will benefit from exposure to this literature. You agree, but you also note some problems with the curriculum as currently written. You are told you may "mold" the unit along whatever lines you wish, as long as students work with myth and epic.

Getting Down to Work

1. Review the entire unit and consider the problem of coupling myth/epic with "folk legends" in the final "expectation." Decide whether to keep folk legends with the unit. The resources list suggests other decisions: Arthurian legends, the *Iliad,* Native American legends, and *Field of Dreams.* Make a list of the materials you plan to use, including any video or film. [Since you don't have the district's anthology, use any 9th- or 10th-grade literature anthology featuring myths/epics.]

2. Look at the match between "expectations" and "suggested activities." You know that outcomes are achieved through a variety of methods, but in this curriculum guide, there's little or no help provided in the "suggested activities." In fact, you

decide to keep only the "write a myth" activity. Once you have developed new learner outcomes, you will develop new activities to help students achieve them.

3. Develop learner outcomes appropriate to the study of myths and epics. Consider not just cognitive outcomes but also those in the affective and basic skills domains.

4. Once you have developed a new set of learner outcomes, speculate on ways to achieve them. Consider that your students are noncollege-bound, reluctant readers who are potentially uninterested in English classes. However, don't ignore the possibility of some motivated, good learners among them. What activities would help students meet your learner outcomes and engage them in the process?

Learner Outcomes and Controversy

In and of themselves, learner outcomes in three different domains (cognitive, affective, skills) pose few problems. As students progress through the English language arts curriculum, they need to develop skills in all three areas. Traditionally, however, cognitive objectives have enjoyed the highest status in education; the student's intellectual development was of primary, if not sole, concern. In such a curriculum, teachers sought materials and activities to develop the student's *knowledge* base. In literature, for example, teachers chose literary readings to increase student awareness and understanding of specific literary periods or genres. Teachers then designed questions and activities to stimulate and enhance cognitive skills. The more students "knew," the better. In the 1970s, however, some educators came to believe that cognitive skills had been overemphasized and advocated that the English language arts curriculum become more humanistic, addressing affective as well as cognitive objectives. Basic skills objectives in reading and writing also became more dominant in the 1970s, and today, basic skills objectives are again in the news.

With the advent of a more holistic approach to English language arts, critics have claimed a loss of basic skills, especially in reading. *Outcome-Based Education (OBE),* another curricular trend, has also caused a controversy in the 1990s. This curricular approach stipulates specific outcomes that students must achieve. Tests match the desired outcomes, and students must achieve a set correct percentage or retake the tests until they do. Often at issue with this approach are the diverse abilities within a single class. What are talented students doing once they pass the test on the first try? And does the chance to redo something 10 times reflect the real world in which students will ultimately work? Do the outcomes reflect important educational goals for all students? These are but a few of the questions that arise in outcome-based education. This discussion of OBE is very simplified, but it underscores the seriousness of learner outcomes.

As an English language arts teacher, you will develop learner outcomes for each language arts area (i.e., listening, speaking, reading, writing, and viewing). Whether you develop outcomes formally (perhaps for district-wide curriculum) or informally (for individual units and lessons) is not an issue. The important issue is that teachers think about what they are doing and why. Questioning the value of learner outcomes is part of your role as a professional teacher. Finally, English language arts teachers need to ensure that curricular objectives and student assessment match. Students who have experienced a mismatch will attest to their frustration and sense of injustice, feelings that affect their learning and motivation for the rest of the course.

Teachers do face a major question in developing learner outcomes: Should they develop them for an entire class or for individual students? Most teachers develop one set for an entire class or for one preparation, perhaps acknowledging individual differences only for the most exceptional students. Given their limited preparation time, large classes, and multiple preparations, it is reasonable to develop one set for an entire class. However, teachers may be challenged by parents who believe the learner outcomes, and subsequent evaluation, fail to acknowledge that students do not all learn in the same way or at the same time. These are legitimate concerns. Providing alternative methods, materials, and assessments may be both a necessary and a sound way of approaching every unit. We'll address this topic in more detail when we talk about individual planning.

THE ROLE OF TEXTBOOKS

In some districts, English language arts textbooks are *the* curriculum. When the texts are congruent with how students learn, allow for diversity, and challenge the learner, this curriculum by default may be a good one. However, it is not unusual for a text series to be uneven (i.e., some grade levels or areas are excellent, others awful). For this reason, teachers may use the assigned text for some units and ignore it for others. If the text runs counter to current research and practice, some teachers may abandon it altogether. In the 1980s, for example, many teachers began to approach composition as a process rather than a product, addressing skill development as part of revision and editing. Many textbooks published in the 1980s, despite new cover designs, were essentially grammar texts. For these teachers, the text became a reference book, perhaps occasionally used when they wished to focus attention on a single concept or skill. New teachers often feel compelled to use the texts supplied for their classroom, but they need to question the texts' validity and usefulness.

Because textbooks represent a major investment, most districts replace old books every five years on average for each curricular area. Therefore, new texts may be unavailable for a number of years, regardless of significant changes in the field. Individual teachers, then, must implement new methods and materials as warranted. At the same time, however, they need to maintain both horizontal (i.e, all English language arts teachers at one grade level) and vertical (i.e., K–12, grades 6–8, and grades 9–12) communication with colleagues. If the school is large enough for a department head, teachers should probably direct their initial questions and concerns at that level. Lacking a department head, teachers can speak with whatever administrator is assigned responsibility for curriculum and instruction in their building.

A district may insist on textbook adoptions across K–12 or, at the least, across grades 6 or 7 through grade 12 largely because it believes such an adoption ensures consistency and continuity. However, if the series is uneven or contrary to what a majority of teachers believe, there is no assurance that any consistency will result. Most districts ask teachers to take part in the textbook selection process, so it's important, despite the hours involved, that new teachers apply their recent education to this critical work.

Textbook Selection Criteria

Selecting a textbook can be a challenging task. Because most of us are drawn to attractive packaging, we need to develop a list of criteria to help us to compare texts on more than just their physical appeal. The criteria emerge from the curriculum itself and from basic principles of language learning, adolescent growth and development, and the specific language arts area or areas addressed in the text. Criteria must also address a pluralistic society, taking account of racial, ethnic, and gender concerns, issues, and contributions. The adoption of a social studies textbook series in California serves as a recent example of issues that can arise in adopting a literature series.

California has a state-mandated curriculum; therefore, the adoption of any textbook is significant. Oakland, which has a predominantly African American population, found itself in the midst of a fierce controversy over the approved text series. Although social studies teachers found the series to be acceptable, balancing historical perspectives among the various races and ethnic groups in the United States, members of the community did not. At a local school board meeting, the argument was disruptive enough that people had to be removed; the final vote was a victory for members of the community—a defeat of the series by one vote. Consequently, social studies teachers in the Oakland district were teaching without any texts, and one seventh-grade teacher noted he had spent over $3,000 of his own money on classroom materials for his students ("Cultural Kaleidoscope"). Although California, as a state with diverse racial and ethnic groups, addresses a pluralistic society in its curriculum and its textbooks, the question of "to what degree and with what accuracy" continues to arise. This is a serious question, one that also faces English language arts educators.

We need to point out here that some language arts areas don't need textbooks. Composition, for example, can be taught without a "composition" text; student drafts become the primary text in a process-oriented curriculum, and only occasionally would students need reference to a text. For this reason, some teachers request class sets of various texts, using them selectively rather than as a primary learning tool. This is also a good way to individualize instruction, to meet the needs of both the most and least capable learners in a single class. Selecting appropriate textbooks and other classroom material is, then, a painstaking process that must be informed by research, effective classroom practice, and the needs of a diverse student population.

Selecting English Language Arts Textbooks

The National Council of Teachers of English helps teachers select appropriate textbooks with a publication by Timothy Shanahan and Lester Knight. They point out the controversy inherent in the decision to use textbooks: Some teachers view a text as a basic tool, as a way to organize and deliver a standard curriculum to all students; others view a text as a prescriptive curriculum, limiting students and weakening teachers' responsibility and authority (1–2). The issue of a standard curriculum is one administrators take very seriously. Craig Hitchens, a district-wide director of curriculum and instruction, defines curriculum as a "set of commonly held beliefs and expectations in the area," and from this perspective, he notes that "all students in the district have a right to a quality *common* curriculum." That is, district teachers have a responsibility to work toward the outcomes stated in the district's course of study for the English language arts.

Each student should be guaranteed, regardless of the teacher, progress toward the stated goals and outcomes. Although Hitchens also believes that a centralized curriculum and standard textbooks may "lock in" some excellent teachers, he nonetheless argues that all students have a right to a minimum set of outcomes in the English language arts and that these outcomes cannot be left entirely to chance. From the perspective of district administration, then, the textbook may be one way to ensure that teachers meet those outcomes.

Shanahan and Knight are quick to point out that their guidelines for textbook selection describe quality language arts instruction and not texts per se. They also caution that teachers involved in text selection need to do some research and keep in mind that the text is only a tool, not a replacement for sound teaching methods. The following guidelines are adapted from Shanahan and Knight and applicable to text selection at any curricular level.

1.   Students gain language skills by using language; therefore, the text should encourage language *use*. Activities should emphasize genuine communicative purposes and encourage students to think about their own language rather than about some artificial samples or exercises supplied by others. A violation of this criterion occurs when students are asked to revise and edit a sample essay or do exercises.

2.   The text should emphasize the social uses of language. The purposes for which we use language and literacy "shape the ways in which we use them." Therefore, students need varied experiences that are genuinely purposeful (e.g., to discover, to imagine, to persuade, to establish identity). Texts violating this criterion are those that ask students to fill in the blanks or give short answers or focus on skills unrelated to actual language use.

3.   The language arts are integrated, interdependent processes, not separate subject matter. Shanahan and Knight note that "combined instruction has often been found to lead to the higher achievement. Despite this, language arts books have more commonly emphasized particular aspects of language learning while ignoring others" (17). Consistent with this guideline are texts that feature writing responses to quality literature or sharing writing orally. Texts that emphasize grammar, which has "little or no relationship to authentic composition" (17) violate this guideline.

4.   Texts should recognize growth and development. Kids change in *what* they know and *how* they come to know. Although, as Shanahan and Knight point out,

many subject areas are able to sequence the content of learning, "the process of reading, writing, speaking, and listening cannot be so easily or accurately divided up into types and sequences of information" (21). In the English language arts, "language processes are more alike than different across developmental levels" (21). That is, a 6th grader and a 12th grader both engage in the same processes when writing an essay; the level of sophistication in handling those processes is the difference, not the processes themselves.

Similarly, Shanahan and Knight argue, their level of sophistication in language itself develops as students create and use language across a variety of settings for diverse purposes—not by adding categories of information. In the English language arts, then, students refine language processes rather than accumulate information (22). Textbooks should reflect this process through activities that encourage students to participate in the language arts, not read about them. Texts should also provide teachers with information on adolescent growth and development and help them model various language processes appropriate to the curricular level.

5. Textbooks should assist teachers in assessing student learning. Shanahan and Knight note that good teachers are always observing and evaluating their students' performance; therefore, a text should help them collect data to evaluate growth (26). Traditionally, texts have supplied purely quantitative measures; however, the language arts are qualitative as well. Texts that help teachers observe and evaluate language in use, implement portfolios, and respond to diversity are better than those using only traditional tests. The teacher's guide should also provide representative student samples, reducing the danger of applying adult standards to adolescents.

6. Textbooks should help kids think. Working with language has the advantage of making our thinking explicit; therefore, text activities should make students more aware of their own thought processes (31). We need and use various means of thinking, and texts should offer students a diverse experience: inventing and creating, drawing on previous knowledge, consolidating new information, problem solving, reformulating knowledge, critical analysis, and evaluating. Activities that depend on cooperative learning groups, for example, foster thinking skills.

7. Textbooks should respect our pluralistic society. We know "different linguistic, cultural, ethnic, racial and gender groups use language in different ways" (36). A literature textbook should contain a balanced selection of representative pieces (not tokens). Teachers should reject a text that ignores culture altogether or negatively portrays, through inference or illustration, a minority group. A language text should address language differences, treating all dialects as variants of equal communicative value, with the goal of enhancing understanding and interpersonal communication. The relationship between our language and our culture should be clear.

8. The centrality of the language arts in all subject areas should be affirmed. Reading, writing, speaking, and listening take place in every discipline; however, each discipline requires or emphasizes slightly different reading or learning strategies. Ideally, teachers in other disciplines would teach these; however, realistically, most schools expect English language arts teachers "to take care of" all areas of language teaching and learning. Given this, texts that provide experience with a variety of subject areas

(e.g., reading nonfiction) or use thematic units that draw on a wide selection of oral and written language activities are preferable. Activities that involve students in cooperative projects are also desirable. Literature texts that contain only fiction and poetry would violate this guideline.

Teachers who would like to see these guidelines transformed into an evaluation chart should consult Shanahan and Knight.

CASE 3–3

A Question of Directions

SAMPLE 1

The following excerpts are typical of those found in annotated teacher editions. This format is representative of the entire text, that is, repeated throughout the teacher edition. What are its assumptions about you as teacher? About 10th-grade students? About the language arts? Even though you have a limited view, how would you respond if told that this text is among those considered for adoption in your 10th-grade English class?

The reading selection is adapted from a Native American legend of a woman chief.

BEFORE READING

Build Background: Remind students of prior reading about Native Americans in the "Introduction."

Use Prior Knowledge: Write the word *legend* on the chalkboard. Ask for an explanation of its meaning. Tell students they are about to read a legend that focuses on harmony among community members.

Make Predictions: Have a volunteer read the introduction. Ask what the woman chief does for her tribal community?

Set a Purpose: Have students determine their purpose for a subsequent silent reading of the legend. Write a variety of purposes on the chalkboard. Tell students to refer to them as they read.

DURING READING

Alternative Strategies for:

Auditory Learners: Read aloud the description of the journey westward. Ensure that students understand the basis of the quarrel.

Kinesthetic Learners: Students may draw a map of the area identified in the selection. They could add the river where events take place.

CULTURE NOTES

LEP/ESL Students: The following concepts or definitions may be unfamiliar:

Page 25: A sapling is a young tree
Page 27: Leggings are leg coverings of cloth or leather.

STUDENT EXERCISES FOLLOWING SELECTION

Summarizing: Choose the best phrase to complete each sentence. Then write the complete statements on your paper.

1. When the chief first ruled the Indian village, _____ (her tribe wanted different chief, strangers caused trouble, people understood each other and lived in harmony).
2. People were upset because _____ (they didn't like the chief, they feared her dog, they didn't understand each other).

INTERPRETING

Interpreting: Write the answer to each question on your paper.

1. Why did the people on the river's north bank spread stories that chief's dog was possessed by an evil spirit?
2. Why did the chief refuse to kill her dog?

For Thinking and Discussing: Do you think that things would have been different if the village had remained small? Explain your answer.

Writing: Imagine that the chief had not drowned, but had managed to swim to the river bank. Write a paragraph that gives the legend a different ending. If you wish, start with this sentence: "The chief and her dog rose to the water's surface."

SAMPLE 2

A colleague has the annotated teacher edition of another literature text under consideration, so you decide to look at the student edition. You choose a segment of Native American poetry to learn how this text directs student thinking, reading, and writing. After reviewing the pre- and postreading directions, you begin to form some definite ideas about how this text would support your teaching. Even though you have not yet seen the teacher edition of this text, what do you expect it to be like? How does this text view you as teacher? What are its assumptions about 10th graders? About the English language arts? Assuming once more that the student questions and activities are typical of the entire text, what would you tell your colleagues about it?

BEFORE READING

Making Connections: In your journal, make a chart like the one below. Then list words or phrases that you believe describe a modern attitude toward nature. As you read the poems, you will complete the chart by listing words or phrases that illustrate the Native American attitude toward nature.

Modern American Attitudes	Traditional Native American Attitudes

THINKING ABOUT THE READING

Responding Personally:

1. When you read these poems, what thoughts and feelings about nature came to mind? In your journal, explore your ideas.
2. Think about the attitude toward nature found in these poems. How would you describe this attitude?
3. As you think about contemporary attitudes toward nature, do you find them more or less appealing than the traditional attitudes of Native Americans? Explain your response.

Responding Creatively:

4. Review the poems once more and listen to the speakers' voices. How might these speakers feel about the taking of human life? What led you to this view?

Responding Critically:

5. You no doubt have some views of Native Americans. What effect did reading these poems have on those views?
6. The views of nature expressed in these poems can be viewed against those of people today who are involved in environmental protection and animal rights groups. Using specific lines from the poems to support your opinion, discuss similarities and differences that you see between traditional Native American beliefs and those of contemporary American activists.

ANALYZING WRITING

Personification: The speaker in the poems addresses the earth and sky as "Mother" and "Father." Why? What is the speaker suggesting about the earth and sky by using these human terms? When human qualities are given to an object, animal, or idea, we call the figure of speech *personification*.

With a classmate, identify at least two more examples of personification in the Native American poems. Also discuss why the poem's speaker uses this technique. What do we gain as listeners or readers?

Presenting Ideas:

1. With one or more classmates, review your charts and share your ideas on modern American attitudes toward nature.
   a. Discuss ways to present your ideas in writing (e.g., poetry, essay, report, editorial, video script). Choose one method and discuss your plans with your teacher. Then, work collaboratively to develop your piece, which will be published.
   b. Discuss ways to present your ideas through mixed media (e.g., art, print, video/audiotapes). Discuss your plans with your teacher. Then, work collaboratively to develop your presentation.
   c. Discuss ways to present your ideas orally (e.g., television "call in" show, panel, informal drama, improvisation). Discuss your plans with your teacher. Then, work collaboratively to develop your oral presentation.
2. Find out more about Native American beliefs about nature and the environment. Choose representative Native American nations from different parts of the United States and compare their views. Use both traditional and contemporary literature, as well as nonfiction, as resources.

Being a Good Scavenger

Teachers can supplement textbooks with acquisitions from the school library, the public library, and used bookstores. The school librarian is often a wonderful resource, not only in providing a constant flow of information about new works of fiction and nonfiction but also in assisting teachers as they develop thematic units. When I was teaching junior high school English in a rural district, the school librarian helped me to pull 20 or more adolescent novels off the shelves to stash in my classroom for several weeks. Similarly, a children's librarian at the nearest public library, once drawn into the unit's theme and goals, prepared stacks of adolescent fiction and nonfiction for my classroom. With their help, I was able to meet diverse student needs and interests, ranging from borderline mental retardation to intellectually gifted in one class.

The public library is also a good source of videos and cassettes, often matching or complementing literary selections. With the abundance of video stores, teachers now also have a low- cost alternative for special films. Used bookstores offer another low-cost source for alternative reading selections. Meeting the diverse needs of students is very challenging, but maintaining a classroom supply of paperbacks and periodicals can ease things somewhat. Even students who appear to dislike everything about school and reading appear to like the *Guinness Book of Records,* books of trivia on sports, cars, music, or any aspect of popular culture, and word games or puzzles. It is not "selling out" to provide materials that appear nonacademic or too heavily representative of popular culture. Through them, you might be able to help some students discover the pleasure of literacy or make the transition to more complex and challenging readings.

Evaluating Software

With the impact of technology in the English language arts classroom, many teachers must evaluate software as well as traditional textbooks. The National Council of Teachers of English's Committee on Instructional Technology, established in 1981, developed a set of criteria that educators could use at all curricular levels. The committee stipulated, however, that no single evaluation form could be applied to all software; thus, they tried to develop criteria "that embraced the most dynamic capabilities of the computer, and at the same time, to take into account the various instructional strategies which could be included in the design of a software program" (n.p.). The committee cautioned that instructional software is still in an early stage of development, so evaluation of it is an imprecise process.

Today, almost two decades after the committee's report, the software industry is still developing and offering a vast array of software for the English classroom. The sheer number of choices makes evaluation a bit more complicated, and with school costs an issue, choosing appropriate programs is a critical teacher skill. The committee recommends that teachers judge software against what publishers claim it can do and compare it to other products attempting to teach the same concepts or skills. The committee further recommends that teachers work through the software themselves and allow students to try it out. The committee believes, as we do, that student response may be the ultimate evaluation of how well the software meets its claims. With a generation of students who have grown up with computers and video games, you may find that they are your best teachers in this arena.

NCTE's *Guidelines for Review and Evaluation of English Language Arts Software* contains five major sections and an addendum for specific software purposes (e.g., word processing/text editing, simulation/problem solving). Briefly, the major sections to evaluate single lessons are these: management features (e.g., recordkeeping system and options for teacher modification); content (e.g., accuracy, value, appropriateness, options for teacher modification); instructional strategy (e.g., practice, examples, logic of sequence, feedback, cognitive value, application); ease of operation (e.g., clarity of directions, student independence); and supplementary materials (e.g., teacher's guide, student material, tests). The *Guidelines* offer specific criteria under each category, the most extensive in instructional strategy.

In the addendum, educators are asked to choose the category description that best matches the software under review. In "simulation/problem solving," for example, the program would be geared to discovery learning and decision making. Thus, teachers would evaluate the software on its realism, relevance to acquisition of English language arts skills, as well as the more procedural aspects of the program. Since word processing and text editing are among the most common software used in English language arts programs, the committee has provided its most extensive list in this section: management features, safeguards, editing, visual presentation, and printing. With these guidelines, teachers can easily add or delete criteria to complement the software under review.

In addition to the guidelines published by NCTE, teachers can check professional journals in the English language arts for current information on educational software. Other journals devoted specifically to computers and teaching (e.g., *The Computing Teacher*) are also good resources. Attending major conferences is another important way to check out the latest programs. Many computer companies give hands-on demonstrations throughout these conferences. And just as textbook representatives come to the schools with their "wares," so do computer specialists. Don't be afraid to ask for on-site demonstrations and sample copies for your students to try out.

ONLINE SERVICES FOR THE CLASSROOM

In the "Software" section of the October 1995 *The English Journal,* high school teacher Sharon Johnston notes the technological maze facing language arts teachers today:

> The media constantly bombard us with intriguing educational possibilities for the Internet, a multiple-layered network that requires time and patience. How do we navigate this information maze? (125)

Johnston goes on to point out that teachers need a helping hand to navigate the Internet but such help is readily available. Despite the complexity of the network and her high school's lack of technology, Johnston undertook a personal journal of discovery, which led her to conclude that the online services themselves are good guides:

> Each [online] service has its own user-friendly communication software that is continually upgraded. To help the customer, experts are available online or by telephone to answer questions about using the software and moving through the network. (125)

Johnston provides journal readers with specific information about the major online services: Prodigy, CompuServe, and America Online. Her review of current services included ease of use, potential as a learning tool in secondary classrooms, potential problems, and costs. Because most services provide a free testing period, she suggests that "teachers begin with a test of several online services to decide which one meets the needs and characteristics of their students and their curriculum objectives" (126). With the services offering a "hand-held" introduction to their resources, even the technological beginner can "develop the online skills needed for navigating the complex Internet system" (126). We'd also suggest that our students do some teaching here. Often, they have amazing knowledge of computer software and services. Asking for their help makes good sense and demonstrates a belief that teachers are learners, too.

NCTE also maintains online services both on the Internet and America Online. On the Internet, NCTE currently has two mailing-list discussion groups, NCTE-talk and English-teachers. These lists are set up so that participants can send E-mail to a central address, from which messages are routed to all other participants. NCTE-talk is open to NCTE members only, but the English teachers list is open to all English language arts teachers. Both lists are devoted to discussion of matters relevant to our profession, including teaching ideas, issues, and questions regarding standards and assessment, and NCTE positions and policies. (Johnston 126)

The use of technology in English language arts will no doubt increase and afford teacher and students alike worldwide communication, data bases previously out of reach for secondary students, and software packages with myriad literary selections. Just as we select textbooks using criteria based on sound principles and practice in the English language arts, we also need to select software and online services with a similar list in hand.

TWO CURRICULUM TERMS: SCOPE AND SEQUENCE

The terms *scope* and *sequence,* as the names suggest, refer to the range or amount of curricular content and its order of presentation. In brief, *scope* tells teachers what content to cover and *sequence* tells them when—the order of instruction. There is no argument about the necessity of understanding appropriate content and sequencing for each curricular level; however, there are questions about how scope and sequence are perceived in the English language arts.

When experienced teachers hear the terms *scope* and *sequence,* they usually picture a detailed chart of concepts or skills to be introduced, mastered, and reviewed at each level of the curriculum. For example, every use of the comma is labeled for distribution at a specific grade level. Students might be introduced to commas that separate parts of dates in the 3rd grade, review this use in 4th grade, and "master" it in 5th grade. In the 10th grade, students would be introduced to commas used with adverbial conjunctions, review this use in the 11th grade, and by graduation, "master" this skill.

A colleague refers to this model as the "language arts auto parts catalogue." The analogy is apt for several reasons. First, language and literature are broken down into discrete parts and labeled, ready to be issued at the appropriate moment. Second the appropriate moment is prescribed: When student X is here, insert concept or skill Y. Third, the underlying assumption is one of a machine not functioning as a whole, not needing all its parts for simultaneous operation. This may be true for cars, but it doesn't work for humans and language. Research in linguistics and psychology, reading, and composition shows us quite clearly that language is a matter of synthesis, of simultaneous operations, not discrete parts in some linear order. We use language holistically; therefore, we should not approach teaching language through discrete parts. Nor can we assume mastery at a particular grade level, or at all, for that matter.

Some textbook series offer an "auto parts catalogue" scope and sequence, a detailed chart showing the introduction, review, and mastery of every concept and skill in the English language arts curriculum. Districts that use such series as the basis of their curriculum thus subscribe to a "part to whole" theory of instruction. Well-informed teachers take issue with this approach, understanding that it violates how students learn in the English language arts, although not necessarily in other subject areas more amenable to a "building block" or linear curriculum.

A SPIRAL CURRICULUM

The language arts do not represent linear learning, or as James Moffett and Betty Jane Wagner put it, growth is not a ladder or stepping stones, metaphors that imply we leave old learning behind as we acquire new. "Most learning is never shed but, rather, becomes assimilated or transformed into more advanced skills and knowledge" (3). A spiral more closely reflects the learning process; it's a concept that has been around for a long time but not generally applied to curriculum in the English language arts. Jerome Bruner, one of the most influential cognitive psychologists of our time, argues that any concept can be taught in an intellectually honest way at any time. In the English language arts we can do exactly that with a spiral curriculum: At every level of the curriculum K–12, we can work with the same concept or skill, regardless of the level of student development. However, we do so with increasing sophistication based on advanced levels of development; we do not, as some textbooks suggest, repeat the same lesson.

Composition is a good example. The concept of audience is quite difficult for primary age students; they simply aren't mature enough to see much beyond themselves. We might refer to audience, asking the child to consider what someone who has never been to the ocean might want to know, for example. But we would not expect the child to handle audience very well. By early adolescence, however, students are much better able to conceive of audience and can entertain more than one point of view. In late adolescence, students can handle multiple points of view, understand the significance of audience in written communication, and can more readily manipulate language to respond to audience, no matter how remote it might be. Our focus, emphasis, and expectations of what students can do with the concept of audience thus shifts.

In parallel fashion, aspects of literature are understood developmentally and returned to again and again. We teach literary character at all levels of the curriculum, but the expected level of response and understanding changes markedly from primary level students to those in senior high. For example, middle schoolers, limited by their experience and maturation, tend to understand characters' actions and responses in rather absolute terms. Juniors and seniors, however, generally can understand and respond to complex characters, an emerging range of emotions and motivations, and consequences resulting from beliefs and behavior. We would choose material, then, based on this knowledge and on the need to return again and again to a more sophisticated handling of character in literature. What we teach changes both in degree and range, and we choose literary materials that match the concepts being taught and that bring students to an increasingly complex level of understanding and response.

Thus, in a spiral curriculum, we return to concepts and skills in developmentally appropriate ways, understanding our students are maturing physically, emotionally, and intellectually. We expect students to grow in independence, to achieve greater control over these concepts and skills, and we gear our materials and teaching appropriately. In evaluating students, we expect the majority to demonstrate greater understanding and to articulate it more clearly and thoroughly than younger students. We would not, however, expect uniform understanding and performance.

CASE 3–4

Is There a Spiral Here?

With a group of classmates, read though the following guide questions and sample curriculum. Then, divide the tasks as if you were members of a committee revising the district's English language arts curriculum. Assume that you represent different curricular levels (i.e., 7th, 10th, and 12th/AP English).

SAMPLE LITERATURE CURRICULUM

GRADE LEVEL: ENGLISH/GRADE 7
UNIT OF STUDY: THE NOVEL
Expectations: Students will be able to:

1. Read and react to the novel as a form of literature.
2. Experience the enjoyment of reading fiction.
3. Experience "life" through reading literature.
4. Interpret and relate what they read to their own lives.

Suggested Activities:

1. Do a prereading/prewriting activity.
2. Do sustained silent reading of the novel.
3. Prepare a chronology or write in journal to highlight the main action or characters.
4. Study vocabulary.
5. Create a chapter.
6. Discuss the novel in groups.
7. "Picture" what they read.
8. React in writing to the reading.
9. Research a topic or issue in reading.

Resources:

The Outsiders S. E. Hinton
The Pigman Paul Zindel
Hatchet Gary Paulson
Julie of the Wolves Jean Craighead George
Island of the Blue Dolphins Scott O'Dell

Evaluation:

1. Teacher observation
2. Checklist
3. Conferencing
4. Student log
5. Objective tests
6. Writing folder
7. Oral report
8. Written report

GRADE LEVEL: SURVEY OF AMERICAN LITERATURE/GRADE 10
UNIT OF STUDY: THE NOVEL
Expectations: Students will be able to:

1. Develop an interest in reading as a leisure activity.
2. Recognize and appreciate literary material that is part of our heritage and culture.
3. Identify the correspondence between literature and historical events.
4. Use literature as a vehicle for understanding prejudices and stereotypes.
5. Improve vocabulary skills by using context clues.

Suggested Activities:

1. Discuss reading.
2. Lecture on novel.
3. Have students keep a list of unfamiliar words in reading assignments; spend a few minutes each day asking about lists and reviewing context clues.
4. Have students compose a description/character sketch of Jem or Scout 30 years after the trial.
5. View the movie version of the novel *To Kill a Mockingbird.*
6. For less capable students, list differences in the plot of the novel and the movie.
7. Include directed historical readings from teacher-made list.

Resources:

To Kill a Mockingbird Harper Lee

Video

Evaluation:

1. Discussion, both teacher-led and student-led
2. Tests
3. Book reports

GRADE LEVEL: ADVANCED PLACEMENT/GRADE 12

UNIT OF STUDY: THE NOVEL

Expectations: Students will be able to:

1. Listen critically during class discussion.
2. Understand the elements of the novel.
3. Understand the novel's themes and universal truths.
4. Understand the motivation of characters.
5. Apply critical thinking skills in discussion.
6. Read a variety of "great" novels.
7. Develop a vocabulary through systematic class and group discussion.
8. Respond to issues and ideas raised in reading and discussion.
9. Use the process approach to writing about literature.

Suggested Activities:

1. Assign novels for summer reading. The first reading is to be completed before the school year begins; rereading is assigned at time of class discussion.

   Pride and Prejudice Jane Austen

   Wuthering Heights Emily Bronte

   Heart of Darkness Joseph Conrad

   An American Tragedy Theodore Dreiser

   Invisible Man Ralph Ellison

   The Great Gatsby F. Scott Fitzgerald

   Fathers and Sons Ivan Turgenev

or others from the advanced placement reading list

2. Lecture and discuss each novel to review its elements and history.

3. Before rereading novel, review the period (e.g., Classical, Romantic, Realism, or Modern) in which each novel was written to develop students' consciousness of language and style.
4. Distribute a vocabulary list for each novel as assigned.
5. Emphasize that students must support their answers with specific passages.
6. Assign a double-entry reading log.

Resources: Novels listed and others from the advanced placement reading list
Evaluation:
1. Class discussion
2. Reading log
3. Objective tests
4. Vocabulary tests
5. Essay test
6. Assigned essay

1. What does the term *spiral curriculum* mean when you consider one of the novels in these units from the perspective of a 7th grader, a 10th grader, and a 12th grader? Does *spiral* have meaning in all three domains: cognitive, affective, and skills?

2. For 7th, 10th, and advanced 12th graders, decide on some basic learner outcomes for a unit centered on a novel. For example, what could you reasonably expect a 7th grader to understand about character development? An advanced placement 12th grader? You'll make some adjustments in these outcomes later. For now, just think in general terms of what you want students to understand about the novel.

3. What do you think of the novels available for each level? Do you see any parallels in themes or plots that would cause you to adjust your learner outcomes? Would you select different novels? For example, the 10th-grade novel *To Kill a Mockingbird* suggests themes of prejudice, injustice, and stereotyping. Will the themes of the 7th-grade novels prepare students for examining these themes in the 10th-grade novel? Does it matter?

4. The question "Does it matter?" probably makes you realize that you don't know the district's overall goals for English language arts. But suppose the statement of goals includes these:

Students will understand major literary themes (e.g., the loss of innocence, rites of passage, prejudice, and injustice).

Students will be able to find relevance in what they read, that is, relate literary themes to their own lives and the world around them.

    a. How does your knowledge of these broad curricular goals guide your instructional choices as you build specific parts of the curriculum at the various grade levels?

b. How does this knowledge guide your decisions about which novels to require and to recommend? Return to the list of novels at each grade level and make your recommendations.

c. How does the spiral curriculum translate into methods (suggested activities)? Into evaluation? Pick one learner outcome and design at least two activities that would allow students to develop the desired knowledge or skills. Then note possible assessment strategies. How will you know if students are making progress toward that outcome?

Keep in mind these simple but effective curricular questions: What are the kids doing? What is it good for? How do you know?

ANOTHER CURRICULAR TERM: TRACKING

However much we might talk about "providing for individual differences," tracking at best exists for the benefit of teachers and the listening/busy work mode. At worst, tracking allows us to blame students for our failure to teach them well—all those low-tracked adolescents of whom we ask and expect less and less. (Atwell 40)

The Dangers of Tracking

Tracking, sometimes referred to as ability grouping, is a serious curricular issue that has a powerful effect on students. There are polarized points of view about this effect, despite research indicating that tracking is largely negative (Oakes; Gamoran and Berends; Good and Brophy; Maerhoff; Berliner and Rosenshine; cited in George n.p.). John Goodlad's study of American schools also pointed to the negative effects of tracking:

Findings revealed significant differences in curricular content, instructional practices, and elements of the student-teacher relationship. They suggest the probabilities of marked inequities among students in regard to access to knowledge and pedagogical practices. (152)

Goodlad goes on to address another issue within tracking, that the distribution of students shows a disproportionately high percent of minority students, especially where they are also economically poor, in low-track classes. Goodlad concludes that these students' access to knowledge is thus considerably limited (159). James Moffett and Betty Jane Wagner agree. In their view, segregating slower students or students whose language or dialect is different from the mainstream also causes *all* students to suffer from a lack of variety in their classes; it also produces negativism among students in the lower track and elitism in the higher track (38). Ernest Boyer's 1983 report on secondary education in America concludes that:

> Putting students into boxes can no longer be defended. To call some students "academic" and others "nonacademic" has a powerful, and in some instances, devastating impact on how teachers think about students and how students think about themselves. (126)

These educators, and others, are not suggesting that students of like interest or ability should *never* be grouped—only that creating a tracking system in which students go for years labeled as "slow," "regular" and "advanced" is a bad idea.

Why Tracking Persists

We can easily understand how this practice not only came into being but sustains itself. Paul George explains:

> Faced with a dizzying array of differences among the students they attempt to teach, educators have struggled with ways to reduce these differences and make teaching more effective. One very common, and "common sense," way of dealing with these differences has been to divide students into class-size groups based on a measure of the students' perceived ability or prior achievement, and then design or deliver differentiated learning experiences to each group. (n.p.)

Despite, as George points out, the appeal and apparent sensible goals (e.g., teaching and learning would be more effective and less frustrating), ability grouping simply doesn't work out that well for most students. Why not? First, because it is very difficult to place students accurately and fairly. Due to their construction and their bias of race, gender, and social class, tests are often poor indicators of actual ability. This is particularly true for language skills.

The Power of Expectations

A second problem with tracking and ability grouping is the lack of expected achievement for students at all levels. Citing recent research studies on academic achievement, George, notes that the "expected benefits . . . simply do not materialize . . . at the secondary level; when differences occur, the results are favorable only to students in the highest tracks" (n.p.).

Research findings indicated that bright students were not held back by being in heterogeneously mixed classes, nor were the deficiencies of less capable students more easily remediated in homogeneously grouped classes (Oakes 8, cited in George n.p.). In addressing the third problem with tracking, George notes:

> If the academic gains from tracking are negligible, we could hope that the affective outcomes are positive enough to justify the practice. Unfortunately, this does not appear to be the case. The weight of the research evidence indicates that the effect of tracking on individuals and classroom groups, affectively, is often *powerfully negative,* especially for students in lower tracks. (n.p.)

Ted Sizer, Director of Research for the Coalition of Essential Schools, believes that because kids are always changing, "tracking flies in the face of rudimentary common sense," and can be both "profoundly cruel and wasteful of talent." His point is well taken when we consider how rapidly middle school students develop within a couple of years and how acutely they respond to a sense of being "different." Self-esteem, once bruised, is difficult to restore. Senior high school students also show remarkable growth between their sophomore and senior years; placing them into a three-year curricular track based on performance at age 14 or 15 is questionable.

Why Tracking Is Unnecessary

Tracking seems particularly unnecessary in the English language arts. If the curriculum is learner-centered, process-oriented, and integrated, students *can* work at varying levels of achievement within a heterogeneous group. Cooperative learning groups provide less capable students the opportunity to learn from their more talented peers in a less competitive environment. Similarly, very capable students can learn important "people" skills within heterogeneous learning groups. All students have talent of some type, and that talent is more likely to flourish in groups where diversity is valued and cooperation is needed to accomplish the task. In an increasingly pluralistic society, students need exactly that perspective.

At times, smaller in-class groups would provide for individual differences. More capable students unquestionably need to be challenged and less capable ones given more time and more assistance. However, these are matters of diverse curricular resources and teaching strategies. Building diversity, flexibility, and reality into lessons is critically important. The expectation that each student can learn from one another and from their teachers is similarly critical.

THE "FEEL GOOD" CURRICULUM*

The expectation that each student can learn is critical for teachers. Both research and common sense tell us that motivation and subsequent achievement depend on the students' belief that they are capable of learning. However, in middle schools, a recent curricular trend, which places excessive emphasis on self-esteem, undermines these commonsense ideas. This emphasis is certainly a reaction against purely cognitive or skills-based curricula; the result has been curricula aimed at students' affective nature. There is, of course, merit in recognizing student interests, feelings, and response as an important factor in learning. We believe in them, too, especially with adolescents. However, a balance among cognitive, affective, and skills-based goals is absolutely necessary. To base nearly all instruction on whether students will "feel good" about themselves while learning is dangerous. A purely affective curriculum, also known as

---

*Adapted from Meiser (29–32).

the "feel good" curriculum, can leave students without the content knowledge, experience, and skills so critical to their academic development and future.

Intuition tells us that kids need self-esteem to succeed in school and in life. Consequently, we must remember that we are teaching kids, not just where to put a comma. However, we believe that self-esteem comes from authentic learning and achievement, both of which are the by-products of an interesting and developmentally appropriate curriculum that involves kids in their own learning. Kids do not need little buttons on their lapels (real or imagined) saying "I am special." Rather, they need well-educated and thoughtful teachers who can design a curriculum that tells them every day "you count."

How do kids know that they count?

- When we design curriculum that stems from their heartfelt interests and concerns as young adolescents
- When we provide them with choices and believe in their ability to make decisions about their own learning
- When we encourage them to work together on assignments and projects, trusting them to share and learn from each other
- When our lessons and assignments challenge them to think and when we believe in their ability to do so
- When we reward them for taking risks and making mistakes, thereby showing them the measure and reality of their growth
- When we let them know that just sitting in a desk and not making trouble no longer counts for a grade, but that achievement in specific content and skills does count.

In brief, kids know they count when their skills are appropriately challenged, when content is not rehashed and boring, and when our lessons consider individual differences and build a scaffold for achievement. Our problem with the middle school "feel good" curriculum lies in its lack of substance, its potential for gimmickry, and most of all, the belief that one cannot simply talk kids into feeling good. Unfortunately, saying "you're special" doesn't make it so, especially in an adolescent's complex inner world or in a home and community that sends some of them to school hungry, tired, abused, scared, and defeated.

Noted educator Alfie Kohn, writing in *Phi Delta Kappan* magazine, addressed this curricular issue in a provocative article entitled "The Truth About Self-Esteem." In it, Kohn noted that research does not support any meaningful relationship between self-esteem and student performance; that is, there's no reason to believe that higher self-esteem causes academic performance to rise. Kohn suggests that the reverse is probably true: Kids feel good about themselves because they are doing well in school. At the same time, Kohn makes an important point. If the evidence doesn't support claims that curricula intended to help kids feel good about themselves are likely to raise academic achievement, it seems equally clear that the Old School approach, "learning is bitter medicine" (which Kohn describes as skills and drills) is even worse.

If neither the Old School approach nor the "I am special" curriculum works, then what does? That, says Kohn, depends on our objectives. If we care about authentic learning, then we should help kids focus on effort rather than ability, to become absorbed in their learning and tasks at hand. Kohn believes we can facilitate learning through the "three C's of motivation: collaboration, choice, and content" (281). And these are part of each teacher's instructional plan for implementing the curriculum.

Kohn states: "Students do not come to believe they are important, valued, and capable just because they are told this is so"; instead, they "acquire a sense of significance from doing significant things, from being active participants in their own education" (282). This, we believe, is the real "feel good" curriculum, one intimately linked to good content. Without content, just what are those "significant things"?

We would argue that few areas lend themselves as well to adolescent growth and development, adolescent interests, and adolescent concerns as the English language arts. Literature written for young adults directly addresses the issues faced by kids: questions of identity, sexual awareness, relationships, and racial, social, and gender differences. Within literature, kids can try out personas, evaluate motivation and action, and weigh decisions. In the most nonthreatening ways, they can delve into the heart of growing up and gain a better understanding of themselves and others. And they have plenty to respond to in their reading—if we give them the chance to say it and choices about how to do so.

Composition is another avenue for adolescents to grow and develop, allowing for collaboration, sharing, and good talk—things close to the adolescent heart. Speaking and listening, informal classroom drama, puppets, and masks all offer many forms for adolescent expression that meet the needs of the shyest to the most outgoing. If adolescent interests and concerns fall largely on themselves and if adolescent needs fall largely on "active," the English language arts curriculum can meet all of these needs—if only we design it with that in mind. As careful and caring curriculum designers and classroom planners, we surely will provide our students with ways to feel good about being a kid in school, a kid that counts. In that sense, we do have a "feel good" curriculum, but one based on authentic content and achievement.

THE INTEGRATED CURRICULUM

Speaking, Listening, Reading, and Writing

A curriculum built on current research and effective practice in English language arts will reflect realities of adolescent growth and development and portray the language arts as active, interdependent processes linked to experience and purpose. Students gain competency and proficiency in language through use. Students who listen, speak, read, and write will gain immeasurably over those who don't. Students who see the language arts as critical to their experience and to the meaning that they themselves are creating will not only use but value them. It is imperative, then, that students do use *all* the language arts in an integrated fashion.

Integrated can be viewed in several ways. Integration of the language arts strands (listening, speaking, reading, and writing) in every lesson, not in separate units, is usually the primary definition of the term. As indicated many times in this text, such integration is essential if we expect students to become competent and confident in their oral and written language abilities. In planning lessons, then, teachers must consciously devise activities that ask students to read, write, speak, and listen, regardless of the primary emphasis in one of these areas. We will address this more fully when we talk about individual planning and thematic units.

The Language Arts and Other Disciplines

Sometimes, when educators talk about integrating curriculum, they are referring to different subject areas being linked with language arts. Writing across the curriculum or language across the curriculum are common applications of this idea. In elementary schools, teachers have an advantage in that they often control all subject areas, thus making integration less complicated. Many middle schools also plan integrated instruction. Teachers from the core areas (e.g., language arts, mathematics, social studies, and science) plan together, consciously blending knowledge and skills from one area with those of another. In math or science, for example, students may be required to keep a journal, to write out their problem solving; in social studies, students may use informal classroom drama as a way of understanding point of view.

Because senior high school teachers most often view themselves as content specialists (i.e., the math teacher, the history teacher), they also tend to view reading and writing as the instructional responsibility of the English teacher. Consequently, integration among content areas in senior high is more often the work of individual teachers rather than a schoolwide curricular design. Sizer, a national leader in school reform, believes the lack of integration in secondary schools is a kind of "intellectual chaos" (n.p.). Students move from bell to bell, hitting the curriculum horizontally in 52-minute snippets. Sizer questions the potential for any authentic intellectual and imaginative work in such a fragmented environment. Sizer argues that in most traditional schools, students experience neither the logical connections among various courses nor a time frame for exploration and reflection.

Some secondary English teachers do an excellent job of bringing history, art, and music into their units, largely because these areas blend so well with literature. Working with science or mathematics, however, is far less common. The language arts offer a powerful means of discovering and applying knowledge and diversifying and individualizing instruction. A curricular goal of integration is one worth pursuing.

BOX 3–4

"STARRY, STARRY NIGHT . . ."

While browsing through some young adult novel titles, you come across one that is linked to art, Bennett's *Deathman, Do Not Follow Me.* The jacket cover tells you that the adventure involves the theft of a Van Gogh painting, *Starry Night,* from the Metropolitan

Museum of Art. When you think about the bold colors and interesting brush strokes of Van Gogh's works, you also think your eighth graders might be interested in them as a basis for descriptive writing. The idea for a unit starts to take shape.

1. How would you use art slides (whether of Van Gogh paintings or those of another artist) in your unit? What kind of activities (viewing, listening, speaking, writing) could your eighth graders do? How would you account for the range of abilities and interests in your class?
2. What fiction and nonfiction might you include in a unit linking art and language arts?
3. How might you also use music in this unit?
4. What kind of creative activities (art, music, drama) might students do? Again, think of the diverse backgrounds, interests, and learning abilities (ranging from gifted to disengaged) of the students in your class.
5. How does linking art with English enhance learning for a diverse group of eighth graders? How does this integration maximize the participation of students with special needs (e.g., disabled, ESL)? How does it challenge the most gifted students?
6. How might you use the expertise of an art instructor?

Student Needs and Interests

Another aspect of integration is placing student needs and interests into the curriculum. How do we know what our students' needs and interests are? How do we find out? Similar questions need to be asked about integrating school with home and community. James Moffett and Betty Jane Wagner explain the significance:

> A human being is made to synthesize all forms of experience into one harmoniously functioning whole. If experience is too incoherent to integrate, we may mentally or physically negate what we can't assimilate, as when some students tune out or drop out of school because they cannot fit it into the rest of their life. (36)

When we think about classes where we tuned out and ask why, several reasons come to mind. Were we consistently bored? If so, the materials and instructional approaches probably weren't connecting with our needs and interests. Were we lost? If so, the materials and instructional approaches weren't connecting with our level of understanding or background knowledge. Then we need to consider how a marginal student would feel. Already disconnected with much of the educational process, this student could quite easily sever the tie altogether. "Marginal," incidentally can refer to students academically gifted, as well as to those academically disadvantaged or disabled in some way.

Moffett and Wagner extend the idea of connecting:

> Schools must accept widely varying dialects, lifestyles, values, and ethnic heritages. A student takes both home and school seriously. If they are made to conflict, he is caught in the middle and has to reject one or disguise the conflict from himself. Either choice is terrible education. (36)

Into a curriculum, we put not only concepts, skills, and topics but also attitudes. If a district ignores multicultural literature, for example, it ignores a body of literature representing many students and fails to prepare *all* students for a world in which diverse cultures must unite to solve common problems and achieve common goals. Districts or individual teachers who refuse to use adolescent fiction are ignoring student needs and interests. Exclusions such as these tell us something about the district, as well as individual teachers. Failure to integrate academic experience with adolescence experience most often translates into students who either skim through the curriculum simply because they are bright and can play the academic game or students who disconnect altogether. Either way, students lose.

BOX 3–5

MADNESS, MURDER, AND MUTINY . . .

As part of a middle school team (English, science, social studies, and math), you are expected to make connections across the curriculum. You find it easy to integrate language arts and social studies, mainly because you know many good young adult novels with a historical base. But these historical novels must speak to the very center of young adolescent life: questions of identity and growing up. How will 1990s adolescents relate to adolescents of other centuries? Very nicely, you think. So you list titles that would be appropriate for middle schoolers and prepare to meet with your team.

1. What kind of team planning would be involved in an interdisciplinary unit?
2. How would you prefer to structure procedures within the group (e.g., with or without a designated team leader)? How do you think an interdisciplinary team would best function? What would be your role as the English language arts teacher?
3. Of the many good historical novels, you really like Avi's novel, *The True Confessions of Charlotte Doyle,* with its female heroine in a totally male world aboard a ship sailing from England to America. Intrigue and action fill every page. Its themes of stereotyping, finding one's strength, identity, and independence will give students plenty to discuss. The social studies teacher agrees that the novel is appropriate for a centerpiece of study about the mid-nineteenth century. Speculate how the two of you would plan.
4. You realize that math and science would also work into the unit. The sailing vessel, voyage, supplies, and stores of food and water could easily lend themselves to concepts in those two disciplines. How would you proceed with planning for the unit at this point?
5. Your team has read the novel. Your concern now is the range of your students' reading abilities. How will you meet that challenge?
6. Your next concern is the group of students who appear consistently "on the fringe." Although some of these students have learning difficulties, many more are simply disengaged from school for reasons that have nothing to do with ability. How can you get these students to participate in this unit? How can working with an interdisciplinary team help you?

A K–12 Perspective

Because we teach specific grade levels, it is easy to forget the importance of viewing the curriculum from a K–12 perspective. For this reason, we have been noting how important it is for a consistent approach to the English language arts. Students who are accustomed to writing in a student-centered, integrated language arts approach, for example, would be jolted by a skill-and-drill approach to writing. A colleague recently told of his nephew's experience with inconsistency. All through junior high school, the student was accustomed to a writing workshop. Global concerns with content took precedence over surface errors; evaluation involved all aspects of composing, not just editing skill. In 10th grade, this student suddenly faced error as the sole determination of his grade. His teacher ignored the development and organization of his work and graded him on his performance in avoiding certain types of syntactical or mechanical errors, usually three per essay. The student was understandably upset and questioned this approach. The response: "Oh, you'll get graded on other things next year."

In a district where teachers work together to develop, implement, and maintain the curriculum, this incongruity is less likely to happen; in such a district, dialogue among teachers in K–12 would bring the various perspectives and knowledge base into focus. Teachers at all levels of the curriculum vary in their level of professional knowledge, creativity, personality, and style. Given these variations, we value some colleagues more than others; we must be careful, however, not to dismiss colleagues at a lower level of the curriculum. The first-grade teacher may provide the best teaching strategies in the district. Respecting every level of the English language arts curriculum and learning the challenges specific to each level can only enhance our own teaching.

Needed Dialogue

In a recent course in a suburban school district, elementary and middle school teachers discussed, debated, and challenged senior high teachers on some critical issues: teaching parts of speech, drills, and diagramming sentences. The middle school teachers in particular were very well informed about research and current practice. The secondary teachers were in a state of dissonance, knowing what they were doing wasn't good practice but not quite ready to give it up altogether. Since none of the teachers had worked on curriculum together, this course was their first K–12 forum. One of the middle school teachers, feeling particularly frustrated, told a high school teacher: "The *only* reason I even use or work with grammatical terms is because you [high school] insist kids know them. Even though it doesn't make any difference in writing and takes up time." The high school teacher was startled by this candid declaration but not offended, and from that point on, real dialogue over a critical curricular issue took place. The middle school teacher couldn't understand why high school teachers insisted on a practice that has been proven ineffective; the high school teachers had no idea that anyone was upset about it. Students deserve a consistent and coherent theory of instruction, from teachers who have figured out what students need to learn and how they will best learn it.

Exploring an Instructional Unit

In previous chapters, we laid the foundation for curriculum and instruction as we discussed just what the English language arts are and how contemporary class-rooms reflect them. We also talked about keeping adolescent needs and interests at the heart of curriculum and instruction. In this chapter, we have painted cur-riculum and instruction with rather broad strokes; we want you to have the "big picture" before we talk about specific planning for units and daily lessons.

But first, we would like you to explore the concepts presented thus far through Amy Henquinet's unit, "A Look into the Future." We have removed Amy's statements about why she chose certain materials and activities, as well as any references to her goals and objectives. We would like you to figure them out for yourself and evaluate Amy's unit for middle schoolers.

As you read Amy's unit, look for the following:

1. What are Amy's goals? Do they address cognitive, affective, and skills areas? Is one area stressed more than others? Is Amy concerned about student interaction?
2. What does Amy want her students to learn, to understand, or to be able to do better as a result of this unit? In other words, what are her objectives or learner outcomes?
3. What material has she selected? What activities has she planned? What princi-ples of teaching English language arts are guiding her decisions?
4. Has Amy provided for students with varying ability levels? Are all of her materials and activities appropriate for the seventh grade? Are her extra resource materials appropriate? Should she include any of them in the unit? Why or why not?
5. Has Amy considered student interests and needs as she planned? How do you know?
6. Has Amy demonstrated awareness of ethnic and cultural differences among her students? How might she use such differences within her theme of "the future"?
7. Does Amy's time frame of two weeks seem about right for the activities planned? Does her sequence of events seem logical for 12- to 13-year-olds?

Amy's unit was developed during one of her English language arts methods courses. She wrote it as a narrative, with a great deal of reflection about why she had chosen certain materials and activities. Because we would like *you* to reflect on these things, we have presented only the bare essentials here, but in Amy's sequence.

A Look into the Future: 2014

Grade Level: Middle School/Grade 7

This unit focuses on the future in terms of how people, including the students, view it and how they fit into it. Not only will students have a chance to analyze their own future and think about where they will be in the years to come, but they will also have a chance to explore how the world could or possibly will be.

Overview: The first week of the unit will deal with the future as broadly as possible. We will begin with a discussion of what the future actually means and continue to explore it through various activities. We will look at all aspects of the future, such as technology, education, recreation, entertainment, government, and more. Then, the last part of the unit will focus on students looking at their own future.

Introductory Activity: Students brainstorm the meaning of the term *future*; they work in pairs before engaging in a whole-class discussion.

Reading: Students read *Timequake* by Robert Lee. Two young adults are caught in a timequake while on a canoe trip and thrown forward to the year 2027. They discover a United States run by state police, where food is rationed and computers design death. The book is 151 pages long and students will have a week to read it.

Writing: Cover metaphors. Teacher mini-lesson with paragraph models (e.g., the future is a giant roller coaster; future is a gigantic dice game). A whole-class brainstorming activity is followed by choice of writing activity: (a) write a metaphor paragraph similar to the models; (b) shape metaphor into a list poem; (c) create a drawing to express a metaphor.

Viewing: View film *2010* (3 class periods); *Star Trek* is another possibility. Compare and contrast book and film ideas of future.

Activity: The book and movie challenge students to think about "what would happen if?" Therefore, the next activity involves students in creating their own "what if?" questions. Students will place questions in a box and draw them out for individual response and class discussion.

Activity: Students will create their own utopia within their classroom, the year 2014 (3 class periods). Allow 30 to 35 minutes of group work and 15 to 20 minutes of whole-class discussion daily. As a class, students will create a map, model, or collage of a futuristic cityscape. Then in small groups of their choice, they will each have a different task (e.g., one group may choose entertainment, another government, money, work, clothing, housing, or technology).

Reading: Each group will receive short stories (*New Destinies* by Jim Baen) of speculation about the future. However, the groups must come up with their own speculations.

Activity: Students will engage in whole-class discussions (15 to 20 minutes) in which each group updates the others on their progress.

Writing: Students will collaboratively write a short story developed from small-group ideas (e.g., one on future government, another on future entertainment, education, and technology). These stories will be published as part of the group's evaluation.

Writing: Students will keep a journal in which they reflect on their own ideas, on the group work, or on other aspects of the lesson. Journals will be checked but not graded.

Activity: Teacher reads *I Had Trouble Getting to Solla Sollew* by Dr. Seuss. Students work in pairs to decide strengths and weaknesses of life in this world or in the future they imagined. A whole-class discussion follows.

Activity: Students role-play concerning some invention. Students will receive informational handouts about inventions that are common today (e.g., forks, cola drinks, chewing gum, zippers, Christmas cards). Students work in groups to develop and present their invention to the class, with all group members actively involved. Evaluation by peers and teacher is based on clarity, interest, and cooperation.

Sample Handout

You are the marketing vice president of a large company, New Age Unlimited. Your group has just developed a revolutionary new item that has the potential for use in many households in the year 2014. You must prepare a description and visual presentation of the product to distribute to the board of trustees at the next national sales meeting.

Be sure to include the following details:

1. Name of product
2. Reasons for inventing the product
3. Extraordinary characteristics
4. Selling points
5. Comparison to other products currently available
6. Production/assembly of product

Be ready to defend your product!

Activity: Students can choose to work alone or in groups of three to invent a product for the year 2014. Each student has a role within the group: production, marketing, or creating ads. The teacher will create a board of trustees (students not in the class if possible) before which products are presented; a prize will be awarded to the top three, each group having decided the award it should win (e.g., candy bar or soda, extra credit).

Writing Activity: Students create a futuristic newspaper (1 week). Students will choose a group based on the type of newspaper role desired: news, editorials, sports, entertainment, advertising/graphics, editing, and design/layout. The teacher will guide each group, ultimately assigning a group grade for the project.

Mini-Lesson: News writing. Models from newspapers and *Omni* magazine.

Activity: Groups will spend one week writing and revising their contributions to the futuristic newspaper.

ADDITIONAL RESOURCES

The following books are examples of fiction that relates to the theme of the future:

A Dark Traveling Roger Zelazny

Fireflood and Other Stories Vonda McIntyre

God's Grace Bernard Malamud

The Integral Trees Larry Niven

My Trip to Alpha I Alfred Slote

Ringworld Larry Niven

The following books are examples of utopias/dystopias:

Fahrenheit 451 Ray Bradbury

Brave New World Aldous Huxley

Animal Farm George Orwell

The Handmaid's Tale Margaret Atwood

The Giver Lois Lowry

QUESTIONS ABOUT AMY'S UNIT

1. All teachers, no matter how experienced, need both self-reflective and peer response. Further, they need student response. Without it, we can't really answer an important question: How am I doing? And that question is linked to others: How are the kids doing? What could be better here? How could I make this unit or lesson more effective? More fun? With this in mind, what would you tell Amy about her lesson? What do you see as strengths? As areas for change? With a partner or small group, evaluate Amy's unit. Provide specific reasons for your comments and suggestions. On what are you basing your praise or "protest"?

2. With a partner or small group, discuss additional resources for Amy's unit. What reading materials might young adolescents enjoy? Are videos available on this theme? Check with your school or public library specialist in young adult literature if you are unfamiliar with this fiction for this theme.

REFERENCES

Assumptions, Aims, and Recommendations of the Secondary Strand. Comp. George B. Shea, Jr. English Coalition Conference. Urbana: National Council of Teachers of English, n.d.

Atwell, Nancie. *In the Middle: Writing, Reading, and Learning With Adolescents.* Portsmouth: Boynton/Cook, 1987.

Avi. *The True Confessions of Charlotte Doyle.* New York: Avon, 1990.

Boyer, Ernest L. *High School: A Report on Secondary Education in America.* New York: Harper, 1983.

Bruner, Jerome S. *Toward a Theory of Instruction.* Cambridge: Harvard UP, 1966.

Committee on Instructional Technology. *Guidelines for Review and Evaluation of English Language Arts Software.* Urbana: National Council of Teachers of English, n.d.

"Cultural Kaleidoscope." *McNeil/Lehrer News Hour.* 28 Nov. 1991.

English Coalition Conference. *The Essentials of Education: A Call for Dialogue and Action.* Urbana: National Council of Teachers of English, n.d.

George, Paul S. *What's the Truth About Tracking and Ability Grouping: Really?* Gainsville, FL: Teacher Education Resources, 1986.

Goodlad, John I. *A Place Called School.* New York: McGraw-Hill, 1984.

Gursky, Daniel. "The Unschooled Mind." *Teacher Magazine* Dec. 1991: 39–44.

Henquinet, Amy. "A Look at the Future: 2014." English 406/606. Spring 1995. Eau Claire: University of Wisconsin.

Hitchens, Craig. Personal Interview. 14 Apr. 1991.

Judy [Tchudi], Stephen. *The ABC'S of Literacy: A Guide for Parents and Teachers.* New York: Oxford UP, 1980.

Kohn, Alfi. "The Truth About Self-Esteem." *Phi Delta Kappan Magazine* Dec. 1994: 272–82.

Lightfoot, Nik. Personal Interview. 8 Aug. 1991.

"Mandated Sex Education." [Letter to the Editor]. *Leader-Telegram* 8 Nov. 1991. Eau Claire, WI.

McNeil, John. "Foreword." Eds. Kathleen M. Wulf and Barbara Schave. *Curriculum Design: A Handbook for Educators.* Glenview: Scott, Foresman, 1984.

Meiser, Mary. "The Feel Good Curriculum." *Wisconsin English Journal* Spring 1995: 28–32.

Moffett, James. *Coming on Center: English Education in Evolution.* Portsmouth: Boynton/Cook Heinemann, 1981.

Moffett, James, and Wagner, Betty Jane. *Student-Centered Language Arts and Reading K–13: A Handbook for Teachers.* 2nd ed. Boston: Houghton Mifflin, 1976.

Shanahan, Timothy, and Knight, Lester. "Guidelines for Judging and Selecting Language Arts Textbooks: A Modest Proposal." *NCTE Concepts Paper No. 1.* Urbana: National Council of Teachers of English, 1991.

Sizer, Theodore R. "School Restructuring. University Summer Forum: What Do We Want From Our Schools?" Madison, WI, 18 June 1991.

Wisconsin Department of Public Instruction. *Guide to Curriculum Planning in the English Language Arts.* Madison: Department of Public Instruction, 1986.

4

Individual Planning

Good teaching consists of the making and adjusting of day to day plans and depends upon a delicate balance between rational order and intuitive spontaneity.

Editorial Staff, *The English Journal*

Effective teachers plan well, laying out units and daily lessons designed to provide their students with a coherent course of study. Despite this, they face days when the reality of teaching and dealing with students with diverse and complex needs defies even the best planning. Teaching is more complex, more unpredictable than we like to admit. As Joseph McDonald, a 17-year teaching veteran, succinctly summarizes it: "Teaching is a messy, uncertain business" (54). McDonald voices what many experienced teachers feel: that experience allows them to cope with uncertainty—not eliminate it. He depicts what he calls a "wild triangle of relations—among teacher, students and the subject—whose dimensions continually shift" at the core of teaching. Consequently, he believes, teachers rarely have "clean evidence" of what is happening both to themselves and to their students. He notes that

> Technique, however proved by research and practice, however skillful the application—is always hostage to so much else: the appearance of spring in the air or a bee in the room, the complicated chemistry of a roomful of humans constructing meaning together, the extent to which the conditions of their lives outside the room that day weigh on any of them that day. (54)

Like McDonald, we believe that "beginning teachers are astounded by these complexities and may try to pretend them away" (54). There is no magic answer to the complexity, other than expecting it.

No matter how well we plan, we cannot eliminate all of the variables in how and when people learn. If we need a rule of thumb for dealing with the inevitable clash between reality and our planning, it would be "go with the reality." Even with 18-year-olds, the sight of a wasp swooping around the lights causes a lesson to cease. The loss of five minutes is hardly cause for alarm. Neither is a lesson that "bombs," for whatever reason. No matter how experienced we become, we will always be confronted with situations that are not planned and certainly not hoped for. Despite good planning, many aspects of teaching are trial and error. The saving grace of that is experience. The more we have, the more confidence we gain. Consequently, we are far less likely to be either totally surprised or devastated by events or people that may sweep in and destroy our carefully designed plans. Sometimes, we unwittingly sabotage our own lessons by not thinking through our expectations against the framework of student interest or ability.

I vividly recall having done just that, despite 12 years of teaching experience. Working with creation myths, I asked students to compare how various ancient cultures viewed the act of creation (i.e., a creator, creation of the world). Although I provided the students with a structure through which to examine the myths, most students had a great deal of trouble, which showed up graphically in their essays. I had overestimated their ability to read and analyze the myths and their ability to convey their understanding in written form. My planning went out the window, lost to reality. However, the more reality we deal with, the more we tend to recall it when we rework or make new lessons or units. I still use creation myths but with far greater oral work and with students supported in collaborative working groups.

VARIABLES WITHIN OUR GRASP

Although good planning is an essential part of success, it is by no means the only part. You can plan well, as I did with the myths unit, and still have an unsuccessful class. And it isn't necessarily your fault. Many variables interact simultaneously in teaching, and you cannot control all of them. Since a class rarely goes awry for a single reason, understanding the major variables affecting the outcome of a class is important—especially when these variables are within our grasp.

Box 4–1

CLASSROOM VARIABLES

1. *Content:* The subject matter of your lesson or unit. What is it? Is it familiar or new material? Does it appeal to student interests, or is it a part of the curriculum that students view as a dose of castor oil? Have students had any choice in the content? How much content is being presented or assigned at one time?

2. *Method:* The way content is delivered to students. Is the content delivered via lecture, seatwork, or discussion? In whole-class or group work? By individuals or pairs? At a computer or a desk? In oral or written activities or both? Led by the teacher or by students?

3. *Time:* The amount of time estimated for the lesson or unit. Do you allow three weeks for a novel? Two days for revision? One week for classroom drama? Two class periods to make paper masks?

4. *Situation:* Time of day or year; might include scheduling classes around special events. Does your class meet the last hour on Friday or the first hour on Monday? Is your class split with lunch in between? Is it a 45-minute class? A 90-minute class? Do you need to schedule around special events such as a basketball tournament, homecoming week, an approaching spring break, prom day, deer hunting season, or winter musical?

5. *Students:* The class mix. Do you have 20, 25, or 28 students? Are they of average ability or above? Do some students have limited English proficiency? Are there students from varying racial and ethnic backgrounds, or are all Caucasian? Are they all college-bound seniors or all very reluctant sophomores? Do you have students with learning disabilities? Do you have most of the football team or the computer whiz kids?

6. *Teacher:* The background and experience you bring to the classroom. Do you have years of teaching experience? What type of academic preparation do you have? What is your teaching style? What is your confidence level? How would you describe your personality?

Playing the Variables Game

Leila Christenbury, an English language arts methods teacher, suggests playing a card game with teaching variables to understand how they interact and affect outcomes (50–52). We'd like you to try it. Here are Christenbury's directions:

> In groups of three, prepare index cards representing each variable shown in Box 4–1. Each group member writes a card for each of the variables. Then, the cards for each category are shuffled together, and each person draws a card from each of the six categories. Each person will end up with six cards, one representing the content, another the method, and so forth. At this point, each silently studies the six cards, perhaps for 5 minutes, and makes a few notes about the mix received, as if this situation were his or her class. Then, go around the group and present your mix, noting what you believe the possible results might be: Do you anticipate any problems? What adjustments might be needed? Would you need to scrap the entire lesson? What might the learning outcomes be with specific students?

As Christenbury notes: "Even if your assumptions and predictions are off-center, it will give you a chance to consider, given the components of a teaching act, what kind of effect this combination of variables might have upon the learning of these hypothetical students" (51). We agree with Christenbury that this is an excellent way to think about variables. It's fun too. Our students tried the game and came up with the variables shown in Box 4–2:

BOX 4–2

SAMPLE CLASSROOM VARIABLES

Content

Selected poems of Robert Frost
The Tempest
Huckleberry Finn
Rime of the Ancient Mariner
Hawthorne short story

Method

Read material for homework and have small-group discussion.
Read material silently in class and use short-answer worksheet.
Read material aloud and have students write short reaction paper.
Read material for homework and have students write a journal entry response.
Teacher lectures.

Time

One class period
Three weeks
Two class periods
One week
Eight class periods

Situation

Early fall, homecoming week, Friday
Winter, last class period, Friday
First period Monday
Class period split by lunch break
Late spring, school musical underway

Students

Class of 31, high ability, 10 African Americans, 3 Hispanics; seniors
Class of 25, mixed ability, 1 ESL; sophomores
Class of 18, average but 2 learning disabled; seniors
Class of 24, mostly boys, mixed ability; juniors
Class of 27, reluctant, juniors

Teacher

Every card had "You"—in other words, the teacher in each situation was a new
teacher with your personal background and traits.

Drawing one set of cards, a student ended up with this scenario:

Very outgoing, fairly confident new female teacher with a class of 24, mostly boys of mixed ability levels. The class meets on Friday during Homecoming week. The teacher has *Rime of the Ancient Mariner* on her schedule, allowing only that one day and planning on lecturing.

Our student quickly decided that this set of variables was a scenario for disaster! And right she was. It is doubtful her class would pay much attention, let alone come away with any knowledge. What could she do? Well, if she were required to use *The Rime of the Ancient Mariner* as part of the district's curriculum, she would first have to link its themes to those of today's adolescents. She would also have to allow more than one class period for this lengthy poem and discard any plans for lecturing. Working with the poem orally in class, using pairs or small-group discussion before whole-class discussion, and assigning some reader response writings would benefit the students. With homecoming week, she might design some projects, giving students a choice among them, and use that Friday as a work day. Or she might have students do some oral work that day, actively engaged in the text and moving about. In any case, lecturing is out.

There's no question that the teaching variables game sometimes results in extreme or bizarre combinations unlikely to occur in a real classroom. Nonetheless, the game forces you to think about variables, options, and changes that are within your control. As Christenbury warns: "Deciding that an instructional pattern just 'doesn't work' is rarely the case. You must try to get an eye for the variables; while the class may not have 'worked,' there may be more reasons or different reasons than you might automatically assume" (52). This is good advice. What's more, you can plan for those special events, days, or weeks when kids' attention is certain to be drawn away from classwork. In other words, plan for the occasional chaotic day.

SOME ACTIVITIES FOR CHAOTIC DAYS

In any semester, we can expect that some days or even entire weeks will be chaotic. Groups of students are suddenly pulled out for testing, a sporting or musical event interrupts the normal schedule, or holiday expectations make students restless. Knowing this, many teachers keep a supply of materials or activities just for those days. Word games and puzzles, trivia books, special interest magazines (e.g., on cars, sports, "beauty," or music) appeal to most students of any age. For some reason, the *Guinness Book of Records* never fails to hold student interest. Another fascinating book is David Macauley's *The Way Things Work*, which explains the workings of hundreds of things from levers to lasers. Even the most physics-phobic student cannot resist the principle of the zipper on their jeans being the same as that which built the pyramids. New forms of puzzles involve students in reading. *Murder Most Artful*, for example, requires reading a short whodunit involving struggling artists, forgery, and upscale galleries, and then, with the clues provided, building the puzzle to solve the murder. *Sonata for a Spy,* as the title suggests, might appeal to the music contingent in a class.

A very different approach to literature can be found in *The Dictionary of Imaginary Places* by Alberto Manguel and Gianni Guadalupi, a guide to more than 1,200 cities, countries, and continents invented by storytellers from Homer to the present. Students could easily become absorbed in this richly illustrated work. Teachers need only examine what's available at bookstores, toystores, and museum shops. Most teachers we know are regular packrats, accumulating instructional materials the way other people collect knickknacks. It's a habit well worth developing, one that can save a class when chaos looms large.

Another habit worth cultivating is that of reading to students. No matter what else is going on, most students respond well to a good tale, especially when they need only listen. Teachers who keep a good supply of short stories or novels on hand, just for those days when students are bound to be restless, will have less trouble maintaining control. At the same time, these activities do involve students in the language arts. Whether they are listening to a story or to a classmate recite weird facts from some book or magazine, they *are* listening. When they work through a word game, they are using thinking skills and often building vocabulary. In solving a puzzle, they are engaged in higher-order thinking and, if working collaboratively, are putting speaking and listening skills to good use. With very young children, we tend to view play as purposeful and necessary; we should consider occasional classroom play at middle and senior high levels in the same way. Planning for it, for the occasional day or week of chaos, makes good sense.

SEEING STUDENTS AS THE HEART OF THE CURRICULUM

"Unteachables"

While working with students considered "unteachable," Larry Johannessen discovered that he was "struggling with a curriculum that seemed to be designed more for the *teachers* than for the students" (73).

> We stumbled through a vocabulary book that was insulting busywork; we plodded through seemingly endless grammar exercises that taught nothing and increased student resentment of me and the school; and we tried to get through Aldous Huxley's *Brave New World,* a task which proved to be an exercise in futility. (73)

Johannessen and a colleague then determined what their students might be interested in reading and selected new materials. He believes subsequent success must be credited to materials that served students' needs and to activities that engaged students in their own learning. Johannessen took issue with another English educator who believed that "any set of materials, any curriculum, if taught by a person passionately, truthfully convinced that it matters for teachers and students—will work" (cited in

Johannessen, 75). We tend to agree with Johannessen. Students who have difficulty reading will struggle with *Macbeth* or *Great Expectations,* no matter how passionately the teacher approaches the readings. *The Outsiders,* on the other hand, will probably touch even the most alienated.

Similarly, students who are presented with exercises rather than opportunities for engaging in appropriate reading, writing, speaking, and listening activities are understandably turned off, even rebellious in the face of language unconnected to their interests. In implementing new materials and methods, Johannessen learned that "remedial students can and will learn if given a chance" (76). He admits that remedial or alienated students can be a trial, making teachers "downright angry," but he challenges those who believe these students are unteachable.

Special Needs

Another group that raises curricular questions is students with special needs. These students often share two curricular worlds, special education and mainstream English language arts, and the curricular models may be very different. We pointed out in the overview of this text that a more holistic approach to teaching and learning offers students a role in their own educational process. As such, we believe it is a better model. At issue, however, is the whole language model for special needs students. Kathleen Strickland states:

> While it is impossible to deny that the traditional paradigm [skills based] is still part of American education, a shift toward the new paradigm is supported by the majority of recent research findings. And yet, for as many educators who have accepted the new paradigm of language learning and teaching, there are still teachers and researchers who still disagree among themselves about methodology . . . The methodology disagreement is especially heated when considering students who have difficulty learning to read and write in school. (16)

This disagreement is not simply one more academic argument: real students will be affected on a daily basis. If your classroom exemplifies the kind of student-centered, holistic learning we are advocating, it may contrast with the skills-based instruction the special education teacher uses. Strickland continues:

> Conventional wisdom holds that students who have difficulty in literacy learning are best helped through the traditional "part to whole" skills approaches. Yet those who have not been successful in school reading programs . . . are more likely than other students to be the victims of too much skills instruction and too much instruction based on behavioral principles. In fact, so much time is spent on remediation that little time is left for actual reading. The net effect of such instruction is that students are led to believe that reading *is* skills [rather than an act of constructing meaning]. (17)

Although skills are involved in reading, as Strickland points out, a singular emphasis on them leaves students without a sense of what reading actually is. From a student's point of view, it is the difference between filling in worksheets and actually reading a story. It is the difference between a mechanistic and a holistic curricular model.

Consequently, you need to know the curriculum and instructional methods of special education teachers in your school. You will need to work with these teachers, in whatever manner possible, to ensure that special needs students receive the best learning environment possible. We suggest that you read some of the emerging texts for "regular" teachers with special needs students; these texts show both why and how a holistic classroom enhances learning, regardless of the students' disabilities. Similar texts are available for working with students such as Larry Johannessen's, who are considered difficult for reasons other than intellectual or emotional problems.

"REGULAR" KIDS

We went straight to the source of curriculum and teaching—the kids themselves—and asked them what they considered a good English language arts class to be all about. An eighth grader, Adam advised, "Have the students read books of their choice." This idea was also popular with senior high students, who extended it to include overall curricular choices:

> Brendan Wenman says, "Don't always go by the book. Vary assignments (book, outside readings, composition, speeches, drawings)."
> Nicole Peters had the same idea: "Have projects that catch students' interests, such as not always doing homework from a book. Variety is good."
> Douglas Luxem believes that "a good teacher doesn't follow a textbook. They can teach the class with their own ideas."
> Glen Wiedemeier agrees, "Avoid just using the textbook."
> Sebastian Janowski adds a reason," Give the students choices. They're not all the same."
> Douglas Luxem echoes Janowski: "Students are different and won't like the same things, so students should have some choice in what they do in class."
> One of our new college freshmen, looking back three months, wanted to tell her high school teachers this: "Please don't use the same material year after year. Vary the material somewhat. Teachers become bored and therefore students become bored with the material."
> Chris Frey, still in high school, had the same advice: "Learn how to keep things interesting and new."

A curriculum centered on students, rather than on teachers, would respond to these students' comments, and the teacher's instructional planning would reflect variety and choice.

PLANNING FOR CLASSROOM INSTRUCTION

> Teaching is the art of blending a conscious agenda with the needs of the students. The best teachers, like jazz musicians, collect knowledge and resources so they can move where meaning beckons. (Vogel and Tilley 47)

In their 1975 English education textbook, Dwight Burton and his colleagues offer a useful framework for planning units and lessons. They ask teachers to consider how they would plan if:

- They had no textbook
- No one was required to be in their class
- They had no school building, only the community
- They had no set curriculum; they had to justify what they use and do by "what can I do to help kids survive, get on, in today's society?"
- Their salary really depended upon how well they can help students solve problems in everyday life
- Their salary depended upon how much they helped the average and below average kids. (37)

In responding to these provocative questions, teachers would be forced to examine their assumptions about teaching and what the English language arts are all about. Twenty years later, these questions are well worth serious thought and response. It's easy to get lost in the demands of day-to-day teaching, forget some basic beliefs in what we do and why, and fail to examine our daily lessons against those beliefs.

Neil Postman and Charles Weingartner, in *Teaching as a Subversive Activity* offer a few questions for daily consideration: "What am I going to have my students do today? What is it good for? How do I know?" (cited in Burton 70). Although these educators provoked the teaching establishment two decades ago, their questions are not outdated or merely rhetorical. They are, rather, at the core of what teachers do every day and should be part of our planning. It is normal for new teachers to sometimes overplan. And at times, they find only by trial and error how long things take or how well certain materials or methods work. In brief, planning and reality do not always match. This shouldn't be upsetting. One thing that teachers do need, however, is a certain predictability about what goes on in the classroom. Lucy Calkins, a teacher and researcher in English language arts, tells us why:

> I have finally realized that the most creative environments in our society are not the kaleidoscopic environments in which everything is always changing and complex. They are, instead, the predictable and consistent ones: the scholar's library, the researcher's laboratory, the artist's studio. Each of these environments is deliberately kept *predictable* and *simple* because the work at hand and the changing interactions around that work are so unpredictable and complex. (12)

CLASSROOM CLIMATE

Aligned with classroom predictability is classroom climate. Climate is just what it sounds like, the atmosphere or environment in which teaching and learning take place. Climate may refer to a physical, emotional, or intellectual environment, or more commonly, a blend of these. Climate has a major effect on what happens, on the success or failure of the plans, and it definitely is something teachers create and control. The rapport that teachers establish with students and the rapport that students develop and maintain with their teachers and with one another are critical. In composition class, for example, a collaborative writing task as a first assignment not only makes students externalize the writing process, negotiating it all the way, but also helps them get to know one another more quickly. They start to feel comfortable sharing their ideas and their writing, the basis for the entire semester's work in peer response groups. They need to feel safe in class, and class must *be* a safe place because they will be asked to share their heartfelt ideas on paper, where they are most visible and most vulnerable to criticism of both substance and form.

The environment is influenced to some degree by the classroom's physical structure and its emotional tone. That degree of influence may depend on the relative wealth and well-being of the district and its schools. Some schools are poor physical environments for learning: dirty, peeling paint, broken desks, and cramped and poorly ventilated classrooms. Teachers in these schools often add whatever they can to brighten up the area; however, the environment still conveys a mood of neglect, reflecting the larger social problem. Nonetheless, we have seen extraordinary teaching and learning in schools that defy normal standards and expectations. Teachers in such schools are often masterful in creating a classroom environment, regardless of the physical surroundings.

Within any classroom, teachers can make important "people" changes relative to furniture and space. Row upon row of desks facing forward, for example, is not very conducive to discussion. Group work can take many configurations, from four desks pushed together to a circle arrangement. Some teachers keep a quiet spot in back of the classroom for students to do independent editing, They may keep a space for a table and a few chairs, where they can meet with students who need individual help, conduct group mini-lessons, or have a student assist a peer. Nancie Atwell reminds us of another spatial relationship: "A curriculum puts limits on learning, kids' and teachers', spelling out what may be covered or orchestrated from behind a big desk" (21).

Atwell's point is well taken. "Orchestrated from behind a big desk" relates to whether teachers see themselves as the sole conductor or not. Staying behind the desk sends a not-so-subtle message of authority and control. This is not to suggest teachers don't need control; they do. But it is a matter of perception and degree. While doing a clinical supervision practicum in one of the nation's oldest independent schools, I learned the difference.

In a seventh-grade classroom, student desks were arranged in various ways but never in rows. There was a single student desk off to the side, which the English teacher used. It was always overflowing with books and papers, and David could never quite keep things in place, including his own adult frame in a small adolescent space. After class one day, I asked David why he used this desk, which was obviously uncomfortable for him in many ways. He didn't respond right away, but then said, "I don't know. Or maybe I do. I guess I don't want the kids seeing me as *the* authority, the person behind the big desk." Verbalized or not, David's personal sense of authority and control had a profound effect on curriculum and instruction in his classroom.

David believed in and practiced cooperative learning, viewing himself as part of that learning circle, the ridiculously small desk a physical symbol. The rigidity of many classrooms was absent both physically and emotionally. These students were trusted with movement, with talk, and were expected to work together productively. And they did, largely because David wasn't worried that they were wasting time or that he would be perceived as less an "authority." David knew seventh graders. He thus knew what environment would capture their restless bodies and minds, at least for an hour.

We need to keep in mind just how powerful classroom climate is. Students know when they are valued by how often we use collaborative rather than isolating, competitive tasks; by how well we listen, rather than just hear; by how well we tolerate the errors and false starts that all of them will make; by how we include the most shy or the most rebellious among them; by how we respond to their diverse backgrounds and abilities. None of these is easy to do; much of it takes time, patience, and experience. The important thing is to teach with clear ideas about what to do, why to do it, and who benefits most from it.

Do It Yourself

> If you don't know where you're going, then any path will take you there.
> (The Cheshire Cat, *Alice in Wonderland*)

The Cheshire cat's observation is an apt one when we consider curriculum from the perspective of individual classroom planning. New teachers often wonder how to determine the amount of time to give to a unit of work or what they should include in a unit. Recent issues of *The English Journal* include advertisements to solve this problem. For $19.95, someone will "Cut your planning and preparation time from hours to minutes!" through literature unit plans "designed to be practical and easy to follow." These plans, available for novels and plays ranging from *Huck Finn* to *Animal Farm, Hamlet* to *The Glass Menagerie,* include: "unit outline, objectives, daily lesson plans (with objectives and activities, reading assignments, writing assignments, study guide questions (with answer key), group activities, extra activities, unit test, bulletin board ideas, and ready-to-copy student materials." We are informed that "many units also include lecture and note-taking sessions, background information, vocabulary or grammar lessons, and miscellaneous helpful hints!"

We have no idea how good these units are; some may contain useful material. Even if they do, we shouldn't use them. Preparing to be an English language arts teacher means deciding what to teach and how to teach it. What's more, one of the most satisfying and pleasurable parts of teaching is the development of units. We shouldn't let anyone, especially a commercial vendor, take that responsibility and pleasure away.

PRINCIPLES OF PLANNING

When educators talk about principles of planning, they generally include value, appropriateness, flexibility, involvement, and feedback and evaluation (Burton et al., 47–48). *Value* refers to the worth of the content—that what we plan to use and do provides students with authentic learning. One 17-year-old questioned this very principle in her world literature class. She accepted that Greek drama was valuable content, but the drama was presented in an English translation, so she and her classmates failed to see the relevance of the added requirement of learning the Greek alphabet. Had they been exploring various language systems, she would have not only accepted but also enjoyed the task. Her small rebellion had nothing to do with the Greek alphabet, which she could easily learn, but with purpose.

Appropriateness, as the word suggests, means the content and activities are suitable for the curricular level; it also suggests consideration of community values, or an understanding of what people find acceptable for teenagers. Although we need to guard against censorship, there is no point in needlessly angering parents and community members by using a novel or movie that flagrantly violates religious or moral beliefs.

Flexibility entails providing for differences in learning styles and learning rates, recognizing that not all students can or need to learn exactly the same thing at the same time or to do exactly the same tasks. Flexibility means planning for learners who are both more and less advanced than their peers.

From a student point of view, flexibility may also extend to varying approaches and time frames. High schooler Nicole Peters would tell new teachers: "Don't use the same approach to learning, like 'now open your book and read three stories for tomorrow.' Throw in a little spice like having each student read an action and discuss it in groups . . . ask for student input on some assignments. We like that. It's easier for us to learn that way." Justin, a middle school student, thinks of flexibility from another point of view. Although Justin confuses the word *standards* in his plea, his point is well taken:

> I think English teachers should seriously lower their standards on writing projects. I think it is wrong to go through every step every time. For example: many English teachers require their students to brainstorm, then prewrite, within a class hour. This is wrong! You can't think of a good idea on the spur of the moment. The real authors get their ideas from the heart, at random, not when an English teacher requires them to do so every couple of weeks.

Justin has hit upon something important: students need time to think, and our plans for assignments and due dates should reflect that need. Karen Bonney, a senior, stresses the importance of time and planning as well: "Give us time. Remember that every student is different and each moves at his or her own pace." Another high schooler, Mindy Vanden Huevel, even selects the word *flexibility* in expressing her belief that students need "flexible teaching." If both middle school and high school students are so aware of their need for flexibility, we surely must note it as a critical component of our planning.

Involvement refers to the type and number of activities students will do, generally a combination of independent, collaborative, and whole-class activities. Darcy Meadows, a senior high student, believes, "It would be best to include a variety of teaching techniques. No one likes to sit through a class that is repeated every day." One of Darcy's classmates, Amanda Harvey, agrees, "The teacher should vary his or her daily activities. Many teachers tend to be repetitive and lose students' interests easily." Another classmate, Chandra Thompson, bluntly advises: "Forget the lectures; they only put us to sleep, and change lesson plans often." And Sebastian Janowski, also a senior high classmate, adds an important characteristic of good teachers: "They tell their plan to the students."

We agree with Sebastian that students should know the plan for the unit and lessons within it. Moreover, they should be involved in some of that planning; many students have great ideas for readings, films, or activities. Students should also be involved in *assessment,* their self-reflection being an important part of the learning process. Also, giving feedback and evaluating student progress is something we plan for, not something that just happens. In working out lessons, we also decide on ways to provide students with response, to let them know how they are doing, and similarly, to evaluate them more formally if necessary.

The Earliest Planning

Most teachers learn what class or courses they will teach when they sign a contract. That is the point to begin planning. What textbooks are customarily used? What freedom is there to incorporate other books, films, or videos? Is there a budget for supplemental materials? What resources are available, not just in the school library and media center but also in the community? What are the district's policies regarding homework, grading, and responses to parents or guardians? What district-wide testing is done? What cultures are represented in the school and to what degree? Will there be any students with limited English proficiency? Will there be students with developmental disabilities? What are the curricular expectations for the grade level? What amount of freedom is there to add or subtract content from the curriculum? These questions, of course, are also appropriate when teachers are considering whether to accept a job in a particular district, not just after they have decided on one.

Once their courses are identified, many teachers start collecting instructional materials: magazines, newspapers, films, videos, art work, and music. Sometimes, the most seemingly insignificant item yields a great class. For example, one teacher learned from a newspaper that a group of Bulgarian diplomats touring Minneapolis were thrown out of a neighborhood store. The owner, believing they were a group of gypsies about to rob him, created quite an incident for our State Department. Without clear plans for using the article, the teacher clipped it anyway. It proved its worth: after students in a composition class read it, they filled the boards with possible writing topics, delineating the difference between those suitable for exposition and for argumentation. The students did a wonderful job of generating ideas, and the goal that they understand how writing purposes differ and how content influences our purpose was met. Because the incident was so bizarre, they also had moments of both laughter and seriousness as they discussed prejudice and stereotyping. All of this grew out of a news item in the local paper.

To increase a personal repertoire of class activities and materials, new teachers can search back issues of *The English Journal* and journals from their state English language arts organization; these ideas from practicing teachers are a rich resource. And when the opportunity presents itself, teachers should attend professional meetings and conferences, not just for the presentations but also for the chance to talk with other teachers informally, to learn what they do and how they do it. Some ideas or methods won't work for us, but unless we hear them and try some out, we won't know that. The important thing is that we build a personal collection.

Instructional Units

As teachers build tentative plans for classes, they need a calendar at their side. Some curriculum guides indicate roughly how much time to allot to given topics; others don't. In either case, individual teachers must determine the number of days or weeks for particular units. A unit is simply an organized block of instruction (like the commercial literature units referred to earlier); it includes goals for the course of study, student outcomes (what we expect them to learn or be able to do as a result of this unit), the materials the teacher and students will use, activities, the sequence of instruction, and ways student learning will be evaluated. A unit varies in length, anywhere from a few days to weeks, depending on the content. Within a unit, teachers also focus on an important concept or theme and select the content to explore it; the material in the textbook does not constitute a unit, although it may be part of it. A unit is something teachers create; within it, they also develop daily lesson plans. These are not elaborate, merely a shorthand version of what they plan to do during each class period. As noted earlier, many schools require teachers to turn in their daily lesson plans on a weekly basis, not just to check on what is happening but also as a guideline if a substitute teacher is needed.

Planning for Reality

When veteran teachers consider their units for the semester, they look at a calendar and ask questions. When are school breaks or vacations? Teachers must ensure that students are not in the middle of a unit when a break occurs. Otherwise, they will spend days reteaching, bringing students back to the point just prior to the break. Some breaks are not on the school calendar but are just as real. For example, in some rural districts, most boys between ages 12 and 18 will be absent for deer hunting season, roughly the week of Thanksgiving. Knowing this, teachers can plan accordingly. Major school events (e.g., homecoming, prom, drama or music productions, or athletic or music tournaments) that will undoubtedly draw energy and attention away from academics also figure into the calendar.

Teachers need to be realistic about these events and plan accordingly, perhaps assigning less homework and more in-class activities during these periods. Other questions involve resources: How far in advance should teachers get supplemental materials for a certain unit, rent a video, or reserve the VCR? How far in advance should they arrange for a site visit in the community or secure a speaker on a special topic? Teachers who plan to take students off campus often need to work through their district administration office and secure parent/guardian permission. Any teacher who has sent forms home knows well that getting them back is a major ordeal; leaving enough time for the return is critical. These are the practical elements of good planning.

Beginning teachers may not know how long any unit or individual lesson may take; even experienced teachers can't be sure. Different classes may necessitate different planning, adjustments, and a need for flexibility. Beginning teachers may feel overwhelmed at times (every teacher does), but planning well can help prevent this feeling. None of us wants to end up with a scheme like the Mock Turtle:

> "And how many hours a day did you do lessons?" said Alice, in a hurry to change the subject.
> "Ten hours the first day," said the Mock Turtle: "nine the next, and so on."
> "What a curious plan!" exclaimed Alice.
> "That's the reason they're called lessons," the Gryphon remarked: "because they lessen from day to day." (Lewis Carroll, *Alice in Wonderland*)

With foresight and a sense of adventure, many teachers begin their planning with enthusiasm. Many wonderful ideas come in and out of our lives, and we urge beginning teachers to capture them in a special folder labeled "Flashes of Brilliance." And yes, we are very sure such a folder will be needed and used. It's the stuff good teaching is made of.

CASE 4–1

Exploring an Instructional Unit

Nancy Koehler, a returning adult student in one of our methods classes, developed a unit centered on one of high schoolers' most persistent interests: themselves. Inspiration for "Generation X: Who Are You and What Are You Whining About?" arose when Nancy was doing her preliminary field work, teacher assisting, at a local high school. Seniors were completing a form for their yearbooks, and among the general autobiographical questions was one asking them how they liked being referred to as "Generation X." As Nancy put it, "That question prompted much discussion in class as students wanted to know where that label came from, what it meant, and who thought of it." Once Nancy started thinking about those questions, her two-week unit emerged.

GOALS TO OUTCOMES

In her introduction, Nancy briefly outlined her goals:

- Discovery learning
- Effective cooperative group work

- Better oral communication skills
- Inclusion of all students in group and whole-class work

Broad goals, as we have pointed out, must translate into specific and concrete student outcomes. In brief, Nancy had to think next about "What are the kids doing?" and "What it is good for?" As she thought about content and skill development, she began that transformation:

Students will

- Discover what they already know about the topic of Generation X; think about what they want to learn about the topic; form a plan to discover additional information
- Have choices in what and how they present the topic
- Work in cooperative groups, where every group member has a specific role both in research and presentation
- Learn how popular culture is portrayed in the media through critical examination of newspapers, magazines, and television programs

Nancy also realized that she had to include another important question in her planning. When she determined "What the kids are doing" and "What it's good for," she had yet to think about the "How do I know?" part—evaluation. Even in the early stages of developing her unit, Nancy began to think about how she would evaluate authentic student learning.

From oral presentations, she would gain a sense of their content learning: just what did they learn about Generation X? She also determined that the presentations would not be successful unless each group member participated, something that is clearly visible. In addition to her own evaluation of each group's presentation, she planned to develop both peer and self-evaluation forms. She also would ask students to reflect on their learning through a journal entry, a way of bringing closure to the unit as well.

SELECTING MATERIALS

Nancy's desire to have students examine how the media portrays Generation X led her to *Newsweek* magazine, where three articles in their June 6, 1994, issue seemed suitable for seniors. She also found an article by Lisa Carver, "Manifesto of Generation L" in *Utne Reader*'s September/October 1994 edition. Placing copies of these articles in a student packet, Nancy noted that these were materials that students could easily read in a class period or two. But she also felt that the unit could be easily expanded and updated with new articles. Thinking ahead, Nancy said: "This is a topic that received a lot of press. There were several magazine articles on the deaths of Kurt Cobain and River Phoenix that I deliberately left out of the packet so individual groups could focus on these issues for their presentations if they wished." She also acknowledged another important factor for student work: "I think it is important to provide all students with the same packet of information as a resource. This levels the playing field of background knowledge to some extent."

Nancy selected the movie *Reality Bites* as the final activity for the unit, so she also noted a need to reserve the VCR. Looking ahead to potential group activities and presentations, Nancy also listed a cassette and CD player, blank transparencies, and an overhead projector as part of her materials planning.

PROCEDURE

As a student herself, Nancy was well aware of the benefits when teachers share their plan with students. As a result, she developed a two-week calendar of the unit and its due dates to distribute and explain on the first day of the unit.

Day 1	Day 2	Day 3	Day 4	Day 5
Introduction to KWL Packet distribution	Divide in groups Distribute choices for presentation	Group work	Group work	Group work

Day 6	Day 7	Day 8	Day 9	Day 10
Group work All presentations due tomorrow	Presentations Peer and self-evaluations	Presentations Peer and self-evaluations	View *Reality Bites*	View *Reality Bites* Self-reflection journal

INTRODUCING THE GENERATION X UNIT

Nancy's first activity is a prereading strategy called KWL. As Nancy describes it, "The 'K' portion of KWL taps into the background *knowledge* of all the students," essentially an oral brainstorming session to help kids discover what they already know about the topic. Also a whole-class brainstorming activity, the "W"—or what students *want to know* or learn about the topic—would be next. The final letter, "L," is the result of student group work and research into some aspect of the topic. "L," *what they have learned* about Generation X, will be presented to the class as part of a group activity.

Nancy would pass out the Generation X information packets and allow students to look them over in whatever time is left. She would also explain procedures for work both in and outside of class time.

CHOICES FOR GROUP PRESENTATION ON GENERATION X

1. Panel discussion on issue relevant to Generation X
2. Manifesto for Generation X
3. Skit demonstrating some aspect of Generation X
4. Song lyrics reflecting Generation X
5. Original idea for group presentation (cleared with teacher)

GETTING INTO GROUPS AND GETTING STARTED

Nancy decided that *she* would determine the groups, mainly because she wanted a heterogeneous mix of ability levels and personalities. A realist, Nancy noted that after students "have stopped complaining about who they are with," she would distribute a list of possible group activities. When thinking about these activities, Nancy realized she would have to do some direct teaching and modeling; students would not be familiar with some forms of writing. These would have to be worked in as mini-lessons.

Because evaluation was part of Nancy's plan from the start, she could provide students with copies of peer evaluation and self-evaluation forms when she presented the activities. At the same time, she could explain that their grades would be determined through a combination of student and teacher evaluation. Nancy indicated that students would also discuss the movie and write reflective journal entries that would bring closure to the unit. She gave this reason for her extensive introduction:

I think it is very important to lay all your cards on the table with students. I want to give them a strong overview of what the unit is all about, what my expectations are of them, why I think it is important they learn about this topic and think critically about it, and the method of assessment that will be used. Speaking as a student, I know I don't like surprises and feel much more comfortable when the expectations are explained to me.

This is an important point: provide kids with the complete picture. High schoolers in particular want and need it.

AT TASK

Cooperative group work forms the next part of Nancy's plan: three or four days of in-class research, decision making, and rehearsal for presentations. Nancy saw her role during this time as circulating among the groups to monitor group dynamics and progress. She would let group members determine their own roles, with a reminder that each person must participate and have an equal role in decision making and the group presentation. Group presentations would follow. Using the forms Nancy developed for evaluation, students would share in the assessment process.

CLOSURE

Nancy is realistic about her final whole-class activity, viewing the film *Reality Bites*. She notes, "[The movie] has to be carefully considered as it might be viewed as controversial in some communities." Despite Nancy's knowledge that "it is a wonderfully relevant film to this unit and students enjoy it very much," she also knows it could not be shown without clearance from her administrator. Again, she is thinking ahead, and if the film violates local community standards, Nancy will eliminate it from the unit.

Her final activity is the self-reflective journal entry. Nancy chose this writing activity because she wanted a forum "where students are encouraged to be honest and analytical about their participation, their feelings about the unit, and to offer any suggestions for improvement of the unit." She also wanted to give them a chance "to air any frustrations they might have had about working within the structure of a cooperative group." Criteria for evaluating this piece of writing rest on the student's sincerity, honesty, and effort, which is an appropriate base for journal writing.

NANCY'S REFLECTION ON THE GENERATION X UNIT

A practice we hope Nancy will take into her own classroom is that of reflection, a critical component of good teaching. Because Nancy had tried some Generation X activities with a senior class, she brought some valuable insights based on her experience to the process of developing this unit. She decided that the unit could benefit from (a) more oral language activities, (b) more time for group work, and (c) a packet of articles as a starting point.

In her reflection on the unit, Nancy noted that students could be easily frustrated if there were too many activities for the time allocated: "When I taught this [unit] to seniors at North High School, I found that these students have tremendous time constraints on them with work, athletics, responsibilities at home, etc. These students have very little time to work on projects outside of class." Nancy had learned something about the realities of a senior class, and on reflection, decided: "If quality work is expected from students, they must be given enough time to work on projects, and they must be given expectations, advice, and encouragement while they are working."

Nancy also realized that the packet of readings was critical: "Providing background knowledge is helpful for students who are not of the majority culture." She also thought about students who might not have magazines, newspapers, or even television available at home; consequently, they might have little or no familiarity with popular culture topics like Generation X. For some of these same reasons, Nancy chose her oral introductory activities: "The brainstorming prereading activities help with [background knowledge], serving to activate schemata in students as they hear each other speak."

With student teaching just ahead, Nancy will have the chance to implement this unit. And she will undoubtedly make more changes based on her experience in a senior high classroom. Her reflection on the unit, along with her willingness to include student opinions, will lead to further refinement.

Although veteran teachers seldom write out a unit in such detail, they do "write" in their heads and make some notes about materials, methods, and procedures. Good planning is essential to good teaching—no matter how experienced one is.

SUGGESTED ACTIVITIES

1. Review Nancy's unit on Generation X. What materials, activities, and tasks would you add or delete? Why? What might you add to her choices for group presentation?

2. Nancy planned her unit around 10 class periods of 45 minutes each. Some school districts have gone to 90-minute periods meeting 4 days a week. What changes would you make in the unit if you had 90-minute periods? What are the benefits of a longer period? What are potential problems?

3. Develop student evaluation forms for Nancy's unit.

4. Examine a series of English language arts texts for three successive grade levels (middle school/junior high school or senior high school) in both a literature series and a grammar/composition series. What are the underlying assumptions of these texts?

   a. Are the language arts integrated in the lessons and assignments?

   b. Are the language arts treated as processes or as subject matter to be divided up?

   c. Are language and learning approached holistically or as bits and pieces, as parts to be assembled?

   d. How is the student viewed—as using language to communicate? as capable of discovering language principles? as a meaning maker?

   e. Is the content of high interest to young people?

   f. Does the content reflect the diversity of gender, race, ethnicity, and social class within our society?

5. Is the curriculum you examined built in a linear (building block) or spiral fashion? Check the teacher's edition for a formal scope and sequence; check content in the text to see how it is approached in each successive year. Read the preface or author's introduction to the text(s). What do you learn?

6. Review Shanahan and Lester's guidelines for selecting texts before making your decision whether not to recommend these texts for district adoption.

DISCUSSION QUESTIONS

1. Ted Sizer, professor of education at Brown University, believes:

   Obviously a low premium is placed on reflection and repose [in the American high school]. The student rushes from class to class to collect knowledge. Savoring it, it is implied, is not to be done much in school, nor is such meditation really much admired. The picture that these familiar patterns yield is that of an academic supermarket. The purpose of going to school is to pick things up, in any organized and predictable way, the faster the better. ("Horace's Compromise 80)

   Is this a fair assessment of today's secondary schools? Does this description fit middle school as well as senior high? What does this portrait have to do curriculum and instruction in the English language arts?

2. In Charles Dickens' *Hard Times,* Master Thomas Gradgrind lays out a curricular plan: "Now what I want are the facts. Teach these boys and girls nothing but Facts. Facts alone are wanted in life. Plant nothing else, and root out everything else . . . Stick to the Facts, Sir! (Signet Edition, pp. 11–12). Is Master Gradgrind correct in his assessment that "Facts alone are wanted in life"? What would you consider as examples of "facts" in English language arts? What would you consider "processes"? Has the English language arts curriculum been guilty of "planting" too many facts and being preoccupied with content and with testing content? Consider the world your students will live in: Would facts or processes be more critical to their well-being? How do you know? What do you envision as critical components of an English language arts curriculum for the twenty-first century? Justify your choices.

REFERENCES

Atwell, Nancie. *In the Middle: Writing, Reading and Learning With Adolescents.* Portsmouth: Heinemann Boynton/Cook, 1987.

Berry, Heather M. "Letter." *Leader-Telegram.* 10 Dec. 1991. Eau Claire, WI.

Burton, Dwight L., Donelson, Kenneth, Fillmore, Bryant, and Haley, Beverly. *Teaching English Today.* Boston: Houghton Mifflin, 1975.

Calkins, Lucy McCormack. *The Art of Teaching Writing.* Portsmouth: Heinemann, 1986.

Carroll, Lewis. *Alice in Wonderland and Through the Looking Glass.* San Rafael: Classic Publishing, 1970.

Christenbury, Leila. *Making the Journey: Being and Becoming a Teacher of English Language Arts.* Portsmouth: Boynton/Cook Heinemann, 1994.

Editorial Staff. "English Journal Focus." *English Journal* 27 Mar. 1981: 27.

Johannessen, Larry R. "Three Offenses to End Despair: A Reply to Daniel Lindley." *English Journal* Sept. 1991: 72–77.

Koehler, Nancie. "Generation X: Who Are You and What Are You Whining About?" English 406/606. University of Wisconsin-Eau Claire, May 1995.

McDonald, Joseph A. "A Messy Business." *Teacher Magazine* Nov.–Dec. 1991: 54–55.

Sizer, Theodore R. *Horace's Compromise: The Dilemma of the American High School.* Boston: Houghton Mifflin, 1984.

Sizer, Theodore R. "School Restructuring. University Summer Forum: What Do We Want From Our Schools?" Madison, WI. 18 June 1991.

Strickland, Kathleen. *Literacy Not Labels: Celebrating Students' Strengths Through Whole Language.* Portsmouth: Boynton/Cook Heinemann, 1995.

Vogel, Mark, with Janet Tilley. "The Dark Within Us All: Stephen Dobyn's "Bleeder." *English Journal* Mar. 1991: 47–50.

5

Oral Language: The Neglected Language Arts

Schools are language saturated institutions. They are places where books are thumbed, summarized, and "revised"; notes are dictated, made, kept, and learned; essays are prepared; examination questions are composed and the attendant judgments made. Teachers explain, lecture, question, exhort, reprimand. Pupils listen, reply, make observations, call out, mutter, whisper and make jokes. Small knots gather over books, lathes, easels, or do nothing in classrooms, laboratories, workshops, craftrooms, corridors and toilets to chatter, discuss, argue, plan, plot and teach one another.

Douglas Barnes

SOME BASIC PRINCIPLES

As Barnes reminds us, oral language is the most pervasive environment of our schools. Not only do we seldom perceive of it in this way, but we also tend to forget that oral language is an important instructional area in the English language arts. At the secondary level, responsibility for oral language has most often been relegated to *the* speech course or fragmented into isolated units. John Fortier, a high school English and speech teacher, reflects on a possible reason for this:

> A number of factors have combined to prevent oral language instruction from achieving the gains that writing instruction has. We sometimes perceive speaking, unlike writing, as a competence which develops independently without instruction. After all, students come to school talking, but few are able to write. (2)

An additional factor may lie in the traditional preparation of secondary English teachers, where written language has been the focus for methods courses. As one of our English education majors put it, "I know it was sort of a shock to some of the methods students to think about teaching speaking and listening skills because they didn't really consider that 'English'" (Lightfoot). Quite often, secondary English textbooks reinforce the notion of the primacy of written expression, which generally appears in two varieties: literature and composition/grammar. Fortunately, a renewed emphasis on an integrated and balanced English language arts program has also brought more resources for teaching oral language.

Before looking specifically at listening and speaking, we need to focus on some very basic oral language principles. Fortier summarizes these:

1. Not all students share the same level of competency in oral language; in fact, some students enter school impoverished by a lack of verbal interaction in the home. The implication for teachers is clear: students do need to talk in school, not "idle chatter, but focused discussion" (3).
2. Similar to other language skills, the acquisition of oral language skills is developmental. We should not expect all students to progress at the same rate or demonstrate the same ability, regardless of similar chronological age.
3. Students need varied and purposeful experience in oral communication, just as they do with written communication. This means shifts from familiar audiences and contexts to more distant ones, as well as opportunities to share feelings, entertain, give information, and persuade. Each of these purposes has its own problem relative to audience and setting; therefore, students would learn to solve diverse communication problems. Our responsibility is to create these contexts, everything from role playing to group activities, from conferencing to public speaking before an entire class.
4. We should not break speaking into subskills, nor should we isolate speaking from the other language arts. Oral language activities integrated with reading and writing, a planned part of every unit and daily classroom interaction, enhances student competency.
5. Since speaking is not totally oral, students need to learn about body language, eye contact, gesture, and so forth. Being aware of how listeners are responding is a critical skill. Similarly, students need to be sensitive to how culturally bound these areas are. For example, in mainstream American culture, eye contact is expected to be direct, indicating honesty and self-confidence. In other cultures, such directness would be ill-mannered. (Fortier 3–5)

TEACHER TALK, STUDENT TALK

The most obvious characteristic of classroom talk is that there is so much of it.
                                                    A. D. Furlong and V. J. Edwards (10)

A. D. Furlong and V. J. Edwards, although referring to British secondary classrooms, characterize our classrooms as well: "The theme is simply 'everybody listen.' For much of the time in classrooms, there is a *single* verbal encounter in which whatever is being said demands the attention of all" (11)

All of us recognize the truth in this, although more recently the use of peer response groups and cooperative learning groups has brought about more varied voices in genuine dialogue. However, the perception still exists in many schools that a quiet classroom is a good classroom, that the appropriate role of the teacher is to speak and of the student to listen. This tradition may be linked to more than just respect for authority and for the teacher as the source of knowledge. Unfortunately, as Furlong and Edwards point out, teachers are judged by their ability "to keep [the class's] collective attention on the matter at hand" (12); that is, discipline is very much a part of classroom talk. Increased student interaction brings with it the threat of loss of control; therefore, some teachers prefer to control most of the talk. Furlong and Edwards put it this way: "Teachers usually tell pupils when to talk, what to talk about, when to stop talking, and how well they talked" (14). Or as Michael Stubbs, another British researcher, noted, "There is a sense in which, in our culture, teaching *is* talking" (12). Research supports this view. In a famous study of classrooms, Flanders learned that in the traditional "chalk and talk" classrooms, teachers talk about 70 percent of the time (cited in Stubbs 12).

A more contemporary classroom would improve this ratio. Students would be involved in far more talk, both structured by the teacher and more informally. The teacher's role would shift from "dispenser of information" to "facilitator of learning." The curriculum would also shift from teacher-centered to student-centered, as the teacher plans activities in which work is no longer a solo, silent affair. Students would interact with one another in pairs or small groups to share or pool information, provide feedback, and develop material together. A truly integrated language arts curriculum, one where listening, speaking, reading, and writing are part of nearly every lesson, demands student interaction. Although teachers structure such interaction by determining tasks and they stipulate whether students should work in pairs or small groups, for example, teachers thereafter function as consultants. Most teachers "drift" around the room, spot-checking the work underway, relinquishing their traditional role as sole provider and controller of information.

Does this suggest that teachers should never lecture or lead discussions? Of course not! In fact, it is critical that we do so, modeling processes and questions that students need to internalize. The issue is one of ratio and balance between teacher talk and student talk. A related concern is classroom arrangements that facilitate more student interaction. The straight, orderly rows of desks seldom encourage interaction and genuine exchange. The flexibility to move into circles, pairs, or small groups is an important consideration of classroom space. Similarly, having a corner where students can curl up with a book or have access to a quiet space for quiet work is equally important.

TALK AND CULTURAL DIFFERENCES

Differences between students' home language and the school language can be a critical factor in student achievement. As Courtney Cazden, former professor of education at Harvard, reminds us: "Ways of talking that seem so natural to one group are experienced as culturally strange to another" (67). School language is, in some ways, strange to all students. However, it is especially strange to students outside the mainstream culture. We need to be aware of this reality, observe our students, and find ways to facilitate their adaptation to this new culture, the mainstream classroom. Lisa Delpit, a researcher in language and literacy, notes: "All students deserve the right both to develop the linguistic skills they bring to the classroom and to add others to their repertoire" (264). Linguistic skills include not only syntax and grammar but also discourse style and language use. How we ask questions, give directions, listen, and interpret are culturally bound. Understanding new ways of using language will continue to be part of the American classroom for student and teacher alike, as projections for the year 2000 indicate the minority school-age population will increase to 42 percent (cited in Duenas Gonzales 16).

LISTENING: NOT THE SAME AS HEARING

Listening is both the most used and the least understood of all communication arts.
Wisconsin Department of Public Instruction (1986, 67)

Considering the percentage of school time in which students are expected to be quiet and listen, we might assume they develop into good listeners. However, this is far from true. To begin with, there are many misconceptions about listening, the first being that listening cannot be taught. Listening can and should be taught, not through talking about listening skills but rather by engaging students in authentic communication. A second misconception is that listening and hearing are the same thing. Given the continual bombardment of "noise" in modern life, we can hardly blame students for tuning out. Nevertheless, as teachers we are responsible for teaching students the difference.

Another misconception is to confuse the statements "you're not listening" with "you don't agree with me; therefore, you're not listening." Parents and teachers often chastise students for not listening when what they mean is the students have rejected what they heard. The implication for the classroom is serious, for it concerns the integrity of speaking and listening as a shared experience. Sometimes, we also fail to differentiate among the varying purposes of listening. There is, however, considerable difference between listening critically and listening aesthetically, for example.

Major Curricular Goals and Classroom Barriers

With awareness of general curricular goals in listening, we can structure lessons to include them. On the most basic level, students should be able to recognize the speaker's purpose, as well as their own in listening—whether to gain information, to analyze, or to appreciate aesthetically. Students must also be aware of the verbal and nonverbal cues that help them understand a verbal text. Their own role in providing feedback in both of these forms is similarly critical. The skill of giving *effective* feedback is learned.

Teachers must also be aware of barriers to effective listening. Unfamiliarity with the vocabulary, syntax, or content may be one cause; dialect and native language differences may be another, but *any* student may face barriers. A much more difficult situation occurs when students simply tune out when lessons involve complex content. Some students choose to not listen to ideas or explanations that demand their full attention. Others may stop listening when they don't agree; usually, they will be framing their rebuttal or preparing some sort of response before the speaker has completed his or her message. Since adolescents are sensitive to situations where *their* words are ignored, some straight, though sensitive, talk about being fair might help.

Structuring classroom activities to encourage or compel students to listen is an important part of teaching listening skills. Although high-interest lessons capture students' attention, we must still consciously incorporate activities that develop good listening skills. Teaching purposeful listening involves two major activities: (a) listening to follow spoken directions and (b) listening to recognize the organization of spoken discourse. The latter is particularly important because students comprehend much better when they recognize "the plan." For example, students who recognize cause and effect or comparison and contrast as the organizing principle will grasp the content far more efficiently. We enhance this ability by giving the students a plan for what they will hear: an overview and an explanation of new or difficult words or concepts in advance.

Listening to oral directions is, of course, a basic part of most classes. However, teachers tend to repeat directions too frequently. Without making an issue out of it, we can help students by not being so generous with repetition. For students who comprehend more slowly, we do need to make adjustments; however, this can usually be done individually as needed.

Listening as Process

Ideally, listening is part of student activities that involve the other language arts. The following listening skills are among the most important in curricular planning:

- Accurately remember significant details and simple sequences of words and ideas.
- Follow oral directions accurately.
- Accurately paraphrase an oral message.
- Follow a sequence in plot development, character development, and a speaker's argument.
- Understand both literal and connotative meanings.
- Understand meaning derived from a spoken context.
- Listen for significant details.
- Listen for main ideas.
- Distinguish between old and new material.
- Distinguish between relevant and irrelevant material.
- Predict outcomes.
- Draw conclusions.

- Identify and summarize main ideas.
- Relate the speaker's ideas and information to their own life. (Devine 5)

Students also need to develop critical listening skills. These skills are perhaps most associated with argument and persuasion; therefore, some curriculum guides list these skills as part of a unit dealing with media. However, students need sustained experience. Sara Lundsteen, professor of education at North Texas State University, notes the most important skills for students:

- Using criteria, distinguish "fact from fancy."
- Judge the validity and adequacy of main ideas, arguments, and hypotheses.
- Distinguish well-supported statements from opinion and judgment.
- Evaluate the use of fallacies (e.g., self-contradiction, false analogy, failure to present all choices).
- Recognize emotional appeals and loaded words.
- Detect and evaluate speaker bias.
- Evaluate qualifications or credentials of the speaker.
- Recognize basic propaganda devices. (60–61)

These skills are, of course, linked with critical thinking. Thus, in devising ways in which students practice listening, teachers are also devising ways to promote higher-order thinking skills.

LISTENING AND COOPERATING IN GROUP WORK

Teachers often offer mixed reviews on group work, along with many myths, but research findings on cooperative group work and learning are generally positive. Virginia O'Keefe, a communications education instructor, provides some reasons:

> Group work produces more actively engaged, task-oriented behavior than when students work alone on "seatwork." The struggling student profits from an interactive situation where he or she receives feedback from peers. And, students at all achievement levels benefit from the opportunity to "rehearse" new concepts as they talk through problems.
> Social cooperation increases as students learn more about each other. They reveal their achievements . . . [and] also admit their vulnerabilities—dropping out of football, failing typing, not winning a debate tournament, and losing parents through death or divorce. That kind of information may not seem relevant to language arts, but those same human experiences are ultimately the stuff of any literary text. (91)

We know from our experience with composition classes that what O'Keefe says is true: Students help one another, find a comfortable niche despite (or because of) mixed abilities, and share both academic and personal ups and downs. As a result, their writing is far richer, as is the class overall, because student cohesion results from sustained group work. And a critical factor in this achievement is listening.

As O'Keefe succinctly puts it: "Improving our relations with others really begins with listening" (91). As we have already pointed out, we listen for different purposes. But regardless of our purpose, we can improve listening through nonverbal behavior, which is critical to the success of working groups. O'Keefe lists the attributes of good listening behavior:

- Maintaining natural eye contact
- Nodding head in agreement
- Leaning forward
- Adopting a pleasant facial expression
- Facing the speaker(s)
- Keeping arms open (not folded)
- Taking position at the same elevation as the speaker (91)

She goes on to note that "if these nonverbal behaviors are choreographed for effect without sincerity, they will have the opposite effect" (91). Kids are especially good at ferreting out nonverbal behavior that doesn't mesh with the speaker or the message, but we also need to "school" them to the importance of nonverbal behavior. Otherwise, they may send unintentional negative messages and impair group relationships.

Whether it is small- or large-group work, students should face one another, preferably in a circle where eye contact is easily gained. And they should learn to give verbal signals, such as a simple nod of the head or a smile, to show they are attending to the speaker. If appropriate, taking notes is another way to signal interest in the speaker's ideas, as is avoiding some listening distractions.

We agree with O'Keefe that "active listening requires conscious effort"—and that the skills and behaviors are indeed teachable (92). But we must see listening both as part of ongoing classroom discourse and a curricular focus.

To improve students' group work, we can provide tangible strategies for listening well:

1. *Be prepared:* Have pens, paper, and materials at hand and have assignments read in advance. For example, if students are dividing up some research, they need to arrive at the group with a sense of the parameters of that research and be ready to discuss their interests and potential tasks. If they are working through a literary text, they need to read it before class.
2. *Set goals:* Plan how group information will be used when students are working on their own. Students need to set a purpose for their listening. If they know that they will have to depend on what they take away from their group, their motivation will likely increase.
3. *Use time well:* Humans think three or four times faster than they speak, so we process messages quickly—faster than a speaker sends the words. What happens in the gap? Mostly distracting thoughts! Students need to know about

this phenomenon and have some strategies to use the gap productively (e.g., take notes, write out questions, reorder information, or find patterns in what is being said).

4. *Minimize distractions:* Students react quickly to all kinds of distractions, whether it is a wasp or a word laden with emotional impact. Teaching them the power of "high blood pressure" words is part of teaching them to be listeners. They need to recognize and control their emotional responses; if they don't, the intellect is turned off. Then, what they get is an argument rather than a discussion. Similarly, kids need to know that developing counterarguments at the same time they are still receiving the message is counterproductive. Remind them how they feel when their parents or teachers appear not to listen or are too ready with a response.

5. *Avoid evaluation:* Although there is a place for evaluative listening and response, such as when someone makes a claim without sufficient support, evaluative listening should be the last part of a process, not the first. That is, students should not say things like "that's dumb" or "it'll never work" in the group. Again, remind them how they feel when their ideas are greeted with such responses.

6. *Use feedback:* Verbal or nonverbal feedback is how a speaker knows group members listened and got the message. Nonverbal feedback, such as smiles, nodding of the head, or laughter, is effective in signaling "understood." Verbal feedback may be a simple "okay" or it may be a question, paraphrase, or request for clarification. Even negative responses, such as "no" or "maybe," provide evidence of listening. (O'Keefe 92–94)

Preparing students to listen, then, is part of the process. Just placing them into groups and telling them to get to work usually results in little work—and leads many teachers to abandon group work altogether. There is, however, more to this process than providing information on how to listen. Understanding how groups should be formed, structured, and conducted is also critical to success.

EFFECTIVE GROUP WORK

Forming Groups

Group work is essentially oral work, and as such, it is vital experience for young people. Whether they pursue some type of postsecondary education or go right into the workforce, they need to know how to work with others. This ability to work cooperatively and effectively depends largely on both oral language and social skills. Some students will be more comfortable than others in group work, depending on personality and learning style, but all students need regular group experience.

A question most teachers face when planning group work is how to construct the groups: Should students choose their own group members? Should the teacher assign them? Should groups be of mixed ability or homogeneous? Should groups be balanced by gender, race, or other considerations? Research findings on these questions are mixed when high-ability students are considered, but the research findings concerning lower-ability students are consistent. Heterogeneous groups benefit less-able students. Explanations from peers improve their understanding, and the more skilled question/answer processes of higher-ability students provide good models and cues. Research has also revealed that group work appears to be especially beneficial for African American, and possibly Hispanic, students (Good and Brophy, cited in O'Keefe 94). Different cultural backgrounds affect oral discourse patterns, so it is not surprising that students flourish in oral situations similar to their home culture.

O'Keefe offers some good suggestions on how to group students. She stresses the importance of talking with students about the group process itself and addressing their fears and expectations. She explains to students that reluctance to speak in a group is a natural reaction, but that their best work depends on the full cooperation of each student. O'Keefe believes that talking frankly about their fears reassures students that their concerns are fairly common. Similarly, letting them know that good participation means listening well and being supportive of others—not "being brilliant" or dominating the talk—helps many students relax. The most apprehensive kids feel less fearful, and their group knows that being quiet has nothing to do with being unfriendly or snobbish. O'Keefe sometimes places students into groups based on her knowledge of their individual apprehension: one student with high apprehension, another with low, and the rest average. To get that information, she administers a self-assessment test (The Communication Apprehension Test PRCA-24, suitable for students in grades 7 through 12; see O'Keefe 101 ff. or request a copy from the Speech Communication Association). However, most secondary teachers know their students' personalities and styles readily without a test.

Another grouping method that O'Keefe recommends is based on sociograms. Teachers need multiple study topics for this group method. Students select three topics of interest and also three students with whom they would like to work. O'Keefe tells them they will get one topic of their choice or one person of their choice, and usually she can give them a topic and at least one person from their list. Students like this method because they participate in the selection process. The process is time consuming initially, so allow several hours for the matching and mixing.

Perhaps best of all, O'Keefe offers suggestions for grouping spontaneously and for improving classroom climate through social interaction. When you need small groups for brainstorming, buzz sessions, or one-class projects, have students count off into groups. Use dyads for responding and devising questions or planning activities; working in twos guarantees that both students will talk and prepares them for larger group work. From dyads, forming groups is easy: Two pairs become a group of four. If the number of pairs is uneven, one group could have six members—but no more. Groups of fewer than five are more productive. O'Keefe notes that "teachers who have not used small groups before find this pairing method a comfortable way to introduce grouping. Neither teachers nor students are placed in vulnerable positions" (95–96).

Training Groups

Working with small groups in a classroom does not come naturally to most students. Even adults usually work in groups only when they share similar interests and goals, and then it takes time for people to become comfortable with others in the group. In a classroom setting, students may experience similar discomfort and must learn and apply behaviors that foster cooperation. Without some training and without a firm structure for their group work, they will flounder—mainly because groups must be self-directed, a skill that requires planning and monitoring.

O'Keefe believes that preliminary activities will build group cohesion. In one such activity, groups choose a name and a logo for themselves, which leads students to explore the talents and interests of each member. Designing shields with sections devoted to each group member is another possibility. When the groups have completed this work, they present it to the class and explain their choices. As O'Keefe notes, "Establishing these social bonds speeds later work because it relaxes defensive behaviors and overcomes listening barriers" (96).

O'Keefe also warns that group work must have specific and clear objectives, or we risk student procrastination and wasted time. She suggests these essential guidelines for teachers establishing group work:

1. *Establish a time limit and stick to it.* For in-class group work, she suggests a 15-minute limit. Some groups will finish in 5 minutes and others won't. Those who finish early can repeat the steps to ensure nothing was missed or they can be asked to explain their work. If needed, grant another minute to those who aren't finished, but return to whole-class discussion. If students know time limits are honored, they are more likely to stay on task.
2. *Assign specific tasks within the group.* Students who don't know what's expected will waste time. Review responsibilities before breaking into groups and be absolutely clear in your directions.
3. *Require a product from the group.* At the end of the stipulated time, students should have something in hand: a list, an outline, questions, an answer, or tasks divided up for research or reading.

If you wish, you can establish a point system for completing the procedural tasks and include the points in the overall evaluation of their work. (adapted from O'Keefe, 97–98)

O'Keefe also specifies roles for group members: Some contribute to the task itself and others maintain the social interaction of the group. For example, a group needs at least one student who knows his or her "stuff" and can provide information, another who can reconcile differences, and yet another who can relax the group through humor. A student who can summarize or integrate information and one who handles notetaking also play important roles in making the group function. When group work is new, students may respond well to having specific roles assigned. As they become accustomed to group work, they will set more of the procedures and roles themselves. The strengths and weaknesses of group members will become clear in the process, and provided the group has good rapport, the students themselves will eventually learn to use one another's strengths to get the work done.

In this text, we cannot go into all the procedures and activities that help establish good working groups, but texts like O'Keefe's provide useful information for teachers committed to student interaction and cooperative learning. We urge you to explore these resources as you begin your teaching career; they will make a critical difference in your success with group work.

SPEAKING: MORE THAN JUST TALK

Speaking is a process, not a series of episodes, units, or courses.
Wisconsin Department of Public Instruction (90)

Speaking has most often been perceived of as "something the speech teacher takes care of," rather than as one of the major strands of the English language arts curriculum. Consequently, in many school districts, a curriculum for speaking translates into a single speech course. When this occurs, speaking is essentially isolated from conscious attention in the development of daily lessons and units in English classrooms. However, speaking is essential in all language arts classes, not only for its own sake but also because it influences the development of other language arts competencies.

Major Curricular Goals

As a curricular area, speaking parallels writing in important ways. Like writing, speaking must be purposeful, serving an authentic communicative need geared to audience and context. Moreover, in both media students need to experience the range of communicative functions. The Speech Communication Association's National Project on Speech Communication Competencies marked the origin of the functional communication approach to curriculum development (see Allen & Brown; Allen, Brown, and Yatvin; Wood 1977). They delineate the *five communicative functions* in this way:

- *Expressing feelings.* This pertains to communication acts that either express or respond to feelings, as well as attitudes.
- *Ritualizing.* This type of discourse is formulaic and culturally determined; it allows people to take part in social interactions and to maintain social relationships.
- *Imagining.* In this type of discourse, people place themselves in imaginary situations. Although we typically think of this discourse as fantasy or story-telling, it also includes communicative acts critical to academic discourse: theorizing, speculating, and dramatizing.

- *Informing.* Informative discourse is, of course, central to schooling. We need to provide information or to seek it. Often, then, we are stating, questioning, explaining, justifying, answering, and demonstrating.
- *Controlling.* This is persuasive discourse, in which people try to control behavior through effective use of language. This function is also central to schooling, where every speech act from permitting to rejecting, from justifying to arguing, from persuading to bargaining are commonplace. (Adapted from Wisconsin Department of Public Instruction, 1986, 90–91)

The major goals of the speaking curriculum are centered in these five communicative functions. The first goal, of course, is that students learn to speak effectively in all five functions. This does not mean that teachers should develop units around them; rather, the goal should be an integrated language arts curriculum in which all four language arts are present in daily lessons. For example, students may be reading novels as part of a thematic unit. Although we would expect and plan for discussion, we would also consciously build in questions and activities that focus specifically on one or more of the speech functions. Asking students to speculate on plot, imagine future character development, or to justify a character's action are different speech functions. Asking students to choose a scene for dramatizing or to write and then perform a scene using characters from the novel draws once more on different language competencies. If we keep the competencies in mind when we plan unit activities, we can be reasonably sure that our speaking curriculum is balanced.

As we plan classroom activities, we also need to consider the different levels of audience—from pairs to small groups to the whole class. Students need varied experiences in developing speaking competencies and audience awareness. Some students may be comfortable in pairs but not in front of a full class; others may feel inadequate in group work. Without consistent experience in all types of speaking situations, they might not develop a level of comfort that will serve them well as adults. Another related goal is competency and comfort among diverse racial and ethnic groups. Teachers fortunate enough to have a diverse student population find that cultural differences in speaking and listening can be easily identified and discussed. Lacking such diversity, we must find ways to increase student awareness of the cultural base of language. All languages express the five communicative functions, but how they do so is a matter of culture.

It might be argued that if students are engaging in these various functions through conversation alone, there is no need to place them in the curriculum. The problem is that student talk *is* culture-bound and, equally important, is not the talk of academic discourse. Moreover, students will not necessarily extend or evaluate talk, or ask good questions, or consider the significance of a message. They are not quick to determine the presence or lack of evidence or evaluate a line of reasoning. Nor are they necessarily aware of language strategies, such as those in argumentation and persuasion, or able to evaluate strategies for social acceptability and civic responsibility. These are critical competencies in a modern, democratic society. We also have another important role: teaching students the responsibility inherent in freedom of speech. Freedom of speech is one of America's most cherished values; however, it can be abused. Students need to understand the difference between the right to express an opinion and the "non-right" to verbally abuse, defame, or denigrate another human being.

All students, regardless of ability level, need classroom experience in speaking. All too often, speaking opportunities and training appear only in honors classes or advanced placement, where teachers view students as future leaders. However, "talk is as essential to thought as exercise is to health" (O'Keefe 15). From this perspective, talk must be at the center of the English language arts classroom. Unfortunately, teachers trained in English language arts generally lack training in oral language; moreover, student textbooks provide little assistance. The occasional discussion section at the end of a reading selection or chapter leaves the teacher trying to figure out how to initiate, maintain, and close a good discussion. But without planned "talk" for students, teachers tend to monopolize classroom talk—a situation that negates a student-centered classroom and integration of all the language arts into units and lessons.

IMPROVING DISCUSSION QUESTIONS

Jane Schaffer gives us a candid appraisal of her skill as a novice teacher:

> In my earlier days, I remember asking such inane questions as, "What about the river in *Huckleberry Finn?*" and then becoming irritated when students did not respond. I figured they had not done their homework or were not really trying hard enough. I look at this question now and understand several problems with it. (40)

Consider this basic principle for classroom discussion: students need to care about the questions. They aren't going to care about questions that are simply a "test" of whether they read the assignment, nor do such questions advance their thinking or oral language skills. Too often, questions at the end of textbook selections are useless, mainly because they are mini-tests of the worst sort: questions that call for facts that students can locate in the text. Such questions are not only mindless but boring. Mainstream students are accustomed to such questions, but non-mainstream students may be baffled by why teachers want them answer to something the teachers already know. As Shirley Brice Heath's *Ways With Words* illustrated, in many cultures teachers don't ask questions to which they already know the answer. We need to figure out what kinds of questions will interest and make sense to students.

Most students respond to questions that relate the material to their own lives. The idea is not to infringe on their privacy, but to link themes or ideas to the contemporary situations faced by adolescents or young adults. Students also respond to interpretative questions for which they know there is no right or wrong answer, where they know their genuine response counts. At the same time, we can train them to support their response by citing references to the text. This is a critical skill, one most lacking in American students according to National Assessment of Educational Progress reports in the past decade. An excellent way to make students better respondents to interpretive questions is to train them to write the questions themselves. Schaffer suggests requiring students to address topics they really want to discuss and to ask for three questions per student. The teacher would then choose several for discussion, dictate them to the class, and allow students time to think about their responses (40). Allowing time for reflection is another critical feature of good discussions. We often tend to avoid silence and call on the first student to respond, thus cutting off thinking time and recognizing the same students too frequently.

Another feature of good discussion is planned closure. All of us have experienced classes where discussion was suddenly cut off in midstream because the class had run out of time. Because we cannot truly recreate the discussion later, it is better to plan for closure. Stopping 5 or 10 minutes before the end of the hour and asking students to summarize, either orally or on paper, is one method. Another is asking them to describe what they learned during that discussion using specific and well-focused comments. Students could also write one question that had not been answered in the discussion (Schaffer 41). All of these activities require good listening skills. For this reason, we cannot initially expect very complete or very good responses, but responses will improve with experience and the knowledge that our request is genuine. If we return to Jane Schaffer's question about *Huck Finn,* at this point, we can probably detect her reasons for calling it "inane." Just what *is* wrong with it?

USING STUDENTS AS TEACHERS

We sometimes underestimate the instructional role our students can play. When this happens, we deny them opportunities to hone their conversational skills and to provide leadership, which also enhance their self-esteem. We are not suggesting just "turning them loose," especially if they are working with younger students. Student teachers need some guidelines, both for their own security and the well-being of the one being tutored. The time initially spent on guidelines and monitoring their progress, however, yields real benefits for all concerned.

Across Grade Levels

Many middle school students are capable of assisting elementary students with their assignments. Their explanations may be the very ones that bridge the knowledge gap. Similarly, senior high students may be excellent teachers of middle school or elementary students. Choose students for their knowledge and skills in any discipline, not just the English language arts. Students with limited English proficiency especially need opportunities for "school talk."

Peer Tutoring

Within the English language arts class, peers are valuable resources. They can read to one another, ask questions to check comprehension, act as audience and respondent in writing, and teach usage and mechanics.

Small-Group Work

Within a group, formally or informally, kids can and do teach other kids. Projects involving cooperation, dialogue, and give and take are important components of a unit. Speaking and listening skills are continually exercised when students have to rely on one another to complete the tasks.

CLASSROOM STRATEGIES FOR FOSTERING AUTHENTIC DISCUSSION

Too often, teachers lead discussions that are really recitation: The teacher asks a question, and the student responds; the teacher asks the next question, and the next student responds. Many textbooks, unfortunately, reinforce this teacher-centered model through the questions at the end of the reading or end of the chapter. Authentic and sustained opportunities for speaking arise when teachers plan them as a matter of course throughout the year. *The English Journal* featured some of these teachers recently, and their good ideas for student discussion are easily adapted for both middle and high schoolers.

Personal Response, Small Group, Large Group

Wilbur H. Sowder, Jr., a teacher at Ridgefield Park, New Jersey, found that techniques developed in his Advanced Placement (AP) English class also work well for his average seventh graders. Sowder uses reading journals (personal response to reading and discussion) as the basis for small-group response. For example, he began a discussion of Zindel's *The Pigman* with a 15-minute journal writing on "Pigmen I have known." Students shared their journal entries with their circle of four or five classmates. Then, as Sowder tells it, from across the room he heard a student read:

> My grandmother had old-timer's disease for six years, and she walked around as if she were searching for a special god. (39)

Sowder noted that the student's entire circle snapped to attention with that line. And that line was the springboard to a whole-class discussion on family relations and the death of a loved one. The progression Sowder followed—individual thinking and response, to focused group discussion, to whole-class discussion—is a good one, regardless of age group or piece of literature. In AP English, Sowder removed the final word, *death,* from T. S. Eliot's "Journey of the Magi" and asked students to complete the poem. Because Sowder uses a reader response approach, the groups are actively engaged and not worried about a "right" response. Later, he gave the class Adrienne Rich's "Living in Sin," without the final image. He found student response so intense that he scrapped plans for only 10 minutes of group discussion. Sowder believes, "A reader cannot seriously attempt to choose the final word for 'Journey of the Magi' or 'Living in Sin' without integrating the poet's ideas and images, without evoking the world of the poem" (40). Benefits of this methodology extend to the teacher. Says Sowder:

> I rely on student ideas, questions, and even misconceptions to promote group and class discussion. I'm becoming a better reader and a better teacher as I learn to see literature through students' eyes. I'd rather respond to their ideas than ask them to grapple with mine. Above all, I want them to be active. (41)

Sowder's success with everything from Hinton's *The Outsiders* to Kafka's *The Metamorphosis* rests on his determination to make students the center of his classroom:

> If I devise thought-provoking, open-ended activities, student momentum often carries discussion further than I ever did in a teacher-centered classroom. I now spend a lot of time preparing questions: unexpected questions, puzzling questions. Questions that ask students to examine their own lives and read literature with a purpose. The students have become the center of my classroom, and I wouldn't have it any other way. (42)

The Fishbowl

In another New Jersey high school, Haddonfield, other teachers are finding similar success. Terry Willis' 11th graders have taken on *Macbeth* and through a "fishbowl" strategy, are having animated, informed discussions (Bolche 30). Classroom chairs are arranged in a "fishbowl," two circles, one inside the other. As students enter the room, Willis assigns students to one circle. The inner circle is then given about eight minutes to discuss the statement: "Men who have been on the battlefield may come home to act like criminals in time of peace." Students are told to relate this statement both to *Macbeth* and contemporary life—an idea that they have already explored in their journals. The ground rules are simple: State an idea and support it with evidence; agree with the speaker and add additional evidence; disagree with a speaker and offer evidence.

Each student in the outer circle spends the eight minutes listening to the discussion and making notes on the interaction of their "fish." Willis provides students with a worksheet to make notetaking easier and more precise:

> Throughout the discussion, students tally each time their "fish" contributes an idea, describes feelings, paraphrases, expresses support or acceptance, encourages others to contribute, summarizes, relieves tension by joking, or gives direction to the group's work. (Bolche 43)

Willis notes that students in the inner circle treat each other with courtesy. What's more, "the positive, enthusiastic acknowledgement of peers has a certain magical quality" (Bolche 43). After eight minutes, students exchange places, those in the inner circle become observers in the outer ring, and those in the outer ring become the inner ring "discussers" of a second focus statement. At the end of class, students reflect on the fishbowl as a discussion strategy. In Willis' experience, students have enthusiastically endorsed it, perhaps for the same reason that teachers employ it: "The best part of this fishbowl is a controlled free-for-all—a spontaneous explosion of ideas with nothing held back—exciting and argumentative" (Bolche 43).

Creative Controversy

Just down the hall at Haddonfield High School, Marilyn Lee Mauger's 10th graders are studying *The Crucible* through a cooperative group technique (Bolche 90). Mauger divides the class into groups of four, and within the foursome, students are paired. Each pair has to build a case, taking opposite positions on the dilemma faced by John Procter in Act IV. For homework, students use the text to build evidence for their positions; in class, the pairs integrate ideas and evidence into a coherent position. Ms. Mauger then has each pair separate and consult others who prepared the same position. Following this sharing, students return to their own partners, assimilating new ideas. The next class period, each group presents its positions. While one pair is presenting, the other pair takes notes. They then ask clarifying questions, request further evidence, and openly challenge one another: "Book pages fly, bodies lean forward, and voices are raised in earnest excitement" (qtd. in Bolche 44).

Mauger notes that following this rather intense discussion, each pair prepares "for what might be the most interesting and challenging phase of this creative controversy—perspective reversals" (Bolche 44). As they switch positions, students have to add at least two new pieces of evidence for the argument, and present the new positions the following class period. Finally, they drop advocacy and strive to reach a consensus. For the final task, the small group (the foursome) presents its decision to the class through oral presentations, written statements, and visual displays. As with most authentic discussion, students are enthusiastic about their experience with this strategy. As one of them said: "It was much more helpful to hear the views of classmates rather than just listen to the teacher" (qtd. in Bolche 44). In a student-centered classroom, such views would be the norm, not the exception.

Teach Each Other

Margo Sorenson, an 8th-grade teacher from Harbor Day School in Corona del Mar, CA, has found "the open-discussion method energizes the classroom and stimulates me to encourage students to challenge themselves" (43). Colleagues report her method has been successful at every grade level between 5th and 12th and with students of all ability levels. Sorenson teaches the format in one class period, beginning with questions about student-teacher discussions. Students readily relate their history with traditional class discussions: boring; never learn anything; teacher does all the talking; a couple of smart kids do all the answering. Sorenson then explains the format and expectations for a discussion unlike those just described. Students will be the center of discussion and will in fact teach one another. At the same time, she explains a bit of reader response to them, emphasizing there are no right or wrong opinions as long as opinions are supported with details from the readings.

There are three rules for open discussion:

Courtesy

Participation grades depend on contributions, and each comment receives a "check," regardless of its merit. Each student calls on another student, with raised hand and a finger signal to indicate if it is the first or second entry into the discussion. Students are expected to keep track of participation and ensure that those who have spoken little or not at all become participants. To encourage silent students, Sorenson teaches the class to do the following:

1. Alert the student who will be called on first by stating that student's name.
2. Give an opinion so the student to be called on has something to react to.
3. Ask about the stated opinion.

"This procedure," says Sorenson, "ensures that no students are caught mentally flat-footed in discussion . . . and promotes the belief that the students really are engaged in helping each other learn" (44).

Don't Look at the Teacher!

Sorenson tells her students that she will not show approval or disapproval, nor will she contribute or ask questions unless it is essential that she clarify some point. She explains that they are a community of learners, teaching one another, and that includes her—and that each year she gains insights and new approaches to literature through her eighth graders.

Tolerate Silence

Explaining that thinking takes time and silence is fine, Sorenson again places leadership within the student group:

> When the discussion on a particular question seems to have ended and no one has anything more to say, or when comments are becoming repetitive, any one of the students may ask "Are we done? Shall we go on to another question?" Students manage their own discussion and end it when they want. (44)

However, Sorenson also helps students with "food for thought" by providing discussion cue sheets. The cue sheets serve as a reminder of thoughts and questions that might otherwise be fleeting:

- What did you like about the previous contribution?
- What new ideas did that contribution give you?
- What puzzled you in that last statement?
- What in the last statement had not occurred to you before?

- How did the person making the statement arrive at that conclusion?
- Can you elaborate, explain, or give another example? (44)

Sorenson also asks students to do some self-evaluation in their journals, using these questions to help them consider their contributions before another discussion:

- Did I contribute to the discussion?
- Did I encourage others to contribute or clarify ideas?
- What would I like to do in the next discussion?
- How can I do this?
- Who contributed the most interesting or valuable comments?
- Who was the Most Valuable Player in keeping the discussion going?
- Who encouraged me the most in discussion? (44)

As further incentive, Sorenson gives some "silly reward" to students named by peers—like a "little gummed gold star (which they promptly stick on their shirts or noses for the rest of the day) or a crazy rubber stamp on the back of their hands and in their spirals" (45). She has found the process "does wonders for motivating students to recognize each other's contributions and do well enough to be nominated next time by one of their peers" (45).

Preparation for discussion begins with journal writes, perhaps responses to some open-ended questions about the literature or developing their own questions. These form the basis of the student-led discussion. Sorenson reports that "the teacher's hardest job is often to be quiet when a 'right' answer seems so obvious and let the students be accountable for their own investigation and inquiry—to teach each other" (46). She also notes that patience pays off as students become more experienced with the format: Insights are deeper, notetaking becomes common, listening habits improve. Students also become skilled at monitoring themselves and capable of assessing when too many similar comments are made or discussion is off track.

Through this discussion method, students make significant gains in both oral skills and analytic skills. These in turn transfer into better writing about literature. Perhaps the most significant aspect of the method lies in students' initiative and responsibility for their own learning—at the core of a student-centered classroom where students build self-esteem and confidence through sustained experience with oral language and an integrated language arts approach.

READER RESPONSE

Although we will discuss reader response in detail in our discussion of teaching literature, it also merits a few words here. We can describe reader response as both an instructional strategy and a form of literary criticism. As classroom practice, reader response invites students to respond to a text, working with it to create meaning. The text does not have a "correct" meaning, and the reader is not laboring to decipher the author's intent. As O'Keefe puts it: "The goal of reader response in the classroom is to facilitate students' perceptions and responses to the text rather than to dictate a specific view" (123). As students look at their own experience and later share their experiences and learned knowledge, they begin to interact with the literary text. "As they discuss and question," says O'Keefe, "they build a bridge of understanding between the text and their own lives in a manner not possible when all the questions originate from the teacher" (123). Thus, argues O'Keefe:

> Classroom talk has particular value for improving reading comprehension. Reading a text aloud, discussing its meaning, and interpreting characters' roles are all activities that fit under the broad category of reader response. Readers shape meaning as they move from concrete personal experience to abstractions of those experiences. This kind of thinking is essential for perceptive, competent readers. And these understandings become more accessible to all students through classroom talk and through dramatic activities. (121)

Each of the discussion strategies just shared by teachers relies on reader response to a certain degree. There is no question that it is a powerful approach to literature, especially for adolescents who are exploring their own lives. When coupled with student-led discussion, reading response reinforces a belief that students *do* have something to say and are perfectly capable of saying it with insight and honesty—if only we let them.

TALKING ABOUT LITERATURE

In *Speaking to Thinking/Thinking to Speak,* Virginia O'Keefe offers many suggestions for integrating oral language activities into the English language arts classroom. These activities can be implemented throughout the year and are easily adapted to whatever literature is studied.

- Students give prepared, short (3-minute) readings from books they have enjoyed.
- Students tape a "Book Program" in which a group discusses one book or reviews related titles. This activity works well with a unit in which students are reading a shared title but also working with supplementary/complementary books.
- Students retell a short extract from a story as a radio play (complete with sound effects and music). Or they could use original scripts based on a piece of fiction.
- Students produce a "sound and light" show to illustrate a piece of literature (poetry also works well), using music, taped or live readings, and projected pictures.
- Groups can advertise their book or complementary texts to their peers via live or taped performance.
- Individuals or groups simulate a call-in program either to characters in a piece of literature or to the author.
- Students pair off to play journalist and author. This exchange is essentially a question-and-answer session about plot, characters, setting, and so forth.

- A group plays out a scenario in which they discuss how they would turn a book into a film (e.g., who would play the leads or what scenes would work well in film).
- Students become characters placed on a witness stand and are cross-examined by lawyers representing other characters or the class community.
- Students retell a story using a Jeopardy-like game. Teams plan questions about story elements and take turns quizzing their classmates. (Adapted from O'Keefe 15–17)

Another of O'Keefe's suggestions for oral language touches social issues and helps students appreciate the underlying meaning in a piece of literature. Students first brainstorm for possible social issues (e.g., for *Wuthering Heights* they might focus on class and race prejudice, alcoholism, women's rights, abuse, and inheritance laws). They then research those issues as they relate to today's society, with each student or group later presenting research findings orally. Each student or group must compile a list of related examples or observations from the literary text, followed by a student-led whole-class discussion of the issue as it relates to the novel. A follow-up written assignment might be an informal journal piece. O'Keefe notes the importance of this kind of activity: "Students can find a 'way into' a text though contemporary issues. This is the kind of discussion that allows everyone to speak and offer opinions, whether about the issue or the text" (18–19).

Pam B. Cole suggests using literary circle discussions to illustrate how an individual response to a piece of literature is not only possible but appropriate. After students have had a few days to immerse themselves in their reading, they meet three times a week to share their responses to the novel. Using their journals as a springboard to discussion, students share their reactions to specific words, lines, or passages. Cole notes that "a more challenging group activity is to have students perform think-alouds" (31). Her teacher directives are as follows:

> Before their groups convene, have students choose passages that depict levels of growth and psychological changes that occur in the characters. When they meet in their groups, have students read their chosen passages to the group and then speculate about the changes that are taking place within the characters. These activities, while encouraging group participation, will allow students to explore their own questions and reactions to the text. (31)

Not only does the literary circle discussion foster good listening and speaking skills, but it eliminates the idea that a single interpretation, especially that of a teacher, is the definitive one.

Literary interviews offer students experience in written and oral language. In a model suggested by Terry Johnson and Daphne Louis, students take on the role of a literary character. They are then interviewed both by a partner and later by the entire class. Although the first questions are based on story information, additional questions can relate to events not in the actual story but which are plausible given the plot and characters. In planning, both partners develop the questions to be asked, but they do not rehearse the responses. As Johnson and Louis note, "The keys to success are well thought-out questions and an interviewee who is able to enter into their chosen character" (134). Students can get some instruction on interviewing skills by listening to radio or television interviews. Then they will be better able to formulate criteria through observation and experience.

Some variations on the literary interview are the "mystery guest," the panel interview, and the "stop-action" interview. The mystery guest is someone who wanders into the classroom, to be questioned by a co-conspirator at first and then by the class. The panel interview involves multiple characters from a story. Or the panel could be inventive and collect characters from different stories who might have some very interesting things to say to one another. The stop-action interview occurs during a dramatization of a story. At prearranged points, the actors freeze. One of them is "unfrozen" by the interviewer, who poses questions regarding the current situation, about other characters, or future plans. The use of this variation, caution Johnson and Louis, should be both infrequent and brief (136).

Mary Ellen MacArthur suggests poetry presentations in place of the more traditional written "favorite author" paper. She helped students make connections between literature and the arts; at the same time, she provided a context for visual and oral interpretation and for performance. She asked her senior high school students to choose a poem from those studied in American literature and incorporate visual, dramatic, and musical elements, or any combination of the arts into an oral presentation. Her students responded with slides, video, computer graphics, cartoons, photos, music, and a variety of props (69–71). This assignment has potential for any grade level and any type of poetry; it also allows students from diverse cultures to explore and present their literary heritage.

ORAL LANGUAGE ACTIVITIES FOR ADOLESCENTS

The following activities, developed by experienced teachers and published in professional journals or texts, are intended to stimulate thinking and discussion. They're not a recipe for instant success. Although working out units and lessons is a highly personal affair, reading about them and listening to teachers talk about what worked well in their classes are important parts of professional growth.

Interdisciplinary

One of the best ways to ensure that oral language activities are purposeful is to integrate them with content area material. This integration ensures that students learn the material more thoroughly and practice speaking and listening skills in a focused but varied environment. Nora Elegreet-DeSalvo and Ronald Levitsky developed an interdisciplinary unit for middle school students that could be adapted for any grade level. Working with material from U.S. history, they chose immigration as the unit theme.

They assigned students to fictitious immigrant families who came to America between 1845 and 1915; they chose appropriate surnames and first names and personal roles within the family, with the only stipulation that there be three generations represented.

Using factual knowledge about immigrants of representative ethnic groups, students developed their roles. They listened to authentic music and then wrote their own songs of farewell. By watching films, they gained a sensitivity to the historical period. They then chose a situation faced by immigrants (e.g., going to a store) and wrote scripts dramatizing each experience. Students then presented these dramatic sketches to the class. The central question that guided the unit was "What is an American?" Students then moved on to discuss the issues facing immigrants in America today.

Verbal Folklore and American Dialects
Verbal folklore is yet another way for students to present their heritage. Folk speech and naming, proverbs, riddles and other verbal puzzles, and rhymes are one aspect; folk poetry, myths, legends, folktales, and folk songs are another. Verbal folklore, which includes drama, dances, and games, allows students of all cultures to present their culture and practice oral skills at the same time (Duenas Gonzales 23). All cultures have an oral tradition, but not all have maintained its primacy. Some students, then, may not be well-versed in their own folklore and may have to do some library work before making an oral presentation.

Oral language activities that promote an understanding of American dialects arise out of literature and the performing arts. Jesse Colquit suggests teachers begin by reading aloud, introducing students to literature, poetry, music, and drama that reflect dialect differences. Colquit recommends the following resources for this purpose:

1. *The Split Cherry Tree* by Jesse Stuart for showing students the beauty of mountain dialect and the diversity of dialect within a single family. Students could role-play or do dramatic readings of various passages.
2. James Russell Lowell's "The Courtin'" compared with Robert Frost's "Mending Wall" to illustrate the Northeast dialect of a century ago and today.
3. *The Friendly Persuasion* by Jessamyn West, a collection of short stories written in the Quaker dialect.
4. "The Heifer Hide" in *The Jake Tales,* Richard Chase's collection of Appalachian mountain folktales.
5. *Huckleberry Finn*
6. Ballads and country music for western and southern dialects.
7. For contrasting black dialect of the nineteenth and twentieth centuries, Paul Lawrence Dunbar's "In the Morning" and Langston Hughes' "The Ballad of the Landlord." Hughes' poetry provides a contrasting voice in black dialect and standard American English (71–75).

A school librarian can help you find other representative titles for illustrating American dialects.

Storytelling

Another oral language activity that works well with students of any age is storytelling. Lynda Williams, a high school teacher, believes that too many teachers have been afraid to experiment with storytelling, perhaps fearing that students will think it is babyish. In her experience, however, high school students love listening to stories; what's more, it changed some of their attitudes toward reading and provided good listening practice (36). For this activity, students must come prepared to listen and suspend disbelief; the teacher must also clue students into listening, perhaps for certain word or concepts, especially if they will be asked to analyze the piece later. The teacher starts by reading a selection of approximately 10 minutes, such as Simon's death in *Lord of the Flies* or Catherine's death in *Wuthering Heights*. In this way, the teacher models the reading performance, which differs from acting. Williams notes that some students may not want to read aloud at first, and that the teacher shouldn't worry about it. What is important is the balance between good oral reading models and experience. Other activities include the use of mystery stories to help students make predictions, asking them "whodunit?" or reading a short story to the class and then asking the students to read it individually and note the differences between the oral and silent readings (Williams 37).

Larry Swartz's *Dramathemes* offers many ideas for storytelling. One activity involves imbuing ordinary objects with importance and a history. As Swartz explains it, each student brings an object and works in a small group to invent a story about it, which he or she then shares with the group. Students could weave their stories from history or cultural folklore (e.g., the jewelry box belonged to Cleopatra; the stone was given to the first Americans on the Great Plains) or even a mythical alien civilization. Students should be encouraged to be very detailed in their storymaking. As an extension, Swartz recommends telling students that these objects belonged to someone important, but now deceased. Each group would build a story about the person, incorporating each of the group's objects into it. Two groups could work together. Another extension would have groups exchange their objects and repeat the exercise; then, they would tell each other the stories they invented for that set of objects (25).

Another storytelling activity recommended by Swartz involves students' working with a novel. The class would be divided into small groups, with each group responsible for conveying important information from one chapter. Each group can dramatize the story in one of the following ways:

- By becoming storytellers
- By telling the story in a role and from that character's point of view
- Creating an improvisation based on a scene in that chapter
- Through tableaux
- Through song
- As Story Theatre (narration, dialogue, and movement)
- As Readers Theatre (reading the text aloud)
- As an interview

- As diary or letter
- As a poem
- As a series of illustrations
- In movement only
- Using sound and movement (Swartz 55)

Swartz also uses fairy tales for storytelling activities. Since fairy tales are familiar to most students, they offer a good springboard for oral work—and fun as well. Since fairy tales are passed down from one generation to the next, students are asked to imagine that one of the characters was able to tape his or her story for future generations. Students could reread a tale they enjoy or try out an unfamiliar one, but in either case, they must retell the story without using the book. The students will tape-record their tales as told from the point of view of any character they choose. They are free to change or omit details from the original story, and perhaps add some details of their own. The tape recordings would be shared with the whole class (77).

High Schoolers, Building Trust Through Stories

Nancy King's *Storymaking and Drama* is an exciting resource for secondary teachers. Because many high school teachers believe that their students will find story activities "kid stuff," they tend to exclude these activities from the curriculum. King, however, believes that old stories are the best way to introduce new ideas: "The experience of telling connects me with the world tradition of storytelling and helps to create an environment that is special, apart from the usual classroom interaction" (26). As a way of beginning, King tells students a story, shown in Box 5–1, she heard from a Thai woman, who told her that she first heard it from her Laotian mother.

Box 5–1

A COMMUNITY OF KNOWING

In former times, the Akha people had letters. One year, all the letters were swallowed by the water buffalo and imprinted on its skin. When the time came to make their yearly move, the people discovered the water buffalo's skin was too big and too heavy for them to move to their new location. The people were perplexed. They did not want to leave their letters, and they could not move the skin.

They went to Headman. He thought about the problems, "If we cannot move the water buffalo's skin, we must eat the water buffalo's skin. This way we keep the letters inside us forever."

And so the water buffalo's skin was cut up into the number of people in the group. Each person swallowed a piece. Thus the letters were kept within the tribe forever. (King 26)

King then takes students through this process:

1. *Write:* On a small piece of paper, write a small bit of information that you would like to see remembered, perhaps to be shared with people you don't know. Don't sign your name.
2. *Pass:* Pass your paper to another person.
3. *Share:* Share the bits of information.
4. *Reflect on the story and the process.* Consider the following: what kinds of information are important? Is hearing the bits of information different from writing it in private? If so, in what ways? (26–27)

The next process King uses is especially relevant given the role of quilts in our past and now in our present, such as those made by AIDS activists, friends, and families. The quilt exercise, shown in Box 5–2, is an excellent way to introduce or remind students of the power of storytelling and the many ways we have to do it.

BOX 5–2

THE QUILT

1. *Consider:* Quiltmaking is part of many cultures' history and artistry. Both AIDS and peace activists have designed and made huge quilts from pieces created by people all over the world. When brought together, the pieces represent lives, memories, dreams, and hopes.
   - In what ways is the impact of a quilt affected if it is made by one person or by one hundred?
   - What might your class consider so important that you decide to work as a group to share your ideas or viewpoint? How do you decide? How do you negotiate differences?
2. *Select:* A theme of interest to everyone in the class. Make it large enough to accommodate many diverse possibilities.
3. *Design:* A class quilt from papers cut into pieces four inches square.
4. *Create:* Using paint, pencil, or crayon, create an image that symbolizes your theme.
5. *Assemble:* Tape together the pieces of quilt.
6. *String:* A rope so that you can hang the quilt with clothespins.
7. *Reflect on the process:* How is your theme affected by being part of an idea quilt? What is the impact when you look at the completed quilt? How does making the quilt affect your connection to the rest of your classmates? (adapted from King, 26–27)

King's text is filled with specific classroom activities that help students conceptualize and build ideas, as well help them build a classroom community through shared experiences. King says:

I realize there are many problems to be faced: large classes; short teaching/learning periods; insufficient planning time; unsympathetic administrations; students who are unable to read, focus or concentrate; unyielding required curricula; and a lack of creative expertise. And yet, there is the human spirit, which thrives on imagery and expression. . . .

Creating stories may appear to be an unusual activity for many students, particularly in classrooms where there are time constraints and academic standards to be met. However, imagemaking is a productive means of evoking stories and drama, all of which improve student understanding of a text. (5)

King offers another important reason for teachers to incorporate storymaking and drama into their literature and language units:

Many of us already feel a sense of isolation, a lack of real community. We live very separate lives, often at great distance from family and childhood homes. We learn to keep our thoughts and feelings to ourselves. Many teachers have told me that they wish their students would be more forthcoming in class discussion. Sharing stories and making drama are excellent ways to build community within the classroom, to create a communal space where students feel safe to express opinions not yet fully formed or clearly understood and to discover the stories of their lives and their society. (4–5)

In a student-centered classroom, "stories of their lives and their societies" is a critical element in student response to literature and language, as well as the taproot of authentic writing.

Using Television

Barbra Morris notes that "students are hungry for serious dialogue about what they see on television" (40). She thus devised some activities to turn students from couch potatoes into informed critics. To teach students to be keen listeners and critics, she asked them to keep individual written logs of a program's content. Their task was to write down as much as they could of what they saw and heard, keeping as thorough a record as possible. Although students initially are frustrated, the results "yield rich firsthand evidence" for class discussion of the elements of various programs. Students are able to discriminate features of programs and make text analyses, leading them to rediscover what familiar programs actually contain. In Morris' experience, as students listen to one another, they soon "realize superficial, unsubstantiated, or unspecific generalizations are a waste of class time" (36).

VCRs give teachers another method of developing activities to enhance both listening skills and critical thinking. They can tape a variety of programs—the *News Hour With Jim Lehrer*, a local newscast, cartoons, sitcoms, sports events, and musical events—and then design preview or postview questions to elicit thoughtful and critical responses. Programs could be divided into various categories (e.g., sports, news, comedy, drama) and given to pairs or small groups of students, with instructions to design questions or prepare oral summaries for exchange with other pairs or groups. Before giving students these tasks, however, teachers should work through one and model the process.

Transforming the Talk Show

Most students have seen various talk shows, such as *Oprah,* and understand the format quite well: prepared questions, ad lib questions, and give and take. This format can be easily adapted for use with literature. One of our students did just that with a popular British talk show hostess, Dame Edna (who is male, by the way). Dale decided that for his oral assignment in Romantics that he would have Dame Edna, whom he played, interview Keats and Shelley. He thus combined a great deal of content knowledge about these poets and the Romantic movement with thoughtful questions. The result was a thoroughly original and humorous oral presentation.

Using Slides

Jack Cameron believes that using slides promotes visual literacy and focused, genuine discussion. He encourages teachers to create their own collection of slides for the following classroom activities: random reaction to literal or implied information conveyed by the slide (e.g., time of day, clues to season); multisensory reaction to nonvisual details suggested by the picture (e.g., if standing by photographer, what sounds, smells, textures, and so forth would one experience?); interpretation of the picture in metaphorical terms; interpretation of the picture in terms of the human condition (e.g., who are these people, what is their relationship?). Cameron notes that students will talk freely about issues, "express what has usually gone unexpressed," and through talk, "make sense of their experience" (14–19). These activities could easily be adapted for writing as well. Students of all ages could develop descriptive sketches, poetry, dramatic monologues, or dialogue for specific slides.

Using Film

Richard Fehlman offers ways to use portions of popular films to develop and foster critical viewing and listening skills. Fehlman urges teachers to choose film segments for their complexity and insight—in other words, an artistic text. These could be used in connection with literary texts. In using only segments, teachers can avoid potential problems with censorship; to avoid legal problems, says Fehlman, be certain to "footnote" the segment you are using, just as you would with a literary text.

One approach to this activity is thematic. Self-awareness, for example, is a popular theme in literature and film. Fehlman notes the opening scene in *Rocky* as one such place to examine this concept, leading to a discussion of the difference between confidence and conceit. Child-parent relationships provide another common and high-interest theme, such as in *Tender Mercies,* the scenes between Mac and his daughter; in *Ordinary People,* the scenes between Conrad and his mother; and in *Cat on a Hot Tin Roof,* the basement scene between Big Daddy and Brick, where attention to the physical setting is critical to understanding the relationship. Film adaptations of books are another way to use film segments. Fehlman suggests using segments that are similar rather than dissimilar. Fehlman points out two such scenes in *To Kill a Mockingbird:* Atticus' summation to the jury and Bob Ewell's attack on the children (84–87). For younger students, *Sounder* provides an interesting view of literary text and film adaptation.

INFORMAL CLASSROOM DRAMA

James Moffett and Betty Jane Wagner note that "*informal classroom drama* covers the *creative dramatics* of elementary school, the *improvising* of secondary, and the *role playing* of both (91). It is differentiated from theatre in that "students invent and enact dramatic situations for themselves" (Wisconsin Dept. of Instruction, 1990, 107). Theatre, by contrast, involves an audience, which necessarily creates different dynamics and accommodations, such as effect and points of view. Moffett and Wagner believe that "theatre is a secondary effect of drama, an outgrowth appropriate in school only for experienced players who ask for an audience" (91).

Informal classroom drama, on the other hand, is a teaching strategy that enhances various academic and social skills. Among these are the improvement of all language skills, analytic thinking, problem solving, and sustained concentration. Betty Jane Wagner points out that "improvisational drama, perhaps more obviously than other oral language activities, ties directly into both literary and nonverbal knowing" (196). John H. Bushman and Kay Parks Bushman concur: "Role playing and improvisation expand the boundaries of experience for students so that they develop a more completed understanding of themselves and of the literature they are reading . . . Students get inside the characters and play out their emotions, making choices and decisions based on the readers' understanding of those characters" (35). Bushman and Bushman go on to argue that young adult novels offer a particularly rich source for drama because "moral dilemma is most often at the heart of the novel's conflict" (35). The analytic and problem-solving skills needed for successful role playing and improvisation based on young adult literature are the same skills most teens need in daily life. Through vicarious experience, teens can safely test their decisions and, without harm, explore the consequences of words and actions. Students involved in classroom drama also strengthen their self-concept and their ability to work cooperatively (Wisconsin Dept. of Instruction, 1986, 108). Because students are both the "inventors and actors," the role of the teacher is one of facilitator.

Informal classroom drama offers a safe place to learn and practice new skills. It also offers a way for growing adolescents to cope with the rapid changes in their emotions and bodies. Anyone who has taught middle school can attest to the "worms in a tin can" phenomenon: The students appear to wiggle all day long. Some senior high school students demonstrate a similar tendency. Kids need movement, and informal drama can provide it. The social aspects are similarly important. Role playing allows students to try out various personas, observe them in other students, and generally gain some insight. Older students also have an opportunity to recognize the complexity of choice and the gravity of consequences, all in a controlled environment. Cognitively, informal drama provides a means of taking abstract ideas and making them comprehensible through concrete expression. Take, for example, the abstract concept "justice." What does it really mean? Is its meaning as simple and clear as the dictionary definition? Through drama, students can enact the meaning and thus deal with it concretely (Wisconsin Dept. of Instruction, 1990, 92).

Wagner suggests using informal drama in various ways: (a) use drama as a whole-class activity in which students pantomime the action as the teacher or a student reads the text aloud; (b) plan a dramatization ahead of time (not reading from script) with two groups of student volunteers to act it out, followed by class discussion comparing the two versions; or (c) dramatize a scene that was *not* part of a story they have just read but which would fit contextually. Wagner believes that "drama in the classroom entails unremitting pressure to develop listening and conversational skill" (197–198). Moreover, students "grow in their capacity to send and receive increasingly complex and mature verbal messages effectively, independently, creatively, and symbolically" (210). What's more, most students enjoy it, which is why Wagner believes its educational importance is often underestimated. Moffett and Wagner make an important point, especially for teachers unfamiliar with informal drama: "Teachers should not feel that time spent on [these activities] takes away from reading and writing or basic literacy. Drama will definitely further such goals" (91).

More specifically, drama serves these important purposes: to foster expression of all kinds, to develop concentration and focus energy, to habituate students to self-directed small-group work, to foster intuitive understanding of rhetorical style, to channel emotions, and to make language in school fun. Further, informal drama can play an important role for students with limited English proficiency; second language acquisition depends on an interesting and lively oral language environment, which informal drama provides (Moffett & Wagner 91–92).

Drama Activities

Johnson and Louis also make an important distinction between drama and theatre: "Drama encompasses every person in the room; there is no stage and no audience. Theatre, on the other hand, involves actors and a passive audience" (162). They also suggest avoiding any type of "star" system or an emphasis on performance. Drama and mime can be used in connection with a story, with students acting out the events. Alternatively, teachers can introduce students to some of the dramatic situations that arise from the narrative before they read the story themselves. This requires breaking the story into a series of dramatic scenarios to which the students would respond. Partner and group work are appropriate here. After students have read the story, they can then dramatize actual scenes.

Readers' theatre is a class activity in which students sit in a group and read their parts directly from a script, as though it were a radio production. Neither movement nor memorization of lines is required. Although the activity works well with prepared scripts, Johnson and Louis believe that students are engaged more fully if they begin with a narrative and transform it into a play themselves (166). Teachers prepare students for this activity by modeling the process: Take part of a story and create a play script; ask the class to examine both and note the changes; then, take a second part of the story and have the class transform it. Finally, students take another part of the story, work on it in pairs, and eventually exchange their work with another pair of students. Students are expected to provide constructive criticism. After this experience, students could work with a story of their own choosing, either alone or in pairs. Johnson and

Louis recommend that teachers go over criteria for story selection first to ensure that students choose a story with ample conversation and several characters (166).

Mask Making, Pantomime, and Improvisation

Although written for elementary students, Bette Bosma's on using folk literature is a rich resource for teachers of all grade levels. Bosma points out that students will "become less inhibited doing pantomime and improvisation when using masks" (56). It isn't that masks hide the student, Bosma notes, but rather that the mask facilitates the student's releasing self into the character. Students could use children's stories or turn to Native American or African folklore, in which masks play a significant role. Bosma suggests consulting *Who's in Rabbit's House?* by Verna Aardema, where Leo and Diane Dillon's illustrations "depict the story as being performed by masked players" (57). Bosma also recommends *Masks, Face Coverings, and Headgear* by Norman Laliberte and A. Mogelon as a resource. After exploring various types of folklore (e.g., myth, fable, legend, fairy tale, folktale), students could write their own and then create the masks for pantomime or oral presentation.

Puppets

Bosma believes that the "sharply drawn characters of fairy tales and animal tales make wonderful puppets. From the simplest paper bag puppet to the most elaborate pâpier-maché model, storybook characters can be easily identified by accentuating particular features" (59). For students who have had no experience with puppets, regardless of age, this might be the best way to start. Writing conversation for the puppets, adding background music, and supplying other props can all be handled by the students themselves, with very little teacher guidance. Puppets could be used for various literary pieces, everything from dramatic poetry to *The Canterbury Tales*. Older students could prepare a production for presentation to younger students, either within the school or within the community, such as in a hospital. It is important to remember that *no* student is too old or too sophisticated for puppetry. Our national love affair with *Sesame Street* and the Muppets should be evidence enough that puppets are for everyone.

EVALUATING ORAL LANGUAGE ACTIVITIES

In traditional English language arts classrooms, teachers found little oral language to observe and evaluate. The contemporary classroom, however, provides many varied opportunities for evaluation. Watching students working in pairs and small groups or listening to student-led discussions, for example, leads to important observations on student participation: Who responds easily and well? Who holds back despite obvious knowledge? Who is reluctant to respond? Who is left out? "Kid-watching" is an important component of evaluating oral language, but there are others. Just as written pieces can be evaluated with holistic or analytic scales, oral language activities lend themselves to similar measures, and students can share in the process. Simple written criteria for evaluating peers can be part of their experience with oral presentations of all kinds, both individually and as groups. Additionally, self-reflection on oral expression, whether class discussion or performance, is important—just as it is with written expression. Chapter 11, which deals exclusively with assessment, contains some examples of oral evaluation. The discussion there will also help you to devise appropriate measures for most oral language activities.

CASE 5–1

Exploring an Instructional Unit

In a previous chapter, you explored language arts concepts and principles of planning through Amy Henquinet's unit, "A Look into the Future: 2014." Here you will explore another student's unit, this one geared specifically to oral language activities. In addition to evaluating the unit's use of these activities, we would like you to review principles of planning and evaluate their application in Mary Beth Koehler's unit, "The Trickster." Each unit, regardless of its emphasis, should reflect conscious decisions about materials and methods. To allow you to discover and evaluate Mary Beth's decisions, we have removed her statements about them. We also omitted her thoughtful and thorough reflection on the process of developing this unit for eighth graders.

As you read Mary Beth's unit, look for the following:

1. What are Mary Beth's goals? Do they reflect all three developmental areas: cognitive, affective, and social? Is one area emphasized more than the others? If yes, why do you think it is? If they are balanced, do you think it would be appropriate in this unit to stress one area more than the others?
2. What does Mary Beth want her students to understand or be able to do better as a result of this unit? What are her objectives or student outcomes?
3. What materials has she selected? What activities has she planned? What knowledge of English language arts is guiding her decisions? Do you think a narrow focus such as this one makes one's decisions more or less difficult? How does her unit reflect Mary Beth's knowledge of both concepts and kids?
4. Has Mary Beth provided for students with varying ability levels? Would students from diverse ethnic and cultural backgrounds be comfortable with this unit? Does she celebrate cultural diversity with this unit?
5. Has Mary Beth considered student interests and needs as she planned this unit? How do you know?
6. How will students be evaluated?
7. Does Mary Beth's time frame of two weeks seem about right for the activities planned? Does her sequence of activities seem appropriate for 13- and 14-year-olds?

Again, keep in mind that Mary Beth's unit was originally written as a narrative with a great deal of reflection about her goals, anticipated outcomes, methods, and materials. To provide you with this evaluative opportunity, we have removed her commentary.

THE TRICKSTER
GRADE LEVEL: MIDDLE SCHOOL/GRADE 8

In this unit, students will work with storytelling. To provide for a common structure, we will concentrate on the character of "trickster" in folk and fairy tales.

Teacher Materials and Resources

Iktomi and the Buffalo Skull
All-Jahdu Storybook
Paper Faces
Paper Masks and Puppets for Stories, Songs, & Plays
Puppets, Methods and Materials
Plenty of Puppets
The Art of Kabuki (video)
The Family Storytelling Handbook: How to Use Stories, Anecdotes, Rhymes, Handkerchiefs, Paper & Other Objects to Enrich Your Family Traditions
American Indian Resource Manual for Public Libraries
Keepers of the Earth

Day 1

Teacher-Led Activity: As students come into the room, I will have dim lights and Native American flute music playing. As they file in, I will whisper and tell them to go to their seats, attempt to sit quietly, and close their eyes. When everyone is in the room, I will help them to imagine Native American life over one hundred years ago.

Discussion Questions:
 1. What did Native American people do for entertainment?
 2. How did Native American people explain natural phenomena?

Story: How the Loon Got Its Red Eyes and Tail Feathers. Demonstration of Menominee Song and Dance/Loon Story.

Student Activity: Journal Response to Loon Story/Song and Dance

Day 2

Teacher Activity: Whole-class discussion from journal writing. Introduce the two-week unit, provide handout with oral project options, and give book talk on the following trickster tale resources:

Keepers of the Earth
The Girl Who Married a Ghost
The Adventures of Nanabush: Ojibway Indian Stories
Why the Possum's Tail Is Bare and Other North American Indian Stories
Teepee Tales of the American Indians
Iktomi and the Buffalo Skull
Iktomi and the Ducks

Iktomi and the Berries
Tricky Rabbit
Favorite Folk Tales from Around the World
Folk and Fairy Tales
Time-Ago Tales of Jahdu
Time-Ago Lost, More Tales of Jahdu
The All-Jahdu Storybook
Anasi and the Talking Melon
Spiderman Anancy

Student Activity: Gain familiarity with resources; begin to select tale for oral project.

Day 3

Teacher Activity: Show and read stories from *Iktomi and the Buffalo Skull* and *The All-Jahdu Storybook*. Encourage students to interact and respond during the reading. Using overhead transparencies, show students how Iktomi's thoughts (and witty asides to audience) are shown in print.

Discussion Questions:
Iktomi—How do the story elements suggest a Native American tale?
How is humor handled?
All Jahdu—What words give a traditional African flavor to the story?
What words give a contemporary flavor to the story?

Student Activity: Brainstorm ways students could retell tales they are interested in and maintain cultural flavor.

Student Assignment: Preparation for guest speaker, Kimberly Blaeser, Ojibway storyteller from White Earth Reservation (also a college instructor). Students will bring five questions on storytelling or the trickster for the guest speaker to answer.

Day 4

Workshop with Ms. Blaeser.

Day 5

Evolve criteria for effective storytelling. Review from workshop and excerpt from *Keepers of the Earth* where authors provide ideas for good storytelling.

Student Activity: Following review and *Keepers of the Earth* work, small cooperative working groups develop criteria.

Whole-Class Discussion: Discuss and merge criteria from the small-group lists into one list for class evaluation/oral project (list to be typed and distributed by teacher).

Conferencing/Peers and Teacher: Select and retell a tale.

Day 6

Teacher Activity: Show taped excerpts from the video *The Art of Kabuki*. Excerpts will feature use of makeup (masks), methods of walking, gesture, movement, and voice.

Teacher Mini-Lesson: Relate Japanese techniques to Native American and African storytelling, emphasizing commonalities in storytelling.

Student Activity: Students will write in their journals on ideas received from tape and mini-lesson on how to adapt some to their own process of storytelling. Share ideas with classmates.

Conferencing/Peers and Teacher: Students' specific tales and plans for storytelling.

Day 7

Teacher Activity: Show students a variety of simple masks, teacher-made from old billboard signs. Give book talk on resources for mask making, asking students to apply the information to their chosen tales.

Conferencing/Peers and Teacher: Mask-making application for students' specific tales.

Day 8

Teacher Activity: Introduce puppetry as a form of storytelling. Give a book talk on resources for making and using puppets, explaining how different styles of puppetry create different tones in storytelling (e.g., simple kid-type masks are lighthearted; shadow puppets are a bit more scary). Encourage student involvement and ask them to apply different mask styles to different types of tales.

Conferencing/Workshop

Day 9

Teacher Activity: Introduce origami in storytelling; explain and demonstrate "Something Special" from *The Family Storytelling Handbook.*

Student Activity: With an excerpt on how to perform "Something Special," work with partners. Practice origami storytelling; focus on criteria for effective storytelling.

Whole-Class Discussion: Origami practice and application for storytelling; comparisons of origami and other storytelling techniques.

Conferencing/Workshop

Day 10

Conferencing/Workshop on individual storytelling projects.

Day 11

Conferencing/Workshop on projects.

Day 12
Student Activity: Performance of storytelling projects.
Teacher Activity: Evaluation based on criteria evolved at start of unit.

Day 13
Storytelling and Evaluation

Day 14
Student Activity: Writing reflection on own experience of storytelling and observation of peers.

QUESTIONS ABOUT THE UNIT

Mary Beth began the "summary reflection" on her unit with this paragraph:

When I did my student teaching in middle school, my cooperating teacher gave me an assignment of creating a speech unit for the students. After spending nights after school and in the library developing lessons and techniques that I thought would help the students create the perfect speech, I walked up to another English teacher and tried to explain step by step what I thought I was going to do with the students. Then I asked what he thought. After my recitations of all the fancy-schmancy things I told him I was going to do, he looked at me and simply said, "I would think the main reason for this would be to make the students comfortable with speaking because most of them are going to be terrified." The next night, I completely overhauled my unit with that in mind, and it ended up a success. I tried to keep that in mind when I created this storytelling unit.

1. Where do you see evidence of Mary Beth's late night middle school education in her unit?
2. Why must you understand the trial and error of unit development if you want to be an effective teacher?
3. Why must you be able to "roll with the errors" and believe in yourself and the second chances we get as teachers?
4. If you were developing a storytelling unit for high school juniors, roughly 16- to 17-year-olds, what might you do differently? Can you think of ways in which the greater independence and self-directedness of older students might influence your decisions? How might working with older students make this lesson more difficult?
5. How could Mary Beth involve other grade levels, parents, or the community in this unit? Why must you be alert to the potential for involvement beyond your classroom?

Exploring an Instructional Unit

Nancy Koehler, a classmate but no relation to Mary Beth Koehler, decided to focus her oral language unit on pourquoi stories or etiological animal tales—folktales. As Nancy explained them in her introduction:

Pourqoui stories, according to Betty Bosma, "explain the origin of certain characteristics. They are written to entertain and are not believed to be true by the storyteller" (57). Often there is an element of trickery in the plot. The characteristics described are not usually attributed to logical or natural causes. (1)

Nancy goes on to say that she chose them because she believes "that almost all students delight in these stories, in their cleverness, and elements of surprise" (1). Nancy also chose middle schoolers as the focus of her unit, and with a similar subject, her unit offers an interesting comparison with Mary Beth's.

Once again, we have removed the author's voice and her many insightful comments and reflections about motives, materials, and methods, although the sequence is presented as Nancy originally prepared it. We would like you to consider what goals and student outcomes Nancy had in mind as she chose the elements of this unit. Similarly, we would like you to speculate on Nancy's philosophy of teaching: What does she believe about kids and English language arts? How do you know? Review the questions that lead into Mary Beth's unit before you read Nancy's unit.

POURQUOI STORIES: HOW AND WHY
GRADE LEVEL: MIDDLE SCHOOL/GRADE 8

Time: Fourteen class periods. Students will each receive a calendar of events and due dates for the unit. The schedule will also be posted in the classroom.

Materials:

Just So Stories
Why Mosquitoes Buzz in People's Ears
Mask-making kit

Mini-Lesson: Characteristics, form, and history of pourquoi stories through reading "How the Leopard Got His Spots" and other stories from Kipling's *Just So Stories.*

Student Activity: Silent reading of both traditional and modern pourquoi stories.

Mini-Lesson: Readers Theatre, criteria for evaluation

Student Activity: Small groups (chosen by teacher), choice of story for Readers Theatre activity, rehearsal.

Student Activity: Performance and evaluation of Readers Theatre performance by peers (form provided).

Whole-Class Activity: Brainstorm ideas for pourquoi stories (e.g., animal characteristics, possible story elements, formats, and possible use of narrator); diversity of animals/cultures (e.g., Kipling's Asian animals, Aardema's African animals).

Student Activity: Small groups, brainstorm ideas for development of an original pourquoi story.

Student Activity: Small groups, following decision of pourquoi story (animals, characteristics), begin mask making from kit materials provided (five days for completion/drying prior to performance).

Mini-Lesson: Story mapping or storyboards; example from Kipling story; preparation for story/script writing.

Whole-Class Activity: Brainstorming, story mapping and formatting of pourquoi stories.

Student Activities:

1. Small groups, writing pourquoi story (use of storyboard or mapping, forms provided); mask-making activities continue.
2. Peer editing of story/script drafts; sharing drafts among groups; mask-making activities continue.
3. Rehearsal of scripts; students may either read parts dramatically or memorize parts for performance.
4. Performance for classmates; if possible, performance for other students or family. Self-evaluation of participation both in writing and performing.

Teacher Activity: Evaluation of each small group on their written product, group participation, and performance.

Student Activity: Self-reflective journal entries on the unit's activities.

REFERENCES FOR UNIT OF STUDY

Aardema, V. *Why Mosquitoes Buzz in People's Ears.* New York: Dial, 1975.

Bosma, B. *Fairy Tales, Fables, Legends, and Myths: Using Folk Literature in Your Classroom.* New York: Teachers College Press, 1987.

Creative Educational Systems. *The New Playmaking: The Latest in Integration of the Arts in Education.* Chicago: Creative Education Press, 1993.

Creative Educational Systems. *Creative Mask-Making Kit.* Chicago: Creative Education Press, 1993.

Kipling, R. *Just So Stories.* New York: Doubleday, 1973.

Rief, L. *Seeking Diversity.* Portsmouth: Heinemann, 1992.

Wisconsin Department of Public Instruction. *Classroom Activities in Speaking and Listening.* Madison: Department of Public Instruction, 1991.

DISCUSSION QUESTIONS FOR UNITS OF STUDY

1. What similarities do you find between Mary Beth's and Nancy's units? Do you think similarities arise because Mary Beth and Nancy share a philosophy of teaching and learning? Or is it simply a matter of similar interests?
2. What differences do you find between Mary Beth's and Nancy's units? What accounts for the differences?
3. Mary Beth had a strong background in theatre and drama; Nancy had one in special needs children. Are their specific interests and talents evident in their respective units? Why is it important for teachers to honor their strengths and interests as well as recognize their weaker areas?
4. How do Mary Beth and Nancy show that who they teach is as critical as what they teach? How are they meshing materials, methods, and learners in appropriate ways?
5. What additions or changes would you make in Nancy's unit? What rationale do you have for making them?
6. How could you use this unit with high school seniors? What adjustments would you make and why?
7. Some senior high school teachers believe that their students are too "old" or "sophisticated" for fairy tales and folklore. How would you respond to criticism that you are using "little kid stuff" as a basis for oral and written language activities with juniors and seniors?
8. Mary Beth and Nancy include both student and teacher evaluation as part of their units. We have not provided you with their criteria or forms because we would like you to devise some. With a partner or small group, choose one unit and develop appropriate criteria and evaluative methods. Review your understanding of Mary Beth's or Nancy's goals and intended student outcomes before evolving criteria. Be sure to keep the age level in mind, and keep things as clear, simple, and fair as possible.

REFERENCES

Allen, R. R., and Brown, Kenneth L. *Developing Communication Competence in Children.* Skokie: National Textbook Co., 1976.

Allen, R. R., Brown, Kenneth L., and Yatvin, Joanne. *Learning Language Through Communication: A Functional Perspective.* Belmont: Wadsworth, 1986.

Barnes, Douglas. *From Communication to Curriculum.* Harmondsworth, England: Penguin, 1976.

Bolche, Linda. et al. "Fishbowls, Creative Controversy, Talking Chips: Exploring Literature Cooperatively." *English Journal* Oct. 1993: 43–48.

Bosma, Bette. *Fairy Tales, Fables, Legends, and Myths: Using Folk Literature in Your Classroom.* New York: Teachers College Press, 1987.

Brice Heath, Shirley. *Ways With Words: Language, Life, and Work in Communities and Classrooms.* Cambridge: Cambridge UP, 1983.

Bushman, John. H., and Bushman, Kay Parks. *Using Young Adult Literature in the English Classroom.* Columbus: Merrill, 1993.

Cameron, Jack. "Promoting Talk Through 35mm Slides." *English Journal* Sept. 1980: 14–19.

Cazden, Courtney B. *Classroom Discourse.* Portsmouth: Heinemann, 1988.

Cole, Pam B. "Bridging *The Red Badge of Courage* With Six Related Young Adult Novels." In J. Kaywell (Ed.), *Adolescent Literature as a Complement to the Classics* (Vol 2, pp. 21–39). Norwood: Christopher-Gordon, 1994.

Colquit, Jesse. "Oral Language Activities for Promoting an Understanding and Appreciation of Dialect Differences." *English Journal* Oct. 1989: 71–75.

Delpit, Lisa D. "Language Diversity and Learning." In Susan Hynds and Donald Rubin (Eds.), *Perspectives on Talk and Learning* (pp. 247–266). Urbana: NCTE, 1990.

Devine, Thomas. *Listening Skills Schoolwide: Activities and Programs.* Urbana: NCTE, 1982.

Duenas-Gonzales, Roseann. "Teaching Mexican American Students to Write: Capitalizing on Culture." *English Journal* Oct. 1982: 20–24.

Elegreet-DeSalvo, Nora, and Levitsky, Ronald. "We Left Our Homeland. A Sad, Sad Day: An Interdisciplinary Approach." *English Journal* Oct. 1989: 62–65.

Furlong, V. J., and Edwards, A. D. *The Language of Teaching: Meaning in Classroom Interaction.* London: Heinemann, 1978.

Fehlman, Richard H. "Quoting Films in English Class." *English Journal* Sept. 1987: 84–87.

Fortier, John. "What to Do Until the Doctor Comes: Speech in the English Language Arts Classroom." *Wisconsin English Journal* Jan. 1987: 2–6.

Henquinet, Amy. "A Look Into the Future: 2014." English 406. University of Wisconsin-Eau Claire, 1995.

Johnson, Terry D., and Louis, Daphne R. *Literacy Through Literature.* Portsmouth: Heinemann, 1985.

King, Nancy. *Storymaking and Drama.* Portsmouth: Heinemann, 1993.

Koehler, Mary Beth. "The Trickster." English 606. University of Wisconsin-Eau Claire, 1995.

Koehler, Nancy. "Pourquoi Stories: How and Why." English 406. University of Wisconsin-Eau Claire, 1995.

Laliberte, Norman, and Mogelon, A. *Masks, Face Coverings and Headgear.* New York: Van Nostrand Reinhold, 1973.

Lightfoot, Nick. Personal interview. Aug. 1991.

Lundsteen, Sara W. *Listening.* Urbana: NCTE, 1979.

MacArthur, Mary Ellen R. "Poetry's presentations: That's entertainment." *English Journal* Apr. 1989: 69–71.

Moffett, James, and Wagner, Betty Jane. *Student-Centered Language Arts, K–12.* 4th ed. Portsmouth: Boynton/Cook, Heinemann, 1992.

Morris, Barbra S. "The Television Generation: Couch Potatoes or Informed Critics?" *English Journal* Dec. 1989: 35–41.

O'Keefe, Virginia. *Speaking to Think/Thinking to Speak: The Importance of Talk in the Learning Process.* Portsmouth: Boynton/Cook, Heinemann, 1995.

Schaffer, Jane C. "Improving Discussion Questions: Is Anyone Out There Listening?" *English Journal* Apr. 1989: 40–42.

Sorenson, Margo. "Teaching Each Other: Connecting Talking and Writing." *English Journal* Jan. 1993: 42–47.

Sowder, Wilbur H. "Fostering Discussion in the Language-Arts Classroom." *English Journal* Oct. 1993: 39–42.

Stubbs, Michael. *Language, Schools and Classrooms.* London: Methuen, 1972.

Swartz, Larry. *Dramathemes: A Practical Guide for Teaching Drama.* Markham, Ontario: Pembroke, 1988.

Wagner, Betty Jane. "Dramatic Improvisation in the Classroom." In S. Hynds & D. Rubin (Eds.), *Perspectives on Talk and Learning* (pp. 195–212). Urbana: NCTE, 1990.

Williams, Lynda. "Storytelling, Oral Literature or . . . Any Other Name Would Sound So Sweet." *English Journal* Nov. 1982: 36–37.

Wisconsin Department of Public Instruction. *A Guide to Curriculum Planning in the English Language Arts.* Madison: Author, 1986.

Wisconsin Department of Public Instruction. *Classroom Activities in Speaking and Listening.* Madison: Author, 1991.

Wisconsin Department of Public Instruction. *A Guide to Curriculum Planning in Classroom Drama and Theatre*. Madison: Author, 1990.

Wood, Barbara S., ed. *The Development of Functional Communication Competencies: Pre-K-Grade Six and Grades Seven—Twelve*. 2 vols. Urbana: ERIC Clearinghouse on Reading and Communication Skills, 1977.

Teaching Composition

What more important service can we perform for ourselves than to write; to write, that is, not to get a grade or pass a course, but to sound the depths, to explore, to discover; to save our floundering selves.

James E. Miller, Jr. (7)

BACKGROUND OF TEACHING COMPOSITION

Writing is a complex skill, and the teaching of writing is therefore multidimensional. We must help students discover their own knowledge and their own voice. We need to help young writers develop the techniques necessary to write their ideas coherently in a form comprehensible and appropriate for others. No one method is best for teaching writing, but the work of educators and researchers over the past 20 years has helped us understand how to improve the teaching of writing.

RESEARCH ON WRITING

Concerns with how we teach composition are not new. From the first issue of the *English Journal* in 1912, teachers have struggled to find the most effective ways of helping students write well. Although the emphasis has changed over the years, many of the same issues that teachers of the 1920s worried about are still with us including writing in other subjects, lessening the burden of grading, balancing the teaching of skills with content, and choosing topics of interest to students (Maxwell 2–4). In the 1930s, the emphasis was on motivating students to write and finding ways to make writing meaningful to them, although correct punctuation was also a concern. Although we may think of journal writing as a fairly new idea in teaching writing, Eleanor Brown introduced journal keeping in 1934 as a way to avoid the stiffness of formal writing (Maxwell 7).

Articles during the 1940s focused on the importance of students writing about subjects that mattered to them. The 1950s reemphasized the concern with errors and ways to help students learn the basics of writing, although many of the *English Journal* authors continued to examine ways of bringing real-life experiences into student writing (Maxwell 9–11).

A growing concern in the 1960s was that, although teaching composition had been an established part of English programs since the early 1900s, there was no comprehensive understanding of how to teach writing. Educators were moving from a concern with the written product to an emphasis on the process of writing, but not until a 1966 conference at Dartmouth College in Hanover, New Hampshire, did process writing become integrated with the teaching of writing in the schools. The Dartmouth Conference emphasized personal growth in both writing and literature, and the participants advocated moving from product to process in the teaching of writing.

John Dixon, one of the participants, described the thinking, discussing, and sharing that went on at Dartmouth in *Growth Through English*. He stressed the need for students to talk about their experiences before attempting to write. "Talking it over, thinking it over, and (as confidence is gained) writing, can be natural parts of taking account of new experiences (cognitively and affectively)" (28). The ideas of exploratory talk before writing and talking in groups as the writing progresses were quite different ways of viewing the teaching of writing.

Traditionally, when writing instruction focused on the product, teachers told students what they did wrong, hoping they would then do it right. Such an approach has the wrong emphasis. Learning is much easier when we are praised for what we do right. If we concentrate on what we do wrong when we are learning to ski, golf, or roller skate, we tend to repeat our mistakes. If we are praised for what we do correctly, we learn more easily because we concentrate on what we do right. We all find learning easier and more pleasant when we receive praise and encouragement.

Writing instruction took just the opposite approach. On Monday, teachers typically assigned a theme, explained it carefully, and asked if there were any questions. The students handed in the themes on Friday, and dedicated teachers spent the weekend going over the papers, noting every error. The model was a negative one—what not to do. As a result, students did not write well, nor did they like to write.

Writing instruction did not improve for the majority of students. The more red ink and negative comments, the less students paid attention to what teachers wrote on their papers. What a discouraging situation for teachers! Students looked at the grade, and without reading the comments, threw the paper away. The situation was just as discouraging for students, particularly for those who had difficulty with writing. They did not know what area or skill to begin working on. Box 6–1 illustrates the frustrations a new teacher may experience even though she uses a process approach to writing.

BOX 6–1

STARTING OUT

Joellen, a first-year teacher, planned on putting the writing process into action in her sophomore English class. She liked to write, especially poetry, and was determined to help her students succeed at writing. She assigned a variety of writing activities and included brainstorming and discussion to help students get started. Before long, Joellen felt completely swamped with the amount of grading she had to do and found she was devoting evenings and weekends to a seemingly endless pile of papers. She considered cutting back on the amount of writing she was requiring, but she felt guilty about that because of her commitment to have students experience a wealth of writing activities. Her students began to complain that they were not getting their papers returned quickly enough, and some rebelled about turning in any more work. Joellen became more and more frustrated with the situation.

How can Joellen improve her teaching of writing? How can she help students become enthused about writing? Joellen's experiences are not uncommon among both new and experienced teachers. Part of the problem is that she is trying to improve students' writing by looking at a finished product, when the main difficulty with the papers may have occurred much earlier—when students were generating ideas for their topic. When evaluation occurs only after the paper is turned in to the teacher, the basic problems may be buried in a morass of red-penned punctuation errors. Teaching writing as a process is an ongoing activity where teachers can help students whenever problems occur.

WRITING PROCESS

Teaching writing as a process means that writers can improve their writing at any or all stages from the first thoughts about a topic to the finished draft. The process is described as loosely fitting into stages: prewriting or discovery, drafting, revising, and editing. However, the writing process is not made up of a series of discrete linear steps leading to a finished product; it is recursive. That is, a writer goes back and forth from one stage to another as the writing progresses. For instance, a writer first considers what to write about and how best to get started. As the drafting, or first attempts at writing, proceed, the writer may return to the discovery stage to rethink what to write or to explore other ideas and feelings. At the revision stage, the writer may return to discovery activities when it becomes clear the writing needs more than minor revising. Throughout the process, writers move in and out of stages as the writing demands. The following diagram illustrates the recursive nature of the process approach to writing.

The Writing Process

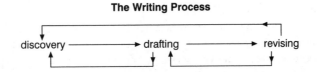

STAGES IN THE WRITING PROCESS

Discovery Stage

The discovery stage is the most important step in writing something interesting, honest, and lively. Various activities help writers discover what they know and what they want to say. These activities might include creative dramatics, films, discussion, reading, or many other kinds of writing. Many people call this stage *prewriting,* but that term does not reflect the many writing activities that occur at this stage.

D. Gordon Rohman coined the term *prewriting* in 1965 when he conducted a study on first-year writers at Michigan State University. He believed students needed time for thinking to develop their ideas and plans for writing. He used journal writing as the prewriting activity and found students improved their writing when given the time and method to discover what and how they would write.

In a 1971 study, Janet Emig found that prewriting was a much longer process when students wrote on self-chosen topics than when writing school assignments. This is true partly because teachers do not provide time for prewriting, but also because students cannot explore their thoughts for writing when the topic is unfamiliar or uninteresting. Allowing time for students to think and talk about writing is essential.

Without discovery activities, writers develop papers that tend to lack a sense of their own voice. The writing also lacks depth and details to make the writing interesting. The papers look more like writing done to fill a required assignment rather than writing that a student cares about. Discovery activities help right from the beginning when students are thinking about a topic choice.

To be successful writers, students must be interested in what they are writing about. This means giving students the freedom to select their own topics. A teacher can provide a general area of topics or a list of possible topics, but students need to have choices. Even with choices, some students cannot think of what they want to write about. Teachers can sometimes think of alternative topics, but other students are often a better source of help. After students select their topic, they meet in groups and the teacher instructs them to talk about their choices—why they think they would like to write about a particular one or what they already know about it. Members of the group help anyone who is having difficulty in deciding on a topic.

After a topic is chosen, several discovery activities help students develop their thoughts. Discussing ideas and getting immediate feedback are a tremendous help. If the general topic is writing about how a character in a novel changed over the course of the story and the reasons for the change, hearing how others perceive the character's development can help someone decide what to write about. The same is true with other kinds of assignments. If students are writing persuasive letters, for example, taking part in discussions about why and to whom a particular letter needs to be written helps generate ideas. Sharing ideas about writing is the most effective way to help writers get started.

A writing classroom is a talking classroom. In traditional classrooms, students wrote in isolation. Opportunities for exchanging ideas did not exist. In the real world, however, we share our writing. When we write a line or paragraph that we believe is particularly good, our first impulse is to read it to someone. We all have turned to someone and said, "Listen to this!" Except for private journal writing (and even that sometimes), writing is meant to be shared.

Another source of ideas for writing is from responses to reading or viewing. In Chapter 7, "Teaching Literature," response writing is discussed in detail. Responding to literature or film is important for many reasons. Instead of remaining passive learners, students become more actively involved in reading or viewing. Also, the comments and questions students write become a rich source of ideas in the discovery stage. They have developed their own private source of writing topics.

Discovery Activities

Depending on the writing task, many discovery activities help students get started. All of the activities need to be modeled for the students, either by the teacher and students or a group of students. Student work from previous classes can be used to illustrate how others used the various discovery activities.

1. *Free writing.* At the top of a page students write the name of their topic or idea—like a person they admire. Then for a specified amount of time, not over 10 minutes, they write everything they can possibly think of connected with that subject. The term *free* means that the writer is free to put down anything that comes to mind and free from any concerns of mechanics or spelling. When the allotted time is up, students read what they wrote and circle phrases and words that seem especially appropriate to them. At this point, if time permits, they can meet in groups and share their writing with others. The next step is to write again, elaborating on the circled phrases, although they can develop the piece any way they want. Free writing often brings thoughts to mind that more structured writing would not tap into, as shown by the following example by a ninth grader writer:

I wish I had a show dog because I like dogs & my friends have animals to show - Skippy would like another dog - small - female - laid back. Mom would object- too much work - ??? Sheltie - really cute - love the long nose -I would clean up after it & it would be good responsibility for me. Sheltie good size - wouldn't be that much work after house trained.

2. *Drawing.* Like free writing, drawing taps hidden thoughts and new connections. One does not have to be very good at drawing for this to be a successful activity. If the assignment is to describe an incident from childhood, drawing a location or scene helps fill in vivid details and spurs the memory into recalling details. When writing a description of my grandmother, I drew a sketch of the pantry in her house. Although I didn't include the pantry itself in the essay, the act of drawing it brought to mind several incidents I had not thought of. When students no longer draw after they leave elementary school, they lose an important way of thinking. The figure below shows a sketch drawn by a student to create a setting for her story. She probably will not refer directly to the plan but can now picture it clearly as her characters and plot develop.

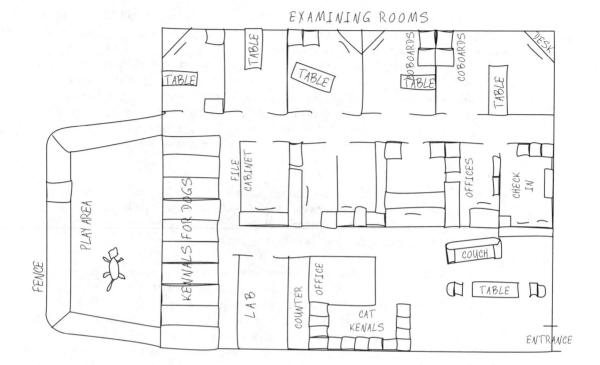

3. *Mapping.* When the writing topic is not familiar to the writers, mapping helps to generate ideas and organization. Mapping is sometimes called *webbing* because the resulting diagram resembles a spider web. By either name, the intention is to generate and connect subtopics. The subject is placed in the center, and topics are added on extending lines as the writer thinks of them. A map on the topic of changing the school calendar might look like the one on the next page.

4. *Outlining.* After the map is completed, students can prepare an informal outline to help structure their thoughts as they begin to write. A more formal outline with the traditional Roman numerals and capital letters can also be used. For some students, though, the structure gets in the way. People have different ways of organizing their thoughts, and teachers need to keep the differences in mind. Because of these differences, when English teachers require a formal outline with the writing assignment, many students write the paper first, then the outline. They cannot plan the whole paper before actually beginning to compose. One writer said, "How can I do an outline when I don't know yet what I'm going to write?" However, everyone would not have that difficulty. Some writers will find particular discovery activities helpful whereas others may not. For that reason, it is best to suggest two or three activities, and let students use the ones that are most helpful to them.

5. *Creative dramatics.* This discovery technique works for many kinds of writing. The definition of creative dramatics includes impromptu acting, role playing, and

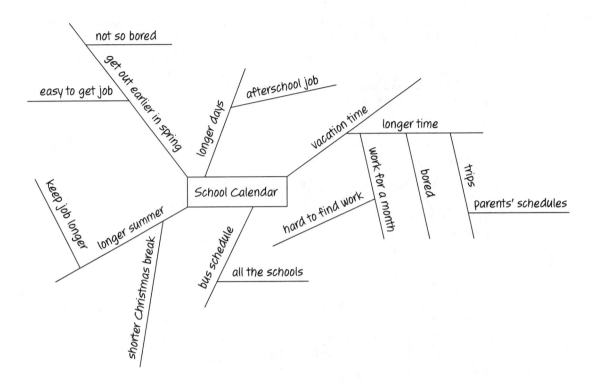

skits, all requiring little preparation time. The audience is the class. The objective is not to put on a performance, but to engage in an activity that promotes better writing. For example, if the assignment is to write a persuasive letter about a desired change in school policy, students could role-play for each other, taking the parts of parents, school administrators, school board members, and other community members. Even though the letters are on different topics, exchanging roles helps to clarify the issues and encourages students to see different sides of the arguments. As a result, their letters are more convincing.

Taking the role of a character in a story helps students to understand the personality and motivation of a character better. The actors do not memorize lines but improvise dialogue. Empathy for and realization of a character's behavior is reflected later in the student's writing. To be successful, creative dramatics should be introduced gradually and always presented as an informal activity.

A creative dramatic activity that always produces enthusiasm is a discovery technique designed to help students write dialogue. In groups of four to six, each group receives a bag of props that the teacher filled ahead of time with an odd assortment of items from home. A bag could contain a hammer, hair clip, copy of Robert Frost's poems, an apple, a feather, knife sharpener, and a pair of safety glasses. The students have about 25 minutes to think up a skit, and then each group performs the skit for

the rest of the class. The one rule is that every prop must be used. During the following period, the students discuss how the dialogue carried the skit along.

This discovery activity provides practice for future writing assignments, but does
not necessarily lead immediately into the writing. A teacher might provide several
activities to help students discover how dialogue can be used effectively before having
students write a short story.

Box 6–2

WRITER'S BLOCK

Students occasionally have difficulty in choosing a topic to write about. How could you
help a student who often has "writer's block"? Think of some assignment-specific ways
and general ways to help.

Drafting Stage

For successful writing, students must realize the importance of multiple drafts. First
drafts should be messy. After the discovery stage, a writer has a great deal to say.
Because the brain thinks more quickly than the hand can write, there is no time to
worry about spelling or punctuation. Helping students to realize that putting down
something worth reading is far more important than putting something down right is
an important lesson at this stage. The need for correctness at this early stage gets in
the way of successful writing. Writers attend to correctness later in the process. Several
suggestions for teachers help students become fluent writers.

1.   Always refer to the writing as drafts. Asking if someone is on a second or
third draft helps establish the notion of multiple drafts. The version students turn in is
called a final draft rather than a final paper because no paper is really ever "finished."
That's not to discourage writers, but to acknowledge that given more time, they could
have polished it even more.

2.   Drafting does not have to proceed from beginning to end; in fact, papers are
usually better if one does not start at the beginning. At one time or another, we all
stare at a blank sheet of paper not knowing where to start. Even when using discovery
techniques, writing that first line is difficult. By encouraging students to not start at
the beginning, we can help students overcome that writing block. Middle school students can actually fold down the top third of the sheet of paper to concretely show
they are not writing the beginning sentence. It is amazing how freeing that can be.
When students complain to a teacher they "don't know what to say," the best help is
for a teacher to ask them what it is they "want to say." Writers can usually articulate
what they want to say, but cannot figure out how to get started. The teacher may
respond, "Why not write what you just said?" Some seem to need permission to write
what they want to write—to be told yes, that sounds good. Often beginnings are best
written after the rest of the paper is done, especially in expository writing.

3. When drafts are first shared in writing groups, no one but the writer actually sees the paper. Authors read their own paper aloud to the other students in the group, so that no one is embarrassed by errors or poor handwriting. The emphasis is on what is being said, which is where it should be at this stage.

Revising Stage

An important point here is that not all writing goes through every stage of the writing process. To get better at anything we must practice, and many practice activities are not revised. Revision is important, but it takes time, and time is in short supply. If all the writing assignments go through the entire process, we cannot teach all of the different kinds of assignments that provide the experiences in writing our students need.

Revision has several steps and purposes.

1. Revision always begins with the writer. We all need help from other readers to improve our writing, but first students need to read their own work with as critical an eye as possible. Reading the piece aloud helps the writer hear redundancies, omissions, and incorrect word choices. Reading the piece oneself is an essential first step before getting help from others. When the revision process is first introduced to students, filling out a memo is a useful strategy (see Figure 6–1). Later, when they are experienced with the three steps, the memo is no longer required. Perhaps this seems more detailed than necessary, but as students are learning the process it reminds them of each step.

2. The second step involves the writing group mentioned in the memo. The groups are fairly large—five or six members—so that each writer benefits from hearing several responses. Groups can be formed in several ways. The teacher may form the groups so that a variety of ability levels is in each group, do a random selection, or select students based on their personalities, such as putting quiet students with more outgoing ones. Many teachers allow students to form their own groups. Perhaps the key to success is to use a variety of ways. Working in groups helps students to get to

Your name_____ Title of writing _____

Date you read this piece aloud and made revisions _____

Date your writing group heard your paper _____

Names of writing group members _____ _____

_____ _____

_____ _____

Date your partner read your piece _____

Signature of writing partner _____

FIGURE 6–1
Revision memo.

know each other; if they always work with ones they know best, they won't expand their circle of friends. On the other hand, students resent always being told with whom they can work. The groups stay together for one piece of writing. With a new assignment, new groups form. Even though students may want to remain in the groups they have worked with, reforming group membership helps develop social interaction and eliminates the problem of cliques.

When students meet in their writing groups, each student reads his or her piece aloud to the others. The others respond with suggestions for improving the writing, which takes some guidance from the teacher. The first time a teacher tries response groups in class, they may not work. One problem is that students will not stay on the task of talking about their papers, which is a natural outcome when friends meet together. A second problem is that students often are overly pleasant to each other. They tell each other how wonderful everyone's writing is, which is no help at all. Again, this is not surprising because everyone has to read his or her paper aloud, and no one wants to be too critical. To make response groups work, teachers need to provide guidance.

One way to help students is have them fill in response sheets, such as the one shown in Figure 6–2, after each writer reads the piece.

A second example of a response sheet intended for informational or expository writing is shown in Figure 6–3.

On the actual response sheet the students receive, spaces are left between questions to allow for written responses. Students respond to all of these questions without actually looking at the paper so they must listen closely. Students often ask the writer to reread a section or repeat a sentence. Usually each student fills out a sheet so

---

Writer's name _____

1. What is the paper about? Sum up in a sentence or two what points the author makes.
2. In what ways is the paper interesting?
3. Where could more detail or explanation be added? How would the additions help?
4. What words or phrases are especially effective?
5. What information is unnecessary?
6. What parts should be changed?
7. What other advice can you give to the writer to make this a better paper?

    Your name(s)   _____

    _____

FIGURE 6–2
Response sheet.

Writer's name _____

1. What is your overall impression of the paper?
2. What is the thesis (implied or stated)?
3. In what ways is it interesting? Where should detail be added? Be sure there is enough detail for you, as a reader, to understand the idea the author wants to convey.
4. In what ways could sentences be improved?
5. Look for transitions, especially between paragraphs. Where should transitions be added?
6. What words and phrases are especially effective?
7. What words are unnecessary?
8. What words should be changed?
9. Sum up in a sentence or two what the paper is about. What points does the author make?
10. How could the author make this a better paper?

Signed _____

FIGURE 6–3
Response sheet for informational or expository writing.

that the writer has five different responses if there are six in a group. Students may also work with a partner and fill one out together, and then both sign. We do not recommend having all of the students work on just one sheet because it ends up being the response of only one or two. They discuss what they liked the best and ask for clarifications so that the writer and responders are all talking together about the paper. The procedure continues for each member of the group. This process takes an entire class period, and a teacher needs to make the groups small enough to make sure everyone has a turn during the same class. Students make revisions, usually as homework, before the next step in the writing process.

Students need to realize they do not have to take all the advice they receive. They should give it careful consideration, but the writer must decide if the suggestions are appropriate for his or her paper. They won't agree with some of the suggestions they receive, but they need to take the suggestions seriously. Students who have trouble writing can offer suggestions that are just as valid as those who write with little difficulty. They know as well as anyone whether a paper is interesting and makes sense.

Sometimes students complain that the response group did not help them. This is partly the writers' responsibility. When they know they have difficulty with a particular area, they need to ask the group for specific help. Someone might be marked down consistently for not using enough detailed description. That student needs to ask specifically for help with including details.

Editing Stage

Editing and proofreading are necessary only when the writing is published—that is, has a wider and perhaps unknown audience. If students work with word processing, they bring a clean copy to the editing session. Otherwise, students do not have to copy the entire piece, but it should be revised and ready to be copied for the final draft. A paper may look messy with corrections written above a word, words crossed off, and other words inserted, but everything should be as correct as possible including spelling and punctuation.

The editing stage is the first time students are allowed to read each other's papers. The students meet in the same group as they did in the revising stage. The first procedure is the same as last time; each reads the revised paper to the others. This time, however, they do not fill out a response sheet, but rather talk about the changes, and the writer usually explains the thinking behind the changes. Often writers make more revisions than the group suggested because once they start revising they see the need for more changes. The writer may jot down notes as the others respond.

After everyone has read the papers, the members pair up and edit each other's papers. With less experienced writers, many teachers use editing guides. These vary with assignments and with the age of the students. The guides are used to focus attention on various problem areas; they are not handed in. At this point in the writing process, students may write on each other's papers. An editing guide for an expository writing assignment for juniors or seniors might look like the one in Figure 6–4.

The points on the editing sheet will change depending on the assignment. Also, students' developmental level affects the direction of editing. An editing guide for middle school students writing a descriptive personal experience paper might look like the one in Figure 6–5.

Student editors, at any grade level, are more effective if they receive guidance in what to look for. Telling students to check everything is too unfocused, and they catch few mistakes that way. Also, giving them checklists is not helpful. It is easy to go

---

1. The paper must support the thesis. Read the paper over and come back to the thesis, making sure it is appropriate.

2. Semicolons are causing problems for some. Check especially for proper use. A semicolon followed by an incomplete sentence is the most common mistake.

3. Transitions between paragraphs are another trouble spot.

4. Borrowed material needs to be introduced. Why is this source being used? Who is this person? Is the source outdated?

5. Any questions about spelling should be answered at this point. Remember that it is better to look up a word than to take a chance if you are unsure.

6. Do a final check on punctuation, subject-verb agreement, and pronoun reference.

FIGURE 6–4
Editing guide for an expository writing assignment.

1. Together check every adjective and verb, making sure the editor knows what the writer means.

2. Look at the sentences. If they all begin with a subject followed by a verb, decide which ones to change.

3. Read for clichés and change to more appropriate comparisons.

4. Check for spelling. Remember to look up words you are not sure of.

5. In the last papers many students had trouble remembering to use commas. Together check each other's papers, reading sections aloud where you are not sure about comma placement.

6. Check over the paper carefully for any mechanical errors. Remember this takes patience and is a responsibility of both the writer and the editor.

FIGURE 6–5
Editing guide for descriptive personal experience writing.

down a list of yes or no questions and not really look for ways to improve the paper. Checklists are particularly useless when writers use them for their own work. The lists are meant to be reminders, but if a writer already believes the paper is in good shape, the questions are answered with a yes, with little thought. The more the editors are involved in the process, the better they will do. Sometimes teachers ask students to copy the writer's best sentence and explain why it works so well. Then they copy the sentence that most needs to be rewritten. Editing guides can focus on specific areas the class as a whole is having trouble with.

Just before the editing sessions, teachers can do a mini-lesson on problem areas with the whole class. A mini-lesson deals with one skill, for example, using semicolons. In about 10 minutes a teacher can cover the uses and show examples. Because the students are going right into editing groups, they can focus on that particular skill, which provides reinforcement.

Students need to bring writing handbooks to class to use as a reference when editing. Without them, they rely solely on the teacher to answer questions of usage and punctuation. We want our students to learn how to function without us, in this case, to know how to write polished papers. A handbook is often underused by most students, and teachers can show them how to use it, much as they would a dictionary. When students ask a question during an editing session, the teacher should help the student find the answer in a handbook rather than supplying the answer. In this way, students learn a skill that helps them to write future papers as well as the one they are working on.

Teacher Help

Teachers are part of the entire writing process, providing suggestions, helping, and listening to writers read their papers to them. But teachers also need to know when to stay out of the student's way. The writing belongs to the writer, and when teachers suggest specific ways to change the paper, they take away some of that ownership. A teacher's opinions carry far more weight than a student's. Teachers are the authority figure; they give the grades. Although we want to be supportive, we do not want to interfere with students finding their own voices. Student papers should never be collected until the final draft. Once the papers are in the teacher's hands, the students are no longer responsible for them. When teachers read and mark rough drafts, they are doing all the work for the writer. The ones who are getting practice in editing are the teachers, when it is the students who should be practicing. When a teacher marks papers with suggested changes, the students have only to make the corrections, and they do not think about why they are making them. Some teachers feel so strongly about the ownership of the writing remaining with the students that they do not hold a student's paper. If a student asks the teacher to read a work in progress, the teacher asks them to read it aloud or reads it over the student's shoulder. The more a teacher takes over, the more students write to please the teacher rather than themselves, and their writing loses vitality and originality.

The Writing Process in Action

As we have discussed earlier, the writing process is recursive; writers move back and forth between the stages as they write. During drafting, writers may come to a standstill and be unable to think of what to say next. The best way to overcome this problem is to go back to discovery activities. Students could brainstorm on what they are trying to say or try mapping with the specific area they are working on or free-write all they know about the topic and move on to drafting again. At the revision stage, writers often return to drafting, rewriting sections or whole pages; here, too, they may use discovery activities again. Teachers need to remind students repeatedly of the recursive aspect of writing. The strength of the process is that writers are learning to improve their writing *as they write,* not after the writing is finished. Two major points are important in teaching writing using the writing process method:

1. The process is recursive. Writers move back and forth among stages as the need arises.
2. Not all writing tasks go through all of the stages—in particular, the stage of editing.

Publishing Student Writing

In some cases, publishing is listed as the final step in the writing process. Although publishing is important for widening the audience for student writers and can be used successfully for many writing activities, students need to write many different kinds of writing and for many different purposes to increase fluency. Also, publishing almost always requires careful editing. At the elementary level, publishing has a different connotation. Putting work up in the halls or around the room is publishing, and because these are developing writers, editing plays a minor role. At the secondary level, however, public expectation is different: Writing that is published should be free from errors. The emphasis for writing, then, is always on a polished final draft. When students know their work is really going public, they are motivated to make the writing error free. The time taken up in editing cuts down on the variety of writing experiences, however. During the year a few assignments can be considered for publication, but not many, so that fluency remains a priority.

Places for publication are plentiful. We can use students' interest in issues to encourage them to write letters to newspapers and school publications. Organizations and businesses usually respond to a student letter asking for information. Many businesses publish student work in their own publications.

The classroom may want to set up its own literary magazine and publish works by student authors. Other outlets for young writers are available. A few examples include:

- *Ebony Jr.,* for ages 6 to 12, published by Johnson Publishing Co. Address: 820 S. Michigan Ave., Chicago, IL 60605.
- *Flip,* published four times a year for ages 13 to 19. Address: 265 E. Emmett, Battle Creek, MI 49017.
- *Highlights for Children,* for ages 5 to 12. Address: 803 Church St., Honesdale, PA, 18431.
- *Jack and Jill,* for ages 4 to 7. Address: 1100 Waterway Blvd., P.O. Box 567, Indianapolis, IN 46206.
- *Just About Me,* for girls, ages 12 to 19. Address: Ensio Industries, 247 Marlee Ave., Suite 206, Toronto, Ontario, Canada M6B 4B8.
- *Kids Magazine,* published for ages 5–15. Address: Box 3041, Grand Central Station, New York, NY 10017.
- *The McGuffey Writer,* published three times a year for ages preschool to 18. Address: 400 A McGuffey Hall, Miami University, Oxford, OH 45056.
- *Merlyn's Pen,* published four times a year for grades 7–10. Address: P.O. Box 1085, East Greenwich, RI 02818. *Merlyn's Pen Senior Edition,* grades 9–12.
- *Prism,* published six times a year for ages 9 to 18. Address: P.O. Box 030464, Fort Lauderdale, FL 33303.
- *Purple Cow: Atlanta's Magazine for Kids,* published for ages 12–18. Address: 110 E. Andrews Drive, NW, Atlanta, GA 30305.
- *Scholastic Scope Magazine,* published for grades 7–12. Address: 50 West 44th St., New York, NY 10036.
- *Seventeen,* for ages 14 to 18. Address: 850 3rd Ave., New York, NY 10022.
- *Skipping Stones: A Multicultural Children's Quarterly,* ages 5 to 15. Address: P.O. Box 3939, Eugene, OR 97403.
- *Stone Soup,* published five times a year for ages 6 to 13. Address: P.O. Box 83, Santa Cruz, CA 95063.
- *Teenage Magazine,* for ages 14 to 18. Address: P.O. Box 948, Lowell MA 01853.
- *Tigers and Lambs,* children's poetry magazine for ages 6 to 16. Address: 2141 E. Waverly, Tucson, AZ 85719.
- *Voices of Youth,* for ages 13 to 18. Address: P.O. Box 1869, Sonoma, CA 95476.

- *Writing!* for ages 12 to 18. Address: 60 Revere Dr., Northbrook, IL 60062-1563.
- *Young Miss,* Address: Parents' Magazine Enterprises, 80 Bridge Road, Bergenfield, NJ 07621.

Submission requirements for these publications are described in the yearly editions of *Writer's Market* (Writer's Digest Books) and *The Writer's Handbook* (The Writer, Inc.). Both of these publications are excellent sources for writers and are readily found in libraries.

WRITING FOR A VARIETY OF PURPOSES

Teachers who believe that writing and learning are inseparable often find themselves in the same situation as Joellen, the teacher described earlier. For teachers who use the writing process and include writing throughout classroom activities, the paper load can become overwhelming. One teacher developed a system of writing levels to alleviate the problem. By developing levels of evaluation to fit the different levels of writing, she simplified the evaluation, thus cutting down on the time required to complete the process. Basing her original work on speech theory, she devised a levels-of-writing approach to use in the classroom (Maxwell xiii).

Many areas of our life are affected by the concept of different levels or standards. For example, we use different levels of eating behavior. How we eat pizza sitting on the floor with a circle of friends as we watch television is quite different from our behavior when eating at an upscale restaurant. One is not better than the other; each is appropriate for the context.

Contexts determine speech levels as well. We use different levels of speech for different purposes and audiences (Maxwell 33–34). Martin Joos describes five levels or scales of language based on the social utility of language and stresses that various scales depend on audience. All of the scales are respectable and have different purposes (4).

Sociolinguist Dell Hymes agrees and explains that the level of speech is determined by the settings and activities surrounding the speech act (43). Within a community, listeners expect and understand a particular linguistic form. A formal speech level can be inappropriate in some settings (57).

Informal speaking is for sharing with a familiar audience. Characteristics of this level are unfinished sentences, slang, and jokes known only by the intimate community that has a shared knowledge (Maxwell 36). Donald Rubin describes such language as elliptical and choppy; he agrees that audience affects the language style (5).

A second level of speech typical in school settings is sometimes formal in style and vocabulary, although still familiar, because it reaches a wider audience than the students' intimate community. The third level, formal speech, is infrequently used and is reserved for an unfamiliar audience or one not known at all. All three levels of speech are important; we need to know not only *how* to use the levels but *when* to use them.

LEVELS OF WRITING

Levels of writing depend on our audience and our purpose for writing. When should we as writers and teachers concern ourselves with correct punctuation and spelling? What determines how formal our writing and speaking need to be? Because of their purpose, the language used in discovery activities is informal, whereas the language in a published article is naturally quite formal. But what about the writing we plan for in school and the writing we do outside of school? By differentiating among writing purposes to establish levels of writing, we provide activities for students that mirror real-life writing. If we want our students to value writing and to see the reasons for writing, then the assignments we make must include all the levels (Maxwell 1996, 33–49).

The levels of writing are related to the functions of speech. *Level 1* is the most casual and informal level because the writer is writing mainly for himself or herself. The writing is shared only with people familiar to the writer, in fact, probably understood only by people close to the writer. The counterpart in speech is talking to close friends where it is often unnecessary to finish a thought or sentence to be understood. The writer takes for granted the interest of the audience regardless of how casual the communication (Martin, Medway, Smith, and D'Arcy 42).

Level 2 is more formal or standard and can be read and understood by most people in the writer's social circle. It is similar to speech used with acquaintances, teachers, and friends, but a wider audience than close friends must understand the writing.

Level 3 is formal writing or speech and occurs in situations where the form is as important as the message, and the audience includes readers the writer may not know. All three levels are appropriate for school writing and are important for helping students improve their writing, although traditionally, level 3 has been used almost exclusively.

Using levels of writing in the classroom cuts down on the paper load for teachers. Evaluation is clearly defined by levels; therefore, much of the writing required of students is graded quickly and easily. Students, parents, and teachers are aware of which type of evaluation fits each assignment. The purpose of evaluation is to help students improve their writing, and everyone involved understands the purposes. In addition, teachers know exactly what elements of writing to look for in the assignments that call for a more formal evaluation. The time involved in evaluation is greatly reduced. Evaluating by levels is explained in detail in Chapter 11.

Writing levels are inherent in any writing assignment. When teachers plan activities or units, the writing is designated with the appropriate level. One advantage to writing lesson plans this way is that a teacher can see at a glance if the balance of levels is appropriate. A second advantage is that students know before completing an assignment what the teacher's expectations are. Anne Elliott, an English education student, wrote a series of writing assignments for a young adult novel, *Crazy Lady* (see Case 6–1). By designating writing levels, she conveys her expectations to her students and establishes the basis for evaluating the writing.

Sample Writing Assignment Using Different Levels of Writing

GRADE LEVEL: GRADE 8 OR 9

UNIT OF STUDY: THE NOVEL *CRAZY LADY* BY JANE LESLIE CONLY, 1993.

Summary: Maxine Flooter (Crazy Lady) is the neighborhood joke, especially for a group of adolescent boys who continually tease her and her retarded son Ronald. Vernon learns that he is closer to these outcasts than he thought. Through his relationship with Maxine and Ronald, Vernon begins to understand his own loss of his mother and to appreciate his own special gift.

Possible Themes: Family relationships, death, love, fear, growing up, and independence.

Writing Assignments:

1. Before reading the book, write in your journals about one thing you wish you could do or could do better. It can be anything you have difficulty with—studying, writing, drawing, speaking, and so on. Is there something you would really love to do but your friends don't know about it? (level 1)

2. Observe your family life for two to three days. Keep notes of your observations in your journal. Notice any family or individual routines such as who cooks at mealtime, who cleans, where people sit, and so on. Make no judgments; just report facts (level 1).

3. Based on the notes you took, describe your family. Write a one-page response about what you observed (level 2).

4. Answer discussion questions based on the book. (Answers are level 2.) For example: Although Vernon doesn't have a lot of parental guidance at home, he is still taken care of. What are some ways he takes care of himself? What are some things the others outside the family do to care for him? Do you think Ronald will be better off at his aunt and uncle's house? Why or why not? Both Vernon and Maxine have experienced the loss of a loved one. Compare and contrast the coping methods each uses and explain which one you think is more effective.

5. Using some of the major themes in the novel, create a five-line poem using the following structure:

Theme
-ing, -ing
adj., adj., adj.,
-ing. -ing
theme

Experiment with as many different themes as you want (level 1).

6. "Crazy Lady" got her name from people in her neighborhood who did not know her. Take the time to get to know a person in school that you do not know, such as new students, faculty members, or school staff. Conduct interviews with that person. After you have gathered all of your information, write a biography of the person (level 3). The level 3 assignment goes through the writing process, incorporating levels 1 and 2. The final biography is a level 3.

EXPERIENCING STUDENT ASSIGNMENTS

Reread and complete Anne's discovery activities 1 and 2, the ones about something you wish you could do better and your observation of family life. Use the sense of family to mean people you are living with now, for example, roommates. The purpose of your doing the activity is to give you a better sense of how a student might respond to the assignment. Share your results with others in your class.

TYPES OF WRITING ASSIGNMENTS

Major research on rethinking types of writing assignments was done by James Britton, Tony Burgess, Nancy Martin, Alex McLeod, and Harold Rosen of the University of London Institute of Education. Britton and his colleagues examined ways to classify school children's writing according to the nature of the task and the demands made on the writer (3). Out of that study some fundamental ideas about writing emerged that shape our present-day thinking and teaching.

Writing has been classified traditionally into the rhetorical categories, or modes, of narrative, descriptive, expository, and argument. Britton and his colleagues explained that using these four categories presents difficulty in teaching writing. The modes are "derived from an examination of the finished products of professional writers" (4). The result is a prescription for how people *should* write, not *how* they write. Britton and his colleagues argued that the categories essentially leave out the writer and ignore the process of writing. As a result, writing evaluation is concerned only with whether the writer uses the collection of rules that rhetoricians in 1828 decided were the "best sorts of things to say in various argumentative situations" (I. A. Richards qtd. in Britton et al. 4).

Through the 1950s, these traditional categories shaped writing in secondary schools. In the 1960s, educators began to distinguish between personal and objective writing, and school writing was dominated by objective writing—in other words, writing that was abstract and generalized (8).

As their study of writing progressed, Britton and his colleagues developed a description of writing based on the function of writing and the sense of audience based on research done on speech (13). They describe three categories of writing based on the intended audience and purpose: expressive, transactional, and poetic.

The most informal type of writing is when writers focus on themselves. Britton and his colleagues used Dell Hymes' term *expressive* to designate language the writer is most familiar with; a writer assumes that the reader is interested in what the writer has to say. Such writing is informal and natural, the kind people like to do.

In the second category the focus shifts from the writer to a listener or a topic and is defined as *transactional*. In this type of writing, the author is trying to interpret, to shape, to represent experience (Britton 41). When writers use transactional writing, they write about events that have already happened from the "role of spectator" as they view past events. The more the writing "meets the demands of participation in the world's affairs, the nearer will it approach the transactional" (83). Transactional language gets things done in the world and is the kind of writing taught in schools, usually to the exclusion of expressive and poetic.

When the focus is on the message or particular words, it is called *poetic*, which is defined as language in art. The purpose of writing in the poetic form is to create a verbal object, an end in itself (Britton 83). Poetry is the most obvious example of the poetic form, but the categories are not exclusive, and poetic writing can occur in any form. Britton and his colleagues explain that the words themselves are selected by the writer to form an arrangement, a pattern (90).

Like Britton and his colleagues, James Moffett also examined categories of writing. He describes the spectrum of discourse as a hierarchy of levels of abstraction: recording, reporting, generalizing, and theorizing. As in Britton's classification, the levels or kinds of discourse overlap. Shifting from one kind of discourse to another, "say, from narrative discourse to that of explicit generalization necessarily entails shifts in language and rhetoric." For example, as the audience changes for students' writings, the form and formality of the writing changes. Moffett explains that language structures such as transitions, organization, and sentence elaboration shift from one level of discourse to another depending on the purpose of the writing and for whom it is intended. Moffett makes a strong point about teaching the language structure in the context of students' writing. They experience a normal growth in sentence elaboration through their actual writing (53). The basic premise of the writing process is that writing can and should be taught as writers write, rather than after the paper is handed in to a teacher.

The personal involvement in writing affects not only the process but also the types of writing students are asked to do. Traditionally, school writing has been transactional writing, and its purpose has been to show what the student knows by repeating or rephrasing information gained through reading or listening (Maxwell 35). In literature, students wrote essays and exams explaining what literary critics thought. In research papers and report writing, they read library material and wrote other people's words and opinions. Students were not allowed to use the word *I* because their own voice and ideas were not considered appropriate.

The types of writing assignments students do in secondary school usually involve expository and creative writing; these might be divided into cause and effect, persuasive, argumentative, classification, analysis, summaries, poetry, and stories. In most cases, informative writing is more prevalent than personal. One characteristic consistent throughout curricula is that personal narrative becomes progressively less frequent at the higher grade levels. Writing for "the real world" takes over composition classes: reports rather than stories, analyses rather than opinions, formal rather than informal. Other serious consequences of the emphasis on expository assignments are the reliance on sources outside the students' experiences, and the omission of *I* in this type of writing. Some teachers tell students they must *never* use *I* in expository writing, yet, in major magazines like *The New Yorker*, first person is commonly used, as are personal experiences to make a point. When the writing must not reflect the identity of the writer, the students' importance diminishes greatly. The message students get is that they do not count, and what they think does not matter.

Although students need to learn how to write a convincing persuasive paper with a strong thesis, major points supported by subtopics, and logical organization, the lines of distinction between expository writing and so-called creative writing are often blurred. Certain elements are unique to a particular type, but many occur in all writing. Descriptions occur in science writing, reports, letters (friendly and formal), essays, as well as in fiction.

As writers we want readers to see and understand what we do. We can achieve this goal by describing in detail the physical appearances of a lake, or chemical reaction, or character, or frog body parts, or a graph, or a battlefield. Using figurative language in these descriptions helps, too, in providing a mind's-eye view for readers. Similes and metaphors work in any type of writing. A letter to the editor or a board member is more effective with personal examples, and political speeches are full of them. As we teach specific ways to write reports, we also need to teach how and when to use descriptive language and personal experiences in report writing.

BOX 6–4

YOUR WRITING HISTORY

Describe yourself as a writer. Do you consider yourself a writer? What kinds of writing do you do and how often? What purposes does writing serve for you? What types of writing did you do in elementary and secondary schools? How might your own experience in writing influence how you will teach writing?

JOURNAL WRITING

Journal writing has a place in every subject and is indispensable in an English class. Because journals are never evaluated, students soon learn to rely on journals for recording thoughts and ideas about a multitude of subjects. Teachers may read students' journals and write comments in a conversational tone, but the comments should never sound negative. The only criterion teachers can use to evaluate journal writing is effort, which is an elusive quality. Counting pages does not help because some students write larger than others. Also, a writer may put a great deal of thought into one page, whereas another could write pages of rambling prose. Reading the journals to see if students did the work is all one has to do.

Journals can have many different purposes: recording thoughts and feelings, organizing plans, figuring things out, observing life. A variety of journals is useful in the classroom.

Personal Response Journals

The most common journal is one for personal response in which students write about anything they want. Janet Burroway explains that journal writing is indispensable to developing fluency:

> There are, though, a number of tricks you can teach yourself in order to free the writing self, and the essence of these is to give yourself permission to fail. The best place for permission is a private place, and for that reason a writer's journal is an essential, likely to be the source of originality, ideas, experimentation, and growth. (3)

An example of a writer capturing a mood and feeling is evident in the following two entries from the same person:

> #1 She was so happy she tried to swallow the smile and it landed in her stomach. The feeling of pride she knew was dangerous. It could grow into a self-satisfaction which might bring a loss of effort, maybe even bad luck. Watch out, she thought as she kept her lips straight ahead in parallel curves. But inside, her intestines were singing to her pancreas, and her stomach was dancing to its own flip-flop rhythm.
>
> #2 The voice that came out was that of an angry gander honking and hissing. It wouldn't stop but continued on for an entire hour. I was a prisoner held by a grinding noise, sound waves pressing me to my chair, held by my eardrums. The group in here murmured a polite chuckle. They must be deciphering some meaning from those sounds that are grating into my ears. He knows. He knows I'm not listening. He keeps stepping closer on the worn wood floor, throwing out words with hand motions.

Students need to write daily. Burroway believes that, "It doesn't matter what you write and it doesn't matter very much how much, but it does matter that you make a steady habit of the writing" (4). Some students, though, have a difficult time thinking of anything to write, and a teacher may provide open-ended questions to help solve the problem (e.g., What I remember best from last year is . . . , What I like least about school is . . .).

List making is also a good place to start:

My ten favorite songs or the ones I dislike the most.
Ten things that could never happen. Choose the one you wish would happen the most and explain why.
Name your three favorite people and describe them.

Name three famous people. Why are they famous?
Name three places you would like to visit and explain why.

One high school teacher writes a quotation on the board each day and students write a response to it. They have the option of writing about something else, but they all have to write.

Even though it takes time, reading student journals is important because they won't put effort into something we don't care about. The following suggestions make the job a little easier:

1. Read journals quickly. Responding every page or two seems to be enough. Students just want the sense that teachers are reading.
2. Stagger the dates students hand in the journals so teachers have journals from only one class at a time.
3. Have students keep a journal for three or four weeks, stop for two weeks, and then start keeping them again.

Project Journals

When students do long projects, a journal helps them remember deadlines, organize tasks, and keep track of where they are. A project journal begins with notes from the teacher's description of the assignment and the dates each part is due. At the end of the project, the journal must be handed in, too. The teacher checks to see that each part is completed. Notes from outside readings, outlines, mapping, and brainstorming are all part of the project journal. When students meet in response groups, they use the journal to jot down notes to use when revising. Keeping a project journal is a great help in staying organized, something students have trouble with.

Language Journals

Paying attention to language in use is one way to appreciate its playfulness and diversity. Talking about language serves the purpose, too, of learning how new words come into our vocabulary, how punctuation patterns change, how language belongs to the people who use it. A language journal might begin with an assignment to look for unusual signs, especially ones that use a play on words. Students note the signs in the language journal and share them in class. Even with a new focus each day, students continue to look for examples of all the suggestions for about a week. We take a few minutes at the beginning of each class period to share what they found. Another suggestion is to use unusual names, including connections between name and occupations. We had a dentist, Dr. Toothacker, and a doctor, Dr. Paine. Students come up with unbelievable examples. They have to be authentic though. Names of businesses provide unusual examples, especially barber shops and hair salons. Advertisements are a rich source, as are newspaper headlines. Overheard conversations can provide examples of clichés. The language journal is a good starting place for discussions about language.

Writer's Journal

The purpose of this journal is to provide ideas for stories and poems. Many students are shy about writing poetry; in their journal they can practice phrases, beginnings, and endings without having to write a completed poem. The same is true of stories. Perhaps they think of a description of a house; that might be all they write. Or they can write a plot outline. If they see an interesting looking person they should write the description in the journal; that person might become a character in a story later. However, the connection between what one sees and, later, writes, may not always be concrete as author Joan Didion explains. She keeps a notebook to record what she sees around her for the purpose of remembering her own sense of self at the time. Although a line or image may appear in her writing, the journal is a private recording of the world as she relates to it (136). Likewise, students can use their journals to recapture a mood, outlook, or frame of mind.

An interesting source for writing is newspaper stories. Students tape the stories in the journal, or even just the headline, and use them for ideas later on. If students have difficulty getting started in noticing the world around them, teachers might provide specific leads. For instance, a teacher can suggest describing someone or something students noticed on the way home from school, unusual signs, bumper stickers, newspaper headlines, scraps of conversation, one side of a telephone conversation, any use of language that catches their interest. Once students begin to notice language use, they are more aware of a wide use of real-world language. Entries in the writing journal are a rich source for sharing in the classroom.

Learning Logs

Journals used as learning logs facilitate learning when related to specific assignments. At the beginning of a unit teachers find it helpful to learn what their students' understandings of concepts and vocabulary are. Learning logs provide a way to do this with no awkwardness for students. When teachers use a familiar word such as *irony*, for example, they cannot assume all students know its meaning even though no one asks for clarification. Asking students to write an explanation of the word shows a teacher where to begin. Students know from experience that journal entries are not graded and, therefore, are willing to risk being wrong. The information helps a teacher plan where to begin and how much detail and what types of examples to use.

Throughout a unit students can use the learning log to record predictions, questions, unknown words, notes from readings and lectures, and any problems they encounter as they study. Most often learning logs are used for projects and are a place for planning and recording. Some teachers may not collect them even for a quick read, but others check the logs to help keep students focused on the work.

WRITING SHORT STORIES

Discovery activities are especially important when students write stories. Plot, characterization, setting, descriptions, and dialogue all combine to create a well-written story. The writer's journal can provide help as mentioned in preceding sections. In addition, a teacher can design many other activities such as round robin stories, developing characters, story strips, and personal narratives.

Round Robin Stories

Round robin stories are one way to get students interested in writing stories, and they work for a wide age span. These stories foster creativity and provide an enjoyable writing activity for students, which is an important result. Once a teacher uses round robin stories in class, students will probably ask to do it again. Because it doesn't take much time, about 15 minutes, it is handy to use when there isn't enough time to begin something else—like the 15 minutes left in a class period after a fire drill. The class is divided into groups of four. Each student has a sheet of paper. At a signal from the teacher, each student begins a story. Sometimes teachers provide the kind of story it must be: mystery, science fiction, or adventure, for example. After a minute and a half, students stop writing. They finish a word if necessary, but not a sentence. They fold the part they've written down except for the last line so that only the last line is visible; this might be one word or a whole line. Then they pass the paper to the right. This time they have one minute to write and follow the same procedure as before. It works well if the stories go around about three times, but the process can be adjusted to the time available. Just before the last pass, students know they have to write an ending, and when they hear the word *stop,* they finish the sentence rather than just the word. Students love to read the stories to their group.

Developing Characters

Students seem to have the most trouble with this area. Plots are the easiest, so most of the time, characters appear in the story to carry the plot along and nothing more. An especially successful way to show students that characters should have personalities is an activity described by David Sudol, a high school teacher. Sudol began by telling his class that characters have to be developed, and he discussed different levels of character development. He places an empty chair in the center of the room and announces that Stanley Realbozo is sitting in it. He explains that the students have to bring him to life. He guides the discussion that follows with these questions.

1. What does Stanley look like? Can you describe him sitting there or doing something?
2. Where does Stanley live, work, and play?
3. What does Stanley think about? What is he thinking?
4. What is Stanley's conversation like? How does he speak?
5. How does Stanley react to people, places, and things?
6. How do others characters react to Stanley? What do they think and say about him?
7. What does the author think about Stanley? (The author is the class.) (64)

When students have discussed all the questions, they put together a composite picture of Stanley. How real he is depends on the amount of detail in the class's answers. As Sudol notes, "But no matter what his level of development, he always comes alive. More than the responses to the questions, he is now an actual member of our class" (65).

At this point the students create a plot for Stanley using five questions as guides.

1. What is the situation of the story? What is happening at the beginning?
2. What is the main conflict of the story? What are the generating circumstances? What gets the action going?
3. What events in the story increase the conflict and push forward the action?
4. What is the climax or highest point of the story?
5. How are the conflicts resolved? (Sudol 63–66)

Sudol used the activity to help his students understand literature better; it can also be used as a discovery activity for short story writing. The first part—describing Stanley—is a whole-class activity; the plot questions help students individually write a story about Stanley. Teachers can adapt this and other activities to meet the particular needs of the class.

Story Strips

As mentioned earlier, most students are fairly good at writing plot, but have trouble with characters and settings. Story strips is an activity that helps them connect all three elements. Before the class activity, a teacher cuts strips of paper about 8½ inches long and 4 inches wide from three different colors. The lesson begins with a discussion of what a setting could be, using examples from stories they read. In some literature, the setting means a great deal and, in others, it makes no difference at all. With help if necessary, students come up with a long list of what settings could include: time of day, season, location, length of time, environment, place, year, month, day. The teacher hands out strips of one color, and they each write a description of a setting.

Next, the teacher discusses how characterization can be described in several ways, such as physical appearance, personality traits, and behavior. Using the second colored strip, students write a character description.

The last strip is used for a single line of plot. At first, students tend to write too much for plot, so it is better to narrow it to one sentence. They might write, "She opened the door slowly," for example.

When students finish the three strips, they place the strips in a hat and choose one strip of each color. Their assignment is to write a story incorporating the information on the strips. Some combinations bring out loud cries of "This is impossible!" "No way will this work out!" But the stories are always interesting and creative.

This activity is an excellent way to teach students how to use flashbacks in story writing. Sometimes a flashback is the only way the writer can weave together dissimilar elements into a coherent story. When they say with despair, "I can't put a guy in a desert in 1834 in the same story as someone taking off in a rocket!" they might be encouraged to consider flashback as one solution (Maxwell 2–3). An example of the three slips that one student had to base his story on is in Figure 6–6.

Setting:	1890s, old saloon with damaged wood floor, good drinks (cheap), regulars sitting around, smoke-filled air, few small tables besides the bar stools, a dog—black with white spots.
Character:	A quiet young adult, about 22 or 23. Heavy heart, melancholy, friendly, but shy, enjoys biking, observant, poor self-esteem.
Plot line:	They suddenly realized the rocket was without fuel.

FIGURE 6–6
Example of story strips.

Personal Narratives

Personal experience and fiction writing go hand in hand. Professional writers often use their own experiences for stories, but we seldom ask students to do that. Students are not easily convinced that it is permissible to change facts when writing fiction. A student once said, "That's lying." But as Ben Logan explains in the afterword of *The Land Remembers,* writers can ignore the facts and capture the truth. When people ask Logan how factual his book is, he explains it is "feeling-level truth" (280). That's what realistic stories are, and we can help students create stories based on their own experiences.

When students begin a personal narrative, thinking about each sense one at a time can help them remember details. Logan explains that "The line between memory and invention is confused" (280). He made up some details to capture an image he knew to be true, only to discover later they were indeed accurate. If writers want to convey an idea to a reader, for example, how cold the day was, they can make up a temperature that conveys the coldness to the reader. A former student wrote a wonderful story about helping out his first-grade teacher, or so he thought, by painting leaves of the classroom plants with shellac. When Mark retells that story now, some of the facts change: the number of plants he shellacked, the grade he was in, and so forth. But what never changes is the image of a little boy trying so hard to please and failing because he did not have an adult's knowledge of the world. Mark is using "feeling-level" truth.

WRITING POETRY

Before attempting poetry, students should be familiar with reading and hearing poetry. Concentrating on poetry writing is often done as a unit for a week or more, but poetry itself should be integrated throughout the year. Once poetry writing is familiar to students, it, too, can be part of many units.

To begin the unit we write a class poem based on Kenneth Koch's suggestion of the "I Wish" poem in *Wishes, Lies, and Dreams.* Everyone in class completes the line that begins "I wish." It is easier to organize the lines if students write them on 3" X 5" cards. All the cards are laid out on a table and arranged and rearranged to create a poem. If the same line or similar lines are written by more than one student, this becomes the refrain in the poem. It is important to put in everyone's line; students look for their own. Even students who are antischool write a line and eagerly anticipate seeing their contribution in the completed poem. Teachers type the poem that evening, run off copies for everyone, and hand them out the next period. Staggering the activity for multiple classes makes it easier on the teacher. The poem always comes out sounding like a "real poem" and impresses everyone. This activity works with students in elementary grades through the graduate students in the writing project. English education students composed the following:

I WISH

I wish there were 40 hours in a day and weekends were 4 days long.
There's so much to do, so many places to go
And so much to experience in this life!
I wish I could travel throughout the world.
I wish that every child could have a peaceful, enjoyable childhood
Free of all abuse, hunger, and drugs.
I wish everyone could accept others as easily
As they accept themselves.
I wish I could read the minds of others
When I'm particularly confused about things they say
Or the way they act.
I wish it was Christmas time all the time
And nobody would ever stop being excited about it.
I wish for long, lazy, fun-filled days with nothing to worry about
Except for long lazy enjoyable evenings in which I'd share
Living and loving with forever friends.
I wish I were a preying mantis so powerful, tall and green.
I wish Coke was still sold in 16 oz. bottles.
I wish the sidewalk between my house and campus
Wasn't under two inches of water.
I wish it was spring.
I wish I was walking on a sandy beach near tranquil waters.
I wish that I could walk to the moon upon silver beams
Reflecting on the still serene waters of Lake Michigan.
I wish the skies were always clear, the weather always warm,
And the grass always green.
I wish for a beautiful multicolored sunset.
I wish for mornings like this one—cool and crisp.
To walk with my friends and enjoy the freshness of the air.
I wish the summer sun would radiate its bright yellow fingertips
Across my grandfather's sparking crystal blue eyes
Just one last time.

The "I wish" poem is a list poem, sometimes called "catalog verse." Larry Fagin suggests many different subjects and types of list poems to use with student writers because they "draw on specific details of everyday experience," and use the rhythms and patterns of everyday speech (2). He suggests beginning with a theme or topic, modeling poems by using a variety of examples, and pointing out characteristics (3). Many of the list poems are collaborative efforts and help to increase students confidence in writing poetry (8).

Writing a poem can be difficult for some people, and using a pattern to create poetry helps them. Fagin suggests beginning lines with a color word as "Red is . . . ," "If I were . . . ," and "I remember. . . . " List poems may be organized around topics as well, such as beautiful things, emotions, definitions, and reasons.

Several explanations and examples of pattern poems are described below. All of the poetry examples used in this section are written by students.

1. *Five liners*
   - Write the name of someone on the first line.
   - Write two adjectives describing the noun.
   - Write three words describing what they do (end in -*ing* or *s*).
   - Write a phrase about the person.
   - Repeat the same name as on line 1 or another name for the same person.

Holden
Confused, introspective
Wandering, wondering, running
Looking for answers
Holden

Gail Servoss

Hester
Spirited, Censored
Sins, Sews, Survives
Nobel brave victim
Hester

Light
Reflect, shimmer
Shinning, sparkling, glowing
Taking away the dark
Light

Becky Olien

Summer
Hot, fun
Swimming, playing, traveling
Free from school
Summer

Jessa Olien

2. *Diamond shape poem.* This poem form is similar to the five liners but has a twist in the middle. The first half refers to the noun on the first line; the second half refers to the noun on the last line.
   - Begin with a noun.
   - Write two adjectives describing the noun.
   - Write three participles referring to the noun on the first line.
   - Write four nouns: The first two refer to the top name, the second two to the name on the last line.
   - Write three participles referring to the noun on the last line.
   - Write two adjectives describing the noun on the last line.
   - Write the second noun on the last line.

Lady Macbeth
Greedy, ruthless
Scheming, controlling, cleaning
Blood, death-king, trouble
planning, killing, worrying
paranoid, superstitious
Macbeth

Laurie Anderson

3. *Concrete poem.* A concrete poem is one in which the words project not only an image but the actual shape of the subject of the poem. These can become trite unless writers use descriptive words, but with creativity they are enjoyable to eyes and ears as in the two students examples shown here:

MY CAR

a customized
window of plexiglass and
bolts. The windshield is graced
with a crack and a scratch from the
stub that was once a windshield wiper a hole in the floor to complement
the heater that works! -- constantly. and a back seat which folds down! --
permanently the ashtray is lost, the seatbelts won't click the radio is falling
out, but who needs the extra noise with the sputtering clanging spft
rattling banging pft
clink clunk t.

— Victoria Gillhouse

Red leaves in the fall
worms and bugs
LIFE big & small
branches big
bird nests with baby birds
Green leaves
green leaves of spring
Beauty
and summer
pine needles on some
WORMS
children climbing on them
birds flying high in the
big strong branches
SQUIRRELS
blossoms
a base of a tree
can lead to...
dirt
water
nutrients
roots

— Jenel Korkowski

4. *Preposition poem.* The poem is seven lines long, each of which begins with a preposition. Authors write about themselves, their feeling and emotions. Giving students a list of prepositions is helpful.

> In a place of wind and sun
> As far as can be seen
> Upon the mind a vision forms
> Of grass and trees and green.
> Throughout the swing I concentrate
> About the ball so white
> Against all odds I hit the thing and sent it out of sight.

Cheryl Mortensen

> Through the azure sky the sun shines
> Upon my waking spirit.
> Before me, the day lies unexplored.
> Into the morning, I step boldly
> In spite of the chill in the air,
> Before the night covers the world
> In a velvet blanket, I shall triumph.

Lisa Willert

5. *Mood poems.* Students begin with a one-word description of the mood they are in at the time or one they felt recently. On the first line they write the mood. The next two lines begin with the word *not,* describing the mood by writing what it isn't. The fourth line is also a *not,* but is stated as a comparison. The fifth line is what the mood is, followed by three lines of description of the mood.

> I'm happy
> Not silly
> Not falling off my chair happy
> Not like the happiest I've ever been in my whole life
> But quietly satisfactorily happy.
> Happy that vacation is starting soon
> Happy that my brother is coming home
> Happy that I'm going skiing with my friends

6. *Found poems.* Poetry defies definition: Some rhyme, some do not; some are long, others short; some tell a story, or evoke a feeling, or describe a single image. The spacing of lines and arrangement of white space can create a sense of poetry. Found poems illustrate that point vividly. A found poem is "found" from any printed material: *TV Guide,* cereal boxes, student handbooks, text-

books, advertising, newspaper headlines, and so forth. Students have fun creating the layout of the words; some are silly, others more serious.

Why Brown Rice?
Brown rice is the most
nutritious
Rice of all.
It's also the least
Processed.
While most rice is
Polished
To remove the bran, brown rice is
Whole
With only the outer hull
Removed.

Kellogg's Kemmei Rice Bran

7. *Bio poem.* A bio poem usually is about oneself, but could also be a character from literature.
   • In line 1, write the first name of the person.
   • In line 2, write four traits that describe the character.
   • Line 3 begins with the words "relative of _____." The student fills in the blank.
   • Line 4 begins with the words "lover of." Then the student lists three things or people loved by the character.
   • Line 5 begins with the words "who feels." Then the student describes three things the character feels.
   • Line 6 begins with "who needs," and the student writes three items.
   • Line 7 begins with the words "who fears," and the student writes three things feared.
   • Line 8 begins with the words "who gives," and the student lists three examples.
   • Line 9 begins with the words "who would like to see," and the student lists three things.
   • Line 10 begins with the words "resident of _____," and the student fills in the blank.
   • Line 11 lists the last name of the character.
8. *Terse verse.* The poem itself is only two or three words, but the titles can be quite long and suggest, almost like a riddle, the subject of the poem. An example by a student, Jennifer Hartzell, follows:

Daring Fungus that Adheres to Dated Vittles
Bold Mold

Experimenting and playing with words becomes the focus of poetry writing. Students, of course, can write haiku, limericks, sonnets, parodies, and so on, but the goal is always to enjoy writing poetry and increase confidence. Writing structured poems helps achieve these goals.

Box 6–5

WRITING POETRY

Write five poems using five different styles. Which ones are the easiest? Which are the hardest? Develop some ways of including poetry writing with literature study and thematic units.

WRITING REPORTS AND RESEARCH PAPERS

Writing reports and research papers can get students into the library to look for information, take notes on what they find, and organize the notes into a first draft. When students self-select the topic, they enjoy writing reports because it gives them a chance to pursue an interest, but problems may occur in locating the information and organizing notes. Writing a report can overwhelm some students, but a structured method helps them keep track of what they are doing. The first time we used this method, students who usually did not complete the longer assignments not only handed in reports on time, but their reports were better organized than others. From then on, everyone used the same method involving these specific steps.

1. *Students choose a topic.* The discovery technique described earlier of meeting in groups to make a selection is used. The teacher may provide broad guidelines to help students think of a topic, but students must be free to explore a topic of their own choosing.
2. *Students use prior knowledge.* After selecting a topic, students write down everything they already know about it, and they know a surprising amount. This is free writing; and they are encouraged to write as quickly as possible, not worrying about spelling or punctuation. They read over what they wrote and devise a list of questions they want to answer.
3. *The following day they bring the list of questions to class and share them in small groups.* Each student explains the topic and reads the questions that will shape the report.

   Without the questions, students go into the library with only a vague idea of what they are doing. Finding answers (information) is difficult if one doesn't know the question—somewhat like going into a room to get something and then forgetting what one was looking for. Finding an unknown is almost impossible.

   When each student shares the topic and questions, the group members make suggestions and provide more questions. If the others aren't responding enough, the teacher asks them to write one or two more questions for each person. As with other revising activities, students decide for themselves if they want to use the additional suggestions, but they have no lack of ideas. Talking over their plans for the reports helps students because, when they start explaining to the others, their own ideas become clearer. By the next class period they have a list of four to six questions for which they need to find answers.

4. *Before starting the library work, they write one question each on a sheet of paper.* If they have four questions, they will have four sheets of paper. Then they take a final piece of paper and title it "References."

5. *Now they are ready for library work.* As they locate a reference, they begin finding answers to their questions. First they record the reference on the Reference Sheet, numbering it 1. Then they jot down notes under the appropriate question and place a 1 by the notes to signify where the material came from. The first reference might provide notes for two or three questions. With the next reference they read, they go through the same procedure, numbering it 2. The question sheets soon will look like this:

If they need help from a librarian, they can be specific about what information they need. When the pages fill up with notes, they staple more on. When the questions are answered, it is time to write the report. Before using this method, students, who had trouble writing reports, never knew whether or not they had enough information; with this method they can see when they've answered each question. If they cannot find information to answer one of the questions. they may substitute another question if they clear it with the teacher.

With notes in hand, they return to the classroom and begin writing the report. Because all of the notes about one area are on the sheet, organizing is no problem. For many students, completing a report is a new experience. This method works for 4th through 12th grade. More experienced writers may not need help with developing questions, although writing questions before looking for references is helpful for *all* writers. All of the students report that keeping track of notes, seeing where more information is needed, and organizing the writing is easier using this method, which can be used with all research papers and reports.

The I–Search Paper

One type of research paper, the I–search paper, encourages students to search for a wide range of information well beyond the traditional sources. Students search for information, compare facts from various sources, and then draw conclusions. The original concept comes from Ken Macrorie and stresses genuine inquiry that the student writer is interested in, as opposed to locating information that has already been collected and summarized. To begin then, the topic must be self-selected by the student.

After students select individual topics, they meet in groups to discuss how to locate resources and to generate possible questions to answer. A summary of Macrorie's advice to students includes thinking about the best way to interview people: what to ask, how to approach them, and what information to know before the interview. He suggests that the statements experts make need to be tested against what other experts say (Nancy Kearns 48). When writing the paper, a good method of organization is for a writer to explain the method of research in the order it was done (Kearns 48).

Because a person is searching for information the writer wants and needs to know, the I–Search method develops lifelong skills in gathering information by listening, interviewing, reading, quoting, reporting, and writing (Macrorie 71).

Difficulties With Research Papers

Although research papers are a common assignment for high school students, many teachers are disappointed with the results. Unlike report writing in which students select and record material from several sources into a coherent whole, the research paper requires, in addition, higher-level thinking skills. Questions that students develop for the research paper cannot be answered simply by looking up material, but require new insights that come from a study of the material, or put another way, from doing research. It goes beyond answering questions with information already published and found in the library.

Many problems occur in research paper assignments. Because research papers require a high level of cognitive ability, usually only students in 11th and 12th grades are able to successfully complete a research paper. Too often, younger students are assigned research projects far beyond their developmental level and consequently are frustrated. Teachers need to be mindful of the cognitive level of the task and the assignment.

Another serious problem is that teachers often do not use the writing process in research assignments. Students work too much in isolation with little guidance from their peers. The emphasis shifts from discovery activities to a stylized format. Only college-bound students could have any use for such a product. Many skills need to be taught and practiced when students undertake a research project. In preparing students for research projects, the skills of paraphrasing, taking notes, summarizing, and documenting all need to be included in class activities.

Many teachers unnecessarily structure the research assignment by limiting the types of sources or specifying a particular number of sources rather than encouraging students to gather information. Robert Perrin, from Indiana State University, explains that students should be encouraged to

> look everywhere and explore every potential source of information. Why shouldn't students use interviews, both personal and telephone? Why shouldn't students conduct surveys when the results would be enlightening? Why shouldn't students use personal experience when it is appropriate? Why shouldn't students use films, pamphlets, lecture notes, records, or television programs when they supply helpful ideas, insights, and information? (51)

Tim Hirsch, a college educator, developed a research assignment for personal decision making that uses many of the resources Perrin suggests. Hirsch believes research should center on a question students care about, one that has personal implications for them. High school students face important questions: Should they go to a postsecondary school? Should they work after school? Should they attempt to get on an athletic team? Hirsch explains that:

> The first step, then, for student researchers is to begin with questions of critical importance to them. The answer to these questions should lead them to action. They should be questions which lead to choices rather than to simple accumulation of information and opinions about a topic. After the question is established, the student researchers need to define the "givens," and establish the criteria they are going to use to answer their questions. (11)

At first, students may think they can't find answers to questions like these in the library, but they can. Hirsch explains that students are more apt to locate library resources when they have a "compelling need for information" (12). Other sources of information are important as well. We all discover information by talking to informed people, watching news broadcasts, or making direct personal observations. Evidence can come from a variety of sources, as long as it is verifiable. Students need to do their own calculations, comparisons, and evaluation (13). When students learn this type of research process, they can apply it to questions in other academic areas or areas of their life. They become lifelong researchers.

COLLABORATIVE WRITING

Students working together to create a single work has many advantages. Writing alone never provides opportunities to see how others figure out what to say and how to say it. In a group, students see what discovery techniques others use: a mapping outline, free writing, listing, and so forth. Brainstorming in a group is more productive than doing it on one's own. One idea leads to another; what one person says makes another think of something else. And working together in a group helps improve social interaction.

Many students loudly proclaim the disadvantages when a teacher brings up collaborative writing. Two areas cause the main difficulties: grades and work load. In collaborative writing everyone in the group receives the same grade. Students who usually receive high grades for their writing worry that their grade will drop. Some students worry that all group members will not do their share. Both are legitimate concerns, but there are ways around them, or at least ways to ease the problem.

Because cooperating with people is a skill we need throughout our life, learning to work with others is a major goal in collaborative writing, as important as writing a well-organized, interesting paper. To make collaborative writing work, teachers need to make sure the students work on both goals. By stressing the need to listen to others and respect what they say, teachers help students work through difficulties.

Receiving the same grade as others in the group bothers some students, and they have to know right from the beginning there will be no other way of weighing the grade. Knowing they receive a common grade encourages students to work at cooperating with the others. When they hand in their final draft, ask them to evaluate individually how the process worked out—for instance, if they thought everyone did a fair share. Often, just having an opportunity to tell the teacher they think they did more work than others is enough satisfaction.

Helen Dale, an English education instructor, sets up collaborative assignments that more evenly distribute the work load. She puts as many students in a group as there are collaborative writing assignments. If she plans three collaborative writing assignments, she puts three people in a group. Each assignment has a primary writer, so the responsibility shifts from student to student. All of the group members contribute to each writing stage, but one person is responsible for collecting the others' work, doing the final polishing, and writing transitions so that everyone's writing blends together, and whatever else needs to be done. For the next group writing assignment, a different member has that responsibility. Obviously the groups have to remain the same throughout the semester or year.

Dale finds that the quality of the papers improves through collaboration. "There is peer pressure to think well and to write well. Students test ideas against each other, so you get their best and clearest thoughts" (14) When she first started assigning group papers, she thought students would write "patchwork prose," but found students "seem to integrate ideas, organization, and style" (15).

Collaborative groups provide firsthand experience in working together, an ability important in our life work. Dale believes that "Wonderful things happen when students are allowed to see other minds at work, puzzle things out, search for the right example or the right word, and arrive at a completed piece of work" (16). Although there are some negative aspects of collaborative writing, the positive outweighs the negative, and with planning teachers can make the experience worthwhile for students.

We have used one collaborative writing assignment in which students write a level 3 paper on the advantages and disadvantages of birth order in a family. The groups are formed on the basis of their birth orders; for example, students who were the youngest in their families work in one group and produce one paper and so on. Our students responded to the experience of working on a collaborative paper:

> I found that working in a group is very different from being on your own. I tend to worry about what they think of my writing and whether or not everyone agrees and is happy with the decisions. In a group you have such different styles and opinions that it can be hard to come to agreement. In our group these differences were evident but not a major problem. I think my role in the group was to help get everyone talking. It took a couple of days to learn and understand each person's style, but I am happy with the experience. There now are six more people I know better. (Shawna Sullivan)

> During the first week of working together some people were a little hesitant to express their opinion or critique someone else's work but as time passed the entire group relaxed and seemed to feel more comfortable sharing their thoughts and ideas. I believe the work load was pretty evenly distributed. Aside from what I learned from the other six people in my group, I learned that it is very difficult collaborating on a paper because there are many different ways a person can approach this type of paper, and with some people in the group it made it more difficult to decide on things—not necessarily because everyone has a different opinion but because one person does not want to make decisions for six others. Overall though it has taught me how to work in a big group on a paper. (Justin Hurd)

> Overall working in a group was a welcome change from writing everything individually. Our group worked well together and we accomplished a lot. The finished product turned out to be a really good paper reflecting various experiences. I think we each shared the workload evenly although Erinn did more on the final draft. We each did different things at different times, which balanced out. Everyone gave input and turned in paragraphs. I learned various things about each group member and their families. I also learned group work is a lot of compromising and combining of ideas. (Dominich Walsh)

COMPOSITION AND THE WORLD OF WORK

Many teachers and business people are concerned about the schools' ability to prepare students for the world of work. Teachers Mitch Cox and Christine Firpo concluded that "the majority of what we were teaching would never make a difference in their lives" (42). They realized they had to identify what their students needed to succeed in the workforce. They learned that managers were concerned with their employees' lack of ability to work on teams (42). They also identified other skills their students needed: to read technical manuals, to maintain records, to write correspondence, and to communicate orally. In addition, they needed creative and logical thinking.

Carol Pope describes five areas of proficiency that students need as they enter the labor force.

1. *Ability to communicate:* Workers must be able to use language effectively in a variety of contexts. They need to function in teams and work in a collaborative setting (38).
2. *Ability to work in a multicultural setting:* Workers need to listen, be empathic, and be knowledgeable and open-minded of other cultures (38).
3. *Ability to adapt:* They need to learn new skills quickly and adjust to changing demographics and cultures of fellow workers. They must know how to learn (39).
4. *Ability to think critically:* Workers need to have "an inquiring responsive mind that sees relationships and considers alternatives, predicts, and analyzes" (39).
5. *Ability to use available technology:* Workers need to be familiar with computers and multimedia so that they can communicate across worlds and be able to deal with various cultures and ideas (39).

English language arts classrooms can, and many already do, facilitate these five proficiencies. To begin, a class structure where students move around the room, where desks are not in tidy straight rows, and where talking is going on is preparing future workers to learn adaptability, accept others, and work in diverse settings.

When the teacher is not the focal point of learning, students learn how to plan for their own needs, where to look for information, and how to find the help they need. Response groups in writing are a good example of creating an opportunity for this to happen. The teacher sets up the situations, but students must take responsibility for the learning.

When students work collaboratively, they are learning how workers write grants and reports and plan for the future. Meeting in small groups to plan a research project teaches the necessary cooperation needed in the workforce. Developing an awareness of audience when composing is an important skill as students learn to consider how to explain information and their own views to others. The entire writing process reinforces the five proficiencies and, in particular, reinforces cooperative learning.

To help students become more self-directed learners, teachers can incorporate the reading/writing workshop into their class structure (Cox & Firpo 43). Within this structure students select what they want to read and write and generate their own writing topics. The students are "encouraged to think of themselves as cooperative team workers" when they collaborate on revising and editing (43).

The more teachers have students work together, the more students realize they learn from each other as well as the teacher and the better able they are to function in the world of work.

In addition to structuring our classrooms to help students achieve the five proficiencies Pope describes, teachers can provide technical writing activities to sharpen student skills in this area. Technical writing is appearing more frequently in high school curriculums as a separate class. A teacher of such a class, Marvin Hoffman, explains the objectives for his course:

We wanted our students to write rich, accurate, precise, objective description; to develop a sensitivity to honest, uninflated language in their own work and the work of others; and finally to demonstrate their ability to synthesize these skills by producing an action proposal on a problem or issue of their own choosing for a real audience. (59)

Hoffman used a wide range of activities to help students develop objective description. Students read a variety of literature and examples of job-related writing throughout the course. Much of the job-related writing was a negative model, and students became adept at rewriting convoluted confusing memos into plain understandable English (61). Hoffman found that some of the "sharpest writing emerges from fields like nature, science, and sports" (61), and he provided many opportunities for students to read from these areas. As a final project, each student chose a problem to research and write about—one that had a real audience. Through library research, interviews, and observations, students wrote their findings and recommendations for a specific audience (62).

In summary, if teachers stress cooperative learning through the writing process and collaborative activities, students learn the essential skills for writing in the world of work. Writing assignments that have real-world audiences and purposes help students understand the necessity of clear writing. Teaching English does not have to seem esoteric to our students.

ADDITIONAL WRITING ASSIGNMENTS

Assignments are related to purpose—the teacher's purpose. What do teachers want students to learn or practice from a particular activity? As teachers plan writing activities, they do so contextually—that is, in the context of a unit or goal. The assignments described in this section appear unconnected, but they are intended for use in different units depending on the teacher's purpose, and illustrate the types of activities teachers find successful.

Checkbook Characterizations

Information about people can come from a wide range of sources, one of which is a checkbook register. With the class, a teacher introduces the idea of describing people through examining their checkbook. In small groups, students write a register of about 10 lines. The groups exchange registers and write a character description based on the information.

A student, Leslie Olmen, wrote the following character description based on a fictitious register:

The owner of this checkbook is very organized. He or she balances the account after every check. Wow! He/she—probably a she because she spent over $100 on hair and clothes. She cares about her appearance, I guess. She's an English major—as determined by book purchase. She should have gone shopping at Ron's or 4-11 instead of ordering Little Caesar's. Perhaps she is a procrastinator. She's a sucker for low-price items because she bought approximately seven items at that junk store. Despite her consistent balancing of money she still goes under or down to the last cent. Maybe she enjoys the good things in life but can't exactly afford them.

Personals

Personal ads in the newspaper make interesting story lines. Tape each one on a 3" X 5" card and hand them out. In pairs or small groups ask students to combine the ads and create a story. Teachers prepare ahead of time for this activity by checking the ads regularly for interesting personals. A few edited discoveries include:

Phony Drivers Licenses
Fool people! For any age, state! Photo! Signature! (No rejection—No proof required) Fast service with cash/money order. Guaranteed! Rush $20

Become an ordained minister. Free ministerial credentials legalize your right to the title "Reverend." Write for information.

SECRET OF LIFE
Guaranteed. Send $2.00

SUPER LOVE SPECIALIST
Prepared astrologer. Indian spiritual. Gifted! Complete satisfaction guaranteed. Send $3.00

28-year-old-man with several positive qualities seeks an adventurous lady for a sincere relationship. Must be attractive and slim.

One-woman Man non-drinker early 40s honest, sincere. Would like to meet one-man lady who is through having children.

Students write stories, either individually or in groups, based on an imagined story behind the ad.

Mystery Packets

Teachers collect an assortment of items and place them in a large envelope. Matchbook covers, imprinted napkins, receipts, ticket stubs, notes, and torn bits of paper are good choices. Each group receives one packet. The contents of the packet represent material found at the scene of a crime. Together, students write a story or police report about the crime based on the evidence.

Many sources for teaching ideas are available to teachers. One in particular that secondary teachers find useful is *Notes Plus,* a quarterly publication from the National Council of Teachers of English and written, for the most part, by teachers. A typical issue includes these topics: "Ideas from the Classroom," "Classic of the Month," "A Writing Assignment of the Month," and "A Literature Assignment of the Month." The next two writing ideas appeared in *Notes Plus.*

1. *Customized holidays.* Begin with a general discussion of holidays. Ask students why they think people create and celebrate holidays. Brainstorm about what holidays students think should be on the calendar, but aren't. Then have students design or create a special day. They write a description of the special way in which this new holiday will be celebrated, and design a logo, slogan, or whatever trimmings it takes to make the new day a complete holiday. The final step is an illustrated poster or commercial announcing the new holiday. As a continuation, ask students to think of special experiences in their own lives that should be celebrated. A children's book, *I'm in Charge of Celebrations* by Byrd Baylor is a great starting point for this discussion. Students deepen their awareness of the value of their observational experiences (Hellman 3).

2. *The rewards of the wanted poster.* To help students focus on what they like about themselves, they design their own wanted poster. Using a form that looks roughly like the real thing, students write information about themselves: name, date of birth, a photo or caricature, physical description, caution, and reward. Students may choose which of their physical descriptions they feel comfortable sharing. Under the heading "caution" students list short phrases that describe problem areas; for example, sarcastic sense of humor, selfish, disorganized. The real focus of the activity is the reward section. Unlike the real wanted posters, this is reserved for a list of positive personal characteristics—a list that highlights how others are rewarded by knowing this person. Many students have trouble with the reward section because they minimize their good attributes. The poster is not complete until their reward section is at least as long as the caution section. This activity can be a real eye-opener for students when they discover that their good qualities outweigh their less desirable traits. (Meisner 7)

The Writing Workshop: Vol. 2 by Alan Ziegler is a rich source of teaching ideas for writing. The following illustrate some activities he suggests:

1. *The most amazing things. . . .* Students first write about the most amazing thing they've *never* seen. They can make up anything they like—"the wilder the better" (26). Then they write about the most amazing thing they've *ever* seen. The subject can't be anything they saw on TV or in a movie. It must be incredible, but true. The assignment could be on heroic acts or beautiful things, and so forth. (27)

2. *The power of words.* Students think of a time when they were affected by what someone said: how they felt about themselves or something that was going on. They describe how they felt. What was the context in which the words were spoken? They write about why the words meant so much to them. (28)

3. *Word combining.* Students write a list of words they have strong feelings about; ones they like or dislike or words that for some reason they happen to remember. They don't have to know the meaning of all the words. Then they

write a short, unrhymed poem (4 to 6 lines) using all the words, in any order they wish (32).

The writing ideas throughout this chapter illustrate the variety of activities teachers can include in frequent writing assignments. Many of the assignments are for practice and not for polished drafts. Writing at all levels should be part of ongoing activities of a classroom.

Classroom Climate

Students will not be able to write well unless they feel comfortable in the classroom. Writing requires mutual respect and trust. To help students succeed at writing, the teacher must establish a rapport with them. The more the classroom is a place students feel at home, the more willing they are to write. A classroom should never look bare, but should be filled with colorful posters that have something on them besides punctuation rules. Part of a wall should be set aside for each class so students have a place to display their work—not the "best" work, but everyone's work. Small-group activities also help to establish a friendly atmosphere, and arranging desks in a circle will enhance discussion. Using a variety of activities helps maintain interest and involvement. Most of all, the sense that the teacher cares about them, listens to them, and respects them as individuals ensures that students become active learners.

CASE 6–2

Exploring an Instructional Unit

Aimee M. Peterson, an English education student, developed a unit on family pressures for seventh- or eighth-grade students. Throughout the unit, Aimee designated levels of each writing assignment. As you read Aimee's unit, notice in particular how she creates student interest for the unit as a whole and for specific assignments by selecting a level of writing suited to the purpose of the writing. Aimee's unit is more thorough than the edited version presented here, but we selected activities to highlight the use of levels and the inclusion of the writing process in planning a thematic unit.

FAMILY PRESSURES

GRADE LEVEL: GRADE 7 OR 8

Objectives: By teaching this unit, I believe my students will feel more comfortable about discussing family pressures that occur in their lives. It is important that they realize everyone has family pressures and to recognize that there are many types of family pressures—positive as well as negative. Also, I want them to gain knowledge about how to handle pressures. It isn't easy to deal with parents and siblings who pressure us to do what they think we should do. I want my students to enjoy the unit and, also, be able to apply what they learn to their own lives.

Introductory Activity: As students enter the classroom, I will hand each one a slip of paper that describes an incident/statement that illustrates a possible family pressure. Examples are "Your mom dislikes your new boyfriend/girlfriend," or "You spent all your allowance getting your hair colored/permed, and when you get home a parent tells you that if you don't change your hair you are not allowed to go to the school dance." Each student reads the statement on the slip aloud, and a class discussion follows led by the following questions:

1. What would you say all of these incidents/statements have in common?
2. What are some ways your family has pressured you?
3. Why did you feel pressures?
4. Think of some conflicts you've had. Why do you think parents or siblings sometimes pressure you?
5. In what ways can pressuring be for our "own good"?
6. Is there such a thing as a good pressure?

Journal Assignment: Write one page describing pressures dealing with your family that you believe are positive and one page you believe are negative (level 1).

Writing Assignment: Using your journal entries, write a short essay comparing and contrasting positive and negative pressures (level 2). The essays will be shared in groups and discussed the following class period.

Literature Assignment: Students choose a book to read from a selection of four, which are listed by level of difficulty:

The War with Grandpa by Robert K. Smith
Cattail Moon by Jean Thesman
Romeo and Juliet by William Shakespeare
West Side Story by Leonard Bernstein

I give a brief description of all four books. Each student chooses one book to read. They have the option to change their minds or read more than one book.

The level 3 assignments are given in the first week so students have a great deal of time to think about what they want to do. The choices are as follows:

1. Find a newspaper article about a family pressure/conflict. This could be a parent pressuring a child, a child pressuring a parent, or something dealing with siblings or grandparents. Write a response to the article in your journal (level 1). Write a story about the article. Include events that led up to the event and explain what happens after it. Use your imagination. Or you may choose to write an article of your own dealing with a family pressure.
2. Write a true story about a time when someone in your family pressured you. Explain using details so your readers can understand how you felt and why.

Brainstorm, web, or free-write to get ideas for your story (level 1). Write a rough draft and share in peer groups (level 2).

3. Compare and contrast the main characters or characters in the novel you read with yourself or with a character from another novel. Include details about the situation of the character and why you chose to examine the particular character(s).

4. Write about an imaginary person. Give them more problems than any character from the novel you read. Write a short story about their life and describe specifically the family pressures your character goes through.

Journal Assignment: Write your thoughts and opinions about the novel you are reading, including whether you are enjoying it or not and explain (level 1).

Music Activity: The students will listen to the song, "Papa Don't Preach" by Madonna. They then will write their reaction to the song and examine the family pressures that are evident (level 1). In groups of four or five, students discuss other songs with a similar theme. Each group is responsible for selecting a song and preparing a short presentation for the whole class that explains the family pressures in the song (level 2).

Literature Activity: Students are placed in groups so that each group represents all four novels. Group members discuss the different family pressures present in their novel. They write a short description of the differences and similarities among the books (level 2).

Literature Activity: Next the students are placed into groups with others reading the same book. Each group creates a skit, reading radio show, or a TV show based on the novel. Each group writes up what it plans to do (level 2). The presentations are done for the whole class.

Discussion Activity: I will read the essay "You Don't Love Me" by Erma Bombeck to the class. This essay is about why parents don't want their children to do certain things. A class discussion follows, beginning with the following questions: What kinds of things do most people do to show their love? How does this essay relate to the positive pressures you have discussed and written about?

Poetry Activities: I will distribute the poem "the drum" by Nikki Giovanni to the class. After reading it aloud, we discuss what being an individual means. Students write their own poem inspired by "the drum" (level 1).

Students are encouraged to bring in and share poems they think represent family pressures or decision making.

Students write an "I Wish" poem expressing their feeling about how they wished things were (level 2).

Students read the following poems and then discuss and write responses in their journal (level 1).

- "The Possessive" by Sharon Olds
- "Legacy II" by Leroy V. Quintans

- "Those Winter Sundays" by Robert Hayden
- "Women's Program" by Marie Luise Kaschnitz
- "Legacies" by Nikki Giovanni
- "The Road Not Taken" by Robert Frost
- "The Other House" by David Wagoner

Non-Print Media Activities: Students view the film *The Three Warriors.* Students write a response to the film (level 1). Using their responses, students write a short essay about the pressures evident in the film (level 2).

We will have a class discussion on TV shows that portray family pressures. Each student writes a list of shows and a short description of the pressures (level 1).

Students watch the film *West Side Story,* and a discussion follows on pressures we may experience from peers and siblings. In journals, they write an entry from each day we watch the film, responding to the film and compiling a list of pressures that are present (level 1). In an essay they compare this film to one of the novels they are reading (level 2).

To conclude the unit, I plan on reading *Parents Can Be a Problem* by Shirley Schwarzrock aloud to the students. There is no assignment planned because the students will be working on their level 3 final paper at this time.

QUESTIONS ABOUT AIMEE'S UNIT

1. In what ways do Aimee's activities reflect her objectives? Write what you see as her purpose in including each activity. Describe how the level of writing matches the objective. Discuss where you might change a level and for what purpose.

2. Aimee's unit is designed for middle school. How could it be adapted for high school students? Aimee included a list of additional readings in her unit. Working in small groups, what suggestions can you make for additional literature selections?

3. Using Aimee's unit as a model, write a letter to Joellen, the teacher described at the beginning of the chapter. What are some ways she could match her goals to assignments using levels of writing?

4. How does Aimee integrate the writing process into the unit? She doesn't explicitly state all of the stages she plans to use. What discovery activities does she include? Where would additional ones be appropriate? Develop a response guide for one of her level 3 activities.

5. Either individually or in small groups, write activities for teaching a topic, theme, or a reading. Plan for at least five level 1 assignments, three level 2 assignments, and one level 3 assignment.

REFERENCES

Britton, James, Tony Burgess, Nancy Martin, Alex McLeod, and Harold Rosen. *The Development of Writing Abilities (11–18)* London: Macmillan Education Ltd., 1975.

Burroway, Janet. *Writing Fiction*. New York: Harper Collins, 1992.

Conly, Jane Leslie. "Unit of Study for *Crazy Lady*." English 406/606. University of Wisconsin-Eau Claire. April 1995.

Cox, Mitch, and Christine Firpo. "What Would They Be Doing If We Gave Them Worksheets?" *English Journal* Mar. 1993: 42–45.

Dale, Helen. "Collaboration in the writing process." *Wisconsin English Journal* 31.2 (Spring 1989): 11–16.

Didion, Joan. *Slouching Towards Bethlehem*. New York: Dell, 1968.

Dixon, John. *Growth Through English*. Reading: National Association for Teaching English, 1967.

Emig, Janet. *The Composing Process of Twelfth Graders*. Urbana: NCTE, 1972.

Fagin, Larry. *The List Poem*. New York: Teachers & Writers Collaborative, 1991.

Hellman, Sally. "Customized Holidays." *Notes Plus*. NCTE. Nov. 1990: 3.

Hirsch, Timothy J. "Student Research for Personal Decision Making." *Wisconsin English Journal* 30.2 (1988): 9–14.

Hoffman, Marvin. "On Teaching Technical Writing: Creative Language in the Real World." *English Journal* Feb. 1992: 58–63.

Hymes, Dell. "Models of the Interaction of Language and Social Life." *Directions in Sociolinguistics*. John J. Gumpetz and Dell Hymes, eds. New York: Holt, Rinehart & Winston, 1972. 35–71.

Joos, Martin. *The Five Clocks*. New York: Harcourt Brace & World, 1961.

Kearns, Nancy J. "I-Search, I-Find, I-Know: A Summary of Macrorie's Alternative to the Traditional Research Paper." *Indiana English* Winter 1995: 47–50.

Koch, Kenneth. *Wishes, Lies, and Dreams: Teaching Children to Write Poetry*. New York: Vintage, 1970.

Logan, Ben. *The Land Remembers*. Minocqua: Heartland Press, 1985.

Macrorie, Ken. *The I-Search Paper*. Portsmouth: Boynton/Cook, 1988.

Martin, Nancy, Peter Medway, Harold Smith, and Pat D'Arcy. "Why Write?" *Writing Across the Curriculum*. Nancy Martin, Peter Medway, and Harold Smith, eds. Montclair: Boynton/Cook, 1984. 34–59.

Maxwell, Rhoda J. "So What's New?" Unpublished essay, 1982.

Maxwell, Rhoda J. "Story Strips." *Notes Plus* Apr. 1987. Urbana: NCTE.

Maxwell, Rhoda J. *Writing Across the Curriculum in Middle and High Schools*. Boston: Allyn and Bacon, 1996.

Meisner, Mark. "The Rewards of the Wanted Poster." *Notes Plus*. NCTE. Apr. 1991: 6–7.

Miller, James E., Jr. *Word, Self, and Reality: The Rhetoric of Imagination*. New York: Dodd, Mead & Co., 1972.

Moffett, James. *Teaching the Universe of Discourse*. Boston: Houghton Mifflin, 1983.

Perrin, Robert. "Myths About Research." *English Journal* Nov. 1987: 50–53.

Peterson, Aimee M. "Family Pressures." English 406/606. University of Wisconsin-Eau Claire. May 1995.

Pope, Carol A. "Our Time Has Come: English for the Twenty-First Century." *English Journal* Mar. 1993: 38–41.

Rohman, D. Gordon. "Prewriting: The Stage of Discovery in the Writing Process." *College Composition and Communication, 16,* 1965: 106–112.

Rubin, Donald L. "Introduction." *Perspectives on Talk and Learning*. Susan Hynds and Donald L. Rubin, eds. Urbana: NCTE, 1990. 1–17.

Sudol, David. "Creating and Killing Stanley Real-bozo or Teaching Characterization and Plot in English 10." *English Journal* Oct. 1983.

Ziegler, Alan. *The Writing Workshop: Vol. 2*. New York: Teachers & Writers Collaborative, 1984.

7

Teaching Literature

I urge us to see our task in schools as helping students read literature to understand the culture, to speculate on the ideas and the imaginative vision, and to speculate on the nature and use of the language that is the medium of the artistic expression.
                                                                    Alan C. Purves (360)

READING LITERATURE

The teaching of literature in secondary schools has undergone a dramatic change in the past 10 years. Emphasis has shifted from the text to interactions between text and reader; that is, what the reader brings to the reading is as important as the words in the text. Texts provide many possibilities for interpretations. Bruce Miller describes reading as a subjective experience because readers bring their own experiences and knowledge to their understanding of a text (19–20). The research behind the reader response approach, which is based on the interaction between reader and text, has been going on for years, but not until recently has this research affected the secondary schools. Although the literature we choose to have students read is of concern, teachers acknowledge that the most carefully selected literature will not benefit students if they do not read it. Students, also, benefit little if they read the selections with no interest or understanding. For students to become lifelong readers—a goal in every curriculum we've seen—they must see reading as an enjoyable activity. As we think of how to help students become lifelong readers, we have two major concerns as educators: how to teach literature and what literature to teach. This chapter examines the methods of teaching literature and Chapter 8 deals with literature selection.

BACKGROUND OF LITERATURE STUDY

A brief review of literary analyses can help provide a perspective for teaching literature in secondary schools. *Historical criticism*—that is, studying literature in the context of the period in which it was written—is a method of learning about literature that has been used since the 1900s. The works were studied in relation to others written in the same time period and were also compared to those written during other periods. By the 1930s, *social criticism,* or literature studied through its reflection of society, became an important way of gaining insights into the works. The work of both Sigmund Freud and Carl Jung also had a strong impact on the way we examine literature. In these traditional approaches, the work is of secondary importance.

By the 1950s, *New Criticism,* which began after World War II, became the dominant method of analyzing literature and remains an important influence. New Criticism is concerned only with the work itself and not with the author, period, or social influence. *Structuralism* and *deconstruction* are based on the same premise—that the meaning and understanding are found in the text itself and that information about the author or social and historical influences have no bearing on the study of literature. It is not within the scope of this text to discuss the various literary critical approaches. Such studies are more appropriate for college literature classes. However, future English teachers do need to consider how these critical approaches influence and inform the teaching of literature to secondary students.

Literary study in middle and high schools has two major focuses. The first is to continue to help students develop an appreciation and enjoyment of literature. In elementary school, students become familiar with a wide variety of literature and have many opportunities to appreciate different styles, story lines, and genres. Generally speaking, the emphasis is on a subjective analysis. In the higher grades, students are introduced to the use of formal analysis, and literature becomes the *study* of literature. Too often, students receive the impression that what they think and feel about literature no longer counts. In *A Handbook of Critical Approaches to Literature,* the authors explain that they do not see a dilemma between teaching literature by subjective or formal analysis. Rather, they believe the "intelligent application of several interpretive techniques can enhance the study of literature" (Guerin, Labor, Morgan, and Willingham 7). However, formal analysis often takes precedence over subjective approaches, creating a rift between the student and the text. In addition, formal analysis can become mired in detail when inappropriately taught to secondary students.

Too often, studying literature meant finding hidden meanings in the text. Students assumed that there was "one meaning" and through careful reading and studying all readers should arrive at the same understanding of the text, regardless of their experiences and knowledge. Most of us have had the experience of thinking that we understood a text only to be told we were mistaken. What the story or poem really meant—the right meaning—was what an authority claimed. A reader's perception, experience, and personality had little to do with the meaning. Such theory established a hierarchy of readers with the renowned critic at the top and the inexperienced student at the bottom. Pedagogy based on this view divides readers into two groups—those who know the right answers and those who don't. For those in the latter group, and there are many, reading is not an enjoyable activity, and so they avoid reading. This approach allows no room for a variety of interpretations even when readers can back up their interpretations with examples from the text. The experiences and knowledge students bring with them when they read don't count in this kind of literature study; what does count is learning one particular interpretation. If students listen carefully in class, they can even "ace" the exam without reading the text! When there is no personal connection between the text and the reader, students don't have to understand or apply what they read. Reading in this way is a passive activity. With such an arrangement, how can we convince students that reading is pleasurable and to be enjoyed lifelong? And how can we help students learn formal analysis if they do not first see connections between themselves and the literature? (Box 7–1 will help you consider your own reading history.)

BOX 7–1

YOUR READING HISTORY

Thinking back to your junior and senior high school years, what literature do you remember? What books did you talk about with friends? In small groups, compile a list of favorite books. Which ones were school assignments? Which ones would you consider teaching?

READER RESPONSE THEORY

The reader response theory is an approach to literature study that stresses the relationship between text and reader. Briefly, students respond to the text after careful reading and develop an understanding of the literature from their own and others' responses. Several scholars and researchers help us understand why the response theory makes sense in the English language arts classroom.

Wolfgang Iser has written extensively about the role of the reader in interpretation. He describes a literary work as having two poles: artistic and aesthetic. The artistic comes from the author in creating a work of art, and the aesthetic from the reader in responding to the art. The meaning of the text is the result of the interaction of the two poles. According to Iser, a meaning is not an absolute value, but a dynamic happening (21). If the meaning is dynamic, then it can change from reader to reader or even with multiple readings by the same person. A reader might have a somewhat different interpretation when reading a text for a second time or after learning what the text means to other readers. Iser dismisses attempts to discover a single hidden meaning in a text as a phase of interpretation that belongs to the past. He believes we have moved beyond the New Criticism, which focused entirely on the text itself, to a belief that each reader brings to a text a uniqueness that shapes the interpretation. Iser quotes Susan Sontag, "to understand is to interpret," and the understanding comes from the reader, not from an outside source except the text itself (6).

Louise Rosenblatt is most responsible for advancing the theory of reader response. More than 50 years ago, Rosenblatt studied how her students responded to literature, and from her research she developed the transactional approach to teaching literature. Her philosophy parallels Iser's; she believes, "The reader counts for at least as much as the book or poem itself" (vi). The interaction between the reader and the text creates meaning. The reading becomes a "transaction": The text provides words and ideas; the reader provides the personal response to the words and ideas; and the relationship between the two creates meaning. Teachers of English language arts teach specific human beings with individual hearts and minds "to seek in literature a great variety of satisfactions" (*Literature* 35) The teacher's job is to help create a relationship between the individual book or play and the individual student (33).

Rosenblatt believes the human experience that literature presents is the primary reason for reading (7). We read through the lens of our own understandings. Rosenblatt explains that the reader "brings to the work personality traits, memories of past events, present needs and preoccupations, a particular mood of the moment. . . . " (30–31).

Robert E. Probst, an educator whose work focuses on implementing response theory in the classroom, explains that readers sometimes discover the need to rethink initial conceptions and revise their notions about the text (31). Students must first feel free to deal with their own reactions to the text. Then the teacher has students share their reactions by asking questions and comparing their reactions with each other in small groups. Creating an atmosphere of security where students are comfortable with each other is essential (33). Through sharing, students examine their responses and come to a deeper understanding of the text. Rosenblatt believes firmly that readers do not stop with the initial responses, but that those responses lead them to reflection and analysis (*Literature* 75). She does not encourage the "uncritical acceptance of texts" (Probst 35). Teachers must help students assume responsibility for their own understandings of what they read. (The activity in Box 7–2 will give you some practice in responding to literature.)

BOX 7–2

RESPONDING TO LITERATURE

Write responses to a book you are reading. Or choose a poem, article, or play to respond to. Share with others in a small group.

IMPLEMENTING THE RESPONSE THEORY

Using Factual Information

If connections between reader and text are the most important things to stress in teaching literature, and we believe they are, what do we do with the literary facts and interpretations we learned in college and high school? Do you remember learning all about Shakespeare and the Globe Theater before reading one of his plays? Rosenblatt describes facts about the author, literary traditions, history of the age, and so forth as "merely secondary and peripheral," and stresses that such facts are "even distracting or worthless unless it is very clearly seen that they are secondary" (33). Knowing the background information is useful when teaching literature, not as lecture material but as supplemental material that comes up naturally in a discussion or in response to a student's question. Admittedly, keeping those wonderful bits of knowledge to oneself is difficult, but telling students too much puts the teacher in the role of holder of the truth and the students as those who know little or nothing. Such an arrangement encourages passive learning. We all remember information better if we either discover it ourselves or acquire it when we actively wonder about it. No matter how wonderful our lecture, it is wasted effort if students are not interested. Our task, then, is to generate interest and convince students that what they know and feel counts in the English language arts classroom.

Writing Responses

Students using a reader response method respond in writing as they read. They can write what the story makes them think about, a particular word or phrase, or a feeling evoked by the piece. In short, they can write about anything the text makes them think of, although they may at first not understand what it is they are "supposed" to write. Students who are not accustomed to responding to literature initially need quite a bit of guidance. Many find it hard to believe that what they think counts, and they try to discover what the teacher wants them to put down. Getting students to trust themselves takes patience. The best way to counteract their lack of faith in their own ideas is to comment positively on the little they do write and encourage them to write more by asking questions that draw them out. Little by little, they learn to believe they do have something significant to say.

A list of questions helps to guide middle school students to respond with some depth. Farnam and Kelly suggest guiding questions that help students think about connections with their own experiences. Also, asking them to respond to the most interesting or important part of a reading requires them to think more carefully about the text (47–49).

In the beginning, questions such as the following might provide the structure students need to get started.

1. What characters remind you of someone you know? In what ways do they make you think of the person or people you know?
2. What experiences in the text make you think of ones you have had?
3. What objects or places make you think of things you have had or places you know about?
4. Perhaps movies or television shows come to mind as you read. Describe the connections, such as similar action, characters, or setting.
5. If you were one of the characters, in what ways would you have reacted similarly or differently?
6. Describe how you feel at the end of the story (or chapter). In what ways does the story seem plausible? If you were the author, what might you write differently?

It is important to avoid yes or no questions as much as possible. We want the students to think about what they are reading, to make connections with the text. Yes or no answers are too simplistic, and students either don't see or ignore the "explain your answer" instruction.

Keep the list of questions short and ask students to respond to all of them if possible. Too many questions overwhelm them, whether they are senior high students or middle schoolers. On the other hand, asking them to write whatever comes to mind might be equally difficult. They need some guidance, especially when responding is new to them. As they become more comfortable with this approach, they write more. Some readers go off on tangents, following a thought or feeling the text evoked; they might write pages without referring directly to the text. Others will follow the text in detail, commenting on a phrase or idea. Both responses are acceptable, as are all the responses that fall between these two.

What is not acceptable is a lack of a response or something so trite it is a nonresponse; for example, "This story is stupid." Talking to the student individually is most helpful. Go over the reading together, asking questions: "Is this a part you didn't care for? What did you think about this? Or how about when the character did this?" Often, students worry that their response is what will be "stupid" and cover up their feeling of inadequacy by giving flip comments. When people are told repeatedly their answers are wrong, they need courage to put themselves on the line again. We have to rebuild trust so students are willing to commit themselves to expressing an opinion.

Responding to literature does not suggest a trite, quick reading. Smagorinsky and Gevinson explain that personal response objectives help students "to respond empathically to literary characters and their experiences" (73). This relating text to their own experiences helps students understand themes, patterns, and archetypes in the literature (73). Rather than reading for specific answers, they read to gain an understanding of the work.

Often in literature class there is no room for students' interpretations. Judith Langer encourages teachers to help students to explore "a horizon of possibilities" (204). We often rethink our first interpretations as our understandings become more complex. Literature is often taught "as if there is a predetermined interpretation" (205), thus leaving no room for students' own explorations. To promote deeper understandings, we need to "link their ideas with what they have already discussed, read, or experienced" (207). (The activity in Box 7–3 will help you practice developing response questions.)

BOX 7–3

DEVELOPING RESPONSE QUESTIONS

Choose a poem or short story and write suggestions that will help students write thoughtful responses. Remember, your ideas are not questions students *must* answer but should be ways of helping them think more deeply about the text and connect the literature with their own experiences.

Using Responses

Students' written responses are an integral part of literature study and may be incorporated into class activities in several ways. Using a variety of approaches will help keep students interested and achieve different results.

1. *Use responses to improve or spark discussions.* Even if students do nothing other than write a response, their discussion skills will improve. When students write about literature, they must think more deeply about it. One substitute teacher's experience illustrates this point. The students had been assigned to read "Neighbor Rosicky" by Willa Cather. Although the regular teacher did not use reader response, the substitute teacher asked them to write about the main character for 10 minutes before they discussed the story. To help students understand what was expected, she suggested they describe the kind of person Rosicky was and whom he reminded them of. After 10 minutes, she asked them to share what they had written. They started out slowly, but soon they had a lively discussion going and talked to each other as much as to the teacher. More than one said, "Well, I didn't write this down, but what she (or he) just said made me think of. . . . " Granted, "Neighbor Rosicky" is an easy story to respond to, but, on the other hand, the students and the teacher didn't know each other, which always make discussion difficult. What got the class involved was the act of writing responses. It allowed students, reluctant to participate, to think through their responses before taking the risk of sharing publicly.

2. *Use responses as a written dialogue among students.* Students write their responses, form groups of four or five, and then each one reads what he or she has written. The teacher tells the students that they can add to their responses after hearing what the others have to say. They do not have to come to a consensus; each individual's responses are respected. Students will challenge each other, however, and ask why someone responded in a particular way. When students explain their responses, they have to start with the text that made them think of the event or feeling they recounted. For example, a student might say, "When he walks away from his father and doesn't look back, it made me think of. . . . or it made me feel like. . . . " They don't defend their responses, but they do explain what part of the reading prompted it.

This way of sharing responses accomplishes three things: (a) Students must read with attention; (b) they learn how others think and read; and (c) they find out what others in the class are writing. Knowing what their classmates think gives students confidence in their own work. Those who are unsure of themselves discover their responses are as valid and interesting as anyone else's. Response writing does not depend on academic ability, provided the students are assigned readings they can handle. In Chapter 8, we will describe ways to accommodate different reading levels in the same class.

Having students write and share responses is an excellent way to keep the students on task for reading. When they meet in groups to share and someone adds nothing, other students complain. Even students who have not read the assignment will often join in the conversation. Although it is obvious they are not prepared, listening to the others talk and adding comments of their own helps them understand the literature at least partially. Sharing responses in groups is far superior to giving a pop quiz to see if students have done the reading. The quiz method, although widely used, only affirms those who did the reading and lowers the self-esteem of those who did not. Exceptions occur, but most of the time the same students read or do not read the assignments. There is nothing motivating about failing yet another test. Students do not read to avoid the embarrassment of failing; that's not how it works for students who have trouble succeeding in school. They either act out, disrupting the class, or withdraw. Every person should be given opportunities to succeed in school, and setting it up so the same kids fail repeatedly is truly unfair.

3.   *Use reader responses to create a dialogue between individual students and the teacher.* The responses are handed in, and the teacher writes comments about the responses. These comments are not evaluations, but rather thoughts that occurred when reading what the student wrote. The teacher's role is similar to that of students in a peer group, not a voice of authority who declares the student is right or wrong. The teacher's support is valuable to students, giving them the sense that their writing is interesting and important. On the other hand, negative evaluations or comments damage the relationship between teacher and student. No one participates easily or works best in a threatening environment.

Students' written responses also give the teacher a sense of how well the students understand and enjoy the literature selections. A student's question, "How come we never get to read a happy ending?" made one teacher realize the need to read something more lighthearted for a change. Even if they don't comment directly, it is not difficult to tell if they are interested in what they read. Also, the dialogue allows teachers to encourage students to respond more fully to the text. Questions can help students expand on their written responses. For example:

- "I would like to hear more about when you. . . ."
- "Your comment about Maya made me think of how I felt when. . . ."
- "What happened after (whatever is appropriate)?"
- "I can really understand how you felt. Have your feelings changed at all now?"

Any comment that supports and encourages is appropriate. Teachers get to know the students better and students get to know teachers better as both share their thoughts and feelings about literature.

4.   *Use responses as a source of discussion questions for the whole class.* As teachers read students' responses, they keep notes on issues that are raised and disagreements students have on motivations of characters, the plot movement, and so forth. It is amazing how different students' reactions can be, and these differences are springboards for discussion. The teacher acts as a moderator, keeping the discussion focused on the text, perhaps playing devil's advocate if students seem too willing to accept an idea. The teacher is not the last word on who is right and who is wrong. Encouraging a variety of interpretations helps students think for themselves.

5.   *Encourage students to use responses when they write papers based on the literature.* As students look through their responses, they can find patterns or themes that suggest

writing topics. Going back to the text for a second reading adds detail and substance to the points they want to make. Because the focus for their paper comes from their own responses, their interest is high and they have a personal stake in writing a convincing paper. The bonus for a teacher is that these papers are much more interesting to read than those where the topic is not student-selected.

Teachers can use any combination of these responses. In fact, it is a good idea to vary activities based on responses. We all become tired of the same routine after a while, and the benefits decrease. The point of reader response is that students' thoughts and feelings about what they read are validated in their study of literature.

COMPREHENSION

Recent research studies have focused on how to implement reader response in middle school classrooms. The most difficult part for teachers in changing over to this approach is to give up their study guides. Teachers fear they won't know whether students are comprehending the material if they are not required to answer specific teacher-made questions.

In *Comprehension and Learning,* Frank Smith describes comprehension as "making sense of information" (10). Students comprehend what teachers want them to know when the new information meshes with what they already know. If the knowledge is completely foreign to their previous experience, they will have difficulty comprehending it. The better we can integrate new information with prior knowledge, the easier it is to not only learn in the first place but to remember (71). When teachers ask, "Don't you see what the author is trying to say?" they are probably asking the students, "Why can't you locate the same kind of information that I do?" (107). Actually both questions are based on the assumption of predetermined meanings that students are supposed to discover, without taking into account their individual responses. When teachers, through reader response, help students connect the text with their own experiences, comprehension is an easier goal to attain. The new information students discover is, right from the beginning, related to their prior knowledge.

The concern about discarding study sheets is a legitimate one for teachers. We want students to know certain information about the text. There is, however, a much better way to arrive at the same goal—better because it is not just busy work for a student, but comes from discussing the work with others in the class. First, teachers are surprised about the amount of information that comes up without teacher intervention in discussions based on students' responses. The students' wide-ranging interests and knowledge touch on most of the points found in a teacher-prepared study guide. A teacher who takes notes on students' discussions knows what is covered and what is not. For example, if the text is *No Promises in the Wind* by Irene Hunt and the setting of the Depression never comes up, a teacher might ask during the discussion, "Does it make a difference when the novel took place?" There is no right or wrong answer to this; the father's behavior might be the same today if he were out of work. The story focuses more on father-son relationships than on the Depression, but some students and teachers believe the novel is basically a way to learn about the 1930s. Who determines what is the correct reading? Through discussion, it becomes clear that the setting is the Depression era, and students remember this fact much longer when the information comes from people arguing whether the setting makes a difference to the reading of the novel than they do from filling in a blank on a worksheet answering, "What is the setting of the novel?" Teacher-posed questions should rarely have one factual answer, but rather, should be couched in "What do you think?" terms. Knowledge arrived at through discussion fits Frank Smith's definition of comprehension.

FORMAL ANALYSES

We have emphasized reader response theory because we strongly believe that this approach achieves the desired results with secondary students. Furthermore, without the connections between reader and text, further analysis has limited effect. This is not to say, however, that no other critical analysis is appropriate. Teachers can use a variety of approaches depending on the developmental stages of the students, as well as the literature being read. A combination of critical analyses works best. Reader response requires close reading of a text as students search for meaning. Close reading is the mainstay of the new criticism. A reader's responses should lead to interpretation of the text.

Recognizing and understanding images is an important skill in literature. However, teachers often have a predetermined list of the images and what they signify, leaving no opportunities for students' own interpretations. Anderson and Rubano suggest that "teachers can introduce a reading selection by asking the students to report the images they recall after having read the piece or even a portion of it" (39). By encouraging students to look for images that relate to their own experiences, they make connections that are often quite different from the usual interpretations, but are insightful and appropriate.

In *Teaching Literature in Middle and Secondary Grades,* Simmons and Deluzain emphasize that older students need to move beyond a mere appreciation of literature to understanding its implied meanings, structure, and form. Teachers, however, must not emphasize information *about* the text more than they emphasize the text itself. Often the best approach is a matter of degree. We mentioned earlier that extensive information about Shakespeare's time is not appropriate for study before reading the play itself, but ignoring the historical implications of a plot during the reading process is not appropriate either.

Some historical or biographical information about the author's life and times or about a major fictional character helps readers understand what is happening. For example, students reading Dickens' *Tale of Two Cities* need background information, but the information must be kept in perspective. One wouldn't read the book to learn only about the French Revolution. The social implications of an author's intentions help students understand Steinbeck's *Grapes of Wrath* or Stowe's *Uncle Tom's Cabin.* Archetypal approaches help students understand the use of motifs, themes, and stereotypes throughout literature. If English teachers use external factors only if they help students understand the works and draw on approaches that best fit the particular text, students are not overwhelmed by the study of literature (Guerin et al. 297). The bottom line is that we are teaching students, not books.

PREREADING ACTIVITIES

Generating interest may involve discussing some of the themes in a story or novel before the students read it. Contrary to what many students believe, there are many themes in a literary work, especially in the longer pieces. For example, *To Kill a Mockingbird* has several strong themes: a father's relationship with his children, growing up, prejudice against blacks, and fear of people different from ourselves. The themes a teacher chooses depend on the age and literary experience of the students. Whatever theme we choose to study, several resources can provide ideas for generating interest as a prereading activity. *Literature—News That Stays News,* edited by Candy Carter, is an example of such a resource. The examples that follow are student suggestions from this text.

1. *Lord of the Flies.* Students do an impromptu writing on "What I would do if I were leader of a group stranded on an island." The following day students share and discuss what they wrote. The teacher encourages students to compare what they came up with to the novel they are about to read (Beem 3–6).

2. "Young Goodman Brown." Students close their eyes and imagine they are in the world's most peaceful setting. They write down as many details as possible, using all of their senses. Then they imagine the most terrifying place and describe it in writing. The responses are grouped on a chart and discussed. The discussion helps students see the similarities in their images, and this helps them to understand the images in Hawthorne's story (Farnam 38–41).

3. *Romeo and Juliet.* The work is introduced with a brainstorming session in which the teacher asks students questions like, "What makes people fall in love?" and "What makes people fight?" Responses are encouraged, and the session ends with questions that lead into the actual reading. For example, "Do people ever decide whom they are going to love or how much they are going to fall in love?" Students keep their notes and refer to them as they read (Christ 66–69).

4. The following activity is from *Structuring Reading Activities for English Classes* (Graves, Palmer, and Furniss). "The Great All-American Cross Country Motorcycle Run" is designed for the "Prologue" to *Canterbury Tales* (11). Before students begin reading the "Prologue," the teacher describes an imaginary present-day trek on motorcycles and then hands out pictures of interesting people who want to participate in the trek. Pictures from *National Geographic* work well. Tape them on brightly colored cardboard and give one picture to each group. Group members write an application letter for their participant. Each letter is read to the class, and students discuss what kinds of problems the travelers might have on the trip, how they could entertain themselves, and which travelers would get along with others and which would not.

The scenario might be something like this: They are going to Colorado to see, for one last time, a beautiful river that will soon be destroyed by a dam project. One student group (Kimberly Paap, Jennifer Ulesick, and Colleen Ahern) wrote:

Dear Sirs:

Momma Mia! When I heard about the trip I knew this is what my late wife, Marie, would have wanted me to do. Being the owner of Anthony's Fish Market, I am aware of the importance of the wildlife of the river and would truly appreciate one last look at this environment.

I would definitely enjoy spending time with a group of people. I have a large group of friends in the old neighborhood and am known as "the entertainer." I acquired this nick-name from my talent as an accordion player and group comedian.

I still have my motorcycle from the old country; the one Maria and I rode around the country on when we were first married. This would be like a second honeymoon for me and my late Maria—although a little less romantic.

Sincerely,
Anthony "Tony" Rossel

5. When teaching *All Together Now* by Sue Ellen Bridgers, the teacher may ask students before they began reading, "What are the characteristics of a good friend?" The responses are listed on the board as the class brainstorms what friendship means. Then students write about the most unusual friendship they have had. Students share these and discuss the responsibilities of friendship. This theme is only one of several in the novel. The prereading activity becomes a springboard for later discussions.

6. A teacher, Jan Sutton, planned a unit on diverse voices and designed the following activity to help students realize that stereotypes still plague our society.

Stereotypes—Small-Group Discussion
Write as many impressions/words as you can think of when you read the following words. Discuss your responses with the other group members.

1. Football player
2. Teacher
3. Student with acid-green hair
4. Women's libber
5. Student with 4.0 average
6. Police officer
7. Fast-food worker
8. Welfare recipient
9. Banker
10. Child molester

In general, prereading activities should generate interest in reading the text rather than provide factual information as "background." Some activities may be related to background, particularly a historical period. However, the discussions are always student-centered and not lectures. The teacher phrases questions in ways that increase student participation and refers to earlier discussions to strengthen the connections between readers and their responses. (See Box 7–4.)

BOX 7–4

DEVELOPING PREREADING STRATEGIES

Choose a literature selection that is appropriate for high school but could be initially uninteresting to or difficult for students. One suggestion is *Great Expectations*, but choose any one you want. Write prereading activities that will increase students' interest and provide any necessary prereading knowledge.

READING ACTIVITIES

Assignments related to the text and given throughout the time students are engaged in reading add interest and understanding. Some activities come from students' written responses, whereas others are not directly related to responses. However, the responses always help students to complete assignments because they have developed clearer understandings of the text's characters, motivations, and outcomes. Activities that link the text with the readers' understanding help to heighten interest.

Activities from *All Together Now* by Sue Ellen Bridges provide an example of connections between text and experience. The main character is 12-year-old Casey, who is spending the summer with her grandparents. Her father is fighting in the Korean War, and her mother is working at two jobs, leaving little time to spend with her daughter. The story focuses on Casey's relationships throughout the summer.

1. After reading the description of Hazard in Chapter 2, describe in your response journal your impression of him. Whom does he remind you of?
2. Casey allows Dwayne to assume she is a boy. What is her motivation? Describe a time when you have told a lie for similar reasons. Assume you were caught in the lie. Write a persuasive letter explaining your reasons for telling the lie and why you should be excused from blame.
3. In Chapter 8, Dwayne gives Casey a gift that means a lot to her. Why is it so significant? Write about a gift you received that was special and explain why it meant so much to you.
4. Pansy and Hazard's honeymoon was not a happy experience. What values and expectations did each have that got in the way of their happiness?
5. In Chapter 11 Marge blows up at Dwayne. What words and images are used to describe Dwayne's feelings. Write about a personal experience when you felt much the same as Dwayne did.
6. Describe your impression of Gwen when you first meet her in Chapter 6. Trace the development of her character throughout the novel, taking notes as you read. Reread your notes and describe how your impression of her changed, using passages from the text to explain.
7. Casey is angry because Dwayne has to spend the night in jail, and she feels the adults have let her down. Describe a time when you felt that parents or

friends let you down. Could the situation have turned out differently? Describe a time when you felt that you let someone down.

8. Point of view strongly influences our opinions of others. Write a description of yourself or someone you know very well; then write how someone else might view that person.

9. By the end of the novel, Casey has learned much about responsibility and love. Describe the changes she has gone through and the results of those changes using passages that illustrate significant learning experiences for Casey (Maxwell 7–8).

Teachers can create many different activities for their students. The following illustrate the possible variety and scope:

1.   Kurt Lothe, a high school student, wrote an article describing the activity his English teacher, Mr. Mead, had the class do for *Crime and Punishment*. He suggested they turn the story into a musical rather than write the usual paper. The students organized committees, and over the next few days worked on dialogue, created scenes, and wrote lyrics. They rewrote some of the scenes to add humor to the story. Showtime was in two weeks. Kurt explains, "What began as an alternative to another paper turned into one of the most memorable things I have done in my high school career. Not only does a musical like this provide an escape from the daily routine of the classroom, but it allows one to explore a character's feelings and emotions that reading alone cannot accomplish" (76–77).

2.   Vicki L. Olson describes several activities for *The Cay* by Theodore Taylor. As students began reading, she had them write predictions to help get them involved in the book. Then students listed three or four things that could happen to Philip and his family now that the Germans had attacked Aruba and brought war to the Caribbean. Students wrote predictions on the chances of Philip and his mother making it to Miami. Then students met in groups to share their predictions and the reasons behind them, later sharing with the large group.

Writing predictions can be used at any grade level and for just about any reading to encourage readers to connect with the text. There is not a right or wrong answer, but students have to defend their ideas by explaining the evidence on which they built the prediction.

3.   Don Gallo suggests a classroom activity that is useful with a variety of stories and novels. Choose a key character from the text. Choose one major problem that character has. Write a letter that your character might write about that problem to Dear Abby. When the writing is finished, place all the letters in a pile. Each student selects a letter and writes a response as Abby might answer. This works well with both serious novels like *Sophie's Choice* or *Death of a Salesman,* and with a humorous story like "The Secret Life of Walter Mitty."

4.   Assignments can build toward an activity that students completed after the literature is read. Karin Cooke, an English education student, devised assignments for "Neighbor Rosicky" by Willa Cather that created the background for such an activity.

a. Before assigning "Neighbor Rosicky," read the poem "Choices" by Nikki Giovanni. Have students write a response to the poem in their journals. They can explain what the poem meant to them or what it made them think of while they were listening.

b. In their journal, students write a poem about either their best friend or someone they value highly. They are encouraged to share their poems with the rest of the class or in small groups.

c. In their journals students write what they feel the word *neighbor* means. They discuss their responses in small groups.

d. After reading "Neighbor Rosicky," students write a short paper about why they think Cather titles the story "Neighbor Rosicky" instead of "Mr. Rosicky." Why was he considered a neighbor? (This is not to be evaluated as a formal paper.)

e. Backed up with examples from the story, students write what they think was most valuable to Rosicky.

f. The teacher divides the class into groups. The groups are the directors and producers for a film based on "Neighbor Rosicky." They use film and TV stars to cast their roles. Then they write a brief description of each character and give the reasons for their casting selections.

g. The final assignment is writing a biography of Rosicky using facts and inferences gleaned from the reading.

Teaching units that use many kinds of literature are discussed in Chapter 14, which is on developing units. Here, we provide one example of teaching a literature selection using an approach that incorporates reader response. The activities tap the students' experiences and knowledge and connect them with the text. *Romeo and Juliet* could become the basis for a unit including other literature selections.

TEACHING *ROMEO AND JULIET*

Barbara Dressler, a high school English teacher, wrote the following three-week unit for teaching *Romeo and Juliet*: Students read the play aloud during class time. Frequent stops are made to clarify questions that arise from the language and vocabulary differences. Then students listen to audiotapes of certain acts to become familiar with the Shakespearean language style. After reading each act, a videotape of parts of all of that act will be shown. Following the videotape viewing, students work in small groups to outline the act. Writing activities follow this group work.

Small-Group Work

Students are divided into groups according to their choice of a minor character in the play (Paris, Tybalt, Mercutio, Lord and Lady Capulet, Friar Laurence, the Nurse, and so on). The groups discuss the traits of the character and how he or she influences the course of the play. Groups then report to the entire class.

Writing Assignments Given to Students

Act One

1. As Juliet, write a letter to a friend telling how you met and fell in love with Romeo.
2. As Romeo, write a letter to a friend telling about your new love and explaining why you've forgotten Rosaline.
3. As Benvolio, write an explanation of how and why you want to help your love-sick friend, Romeo.
4. As an attendant of the Prince, write a description of the street fight.

Act Two

1. Write a description of Friar Laurence. Tell why Romeo turns to him for help.
2. Write Tybalt's letter to Romeo.
3. Write a description of scene 4 through the eyes of Peter.

Act Three

1. Imagine Juliet has asked you for advice. Write her a letter telling what you think she should do at this time.
2. As the Prince, dictate a letter to your secretary explaining your banishing Romeo.
3. Write a speech for Lord Capulet to give at Juliet's wedding.

Act Four

1. Write what Lady Capulet would say if she discovered that Juliet was planning to take the potion.
2. Write what Lord Capulet would say if he discovered that Juliet was planning to take the potion.
3. Write a letter from Friar Laurence to Romeo.

Act Five

1. As the page, tell what happened between Paris and Romeo.
2. Write a persuasive speech Friar Laurence could use to try to convince Juliet to leave the tomb with him.
3. As Friar Laurence, explain your involvement in this affair to your superior.

After reading and discussing the entire play, students select from the following assignments:

1. Using the play's prologue as a model, write an original epilogue for *Romeo and Juliet*.
2. As Romeo or Juliet, write a diary entry for each of the five days of the play.
3. As Juliet, write two letters to an advice columnist. As the columnist, write a letter in reply to each of them.

4. Rewrite the ending of the play as it would have been if Friar John had not been quarantined but was able to deliver the message to Romeo.
5. Write a front page news article that could appear in the newspaper the day after Romeo and Juliet were found dead.

There are many assignments a teacher can use for any work of literature. What is important is that the assignments occur throughout the reading, especially in longer works. The activities should be designed for individual work, small groups, and the entire class. Discussion is vital to provide students with opportunities to interact and discover what others are thinking and writing.

Romeo and Juliet is the most widely taught work of literature at the secondary level. Using activities that involve students as the ones Dressler described helps students who may have difficulty reading this selection. One teacher, Pamela E. Adams suggests that one way to help students see connections between their lives and the play is through a preview. Adams explains that students "need to spend much effort understanding the antiquated English and often get bogged down at a literal level and fail to appreciate the humor, puns, and story line" (425). To alleviate this problem, she suggests a text preview that builds information with questions for discussion, synopsis of the story, and vocabulary introduction. The preview's purpose is to help students understand and enjoy the play, not to test them on what they learned. (The activity in Box 7–5 will give you some practice in teaching a Shakespearean play.)

BOX 7–5

TEACHING A SHAKESPEAREAN PLAY

Choose a Shakespearean play other than *Romeo and Juliet* and design activities to help secondary students enjoy and understand the play.

TEACHING SHORT STORIES

Teaching short stories is not appreciably different from teaching novels. However short stories are often overlooked when designing thematic units. Too often, short stories are taught, one after another, with little or no connection among them. The beauty of short stories is quite simply the length. For some students, a novel is overwhelming and they avoid even beginning one. As with other literature, teachers can find in short stories a wealth of subject matter, variety of settings, complex characters, and intricate plots. Stories themselves are an important part of our lives. All families share stories, and telling stories has a long, rich tradition. Using response activities with stories we assign students can help them connect school texts with their family stories. (The activity in Box 7–6 encourages you to record your own family stories.)

BOX 7–6

STORIES FROM OUR FAMILIES

Recall as many of your family stories as possible. Which ones were repeated over a period of time? Why these and not others? Jot down some of your stories and share them with your future students.

Short Story Activities

The following student assignments were written by Anne Elliott, an English education major, to accompany "The Secret Life of Walter Mitty" by James Thurber.

1. Write a synopsis of the story as if you were describing it to a friend. Try to condense the story into a few sentences.
2. Pretend this story is going to be a TV series. Write a television announcement to advertise it. Include who will play the leading roles as well as what the series will be about.
3. Think about other books you have read, television shows you've watched, or stories that express a great deal of imagination. How do they compare to "The Secret Life of Walter Mitty"?
4. Many of Mitty's fantasies are interrupted. Choose one and finish it for him.
5. Before reading the story, students form groups of four or five. The teacher begins each group by reading one line from the story, and students create their own story by each contributing one sentence at a time. After reading the story, students compare their versions with Mitty's version. Discuss the power of the imagination.
6. Recall one event from your life and then write an exaggeration of it to create a tall tale. Then write the event as it actually happened.
7. Write a character description of Walter, including how he looks, acts, and sounds. Pantomime your description for the class or draw an illustration.
8. In a small group, act out one of Mitty's fantasies, changing the ending as you wish.

A second group of activities is written by Renee McCarthy, an English education student, and is based a collection of short stories, *Baseball in April.* written by Gary Soto. This book is an excellent choice for middle and high school students. The stories reveal day-to-day life of Mexican American youth in Fresno. The issues in the book include love, friendship, family, youth and age, success, failure, and self-esteem. Students write in a journal following every story or reading.

1. The first activity is for prereading. Answer the following questions in your journals:

What does it mean to be attractive? Does it mean physically beautiful or can it mean something else? Explain what you mean.

What does it mean to be popular? How does one get to be popular and whose decision is it? Do you think popularity is important? Explain your answer.

2. The second activity is done throughout the book, starting with Chapter 1. After each chapter write in your notebook the main points from the story you just read. What experiences in your life does it remind you of?

3. This activity deals only with the chapter on the Barbie doll. The issue in the story is self-esteem and self-perception, important concepts at this age. Write an essay about Veronica's treatment of her two Barbie dolls. How does she treat them differently? What does this say about the way people treat one another?

4. The final activity: Imagine you are asked to write an essay to a governor who does not support learning foreign languages in middle school. Explain why you think it is helpful to learn about another culture and its language. Use at least three examples from the book.

Short stories should be included in the literature program not as a separate unit but integrated throughout the curriculum. As with other literature selections, the teacher offers choices to students and needs to have resources of interesting short stories available for them. Many of the following selections are written by authors popular with young adult readers.

- *8 Plus 1* by Robert Cormier
- *Dear Bill, Remember Me?* by Norma Fox Mazer
- *Athletic Shorts* by Chris Crutcher
- *Baseball in April and Other Stories* by Gary Soto
- *The Illustrated Man* by Ray Bradbury
- *Angels and Other Strangers* by Katherine Paterson
- *Coming of Age* Edited by Bruce Emra

TEACHING POETRY

Activities for poetry follow the same guidelines as those described for short stories and novels. Students' reactions to reading poetry are often "I don't get it," as if there is a hidden meaning. Student responses are as valid here as for other types of literature, and the same general guidelines are appropriate. Poetry is meant to be heard. When teachers share a poem with students, it is important to read the poem aloud as students follow along with a printed copy. The teacher asks them to allow their minds to react to the words, letting thoughts flow freely, and not to think about what the poem "means." Students then write responses without talking to anyone else. A teacher may want to provide suggestions if students have difficulty responding.

- What images do I see as I hear the poem?
- What do the words remind me of?
- What feelings have I had that are similar to the ones expressed in the poem?

Students compare their responses and discuss the similarities and differences. Poetry, more than prose, elicits widely different comments. For example, when students read Theodore Roethke's "Papa's Waltz," some students believe the poem represents a joyful romp of a father with his son, whereas others see it as the father's abusive behavior, probably caused by alcohol. The differences arise out of different experiences of the students. Also, many of the young women believe the father is dancing with a daughter, and images of themselves as small children come back strongly. Both views are "correct," and students can point to specific examples in the poem to back up their interpretations.

In a study of student responses by Robert Blake and Anna Lunn, students read a poem and responded with no restrictions. In fact, the responses were done outside of a school setting to further remove any sense of a threatening or structured expectation. The findings of the study have important implications for classroom teachers (72–73).

1. Reading a poem is not a simple or linear process. Readers need time to read over particular lines and to think about the poem, to not be rushed through the process. A poem "needs to grow on us—adults and adolescents alike" (72).
2. When students say they do not like a poem or poetry in general, they generally mean they are afraid they cannot understand the meaning. Further, they believe the teacher does know the "meaning."
3. Adolescents read and respond differently "from English majors and experienced teachers in many immensely important ways" (72). This does not mean that adolescents do not read poetry successfully, but they bring to the reading different backgrounds and experiences; few have acquired the critical techniques that took us years to understand.
4. Within the limits of meanings held by class members and the larger community, there are as many responses to complex poems as there are students in the class. It takes time for students to learn how to read and respond to poetry. Students need many opportunities to develop confidence that they can respond in meaningful ways to complex poetry.

One of the problems with teaching poetry is that students often have had little experience with poetry since elementary grades. Moreover, it is usually taught in a separate unit pulled out of the regular context of literature. If students become more familiar with a wide variety of poetry, responding to it becomes easier. Poetry is best taught throughout all thematic units. Regardless of the day's activity, try to read a poem to the students, not to "study" it, but to enjoy it. (Box 7–7 offers some suggestions for enjoying poetry in your classes.)

Richard Beach and James Marshall, English educators, suggest the following guidelines for successfully teaching poetry:

- Never teach a poem you do not like.
- Teach poems you are not certain you understand.
- Teach poems that are new to you.
- Read poems daily in your life outside of school.
- Give students the freedom to dislike "great poetry." (384)

BOX 7 7

ENJOYING POETRY

Immerse yourself in poetry for a week. Read children's poetry, which is often in a pictu book format. Read funny poetry like those found in Shel Silverstein's books, poems current magazines written by novice writers, award-winning poetry, poems written by e mentary school children, and poems by minorities. Think about them; roll the wor around in your mind. Bring your favorites to class to share.

ACTIVITIES FOR TEACHING POETRY

1. Teacher John T. Kell, Jr., devised a lesson that helped his 10th-grade students understand how description is used in poems to create images. He wrote a short descriptive poem based on a picture of Alaska. Without showing students the picture, he gave them copies of the poem. As they listened to the poem and read it to themselves, they drew a picture of what they thought the poem described. After completing their drawings, they circled words and phrases from the poem that helped create the images they drew. (66). In discussion, help students see that the circled words created the images so that in future readings they can recognize imagery and understand the deeper meaning in their individual readings.

2. A similar assignment for developing student abilities to see images in poems comes from Linda Wall, a middle school teacher. One way to help students see images in poems is to help them realize that imagery is language that appeals to our five senses. "Students can understand poetry through the pictures we see, hear, touch, taste, and smell" (9).

   Wall begins by handing out peppermint candy. Students write words or experiences that come to mind as they eat the candy, identifying what sensory impression they are reminded of. Students could later apply this technique when reading a poem.

   Another approach Wall uses is to have students draw pictures or images they recognize from a poem. After hearing and reading the poem, they draw as many images as they can. The activity can be reversed by having students first draw pictures based on a sensory image, then write a poem based on the picture.

3. To help students recognize tone in poetry and, consequently, to come to a deeper understanding of the poem, Renee McCarthy, an English education student, developed a list of questions to guide students when they read "Hermana" by Gary Soto.
   - What type of tone does this poem have? In other words, how does it make you feel? Is it uplifting, inspiring, melancholy, or depressing? Give examples from the poem that make you feel this way. Quote a line that made you feel the way you did.
   - Who is the voice in the poem? Is she or he young or old? How do we know? Is this individual feeling pain? Why? Who else is affected by the father/brother-in-law's behavior? What types of problems are these people experiencing and how might they be helped? How would you act if you were a member of this group? Explain the living environment for the children and explain how justice could be found.

4. English education students brainstormed questions and activities they could use in a secondary English class after assigning the poem "The Belly Dancer" by Diane Wakoski.

   To begin, place the poem on an overhead, cover the title and read it together, line by line. Have students write reactions to each line as it is read. They write a summary of reactions after completing the reading. How did their reactions change after they read the title?
   - Write a list of words from the poem that appeal to our senses.
   - Discuss attitudes toward the body as exhibited in the poem.
   - What does the poem say to you about relationships between men and women?
   - How does the poem use sounds to create meanings?
   - How does the snake image function within the poem? Why a snake and not a different animal?
   - What do you think is the tone of the poem? Specifically what words or thoughts provide the tone?
   - Discuss the women's fear. Why are they uncomfortable in the presence of the belly dancer?
   - What do you picture as the setting of the poem? If it were changed, would your reaction change?
   - Think of another type of dance and write a list of words to describe it. Compose a poem based on these words.
   - Explain with examples from the poem whether you feel the belly dancer presents a positive or negative image.

   Although a teacher would not use all of these ideas or suggestions in guiding students to a deeper understanding of a poem, the list illustrates the many possibilities teachers have when we want to encourage students to read more closely and to explore a variety of meanings.

5. An activity that includes a poem and a short story helps students recognize common elements in different genres and may make poetry more accessible to them. Ella Shaw, a high school teacher, asked her students to read the story

"Two Kinds," an excerpt from *Joy Luck Club* by Amy Tan, and the poem "Thanking My Mother for Piano Lessons" by Diane Wakoski. Both works focus on the a relationship between mother and daughter and piano playing as a major force.

Shaw suggests the following: Have students list characteristics that describe first Wakoski's mother, then Tan's mother. After generating the lists, students discuss in what ways the two mothers are similar and in what ways different. Next they compare and contrast the tones of each piece and find examples in the texts. Their findings are turned in as group writing products. The following are questions for individual students to consider:

- What attitudes do Wakoski and Tan seem to have toward their mothers?
- How are their feelings about the piano as adults different from their feelings as children?

Students write a short essay discussing these questions and other points they want to include when comparing the two texts.

Box 7–8 offers a suggestion for teaching poetry.

Box 7–8

TEACHING POETRY

Select a poem you found in Box 7-7 and write as many ideas as possible that you could use if you taught the poem in class. How could the poem relate to other literature you are having students study?

POETRY RESOURCES

Poetry is not difficult to find, but beginning teachers should not use poetry that they studied in college literature classes for two reasons:

1. Many of the selections are too difficult for young adult readers. The difficulties may come from vocabulary, allusions, content, word choice, and syntax.
2. Because you studied them in a college class, you may have learned only one way of understanding the poem, thus making it difficult for you to accept the various meanings your future students will find.

Rather than resort to teaching the same poems you were taught, try to explore the wealth of resources available to us. Bushman and Bushman suggest the following texts, as well as others, for secondary students:

- *Reflections on a Gift of Watermelon Pickle and Other Modern Verse* edited by Steve Dunning, Edward Lueders, and Hugh L. Smith
- *Class Dismissed!* and *Class Dismissed II* by Mel Glen
- *Postcard Poems: A Collection of Poems for Sharing* by Paul Janeczko
- *Rainbow Writing* by Eve Merriam
- *A Fire in My Hands* by Gary Soto
- *Now Sheba Sings the Song* by Maya Angelou (45–46)

Beach and Marshall list several poetry collections, of which a small sampling is included here:

- *Celebrations: The Poetry of Black America* by Arnold Adoff
- *I Am Phoenix: Poems for Two Voices* by Paul Fleishman
- *To Look at Anything* by Lee Bennett Hopkins
- *Bring Me All Your Dreams* by Nancy Larrick
- *I Like You, If You Like Me: Poems of Friendship* by Myra Cohn Livingston (403–405)

WHOLE LANGUAGE

Whole language is both a theory about how students learn language and a set of guidelines for classroom practice. It contrasts with the traditional way of teaching by expanding learners' roles in choosing literature, writing activities, and being involved in their own learning. Educators explain that the whole language movement is based on a social-constructivist viewpoint (Lamme and Hysmith 52), which means simply that students take an active role in learning. The teacher's role changes from a dispenser of information to a facilitator of student-centered learning. The classroom has a cooperative rather than a competitive atmosphere (Lamme and Hysmith 52).

Learning is based on strategies rather than isolated bits and pieces, such as skill sheets with no connection to what students are writing. The idea of viewing a students as constructing their own learning changes the curriculum. Teachers create opportunities for students to learn with reading, writing, listening, and speaking activities and provide general guidelines; students chose what they want to explore and create to reach the learning goals (Lehr 13).

A major emphasis in whole language is that students are allowed to make choices. Students are also given lots of good literature from which to choose; they write frequently, and reading-writing connections are encouraged (Willis 3).

Anne Genevieve Whitt explains what whole language means in her high school classroom: "Reading becomes a process when students brainstorm what they know and what they would like to know or what they expect to discover from the reading before they read" (488). She began using the whole language process when she could not locate any reading selections by Florida authors, and she turned the project over to the students. They assignment was to create a book on Florida authors that future students could find useful. The students selected their own authors to study, chose what they wanted to know about them, and made judgments about what they thought others would want to know (489). The students read and wrote with enthusiasm because they had a strong purpose and were self-directed. The project worked because the students had choices but also because they had direction and guidance from the teacher.

TEACHING LANGUAGE IN LITERATURE STUDY

The study of tone, diction, imagery, and style is appropriate for older students, juniors and seniors, who are capable readers and are enrolled in a college-bound or advanced placement English. If teachers stress these language elements for younger students, however, literature becomes a study of facts at the expense of reading, enjoying, and learning about ourselves and others. Even with the advanced students, teachers must present the study of language elements in an interesting and appropriate way; not the way college students are taught. Two experienced teachers share lesson plans to illustrate how they accomplish this goal.

"A closer look at tone" (Jean Moelter)

1. To begin, we have a class discussion to define what is meant by tone. How do you decide what type of clothes to buy—style? color? size? What does your style say about you? What does it mean when someone says, "Tone down your color"? What can tone of voice convey? Compare two versions of the same song by different artists. Discuss the differences between tone and style even though it is the same song.
2. Read "We Real Cool" by Gwendolyn Brooks and "The First Confession" by X. J. Kennedy. What is the message each writer is trying to convey? How do you know? How does tone create meaning? How does the tone in the poem support the meaning?
3. Students look at how a stereotyped group is portrayed from the movie *Grease* or a similar one. How did the director create tone to get the meaning across? After discussion, students model either Brooks' or Kennedy's style to write a poem or narrative that has a strong tone conveying meaning.

Metaphor Focus (Andrea Kramer)

Before reading Hamlet:

1. Students listen and respond to "I am a Rock" by Simon and Garfunkel. Why does this voice identify himself as a rock and an island? Have you ever felt this way? When? Are a rock and an island good things to be when a person has had a struggle with a loved one or a friend? Why? What other choices would also work to describe a person in this mental state?

2. Students bring in lyrics of a song containing a metaphor. Together we analyze whether the metaphors "work." Is the comparison appropriate? Are enough connections drawn? What other words could they choose instead to create that metaphor?
3. Students listen and respond to "An Old Pair of Shoes" by Randy Travis. How is this comparison similar to and different from "I am a Rock"?
4. Discuss the use of imagery and puns to create metaphors; use "An Old Pair of Shoes" to begin the example. Other examples from literature are also used.
5. Students write a personal metaphor or lyric form with the option of performing their metaphor in some fashion for the class.

During the Reading of Hamlet

6. Demonstrate the concept of extended metaphors with "Whose List to Hunt" (and other sonnets) and the disease imagery in *Hamlet*.
7. Students keep a list of words associated with imagery that continue the unweeded garden and disease metaphors.
8. Students brainstorm a list of words appropriate for creating a personal metaphor for Hamlet. Use that list to create a diamante poem for Hamlet; then choose one to further develop in essay form.

These two lessons involve students in their own learning rather than being told in a lecture format what style, tone, and metaphor are. (Box 7–9 encourages you to practice planning other lessons on literary devices.)

BOX 7–9

PLANNING LESSONS ON LITERARY DEVICES

Select another literary language device such as diction, irony, connotation, mood, or any other. Develop a lesson plan that is creative and interesting. Use any literature you like, but the lesson must connect to specific literature examples.

VOCABULARY STUDY IN READING

Vocabulary study has several purposes, and how we teach vocabulary depends on the specific purpose. Teaching reading vocabulary does not require pronunciation or spelling. Spelling has nothing to do with speaking, listening, and little with reading. Pronunciation is important only when speaking, and further, we know the meanings of many words that we neither speak nor write.

Vocabulary in reading has two purposes: to learn the meanings so the present text can be understood and to increase reading vocabulary so that meanings in future texts will be understood. It is important to realize that none of us needs to know the meaning of every word to comprehend what we read. Without thinking about it, we skip over many words when we read, inferring the meaning from the context. To stop and look up each word slows readers down so much that they lose interest. Occasionally, readers might write down words they don't know, but they often keep right on reading and look them up later. The only reason for doing this is a love of words, not a need to understand the story better.

Words are never to be taken out of context, either for learning or for testing. We know how important context is in figuring out meanings, and it goes against all common sense to give students a list of words to learn, ask them to look up the words in a dictionary, and use each in a sentence. To illustrate, a teacher assigned a list of words from a short story by Poe. A very competent student looked up the word *dank*. Learning that it meant moist, she wrote, "My, these brownies are dank." When the teacher explained the connotation to her, she thought it so funny she shared it with the rest of the class. After that, every time we ate brownies someone would say, "Mmmmmm, good—so dank." Although that turned out to be a shared joke, the teacher learned students must have context to understand connotations and never gave them words in isolation again.

Another experience involved a student who struggled with reading. While taking a vocabulary test, he commented that the teacher forgot to include the meaning of a particular word. The test was one where students were to match words to appropriate meanings. As she looked at the paper, the teacher could see the meaning he was supposed to choose; of course she wrote the test and knew all the answers. She asked him what he thought the word meant, and in his own words he gave a reasonable definition. The teacher told him she had forgotten to include that meaning and wrote it on his paper. Many students could generalize the meaning supplied for the test and come up with the "right" answer, but she was penalizing those who could not. Yet, these students did know what the word meant. The tests were more "guess what meaning the teacher has in mind" than tests of vocabulary knowledge.

Because words must remain in context, one way to identify the ones the teacher has chosen for study is to give the line and page number of each word. Another method is to reprint the sentence or part of a sentence on a handout. For example: "He usually agreed with her in earlier years, sometimes grudgingly, but without *rancor*." (from *No Promises in the Wind*) The directions to students are to write what *rancor* means in the context. To help them use context, they first write what they think the word means, and if unsure or just want to check, they look it up in a dictionary. The students meet in groups to go over the meanings and use dictionaries to solve arguments.

If a teacher wants to test students on reading vocabulary, the same sentences appear in the test as were on the handout, perhaps in different order. In their own words, students write the definition of the word as used in that sentence. Spelling should not be evaluated, nor do students need to write complete sentences because that is not what is being tested. Rather, teachers look for accurate meanings of the words in the context in which they appeared in the text. Grading time is minimal, guessing doesn't help students, and the test is true to the principle that context provides clues for word meanings.

Words in the text are often esoteric or specialized, such as foreign phrases or words that are not commonly used, and students need not remember them beyond the passage they are reading. For these words, a teacher can simply tell students the meaning.

SHARING BOOKS

This section might be called "Book Reports," except we are strongly opposed to them as they are generally used. Having students fill out a book report form or follow a particular format wastes the teacher's and the students' time. When asked why they require the reports, teachers usually respond, "So I will know if the students are reading." Ironically, book reports do not provide that information. It is too easy to write a report without actually reading the book, which makes it difficult to know who reads and who does not. And book reports are boring. Teachers try to make them more interesting by providing options to the standard report, but generally the options, although more fun, can also be done without reading. Teachers cannot be sure students actually read the books unless they ask, and students are surprisingly honest.

Sharing books, though, is a vital part of a literature class. Most of us like to read; after all, teaching English is our chosen field. When we read something we especially enjoy, we try to think of someone who would also like it. Friends and family pass books around, usually with the comment, "You have to read this! You'll love it." We can replicate that enthusiasm in the classroom if we provide the opportunities.

Students pay attention to what other students read, which can be frustrating for a teacher who takes time to suggest books to a student who then ignores the advice and chooses a book a classmate casually recommends. The solution is to structure time so that students can share, and this can be done in various ways.

The most informal, and often most successful, way is setting aside part of a period to talk about books. Students know ahead of time when this will be, but they do not have to prepare anything. Not everyone has to talk about a book, although everyone is encouraged to do so. Some share information about a magazine article they read, which is fine. The requirement is that it must be reading material as opposed to a TV show. The teacher, too, shares reading of interest to the students. The discussions are casual, and students stay seated when sharing. Student show high interest in the discussions; questions and conversations are common.

One time in a book-sharing session, one student walked out of the room. A few minutes later he reappeared with a book under his arm. When the teacher asked where he had gone, he explained he left to check out the book one of his classmates was talking about. He said, "If I waited until class was over, I was afraid someone else would get it before I did." Such eagerness to read is precisely the objective of book sharing.

A more structured way to create book-sharing time is for students to form groups based on the type of book they read. After students select the book they want to read, they jot down the genre (e.g., biography, mystery, adventure,), and the teacher forms the groups, so that the mystery buffs talk about mysteries together, the biography readers talk together, and so on. The reason for doing this is that readers with a strong liking for one kind of book enjoy talking to others who share their reading tastes. This is especially true of science fiction fans, but everyone likes to share a common interest. The students meet in groups after they read the books. This grouping is appropriate only once in a while because, of course, we want to increase the variety of books students read, but interest groups are popular with students, and they increase reading enjoyment.

As a spin-off on the interest grouping, each group can create a skit involving characters from the books each student reads. Students perform the skits for the class, and it is a good idea to videotape them and have them available on Parents' Night. We've had talk shows with characters across historical times and from different fields; in one Joan of Arc and Einstein held a discussion about taking responsibility for making the world a better place. Another time students dressed in gym clothes dribbled and passed a basketball around while discussing feats of the various sport figures they had read about. Admittedly, students could do these without reading the whole book, but the activities provide opportunities for informal dramatics and are based on literature and are therefore well worth the class time.

Another way to share books is to keep a card file in the room with student-written summaries and information about the books they have read. They include their name so others can ask more about the book if they care to. Many of the students use this source instead of browsing in the library when looking for a book to read. This also provides a way for shy students, who may be reluctant to speak in class, to share their reading.

At the end of the year, all students write a paragraph about a book they would highly recommend for others to read over the summer. Every student goes home for the summer with a copy of all the book descriptions.

A middle school student (D. Stevens) wrote:

Lord of the Flies by William Golding
    When they land the boys are overjoyed to have no grownups. But soon work has to be done: the fire kept burning, the huts built, the hunting done. There is Piggy. He is fat and very grownup. He knows how to do things but the crowd rejects him. He gets killed by a rolling rock that cracks his skull open. Ralph is the "leader" because he blew the conch first. On the other hand, Jack, though he doesn't know at first, is bloodthirsty!

Many teachers believe that reading in class is a waste of time, but Larry Johannessen believes that if students begin a reading assignment in class that this "significantly increased the likelihood that they will continue and finish the reading outside of class" (69). In addition, giving students class time to read promotes the idea of reading being an integral part of English class. That sounds obvious, but some students brag about their ability to never read a book and yet pass English courses.

To increase reading enjoyment and come closer to the goal of helping students become lifelong readers, reading and talking about books must become an integral part of the class. The groups work well because they focus the activity, but talking about books needs to be a common, almost daily, activity. Teachers can set the stage for this to happen by talking about books they themselves read. At first, students may seem surprised that teachers know about, let alone read, romance novels, Stephen King, or any contemporary popular authors. The same is true for magazine articles. When teachers first share articles from *Road Rider* or *Rolling Stone,* they may be met with looks of disbelief, but students do begin to talk more freely about what they read. Book sharing increases enjoyment in reading and makes the goal of helping students become lifelong readers more attainable.

How we teach literature is vitally important for our students. Your future classrooms will not be filled with students who feel the same way you do about literature. Our job as teachers is to make literature accessible and enjoyable for *all* our students. Arthur N. Applebee believes that "when books are taught well they will invite exactly the kinds of thoughtful discussion, reflection, and debate that we most need to foster" to help our students become responsible citizens (46).

CASE 7–1

Exploring an Instructional Unit

Stan Nesbit, a high school English teacher, developed a unit on the American dream for the 10th grade. He has chosen a theme commonly taught at the secondary level, but his presentation of the material is strikingly different from a traditional approach. He incorporates introductory activities to develop student interest and to broaden the concept of an American dream by including texts that represent the voices of American women, men, and children. His planned activities include not only reading, but writing, listening, and speaking. What follows is an abbreviated version of Stan's unit listing only the activities.

THE AMERICAN DREAM

Activity 1: As students enter the first day of the unit, I will play the song "Born in the U.S.A." by Bruce Springstein. To introduce the unit I will ask students to respond in their journals to the question "What is the American dream?" I will ask students for examples of this dream. Students share their individual responses in small groups, and then each group writes a level 2 paper on the discussion. I will collect their individual responses and keep them on file for a comparison/contrast activity at the end of the unit.

Activity 2: I will ask students to do some research at home. They have one week to ask parents, grandparents, and friends about their family's immigration to the United States. Students then choose one of the stories they hear and write a paper in first person. These papers will be shared orally in pairs for a peer response activity and handed in as a level 2 paper.

This assignment is followed by reading a selection from the autobiography *Stelmark* by Harry Petrakis, a Greek immigrant. Students write a response in their journal about the relationship between the main character and the old Greek man, the work ethic portrayed, and the relation to the theme of the American dream.

1. From these assignments what can you deduce about Stan's objectives? What in particular is he accomplishing?
2. What was his point in having students write the stories they heard in first person?

Activity 3: Next we watch segments of a video recording of speeches by presidential candidates, all of whom claim to deliver the American dream to everyone. Students respond in their journal, stating first why the candidates all refer to our theme and then explaining which person they believe gave the most believable speech and why it was effective.

Activity 4: While the students do research for activity 2, we will read several early works of American literature to observe the establishment of the American dream and the effect of this ideal on our history.

The first text we read is the "Description of New England" by Captain John Smith. Students respond in their journals to the following questions: Who is Smith's audience? What do you think Smith's audience is looking for in a new world? How does Smith sell America in this selection? How does this relate to the American dream?

After the journal entry, we review advertising techniques (bandwagon, testimonial, name-calling, transfer, and so on). Students form groups, and each group is assigned a technique to use in writing an ad to sell the New World to the English back home. Each group presents the ad to the class, and the whole class tries to determine which technique was used.

Activity 5: As a prereading assignment to the next activity, we read two letters from Abigail and John Adams. In these letters, Abigail encourages her husband to "remember the ladies" when he helps establish the laws of the new nation. Students write a journal entry guessing what Abigail's response will be to John's letter. Students share their entries with the whole class.

Stan has the activities flow from individual to small group to whole class. What is his purpose in organizing the time this way? How does this affect the learners?

Activity 6: As students enter the classroom, I will play the song "Pink Houses" by John Mellencamp. Together as a class, we will read aloud and discuss Jefferson's "Declaration of Independence." Then each student reads Elizabeth Stanton's "Declaration of Women's Rights." We will compare and contrast these two documents. Following the reading and referring back to the persuasive techniques we learned in activity 4, students write their own "Declaration of Independence" from adults, parents, teachers, administrators, or whomever they choose. We will have peer response groups for this level 2 assignment. Students must consider the whole audience as did the framers of the U.S. Declaration and make this a persuasive document.

Activity 7: As students enter the classroom, I will play the song "My Hometown" by Bruce Springstein. To introduce selections from Ben Franklin's *Autobiography* and *Poor Richard's Almanac,* we will define the term *aphorism* and brainstorm a list, followed by a class discussion. Then using *Poor Richard's Almanac* students choose two aphorisms that mean the most to them, paraphrase each one, and write a personal experience that illustrates the concept (level 2).

---

1. What is Stan's purpose in playing the music at the beginning of class periods? Do you think it is effective?
2. What other selections might fit into the theme?

Activity 8: Activities 8 and 9 are transitions to the "dark side" of the American dream. I introduce the idea that nothing comes free, that every step we call progress carries with it a price. Students write a journal entry on the costs of the American dream. Next we watch a videotape of Dr. Seuss' *The Lorax;* students also have a hard copy. In discussion, they relate the poem to loggers and the proposed mines in northern Wisconsin. We will discuss the name "Once-ler," the chain of events in the story and other points the students contribute.

Activity 9: As an introduction to "Under the Lion's Paw" by Hamlin Garland, we will discuss economic hardships and question the myth that we can achieve our dreams if we work hard enough. Students write in their journal guided by the following prompts:

1. Is Bulter an evil man or is he simply a shrewd businessman trying to achieve his own dreams?
2. Why doesn't Haskins kill Bulter? What does this show about his goals for his children?
3. Does this story present a realistic or romantic view of life? Support your answer with evidence from the story. Journals are shared in large group.

Activity 10: I will ask students to brainstorm a list of Americans to whom the American dream is difficult or impossible to attain. Also, what Americans may reject the dream entirely? Students read several poems showing the variety of attitudes toward the quest for a satisfying life in America. The poems include these: "America" by Claude McKay, "From the Dark Tower" by Countee Cullen, "Weekend Glory" by Maya Angelou, and "The Bean Eaters" by Gwendolyn Brooks.

Students relate the poems to earlier definitions of the American dream and write a level 2 paper on their response. Students listen to songs by Tracy Chapman, especially "Fast Car."

What other poems might fit in this activity?

Activity 11: Students read "The Man Who Saw the Flood" by Richard Wright. Then they write responses to the following statements:

1. The African Americans portrayed are fundamentally still slaves.
2. Some Americans today have no more opportunity to realize the American dream than Tom and his family did. Compare Burgess in this story to Bulter in "Under the Lion's Paw." Students should support their responses with reason and evidence.

Activity 12: We view Martin Luther King, Jr.'s "I Have a Dream" speech. I will encourage students to pay attention to the rhetorical devices King uses to persuade his audience. Students then write their own "Dream for the Nation" using King's rhetorical devices as a model. I will remind students that their dream must be for the good of the nation.

We have not included all of the transitions Stan uses to introduce each activity and to create interest. For the last two activities, what might a teacher do to create good discussions and involve students in the issues?

Activity 13: We will read two poems by Langston Hughes, "Freedom" and "Dream Deferred," and discuss a person's responsibility for achieving one's own dreams. In a response journal, students respond to Hughes' question: What happens to a dream deferred?

Stan usually gives students prompts to answer for journal entries. Discuss whether you agree with this technique. What else might a teacher do?

Activity 14: Students view the video *A Raisin in the Sun* by Lorraine Hansberry. Following the video, they write a journal response using these questions as a guide:

1. Identify the dreams of the main characters in the play. Then consider this character in light of Hughes poem "Dream Deferred."
2. Compare the dreams of a character in the play to those described in King's speech.
3. Write a dialogue between Joseph Asagai and George Murchison that shows their different dreams, lifestyles, and perceptions of America.
4. In what way has Walter come into his manhood at the end of the play? In what ways will the change be favorable and unfavorable?

The writing assignment will be level 2 and revised in peer groups.

Activity 15: I will play "Signs" by Tesla as the students enter the room. Students read "Stupid America" by Abelardo Delgado, a Chicano who expresses the clash between the American idea of progress and the Chicano way of life. Students respond in their journals to the following questions:

1. What is the source of misunderstanding between the man and "America"?
2. What is the source of frustration for the man?
3. What role does art play in the Chicano's life?
4. What was your emotional reaction to the title? To the poem itself?

After large-group discussion, we read the poems of the Chinese Americans of the "Town of Iron," the Angel Island Detention Center where, from 1910 to 1940, Chinese immigrants were imprisoned and interrogated. For a level 2 assignment, students are assigned a flag, either China's or Mexico's, to designate their native country (These are assigned because we do not choose our birthplace). Students write a letter to a friend or family member back home telling about their life in the New World. The letter should end with a recommendation of whether or not the person should come to America, too.

Activity 16: Class begins with a discussion of the history of immigrants who have come to America and have been victims of prejudice, such as the Irish, Swedish, and Italians. Students watch *The Blue Hotel* by Stephen Crane and respond in their journals to who and what are responsible for the death of the Swede. In groups, students discuss their responses and write a level 2 group paper.

Activity 17: Students read "The Sculptor's Funeral" by Willa Cather and then write a short level 2 assignment comparing the values of the town with those of the sculptor and his friends.

Activity 18: I will read aloud a selection of Native American myths to help students understand that with their diverse beliefs and environments many Native Americans live satisfying lives without the idea of personal or national progress. Students then read selections from *Bury My Heart at Wounded Knee* by Dee Brown. They write responses in their journals.

What suggestions can you add to Stan's unit to help students respond with depth and understanding?

Activity 19: Students will read *The Great Gatsby* by F. Scott Fitzgerald. I will play selections of jazz classics and give students some background about the Jazz Age. Students select from a list of possible topics to write a level 2 assignment:

1. Write two biographies with time lines: one for Jay Gatsby and one for James Gatz.
2. Supply the dialogue between Gatsby and Daisy, the one Fitzgerald discreetly omitted from Chapter 5.
3. What is Gatsby's dream? What did he do to achieve it?
4. Contrast Gatsby's dream relationship with the real one that developed. How do you account for the differences?
5. Ben Franklin and Gatsby each had detailed plans for becoming successful. Write your own plans in detail. Students also complete a level 3 assignment by writing a comparison paper for any two characters or people we have read about during this unit.

Activity 20: As a closure activity, students examine what it means to be an American. First they read "What Is an American" by Jean Crèvecouer and then the preface to *The Pursuit of Loneliness* by Philip Slater. Students write their definition of an American, taking into account all of their readings. Then I hand back their definitions from the first day of the unit, and we discuss the differences in large group.

1. What do you think Stan's students learned from the unit? In what areas might some students have difficulty with the material? What could a teacher provide for these students?
2. The unit is designed for the 10th grade. Would it or parts of it be appropriate for other grade levels?
3. Stan noted that he had trouble finding works by female writers whatever the culture. What additions can you suggest?
4. He wondered if the American dream is more of a male pursuit than a female one. What do you think? In groups, plan a unit on a more female pursuit.
5. What would you add or delete in Stan's unit?

REFERENCES

Adams, Pamela E. "Teaching *Romeo and Juliet* in the Nontracked English Classroom." *Journal of Reading,* 38.6 (March 1995): 424–432.

Anderson, Philip M., and Gregory Rubano. *Enhancing Aesthetic Reading and Response.* Urbana: NCTE, 1991.

Applebee, Arthur N. "Literature and the Ethical Tradition." *Vital Signs 1.* Ed. James L. Collins. Portsmouth: Boynton/Cook, 1990. 39–47.

Beach, Richard, and James Marshall. *Teaching Literature in the Secondary School.* San Diego: Harcourt Brace Jovanovich, 1991.

Blake, Robert W., and Anna Lunn. "Responding to Poetry: High School Students Read Poetry." *English Journal* Feb. 1986: 68–73.

Bushman, John H., and Kay Parks Bushman. *Using Young Adult Literature in the English Classroom.* New York: Macmillan, 1993.

Carter, Candy, ed. *Literature—News That Stays News: Fresh Approach to the Classics.* Urbana: NCTE, 1985.

Elliott, Anne. "Stereotypes: The Root of Aggressive Behavior." Unpublished paper. ENG 404, 1995.

Farnam, Nancy, Patricia K. Kelly. "Response-Based Instruction at the Middle Level: When Student Engagement is the Goal. *Middle School Journal* Sept. 1993: 46–49.

Guerin, W. L., Labor, E. G., Morgan, L., & Willingham, J. R. *A Handbook of Critical Approaches to Literature.* New York: Harper & Row, 1979.

Graves, M. F., Palmer, R. J., & Furniss, D. W. *Structuring Reading Activities for English Classes.* Urbana: ERIC, NCTE, 1976.

Iser, Wolfgang. *The Act of Reading.* Baltimore: John Hopkins University Press, 1978.

Johannessen, Larry R. "Enhancing Response to Literature: A Matter of Changing Old Habits." *English Journal* Nov. 1994: 66–70.

Kell J. T., Jr. "Illustrating Imagery." *English Journal* Apr. 1995: 66–67.

Lamme, Linda Leonard, and Cecilia Hysmith. "A Whole-Language Base for Theme Studies in the Social Studies Curriculum." *International Journal of Social Education* Autumn 1993: 52–65.

Langer, Judith A. "A Response-Based Approach to Reading Literature." *Language Arts* 71(Mar. 1994): 203–211.

Lehr, Susan. "Reading, Writing, Speaking, and Listening." *Whole Language.* Ed. Robert W. Blake. Schenectady: New York State English Council, 1990: 1–15.

Lothe, Kurt. "Crime & Punishment, The Musical." *Wisconsin English Journal* Fall 1990: 76–77.

Maxwell, Rhoda J. "Exploring Characters in *All Together Now.*" *Notes Plus* Jan. 1989: 7–8.

McCarthy, Renee. "Teaching Activities for *Baseball in April* and 'Hermana.' " Unpublished paper, 1995.

Miller, Bruce E. *Teaching the Art of Literature.* Urbana: NCTE, 1980.

Nesbit, Stan. "The American Dream." Unpublished paper, July 1992.

Olson, Vicki L. "Connecting With Literature: Activities for *The Cay* and *The Bedspread. Literature–News That Stays News: Fresh Approaches to the Classics.* Ed. & Chair of the Committee on Classroom Practices, Candy Carter. Urbana: NCTE, 1985: 19–25.

Probst, Robert E. *Response Analysis: Teaching Literature in Junior and Senior High School.* Upper Montclair: Boynton/Cook, 1988.

Purves, A. C. (1993, September). "Toward a Reevaluation of Reader Response and School Literature." *Language Arts* 70 (Sept. 1993): 348–361.

Rosenblatt, Louise M. *Literature as Exploration.* 3rd ed. New York: Barnes & Noble, 1976. Original work published 1938.

Rosenblatt, Louise M. *The Reader, the Text, and the Poem.* Carbondale: Southern Illinois UP, 1977.

Shaw, Ella. "Activities for *Two Kinds* and *The Joy Luck Club.*" Unpublished paper, 1994.

Simmons, John S., and H. Edward Deluzain. *Teaching Literature in Middle and Secondary Grades.* Boston: Allyn & Bacon, 1992.

Smagorinsky, Peter, and Steven Gevinson. *Fostering the Reader's Response.* Palo Alto: Dale Seymour, 1989.

Smith, Frank. *Comprehension and Learning.* New York: Holt, Rinehart & Winston, 1975.

Wall, Linda. "Seeing Is Believing: A Method for Teaching Imagery in Poetry." *Notes Plus* Mar. 1994: 9–10.

Whitt, Anne Genevieve. (1994, March). "Whole Language Revitalizes One High School Classroom." *Journal of Reading* 37.6 (Mar. 1994): 488–493.

Willis, Scott. "Whole Language: Finding the Surest Way to Literacy." *Curriculum Update* Fall 1995. Washington: ASCD.

CHAPTER

8

Selecting Literature

Every time we select a piece of literature to read, we are exposing ourselves to a vision: a vision of people and places and things; a vision of relationships and feelings and strivings.

G. Robert Carlsen (201)

OBJECTIVES FOR TEACHING LITERATURE

Deciding what literature to teach seems to be relatively easy at first glance. School districts may have decided who reads what when, and new teachers have their literature notes from college. A closer look at why we teach literature and what we want to achieve in teaching it reveals that literature choices may be difficult.

In general, teachers want students to read, to think about what they read, and to enjoy the experience. More specifically, a list of objectives could include the following:

1. Develop an enjoyment of reading so that lifelong reading is realistic.
2. Understand the past by becoming more knowledgeable about not only what people did, but how they felt.
3. Understand one's own experiences and how they may or may not fit with those of others.
4. Know and appreciate a wider view of life, both different cultures and different circumstances.
5. Learn how to make critical judgments about literature and to understand literary devices.

Only by using a wide variety of literature can we achieve these goals. One of our purposes in teaching literature is to help students read well; because students have different personalities, experiences, and abilities, we must provide as wide a range of literature as possible.

Many new teachers teach the literature they recently studied in college classes because they are most comfortable with it and know the most about it. Some of these selections may be suitable for high school seniors, but the way the literature was taught is never appropriate. The gap in maturity between high school seniors and upper division college students prohibits use of the same teaching material and approaches. The wealth of literature from which to choose leaves no excuse for not choosing selections appropriate for secondary students.

The literature we select for students to read has both social and political implications and far-reaching consequences. One may think it is not difficult to decide what to ask our students to read, but a serious problem is what we do *not* ask them to read. For years the literature of minorities has been ignored in the schools, and only recently have women authors been included in anthologies. In collections of American poetry, it is not uncommon for Emily Dickinson to be the only woman represented. By omission, the impression is created that great works are written only by white males. Northrop Frye calls literature an organization of human experience. The question is, whose experience? Because we can't teach everything, we make selections, and those selections determine if we are providing opportunities for students to become truly literate.

Being literate means having the ability to use knowledge to better understand the world and ourselves; it is not decoding words. Frank Smith, who has written many books and articles on language and learning, in "Overselling Literacy" describes what literacy is and is not and examines how our understanding of literacy affects how we teach literature. His main point is that the press makes too much of illiteracy and assumes too much for literacy. He writes that literacy "doesn't generate finer feelings or higher values. It doesn't even make anyone smarter." He further explains that "people who can't read and write think just as well out of school as people who can read and write, especially if they are members of a culture in which strong oral language traditions have prevailed" (354). The important point here for teaching is that literacy is not just a set of skills but an "attitude toward the world." "Individuals become literate not from formal instruction they receive, but from what they read and write about and who they read and write with" (355). Seeing their teachers read with pleasure goes far to convince students that they too can enjoy reading. Trying to talk students into believing that they will enjoy a piece of literature is usually not successful. Smith suggests the following:

> They [teachers] can promote interest by demonstrating their own interests. Nothing attracts young people more than activities, abilities, or secrets that absorb adults; they want to know the things that we find worth while. Demonstrating the imaginative possibilities of literacy and collaborating with students should be a classroom delight for teachers and students alike. (358)

Smith's statement emphasizes the responsibility teachers have to select literature that interests the diverse group of students we find in our classrooms. Being literate does not mean that students have read a particular list of titles, but rather that interest and understanding were generated when students read literature they could relate to (see Box 8–1).

BOX 8–1

PERSONAL LITERATURE CHOICES

What literature did you study in middle and high school? What were your favorites? What books did you read on your own? What literature selections are middle and high school students reading? Visit a local school and check out the paperbacks the students are reading. If you have the opportunity, ask them what they like to read. Discuss your findings in class.

On what basis do we select literature? A strong influence is the society we live in. Northrop Frye writes that every society produces a social mythology or ideology, and he describes the two aspects of this mythology. One is a body of beliefs deeply held by a society. For Americans, those beliefs are self-reliance, independence, democratic process, and tolerance. All are important values for creating the kind of society we want to live in. The second is an adjustment mythology by which our ideology is learned by the society's citizens. One function of education is to teach this adjustment mythology, and we do so, Frye explains, by keeping alive a nostalgic version of the American past, relying heavily on Washington's honesty, Lincoln's concern, and stories about pioneers, hunters, and cowboys (16). Such a design is not intrinsically wrong; we value certain ideals and we want future generations to value them as well.

When the adjustment myth becomes perverted, however, some groups of people in society become subordinated. For example, in Victorian times women were thought to be exceedingly delicate—a perverted myth. Protecting women was taught as a social value. As a result, women were actually deprived of equal participation in society (Frye 22). For a variety of reasons, some more vicious than others, minority groups have remained outside the mainstream of the adjustment myth education. When bravery is studied in the classroom, for example, the literature chosen is still, too often, a story of whites fighting Native Americans or men defending helpless women. There are exceptions, of course, but the multitude of literature selections available leaves no excuse for promoting such stereotypes. Becoming aware of this situation and realizing that the literature we choose can help students develop an imaginative social vision make our society a better place to live—for everyone.

CANONICAL LITERATURE

In the late 1980s a movement called cultural literacy gained popularity when William Bennett, then Secretary of Education, argued that students need to read particular authors and works that represent great Western literature. The movement affected the public's opinion about what students should know. Cultural literacy gained momentum when E. D. Hirsch, Jr., wrote *Cultural Literacy,* in which he listed the titles of texts that all students should read. One difficulty with Hirsch's list is that he sponsors only the cultural literacy of rich and educated white Anglo-Saxon Protestants of the

19th and 20th centuries. At a time when our country's population is nearly 40 percent minorities, Hirsch's cultural literacy is too narrow in scope and limited in perspectives to adequately meet the needs of teachers and students.

A second difficulty with Hirsch's concept of cultural literacy is its simplistic view of learning. Peter Elbow in *What Is English?* describes Hirsch's list as ideal for learning chunks of information that have right or wrong answers, but leaves no room for interpretative imagination or the ability to create meaning from reading texts (163). Hirsch has a specific plan to encourage the teaching of his list—a test of general knowledge for 12th grade. He is planning to write tests for 3th, 6th, and 9th grades. For Hirsch, then, knowledge is a set of memorizable facts.

However, as Chris Anson explains in an article in *English Journal,* knowing about something is not the same as integrating content into prior knowledge, perceptions, and beliefs, or even more important, knowing how to know (17). We want to provide learning situations that encourage students to explore many varieties of discourse. This is a very different kind of learning from what Hirsch proposes. The best argument against such an approach to teaching literature is a well-thought out philosophy of one's own (see Box 8–2). Teachers need to take literature selection into our own hands by first establishing goals and then choosing literature that facilitates those goals. If we don't, we run the risk of someone else deciding for us.

Box 8–2

DEVELOPING A PHILOSOPHY FOR TEACHING LITERATURE

Individually make a list of what you believe is important in literature study for secondary students. What selections do you think are important for them to read? What do you want them to learn? Remember your future students will have different interests and abilities than you do. In small groups, discuss what you wrote. Develop a philosophy for teaching literature.

Current literature anthologies include more selections by women and minorities than they did 10 years ago, but many still contain writings by a disproportionate number of white male middle-class authors. For example, in a 12th-grade British literature text published in 1989, only 15 women authors are featured among a total of 102. Our literature curriculum should reflect the multicultural nature of our society. We need a variety of forms and perspectives. If the anthology does not provide such a spectrum, then we must supplement it with paperback books and copies of stories and poems that give students reading experiences that reflect the lives of all.

Making Choices

Because teachers know the abilities and interests of their students, as well as the units of study where particular themes are appropriate, they should control the literature program for their school. We want to choose "good" books for our students to read, but what criteria do we use? In *Experiencing Children's Literature,* Alan Purves and Dianne Monson suggest that teachers use three questions to judge the quality of a book:

1. Did the book arouse my emotions? (Are the emotions trite or realistic? Is it interesting?)
2. Is the book well written? (Are characters believable and is the language appropriate to the theme?)
3. Is the book meaningful? (Is the audience respected? Is the theme treated seriously?)

In addition, the book should appeal to both student readers and the teacher.

ORGANIZING LITERATURE STUDY

We don't believe that particular types of literature should be taught at specific grade levels. Rather, teachers should select literature based on what they believe are important considerations for a unit or theme designed specifically for their classes. In many curricula, tall tales are designated for only one grade level, and fables for another. Instead of attaching a grade level to a kind of literature, teachers should consider the developmental level of their students and what literature best meets this purpose. For instance, it is appropriate to use Dr. Seuss books and Shel Silverstein's poetry at the senior high level when discussing how authors can integrate morals into literature or to understand the creativity of language play. Tall tales, myths, and legends can be used at any grade level because readers bring different levels of sophistication to their responses.

Literature study is often organized by genre. Our university, for example, offers courses in the short story, drama, novels, and poetry. Or the literature is organized by historical periods and geographical locations, such as British literature before the 18th Century or American literature after WWII. We strongly believe that if we want to interest secondary students in literature we should not use these divisions. Students have little interest in literary periods, and this approach relies heavily on the "teacher" knowledge discussed in the previous chapter. Literature tied to a unit in social studies or history is certainly appropriate; however, historical facts become more "real" to students when they understand them through the feelings and thoughts of people who lived at that particular time. But teaching John Dryden because he wrote before Oliver Goldsmith and after John Donne does not turn students on to reading. Providing literature by genre is just as troublesome. Rarely in the real world do we read only poetry for several weeks. The same is true for any genre. We mix forms, styles, and periods, and we believe the same should be true in the classroom.

Jodi Resch, an English education student, illustrates the richness possible when a unit includes several genres. She wrote a unit on Mexican culture intended for 12th-grade students.

Exploring an Instructional Unit

Week One

The unit begins with a short story, "Un Drama de Familia" by Heriberto Frias. The theme is that although the family has no money, they still have each other—the most important thing in the world to them. The students write responses as they read (level 1 writing) and also jot down any vocabulary words they have difficulty with. Students meet in small discussion groups to exchange views on the story then write an in-class essay on the choice Antonia made and her reasons behind it. During the week students read two poems: "The Men of Dawn" by Efrain Hueta and "Humbly" by Ramon Lopez Velarde. Both poems are about labor on a ranch. Students write their own poem on a cultural aspect of Mexico (level 2 writing).

Week Two

Jodi shows the students slides and crafts from her travels to Mexico. They discuss the environment, people, and activities shown on the slides. Students follow up with a one-page paper of a description of a Mexican setting (level 2 writing). Next students read a poem by Jaime Sabines, "la Casa del Dia." Students write a response to the poem (level 1). She assigns the story "Rosamunda" by Carmen Laforet, followed by nonfiction material from *Mexico: Civilizaciones y Culturas* by Luis Leal. After discussion of the readings, students write a short paper comparing an aspect of Mexican culture to an aspect of U.S. culture (level 2).

Week Three

Students read two poems: "Don't Talk to Him about Love" by Amado Nervo and "The Southern Cross" by Jose Juan Tablada. They compare these poems to "Rosamunda." Jodi shows a video she made in Mexico that is a collection of interviews she conducted with people from many classes and life-styles.

Week Four

Students write a level 3 research-type paper on a cultural aspect or issue in modern-day Mexico.

By including short stories, poetry, nonfiction, slides, a video, and firsthand experience, Jodi provides her students with an interesting and compelling view of Mexico.

ORGANIZING AROUND A THEME

Organizing around a theme has many advantages. First, several types of literature can be included, providing for a variety of reading levels and interests. Second, the choice of themes can include current issues, developmental stages, and selections from an anthology. In choosing a theme, teachers can keep their students' interests and ages in mind, but they also rely on their own enthusiasm for a topic, as Jodi did. A teacher's special interest in travel or sports can be the foundation for a successful unit.

The first unit a teacher designs is time-consuming and may be somewhat overwhelming, but once unit planning gets underway, it becomes easier. A large file for each unit enables teachers to add material as they find it. For instance, when teaching a unit on heroes to middle school students, a teacher might want to convey the idea that many ordinary people are heroes, and therefore collects newspaper articles that describe heroic deeds over a period of several weeks prior to teaching the unit. Then, during the unit, several current nonfiction selections can be made available to students. After the unit is finished, teachers continue to add new material and suggestions, so that the development of units is continual.

Thematic units work well in classrooms for both middle and high school for several reasons:

1. *They promote student interest.* Students are more likely to be interested in learning about "what is a hero" or "high adventure" than reading a single book title, even though that title may be included in the unit. Reading one book after another with no connection among them makes it difficult to compare books or develop serious discussions on, for example, relationships with parents. By using a variety of sources, students better understand the complexities of issues. Because units contain a wide variety of material, students are more likely to bring in suggestions and reading material for the class; in other words, they become more involved in their own learning.

2. *They integrate genre.* Choosing a variety of poems, stories, novels, plays, and nonfiction related by themes introduces forms of literature to students in a natural way. Students are not required to read a poem because it is the week to study poetry, but because the poem provides insights or other ways of looking at the theme. For example, in designing a unit titled "Who Am I?" eighth-grade teacher Liz Rehrauer included the following literature: a novel, *The Light in the Forest* by Conrad Richter; the short stories "The Moustache" and "Guess What? I Almost Kissed my Father," both by Robert Cormier, and "Raymond's Run" by Toni Cade Bambera; and several poems—"Me Myself, and I" by Eve Merriam, "The Ballad of Johnny" by May Sarton, "Sometimes" by Eve Merriam, "Speak to Me" by Calvin O'John, "Celebration" by Alonzo Lopez, "The Question" by Karla Kuskin, "Self-Pity" by D. H. Lawrence, and "Will I Remember?" by Richard J. Margolis. Rehrauer also included a list of novels for young adults that students could choose from for further reading.

Including many forms of reading materials broadens students' concept of "school learning." For example, a comic book may provide an excellent model of one type of hero to begin a discussion on the attributes of heroism. This could be the basis for comparing heroic character traits in other forms of literature. Students then can develop their own definition of heroism.

3.   *They provide for different reading levels.* Some thematic units are more appropriate for one level than another. The "Who Am I?" unit mentioned above is an excellent choice for middle school; a unit on war might be more appropriate for high school. Many themes can be used at any level, but the literature selections should always reflect the level of the students. The following list provides a few suggestions for topics that might be used in grades 6 through 12:

- What is it like to grow old?
- Fantasy
- Choices
- The American West
- Friendship
- Values
- Love
- Heroes

Because students read a wide variety of literature in thematic units, the whole class does not have to read the same material, or they may read the same material but not at the same time. If the unit includes three or four novels, the teacher devotes a class period to introducing all of the novels by explaining a little about each. All of the novels are related by theme, but the reading levels are different. For example, a unit on family relations might include *Home Before Dark* by Sue Ellen Bridgers, *Ordinary People* by Judith Guess, and *Tell Me a Riddle* by Tillie Olsen, listed in order of difficulty. Students are free to read all three novels and many do, especially the better readers, but they are required to read only the one assigned to them. It is wise to tell students during the time the books are introduced that they can read as many as they want but not to mention reading level. It is important to avoid any stigma attached to who reads which book first.

General class discussions based on issues related to the theme involve all students. Students also meet in small groups to discuss their assigned book. Group projects might be based on just one of the novels, or two, or all three. Everyone in the group will not have to read all the novels because each one can make contributions based on one book. In this way, students of varying abilities can work together. (See Box 8–3.)

Box 8–3

SELECTING THEMES

Make a list of topics you are especially interested in that could be the basis for a unit, perhaps countries and cultures similar to Jodi's unit or a hobby or interest you can share with your future students. Share your list in small groups and brainstorm literature selections appropriate to various themes.

READING LEVELS

The literature we select for students depends on many factors. The most obvious, of course, is the grade we teach, but we must also consider our students' age, interests, and developmental stage, as well as our own interests.

Reading levels are rarely considered in secondary schools. Students are handed *Hamlet;* if they can't read the text, they watch the film. We believe this practice is grossly unfair to students who have trouble reading difficult material. If we do not give them material they can read, their reading ability does not improve. Secondary school teachers must be as concerned with reading levels as elementary school teachers.

Reading levels vary greatly across a grade level. A rule of thumb in determining the span of reading levels in an "average" class is to divide the grade number in half, subtract that number to establish the low end and add that number to predict the high level. For instance, in teaching 6th grade one can expect reading levels to range from 3rd to the 9th grade. The higher the grade, the greater the differences; 12th-grade levels range from 6th grade to well beyond a college education. We often think of reading problems as a concern of elementary grade teachers only, but it is also a major cause of problems in school for older students. Secondary teachers also must be concerned, and make their classrooms a place where more students can succeed. One way to achieve this is to choose literature that is interesting but at a lower reading level. Young adult literature is a good choice.

YOUNG ADULT LITERATURE

Young adult literature deserves a solid berth in the literature programs of secondary schools. A growing number of talented authors are writing for adolescents. Writers such as Maya Angelou, Chris Crutcher, M. E. Kerr, Sue Ellen Bridgers, Cynthia Voigt, Ursula Le Guin, Robert Lipsyte, Emily Cheney Neville, Katherine Paterson, Gary Paulsen, Sandra Scoppettone, Ouida Sebestyn, and Brenda Wilkinson, to name just a few, hold their own with respected authors of adult fiction. As with literature for adult audiences, some pieces are trite or poorly written, but others receive critical acclaim. Intricate plot structure, multifaceted characterizations, interesting and various settings, symbolic interpretations, and artistry of language can all be found in young adult literature. Writing for a teenage audience is a serious undertaking for many fine writers. The results are important contributions to the study of literature in the secondary schools.

Young adult literature didn't come into its own as a genre until the 1950s. Since that time, novels for adolescents have become increasingly realistic. Young adult books cover a wide variety of topics: murder, theft, child abuse, mental illness, fatal illness, abortion, pregnancy, self-esteem, relationships, and responsibility. The protagonists are always teenagers and the stories are told from their point of view. Although the themes are as varied and universal as those in adult fiction, the stories are about the adolescent experience; it is this characteristic that defines the genre rather than a particular plot.

The study of young adult literature enhances students' understanding and appreciation of more difficult works. By including young adult literature, we can assure greater success in meeting the goals of teaching literature: to gain an understanding of themselves and others, to learn of a wider worldview, and to become lifelong readers. Specifically, we believe teaching young adult literature will achieve the following outcomes:

1. *Students learn to make critical judgments about what they read.* It is difficult for students to critically analyze the more sophisticated works, yet the skill of analyzing literature—that is, critically thinking about what they read—is important. By using young adult literature, students can more easily understand the motivation behind characters' actions. Students not only can discuss how fictional teenagers react to a situation, but they also can sense the validity of the author's perception. These books speak to experiences they know something about. As students consider cause and effect—that is, the relation between plot and characterization—they gain understanding beyond the work itself. Once students gain skill in analyzing fiction, they are better able to look critically at more difficult works.

2. *Students learn to support and explain their critical judgments.* The simple vocabulary and sentence structure in most young adult literature allows students to understand the text better. The National Assessment of Educational Progress (NAEP) 1979–80 test results showed that students have a difficult time using material from the text to document judgments they make from their reading. Even when they make appropriate judgments about the reading, they often cannot explain and defend their opinions. This inability mandates that teachers reexamine the way they teach literature and what literature they teach. In the preceding chapter, the discussion of response theory described ways to help students understand what they read. Using literature with easier vocabulary and style helps students get beyond surface elements. Archaic language often has a beauty of its own, but it can interfere with comprehension. Because young adult literature uses simpler vocabulary, it is an excellent source for teaching the difficult skills of documenting judgments because the language does not interfere.

3. *Students will gain an understanding of themselves and others.* Adolescence is a time when young people critically examine their own beliefs and values. As they grow away from dependence on their family, they are often confused by anxieties and uncertainties. The teenage fictional characters in young adult literature mirror the readers' experiences and provide helpful insights. The characters are realistically portrayed so readers relate to their concerns of physical appearance, family relationships, and sexual experiences. Teenagers feel reassured to discover through young adult literature that others have the same concerns they do, and in the process of understanding the fictional characters, they gain a better understanding of themselves. Maturity is enhanced as they learn more about themselves and others.

4. *Students learn about a wider view of life.* Young adult literature covers every historical period and country in the world. Because the teenager's point of view is central to the novels, the reader is likely to respond personally and reach a better understand-

ing of historical concepts and different cultures. The vicarious experiences broaden students' views. Young adult literature celebrates the uniqueness of individuals. The central character must often overcome obstacles and prejudices. Accepting one's own disability or relating to people with disabilities is a popular theme. Because ignorance fosters prejudice, the more knowledgeable students become, the more they will accept and understand individual differences.

5. *Students' enjoyment of reading will increase.* Because the protagonist is a teenager and the plot involves problems teenagers encounter, young adult literature provides high-interest reading. Every literature curriculum contains the objective of helping students to enjoy reading. Motivation occurs naturally when teenagers can read about situations they are knowledgeable about and interested in. Young adult literature does much to establish the habit of reading for pleasure. (See Box 8–4 for an activity on identifying themes in young adult literature.)

Box 8–4

READING YOUNG ADULT LITERATURE

Read a young adult novel published since 1990. What themes are present in the novel? What grade level would enjoy the book? Choose a theme, either one present in the book you read or one you have a particular interest in and find another young adult book with this theme.

WORLD LITERATURE

Awareness of other cultures becomes increasingly important as the world shrinks via television. Yet most secondary students know very little about cultures other than their own. Teachers need to become aware of literature that helps students develop a wider worldview. Prejudice and fear come from ignorance; literature can do much to increase awareness of other people—their hopes, their fears, their dreams. Studying world literature helps students see not only the differences among cultures, but also the similarities. And by learning about other people, we learn about ourselves and the part our culture plays in shaping an individual's life.

Including world literature in English language arts classes generally means selecting literature from Third World countries. Students and teachers know little about this body of literature, which is why we should include it. Teachers and students learning together creates a dynamic class. Contemporary Third World authors are concerned with the tension between traditional values and ways of life and the changes the new life brings to their country; their themes often involve struggles between the old and the new. Young adults understand such struggles and find they have more in common with Third World people than they may have thought. Also, much of the literature is reminiscent of early American concerns as these countries work to develop strong independent governments.

In the introduction of *Guide to World Literature,* editors Warren Carrier and Kenneth Oliver make the case for including world literature in English language arts classes.

> As we move into multi-national economic, ecological, and cultural enterprises and inter-dependencies, it becomes increasingly important for students to recognize national similarities and differences, but above all to recognize our common bond, our common lot. A study of world literature contributes much to an appreciation and understanding of the heritage we share. (3)

Teaching world literature brings a special set of concerns. We rely on the same practices as we do in teaching any literature: encouraging responses, valuing students' opinions, helping students to think beyond the obvious. But how do we select the literature and organize it for teaching? Teachers offer a variety of suggestions.

Thematic Approach

Carrier and Oliver believe the thematic approach is the best way to teach world literature. The thematic approach works for all literature and is especially important when reading about other cultures. When studying one country's literature apart from other cultures, we might emphasize differences between them. Although great differences may exist, we want students to realize they have more in common than may be apparent. Carrier and Oliver suggest themes of love, injustice, conflict, separation, and war, among others (3). They give as an example the theme of time. In *The Great Gatsby* by F. Scott Fitzgerald, Gatsby tries to recapture time. In a Japanese novel *The Sound of the Mountain* by Yasunari Kawabata, the hero is very aware of the passing of time. The transience of time is also a theme in *My Mother's House* by Colette (French), *The Tale of Genji* by Murasaki (Japanese), and *Lucy Gayheart* by Willa Cather (American) (4). Selections can come from a variety of countries and be grouped around a common theme.

Studying One Culture

A teacher may want to focus a unit on one particular culture if the area of study is largely unknown to students. An intense study of the literature is an excellent way to acquaint them with that culture. Alan Olds, a high school teacher in Colorado, explains in a recent article that he taught Chinese literature to his students to help them understand China's rich heritage. To understand our own culture, we need to understand ideas and traditions from other voices (21).

> I constantly remind my students (and myself) that we are visitors, not tourists, when we read literature from other cultures. We try to prepare for our visit, so that we do not stumble about in an unfamiliar setting. We are not reading these writers to check them off our list of books, the way a tourist checks off destinations without really tarrying to see beyond the surface attractions and rushes on to see the next stop. Instead,

we intend to arrive informed and sensitive to a new culture, open to its wonders. We want to stay long enough to see beyond the clichés. If we are lucky, our visit will broaden our sense of what it means to be human. (21)

Olds wants his students to be able to read Chinese literature with an Eastern viewpoint. The article contains a rich variety of sources and a description of how he teaches the unit.

In writing about teaching South African literature, Robert Mossman, a high school teacher in Arizona, warns of the danger of choosing only one representative novel from a culture.

> A study of South African literature in an American classroom, to be valid and legitimate, cannot consist of merely one work and be successful. By the very fact of the polarized nature of the apartheid system and the literary responses to it, students must encounter and examine works which represent viewpoints from different racial perspectives. Reading only one work may do a disservice because it inevitably provides only one perspective. The richness and complexity of South Africa's literature deserves better (41).

Mossman explains the problems occurring when *Cry, the Beloved Country* is the only South African literature taught in English classes. Students read and learn only one perspective which, particularly in South Africa, creates a false impression. "If *Cry, the Beloved Country* must be taught in the curriculum, then it should be taught in conjunction with *Mine Boy* by Peter Abrahams" (42). Mossman suggests six other pairings of South African literature that offer different perspectives.

Resources for World Literature

An excellent resource for selecting African literature is *Teaching African Literature* by Elizabeth Gunner. Her handbook contains teaching suggestions, information about the novels and authors, and an extensive annotated bibliography of books, films, and recorded sound. In the introduction, Gunner emphasizes the importance of including African literature in the curriculum. "Texts by African writers often provide an alternative view of history, or illuminate an aspect of history and individual experience previously not available to a particular pupil or group of pupils" (v). In addition to the teaching ideas for individual novels, Gunner describes thematic units that include novels, poetry, and films. For teachers not well acquainted with African literature for secondary students, this book is invaluable.

Another book in the same series is *A Handbook for Teaching Caribbean Literature* by David Dabydeen. The format is similar to Gunner's and provides information about the authors and literature as well as teaching ideas. Dabydeen describes 12 units, each dealing with a particular novel or a set of poems. He includes related readings and audiovisual resources.

LITERATURE BY WOMEN

Gender imbalance in literature choices for student reading continues in spite of numerous articles, reports, and editorials arguing for a change. One reason for the lack of change is that teachers often do not challenge the lists of required reading and do not reexamine literature choices; they teach what has always been taught. A second reason is that the literature canon is perpetuated by agencies that carry a voice of authority. Patricia Lake, a high school teacher, reports that the Advanced Placement Course Description published by the Educational Testing Service includes few women authors. Lake found that, "According to the guide book, only fourteen women (versus eighty men) have written prose of sufficient merit to warrant its study" (36). ETS is a powerful influence on literature selections for advanced placement English classes. Lake asks,

> Why then is there continued propagation of such severe gender imbalance in the reading lists provided by ETS? High-school literature courses should be broadening students' perspectives, not directing them into predetermined stereotypical channels which, by their exclusionary nature, actually prevent students from reading about life in other than traditional contexts. (36)

Often lists of books taught in secondary schools are interpreted as a list of what *should* be taught. Teachers need to critically examine such lists because important authors are ignored and the lists give an erroneous message to young people. Lake explains,

> If we do not work for a greater gender balance in teaching literature, we present a distorted picture of our literary heritage and the society which spawned it. We do a wonderful job of showing that indeed men did—and do—receive most of the recognition, but we also suggest that there were no women doing anything of scholarly or literary merit. (37)

Another danger for the young women in our classes is that, when they read male authors almost exclusively, they develop a male perspective of understanding the women characters. They have no choice when both the authors and the critics are male. The readings need to be balanced to give young women a better sense of the value of their own experiences. Literature by women is as rich and varied as literature by men. We owe it to our students (and ourselves) to provide a gender-balanced literature curriculum. (See Box 8–5.)

The National Council of Teachers of English publishes a pamphlet "Guidelines for a Gender-Balanced Curriculum in English, Grades 7–12." It suggests how a teacher can create a gender-balanced curriculum and includes a list of literature selections. The pamphlet is free upon request and may be copied without permission. Ask for #19654 from NCTE, Order Dept., 1111 Kenyon Road, Urbana, IL 61801.

Box 8–5

LITERATURE BY WOMEN

Male authors in any culture are published and recognized before female authors. Why is this the case? During your middle and high school years, what works by women authors did you read? Which ones would you teach?

MINORITY LITERATURE

The population of the United States is shifting from a predominately white culture to one with an increasing number of people of color. Nearly one out of every three Americans is from a non-English-speaking home. The Hispanic population is the fastest growing and is around 17 percent of the total population. African Americans comprise 16 percent. Mary Sasse, a high school English teacher, stresses the importance of teachers gaining an understanding of the term *ethnic*.

> With those understandings comes an acceptance of the universality of human experience, which teachers can use as a bridge between themselves and other ethnic peoples and as a recognition of the richness and diversity of American ethnic literature. (171)

She provides three criteria for selecting minority literature:

1. Selections should be by minority authors, not just *about* minority people; otherwise, stereotyping can be a problem.
2. Selections must represent the total dynamic nature of an ethnic group. Historical accounts should be balanced with contemporary ones. Both urban and rural experiences need to be represented.
3. Selections should represent a broad spectrum of experiences to avoid romanticizing or stereotyping (170-171).

Teaching minority literature is vital if we are serious about reaching all of our students. Roseann Duenas Gonzalez, a teacher at the University of Arizona, explains that classrooms have changed dramatically in the past 10 years. Our students come from widely diverse backgrounds, both culturally and linguistically, and "are fast becoming a significant proportion of the school-age population" (16). We are not meeting the needs of these children. If these culturally and linguistically different children do not stay in school and receive an adequate education, "our society incrementally loses the productive capability of an entire generation" (16). Gonzalez discusses the problems teachers have in teaching minority literature and presents recommendations. Minority literature should not be taught as "special," but should be discussed in terms of the same criteria as any other literature: style, honesty, and language. To fail to do so sends a message to students that this literature is inferior and will not stand up to critical analysis (19).

It is difficult to select literature with which we are unfamiliar. The following resources provide annotated bibliographies for selecting appropriate literature.

- *Booklist,* an American Library Association publication
- *Bulletin of the Center for Children's Books*
- *The English Journal,* a National Council of Teachers of English publication for secondary school teachers
- *The Horn Book Magazine*
- *Interracial Books for Children Bulletin*
- *Journal of Reading*
- *Media and Methods*
- *School of Library Journal*
- *Wilson Library Journal*

Searching for appropriate books does take time, but the time is well spent and the books are interesting. Not taking the time ensures that teachers will continue to use the same books that have been used for the last 25 years with no changes. Arthur N. Applebee, Director of the Center for the Learning and Teaching of Literature, did a study in 1989 to determine what book-length works were most commonly taught at secondary schools. The 10 most commonly taught books included few by women and minority authors, and classics dominated the lists. While we should continue to teach classics, we need to make room in the curriculum for literature that all students can identify with and appreciate.

Native American Literature

A study of Native Americans is an essential part of our American past and does much to enrich our curriculum. Because of the Native Americans' oral traditions, students learn a great deal about the nature of language; the songs and chants provide beauty and meaning, helping students to understand the importance of lyrical quality. The themes carried through Native American literature are of special interest and importance to adolescents: developing self-identity, establishing values, understanding a relationship with nature, making decisions that are often at odds with the majority.

Not long ago, Native Americans were portrayed in negative or outdated stereotypes, which may persist in many students' minds. To discover what knowledge students have of Native Americans, a teacher can ask them to write everything that comes to mind when they think of Native Americans. The results are usually shocking, from comments that are ludicrous, such as they live in tents and wear feathers all the time, to negative and cruel, such as they are lazy and drunkards. The contrast between such misinformation and actual Native American beliefs and behavior is startling. Students have much to learn from Native Americans: the spiritual nature of the universe, respect for the land, importance of ritual and ceremony, oneness with nature. Using literature by Native Americans, we can dispel erroneous impressions and replace them with understanding, knowledge, and empathy.

Excellent literature written by Native Americans is not difficult to find. Particularly appropriate books for middle and high school students include *The Education of Little Tree* (nonfiction) by Forrest Carver, *Tracks* by Louise Erdrich, *The Indian Lawyer* by James Welch, all of Tony Hillerman's books, and *Night Flying Woman: An Ojibway Narrative* by Ignatia Broker.

Hispanic Literature

Hispanic literature is poorly represented in anthologies, more so than other minority literature. For example, a 1989 anthology of American literature published by a major company contained over 1,000 entries but had no literature about the Hispanic experience in the United States. What message does this give to our Hispanic students? If a particular literature is not included in a new anthology, it must not be important. Two teachers, Patricia Ann Romero and Don Zancanella, explain why they include Hispanic literature in their program:

> We believe that outside the traditional American canon lie works by less familiar names—classics of the future, we would argue—demonstrating to our students that the American story becomes much richer when we hear it told in all its voices. For example, alongside the traditional American anthology pieces, we place the works of contemporary Hispanic writers. (25)

Romero and Zancanella believe it is important for students "to read literature that validates their own experience and know that authors and artists of substance and value have come from their culture" (29). Teachers who are fortunate enough to have cultures outside the mainstream represented in their classrooms can enrich the learning of not only these students but all their students by including authors from the various cultures.

African American Literature

Many high school graduates are familiar with African American male writers, such as Richard Wright, Ralph Ellison, and Langston Hughes. In recent years, African American women writers have been included in college literature classes but are not likely to appear at the high school level. There are, however, many wonderful selections to choose from, such as *Their Eyes Are Watching God* by Zora Neale Hurston. The story centers on a young woman who, in spite of immense difficulties, develops a strong sense of self, an ideal topic for adolescents. In addition to a good story, the book has an incredible lyrical quality, and Hurston's use of figurative language stays with a reader long after the book is finished. Other outstanding African American authors include Maya Angelou, Virginia Hamilton, Alice Walker, Mildred Taylor, Terry McMillan, J. California Cooper, Nikki Giovanni, and Toni Morrison. Teachers need to include both male and female writers from different literary genres and sources.

Asian American Literature

The term *Asian Americans* includes Chinese, Japanese, Filipino, and Korean Americans, as well as immigrants from Laos, Cambodia, Vietnam, and Thailand. Ogle Duff and Helen Tongchinsub describe the thematic concerns of modern Asian American writers as love, personal liberty, injustice, and inner struggles. However, when Asian Americans were first published, their writing tended to be nonthreatening, nonassertive, and self-negating because otherwise their work would not have been accepted. An example of this type of writing is Jade Snow Wong's *Fifth Chinese Daughter,* published in 1950. Although the story denigrates certain Asian values, it was often included in secondary literature anthologies. Although some contemporary Asian American literary critics are critical of the story, others like it (222). In choosing literature, teachers need to look for accurate portrayals of other cultures. A balanced representation of positive and negative characters struggling with contemporary issues is important in literature selection to assure a honest view and to avoid stereotyping (238).

When selecting Asian American literature, teachers have many choices. Ellen Greenblatt in *Many Voices* suggests combining the reading of *Joy Luck Club* by Amy Tan with the more difficult *The Woman Warrior* by Maxine Hong Kingston. *The House of the Spirits* by Isabel Allende, a Chilean writer, could also be a companion reading with *Joy Luck Club*. Another suitable book by Tan is *The Kitchen God's Wife*. *The Sound of the Waves* by Yukio Mishima, a book about forbidden love, could be paired with *Romeo and Juliet*. Greenblatt highly recommends *A Boat to Nowhere* by Maureen Crane Wartski, a novel of the boat people's desperate flight from Vietnam (7).

Readers and Literature

We are not suggesting that traditional literature from the white male Protestant perspective be excluded. But to accurately present the American experience, the literary canon needs to be redefined and expanded to include American minority authors. At one time, the difficulty of finding literature by minorities, women, and Third World authors created a serious problem for teachers. Now, however, many readily available bibliographies and articles provide annotations of titles; a list of resources appears at the end of this chapter.

Should we teach literature from the cultures represented in our classrooms? Regardless of the cultural makeup of our class, should we teach literature from other cultures? The answer to both questions is yes. We live in a pluralistic society, and our literature selections need to help our students better understand and appreciate the multiple cultures in the United States and the world. Students may have difficulty understanding references and idioms from cultures other than their own. Even though the same can be said for Chaucer, teachers believe that the value of helping students understand *The Canterbury Tales* far outweighs any difficulties students have with its language. That belief should transfer to teaching a wider spectrum of literature than the canon.

Sharon McElmeel, a library media specialist, agrees: "*All* children should be exposed to a diversity of cultures and heritages—that is how they grow, become tolerant of differences, and learn to respect others and their ideas" (50). McElmeel argues that teachers and librarians must provide up-to-date multicultural books for students. Otherwise the images students remember from their reading too often depict Native Americans as wearing feathers and face paint, African Americans as making their mark only by playing sports, and all Hispanics as migrant workers. We must not limit our cultural awareness by using only folktales and ignoring modern-day, realistic images. We need to "show the faces of the real America" (50).

When we think of teaching multicultural literature, we must realize that "individuals do not belong to single, clearly identifiable cultures" (Fishman 75). Each of us represents several cultures, and at different times we represent different cultures. For example, a student might be identified at one time by her age and background, another time by her race, or another time by her occupation or political beliefs—all different cultures overlapping and combining (75). No one person can represent a single cultural group, and no one literature selection "effectively represents any single cultural group" (79).

RECOMMENDED BOOKS BY OR ABOUT MINORITIES

What follows are personal choices or those recommended by other English teachers. (Special thanks to the Cooperative Children's Book Center, University of Wisconsin-Madison.) The list is in no way comprehensive but is perhaps a starting point for those not familiar with minority literature.

NATIVE AMERICAN LITERATURE
When the Legends Die by Hal Borland
Anpao: An American Odyssey by Jamake Highwater
Ceremony by Leslie Silko
The Man to Send Rain Clouds: Contemporary Stories by American Indians edited by
    Kenneth Rosen
House Made of Dawn by N. Scott Momaday
I Heard the Owl Call My Name by Margaret Craven
Brothers of the Heart: A Story of the Old Northwest, 1837–1838 by Joan W. Blos

AFRICAN AMERICAN LITERATURE
I Know Why the Caged Bird Sings by Maya Angelou
The Women of Brewster Place by Gloria Naylor
In Search of Our Mothers' Gardens by Alice Walker
Blue Tights by Rita Williams-Garcia
Trouble's Child by Mildred Pitts Walter
Marked by Fire by Joyce Carol Thomas
Let the Circle be Unbroken by Mildred D. Taylor
Scorpions by Walter Dean Myers
Out From This Place by Joyce Hansen

Sweet Whispers, Brother Rush by Virginia Hamilton
Rainbow Jordan by Alice Childress
Cotton Candy on a Rainy Day (poems) by Nikki Giovanni

CHICANO LITERATURE

Bless Me, Ultima by Rudolfo Anaya
The Road to Tamazunchale by Ron Arias
The Day the Cisco Kid Shot John Wayne by Nash Candelaria
The Last of the Menu Girls by Denise Chavez
The House on Mango Street by Sandra Cisneros
Across the Great River by Irene Beltran Hernandez
Schoolland by Max Martinez
The Iguana Killer: Twelve Stories of the Heart by Alberto Alvaro Rios
Kodachromes in Rhyme by Ernest Galarza
The Crossing by Gary Paulsen
Black Hair (poetry) by Gary Soto
Nuyorican Poetry: An Anthology of Puerto Rican Words and Feelings edited by
    Miguel Algarin and Miguel Pinero
Chicano Voices, edited by Carlota Cardenas De Dwyer

ASIAN AMERICAN

Many of these selections are recommended by Duff and Tongchinsub.

Tule Lake by Edward Miyakawa
Woman from Hiroshima by Toshio Mori
Citizen 13660 by Mine Okubo
Nisei Daughter by Monica Sone
Homebase by Shawn Hsu Wong
Child of the Owl and *Dragonwings* by Laurence Yep
Woman Warrior: Memoirs of a Girlhood Among Ghosts by Maxine Hong Kingston
The Joy Luck Club by Amy Tan
Asian American Authors, an anthology edited by Kai-Yu Hsu and Helen Palubinskas
Aiieeee! an anthology of Asian American writers edited by Frank Chin, et al.

OTHER SELECTIONS

Waiting for the Rain: A Novel of South Africa by Sheila Gordon
Somehow Tenderness Survives: Stories of Southern Africa, selected by Hazel
    Rochman
A Thief in the Village, and Other Stories by James Berry (Jamaican)
The Honorable Prison by Lyll Becerra de Jenkins (South American)
The Return by Sonia Levitin (Ethiopian)
Rebels of the Heavenly Kingdom by Katherine Paterson (19th century China)
So Far From the Bamboo Grove by Yoko Kawashima Watkins (Japanese)

The Third Women, edited by Dexter Fisher includes selections of Native America, Chicano, and Asian American literature

Invented Lives: Narratives of Black Women, edited by Mary Helen Washington

Breaking Ice: An Anthology of Contemporary African-American Fiction, edited by Terry McMillan

Jews Without Money by Michael Gold

Call It Sleep by Henry Roth (Jewish)

Bronx Primate: Portraits in a Childhood by Kate Simon (Jewish)

BOX 8–6

SELECTING LITERATURE FROM A VARIETY OF CULTURES

Select several books representing a variety of cultures that were published in the last two or three years. Decide what grade levels they are appropriate for. Share your findings with the class.

PUTTING IT ALL TOGETHER

Literature selections are appropriate in several different thematic units depending on what aspect or theme a teacher wants to emphasize. For instance, *Summer of My German Soldier* could be used in a unit on family relationships, war, or on the need for acceptance. The groupings of literature that follow are examples of how some teachers combine their selections.

Mary Beth Koehler, an English teacher, created a unit on self-expression using Native American resources. Her rationale for the unit is based on her knowledge that the United States is a country of diversity. In any class in her school district, a teacher might have students representing three types of Asian cultures; African Americans from inner cities and blacks from other countries, such as Nigeria; and Native Americans students from as many as five different tribes as well as Caucasian students. Teaching to single Anglo-American background makes no sense. Mary Beth designed her unit using culturally specific literature and resources. She explains that using this approach helps students to understand the experience and concerns of a culture different from their own and learn how to express their own individuality through the use of what's called "minority or ethnic" literature (2). Mary Beth's categories are music, dance, poetry, storytelling, and novels in the unit.

 The groupings include novels at different reading levels, novels by minority authors, and a balance of male and female writers. Many selections are included to highlight the variety of literature available to teachers. The final chapter in this text describes detailed units with lesson plans and specific teaching ideas relating listening, speaking, writing, reading, and creative dramatics for a comprehensive view of how the units work.

Selections for a Unit on Family Relationships

NOVELS

Home Before Dark by Sue Ellen Bridgers
Summer of My German Soldier by Bette Greene
Everywhere by Bruce Brooks
The Disappearance by Rosa Guy
Ordinary People by Judith Guest
Family Reunion by Caroline Cooney
A Fine Time to Leave Me by Terry Pringle
Unlived Affections by George Shannon
Thief of Dreams by John Yount
IOU'S by Quida Sebestyen
Sarah, Plain and Tall by Patricia MacLachlan
But in the Fall I'm Leaving by Ann Rinaldi
Cold Sassy Tree by Olive Ann Burns

POETRY

"My Papa's Waltz" by Theodore Roethke
"Those Winter Sundays" by Robert Hayden
"Blaming Sons" by T'ao Ch'ien
"Fifty-Fifty" by Carl Sandburg

Selections for Coming of Age or Developing a Sense of Self

STORIES

"Train Whistle Guitar" by Albert Murray
"The Tree in the Meadow" by Philippa Pearce
"Thank You, Ma'am" by Langston Hughes

NOVELS

Anywhere Else but Here by Bruce Clement
The Catcher in the Rye by J. D. Salinger
Come Sing, Jimmy Jo by Katherine Paterson
Far From Shore by Kevin Major
In Summer Light by Zibby Oneal
The Moves Make the Man by Bruce Brooks
Notes for Another Life by Sue Ellen Bridgers
Long Time Between Kisses by Sandra Scoppettone
I Will Call It Georgie's Blues by Suzanne Newton
A Place to Come Back To by Nancy Bond
A Day No Pigs Would Die by Robert Newton Peck

Lily and the Lost Boy by Paula Fox
Spanish Hoof by Robert Newton Peck
The Crossing by Gary Paulsen
To Myself by Galila Ron-Fender
Permanent Connections by Sue Ellen Bridgers
The Moonlight Man by Paula Fox
A Solitary Blue by Cynthia Voigt
The Birds of Summer by Zilpha Keatley Snyder
My Antonia by Willa Cather
A Portrait of the Artist as a Young Man by James Joyce
Member of the Wedding by Harper Lee

POETRY
"Well Water" by Randall Jarrell
"Curiosity" by Alastair Reid
"Dreams" by Langston Hughes

Selections for Heroes or Courage

NOVELS
Chernowitz! by Fran Arrick
Eyes of Darkness by Jamake Highwater
Ganesh by Malcolm J. Bosse
The Autobiography of Miss Jane Pittman by Ernest Gaines
If Beale Street Could Talk by James Baldwin
M.C. Higgins, The Great by Virginia Hamilton

POETRY
"They Tell Me" by Yevgeny Yevtushenko
"Wild Horses" by Elder Olson
"Icarus" by Edward Field

Selections for a Unit Focusing on Women and Women Writers

These selections are provided by Dennis Crowe, a high school teacher.

Anne Bradstreet, selected poetry
Nathaniel Hawthorne, *The Scarlet Letter*
William Luce, *The Belle of Amherst*
Emily Dickinson, selected poems and letters
Virginia Woolf, *A Room of One's Own*
Tillie Olsen, "Silences in Literature"
Beryl Markham, *The Splendid Outcast* or *West with the Night*
Marianne Moore, selected poetry

Amy Lowell, selected poetry
Gwendolyn Brooks, selected poetry
Zora Neale Hurston, *Their Eyes Were Watching God*
Maya Angelou, *I Know Why the Caged Bird Sings*
Annie Dillard, *Pilgrim at Tinker Creek*
Judith Freeman, *The Chinchilla Farm*
Bobbi Ann Mason, *In Country*
Louise Erdrich/Michael Dorris, *Crown of Columbus*
Barbara Kingsolver, *Animal Dreams*

MEDIA IN THE ENGLISH CLASSROOM

Movies

Young adults like to go to the movies; movie studios make more money from teenagers than any other segment of the population. Harold Foster, a high school English teacher, believes that ignoring movies in the English classroom prevents us from helping students to become aware of how movies influence them (86). Objectives for teaching about movies are similar to those involving advertising. We want students to become more objective and to understand how they are influenced. Not all advertising is bad, nor all movies poor, but teachers must help students learn to tell which are and which are not. Foster suggests the following goals: (86)

1. Transform students into discriminating viewers who can distinguish good from bad, exploitation from communication.
2. Sensitize students so they perceive how these films are designed to influence and manipulate them.
3. Educate students to understand films visually and thematically, so they can analyze and critique films they see.
4. Develop critical awareness so students will occasionally pass up the worst of these films and stay home and read a book.

To achieve these goals, we need to discuss current films in the classroom and use videos in the literature units. Visual literature can be powerful; we and our students benefit from this added dimension.

Television

Television is a major influence in our lives, yet rarely are TV shows discussed in English class unless we tape and show something like *The Nature of English*. Many of the same goals for movies apply to TV. We want students to become more objective observers and to make critical judgments. Television is a showcase of American life and an excellent vehicle for making students aware of stereotypes. Teachers can move them away from passive viewing and into critical analysis.

To accomplish these goals, students choose an area to focus on and then write questions to guide their viewing. For instance, begin a class discussion of favorite or not so favorite TV shows. Ask why students like or dislike a show. Conversation will be lively, with strong opinions, and students will interrupt each other frequently. Students then choose a series, type of show, or commercials shown during particular shows. Individually they write three of four questions that will guide their viewing: Are there consistent stereotypes? Are stereotypes more apt to be of minorities or women? What image is portrayed of children, parents, and their relationships? What audience is the show or commercial geared to? Do the commercials and shows complement each other? Are sport announcers biased, and if so, in what way? In small groups, students share questions and help each other refine the questions and generate new ones.

To be effective critics, students must keep track of what they view. Taking notes while watching is almost impossible, but students can write notes at every commercial break. And when they get used to keeping a pen and paper handy, they become better at recording dialogue and action. Students see things they never saw before and become much more objective.

We owe it to our students to help them become more critical viewers, which leads to their becoming better critical thinkers. Discussing whether violence is essential for the show, whether humor is appropriate, and whether people are portrayed honestly also helps students grow confident that they have something important to say. Sometimes the confidence transfers to discussing similar elements in literature, but even if that doesn't happen, they gain knowledge and objectivity.

Videos

Because they are so easily obtainable and because their visual aspect appeals to students, videos are an important addition to the study of literature. Videos make some literature selections accessible in ways that a book cannot. A common way to use a video is to have students read a novel or play and then see the video; however, teachers use videos in class in other ways as well.

1. Instead of showing the video of the book students read, select a different title, but one on the same theme. Harold Foster, a high school English teacher, suggests that for a thematic unit on "Coming of Age" *Sixteen Candles* is a good choice. Also, *The Alfred G. Graebner Memorial High School Handbook of Rules and Regulations* fits in very well, describing with humor what life as a high school freshman is like (87). Many videos on the popular theme of growing up are available and can be ordered from the school's catalogue. Teachers do need to plan ahead because it takes several weeks for the films to arrive, and popular ones are booked up early. We found it best to order the films for the following year in the spring.

2. Show a video different from the novels read, but select one based on a novel that is too difficult for all or most of the students. Seeing the film first does not detract from their enjoyment of reading the novel later. In fact, students report

they liked and understood the novel better because they saw the film first. Our students do not always need to read the book. We can greatly broaden their literary experience by showing the film only and discussing it in class.

3. The visual interpretation of literature is always different from the printed form, and helping students learn how to analyze these differences deepens their understanding of interpretations. "The Revolt of Mother," based on a short story of the same title by Mary E. Wilkins, is an appropriate choice for secondary students. Observing expression and actions brings a different dimension. These questions might be posed:
   • Where do the two versions differ?
   • Is the film true to what students believe the author presented?
   • Why are changes made?
   • If you made a film based on this or another story, how would you film it?
   • How do music, shadows, and light affect the meaning?
   • In what ways does camera angle make a difference?

   An offshoot of this activity is to have students choose well-known TV or movie actors for the characters in a literature selection and explain why they made the particular choices. Characterizations often become clearer when they think about matching a fictional character with an actor.

4. Classic films like *Stagecoach, The African Queen, Wizard of Oz,* and *Gone with the Wind* are excellent for analyzing the use of prototypes, directing techniques, and story line. A unit on a film or films is appropriate in an English class. Incidentally, comparing the novel *The Wizard of Oz* to the film version is interesting because the two are quite different; yet the intended audience for both is children.

CENSORSHIP

One cannot think about literature selections without considering censorship. The basic premise in censorship cases is that reading certain material results in a change of values, beliefs, and/or behavior. For years, researchers have been trying to prove or disprove the connection between books (or television) and behavior. If children see or read violent actions, will they then be more apt to perform violent acts? No clear conclusions either way emerged from the studies.

For parents, school boards, and teachers who believe books should be censored, the results of such studies make no difference. If they believe a book is harmful, teachers must deal with that belief. Although a few teachers around the country refuse to teach certain books or want them removed from library shelves, teachers on the whole are in favor of having students read the books that continue to be the most common targets in censorship cases. A look at the books most often censored will explain why. Lee Burress, who has long been involved in censorship issues, lists the 30 most frequently attacked books since 1965, according to six surveys: (180–181):

- *The Adventures of Huckleberry Finn*
- *The Diary of a Young Girl* (Anne Frank)
- *Black Like Me*
- *Brave New World*
- *The Catcher in the Rye*
- *Deliverance*
- *The Electric Kool-Aid Acid Test*
- *A Farewell to Arms*
- *Go Ask Alice*
- *The Good Earth*
- *The Grapes of Wrath*
- *A Hero Ain't Nothin' But a Sandwich*
- *If Beal Street Could Talk*
- *I Know Why the Caged Bird Sings*
- *Johnny Got His Gun*
- *The Learning Tree*
- *Lord of the Flies*
- *Love Story*
- *Manchild in the Promised Land*
- *My Darling, My Hamburger*
- *Nineteen Eighty-Four*
- *Of Mice and Men*
- *One Day in the Life of Ivan Denisovich*
- *One Flew Over the Cuckoo's Nest*
- *Ordinary People*
- *Our Bodies, Ourselves*
- *The Scarlet Letter*
- *Slaughterhouse-Five*
- *To Kill a Mockingbird*

Burress compiled a list of the reasons people objected to each book. Sex and obscene language were the most common complaints, but people also objected to references to God, comments they perceived as being un-American or Communist propaganda, references to homosexuality, and depressing story lines. It is important to note that 40 percent of the books most often attacked are written by women and minorities. A hidden agenda of keeping works of these authors out of the schools is certainly a possibility.

The American Library Association (ALA) points out that banning books just makes teenagers want to read them. When a book is challenged, the number of students reading it goes up because, as one teenager explained, they are at the age when they want to be independent and do not want adults telling them what they can't read. The ALA publishes a list of books banned or challenged each year and the reasons cited. An abbreviated list was published in the newspaper.

- *A Thousand Acres* by Jane Smiley. Reason cited: No literary value.
- *The Little Mermaid* by Hans Christian Andersen. Reason cited: Illustrations showed bare-breasted mermaids and was pornographic and satanic.
- *Little House on the Prairie* by Laura Ingalls Wilder. Reason cited: Some statements derogatory to Native Americans.
- *Complete Fairy Tales of The Brothers Grimm* by Jacob and Wilhelm Grimm. Reason cited: Excessive violence, negative portrayals of females and Jews.
- *The Chocolate War* by Robert Cormier. Reason cited: Themes of rape, masturbation, violence, and degrading treatment of women.
- *I Know Why the Caged Bird Sings* by Maya Angelou. Reason cited: Pornographic, encourages premarital sex and homosexuality.
- *Bridge to Terabithia* by Katherine Paterson. Reason cited: Offensive language.
- *The Autobiography of Miss Jane Pittman* by Ernest Gaines. Reason cited: Racial slurs.
- *Private Parts* by Howard Stern. Reason cited: Obscene.
- *The Adventures of Huckleberry Finn* by Mark Twain. Reason cited: Racial slurs and bad grammar. ("Book Bans" 3A)

From the reasons cited one can see that many different viewpoints are reflected. Some of the books clearly reflect the common prejudices of the time in which they were written, and students need to understand that, but banning the book prevents any discussions that would correct misconceptions.

Teachers' best defense against censorship is to know why they are teaching a particular book. Sometimes teachers think they can avoid trouble for themselves by not teaching a book someone might object to. But self-censoring is wrong because it is driven by fear and emotional response. Our reasons for teaching a book must come from our knowledge of literature, our desire to teach students about the diversity of America's culture through a multitude of voices, our ability to help our students learn about other ways of life, and a wider worldview. Of course, teachers make choices based on personal preferences as well; we can't teach everything. However, choices should not be based on fear but on meeting our objectives for teaching literature.

Parents may initially question a literature choice but, after hearing the reasons for teaching it, be satisfied. Teachers can always select an alternative book for a student as long as it is on the same theme. Teaching thematic units with two or three selections makes this an easy solution. An important point in the censorship issue is that parents do have a right to influence what their children read; however, they do not have the right to decide what other children read. Teachers must be prepared to provide options.

Elizabeth Noll, a former English teacher, is concerned with the ripple effect of censorship cases that compel teachers to self-censor the choices they make when selecting literature for their students (59). School censorship is on the rise and is not limited to a geographic region or a particular grade level or instructional area; therefore, every teacher is affected by censorship. Some teachers avoid the problem by offering students a choice of reading material. When the curriculum is based on units of study, the choices, although broad in scope, can still be on the same theme. Noll reports that one teacher tells her students when she assigns a book that may cause a problem. She tells the students that if they or their parents object to any of the material, she will substitute something else that fits into the unit (62). Many teachers have a lengthy list of related materials and allow students to freely select what they want to read.

Although censorship usually comes from outside the school, Dorothea Hunter and Winifred Madsen, both librarians, experienced censorship pressure from within their school when a library supervisor ordered eight titles to be removed from the school library. The district had established procedures for examining books that were called into question, but this 20-year-old policy was ignored. Hunter lost her job, and the entire book selection committee was dismissed. After two years of effort, the books were finally reinstated. Hunter and Madsen received help from People for the American Way and the American Civil Liberties Union. "Both organizations fight for intellectual freedom and can give you crucial outside support, including legal assistance" (140).

Susan B. Neuman, a teacher at Eastern Connecticut State University, explains:

> Censorship is negative because it eliminates choice and discourages reading. It does not encourage or create opportunities for positive reading experiences. Further education, rather than censorship, can lead to an informed citizenry. That is the goal educators must emphasize. (49)

Because censorship problems occur all over the United States in every school district, all teachers are affected. We do not have to fight censorship problems alone, however. State departments of education, universities, the National Council of Teachers of English, and the Office for Intellectual Freedom of the American Library Association can provide assistance.

The National Council of Teachers of English passed a resolution in 1981 that reaffirms the students' right of access to a wide range of books and other learning materials under the guidance of qualified teachers and librarians. To help teachers resist censorship, Geneva T. Van Horne wrote "Strategies for Action" for the NCTE publication *SLATE*.

Strategies for Action

I. Develop and promote, on a regular basis, good public relations and communication with community groups and parents about the school's philosophy and goals, the English language arts educational objectives, the curricula, and classroom and library media programs.

II. Distribute the NCTE booklet, *The Students' Right to Read,* to all faculty, school board members, administrators, and community and parent groups.

III. Prepare, and have adopted by the school board, a written selection policy for all media, print, and audiovisuals. Include a well-defined procedure for handling challenged materials. Coverage should include:

A. Philosophy and goals of the school system

B. Goals and objectives of the instructional program

    C. Responsibility for selection of instructional materials

    D. Criteria for selection of instructional materials

    E. Standard professional and current selection tools to be consulted (e.g., Elementary School Library Collection, W. H. Wilson Company Catalog Series, Book Finder, and NCTE booklists.)

    F. Procedures for reconsideration of instructional materials

       1. Statement of policy

       2. Guiding principles

       3. Specific procedures

          a. Informal resolution

          b. Formal resolution

       4. Forms would include:

          a. Instructional objectives rationale form

          b. Reconsideration of instructional materials form

          c. Reconsideration of nonfiction instructional materials form

          d. Reconsideration of fiction instructional materials form

IV. Follow the procedure for handling challenged materials without deviation.

    A. Attempt to resolve the challenge informally but if, at the end of the meeting, the complainant still wishes to challenge the material, a form for reconsideration should be provided.

    B. Only when the written request for reconsideration has been filed should the formal review process commence as outlined in the selection policy.

    C. Adhere to the policy established for reconsideration of instructional materials. There should be no restrictions or curtailment of use of the questioned material while it is being reconsidered.

    D. Follow the time line established in the policy. Complete the process with the written report.

    E. Consult your NCTE state president, local English supervisor, and English language arts state department consultant for further assistance and advice.

V. Acquaint the faculty, administrators, and parents with all aspects of the selection policy and the challenged materials procedure through inservice programs and workshops yearly so there is no question of what is involved or what is to be done.

VI. Keep on file a written faculty rationale, an explanation of the controlling principle, for any materials students read or study in common or that are most often censored.

VII. Permit students to have an alternate assignment or allow them choices when developing course assignments and objectives.

VIII. Provide a variety of books and materials addressed to different levels of readability, maturation, and interest.

IX. Honor a parent's right to exempt his or her child from content or assignments to which he or she objects.

X. Use standard and current professional bibliographies when selecting materials to support the instructional program.

XI. Include a clause in the bargaining contract protecting academic freedom. Work for Board adoption of grievance procedures to protect teachers' due process rights.

XII. Consult current references on censorship available from NCTE, American Library Association, and other professional organizations.

John Kean, a member of the NCTE Committee Against Censorship and the Commission on Intellectual Freedom, stresses the importance of teachers being prepared to explain their choices of literature and methods to critics. "The teacher needs to know what the district's goals are and what the expectations are for the English curriculum" (136). Schools need to have a policy in place, and teachers need to be well informed about the policy. Kean offers this advice:

If you anticipate that some aspect of your program or material has the potential for controversy, discuss it with colleagues and administrators to ensure that they understand what you are doing or using and why you are using it. Although it is possible to invite trouble by such consultation, it forces you to think through your own curriculum carefully and is likely to lead to a more supportive environment in which to work. (141)

Kean's advice is especially important for new teachers as they work at balancing literature selections with the community's concerns.

CASE 8–2

Exploring an Instructional Unit

Anne Elliott, an English education major, developed a thematic unit on "Stereotypes: The Root of Aggressive Behavior." She planned the four-week unit for 10th or 11th grade students. As with other instructional units we are using, Anne's explanations, objectives, and rationale are omitted here. Why might Anne have selected this theme? Before reading the unit, what literature and other resources can you think of that would fit this theme?

STEREOTYPES: THE ROOT OF AGGRESSIVE BEHAVIOR

WEEK ONE

Introduction: Students are in groups of four with one person designated as a recorder. Every few seconds I will write a word on the board; for example, *drug addict, athlete, police officer, honor student,* or *nurse.* As each word is added to the board, students in the groups tell the recorder every image that comes to mind in associated with the word. When the activity is over, students answer these questions:

1. Has your group made any stereotypes?
2. What effect do these labels have on people?

Before discussing their responses, I will provide students with the dictionary definition of *stereotyping* and give them time to rethink their responses to the questions. We will discuss what the differences are among stereotyping, prejudice, and racism. Students read Chapter 5 in *I Know Why the Caged Bird Sings* by Maya Angelou. They respond to the chapter in their journals. Later journal responses are shared in class, guided by the following questions:

1. How do you think people feel when they are labeled?
2. How have you reacted when you've been labeled?
3. How does Momma resist insulting behavior?
4. What are some strategies for dealing with insulting behavior?

Throughout the unit we consider strategies for coping with stereotype labels.

We will read the poem "Indian Blood" by Mary Tallmountain. Students respond in their journals to the following questions:

1. In the poem, the girl uses the words *stumbled, crouch,* and *trembled* to describe her actions. How do you suppose she felt that day on the stage?
2. Why do you think she waits until "late in the night" to draw her "Indian blood"? Do you think she is celebrating or resenting her heritage?

---

1. What are Anne's objectives for this unit?
2. How might she prepare her students for the literature circles?
3. Although Anne assigns some literature, she has built into the unit the students' responsibility for choosing literature. What are the benefits of this? Are there any potential difficulties?

WEEK TWO

Students meet in their groups and define *stereotyping,* giving specific examples. Also, they discuss if they think stereotyping will ever be eliminated and why they think it exists.

They read the short story "Learning the Language" by Haruhiko Yoshimeki. Students may choose one of the following questions to write a one-page response (level 2).

1. Find two or three examples of people of one race making comments about other races. Decide if you consider them racist. How do you define racist?
2. Yoshimeki describes his experience of coming to terms with a culture different from his own. Think of all the ways we encounter cultural differences and compare to Yoshimeki's experience. Reach a conclusion about how racial attitudes are culturally determined.

I will introduce the selection of novels they will read: *Pickle and Price* by Pieter Van Raven, *Night* by Elie Wiesel, and *The Bluest Eye* by Toni Morrison. The books represent different levels of difficulty. Students choose which one they want to read and may change their selection if they wish. As a prereading activity, I will hand out a page of quotations from all three books, and the students guess which book each one comes from.

---

1. What are Anne's objectives for the activities in week two?
2. How might a teacher introduce the books and help students decide what they want to read?
3. What additional literature selections could one add?

WEEK THREE

As students are reading their books, other activities and discussions are ongoing. I do not plan to give tests or quizzes to make sure students are keeping up with their reading. The class will work on a definition of culture. As an assignment, students will make a family tree to discover the many cultures that exist within their own family. Students will read "Nikki-Rosa" by Nikki Giovanni. Students will respond to one or more of the following quotations from the poem: "Black love is Black wealth," "biographers never understand," and "all the while I was happy." Also, they will read "Thank You, Ma'am" by Langston Hughes. Students respond in their journals.

To help students realize how easy it is to make generalization I will use the following artwork and ask the accompanying questions:

1. "Mother Courage" by Charles White. Why did White entitle this work "Mother Courage"?
2. "Sunny Side of the Street" by Philip Evergood. What associations do you make from this work? What kind of emotional response do you have?

The final activity for the week is role playing. Each small group has a counselor role, and the others have been confronted with hostility, insulting behavior, labeling, or stereotyping. They discuss what has happened with the counselor who explains a process for dealing with the dilemma. Students take turns playing different roles.

---

1. How might Anne monitor the students' reading progress?
2. What are the students learning?
3. What are Anne's goals?

WEEK FOUR

Students finish their novels and work on a level 3 assignment. The final discussion is on how people respond to stereotyping. The discussion should be based on all the activities they have done during the unit.

The final project is to develop a conflict-resolution program for our own school. Some possibilities could include increasing awareness by creating announcements, posters, handouts; organizing a culture club to discuss diversity issues; or developing a peer mediation group to intervene in disputing parties. Students may create any project; they can work in a group, with a partner, or individually. This project will not end when the unit does. For this reason students set their own completion dates. They must turn in a written plan and purpose of their program. Also, they need to turn in a written weekly update.

Anne plans to integrate this theme into subsequent units. How might she do this? How would the theme fit into units you are thinking of creating?

Anne states at the conclusion of her unit, "Aggression in American schools manifests itself in attacks on teachers and students as well as in vandalism and property damage. The trend has serious implications for our children as well as for our schools. A unit on stereotypes seems not only appropriate but necessary."

Cassie Scharber constructed a thematic unit for an English education class from a different starting point than Anne. Cassie first selected the play she wanted to teach (*Our Town* by Thornton Wilder). She then decided to focus on one of its themes, the importance of simple pleasures, and finally selected other literature and activities to develop the thematic unit. Her unit is planned for four weeks and intended for 11th grade students. As with Anne's unit, only part of Cassie's is included here.

Exploring an Instructional Unit

SIMPLE PLEASURES

To begin the unit, the students form their groups when they come into the classroom. I give each group a container of green goo (Oobleck) that I've mixed up. My directions are simple:

1. Play with it.
2. Please keep their goo to themselves.
3. Think of reasons why you like/dislike the goo.

After about 20 minutes playtime, I tell them the story behind Oobleck (a Dr. Suess book) and ask them why they think I had them play with it. (I want them to remember how it feels to play, to have fun, and to laugh.) After the discussion, I will read the children's book *Peach and Blue* by Sarah S. Kilborne aloud to them. We then discuss the story. By the end of the unit, I want them to see things differently and notice things they never saw before; I want them to appreciate the simple pleasures of life.

What do you think of Cassie's objective? What about her introduction?

The first assignment is to read "The Trashman" by John Coleman (journal/nonfiction). Students discuss the story, using the following questions as guides:

1. Why do you think Dr. Coleman went to work as a trashman?
2. What did he like about his job?
3. How might this experience make Dr. Coleman a better person?
4. Would you ever want to be a trashman? Explain your answer.
5. How did a change of perspective affect Dr. Coleman?

Because this story deals with changing perspectives, the next activity puts students in someone else's shoes for awhile. Students pull a slip of paper from a hat that I pass around the room. Each slip has an occupation or situation written on it. Students write a couple of paragraphs that describe a day in the life of whatever is on the slip. I will encourage them to think hard about this and try to visualize becoming the person their slip identified.

The next literature selection is *Walden* by Henry David Thoreau. I will provide just enough background material to help them understand the readings. The next few days in small groups we discuss Thoreau.

1. Why does Cassie use small groups rather than a large group discussion?
2. What other literature selections might a teacher use at this point in the unit?

I will give students a discussion guide that lists some points they might talk about. For example:

1. Why did Thoreau go into the woods?
2. Explain the word *deliberately* as used in "I went to the woods to live deliberately."
3. What does he mean by "To be awake is to be alive."
4. What is Thoreau's perspective on life?
5. What are some of the simple pleasures in his life?

Students also keep a response journal on all their reading.

For the next literature selection, students can read either "One Last Time" by Lori Russell (fiction) or "The Old Ones of New Mexico" by Robert Coles (oral literature written down). They may read both if they want.

The following day is a field trip to a senior citizen home to learn something about the senior citizens' perspectives. The students write in their journals about the day.

The next assignment is to think about their own simple pleasures. They define themselves by designing a poster of the simple pleasures in their lives. Students share their posters with the class, and then I will put the posters up in the room.

Although not included here, Cassie explains in her unit why she gives this assignment and what the students gain from it. What do you think the reasons might be? What purposes do the posters have?

I read the poem, "If I Had My Life to Live Over" by Nadine Starr. After a discussion, I want them to think about a couple of things. First, what would they change in their lives? Second, how do they want to live their lives? Keeping these questions in mind, they are to write a poem, either on "If I Had My Life to Live Over" or "For the Rest of My Life I Am Going to . . . "

Students will write a journal of simple pleasures everyday for the rest of the unit, recording things they noticed that day that made them happy. As a result of writing them down, they remember simple thing that made the happy—if only for an instant. Maybe for a few weeks they will "awake." In addition to recording the pleasures, students need to briefly explain why each notation made them happy.

After explaining this assignment, I will hand out a copy of the poem "Barter" by Sara Teasdale. One of the students will read this poem aloud, and then the class will discuss it. Some things that might be covered are the author's favorite things, a celebration of life, and the price of loveliness. As we consider how people live, the discussion will lead us into *Our Town*. Do they generally live the same? What are some similarities in life around the world?

---

1. Cassie has come to the major reading that she built the unit around. What do you think of the activities that lead up to *Our Town*? In what ways do they differ from the usual introduction to reading a literature selection?
2. What can you surmise about Cassie's objectives and goals based on her planning?

Note: What follows is an abbreviated version of Cassie's plan for the unit. We list the sequence of activities, but not the transitions between activities or reasons she states for her planning.

I will briefly introduce the play and assign Act 1. The next day we discuss Act 1 in small groups. Each group reports to the whole class at the end of the period.

The students' writing assignment is to write the titles "Celebration of Life," "Uniqueness of Each Person's Experience," and "Timelessness of Human Experience" at the top of three different pieces of paper. As they read the play, they keep track of ideas that fall under each title.

Students continue to read, discuss, and record.

I will have the class design a cornerstone. First they brainstorm about what might go into a cornerstone. Then each student writes on strips of paper one or two suggestions to include in the cornerstone. I will read the collection aloud to the students.

During the reading of the play, students will act out key scenes, for example, the wedding of Emily and George. Also, students will discuss quotes that they believe are significant. The students will also read "A Drum Major for Justice" by Martin Luther King (nonfiction/speech). After they read the speech, I have them compare Emily's and Simon's good-bye speech to King's. Students then write their own good-bye speech based on how they would answer one of these questions: What would they like to be remembered for? or What would they write in a speech that says good-bye to the world? Following this activity, I will read a short story from *Random Acts of Kindness*.

Students are required to write a level 3 paper for the unit. They may choose from the following ideas or come up with their own:

1. Write a children's book that has a theme of simple pleasures.
2. Consider this quote from *Walden;* "To be awake is to be alive." How does this quote relate to the themes in *Our Town*?
3. What has the unit meant to you? Use your journal of simple pleasures and the unit as a whole.
4. Develop a character who would fit into the life portrayed in *Our Town*. The person can be fictional, yourself, or someone who is alive today. Describe the person fully and what he or she learned from living in Grover's Corners.
5. Write a letter to the world that explains why life is wonderful. It can be of a time of sadness or joy. Use references to some of the literature we read during the unit. The paper goes through all of the steps of a writing process. After the papers are turned in, the unit will conclude with a video of *Our Town*.

---

1. What does Cassie want the students to learn from the unit? In what ways do her activities develop her objectives?
2. What other selections could Cassie use?
3. Do you think she has a good balance of genres, minority authors, and time periods?

REFERENCES

Anson, Chris M. "Book Lists, Cultural Literacy, and the Stagnation of Discourse." *English Journal* Feb. 1988: 14–18.

Applebee, Arthur N. *A Study of Book-Length Works Taught in High School English Courses.* Albany: National Research Center on Literature Teaching & Learning, 1989.

"Book Bans for Teens Backfire, Group Says." Associated Press. *Leader-Telegram* 14 Sept. 1995: 3A.

Burress, Lee. *Battle of the Books.* Metuchen: The Scarecrow Press, 1989.

Carlsen, G. Robert. "What Beginning English Teachers Need to Know about Adolescent Literature." *English Education* 10 (1979): 195–202.

Carrier, Warren, ed., and Kenneth Oliver, associate ed. *Guide to World Literature.* Urbana: National Council of Teachers of English, 1980.

Crowe, Dennis. "Women and Women Writers." ENG 703, Teaching AP English. University of Wisconsin-Eau Claire, 1993.

Dabydeen, David. *A Handbook for Teaching Caribbean Literature.* London: Heinemann, 1988.

Duff, Ogle B., and Helen J. Tongchinsub. "Expanding the Secondary Literature Curriculum: Annotated Bibliographies of American Indian, Asian American, and Hispanic American Literature." *English Education* 22 (1990): 220–240.

Elbow, Peter. *What Is English?* New York: Modern Language Association of America, 1990.

Elliott, Anne. "Stereotypes: The Root of Aggressive Behavior." ENG 404, Teaching AP English. University of Wisconsin-Eau Claire, 1993.

Fishman, Andrea. "Finding Ways In: Redefining Multicultural Literature." *English Journal* Oct. 1995: 73–79.

Foster, Harold M. "Film in the Classroom: Coping with Teenpics." *English Journal* Mar. 1987: 86–88.

Frye, Northrop. *On Teaching Literature.* New York: Harcourt Brace Jovanovich, 1972.

Gonzalez, Roseann Duenas. "When Minority Becomes Majority: The Changing Face of English Classrooms." *English Journal* Jan. 1990: 16–23.

Greenblatt, Ellen. *Many Voices: A Multicultural Bibliography for Secondary School.* Berkeley: Bay Area Writing Project, 1991.

Gunner, Elizabeth. *A Handbook for Teaching African Literature.* 2nd ed. London: Heinemann, 1987.

Hunter, Dorothea, and Winifred Madsen. "The Enemy Within." *School Library Journal* 39.3 (Mar) 1993: 140.

Kean, John M. "The Secondary English Teacher and Censorship." *Preserving Intellectual Freedom.* Ed. Jean Brown. Urbana: NCTE, 1994. 133–142.

Koehler, Mary Beth. "Native American Resources as a Catalyst for Self-Expression in the Language Arts." Unpub. Paper, 1994.

Lake, Patricia. "Sexual Stereotyping and the English Curriculum." *English Journal* Oct. 1988: 35–38.

McElmeel, Sharon L. "Toward a Real Multiculturalism." *School Library Journal* Nov. 1993: 50.

Mossman, Robert. "South African Literature: A Global Lesson in One Country." *English Journal* Dec. 1990: 41–46.

Neuman, Susan B. "Rethinking the Censorship Issue." *English Journal* Sept. 1986: 46–49.

Noll, Elizabeth. "The Ripple Effect of Censorship: Silencing in the Classroom." *English Journal* Dec. 1994: 59–64.

Olds, Alan. "Thinking Eastern: Preparing Students to Read Chinese Literature." *English Journal* Dec. 1990: 20–34.

Purves, Alan C., and Dianne L. Monson. *Experiencing Children's Literature.* Glenview: Scott, Foresman and Co., 1984.

Rehrauer, Liz. "Who Am I?" ENG 702, Literature for Teachers. University of Wisconsin-Eau Claire, 1994.

Resch, Jodi. "Mexican Culture Unit." ENG 404, Literature for Teachers. University of Wisconsin-Eau Claire, 1995.

Romero, Patricia Ann, and Don Zancanella. "Expanding the Circle: Hispanic Voices in American Literature." *English Journal* Jan. 1990: 24–29.

Sasse, Mary Hawley. "Literature in a Multiethnic Culture." *Literature in the Classroom: Readers, Texts, and Contexts*. Ed. Ben F. Nelms. Urbana: National Council of Teachers of English, 1988. 167–178.

Scharber, Cassie. "Simple Pleasures." ENG 420, Composition for Teachers. University of Wisconsin-Eau Claire, 1995.

Smith, Frank. "Overselling Literacy." *Phi Delta Kappan* Jan. 1989: 353–359.

Van Horne, Geneva T. "Combatting Censorship of Instructional Materials." *SLATE Starter Sheet* Feb. 1983.

Improving Writing Skills: Usage, Syntax, Mechanics

I think we teach too many skills and not at the right time. We succumb to the temptation to cover English "content" because the surface features of written language are so obvious, teachable and testable. (144)

Nancie Atwell

A FRAMEWORK FOR IMPROVING WRITING SKILLS

Writing skills generally improve when students care about their writing. For as simplistic and full of common sense as that idea sounds, it is nonetheless easily lost in a context of teaching and testing. Textbooks, curriculum guides, and standardized tests have consistently presented skills as a world unto themselves, separate from student writing. Writing skills— usage, syntax, mechanics—are part of the process of developing a written text, of making meaning; they are part of revising and editing.

Writing is a complex process. Often, we discover what we want to say in the very act of writing; thus, early concern about correctness may block the discovery. At the point where we generate ideas and draft, we need to think of what it is we mean, the content, and save the urge to correct for later in the process, when editing and proofreading are appropriate. As Tom Romano reminds us:

> We [teachers] must strive to keep editing skills in perspective—a part of the writing process. Countless people have had their attitudes about the creative act of writing permanently darkened by a teacher who emphasized perfection in editing to the point that all other parts of the writing process did not matter. (74)

Dan Kirby and Tom Liner also support keeping skills in perspective, suggesting that we:

> Treat proofreading as something to be done quickly and efficiently, rather than as a climatic step in the process of composing. Only when proofreading is made a mysterious and complex part of the mastery of standard English does it become intimidating and therefore difficult for students. (235)

Writing skills need to be linked to the act of writing; further, they need to be kept "in their place." There is no argument over the need for the skills or for students learning standard usage, syntax, and mechanics as part of their versatility with language, as one of the dialects they command. However, a useful perspective for both teacher and student comes from Emily Meyer and Louise Z. Smith: "Standard written English is a dialect nobody speaks" (219). Given this, it is even more important that students view writing skills as a critical part of their own written expression, not as lessons to get out of the way as quickly as possible.

THE TEACHER'S ROLE

With movement to a more process-oriented approach to writing, the teacher's role had to be redefined. In the traditional model, a teacher was often the giver of information and the hunter of errors, the examiner. A more contemporary approach views the teacher as facilitator. Letting students write is the first step in gaining mastery over writing skills; allowing time for the entire writing process is the second. Teachers need to validate the importance of revising and editing, not through using red pens but through allowing in-class time for these processes. Another aspect of teacher as facilitator involves modeling revising and editing, not the old marginal, a more distant, command of "Fix!"

Modeling

Modeling is best accomplished through student drafts on overhead transparencies or duplicated copies for use with an entire class; it may take different formats, however.

TEACHER-LED DISCUSSION.   Ask students what changes need to be made, make the changes, and briefly discuss the rationale or reason behind each change; limit the focus to only a few errors, prioritizing them.

STUDENT/INDIVIDUAL.   Ask students to proofread a paper individually, prior to group work on the same piece. A collection of papers from previous or other classes, without names or other identifying factors, provides experience with full discourse proofreading or editing.

STUDENT/GROUP.   Ask a small group to pool their knowledge, decide on correction, and determine the reason for the correction; then follow with full class discussion.

STUDENT/GROUP.   Ask a group to generate a checklist, perhaps assigning different groups different areas (e.g., usage, mechanics, sentences); follow with a whole-class discussion, talking about errors that derail the reader and errors that are less serious but nonetheless irritating to many readers.

MINI-CONFERENCES.   Briefly focus on editing skills at a table with one or several students or over a student's shoulder; your questions are the modeling part of the process and are the type of questions teachers want students to internalize and apply on their own.

PEER CONFERENCES.   Give students guidelines for holding peer conferences; if students are unfamiliar with peer conferencing, provide models, questions, and procedures. Establish rules: The author has first responsibility for proofreading, peers second; peers are not to make any corrections on paper without discussing it with the author; when making a correction, peers initial it (in this way, teachers are able to see what students know). Peer conferences can be done in pairs or small groups.

MINI-LESSONS.   Limit the lesson to less than 10 minutes and use student draft material. Done throughout the year, mini-lessons offer some assurance of covering all the basic skills. These lessons can involve the entire class or a small group. Analyses of student error logs help determine which errors to focus on first and whether whole-class or small-group instruction is appropriate. The important thing is that students need to apply the lessons to their own work. The lessons should not become a facsimile of the skills section of textbooks.

DAILY ORAL LANGUAGE.   Developed by Neil Vail and Joe Papenfuss, two educators in the Racine (WI) school district, *Daily Oral Language* (DOL) provides students with two or three sentences with various errors in usage and mechanics. Vail and Papenfuss have prepared plenty of sentences for use at junior and senior high school levels, as well as a teacher's manual. Most teachers put the sentences on the board or a transparency and ask students to make corrections in their journals; full-class discussion of corrections and the reasons for them follows. This process takes no more than 5 or 6 minutes. The value of DOL is its brevity, immediate correction, and oral discussion. However, it should not be used as a test nor should teachers "over-do" it.

TEACHER'S MODEL.   Using a short piece of their own, teachers talk students through revision and editing, pointing out why they make certain choices, what questions or problems they have to solve. This strategy is important not only for the modeling but also because teachers who share their own writing are generally perceived differently; they are writers, not merely critics of other people's writing.

Self-Editing

Students can self-edit through individual lists maintained as part of their writing folder. Although it is possible to be superficial and mechanical about this task, asking the students to both maintain and consult their individual skills list places the responsibility with the right person, the student. Students will need familiarity with strategies that help them focus on proofreading:

- Reading one line at a time, ignoring meaning; students need to understand that we find it easy to read over errors because we carry the intended meaning in our heads.
- Pacing the writing, leaving the piece alone for at least 24 to 48 hours and returning to it "cold"; again we need to help them understand why this is important.
- If the draft is handwritten, we can ask them to type a subsequent draft, where it is easier to spot errors; the professional sense of finishing a product also helps to reinforce the need for proofreading.
- Students write their most persistent error (or perhaps two) at the top of each page and read through for that error(s) and that error(s) only. Limiting students to one or two errors helps them focus on a problem area and prevents early discouragement with the process.
- Students use a ruler or a blank sheet of paper, blocking out everything but one line, and read through with a focus on one line only.
- Students read their text backward to proofread for spelling errors, thus reducing any interference from content and meaning.

Self-Help

We can create a corner of the classroom where self-help is available: different types of dictionaries; one-page handouts to help with the most common mistakes; simple explanations/examples. Students can also create their own "handbook" for the corner. Many student handbooks are not only obtuse but difficult to access.

If the teacher is a facilitator rather than an error-hunter, students are given what they need most, the chance to internalize skills through guided experience. Too often, we have been neurotic about errors, focusing on them to the exclusion of everything else. This is not to suggest that we ignore errors; as we pointed out earlier, this simply leaves students more powerless. Establishing a classroom model that provides them with time, strategies, and experience will go far in developing self-reliant students.

The Normality of Errors

Although we discuss student errors at some in length in Chapter 10, the importance of the issue merits a word here as well. Writing skills take time to develop and to become routine. In this way, they are no different than skills such as those in athletics or music. Teachers also need to keep in mind that "mastery" does not occur all at once. Students will show varied competency or proficiency on a range of writing skills; further, regression is normal. The more complex the writing task, the more a student has to concentrate on making meaning; at such times, some skill may "drop out" momentarily. Similarly, the more complex the sentence structure, the more likely the mechanics within it will go awry. These are good errors, signs of development. Teachers who maintain this view and make their students aware of the nature of developing writing ability provide a good writing environment. If we learn through trial and error, we also depend on tolerance for the motivation to make it through the process. We don't want to penalize students for taking risks as they try out more complex structures and more sophisticated punctuation.

Skills As Purposeful

We need to maintain the relationship between skills and genuine communication: We write to convey meaning, and the use of appropriate conventions helps us do that. Teaching skills for their own sake, unrelated to creating a meaningful text, or worse, for taking standardized tests is a waste of time. Students need good skills, and the only way most will acquire them, internalize them, and apply them is in pursuit of communicating something *they* want to say.

The Responsible Student

Students, not teachers, should hold primary responsibility for correctness. This notion makes some teachers nervous: They distrust student ability to self-correct; they see their own role as "the corrector." As noted earlier, students will never learn to self-correct if they are not given, first, the understanding and strategies to do so, and second, the sustained requirement to do it. Dan Kirby and Tom Liner put it bluntly:

> Leave proofreading to the students. In every class there are some students who have mastered most of the proofreading skills. Often such students are simply "good spellers" or "intuitive punctuators." Acknowledge their skill by setting them up as proofreading consultants to the class. (234)

Most teachers will admit that most students learn well from their peers. Peers often have a facility for translating academic material into peer language, a facility that can be used in our classrooms. We can train some of those "masters" to ask questions, to work inductively—and not simply give the right answer. When students have had the benefit of teacher and peer explanation, they should take over proofreading and be held responsible.

In the discussion of error, we noted that little is gained by a teacher-marked and corrected paper. As much as teachers don't like this news, it remains true: Students don't pay much attention to teacher marks. If the paper is laden with them, students will simply give up, having determined that they do nothing right. The students may not find every error, but unless they try, little will be gained.

To avoid worry about unedited papers making their way into hands of parents, other teachers, or administrators, some English language arts teachers invest in a rubber stamp that says something to the effect of "under construction." Before a draft leaves the classroom, it is stamped. Also, teachers who discuss their methods with parents or caretakers seldom run into trouble. If people understand that the emphasis on correctness shifts to final stages of writing and that we do expect standard written English on final drafts, the chances of a problem are very minimal.

ACTIVITIES TO IMPROVE USAGE

"Bad grammar" usually refers to deviations from standard usage: *he do* for *he does; me and her* for *she and I; them books* for *those books.* There is no question of misunderstanding the meaning here; thus, we are talking about conforming to a single form designated as "standard" usage. The acquisition of standard usage, perhaps more than any other skill, is linked to motivation—to the benefits it provides for the student. For this reason, fault-finding doesn't work other than to strengthen student notions of us as eighteenth-century grammarians.

Understanding Usage

First, we need to establish a language environment through books, film, video, music, and other resources. We need to build student interest in language. One of the most valuable viewpoints the English language arts curriculum can provide is that of language diversity. American regional dialects are a good starting point; they function as a lens through which to view usage. Discussing usage in terms of dialect and versatility with language and in terms of the various subcultures in which people live their lives will make sense to most middle school and senior high students.

Using Literature
Young adult fiction is rich with language variation. Novels that portray the regional and cultural settings of American dialects offer a forum for discussing variation. Black poets such as Langston Hughes, Paul Laurence Dunbar, and Gwendolyn Brooks demonstrate the versatility of voices that use both standard and nonstandard dialects; comparing works of these poets can reinforce the concept of appropriate usage linked to audience and purpose.

Using Video
Today, teachers can access regional dialects easily through the many movies that use them. Boston, New Orleans, New York, Texas, Chicago, Los Angeles, Nashville, and Maine are but a few settings that provide different American voices. Taping portions of television shows, particularly call-in shows, also offers a rich source of American voices.

If the school district does not have access to commercial videos such as *The Story of English* or *American Tongues,* the public library may have them. A regional college or university is another resource for these excellent productions.

Using Television
SPORTS.   Students can collect data on standard and nonstandard usage from listening to sports broadcasters and athletes from across the nation.

POLITICAL FIGURES.   Students can collect data from the nightly national news. Prominent African Americans, Hispanics, Asians, and Caucasians from every region of the country provide a rich linguistic field. Students should speculate about the use of dialect: When do people use their "home" dialect and when do they use their "public dialect"? What conclusions can be drawn about standard and nonstandard usage?

CALL-IN SHOWS.   Popular call-in shows feature people from all regions of the country speaking naturally. Students should keep a journal of usage variation, noting their emotional response to the language itself.

ADVERTISEMENTS.   Students can work in groups to collect language data through advertisements on specific products. Ask them to identify the audience for their ads and the effect of audience on usage. They can also use print media for this purpose.

Using Music
LYRICS.   Most students have access to many varieties of music. They might listen to the lyrics across several varieties (e.g., rap, country-western, rock, ballads) and identify changes in usage; they might also speculate on reasons for changes.

Using Graffiti
WALLS, DESKS, AND OTHER SURFACES.   Graffiti is a rich source of language variation and economy. Students can work in pairs or small groups to gather data, analyze it, and report on what usage means to the authors of graffiti.

Manipulations: Language Activities

For students who learn well through visualization and physical activities, activity cards work well. Using different colors for different word classes (e.g., noun, verb), make stacks of subject and verb cards, both singular and plural. Include the types of usage problems most common to the grade level and to speakers of other dialects or languages. Students can work in pairs to match cards and solve usage problems.

A "spinner" card of subjects is another manipulative strategy. Students spin for their subject and then add an appropriate predicate, either oral or written. "Spinner" cards that exploit various usage problems provide good experience in a nonthreatening way.

Investigating Basic Language Relationships

Provide students with sufficient language samples in which to isolate problem areas associated with standard usage (e.g., subject-verb agreement, pronoun agreement, pronoun case, possession). Students work in pairs or small groups, analyzing the text and determining what constitutes standard written usage. Follow their investigation with a teacher-guided discussion on their findings.

Daily Oral Language

Use only two or three sentences per day, written on the chalkboard or a transparency, and ask students to correct the sentences in their journals. Then using only five minutes of class time, ask for their changes. The value of this activity lies in students hearing the standard forms and discussing them orally and briefly. We need to remind ourselves, however, that this exercise can become as mindless and useless as any exercise. Further, grading will destroy its effectiveness. Many teachers use DOL as a "settling down" activity, students doing their journal sentences while teachers take roll.

Working from Student Drafts

Usage needs to be linked to student writing, where students proofread as a matter of standard procedure. Using student drafts on transparencies, teachers model the process. Teachers need to help students shift their perception from writer to reader through a more systematic and detached reading of the text, a line-by-line reading. We can raise student awareness of spots where usage errors are likely to occur (e.g., separated subjects and verbs, pronoun case). Students need to learn to identify problems as well as to solve them.

Mini-Lessons

The mini-lesson, like *Daily Oral Language,* is brief. Focus on a single problem, like the mix-up between *lay* and *lie,* and return immediately to writing activities. Since application is the point of the lesson, draw the usage problem from student writing as often as possible, using the whole class or small groups as appropriate.

Example: Pronoun Case
Don't use terms such as *case, nominative,* or *objective.* They scare students and only convince them that their own language is arcane and unavailable to them. Show students how to test pronoun use by adding or eliminating words:

> John threw the ball to Paul and I.
> John threw the ball to —- I?
> John and me went to the game.
> —- me went to the game?
> John is taller than me.
> John is taller than me —- is tall?

Most native speakers with standard dialects will recognize which form is correct when they hear and see it in this context. We can use this lesson to underscore that standard usage has nothing to do with understanding or meaning per se. Otherwise, students are likely to remind us of that reality.

Keeping Logs or Analysis Charts

As part of the writing folder, include a log or chart of the most common errors. The category names should be accessible and reasonable; the students should be responsible for maintaining their own chart. Typical categories include word ending errors (e.g., omitting *-ed*); subject-verb agreement; pronoun agreement; pronoun case; wrong word (e.g., *lie/lay*). Using information from their error logs, students can work in small groups to assist and teach one another.

For speakers of other dialects or languages, prepare a more descriptive log, such as this:

Personal Usage	*Written Usage*	*Reason for Difference*
Three boy went	Three boys	plural marker *s*
He done found him	He found	*done* is extra, used for emphasis in home dialect

In introducing students to the chart, stress that we have a variety of personal grammars but that we need to use them appropriately depending on our purpose and audience.

Error Analysis

Teachers need to judge their students' ability to analyze their errors; however, eventually students need to take over this task. Teachers, nonetheless, must find the pattern and determine its origin: a lack of understanding or a performance error (e.g., overgeneralizing some rule, carelessness, native language interference, dialect).

Atwell's System

Nancie Atwell suggests a systematic approach to student editing and proofreading. Students are the first editors of their work and are expected to do the best possible job. They then submit the draft to the teacher, who corrects whatever was missed. The teacher chooses one or two high priority errors for an individual conference the next day, applying them to the piece of writing at hand. The writer adds the error(s) to the personal chart stapled in his or her writing folder. After teacher explanation, the student assumes responsibility for editing. In Atwell's system, three pen colors—original text, student editing pen, teacher blue editing pen—indicate who has done what work on the draft. Atwell also maintains a separate in/out basket for this editing procedure and a supply of tools of the trade—white-out and a supply of editing pens (106–07).

The editing procedure takes place only after content is set. Atwell notes: "Asking students to edit before the content is set reflects a misunderstanding of what writers do" (106). Thus keep in mind that this process is for editing only. In a writing workshop environment, the teacher has already commented orally on student's content.

Grammar Grams

Stephen Tollefson's *Grammar Grams,* as the name suggests, offer students a very brief explanation of a single point of usage or punctuation. The brevity, clarity, and humor of a grammar gram allow senior high students to process the information easily. Teachers can also make their own grammar grams by adjusting for class level or asking some of their most capable students to make some. Like *Daily Oral Language* and mini-lessons, the grammar gram idea derives its power from a clear, single focus. Grammar Grams or some other brief explanatory lessons could be part of a "Correction Corner," where materials are placed for student use at the editing and proofreading stage. Again, the student must learn to take responsibility for these parts of the writing process.

Publishing

When students know their work is *really* going public, they have more motivation to check usage, mechanics, and spelling. We need to use student interest in issues that affect them for letter writing; we need to encourage them to contribute to school publications. We might find out which businesses and factories have their own publications and see if students can contribute (e.g., Uniroyal published essays of students whose parents worked for them). We can find out if clinics or medical offices would put a student anthology in their waiting areas or if nursing home residents would welcome student work or correspondence. The National Council of Teachers of English sponsors writing contests for students in middle and senior high school. Various national publications for young people also solicit original writing.

Summing Up

Usage is intimately connected with the communication situation at hand; appropriate usage is relative to audience and purpose. When students view usage in the context of flexibility with language, as empowering them across many communication situations, they are far more likely to adopt standard usage as one of their dialects. In working with student errors, we should focus on only a couple at a time that most derail the reader or irritate the listener. Once we have explained the problem, the student can take responsibility for corrections. With non-native speakers or speakers of other dialects, we need to allow more time for assimilation of a usage rule and ask them to apply it to ensure they have grasped the concept. In some cultures, students are not accustomed to asking questions of their teachers or elders. Moreover, some non-native speakers may be too shy or embarrassed to indicate they don't understand. We can't expect that one explanation or demonstration will do it, especially if the student comes from a weak literacy background.

BOX 9–1

PUT YOUR BOOK AWAY . . .

The annotated edition of your grammar textbook may say something similar to this:

> *Some students use objective case pronouns as objects of prepositions, especially if compound objects are used.*

To help students understand this rule, write these sentences on the board or transparency and ask which is correct.

Wait for Lyn and I.
Wait for Lyn and me.

Show students that by leaving out the first object of the preposition and the conjunction, they can tell which word, *I* or *me*, sounds right.

1. When would students have trouble with the "it sounds right" approach to usage? What can you do to help students develop a better ear for standard usage?
2. What would happen if a teacher used "grammar language" to explain the problem or solution here?
3. How would you explain the following usage error to a sixth grader? Me and Tina left the party before midnight.

BOX 9–2

GERUND? HUH? ANY RELATION TO GERBIL?

Senior high "composition" textbooks continue to present students with a maze of mostly unhelpful information. For example:

The Gerund

A *gerund* is a verb form ending in *-ing* and used as a noun.

Subject: Fishing can be fun.
Predicate Nominative: My dad's hobby is fishing.
Object of Preposition: Shut off the TV before leaving.
Direct Object: Did you like fishing?

Don't confuse the gerund with a present participle.
Example: Looking both ways, the quarterback was searching downfield before releasing the ball.
Looking is a participle modifying quarterback.
Searching is part of the verb phrase.
Releasing is a gerund, the object of the preposition.

1. Do 11th graders need this information? What do you believe they need to know about gerunds and their uses? How can you explain gerunds in "kid language"? How much, if any, explanation does a native speaker need to use gerunds?
2. The textbook states these learner outcomes: (a) to identify and classify gerunds, (b) to write sentences using gerunds, and (c) to write a conversation by using gerunds. What is your opinion of these outcomes? How would you state learner outcomes regarding gerunds and their appropriate use?
3. The exercises for the chapter on gerunds follow this pattern:

Find the gerunds in the following sentences and identify each as a subject, predicate nominative, direct object, or object of a preposition. If the sentence has none, indicate this.

a. What does your background in the English language arts tell you about this type of exercise? What does your knowledge of adolescent development tell you?
b. How would you respond to a parent who firmly believes that students lack basic skills because they have failed to do these types of exercises?
c. What could you do to improve 11th graders' knowledge of gerunds and their usefulness in writing? How do you involve the kids in this learning process?

BOX 9–3

WHAT'S "USAGE" ANYWAY?

Fifteen-year-old Brian knows something about Nintendo, but much less about standard English usage. His good ideas are affected by his inability to edit for usage problems (and a few other problems as well). How would you help him with his essay on "The Junkie"?

To most a Nintendo Entertainment System is just a toy for kids, but to others this "toy" is his life. Nintendo junkies are a rare breed and there is no doubt that you will know one when you see them. These junkies are rarely seen in public, because they spend most of their tie in front of a TV. Most junkies have specific physical characteristics, a strong thumb is one characteristic he has. Their thumbs are strong because of the constant moving of it done when he is playing. They also usually have very pale skin. This is due to staying indoors to play the games. Every junkie has poor eyesight after staring at a TV for numerous hours a day their eyes just start to get worse. If you know anyone with these characteristics ask them if he would like to play some Nintendo.

UNDERSTANDING AND IMPROVING SYNTAX

Yet just as complete sentences do not necessarily reflect a wholly rational and coherent mind, so fragments do not necessarily reflect a fragmented and incoherent one. (87)

Rei Noguchi

Syntax can be defined as a system for indicating relationships among the words in a sentence. Syntax errors are usually considered serious, mainly because they keep the sentence from being understood clearly or easily. Although native speakers have an intuitive understanding of sentences, the difference between the sentences we utter and those we write is considerable. Speech generally lacks the complexity of written language; speech also conforms to normal word order and carries a high level of redundancy. Writing, by contrast, demands consolidation through coordination and subordination and generally penalizes redundancy. It also requires certain conventions. All too often, students reduce their writing to short, simple sentences because they know that more complex sentences require punctuation and hold greater potential for making errors. Talking, on the other hand, holds fewer dangers and seldom needs "revision." Understandably, some students avoid writing as much as possible, especially if their confidence has been undermined through excessive marking.

Revising Sentences: Harder Than It Looks

Revision of sentences is a fairly complex task, especially for inexperienced writers. Mina Shaughnessy summarizes the processes:

> The ability to re-scan and re-work sentences . . . assumes several things: a memory for unheard sentences, an ability to store verbal patterns visually from left to right, as in reading, and beyond this, an ability to suspend closure . . . until, through additions, deletions, substitutions, or rearrangements, the words fit the intended meaning. (80)

Scanning sentences and making judgments are cognitive acts that are more difficult than we assume when we write AWK or FRAG or SPLICE in the margin. Further, most students are simply not used to examining their sentences to understand how they work rather than what they mean. For this reason, sentences are best taught from the perspective of function—of how the parts work together to express meaning.

This perspective also explains why textbook or worksheet exercises fail to help students gain control of sentence structure. First, students create sentences that are more complex and ambiguous than those found in exercises. Second, we make choices about sentences based on what we have already said and what we are planning to say, which most exercises fail to consider. Third, trying to untangle our own sentences to express the meaning we ourselves want is at heart of composing. When students have no investment in the sentences, the work appears nothing more than busy work. Sentence combining exercises, although valuable, also suffer from this third important consideration. Also, giving students pages of exercises with sentence errors may actually reinforce the error. For example, students who initially had no trouble with fragments may start writing with them; students who do have trouble with sentence boundaries may be even more confused. Further, students have to become readers of their own text and habitual reviewers of their own sentences in their own essays.

From another perspective, reading experience is critical. Erika Lindemann points out the connection:

> Some students have troubles with sentences because they can't depend upon the eye or ear to help them identify prose rhythm. If they read poorly, have rarely been read to, infrequently converse with adults, or passively watch a great deal of television, they may have a limited repertoire of comfortable sentence options. (132)

Moreover, students who seldom engage in any language except with peers, where shared backgrounds allow almost elliptical expression, may lack knowledge of a range of sentence types, especially those most used in academic writing. Even if they have knowledge of them, they may have had little practice in constructing them. Other sentence problems result when students are trying to sound "academic" and use lengthy constructions and unfamiliar vocabulary. The result is wordy, garbled, and at times, pompous prose.

Vocabulary itself is another area related to sentence problems. Students who lack an adequate vocabulary often compose lengthy, imprecise sentences. Moffett offers a striking example: a person who has not learned the word *dregs* must use "what is left in the cup after you finish drinking" (qtd. in Shaughnessy 73). Sentence problems may result from three different vocabulary problems: not knowing a word; not knowing the right grammatical form of the word; or not knowing the appropriate context for it. Unfortunately, vocabulary problems are difficult to solve. Our vocabularies grow slowly, and understanding the allowable contexts of words usually occurs through trial and error, not through word lists.

Improving Sentences

When we've asked secondary English teachers which sentence problems they see most often, their response is remarkably close to the problems we see in college composition. This isn't surprising, for learning to construct effective sentences takes time and experience. Consequently, the most obvious way to improve sentences is through guided experience, both in reading and writing. Major problems of secondary students include these:

- *Tangled, confused sentences.* Students try to say too much in one structure and thus lose focus, meaning, and emphasis.
- *A series of short, choppy sentences.* The sentences are unconnected and often redundant.
- *More than one idea.* The relationship between ideas is unclear.
- *Non-sentences, fragments.*

As students mature and their cognitive abilities increase, their linguistic potential to express more complex ideas increases as well. For this reason, students need to know how to condense, simplify, join, and combine; they need to understand various ways to connect ideas through punctuation and connective words. Such instruction can and should be done through various means, and in all cases, with a minimum of grammatical terms. Subject, verb, modifier, and connector are probably all that is needed. Although *sentence* is often not technically correct, it serves just as well as *clause* and has been part of student vocabulary for many years. There's no reason not to use terms like *adjective* and *adverb* in the context of actual writing, but for the most part, *modifier* works just as well. Teaching from a perspective of function, we ask these kinds of questions: How does this word or word group work in this sentence? What does it do? How does it help the reader? Students don't need to know *nonrestrictive relative clause* to understand its function or accompanying punctuation, for example.

Modeling

Teachers should respond to student sentences through questions and model the process that students need to internalize:

- How many ideas are in this sentence?
- List the ideas separately.
- What is the relationship between this idea and this one?
- How can you show this relationship? What word, what punctuation mark, and what options do you have? Why?
- What's happening and to whom? How can you make this clearer?
- What's another way of saying this? What single word would mean the same thing?
- What punctuation mark is needed here? Why? How does it help the reader?
- What is the relationship between meaning and punctuation here?

Punctuation should be taught as part of syntax, not as a separate skill area, because very few marks are unrelated to syntax. Some students avoid various constructions because they know a comma belongs in them somewhere, thus limiting their versatility considerably. We address this problem in more detail when we discuss sentence combining.

Manipulating for Meaning

Students need to understand the concept of sentence from a written, not oral, sense. Various activities provide some experience and insights into what a sentence is. R. Baird Schuman suggested many of these (71–71):

1. Give students word groups to arrange into sentences. A variation on this activity: List the words alphabetically. After they have arranged them in one sentence, ask them to change the sentence without adding words—that is, to do variations. Then ask them to rank their creations and discuss which they liked best. You can also ask students to bring in the word lists, limiting the list to 20 words.

2. Isolate typical sentences from a social studies text (or any content area text-book). Make a placard of each word or word group in the sentence and distribute them to students. Ask them to find a word they can "attach to" (e.g., adjective searching for a noun; auxiliary searching for a verb). Once students have arranged their placards into an acceptable sentence, discuss it. Question them about the functions of the sentence parts, if the part can be moved, if so where, and so forth.
3. Give students "jabberwocky" sentences in which they can demonstrate their knowledge of how English sentences function and carry meaning. This is a good way to reinforce the notion of noun and verb markers, tense, suffixes, and word position.

These suggestions work well with native speakers but are not appropriate for non-native speakers. Students for whom English is a second language may not understand what a complete sentence is as we typically use it. The concept is not a language universal. For example, some languages omit the subject or a linking verb and rely on contextual understanding. In English, only the word *you* is omitted and understood as the subject of a sentence.

Sentence Combining and "Decombining"

Sentence combining helps students build fluency; however, it is also important to remember that cognitive and linguistic maturity is a fundamental part of syntactic maturation. William Strong, an early advocate of sentence combining, cautions that the ability to "tighten up" sentences is a later psycholinguistic development than expanding them; therefore, teachers need to delay this work until the upper levels of high school (18).

Sentence combining should always first be done as a whole-class activity, with the teacher modeling the process and asking questions. The value of the exercise lies in discovering the range of options in constructing the sentence. Usually it not a matter of right or wrong, but of improved effectiveness or clarity. If some sentence parts are wrong, usually because a modifier is in the wrong place, we are able discuss modifiers from the perspective of "what is happening here?" Following whole-class experience, sentence combining can be an individual, paired, or small-group activity as well. Asking groups to work on a "problem" is a good way for students to learn in a risk-free environment. For this reason, sentence combining work should not be graded.

Although students need sustained work to ensure an effect, sentence combining exercises that are given too frequently can lead to boredom and a perception of busy-work. Consequently, students must be directed to the potential for sentence combining and decombining in their own drafts. Strong reminds us that:

A basic aim of intelligent sentence combining is to make good sentences, not merely long ones. It follows that "decombining" may be at least as important as putting sentences together. (18)

Guided instruction in untangling and tightening sentences is important, then, at the upper levels of high school or with advanced students at any secondary level.

Coordinating and Subordinating Sentences

Some general activities for either coordinating or subordinating involve students in creating, analyzing, and discussing sentences.

- *A series of phrase, connector, and punctuation cards.* Make cards containing noun and verb phrases, coordinators or subordinators, commas, semicolons, and periods. For older students, add the colon. Have students arrange the cards and then discuss the arrangement and punctuation. Focus on meaning, clarity, and effectiveness.
- *Models from literature.* Choose poems or prose passages that illustrate effective coordinating or subordinating. Discuss how the author achieved a certain effect through manipulating sentences. Ask students to write their own poem or sentences, concentrating on patterns that will achieve an effect suitable to their subject.
- *Madcap or maddening sentences.* Take sentences that drag on and on and write them on large sheets of paper. Ask students to cut the sentences apart, literally, and come up with a clearer, more effective sentence.
- *More models from literature.* Use children's literature to demonstrate differences between sentences meant to be read orally (oral tradition versus written), those meant to be recalled easily, and those that aren't. *Why Mosquitos Buzz in People's Ears, One Fine Day,* and *Where the Wild Things Are* are good texts for this purpose.
- *Gathering Data.* Ask students to compile a list of connectors for joining sentences by examining popular magazines, textbooks, and other sources. They will no doubt get all of the coordinators and most of the subordinators; those used for embedding—*that, who, whose, which, whom*—will be less obvious.

Coordinating Sentences

Work with the most common coordinators first—*and, for, or, but,* and *yet*—and add the appropriate punctuation lessons at the same time. Ask students to indicate the relationship between the two independent sentences and the meaning carried by the connector. Ask them why the comma is used before the connector. Explore the idea of punctuation acting as voice. If there is anywhere students half-learn a comma use, it is with coordinated sentences. Some swear their teacher told them to always put a comma **after** *and* or *but.* To avoid this problem, keep student attention on the function of the comma and its relationship to the sentences. When you feel confident that most students understand coordinated sentences, focus on coordinated sentence parts. You will need to reinforce earlier teaching on the comma because, again, some students will insist they have been taught to put a comma with every *and* they write.

Depending on the level of students, add a second group of coordinating connectors—*however, consequently, nevertheless,* and *therefore*—and again discuss how punctuation provides voice and aids the reader.

Punctuation marks functioning as coordinators—the semicolon and colon—would be the next focus. Most secondary students, even those at lower levels, can use the semicolon effectively. The colon, however, is a somewhat sophisticated mark, better introduced at the upper levels and only with students who already demonstrate good sentence knowledge and control. In both cases, always link the mark to the relationship between the sentences it separates.

Using Student Competency

Because native speakers have a good intuitive sense of sentences, use inductive means of instruction. Give students a passage with a considerable amount of coordination of all types. Let them analyze and discuss it, working in groups before whole-class discussion. Provide them with sentences that will form a single, meaningful paragraph or passage if combined appropriately. Although you may wish to start with sentence groups that are unrelated to one another, move on to sentence groups that will meld into a single paragraph or passage. Another strategy for coordination is based on student sentences that have been overcoordinated. Ask students to rewrite the faulty sentence, but provide them with a certain word, phrase, or punctuation mark as the initial starting point for their revision. This practice helps students internalize syntax and draw on their existing competency.

Subordinating Sentences

We use many varieties of embedded sentences, and students need to understand why versatility is so important. A brief demonstration of how subordination helps us establish clarity and extend meaning should accompany any formal work with this sentence strategy.

Ask students to assemble a list of common connectors (ignoring the coordinators this time) and determine the subordinator's role in the sentence. Most likely, students will emerge with those related to time, condition, reason, and cause and effect. More mature and knowledgeable students may recognize relative clauses or may be led to them through teacher questions.

Establish the role of the comma through observation, not through grammatical terms and rules like "when the dependent clause comes first." Reinforce student understanding of how commas function and relate to meaning. This is also the time to talk about how fragments occur, explaining their logic and their relationship to oral language. This discussion can and should be reinforced through using actual student writing and commonsense questions. With a college-bound senior class, teachers can talk about dependent and independent clauses as they work with them. You can assume an appropriate level of development, motivation, and interest. But for most students, the notion of a complete or incomplete *sentence* is more important than the technically correct *clause*.

Keep in mind that in subordinating, we are adding to a base sentence, which is a cognitive act. This addition requires the writer to suspend one part of the sentence and hold it in mind while completing the second part. This act requires, as Shaughnessy reminds us, a memory for written words or grammatical structures that inexperienced writers may not have (80). That is, they may just plain forget what they have already written, thus causing a problem in the rest of the sentence. The problem is compounded by this same inexperience: Most students don't review their sentences and thus fail to catch inconsistencies or errors that an experienced writer would catch in a second reading. For this reason, students have to become readers of their own text as a matter of habit. Sentence revision or correction must be part of the editing process.

Embedding: A Special Problem
The most common problem with embedding occurs with the decision of whether that information is essential and whether to add commas. A textbook gives rules for punctuating restrictive and nonrestrictive clauses, but this concept, one that befuddles even college freshmen, seldom takes hold easily or firmly. The problem often lies in textbooks and handbooks where students are given rules rather than observation and questions about function and meaning. Students who can pick out a nonrestrictive clause in an exercise often fail to note one in their own writing, where the language is more complex. It is no wonder that there has been nearly universal confusion and noncompliance with the rule. Take these two sentences as examples:

Boys who put snakes in the teacher's desk should be expelled.
My brothers, who put snakes in the teacher's desk, should be expelled.

For many students, the distinction between these two sentences will be unclear, at least as it relates to essential information. You will need a thorough discussion, with ample examples drawn from student writing, of how meaning is affected with or without the clause. At the same time, you will need to underscore the meaning of *essential information*—information that is needed to identify someone or something and without which the meaning of the sentence would change. Students have to understand that removing *who put snakes in the teacher's desk* not only removes identification of the boys but also changes the intended meaning of the sentence.

BOX 9–4

PADDING WITH PURPOSE

In reading student drafts, you realize that your 11th graders would improve their writing if they used more appositives and relative clauses. You know that embedding is a late-developing skill, so you have to teach it in very concrete ways. Knowing that most students won't see the similarity between these structures, you decide to develop some mini-lessons. Which structure would you teach first? How would you present the required punctuation?

With a classmate, prepare a mini-lesson on these structures. Each of you might prepare just one, but work together to ensure that students have coherent bridges from one lesson to the other.

BOX 9–5

THE ACTIVE APPOSITIVE

Your class has a number of students who respond best to kinesthetic methods, that is, to movement and action. You also have two students with learning disabilities who seem to do better when "action" is part of explanations. How would you help these students understand the appositive as a useful structure for their writing? Think in terms of physical objects, color, shape, and manipulation of parts.

With a small group of classmates, design an activity that helps these students in particular, but that also appeals to all students in the class.

Major Sentence Errors: Run-ons, Comma Splices, and Fragments

Sentences that run together (called *run-on* or *fused* sentences) or are separated by a comma (*comma splices*) are common sentence errors. So are fragments, parts of sentences punctuated as though they are complete. Although most readers are not derailed by these errors, the errors are considered serious, perhaps signaling some sort of illiteracy to the reader. To many English teachers, the errors are grave indeed, and since these errors occur at every level of the curriculum, many teachers spend considerable time worrying about them. Unfortunately, these same teachers often fail to figure out why the errors occur in the first place and why textbook explanations fail to change student performance.

As Rei Noguchi reminds us, traditional definitions of sentences are either opaque or vague, leading to even more confusion. For example:

> Defining a sentence as a sequence of words having a complete thought only shifts the problem to the equally perplexing task of defining "a complete thought." Defining a sentence as a unit with a complete subject and predicate (or, alternately noun-phrase subject and a verb phrase), necessitates defining "subject" and "predicate" (not to mention the notion of "complete"). . . . (65)

Thus, what may start out as a seemingly straightforward definition ends up in a labyrinth of related definitions necessitating a high level of grammatical savvy. Rather than get lost in definition, you can explore how the errors occur. Then link this knowledge to student competency, the intuitive knowledge native speakers bring to sentences.

Carelessness and poor proofreading aside, many errors are most likely linked to the differences between oral and written language. The boundaries of oral language are marked by intonation and pause, whereas in written language, they are marked by capital letters and end marks. These two systems, one oral and one written, do not always correspond. If students have trouble writing, they may be letting the oral system take over. Because the oral system is semantic, linked to meaning in the writer's head, writing becomes easier (Noguchi 68, 73). But students produce errors because of variance between oral and written systems. In Noguchi's opinion, run-on and comma splice errors, "far from being mere instances of random error, reveal writers' efforts to organize meaning," regardless of violating written conventions for marking sentence boundaries. If this is so, then teachers need to work from what Noguchi believes is a latent but "powerful semantically based system for punctuating sentences" (73). In other words, we can profit from the knowledge that native speakers chunk sequences of words based on meaning, not on syntax. From that perspective, we can approach run-ons and comma splices with questions that allow students to understand both the error and its correction.

Noguchi believes that fragments are not only natural, but useful. Our speech is peppered with fragments, mainly because the face-to-face context allows us to use them; moreover, the speed of speech and our interactions make fragments desirable. We couldn't hang on to everything in long, complete, and complex sentences. Thus, in speech, fragments are acceptable. In formal writing, however, they are not—at least not when they are unintentional. Nonetheless, the pervasiveness of our oral culture has affected our writing to the point that researchers have found that fragments are more frequent today than 20 years ago. Noguchi also points out that intentional fragments can enhance our writing, providing voice, liveliness, and a sense of spontaneity to what might otherwise be cold prose (85–87).

Similar to comma splices and run-ons, fragments reveal what students *do* know about their native language. Thus, teachers can capitalize on intuitive linguistic knowledge. For example, native speakers of English characteristically create fragments at predictable boundaries:

- Ms. Witchit made me wash the board. Which was really unfair.
- Rudy missed the bus. Because he was too lazy to get up.
- I saw her. Last night at the mall when I went to the movie.
- Whenever you make that soup. Be sure it is less salty.

Thus, what may seem at first to be an impossible teaching situation really isn't. Work with the students orally, asking them to analyze the fragment: How is this information related to another sentence? Where should the fragment connect? Why? If the students have trouble identifying the structure as a fragment, they are probably "thinking in oral." Isolate the fragment from its context and ask the students if it can stand alone as a piece of information. Teachers need to discuss the differences between oral and written language again and again, so students understand that written language is not just speech "written down." If you have discussed dialects with your students, you can refer to written language as "the dialect nobody speaks" (219), as Emily Meyer and Louise Smith so usefully termed it.

If They Know Sentences, Why the Errors?

This is a good question, and as we've noted before, there are two good reasons for the persistence of run-ons, comma splices, and fragments in student writing. First, many students have had little experience with reading and writing; they simply don't know the conventions of writing well. What's more, oral language permeates our world, and oral language allows for running sentences together and omitting whole sections of sentences. Until students have enough experience with written language and understand the written code for marking sentence boundaries, their writing will no doubt contain sentence errors. Second, some students make sentence boundary errors for the same reason they make any other error: They may be careless, or in some cases, lazy. For this reason, teachers have to determine the source of the problem. Most often, however, the problem relates to student inexperience with written language.

If students have been doing workbook or text exercises rather than composing, they lack experience with written language. Correcting isolated sentences is a simplistic act, nowhere near as complex as reading and judging one's own sentences in a web of related meaning. For this reason, sentence work must be part of the writing process, where students are working with genuine discourse.

John Fortier, a veteran senior high English teacher, offers a valuable perspective on student errors: a developmental pattern. The first sentence errors are usually run-ons, probably a "response to outside suggestions or inner feelings that ideas should be combined." Fortier believes that students who are not developmentally ready for complex transformations simply run their sentences together. The next developmental error occurs when students begin to subordinate sentences, but maintain the punctuation for independent sentences. The result is a fragment. Correcting the fragment, speculates Fortier, may result in yet another error, the comma splice. We tell students to attach the fragment but separate it with a comma. If students overgeneralize this concept, they may produce sentences separated by commas. Fortier concludes: "This predictable pattern of error suggests normal linguistic development for many students and may emerge earlier or later, depending upon the individual student" (n. pag.). Fortier's analysis, based on years of teaching, illustrates the importance of teachers *thinking* about student errors and the logic behind them. Knowing that some errors are part of normal development and that students have an individual pattern of development can be comforting both to teacher and student.

BOX 9–6

UNTANGLING SENTENCES

Each of the following student sentences needs revision. Determine where the problem or problems occur. Then decide how you would work with this student on sentence revision. Approach the problem from a functional perspective and use these questions to guide your analysis:

1. Where is the reader derailed and why?
2. What is the main idea?
3. What information is missing?
4. What can you do to help the reader understand the intent?
5. What options do you have to repair the sentence?
6. What punctuation is needed and why?

Remember: Help the student through questions. These sentences were written by 18-year-olds, and you can assume they are capable of thinking about syntax and making appropriate revisions.

1. For example in football I had a coach who wanted me to gain 30 pounds on the off season and when he found out that I wasn't even going to try he had a long meeting with me about the poor attitude in sports.
2. But for more than eight days before this weekend the maintenance employees had not even touched the roads and sidewalks with any effort to clear the ice, except with a machine that has a brush type roller which brushed the snow off the ice.
3. Another point about athletics is is for all types of people.
4. As you can see owning a car can be very expensive. Especially if you are going to school.
5. A car can be a pain at school. For many different reasons. Like people borrowing it and costs to the owner.
6. An example of this is somewhat like a mutual relationship. When you do things together and have some fun.
7. The frustration would consist of not having money, no transportation and no time, I wouldn't like that.
8. The solution to the problem was that he thought what he wanted the most, if his friends didn't want to share in what he wanted, they shouldn't have to.
9. After careful consideration of these reasons my decision was made, it was not easy to do.
10. The reason I remembered this is because of the way it looked (reference to a candy bar).

Punctuation

Punctuation marks, when used correctly, only sometimes have a noticeable effect; when used incorrectly, they almost always do. 46

John C. Schafer

Keeping Punctuation in Perspective

Punctuation is a response to sentence structure; therefore, punctuation should be part of sentence work. The codes, once mastered, seem easy. However, we need to keep a perspective of just how long it takes for "mastery." We also need to keep motivation in mind. Students should know why punctuation is useful: to signal intonation, vocal nuance, and pause and to help readers predict grammatical structures. Although it's tempting to think that all punctuation errors stem from student carelessness, we can't. Some punctuation errors certainly occur because students don't think marks are important or don't take the time to proofread. But with inexperienced writers, errors are seldom a lack of care. Students gain control over various aspects of writing over a very long time, achieving control gradually and unevenly. This means they are juggling various skills areas when they write, and all areas will be in different stages of development and competency.

Telling students to proofread doesn't help. We have to help them understand the various marks and how they function. There are punctuation marks many students aren't even aware of, marks that bring voice to their writing, such as dashes and ellipses. There are also marks they are well aware of and often misuse: commas, periods, quotation marks, and apostrophes. Because of an overemphasis on rules, students half-know and half-apply those rules. They know, for example, that punctuation helps to connect and separate ideas, so it's not uncommon for them to ignore sentence endings altogether and run sentences together without punctuation or with a mess of commas. Or they may end up with the opposite effect, breaking sentences into fragments. As indicated earlier, fragments may occur because students have not had enough experience with embedding (subordination) and find it hard to keep all the sentence elements in mind. We tend to work ahead, thinking of what's coming, and if we fail to review where we have just been, errors may result.

Punctuation needs to be aligned with work in sentence structure, where students learn the role of the marks rather than the definitions. Handbooks and textbooks often act as though fixing punctuation errors is a mechanical problem rather than what it most often is, a conceptual one. We also need to avoid punctuation as "rules for rules' sake," which handbooks and texts seem to imply and which students tend to resent. When punctuation is viewed as critical to voice, style, and clarity, students will find it an essential part of making meaning—their meaning.

Examining the Marks and the Confusion

COMMAS.   Commas used with relative clauses, appositives, and participial phrases most often mark descriptive or qualifying information. When students see the connections and understand the function of the comma as *the same function* in these constructions, their grasp of them usually increases significantly. They are not learning six different rules; they are learning one, by function. Some commas are simply convention, such as separating the parts of dates and places within a sentence. Most students do fine with commas separating month from year and city from state but fail to add commas to separate year or state from the rest of the sentence.

SEMICOLON AND COLON.   Students need to understand what the marks mean. A semicolon equals an implicit *because*. A colon equals an implicit *for example*. Stressing the relationship of the mark to meaning, to its role between the sentences, is critical.

DASH.   We tend to sprinkle our informal writing with dashes, so students should learn the power of the dash and use it sparingly. They can determine its effect, how it calls attention to a word or word group, through observation of texts that use them.

PARENTHESES.   We also tend to freely use parentheses without considering their function of "playing down" information. Older students may find them a useful device.

ELLIPSES.   These marks may be used dramatically, in personal expression or fiction, or in their traditional research role, signaling material omitted from quoted material.

QUOTATION MARKS.   Even young writers understand and use these marks in personal expression or fiction writing; older writers also use them in research writing. Most students are plagued not by the quotation marks themselves but by punctuation setting off the speaker: which punctuation mark to use and if it goes in or outside of the quotation marks.

APOSTROPHE.   Inexperienced writers often misplace or omit this mark altogether. In Black dialect, the possessive is omitted in speech (e.g., *Tom hat on table* is understood as possessive). Thus, we have to draw attention to the physical mark and the pronunciation of *s*. Since many students, regardless of dialect, omit the apostrophe, you need to teach it. However, how you do it is important. Thomas Friedmann offers a particularly helpful view of the problem, noting that most texts and all handbooks lay out every possible use of the apostrophe all at once. Students are told in quick succession that they need the mark to indicate ownership, contractions, and use of plural (e.g., *A*'s). Explaining all of the uses at once can cause confusion because students associate a plural with the letter *s*. Then they are told to add '*s* for the possessive form and -*es*' for plural. Friedmann notes that for students who don't notice the apostrophe at all, it all appears absurd (111). If students do understand that they need the apostrophe for ownership, we can expect that some will extend that notion to *hers*' *his*'. This overextension of the rule shows students actively thinking about how the language works. This is a "smart error," an error of growing competency rather than regression.

Contractions offer another opportunity for confusion. When students hear a teacher say: "*It's* means *it is* and *its* means *ownership*, they are hearing identical sounds, which doesn't help them at all. Working graphically, in print, is important here. Contractions are nearly as mysterious as possessives because students may not understand the fusion of two words and role of the apostrophe. Thus, they may omit the apostrophe altogether or place it incorrectly (e.g., *did'nt*) They assume the apostrophe has something to do with the juncture of the words rather than with an omission.

Working With Punctuation

As noted earlier, texts and handbooks have a fatal flaw: teaching the exceptions rather than the rule. But when children learn their native language, they learn to make a plural by adding -*s* or -*es* and applying that rule, no matter what. Most of the time, the child is right, but "*tooths* and *foots*" pop up now and then. No one seizes the moment to give the child all the exceptions to the plural rule (Friedmann 112). Students should master the rule of most frequent occurrence first; later, we can add the exceptions, as they present themselves in student writing. Textbooks that state a basic punctuation rule and then follow with a list of every exception possible are better left on the shelf.

The Writing Connection

First, link punctuation marks to the various forms of writing in which they occur most often, such as quotation marks for interviews and dialogue and commas for description. Using quotation marks for research should be limited to those students capable of undertaking formal research writing. Provide these students with peer essays that have used quotation marks correctly and effectively.

Literature

Call attention to effective punctuation during discussions of literature. Ask students to find passages that affected them and to determine what role punctuation played. Use children's literature to demonstrate how punctuation aids reading, promotes meaning, and adds voice. Use fables for an enjoyable experience with quotation marks in dialogue, reading some of the classics, and then writing original fables. The more often students use the marks in authentic writing, the more likely they are to recall just when and how to use the marks.

Driving Home the Point

Take an article or a section of a textbook and omit all punctuation. Let students work on it in pairs or groups, restoring meaning and clarity.

Trying Out the Marks

Sentence combining is a good way to try out different marks, to understand them through trial and error without penalty. Let students work in pairs or groups before whole-class discussion of the options. In discussion, the link to rhetoric—to effective sentences rather than simply correct sentences—can be made.

Student Drafts: The Ultimate Teacher

Most of all, relate punctuation to student drafts, where intent and meaning are vital components. Let groups or pairs work on a draft and follow with whole-class discussion. Use transparencies to illustrate the options and problems. Contrary to some of our fears, most students like their work discussed publicly. Even when we have gone out of our way to obscure ownership of draft material, students often verbally claim it in class.

The Elusive Apostrophe

For students having difficulty with apostrophe use and the concept of possession, transforming the long form into the shortcut may help. For example: the cat of the witch = witch's cat. Don't overdo the exercise, however. Also teach different uses of the apostrophe at different times.

The Fallible Ear

Remind students that punctuating "by ear" is not infallible. There is no one-to-one relationship between how we pronounce and pace and how we punctuate.

Teacher's Tip
Analyze the types of error you find in student drafts. You need to determine what assumptions the student is making, which may require asking the student some direct questions about the reasoning behind a mark.

BOX 9–7

PERSONALIZING PUNCTUATION

Lisa has a good example in her essay about judging people, but she also has punctuation problems. How would you help her to recognize and correct the punctuation in this essay? Look for patterns among the errors.

Judging a Person

You cannot judge a book by its cover. Many do not take this cliche seriously. When a student is assigned to do a book report he will most likely look for external features such as the books length. He should actually be concerned with the content something that is not evident at first glance. People judge individuals in the same manner they judge books. When a person is judged he is judged on his physical features instead of his personality.

On October 23, 1990 at 11:00 am I was watching Geraldo on the television set. While I was looking at all the guest speakers on the stage I noticed a woman was wearing only half a shirt and a short mini skirt. Geraldo introduced the womans name and her profession which was modeling. She looked like a model to me and also looked like the type of woman who would sleep around. After the commercial break Geraldo introduced the topic for the day.. It was on chastity. People sitting in front of him, belonged to a group who believed in chastity. The woman I described to you was one of these people. I could not believe this woman believed in chastity but you see I was judging the woman on appearance not personality. In this example, I showed that I am guilty of judging people by their cover.

CAPITALIZATION

Again, one of the best ways to proceed is through inductive teaching. Bring in materials that are "heavy duty" in terms of capitalization, and let the students devise the rules governing when we capitalize. Linking capitalization to materials from history, literature, art, and music is another way to reinforce the skill. Similarly, linking it to commercial products that students like will make the point faster than any textbook can. Ask students to make directories of places where they "hang out," buy things, or go for entertainment. Having students compose "Capital Stories" will involve proper nouns, titles, and dates. Older students could draw on Washington D.C. and national politics as a source for plot lines; younger students could use their own town. Working with news stories is another way to provide students with experience in capitalization.

Most students have no problems with capitalizing names of people but have a great deal of trouble with race, ethnicity, religion, and politics. Ensure that they receive ample exposure to readings that will visually reinforce capitalization in these areas; lead them in a discussion of why capitals are used. School subjects is another area of trouble. Most students take a cue from English and generalize to other subjects, capitalizing everything from math to chemistry to art. You will no doubt have to explain why English is capitalized, why Algebra II is capitalized, and why algebra is not. Avoid giving them too many different rules at one time.

SPELLING

Learning to spell is learning about words—their meanings, forms, and uses in communication. (15)

Richard Hodges

Spelling errors tend to be publicly offensive errors, the ones most damaging to the writer's reputation. A paper may have far more serious errors, yet spelling mistakes stand out as the most prominent feature of the paper—one that may mark the writer as "careless" or "dumb." Mina Shaughnessy believed that the public views correct spelling as the hallmark of an educated person, and that failure to meet that standard causes others to question both the quality of the writer's education and native intelligence. Despite this, noted Shaughnessy, out of all the writing skills, spelling is viewed by most teachers and students as the one most resistant to instruction and least related to intelligence: "It is the one area of writing where English teachers themselves will admit ineptness" (161–62). Regardless, secondary English teachers often experience frustration when faced with students who cannot spell, mainly because they didn't expect this problem, and they are not sure how to deal with it. Yet, as Richard Hodges points out:

> Individuals make few, if any, random spelling errors. Each incorrect spelling has a cause, whether from carelessness or from insufficient or erroneous knowledge about the written language. (13)

Moreover, says Hodges, some aspects of spelling are learned best at the secondary level, when students have both greater intellectual maturity and life experience (13).

Spelling Without Panic and Despair

Students who are disabled spellers have most likely been told, for years, that they must "do something about spelling." Consequently, these students dislike writing and fear putting anything on paper, where each new word opens up more potential for making errors. However, it is critical that they write, for it is within the context of their original writing that spelling instruction must take place. Forget the textbooks and handbooks, forget the gimmicks offered by various commercial vendors, and stick to student drafts. In the first place, drafts have words that students want to use—in context and with a purpose. In the second, spelling can be put in its appropriate place, as the final concern for correctness. Students need to separate composing from editing, composing well from spelling well. For students who have been lost in a fog of errors, this is no small consideration.

Elizabeth Grubgeld offers some useful suggestions for helping students emerge from the fog:

1. Analyze the errors as they emerge in student drafts, "find clues to the hodgepodge of rules, visual memories, and systems of logic" by which students make spelling choices (59).
2. Once you have imposed order on the chaos of errors, provide the student with a limited number of words for proofreading, allowing the student ownership and control of the words.
3. Help the student see structures within their words that provide keys to words with similar structures.
4. Isolate words with similar structures and let the student work inductively to discover the patterns and principles.
5. Consider various alternatives for ways in which students can describe their own spelling rules: Write a series of conditions (questions) that help to examine the word in question; conversationally write an answer to the question "what confuses me about this word?"
6. Forget the common practice of teaching confusing words together (e.g., *there* and *their*—put *there* with *here* and *where*).
7. Teach students the concepts of syllable, root word, and affixes, so they see words as divisible rather than as an arbitrary groupings of letters.
8. Suggest that the student "read as slowly and with as much choppiness as someone who can barely read" to increase the ability to hear unstressed syllables.
9. Combine oral reading with practice in visual recognition of the grapheme-phoneme correspondence (i.e., written letters to sound).
10. Establish ways to emphasize blurred pronunciations, such as associating *major* with *majority* to prevent spelling *majer.*
11. Develop spelling cards: Punch holes in the top of index cards and put rings through them (or buy a set of cards that are prepared that way for research writing). Have students list their spelling words alphabetically, using large handwriting or printing; they write only the correct version of the word, underlining the confusing part. If the confusion came from not hearing syllables, they leave a space between the syllables. Next to the word, they write why this particular word gives them trouble, and finally, they record some means of remembering the correct spelling. Occasionally check the cards, note error frequency, and provide extra work on problem words as warranted.
12. Encourage students to tape-record their words and then take dictation from the tape. (48–50, 58–61)

Grubgeld notes that this method is time-consuming and slow and that one semester or even one year may not correct the errors. However, she believes that students become critical readers in the process, recognizing spelling errors as they proofread (58–61).

Spelling and the Average Error-Maker

Although many of Grubgeld's suggestions work as well for average students, you can expect more autonomy and responsibility from students who are not truly disabled in this area. Ask students to self-edit first. Have them edit in a color other than that in which they wrote, circling any word that appears strange to them. They should then check a dictionary or other spelling aid. Students who use a computer may have the advantage of a spell checker. However, they must understand that not every writing situation allows them such freedom and that they need to have a good grasp of spelling, regardless.

Improving Spelling

Richard Hodges' monograph *Improving Spelling and Vocabulary in the Secondary School* has many suggestions for increasing student awareness and proficiency with language. Herbert Kohl's word books offer a similar resource for secondary teachers. Using a variety of word games and puzzles helps to keep student interest high. Commercial games such as *Scrabble, Probe,* and *Wheel of Fortune* offer endless hours of experience with words. Vocabulary development is critical to all aspects of the English language arts. However, don't give students lists of words to memorize or match to definitions. This approach does little or nothing to improve students' vocabulary, mainly because the words are decontextualized and the routine is rote and meaningless. As with any learning, students need context and motivation, a genuine purpose. Thus, reading and writing are central in the acquisition of new words.

The study of words (e.g., roots, commonalities, affixes) can be fascinating and purposeful if students apply this knowledge in their writing. Poetry is an excellent way to explore and exploit the power of vocabulary. Working with vocabulary from students' other courses is also important. Content area teachers often fail to teach their students about discipline-specific vocabulary, despite students' need to understand the web of definitions found in texts and related materials. William E. Nagy's monograph, *Teaching Vocabulary to Improve Reading Comprehension,* is an excellent resource for teachers who wish to learn how to link vocabulary study to students' prior knowledge. Nagy explains why traditional methods either fail or create problems and offers strategies for more effective instruction.

We need to remind ourselves how students learn to spell. Hodges sums it up nicely:

> One learns to spell by having opportunities to generate useful "rules" about the written language, an outcome that becomes possible only through a rich interaction with written language in numerous and varied settings. Every instance of writing and reading is a potential moment for learning more about the properties of spelling. (13)

Spelling, then, is a contextual activity, not lists of words and a Friday test. Hodges also makes an important point about spelling errors: "Individuals make few, if any, random spelling errors" (13). It is up to us, through talking with students, to determine the cause.

Staying Calm and Answering Questions

Teaching English sometimes seems like a risky business. Our "products" are visible in a way few other subject areas are: They are speaking and writing in the world at large. It's important, then, that we understand why some errors persist, why these errors continue to be in the public's eye (and critical voice), and how we can respond. The more completely we understand and articulate how we acquire various language skills, how much time instruction takes, and what type of environment we need to do so, the more easily we can quell parental fears or uneasiness about new methods in teaching writing skills.

Box 9–8

ON THE LINE . . .

Alan's passion is football, not English class. He has turned in the following essay, and you schedule a conference with him. How would you approach the problems?

> *Wide recievers and lineman are two different kind of people. One is a alusive and quick person and the other is purely brut strength. The wide reciever has to relay on his fleet feet and his ability to get open for a wining TD. The linemen has to block his man so he doesn't get to the quarterback.. He has to go threw endless pain. The obvious difference between the two are there role in the game. The wide reciever gets all the glory. He makes the spectaculer catches with no time left. A wide reciever is thought as an artist in a game of violence. The linemen gets no reconition. I am happy I choose to be a wide reciever in high school.*

REFERENCES

Atwell, Nancie. *In the Middle: Writing, Reading, and Learning With Adolescents*. Portsmouth: Boynton/Cook Heinemann, 1987.

Fortier, John. Letter to the author. 15 October 1991.

Friedman, Thomas. "Teaching Error, Nurturing Confusion: Grammar Texts, Tests and Teachers in the Developmental English Class." *College English* Apr. 1983: 390–99.

Hodges, Richard E. *Improving Spelling and Vocabulary in the Secondary School*. Urbana: National Council of Teachers of English ERIC, 1982.

Grubgeld, Elizabeth. "Helping the Problem Speller Without Surpressing the Writer." *English Journal* Feb. 1986: 58–61.

Kirby, Dan, and Tom Liner. *Inside Out: Developmental Strategies for Teaching Writing*. 2nd ed. Portsmouth: Boynton/Cook Heinemann, 1988.

Lindemann, Erika. *A Rhetoric for Writing Teachers*. 2nd ed. New York: Oxford UP, 1987.

Madsen, Alan L. "Language Games and Usage." *English Journal* Oct. 1987: 81–83.

Meyer, Emily, and Louise Z. Smith. *The Practical Tutor.* New York: Oxford UP, 1987.

Mitchell, Arlene Harris, and Darwin L. Henderson. "Black Poetry: Versatility of Voice." *English Journal* Apr. 1990: 23–28.

Newkirk, Thomas. ed. *To Compose: Teaching Writing in the High School.* Portsmouth: Heinemann, 1986.

Nagy, William E. *Teaching Vocabulary to Improve Reading Comprehension.* Urbana: National Council of Teachers of English ERIC, 1988.

Noguchi, Rei. *Grammar and Teaching Writing.* Urbana: National Council of Teachers of English, 1991.

Romano, Tom. *Clearing the Way: Working with Teenage Writers.* Portsmouth: Heinemann, 1987.

Rosen, Lois Matz. "Developing Correctness in Student Writing: Alternatives to the Error Hunt." *English Journal* Mar. 1987: 62–69.

Sanborn, Jean. "Grammar: Good Wine Before Its Time." *English Journal* Mar. 1986: 72–80.

Schafer, John C. "Punctuation and Process: A Matter of Emphasis." *English Journal* Dec. 1988: 46–49.

Schuman, R. Baird. "Seeing and Feeling Sentence Structure." *English Journal* Jan. 1990: 71–73.

Shaughnessy, Mina. *Errors and Expectations.* New York: Oxford UP, 1977.

Tabbert, Russell. "Parsing the Question: 'Why Teach Grammar?'" *English Journal* Dec. 1984: 38–42.

Tollefson, Stephen. *Grammar Grams.* New York: Harper, 1990.

Strong, William. *Creative Approaches to Sentence Combining.* Urbana: National Council of Teachers of English ERIC, 1986.

Vail, Neil, and Joseph Papenfuss. *Daily Oral Language.*

Evanston: McDougal Littell, 1989.

Van DeWeghe, Richard. "Spelling and Grammar Logs." *Non-Native and Nonstandard Dialect Students.* Ed. Cindy Carter et al. Urbana: National Council of Teachers of English, 1982.

10

Understanding Grammar

It appears that the teachers of English teach English so poorly largely because they teach grammar so well.

Linda Enders, high school student

Grammar is perhaps the most contested and the least understood area of the English language arts curriculum, despite being the area most taught in U.S. schools. Many people associate English classes with grammar: learning terminology and rules, diagramming sentences, filling in blanks and worksheets, and taking quizzes. Presumably, these activities enable students to speak and write acceptable English. The presumption, however, is false. Considerable research and classroom practice have shown that these activities have little or no effect on student competency and performance (Braddock et al.; Haynes; Bamberg; and Hillocks).

Researchers continue to tell us what many classroom teachers already know: Practicing skills in textbooks or worksheets doesn't work. The skills fail to transfer when students are engaged in the messy business of composing a full essay. A student who has done 10 exercises and passed a quiz on a specific skill may make errors in that skill on the very next essay. There are several reasons for this. First, the isolated study of language skills has little or no effect on that permanent language knowledge we carry in our heads. Second, we make choices about language through the context in which we use it; a drill sheet has no context, only unrelated sentences. Third, the "dummy runs" in texts and worksheets are far less complex than the students' own language. If students don't learn to untangle their own language and judge effectiveness and correctness in an entire piece of writing, they will gain little or no proficiency. But even more damaging is the time factor: Students who are doing exercises are not writing. They are not learning about standard usage, appropriate mechanics, and correct spelling in the one context where these skills are both meaningful and mandatory: real communication. Student drafts provide ample opportunities for teaching the various language skills as they relate to communication, to what students themselves want to express.

Because grammar evokes personal, and even emotional, responses, teachers need to understand the diverse meanings applied to the term *grammar*. When teachers say they are going to do a "grammar unit," they usually mean they are going to concentrate on some aspect of standard American usage, such as conventions or sentence patterns. For example, they will block out two weeks to cover subject-verb agreement, three weeks to study comma use, or two weeks to work on sentences with a subject-verb-object pattern. Even though the notion of a grammar unit is outdated, many teachers, nonetheless, persist in it. An examination of school curricula and textbooks demonstrates its resistance to change, despite research that refutes teaching skills as isolated units.

WHAT IS GRAMMAR?

As noted earlier, controversy and confusion arise when the word *grammar* is used. People usually give three reasons why they think students must study grammar: students can't put a sentence together; students don't know a noun from a verb; students can't speak or write without making mistakes. In exploring these reasons, we can find underlying definitions of the term *grammar.*

Students Can't Put a Sentence Together

In this context, grammar refers to the set of rules native speakers know intuitively, the rules we acquired without lessons, as we acquired our native language between birth and age 6. Grammar here is tacit, unconscious knowledge. As native speakers of English, we know how to form words and sentences, no matter how simple or how complex, and we do so without making any conscious decisions about word order, word endings, and so forth. In brief, we know the grammar of our native language.

Assuming normal development (that is, no damage to the brain and capacity for language), all native speakers know the grammar of their language. They recognize non-grammatical English sentences immediately. For example, the construction

    sees boy the ball red

would be rejected by every native speaker of English. Teachers and others may not like some students' sentences, which may be poorly constructed, awkward or unclear, suffer from weak vocabulary, or punctuated incorrectly. However, these weaknesses are not grammar problems, at least not to teachers who understand grammar as the system of language we learn as native speakers.

Students Don't Know a Noun From a Verb

In this context, the term *grammar* refers to the ability to talk about the language system; it is our conscious knowledge about our native language. In the United States, tradition has dictated that educated people know some basic language terms, such as noun, verb, adjective, adverb, and sentence. An understanding of these terms is not acquired naturally, the way the language itself is. We have to learn the terms through instruction, thus the heavy emphasis on them at every curricular level. In reality, few students learn all the terms. Their textbooks often define the terms poorly, probably because the concepts they represent are far more complex than people like to believe. For those who do learn the terms, the knowledge is often fleeting, largely because students quickly realize that labeling nouns and defining verbs does not make a significant impact on their lives. As one 10th grader recently remarked:

> Does anyone really believe that we have to know this stuff, that someday a person will jump out from behind a tree and say "Tell me what a verb does"?

Students' aversion to learning terms for terms' sake is supported by research; understanding the function of language is more important than memorizing terms and definitions. However, English teachers persist in their belief that "doses" of such directed study do improve language skills, especially writing. As Rei Noguchi puts it: "Like the near mythical omnipotence of cod-liver oil, the study of grammar became imbued with medicinal power it simply did not possess, particularly with respect to writing ills" (15).

Thus the labeling of parts of speech, the diagramming of sentences, and other activities designed "to name" language rather than to use it, continue. The same 10th grader who questioned the validity of studying terms also commented on their domination of the curriculum: "Different cover, same old stuff." We do expect an educated person to have literacy skills, that is, to be able to read and write competently, but these abilities are not the result of knowing the parts of speech. Moreover, forcing such knowledge before students have a reason for knowing or the cognitive maturation to understand is futile.

Students Can't Speak or Write Without Making Mistakes

Here grammar refers to rules of language etiquette or verbal manners: We adhere to a standard use of language in the academic or business world. This standard has nothing to do with communication, for nonstandard forms communicate meaning as well. For example, there is no confusion of meaning when we hear nonstandard forms such as *she's taller than me* or *he can't hardly talk,* just as there is no confusion when we read *them boys did pick a fight.* What is involved is a continuum of verbal manners. Many people would not notice the error in *she's taller than me,* but few would fail to notice the deviations in *them boys did pick a fight.* "Mistakes," then, translate into a view of what does or does not constitute standard American English, the dialect used in the world of formal communication and taught in schools, the dialect of social prestige.

Since standard dialect is the dialect of schools, English language arts teachers want students to use it. Most parents, similarly, want their children to know and use it appropriately. The key, however, is flexibility and appropriateness to the communication situation. Teachers sometimes assume that all "mistakes" are equally serious and all rules applicable in every type of communication. This is simply not the case. Some mistakes derail readers, causing them to go back and sort out the meaning; these errors are serious because they interfere with meaning. Others errors, however, may irritate the purist but cause no confusion for the general reader. The issue of "mistake" is serious nonetheless. Teachers face a challenge in presenting students with a standard dialect and, at the same time, honoring other dialects used at home and in the community.

Patrick Hartwell offers a cogent explanation of the two grammars that get lumped together under the term *grammar*:

> School grammar. This grammar is the one of school textbooks. Although linguists cringe at fuzzy definitions (e.g., a sentence expresses a complete thought), school grammar makes no claims of scientific accuracy. School grammar presents the student with parts of speech, sentence patterns, standard usage forms, conventions of writing and spelling. Another name for school grammar is traditional grammar.
>
> Grammar-as-etiquette. When speakers or writers deviate from certain forms or conventions (those taught in school grammar), they are accused of having "bad grammar." This grammar refers to standard American English, the dialect of school and business.

The basic controversy and debate over grammar are found in school grammar and grammar-as-etiquette. Does school grammar improve grammar etiquette? Researchers have tried to determine whether instruction in traditional grammar improves student writing. That is, do grammar exercises or drills make any difference? To date, the findings suggest they do not, mainly because this approach does little to affect the internal language system.

What does affect it is the use of authentic language: students listening, speaking, reading, and writing standard English; students manipulating language, their own language. English language arts teachers who recognize and teach standard usage and sentence clarity as products of revision enter into a process which, over time, affects the internalization of language. There is no debate over the basic issue—that students can and should become more effective and flexible users of their language—only over the method by which to achieve it. Few curricular areas are as visible or as open to criticism as grammar. Given this, the issue will no doubt remain a force in the English language arts curriculum.

Grammar study as a means of improving students' language is a major reason for its place in the curriculum. Other reasons also exist, associated with everything from studying language for its own sake to preparing students for standardized tests. Teachers need to be aware of these reasons and be prepared to discuss them with colleagues, administrators, and parents.

STUDYING GRAMMAR FOR ITS OWN SAKE

Language is a uniquely human phenomenon; as such, it is worthy of study. However, studying English grammar at the expense of time for listening, speaking, reading, and writing costs most students dearly. To solve the dilemma, many high schools offer an elective course in English grammar at the junior or senior level. Such courses validate the study of language but reserve it for those students who are motivated and capable of undertaking such a study, a study that demands advanced cognitive and analytic skills. A grammar course should in no way replace English courses that offer students a well-balanced experience in the language arts.

Why Grammar Units Persist

Why does grammar dominate the English language arts curriculum? Cultural mythology is one reason. People tend to believe that studying grammar contributes to their ability to use language correctly and well. They either forget or ignore the fact that effective language skills arise out of a great many language activities and a supportive environment. People may also associate grammar study with "real" schooling, their own school days when the "3 R's curriculum" was the standard for literacy. This is, of course, a simplistic—indeed romantic—notion of schools. These schools educated fewer students in a less complicated society and dealt with fewer social ills. Even then, literacy skills came from active listening, speaking, reading, and writing; literacy came from a motivation to become literate and an environment that supported it.

A second reason for the persistence of grammar study lies in English language arts teachers' convictions about themselves. They reason that their own language skills came from studying grammar, diagramming sentences, and so forth. If we think for a moment who the English teachers were, we quickly realize the falseness of their reasoning. Today's English teachers were students for whom reading and writing were constant companions; they were students who liked playing with language. They were highly motivated and probably reinforced continually. A secondary classroom often has at least one student with an aptitude for language in the same way someone else has an aptitude for and intense interest in math. In brief, English teachers forget that they were the exceptions throughout their own schooling.

A third and pervasive force in maintaining traditional grammar lies in texts and workbooks. Here explanations, exercises, and drills come nicely packaged and easily tested. Publishers continue to give teachers what teachers expect; thus, it is fair to say that most textbooks are written for teachers, not students. It is no wonder, then, that language texts seem straightforward and easy to teachers and obtuse to their students. Many English teachers like grammar, like teaching it, and continue to choose texts and other materials that keep this model alive. It is not surprising that grammar still dominates the curriculum. The problem is that grammar study has not and will not solve literacy problems, nor does it enhance the skills of our best students, at least not as long as it is taught as a subject to be mastered. As Rei Noguchi points out, there is considerable difference between "teaching grammar as an academic subject and teaching grammar as a tool for writing improvement" (15). Unfortunately, many teachers are unaware of this difference. Thus the cycle continues.

WHAT TEACHERS NEED TO KNOW ABOUT GRAMMAR

Historically, the English language arts curriculum has shifted back and forth among different notions of teaching grammar. In the late 1960s, many educators turned away from traditional grammar; structural and transformational grammars became the new base of instruction. It was not uncommon in the 1970s to find junior high school texts worthy of a college English major taking a course in structural-transformational grammar. However, these new grammars worked no better than traditional grammar in producing more effective writers. With the perception of an impending literacy crisis, people determined that if the new linguistics had not worked and had perhaps added to the problem, then traditional grammar should be revisited. Thus, the emphasis on formal grammar and correctness in the 1980s reflected a more conservative view of education after the turbulent 1970s.

It is not surprising that veteran teachers are skeptical of any claims related to grammar and language improvement. However, the 1980s also brought advances in our knowledge of how people acquire, process, and improve their language abilities. Studies of students and classrooms, such as those done by Donald Graves, Lucy Calkins, and Nancie Atwell demonstrated the difference between talking about grammar and applying grammar. The Bay Area Writing Project, under the direction of James Gray, also promoted teaching standard usage and conventions through student writing; as state after state initiated a writing project, more and more teachers became convinced of the value of teaching grammar contextually. At the same time, teacher-researchers such as William Strong and Donald Daiker applied principles of transformational grammar and developed sentence-combining to improve syntactic fluency. Most textbooks today reflect, even if briefly, the contribution of this new grammar. However, they also cling stubbornly to the old, causing dissonance for many teachers educated with a writing process approach to grammar and mechanics.

English language arts teachers should be acquainted with all descriptions of grammar: traditional, structural, and transformational. We may be called on to respond to concerns of parents, administrators, and other teachers to explain what we are doing and why, to make informed decisions on materials and methods, and to evaluate our school curriculum. A good grammar background also enables us to help our students make effective language choices and to determine the source of language difficulties.

TRADITIONAL GRAMMAR

The English grammar that we call "traditional" was modeled on the classical languages of Greek and Latin. Roman scholars took both the terms and descriptive methods of the Greeks and applied them to Latin. Because there are some similarities between the two languages, the application was fairly successful. This is not the case when these same terms and methods are applied to English; the result is a distortion of English. For example, one of the rules of Latin grammar was never to split an infinitive, a rule still found in English handbooks today. A sentence such as "To fully appreciate this movie, you need some background in African history" would be judged flawed because the adverb *fully* is placed between parts of the infinitive *to appreciate*. Not splitting an infinitive in Latin made sense because it meant splitting a one-word verb; however, there is no reason not to split an infinitive in English. Sometimes, the rhythm of the sentence makes splitting an infinitive exactly what a writer *should* do. The admonition not to do so is the result of applying Latin grammar to English.

From models of classical Greek and Latin, English grammar moved into medieval times and acquired yet another emphasis that persists today: to "fix" the language, to stop its degeneration, and to eliminate error. This view of grammar matched the focus and instruction of the medieval church. Again, in the eighteenth century, the emphasis on correctness and rules was reinforced in an Age of Rationalism. Today, therefore, traditional grammar is Latin-based, rules-oriented, and prescriptive. Despite the fact that English is structured differently from Latin or Greek, the tradition of teaching the parts of speech is almost unchanged. Since Latin had more word endings than English, we ended up with more categories than we needed, along with rules that were equally inappropriate (Weaver 101).

The insistence on rules and a belief that learning rules will teach students to write correctly is another part of this heritage. Rules such as "It is I" rather than "It is me" exist because Latin takes the nominative form *I* in a mathematical equation: *it = I*. We are to utter "To whom do you wish to speak?" rather than " Who do want to talk to?" because "To whom do you wish to speak" is the base, and prepositions take the objective form *whom,* not the nominative form *who*. Following Latin dictates, definitions became singularly unhelpful and downright obtuse, as this passage from a 10th-grade textbook demonstrates:

- An adjective is a word that modifies a noun or pronoun.
- An adjective clause is a dependent clause that functions as an adjective.
- An adjective clause may be introduced by a relative pronoun or by a relative adverb.

> When Nora arrived later, the old playground—empty and unkempt—shimmered in the heat of the Hawaiian afternoon. Crushed cans and paper cups littered the brown grass. The swings rocked slowly, creaking their rusty chains. The pond was dry.

Adjectives are not the only words that can modify nouns. For example, the second sentence above begins with the phrase *Crushed cans. Crushed* would appear to be an adjective, modifying *cans,* but it is not. It is a verbal—specifically a past participle—which functions in the same way that an adjective does. (Laidlaw Language Series, 1985)

It should be clear that students learn little from this type of textbook and the heritage of Latin grammar—other than a firmer conviction that this work has nothing to do with them, their language, and their world. Learning to work with adjectives and verbals is important in the world of making meaning and of seeing options, but not as a study of arcane terms. When some college composition instructors complain that freshmen don't know gerunds, they place pressure on secondary teachers to teach terms. When some secondary English teachers express shock that students coming to their classes can't define adjectives, they place pressure on elementary teachers to focus on definition rather than function. Teachers themselves thus drive the English language arts curriculum back through the centuries and revive a long tradition of parsing sentences and hunting down errors.

The preoccupation with defining and classifying words and labeling and diagramming sentences also left us with some strange definitions:

A verb is a state of being.
An adverb modifies another adverb.
A noun is the name of a person, place, or thing.

Most of us memorized these and similar definitions, and because we liked English, we had little trouble with them, nor did we resist such tasks. However, they did little to improve our writing skills. Being bookworms and closet writers did that. Many of our classmates, however, those less thrilled about English, not only had trouble with the definitions, but also developed negative attitudes about English class in general. That seems a high price to pay for definitions that are unhelpful and unnecessary for authentic language activities.

Traditional Grammar in the Classroom

Of what use is traditional grammar? For one thing, there is no reason to invent a new vocabulary for nouns, pronouns, verbs, adverbs, and adjectives. As Connie Weaver notes:

Traditional grammar is important, if only because its terminology is widely known and because its appeal to meaning is often vital in determining the precise function of a grammatical unit. (105)

There is nothing wrong in using traditional names when we speak to students about their own writing. Pointing out, for example, that a certain verb doesn't provide the reader with a good sense of the action or that an adjective conveys just the right sense of description *within the context of the student's draft* provides a common vocabulary without drilling labels. The extreme, of course, would be terms such as *gerund,* which students really don't need to know.

Do students have to learn every part of speech? No. The most common categories of noun, pronoun, verb, adjective, and adverb will do. Some teachers collapse adjective and adverb into *modifier* and find that it works just fine. Rather than teach prepositions, teachers can concentrate on the function of prepositional phrases, how useful they are in adding detail, for example. The same holds true for adjective and adverbial clauses, and again, the term *modifier* helps students to see function. However, native speakers can discern for themselves the function of these clauses; they need neither a label nor a lesson in underlining them. Students at all curricular levels benefit from sentence analysis of function: Just how does that word or word group contribute? Is it in the right place? Is it in the most effective place?

Some teachers wonder if they should use the more accurate term *clause* rather than *sentence*. Because *sentence* is the common term, the traditional descriptor, we believe it's fine for student use. Teachers do need to understand *clause* and the difference between a grammatical sentence and a rhetorical one. Weaver provides us with workable definitions:

> *Grammatically,* a *sentence* consists of an independent clause plus whatever dependent clauses may be attached to it or embedded within it.
>
> *Rhetorically,* a *sentence* may be defined as whatever occurs between the initial capital letter and the final period, or between the onset of speech and the utterance's final pause. Hence a rhetorical sentence may be as short as a single word, or as long as several hundred words. (118)

Sometimes, teachers need to explain to students why their "sentence" is not a sentence. The definitions, as just given, would be unsuitable, but the idea of "rhetorically correct," as well as some discussion of the differences between oral and written language, would be very helpful. As noted earlier, a great deal about traditional grammar is unhelpful, if not downright confounding, but English language arts teachers can view it as part of their professional background and draw on it for commonsense applications.

STRUCTURAL GRAMMAR

Whereas traditional grammar was prescriptive, telling us what we should or shouldn't do, structural grammar attempted to describe language as it exists. Thus, structural linguists divided language into three levels: (a) individual sounds (phonology) (b) groups of sounds with meaning (morphology), and (c) arrangement of words, relationships among parts (syntax). They also classified words differently. For example, *gangsters* is a noun not because it is the name of a person, place, or thing but because its inflection -*s* marked it as a noun. This suffix belongs to nouns, marking a plural in English. *Gangster* is a noun because of another suffix that marks nouns, -*ster* (cf. *youngster*). And finally, the placement of *gangster* in English sentences marks it as a noun: The *gangsters* were put in jail. I saw *the gangsters*. Nouns lead off most English sentences; nouns often have *the* or *a* in front of them; nouns are in predictable places in English sentences.

We can see how this system works by examining what native speakers do:

1. The + kitten + s + jump + ed + play + ful + ly.
2. The + kit + tens + jum + ped + pl + ayfully.

No native speaker of English would divide the sentence as in 2 because the system of affixes carries meaning to a native speaker: -*s* = plural on noun; -*ed* = past tense on verb; and *-ful* + *-ly* = adverb. This knowledge is part of the internal grammar, the tacit knowledge, of a native speaker. A few irregular forms aside, we automatically add an *-s* when we want to make nouns plural, *-ed* when we want to make verbs show past tense. Structural linguists used this knowledge as the base of their description of the language.

In English, the flexibility of affixes is characteristic:

green greener greenest   earn unearned
soft softer soften   visual vision visible

These are derivational affixes—changes in the form of the word that may change its function in the sentence. For example:

She will sweeten her coffee with sugar.
Do you have a sweetener here?
I find the sweetness sickening, but I will sweetly comply and bring the sugar.

There are also inflectional affixes:

for plurals: boy boys   church churches
for tense: work worked

These characteristics, then, became part of structural linguists' attempt to describe English as native speakers know and use it. Structural linguists also looked at sentence patterns. These are the most common in English:

Subject	verb	direct object
The boy	hit	his neighbor.

Subject	verb
The boy	lies.

Subject	linking verb	complement
The boy	is	angry.

Subject	verb	indirect object	direct object
The boy	gave	his neighbor	a black eye.

Sentence features such as noun and verb markers were also identified: *a, an,* and *the* are common noun markers; *can, should, would, will,* and *might* are common verb markers. A native speaker can recognize the role of a nonsense word because of these features, the affixes, and the word order common to English sentences. For example:

The wibbels ruped lifly on the jip.

Any native speaker would indicate that *wibbels* is the subject, a noun. *Wibbels* is placed between the noun marker *the* and a word recognizable as a verb (*-ed* marking its tense). The *-s* on *wibbels* indicates plural form, a sign of a noun. The verb *ruped* is marked by the *-ed*. *Lifely* has an *-ly* to indicate how the wibbels ruped. And the phrase *on the* marks *jip* as place, another noun. Even in nonsense, a native speaker of English can identify how the parts fit together.

The flaw in this description of English, as other linguists have noted, is its inability to account for the creative use of language. As native speakers, we produce thousands and thousands of sentences never before uttered or written, yet understood perfectly by other members of the language community. When linguists asked how we can do this, transformational grammar took its place among the English grammars.

Structural Grammar in the Classroom

Structural grammar is important, says Weaver, because "it lends precision to definitions and to procedures for identifying grammatical units and their functions" (105). Whereas traditional grammar defines a noun somewhat vaguely as "name of person, place, or thing," which can get teachers into all kinds of trouble, structural grammar identifies a noun by certain endings, such as a plural or a derivational affix. Verbs, traditionally defined as words that "express an action or a state of being," are defined structurally by their endings or a distinctive verb form (Weaver 111). Trying to explain "state of being" to a 12-year-old is something most teachers never want to do; in fact, we're not even sure what it really means. On the other hand, verbs can be identified by the inflectional endings we use to show tense. The verb also functions as the beginning word, or *headword* of a predicate; it's essential to meaning. Structuralists identify adjectives and adverbs similarly, both by characteristic endings and by function. Youngsters can relate to concrete endings and function more easily than to definitions, which may fail them in complex sentences.

By the time students enter middle school, they have been very successful communicators, using nouns, verbs, adjectives, and adverbs at will, stringing them together in very acceptable sentences. The problems occur as students enlarge their vocabulary and their capability for more sophisticated syntax and increasingly have to deal with written rather than oral language. Recognizing endings, understanding the flexibility of English words, and recognizing the function of words or word groups can help them make this transition. They don't need to practice sentence patterns; they already know them. However, teachers usually have to bring this tacit knowledge into consciousness. Through questions that make students analyze their own words and sentences, teachers are encouraging independence and empowering students. They soon realize how much they already know about their language. Structural grammar, then, has a place in the classroom.

TRANSFORMATIONAL GRAMMAR

Transformational grammar attempts to explain the production of sentences through a number of basic (kernel) sentences that transform or expand into various patterns. Whereas the base of structural grammar was empirical, based on what native speakers actually say, the base of transformational grammar is theoretical. No one actually knows if these language structures exist or work in the way presented by linguists. Transformational grammar assumes the existence of deep structures that lead to surface structures, or what is actually said or written. According to transformational grammar, we have two basic sentence types: kernel and transformed.

A kernel sentence: John is my friend.

A transformed sentence could be

A negative: John is not my friend.
A question: Is John my friend?
A passive: The ball was hit by John.
Embedded: John, who is my friend, hit the ball.

According to linguists, we access these patterns in producing sentences, automatically and effortlessly in the case of speech. Noam Chomsky, whose work in transformational grammar was revolutionary, claims that we are born "wired" for this language activity, that we learn a set of rules and learn how to transform sentences, all without instruction. With this ability, we are able to create endless numbers of sentences. Transformational linguists devised a set of rules, called phrase structure rules, to describe how we form and transform sentences. They represented sentences in symbol strings:

NP + pres + Be + NP
John   is   my friend

Transformational grammar shows the patterns of English at work, how native speakers construct novel sentences out of basic patterns. For students of language, this was a useful view of the creativity of language, of process rather than product.

Transformational Grammar in the Classroom

For many English language arts teachers, transformational grammar was a revelation, a means of viewing English from a very different perspective. When viewed as product, the language appears static, and teachers are often hard pressed to explain how certain sentences got that way or how the language was working. With an understanding of embedded sentences and transformations from one sentence form to another (e.g., to negative, to question), teachers found a useful classroom tool. Sentence combining became the most visible and applied means of transformational grammar. Indeed, this instructional strategy remains one of best ways to improve student awareness of syntax, rhetorical effectiveness, and function of punctuation.

WHY THE DIRECT TEACHING OF GRAMMAR FAILS

The Nature of Kids

Teaching grammar directly fails not only because of flawed methods but also because of the inherent nature of language and of our students. The study of any grammar involves the study of an abstract system, a set of abstract rules about the nature of language as described by various linguists. This calls for both well-developed analytic skills and high motivation. Our students, almost without exception, lack both. As pointed out, students already know grammar—intimately and thoroughly, possessing nearly total competence to express meanings they themselves understand. Consequently, they see little reason to take sentences apart, label parts of speech, fill in blanks, and diagram sentences.

Student attention, if focused at all, is usually on the wrong thing. As one 16-year-old remarked on leaving her high school English classroom: "I *know* I got it straight; I used a ruler." So much for the importance of diagramming. Students also fail to see why a teacher or parent is upset with a statement such as "He ain't there." It communicates meaning, which is, after all, the point. And students fail to be enthused about a course that tells them that "It is I" is any more useful than "It's me." As teachers, however, we can provide needed lessons about the varieties of American English, about audience and purpose, and about choices in language. Only then might we convince a student of the unsuitability of "He ain't there." Lectures on rules, dozens of exercises, or weekly mastery quizzes merely reinforce the students' sense of "no concern to me, not my world."

Improving Student Skills

What's more, teaching students to break down sentences will do nothing to improve their capability to create and improve sentences. Syntactic maturity—the ability to write more complex and varied sentences—comes with cognitive and linguistic development, not from learning rules or memorizing sentence patterns. What is important is providing sustained experience in all the language arts; students will improve their language through using language. This notion appears so simplistic that people sometimes resist it, yet it is the basis for competency. Rather than breaking down and labeling sentences, students need experience in building them. Through creating, changing, and manipulating sentences, students gain fluency and flexibility, much as a musician does when practicing finger exercises. Once students understand that syntactic control is linked to making meaning, to what they themselves wish to convey, sentences take on a new significance—one certainly not appreciated in isolated exercises.

Making Useful Distinctions

As teachers, we need to keep the distinction between grammar and usage very clear. We have a native ability to create and comprehend sentences; this is our internal grammar. Usage, on the other hand, is linguistic etiquette, a set of socially acceptable styles of language. Problems arise when we insist on one standard usage as an absolute, the only way to say or write something. English permits many forms of language, a range of choices dependent on situation and audience. Approaching usage from this perspective allows students to maintain their many voices. Often usage is extended to mean mechanics as well—punctuation, capitalization, and so forth. Again, the notion of an absolute standard causes both student difficulty and apathy. For example, students partially learn a comma rule for *and*; then they add a comma every time *and* pops up on their paper, incorrectly breaking apart phrases most of the time. If, instead, students learned that commas function to help us read more easily and comprehend more quickly, the world would be blessed with fewer commas and less red ink.

We also need to help students see the distinction between speaking and writing, that writing is *not* speech written down. Again, the more useful lessons about varieties of English come into play. Students do know their native language grammar orally but may be inexperienced with manipulating it on paper or even seeing it on paper. If their vocabulary is impoverished, they struggle even more. If we work from a perspective of native language competence, from what students *do* know, we can influence student performance and their language use in everyday life. Teachers who substitute grammar drills for experience in oral or written language, on the other hand, will seldom have that pleasure. Grammar is alive, something we use—not a subject to be taught.

DEMYSTIFYING GRAMMAR

We need to demystify language. No matter which grammar one is talking about, the grammar is arcane knowledge, part of a teacher's repertoire. Students perceive it as a mystery, as something they aren't very good at, and perhaps as a rite of passage. Too many adults' only remembrance of English classes is grammar. Since students usually don't understand the abstract grammar system, they survive by learning some rules, memorizing others, and doing the exercises as assigned. With minimal motivation, most students can get by. The problem is that they are not internalizing anything; the activity has no real effect on their language patterns and behavior. Thus, teachers should not be surprised when students make mistakes in composition, when the very skills drilled and tested turn up as errors in full discourse.

If these teachers stopped to think about it, one mystery might be solved. Students who have had a steady immersion in grammar arrive every fall with little or no knowledge; every teacher more or less starts from scratch in teaching grammar. Why? Because for most of their academic lives, students lack the cognitive skills to understand analytic grammar. Furthermore, most lack the motivation. Studying grammar in the context of their writing is valuable and necessary, and when students see grammar linked to making meaning, their motivation increases. But when English language arts teachers take grammar and turn it into another bit of content knowledge to be memorized and tested, grammar becomes disconnected and disliked.

UNDERSTANDING STUDENT ERRORS

Novice Writers

In her masterful exploration of unskilled writers, Mina Shaughnessy offers some of the most cogent explanations of student error. Shaughnessy first reminds us that "errors count, but not as much as English teachers think" (120). Teachers, she notes, are trained to evaluate students by absolute standards rather than by developmental standards. Teachers forget that their students, for the most part, *are* novice writers. Thus, serious grammatical errors may stem from a lack of experience in academic writing rather than a problem with the language itself. Shaughnessy also argues that if we view novice writers in the same way we view foreign students learning English, where errors are accepted as part of normal development—and not as evidence of their incapability of learning, their inability to be educated—that we, and the students, would be better off (90). This view does not suggest that teachers ignore errors. Allowing students to write in a fashion in which we merely "catch the meaning" is irresponsible. However, as Shaughnessy suggests, many teachers embark on an error-hunt that fails to distinguish between the important errors, those that seriously impair our ability to comprehend, and the merely irritating, those that bother only the English language arts teacher.

Expecting Too Much

Shaughnessy raises another issue in asking us to consider whether it is realistic to expect unskilled writers to learn what we set out for them in the time allocated. The acquisition of writing skills is highly individual, and for students lacking a good background in reading and writing, the process takes time. Moreover, students from homes where literacy is lacking and poverty is commonplace are disadvantaged to begin with. We cannot expect them to meet timetables based on some mythical average student or laid out by publishers unconcerned with adolescent growth and development or societal problems. Inexperienced teachers often have unrealistic expectations of student learning, which may bring frustration both to teacher and student.

Textbooks can reinforce these expectations, especially if they present chapters of separate grammar skills, a linear plan that is contrary to how we actually acquire and process language. Further, cognitive and linguistic maturity limit what we do, when we do it, and with what degree of competency or proficiency. Another human reality lies in the gap between cognition and production, between the time in which we comprehend something and when we can produce it ourselves. This gap between cognition and production parallels the way we acquire oral language. We could understand far more than we could produce, a problem that time and sustained language experience solved. Thus student failure to correct grammar errors immediately is not necessarily a reason to repeat the lesson; rather, students may just need more opportunities to apply the lessons in original writing (Shaughnessy 120).

Smart Errors

Another view of error, but one seldom discussed anywhere, is a positive one: Many errors are errors of competency, a demonstration of student progress toward more complex language. This phenomenon is perhaps recognized more often with second-language students, but it occurs in native speakers as well. In middle school, for example, students begin to use more complex syntax, thus increasing their potential for error. The errors are the result of progress, not regression; they're really "smart" errors. Kids need to know that.

TRIAL AND ERROR

To learn to write, one has to write and to make mistakes. Errors are a normal part of the process, or as James Moffett puts it, "trial and error":

> Now, trial and error sounds to many people like a haphazard, time-consuming business, a random behavior of children, animals, and others who don't know any better . . . Trial and error is by definition never aimless, but without help the individual alone may not always see how to learn the most from his errors. (198–99)

In Moffett's opinion, teachers should present students with meaningful trials (assignments), in meaningful order, and provide "feedback that insures the maximum exploitation of error" (199). Even more important in Moffett's view of student error is his contention that the "teacher does not try to prevent the learner from making errors" through preteaching (199). If, according to Moffett, a teacher does preteach, the student approaches the writing task with "good" and "bad" in the head, trying to keep them separate. In this way, errors are viewed as "bad" rather than what they are—part of trial and error, part of growth. Responding to those who might ask if this is not a discouraging way to learn, Moffett says:

> For one thing, trial-and-error makes for more success in the long run because it is accurate, specific, individual, and timely. For another, if the teacher in some way sequences the trials so that learning is transferred from one to the next, the student writer accumulates a more effective guiding experience than if one tried to guide him by preteaching. (200)

Moffett stresses the importance of plentiful and informed feedback that is given in the process of writing and not after the fact. Within this context, error carries no stigma. If students view errors as normal and see themselves as capable of correcting them, motivation to do so should remain high.

Unfortunately, this view is uncommon in many secondary classrooms, especially in school systems where less able English students are routinely assigned to remedial classes. These classes are often designed on the deficit model, a model that assumes students are incapable of recognizing and self-correcting language errors. This model also elevates the status of error; entire courses are built around stamping out various errors of syntax, usage, and mechanics, usually through rote drill and exercise formats. We are not suggesting that students in remedial English courses have no deficiencies, for they do. However, these deficiencies lie in written language only and relate to inexperience in reading and writing—not to native language competency. Thus, many remedial courses fail to build on what students *do* know, thus continuing a cycle of discouragement and frustration for all involved.

In *Errors and Expectations,* Shaughnessy speaks of student capabilities:

> Students themselves are the best sources of information about grammar. Despite difficulties with common errors, their intuitions about English are the intuitions of the native speaker. Most of what they need to know has already been learned. What they have not learned and are not used to is looking long and carefully at sentences in order to understand the way in which they work. This involves a shift in perception which is ultimately more important than the mastery of any individual rule of grammar. (129)

In this view, remedial courses would be built around a great deal of oral and written language experience; error would take its place as a normal part of learning to write academic English. Texts and exercises focused on error would vanish; texts that proceed deductively would vanish. In their place would be time and an environment that allows for inductive learning, for Moffett's trial and error.

SOURCES OF ERRORS

When teachers are confronted with student errors, they must make certain assumptions about the source and then consider the implications for teaching. Three basic assumptions are common:

1. That the learner doesn't know the grammatical concept
2. That the error is due to a lack of information and habit
3. That errors are developmental

We would be wise to limit the first assumption, that the learner doesn't know the grammatical concept, to students for whom English is a second language. For these students, a particular concept may not exist simply because their native language lacks this feature (e.g., tense, articles). To assume this situation with speakers of American dialects, however, is wrong. A student whose first dialect is Black English Vernacular understands grammar and has a grammar very similar to standard dialect. Some of the surface features do differ from standard dialect, including pronunciation. Therefore, we need to know these features to avoid error judgments when students are merely "translating" the standard printed dialect into their spoken dialect. For example, in reading, a student may turn *John's hat* into the oral *John hat,* indicating she does understand the concept. In her dialect, *'s* is not needed.

There may be times when our least experienced readers and writers do not understand the grammatical concept, but these will be infrequent with native speakers of English. If students don't understand the concept, we have to break it down, analyze its parts, and then present it to them in a way that allows them to see the function. Subject-verb agreement, for example, relies on an understanding of singular and plural. We need to start there, not with agreement itself.

If a lack of grammatical concept is seldom a source of error, then what is? Some errors may stem from a lack of information or a language habit. In this view, language equals behavior, and that "bad" behavior can be fixed. This notion often leads to intense correction of oral and written language, the fate of students labeled "remedial." The first problem with this approach is its lack of judgment about which errors count most. Some teachers attack every error as though each were equally important in derailing meaning. This shotgun approach to error usually overwhelms students and contributes to further confusion, indifference and, in some cases, hostility. Moreover, the approach takes on a life of its own if worksheets and workbooks are around. Such practice doesn't transfer when students do their own writing, where they are not told what to pick out, label, or underline. Shaughnessy puts it this way:

> It may well be that traditional grammar-teaching has failed to improve writing not because the rules and concepts do not connect with the act of writing but because grammar lessons have traditionally ended up with experiences in workbooks, which by highlighting the feature being studied rob the student of practice in seeing that feature in more natural places. (155)

"In more natural places" refers to genuine discourse, people involved in communication and making meaning. Because habits of any type involve a will to change, we need to link language habits to genuine discourse. Students need a reason to edit and proofread.

ERROR ANALYSIS

Error analysis, a more developmentally based approach, asks us to discover the pattern and frequency of errors in student writing. Because it asks for an explanation of what is happening, the approach is more aligned with language acquisition than with behavior. We discover that some errors are performance errors, which students should be able to correct. An oral check quickly sorts these out, for they are the types of error most associated with editing and proofreading. These errors often form the basis of mini-lessons linked to student writing; the errors mar the final product but don't interfere with meaning. A grammar-based error, one for which the student lacks the information to self-correct, is best handled in a one-on-one teaching situation. In any event, error analysis assumes that one keeps a record of errors: types, where most pervasive (i.e., in which types of discourse), and frequency.

Another view of error, but one seldom discussed, is that of avoidance. We can't assume that the absence of grammatical or mechanical errors means mastery. Some learners simply avoid certain words and constructions, knowing that they have had trouble with them in the past. Students, for example, who have had trouble punctuating descriptive clauses may not try to use them. College freshmen often admit to this "play it safe" approach to writing when confronted with questions about their "look-alike" sentences. Thus, the absence of error does not necessarily mean competency or proficiency, especially among some of our best students. They may be afraid to take risks and need to learn about "good errors," about growth through errors.

TAKING ON ERROR

Shaughnessy warns us about ignoring errors for fear of inhibiting students, a non-helpful approach with students who already feel helpless (127-28). Students are well aware that they make errors and lack knowledge about academic writing. Thus, ignoring errors, either from a sense of "kindness" or a sense of "not that important," does nothing to help students. We need to convince them that they can take on errors and, most importantly, we need to provide them with the strategies to do so.

Errors: For Editing Only

Shaughnessy also reminds us that "correcting errors is an editorial rather than a composing skill and requires the writer to notice features of a sentence he would ordinarily have to ignore during composing " (128). Given this, students must learn to look at their own sentences analytically. If they do a great deal of original writing and take the writing process through editing and proofreading, they will get this experience. However, they need strategies to guide them. We discuss these strategies in Chapter 9.

Errors cause so much trouble with novice writers because, as Shaughnessy notes, they "seem to demand more concentration than they're worth" (123). Students have been communicating successfully for years, something they have learned to do without direct instruction. Writing correctly is a learned behavior, requiring them to shift vision and analyze, something they don't normally do in informal speaking.

Errors and the World at Large

For some minorities, the situation is more complex. Many cannot identify with standard dialect, the majority dialect and its culture. Error thus takes on an emotional dimension as well, a perspective that might be shared by other students as well, but for very different reasons. Even excellent students can be motivated negatively by error. For them, errors are to be avoided at all costs because the emotional costs are also high, with penalties of low grades and reduced social status. For many other students, errors bring ambivalence at best.

Young people carry a false notion that writing is not all that important; after all, the world seems linked by cellular phones, television satellites, and other wonders of modern communication. Given this view, we must make a case for the mastery of standard written English; it is the language of public communication, public transactions, school, and business. "Getting on in the world" and having choices are linked to language. Against a background of pragmatism, of respect for various American dialects, and of linguistic versatility, we can make a strong case for standard written English.

SUGGESTED ACTIVITIES

1. As the most recently hired English teacher in your school, you have been asked to update your colleagues on research in teaching grammar. With sinking heart, you agree. You know some teachers are using methods and materials that do not reflect current knowledge about how students learn language, and you risk alienating them regardless of how carefully you frame your presentation. You face an ethical dilemma: You need to be accepted as a colleague, but you also need to be honest about the state of the field and promote the best possible learning situation for students in your school. What will you say? Prepare an outline of your remarks.

2. "Back to Basics" is a familiar theme among proponents of a traditional curriculum, especially grammar. However, as the centerpiece of the writing skills curriculum, traditional grammar is indefensible. You need to bring your knowledge of language acquisition, writing processes, cognition, and adolescent development into play when you take that position—and explain why contextual grammar instruction has taken the place of drills, memorization, and dummy runs.

   Choose one of the following situations, and in a one-page piece, present your position. Consider the background of your audience carefully. You cannot assume knowledge nor can you underestimate the force of tradition, especially with parents and the community.

   a. You are teaching in an essentially rural school fed by several small communities. The students' backgrounds are diverse, some from professional families and many from farm or small business families. School activities, especially in music and athletes, are the centerpiece of the community, and most parents are interested in what goes on in the school. When you took over the English 10 course, you discovered the textbooks, although relatively new, contain sentence diagramming, many subskills exercises, and so forth. Consequently, you decide to leave the texts on the shelf other than for occasional, limited use. Some of the students tell their parents that they like your class because they don't have to do grammar anymore. As a result, a few parents decide to find out why you have dumped what they see as an essential part of the English curriculum. Instead of calling you, they call your principal. She tells you to prepare a letter to the parents of English 10 students to explain what you are doing and why.

   b. You will teach an English 12 college prep class. The course description indicates that students will learn traditional grammar as part of their preparation for college composition. You know that college composition does not require knowledge of traditional grammar, nor do standardized college admissions tests. You also know that the best preparation for college composition is revising, editing, and a good vocabulary. Since English 12 has excellent students, you know they could learn traditional grammar quite easily, but you don't want to spend time on it. You also know their parents will be interested in what you are doing, so you just can't "shut the door" and ignore the district's curriculum guide. How would you change a curricular emphasis in traditional grammar? Write a curriculum proposal that will go to your department chair (a traditional grammarian, greatly respected in the district) and curriculum coordinator (a generalist, not specifically for English language arts).

REMEMBER: Your task is not only to indicate why you don't support a traditional approach; it is also to present a contemporary approach in down-to-earth language. Further, keep the kids at the center of your proposition.

3. You have been assigned to the committee that is to recommend an English language (composition and grammar) textbook for district adoption. Your task is to examine an English language textbook series for three consecutive grade levels (either middle school/junior high school or senior high school). First, your committee must determine the criteria for selection. On what will you base your recommendation and why? Make a list of the criteria. Then, you must apply the criteria to the texts themselves. For example, if one of your criteria says that students should work inductively, drawing their own conclusions about the way their language works, then you will evaluate student activities to see if they are based on inductive learning. When you complete your evaluation, write a brief, informal memo telling the rest of your committee whether you would recommend this text series.

4. Your 11th-grade composition and grammar textbook has the following explanation of the adverb phrase: *An adverb phrase is a prepositional phrase modifying a verb, an adjective, or another adverb.* Although you want your students to use adverb phrases correctly and well, you see nothing but trouble ahead as you scan the examples given in the textbook:

EXAMPLES:

The fire moved like dancers.
The hat looked strange on her head.
Leo arrived late at night.
Ms. Jones has lived there for 10 years.

An adverb phrase may come before or after the word it modifies.

EXAMPLES:

The reporter interviewed the attorney before the trial.
Before the trial, the reporter interviewed the attorney.
More than one adverb phrase may modify the same word.

EXAMPLE:

On October 2, the space shuttle Pegasus was finally launched into space.

EXERCISE 1: IDENTIFYING ADVERB PHRASES

Each of the following sentences contains at least one adverb phrase. Identify each and the word it modifies. [Twenty sentences follow these instructions.]

a. You shut the book and decide to develop your own lesson on adverb phrases. One of your colleagues stops in just as you utter a large sigh, and he wants to know what the problem is. What do you tell him?

b. The two of you decide to develop this grammar lesson together. Your classes are comprised of native speakers of English, but they also have a range of skill levels—and a number of very uninterested students. Sketch out a plan. What activities will you include and why?

REFERENCES

Atwell, Nancie. *In the Middle: Reading, Writing, and Learning with Adolescents.* Portsmouth: Boynton/Cook, Heinemann, 1987.

Bamberg, Betty. "Composition in the Secondary English Curriculum." *Research in the Teaching of English* Oct. 1981: 257–66.

Braddock, Richard, et al. *Research in Written Composition.* Urbana: National Council of Teachers of English, 1963.

Hartwell, Patrick. "Grammar, Grammars, and the Teaching of Writing." *College English* Feb. 1985: 105–27.

Haynes, Elizabeth. "Using Research in Preparing to Teach Writing." *English Journal* Jan. 1978: 82–88.

Hillocks, George. *Research on Written Composition.* Urbana: National Council of Teachers of English, ERIC, 1986.

Moffett, James. *Teaching the Universe of Discourse.* Boston: Houghton Mifflin, 1968.

Noguchi, Rei. *Grammar and the Teaching of Writing.* Urbana: National Council of Teachers of English, 1991.

Shaughnessy, Mina. *Errors and Expectations.* New York: Oxford UP, 1977.

Weaver, Constance. *Grammar for Teachers: Perspectives and Definitions.* Urbana: National Council of Teachers of English, 1979.

11

Evaluating English Language Arts

Practitioners must educate the public that strong correlations exist between qualitative measurements—student artifacts, exhibits, projects, portfolios, experiments, and other creative products—and workplace demands for self-directed, collaborative workers. (11)

Jim Abbott

AUTHENTIC ASSESSMENT

Many teachers are changing what they teach and how they teach in response to John Goodlad's description of the curriculum in most schools as being dull and lifeless, filled with teacher talk and uninterested students (*A Place Called School,* 1984). Classrooms have become more student-centered as students are allowed and encouraged to self-select topics for writing and texts for reading. Small groups provide more opportunities for interaction among students. As teacher talk declines and student input increases, interest and enthusiasm heighten student learning. However, too often, the students are evaluated with the same old tired tests and quizzes. Abbott explains that "Quantitative measurements, such as multiple choice, norm-referenced tests, reveal only a small portion of a child's knowledge" (11). How teachers evaluate their students' progress deserves a closer look.

Authentic assessment is the fair assessment of what students know. The problem with standardized tests and other tests that require one correct answer is that students may know the information called for, but the question may be worded in a way that does not make sense to them. This is especially true for ESL students or students of limited language proficiency. Often, to get a correct answer, students must guess what the author of the test was thinking rather than show that they actually know the information. For this reason vocabulary, comprehension, and short-answer tests should allow students to answer in their own words rather than include formats such as matching columns or selecting multiple-choice or true/false answers. Students then can explain in their own way what they know.

Larry Johannessen explains that teachers continue to use the same tests because of habit; they have given the tests for years and feel comfortable with them (66). "The trouble is that most of us give quizzes without thinking about why we are giving them; and most important, we don't think about what the effect of giving them will be, especially over a long period of time" (67). Teachers must consider what their purpose is for each quiz and whether it really tells them what they want to know. For example, teachers give pop quizzes because they want to make sure students do the required reading. The problem is that pop quizzes do not serve this purpose. The threat of a pop quiz does not encourage students who read with difficulty or those not interested in the required selection to read; consequently, they receive yet another F. They become discouraged and lose even more interest. Students who excel at reading often finish the literature far ahead of the others and when given a pop quiz have difficulty remembering the literal information required for these tests. Quizzes do not tell teachers how well students interpret literature or learn an interpretive skill or strategy (Johannessen 68). All students view them as unfair, even those who do well because they have no input into the content or timing.

Students need to have a voice in the assessment process so they know what its purpose is, what it tells them about their learning, and what the teacher will use it for. "Assessment should teach students something, not just take time away from teaching" (Sandra Murphy 151). Both students and teachers need to learn something from evaluations other than a meaningless number or percentile. The criteria for evaluation need to be "explicit to students, so that they can begin learning how to do it for themselves" (151). Assessment does not have to be something teachers "do" to students, but rather a process in which teachers can improve their teaching for individual students and in which students discover what they need to focus on in their learning.

PLANNING FOR EVALUATION

Evaluating students' work can be a teacher's most difficult task. Should one pay more attention to content or mechanics? How do we give credit for creativity? How does the evaluation of a research paper differ from an evaluation of a short story? The answers lie in the teacher's purpose for assigning the particular activity. Or put another way, what did the teacher want the student to learn? Evaluation means deciding if something worthwhile happened, not just measuring a skill. Consequently, teachers must be clear and specific about what they expect to happen when they give students a particular assignment.

Box 11–1

ADAPTING GOALS FOR ASSIGNMENTS

What goals might a teacher have for assigning a written report to 7th graders? How would the goals change for written reports for 11th graders? What goals would one have for writing poetry?

PURPOSES OF EVALUATION

Evaluation is not the same as measurement. We evaluate to see if something worthwhile was accomplished. We might evaluate our teaching methods or our students' learning. In *The Evaluation of Composition Instruction,* Davis, Scriven, and Thomas describe two purposes for evaluation: formative and summative. Formative evaluation is used to discover how writing can be improved; that is, what specific areas do students need to work on to become better writers. Summative evaluation is used to report the overall quality of the writing (3–4). Both forms are useful when used appropriately. When teachers want to know if their teaching methods are improving student learning, summative evaluation provides that information. When teachers and students want to identify particular strengths and weaknesses, formative evaluation gives them that information. Holistic evaluation is an example of summative evaluation and is commonly used to assess the success of a curriculum. For example, a school district may collect student writing samples in several grades and evaluate the writing holistically to determine the effectiveness of the writing curriculum. This type of summative evaluation does not supply information on individuals, only on the program as a whole. Analytical grading scales are examples of formative evaluation that furnish information on weaknesses and strengths of students' writing. Because of the amount of time needed for formative evaluation, it is used more often in individual classes than in large-scale assessment.

ASSESSMENT

Most school districts have some method of assessing how well students do in reading, math, and writing. Assessment of writing can be either direct, as in a writing sample, or indirect, as in an objective test. Objective tests are editing tests in which students read test items to identify errors in punctuation, subject-verb agreement, pronoun-noun agreement, and other conventions of language depending on the grade level tested. However, direct assessment more closely reflects what is taught in the classroom and provides a clearer idea of what needs to be improved. Our goal is to help students become better writers, and objective tests are not a good measure of that. A student may be able to pick out writing errors, but not be capable of thoughtful, interesting writing, and the reverse may be true as well. Unless large-scale assessment and classroom grading reflect the teacher's purpose in teaching writing, the evaluations provide no useful information, and, in fact, can be harmful to teachers and students because the information is misleading.

Box 11–2

PURPOSES OF EVALUATION

What are the similarities and differences among assessment, evaluation, and testing? As a teacher, when and how would you use each one? What would the goals of using each be?

EVALUATING LITERATURE

What matters to students is not the details of knowledge they pick up when studying literature, but the "internalized concepts that help them to cope with the problems they encounter in the world outside of school and throughout their lives" (Schuman 55). Because of this emphasis, educators are less interested in objective testing and are looking for ways to assess interpretive skills. When literature is presented through a whole language approach, the scope of reading sources widens greatly. Many teachers are uncomfortable with whole language because their students are reading books they themselves have not read (55). However, if teachers limit students to reading selections the teachers have read, they are narrowing the scope of reading experiences. When teachers use the whole language approach, the works themselves are not as important as the way students analyze the works.

Using reader response for literature study invalidates the true/false, multiple-choice, and even the short-answer tests. This doesn't mean that we can't evaluate students' knowledge and understanding of literature, but it does mean that we must truly test students' knowledge and not force them to guess what the teacher is thinking.

In "Testing Literature: The Current State of Affairs," Alan C. Purves summarizes a longer report of a study funded by the U.S. Department of Education. He explains that tests published for secondary school students are, for the most part, multiple-choice questions that focus on comprehension at a relatively low level of understanding. The questions are based on the meaning of specific parts or the main idea of a passage and test literature as if it were the same as encyclopedia articles or research papers. Little attention is paid to the artistic characteristics of literature, such as language, structure, and point of view. Purves' report recommends not using purchased tests and encourages teachers to create their own methods of evaluation.

Teachers can create their own evaluation methods in several ways. First, it is important to realize that not all assignments should be graded. For instance, response writing would be checked only for the effort the student made in reading and responding. The same is true for any journal writing, even when we give fairly specific assignments for journals. Length is not an accurate measure of the effort, but teachers can evaluate the extent of the reader's involvement with the text.

Another important area of literature study is discussion. However, keeping track of who answers questions in class is tricky and an unreliable way to assess interest and involvement. Some teachers believe that noting when students respond to a question motivates discussion, and occasionally that may indeed be the case. The danger, though, is that only high-achieving students will care about the discussion grade. Also, shy students may find it very difficult to talk in class, and it would be wrong to penalize them. Response and discussion are crucial to active class participation, but they are informal activities and, as such, do not need to be evaluated with a grade.

Many assigned activities can be graded on a more formal basis, but a teacher should clearly state the purpose of the assignment and grade accordingly. For instance, if the activity is to write down characteristics that will help readers understand character's motives, the evaluation should reflect that purpose. That is, did the student describe the characteristics? Too often, teachers grade all activities alike, even though the purpose can be quite different. The teacher may count spelling, punctuation, and grammar, for example, even though the assignment was to discuss viewpoint. The levels of writing described in Chapter 6, "Teaching Composition," clarify the connection between purpose and evaluation.

Box 11–3

CONNECTIONS BETWEEN PURPOSE AND EVALUATION

Describe the purposes for assigning a poem to be written at each of the three levels. Write an evaluation plan for each of the three levels.

Over the span of time that students are reading a text, the teacher may use questions to guide their understanding. Students often answer questions as homework assignments, discuss their answers, and hand them in the following day. Questions, of course, depend on the literature, but as a guide, one might use questions like these:

What factors influenced the actions of the characters?
How did relationships between people influence actions?
Why do you approve or disapprove of a character's action?
Why do they behave the way they do?
In what ways are their actions realistic or unrealistic?

Students' answers will vary, but as in responses, a teacher can tell if a student has read the material. Because these are more formal than responses, they are graded more formally. A point system works well, such as five points for each question; the total score rather than a letter grade goes on the paper. Using points more clearly specifies acceptable and unacceptable answers for each question rather than assigning a grade for the work as a whole.

A more formal evaluation is the essay exam. New teachers are often tempted to use a test written by either another teacher or a publishing company. But students don't always understand the questions even if they did understand the novel. Because the exams do not necessarily test what was covered in class, a teacher who wants to be fair to the students should teach the test material, whether it seems appropriate or not. Ready-made tests cannot reflect the dynamics of the classroom discussions and learning. Short-answer, true/false, and matching questions all test lower level comprehension, and that is not what we want to test students on. Instead, we want to see if they grasp connections between ideas, make inferences about motivations and outcomes, analyze points of view, and judge a work's effectiveness; in other words, we want to test higher order thinking.

Teachers often express two objections to essay exams. First, some believe that the evaluation of essay answers is not objective. On a multiple-choice or true/false question, the answer is either right or wrong, and the teacher needs only to count up the number of correct answers and convert that number to a grade: 80 percent right is a B, 90 percent an A. The numbers make us believe we are being objective, and therefore fair. However, the test itself is subjective and unfair, even though we can count correct responses. It is difficult, if not impossible, to write multiple-choice, true/false, and matching questions that are not misleading. Short-answer questions test recall, the lowest stage of critical thinking. When teachers or unknown test makers create a test, they decide what is important for students to remember and learn. That's where the subjectivity comes in. By giving students more latitude in explaining what they know and understand, we give them a more objective test, that is, one that is not as tied to the teacher's way of stating information. A true test of our understanding comes from our ability to explain in our own words.

The second objection is that essay exams take longer to grade than op-scan sheets or short-answer tests. Yes, they do. However, it is not an impossible amount of time. As teachers read the answers, they have a clear idea of what they are looking for, even though it may be expressed in a variety of ways. It is best to evaluate one question at a time on all students' exams. That way teachers get a good idea of how the responses compare in the development of ideas and the use of details and examples. Then, they shuffle the papers before reading the second question. This method ensures that teachers are not influenced as much by the paper they read just before. Several studies have shown that the order in which essays are read does affect our evaluation. If we read a strong essay followed by a weaker one, the second one suffers by comparison. Also, the 20th essay will probably seem less wonderful than the 2nd one did, even though they are similar. It does take time to read essay exams, but they promote learning and give students opportunities to express ideas in their own words, and that makes them well worth the time.

It is also important to remember that students write the exams in class where time and test anxiety are factors, and students may not use correct punctuation or spelling. Therefore, it is inappropriate to consider these skills when evaluating. We are looking for understanding of the literature, and that is all we need to pay attention to. When students are concentrating on thinking, the most common word can be misspelled. Mechanics are important, but not in a testing situation.

CONSTRUCTING TESTS

In a student-centered classroom, evaluation covers both academic and personal competence because teachers want students to learn not only material and strategies but also how to continue learning without a teacher's guidance (Everly 193). Testing for academic competence gives students opportunities to show they have subject area knowledge and understand structures for learning in an area. Testing personal competence includes showing that they can manage their time to reach goals and take responsibility for their work (193). A test that covers these areas must clearly define the required task, provide guidelines, and allow students to manage their work time on their own. Everly designed a test that resembles a unit; one that is a "complex, authentic task that requires one to two weeks of constant class time work to complete" (194). Peer tutoring and review are encouraged, but the teacher does not help except for procedural questions. Figure 11–1 shows an adapted version of Everly's test.

Editing guides, response sheets, and the grading criteria for this assignment are available for students. Everly publishes the stories so students have a clear sense of audience as they compose. Exams of this type evaluate subject knowledge, ability to use time wisely, and knowledge of how to organize a task—important skills for a lifelong learner.

Evaluation can take many forms besides an exam. Teachers often require papers as a final project instead of an exam. Group projects are also valid ways of evaluating if students understand the literature. We believe it is wise to use a variety of evaluation methods to accommodate different learning styles and to encourage interest in class activities. We need to be as creative when evaluating as we are when providing choices of writing assignments, topics, and projects.

Your assignment is to write a short story using what you have learned about the writing process and literary forms and techniques. Your story will be published in a class literary anthology and distributed at the end of school. You may choose the subject and format of your story, but you must include the following:

1. At least two well-rounded characters

2. A conflict

3. Direct and indirect characterizations

4. A believable setting

5. A developed plot

6. At least two techniques for building suspense

FIGURE 11–1
Adapted version of Everly's test.

Evaluating Writing

Teaching writing through a process approach means that the purposes of activities vary. For example, the purpose of a discovery activity in which students practice how to develop a character is different from a library activity that acquaints students with Newsbank. The purpose of an assignment to practice dialogue is different from that of an assignment to write a story including dialogue. The differences in purposes of assignments shape evaluations. What we want students to learn determines how we evaluate.

Creating the assignment and deciding how to evaluate it should happen at the same time. If this connection is not clear in the teacher's mind, and therefore not clear to the students, evaluation can be troublesome. Students have the right to know how their work will be evaluated before they hand it in. Shelly Smede, a junior high school teacher, agrees: "Part of assessing student work fairly is to let them know exactly what you expect before they begin" (93). If teachers evaluate using levels, students know the teacher's expectations and never have to ask if spelling or neatness counts.

Evaluation by Levels

By using levels of evaluation, teachers focus the grading and students know how their writing is to be evaluated. Parents, too, need to know how the students' papers are evaluated. With the process approach to writing, students have papers that contain mechanical errors, yet receive comments of praise and, perhaps, a high grade. When parents understand the three levels used to evaluate their children's writing, they are much less likely to criticize because they understand the evaluation procedures. To create the home/school connection, teachers write letters to parents at the beginning of the school year explaining the levels of writing and emphasizing their expectations for each level. Also, at the beginning of the year, students write the level of the assignment on the paper. Then, when parents do read their child's work, they are more likely to understand the purpose of the assignment and evaluation.

Level 1

For level 1 assignments, the teacher's purpose is to provide a wealth of activities for ideas and practice. Teachers want their students to engage in a wide range of thinking, such as brainstorming; making connections between thoughts, as in mapping; or practicing a variety of kinds of writing. If teachers add the layer of correctness to such activities, the purpose is lost. First drafts and journal writing are also level 1. Here students concentrate on getting ideas down; if they stop to look up a word or even to consider how a word is spelled, their train of thought is interrupted. In level 1 writing, the writer should be free from distractions as much as possible. The purpose is to get thoughts on paper and to try new forms of expression. Notetaking is also level 1; writers jot down notes to help them remember, and that is the only purpose.

The audience for level 1 is, first and foremost, the writer. The writer may be the only one who hears or reads the writing. However, peers may also be the audience when the writing is shared in groups. An example of using peer groups for level 1 could be when students are thinking of questions to use for a report or when they share ideas for a collaborative story.

To evaluate, teachers may read the writing and make a comment or a checkmark to show they read the work. Often, though, the teacher does not read this level because it is not handed in. Students may keep it in a notebook or folder, but no evaluation is necessary. Level 1 writing is the foundation for all other writing and is therefore assigned the most frequently, even daily. In level 1 writing, students practice writing, try out ideas, take notes, write in journals, and respond to reading or listening. The major focus is on content; the main audience is themselves.

Level 2

A level 2 assignment is somewhat more formal. The purpose of these assignments is to explain, inform, or to further develop a discovery writing activity. Teachers assign level 2 writing to see if students understand ideas and concepts. Examples of this level are homework assignments, essay tests, and multiple drafts students are working on. The audience is the writer, the teacher, and peers. The audiences are always known, and the writing is often read by others, not only shared orally. Because people other than the writer read the writing, a certain amount of formality is required. Writing conventions need to be adhered to so others can understand the writing. On the other hand, level 2 is not intended as a final draft and is not evaluated as such. A teacher evaluating a level 2 assignment expects correct spelling of common words and the correct use of most punctuation marks. However, if a student uses an uncommon word and spells it incorrectly, the error is not noted. When teachers overemphasize spelling, students do not expand their vocabulary. Instead, they use a word they know how to spell rather than one that captures the connotation they want. In an essay test, a teacher may circle a misspelled word, but spelling errors should not be included in the evaluation. The teacher's purpose is to see if students understand the material, not to check their spelling ability. Level 2 assignments should reflect knowledge of common conventions of punctuation. The appropriate conventions depend on the abilities and grade levels of the students.

Organization is another area not evaluated highly at level 2. Thinking is not a highly organized activity, and students often think of other ideas and points too late to make coherent organization. For example, in an essay exam, students may write in the margins or crowd words in between lines because they are thinking hard about the subject and remember additional information.

In homework assignments, the intensity seen during essay tests is not present, but if students make an effort to organize their thoughts, that is sufficient. Again, teachers want students to add new ideas even if the paper looks messy because of the additions. Level 2 assignments are rarely recopied. The emphasis is on content with a common level of correctness. Level 2 writings are assigned two or three times a week.

Level 3

Level 3 assignments are the most formal. The purposes for these assignments are to give students an opportunity to write for audiences outside the classroom, to organize thoughts into a coherent form for readers outside the writers' circle of friends, and to learn the value of creating error-free writing when the occasion calls for it. Level 3 writings are always polished drafts that students carry through all of the stages of the writing process. Examples of assignments include research papers, reports, stories, letters, plays, poetry, and essays. Length is not a factor in determining levels. Level 1 might be the longest, such as journal writing; level 3 might be one page or less when writing a poem.

The intended audience is oneself, the teacher, peers, and unknown readers. Level 3 writing might be for a class or school anthology, the school or city newspaper, a gift for family or friends, and used any time a writing needs to be the best possible. The teacher's purpose is to help students learn how to carry a piece of writing through revising, editing, and proofreading to create an error-free paper that is well organized and interesting to read.

Evaluating a level 3 writing is similar to traditional grading of writing. Because the paper has been taken through all the writing process stages, a teacher can expect it to be the writer's best work. However, the mechanical aspect of writing never outweighs the value of the content.

Students are more likely to value creating a polished piece of writing when the purpose is clear; if teachers require "perfect" papers every time a student writes, students lose interest in that objective. No one writes perfect papers all of the time because no one needs to. Writing done in the world outside of the classroom is largely at levels 1 and 2, except for occasional reports. List making, notes to oneself, telephone messages, journal writing, and class notes are all level 1. Letters we write to people we know are level 2. College students write more level 3 papers than anyone else, far more than they will after graduation. Secondary students learn how to produce a polished draft if teachers assign a level 3 no more often than once every four to six weeks. Going through the entire writing process takes a great deal of class time. That in itself is not a negative aspect, but running out of time to include a wide variety of writing forms and activities is. Teachers never have enough time to carry out all their ideas, and assigning a level 3 writing more than once a month can eliminate creative dramatics, independent reading, discussions, and other activities.

Figure 11–2 summarizes the three levels of writing.

Box 11–4

LEVELS OF EVALUATION

Discuss the importance of writing levels in improving student writing. Describe how the purposes would be different for an assignment to write a short story at level 2 compared to one written at level 3.

	Level 1	Level 2	Level 3
Style	Informal	Semi-formal	Formal
Audience	Writer, teacher, and classmates.	Writer, teacher, class-mates, and parents.	Writer, teacher, class-mates, and parents. May have an audience outside the classroom.
Function	Thinking, organiz-ing, generating ideas, fluency, and study skills.	Organizing, develop-ing ideas, explaining, and informing.	Recognizing the value of error-free products, editing, and proof-reading for a wider audience.
Form	Notetaking, journals, responses, lists, and mapping.	Exams, homework, drafts, reports, and summaries.	Letters, reports, poetry, books, and final drafts.
Evaluation	Content only. Often not evaluated.	Content and appro-priate conventions.	Content, form, skills, word choice, neatness, and typed format.

FIGURE 11–2
The three levels of writing.

METHODS OF EVALUATION

Depending on the purpose of the writing assignment, evaluation varies from formal to informal. Evaluation does not necessarily mean a grade is assigned. We evaluate to see if students are learning what we want them to learn. A variety of methods can supply that information. In fact, teaching writing by the process approach requires many different evaluation techniques, depending on the stage or level of the writing.

Impression Grading

Discovery activities are always evaluated with impression grading; that is, the teacher reads the writing quickly to see if the student put effort into the writing. Teachers may write comments on the students' papers but not evaluative ones. When reading journals, teachers respond in writing as an adult friend, someone who listens and nur-tures. Other discovery activities may require only a short comment: "good start, cre-ative, interesting." Or the comment can encourage students to expand their thinking and writing: "tell me more about . . . , how did. . . . happen?, what did you think of the part where . . . ?" If teachers ask specific questions, students have an easier time expanding on what they wrote. In some cases, a simple checkmark at the top is suffi-cient to let students know the teacher read their work and approved. Sometimes students ask if these discovery activities "count." Because discovery activities are essential to good writing, we want to make sure students value their work at this level, but we do not want to evaluate on a more formal basis. Informal grading and following up if a student does not turn in an assignment help students realize the teacher values their work, so that they, too, will come to value it.

Holistic Grading

Holistic grading gives an overall evaluation without identifying the particular weaknesses or strengths of the writing. Papers are evaluated on the overall success of the writing, not on specific elements. Papers are read as a "whole" piece, and the evaluator decides if the writing is competent or not. Because this type of evaluation is quite reliable and quickly done, it is useful for large-scale assessment, such as evaluating writing in an entire school district. In the classroom, holistic grading may also be used as an assessment tool when a teacher wants to know, in general, how well the students write or if teaching methods are effective. At the beginning of the year, a teacher assigns a writing task and evaluates the writing holistically. Then, later in the year, the teacher gives a similar writing assignment and evaluates it in the same manner. By comparing the two pieces of writing, teachers monitor students' progress.

Writing used for holistic evaluation is usually done during one class period, or it can go through the stages of the writing process. In either case, when assignments are holistically evaluated, the final draft is not returned to the student because the teacher makes no comments and the grade is only a number. Such evaluation, although useful to the teacher, means nothing to students. Receiving a holistic grade does not help students improve their writing because they do not know what specifically they did right or wrong.

When evaluating holistically, evaluators spend about two minutes on each paper and use scoring guides to decide the category of competency for each paper. Using an even number of categories works best because the top two describe acceptable writing and the lower two, unacceptable. For instance:

4	3	2	1
acceptable			unacceptable

If an odd number of categories is used, the middle area becomes confusing: 5, 4, 3, 2, 1. Would papers that fall into the middle be considered competent or not? Evaluators tend to score near the center of the scale. Providing a middle number increases the chances of that happening. Holistic grading requires that decisions on the quality of writing be made quickly and decisively.

Scoring guides describe what is expected in each category. Criteria include the amount of detail, the extent the writing reflects the writer's own experience, organization of ideas, and control of the conventions of writing. Holistic evaluation determines overall fluency. Grammar, punctuation, spelling, organization, and expression of ideas together form a sense of fluency. Even the best papers contain errors; in fact, good writers tend to write longer papers and, therefore, may have more errors. Also, if the students had to produce the writing in a certain length of time, which is usually the case when collecting writing samples from a large number of students, the writing will contain more errors. The quality of writing is lower than if students wrote in a less stressful situation. Students may have time to read over what they wrote, but the writing looks more like level 2 writing than level 3. The scoring guide needs to reflect the limitations of timed writing.

Analytical Scales

Analytical scales evaluate the parts of a written piece. Because this method is slower than holistic evaluation, it is seldom used in large-scale evaluation but is a valuable tool in the classroom. Paul Diederich and associates at the Educational Testing Service (1974) developed a grading scale used for scoring SAT essay essays. (see Figure 11–3). The scale emphasizes ideas and organization. The first four factors in the scale are on "general merit" and the last four on "mechanics" (54). Analytic scales are useful evaluation tools. Teachers can adapt the scale to fit the assignment, the grade level, and the recent focus of teaching. Using such a grading scale ensures a fair weighting of all the elements that create the final grade for a paper.

The content of a paper should always be at least 50 percent of the total grade. If a student makes several errors in spelling, and spelling errors are designated as 10 percent of the grade, then regardless how many words are misspelled, only 10 percent of the grade is affected.

Quality and development of ideas	1	2	3	4	5	
Organization, relevance, movement	1	2	3	4	5	
						_____ × 5 = _____
Style, flavor, individuality	1	2	3	4	5	
Wording and phrasing	1	2	3	4	5	
						_____ × 3 = _____
Grammar, sentence structure	1	2	3	4	5	
Punctuation	1	2	3	4	5	
Spelling	1	2	3	4	5	
Manuscript form, legibility	1	2	3	4	5	
						_____ × 1 = _____

FIGURE 11–3
Diederich rating scale.
Source: Diederich (1974): 54.

Correct form (5)   _____

Sense of audience (2)   _____

Clear information (3)   _____

Mechanics (5)   _____

_____

Total points (15)   _____

FIGURE 11–4
Sample analytical scale for evaluating a resume.

The scale represents a contract between a student and the teacher. Before students write their final draft, they have a copy of the scale and know exactly how the paper will be evaluated by the teacher. The scale is also used during peer response groups, particularly at the editing stage. The criteria on the grading sheet is the focus for the student editors.

We assign point values to each criteria rather than using the multiplication technique in Diederich's scale. The criteria and point values differ greatly from one assignment to another. The criteria reflect what the teacher wants students to achieve in each assignment. For example, form might be important in one assignment and not in another. When the assignment is for seniors to practice writing a resume, the points might be divided up as shown in Figure 11–4. The number in the parentheses represents the possible points for each criterion. The number of points actually received by the student is noted on the blank line. Students know exactly why they receive the grade they do.

For longer level 3 assignments, the analytic scale is more detailed to reflect the amount of time available for students to work on the writing and the effort they put into it. Figure 11–5 is an example of a scale for a research project intended for juniors and seniors. The first five items relate to the content of the paper and are 50 percent of the total grade. The reason the conventions count for so much in this assignment is that a main purpose is for students to learn how to use documentation. Several smaller assignments at levels 1 and 2 gave students opportunities to learn these skills. The final draft went through a response group, an editing group, and a proofreading session.

Using scoring guides helps teachers to more accurately evaluate. We all have biases about certain errors. Someone may be really bothered by incomplete sentences, another by subject-pronoun errors. Mistakes should be noted for a paper that went through all of the revision steps, but every error should be counted in fair proportion to the rest of the paper. A scoring guide makes it easier for a teacher to grade in an unbiased way.

The scoring guide in Figure 11–5 was used with students who were familiar with analytical scales. When students are not used to this type of grading, descriptions of the items are helpful. For example, students would not necessarily know what "Organization of subject clear" means. A description of organization might include the following:

Name _____

Thesis clearly stated	(5)	_____
Organization of subject clear	(10)	_____
Major points clear	(10)	_____
Supporting details and examples well developed	(15)	_____
Introduction and conclusion clear and concise	(10)	_____
Correct word choice	(10)	_____
Transitions clear	(5)	_____
Punctuation acceptable	(10)	_____
Spelling accurate	(10)	_____
Introduced borrowed material	(5)	_____
Correct documentation	(5)	_____
Accurate work cited page	(5)	_____

Total Points (100) _____

Comments:

FIGURE 11–5
Sample scoring guide for a research project.

Transitional words connect paragraphs. Paragraphs are in a logical order. Ideas in each paragraph are related. The paper as a whole has logical sequencing. Major points are supported by examples and support.

When scoring guides are used, we do not mark on the students' papers. A checkmark in the margin calls attention to a particular place, but the comments go on the guide. When papers are unmarred by teacher's comments, the students can make revisions and hand the paper in for further evaluation. If teachers make all the needed corrections, students lose ownership of the paper. They just go through the motions when they revise, not thinking about how and why to make changes.

Some Final Points to Remember

- Scoring guides are a type of formative evaluation designed to help young writers improve their writing.
- The guides differ from one assignment to another and reflect the development age of the students.
- Students are familiar with the scoring guide before they turn in final drafts to the teacher.

	Needs improving			Very good	
Strong major points	1	2	3	4	5
Supporting vivid details	1	2	3	4	5
Lively specific language	1	2	3	4	5
Clear organization, easy to follow	1	2	3	4	5
Transitions provide unity	1	2	3	4	5
Mechanics and grammar	1	2	3	4	5
Overall impression of the piece	1	2	3	4	5

FIGURE 11–6
Sample checkpoint scale.

Box 11–5

SCORING GUIDES

Write a scoring guide for a report written by 7th graders. The report is worth 100 points and is a level 3 assignment. What changes would you make in the scoring guide if it were a 12th-grade assignment?

Checkpoint Scales

Checkpoint scales include specific criteria and an overall impression of the paper. Teachers need to develop their own guides and vary them depending on grade level and assignment. The advantage of checkpoint scales is that they can be used quickly. Besides providing an in-progress evaluation, the guides suggest ways to improve the writing without actually doing the revision for the students. An example of a checkpoint scale is illustrated in Figure 11–6. Using a checkpoint scale is a quick way to help students gain a sense of "how they are doing"—something young writers often need for assurance.

SELF-EVALUATION

First and foremost, writing must please the writer. No matter who finally evaluates, if the writer is not pleased with the piece, the writing will lack spirit and flair. The more involved students are with the whole process, the more they personally care about what they wrote. Too often, however, evaluation comes from a source outside the process.

With help, students learn to be a good judge of their own writing. Criteria for judging writing are developed by the whole class. Students tend to be critical when they discuss writing in the abstract. They often describe criteria far too difficult to achieve. Through discussion, teachers can help them understand what is important at each stage of the process and at each writing level. The list of agreed-upon criteria then guides the self- evaluation.

The list should not be a checklist or a series of yes or no questions. Checks do not engage one's mind because it is too easy to just check yes for each item without really thinking about it. Student textbooks commonly include checklists to help students with their own editing, but such lists do not require a thoughtful response. Students do a better job if teachers give them opportunities to slow down their reading and think about the writing. Items on a checklist can be turned into directions that help students locate errors or into questions that require answers other than yes or no. For instance, "Did I spell all the words correctly?" can be changed to a more helpful suggestion: "Read your paper slowly, looking only for misspellings. Circle any word you are not sure of, and after reading through the paper, look up the words you questioned." Or on the subject of description, "Where is your best descriptive phrase? Where else might you add descriptive details?"

Assignments selected for self-evaluation should not then be evaluated by the teacher. Self-evaluation means assigning a summation comment or grade to one's own paper. This is different from reading over one's own work before receiving help from a response group or turning a paper in for a grade. Self-evaluation is a way of helping students understand what it means to evaluate, and the experience improves their own writing. Self-evaluated papers may go into a writing folder, or the teacher may record the grade and return the papers to the students.

EVALUATION OF ORAL LANGUAGE

In a classroom, the setting for oral language is often small groups. Discussion group responsibilities can be described and used as evaluation techniques for teachers and students. Les Parsons in his book *Response Journals* organizes the skills needed for effective group discussions into five areas:

1. Sharing with others (speaking up, listening to others, giving facts and reasons)
2. Replying to others (asking clarifying questions, replying to others, sharing equally in the talking)
3. Leading others (suggesting ideas, problem solving, keeping on topic)
4. Supporting others (helping others have a turn, acting interested in what others say, giving others credit)
5. Evaluating in a group (indicating if you agree, considering how to make the group work better, adjusting own ideas after listening to others)

Parsons suggests focusing on only one or two of these areas during a discussion. After the small-group discussions, students record in their journals whether they used a particular skill, how well they succeeded, and what they can do to increase their competence (58–59). Teachers can use the same criteria to evaluate an individual's group participation.

EVALUATION OF UNITS

Evaluation occurs as students progress through the unit. Teachers evaluate journal writings as a level 1 task and mark a checkmark in a recordkeeping book to indicate a student completed the work. The same method is used for much of the group work. Collecting the work and responding to it is important. Students need to know the work "counts," and when a teacher writes a response or comment on their work, it gives them the sense that it was important. Level 2 writing, such as homework and some group work, deserves a grade or numerical evaluation. Level 3 writing, the final project for the unit, requires evaluation based on a grading scale described earlier. If the final project is not a writing assignment, then a different type of evaluation is required, one in which students help develop the criteria and know about well before they perform or hand in the project.

Middle school students, in particular, need frequent evaluations as they progress through a long-term project. Individual conferences with students help keep them on track and aware of how they are doing. Students, for the most part, do not manage their time well, and teachers can't assume they are completing their work when the units extend over time. However, with help and encouragement, students can be taught to assume more responsibility for their own learning. Frequent checkpoints by a teacher and group work, where students are responsible to each other, help students stay on task and complete their work.

Evaluating Oral Activities

Teachers are sometimes puzzled about how to evaluate oral language activities. However, when we consider the similarities between oral and written expression, we see the potential for evaluation of oral work. Just as in written work, it is important to realize that not all oral activities are evaluated. Evaluation is based on the formality and purpose of the activity, in other words, according to the intended level. Practice is vital for increasing students' self-confidence and ability, and as in writing, practice is never formally evaluated.

Analytical grading scales are important, as they are in writing, to help students. Without the specific information students learn from the scale, it is difficult to improve, especially in speaking where there is so much to attend to. Items on an oral activity grading scale include vocal and physical delivery, organization, and presentation of the material. What is emphasized depends on the type of activity: informational, storytelling, dramatic, explanatory, persuasive, or humorous.

Peer critiquing is important to include, much as peer groups work in revising writing. Response forms that reflect the evaluation scales help direct students in making worthwhile comments and suggestions, as well as keeping them on task. Speaking and listening are linked activities, and learning to listen in order to make judgments about another's speech helps both the speaker and the listener.

Portfolio Evaluation

Portfolio evaluation is not a new way to evaluate student work. Artists have used portfolios for years to show employers the depth and breadth of their work. Only recently, however, have schools begun to use portfolios to evaluate student writing. The major advantage to portfolios is that teachers can look at students' work over a period of time. Too often we are judged on a one-time evaluation: SAT scores, unit test, musical performance, writing sample, and term paper. The thinking, planning, and effort that went into creating the final product is ignored in the evaluation, as is the possibility of not feeling well physically or emotionally the day of the test. The restricted time allowed for writing greatly affects the product. As Sandra Murphy notes, portfolios show what students do in a variety of situations, giving teachers a "broader and more accurate picture of student performance" (143). Because portfolios include writing intended for different audiences and purposes that draw on different strategies and skills, portfolio assessment is more fair to students (144). The overall evaluation of portfolios gives a much clearer picture of students' fluency and progress in writing.

Peter Elbow, a university educator, supports portfolio evaluation because of improvement in student's effort and interest. Students are more willing to revise their work because they receive credit for their effort. They are more likely to "try for what is exciting, not just what's acceptable" (*What Is English?* 167). Portfolios give students the chance to show their "best" work and to say, "Look how hard I worked," providing a more complete picture of student abilities than one piece of writing (Maxwell 143).

In *Portfolio News,* Martha Johnson, a director of a cooperative writing program, lists several positive attitudes and behaviors that portfolios encourage in students:

- To take more responsibility for their work
- To see themselves as apprentices
- To value daily work as a meaningful part of learning
- To see mistakes as opportunities for learning
- To see revision as an opportunity to succeed
- To spend more time thinking about their teacher's response
- To spend more time conferring with classmates
- To spend more time reconsidering and improving their work
- To be more creative, to feel more confident, to be more productive
- To take pride in their work, to perform, or display what they know (2)

Johnson's claims for portfolios might sound somewhat ideal, but involving students in evaluation does improve their attitudes toward writing.

Writing folders and portfolios serve different purposes. The difference lies in what each contains. Students keep *all* of their writing in a folder, but they select only the best pieces of writing for placement in their portfolio. Depending on the grade level, a teacher may keep the writing folders in the classroom. Older students keep track of their own. Teachers encourage or actually require that students keep everything they work on. In addition to portfolio selection, students may want to revise a paper they did several weeks ago or use one of their papers for a reference in a later assignment. The folder does not involve any self-selection on the part of the student, but the selection process is essential for portfolios.

The physical appearance of portfolios can vary considerably. Some teachers require neatly organized notebooks; others have bulky folders or expandable files. Some portfolios are covered with student artwork or handmade covers. Whatever their appearance, they share the common philosophy that teachers value what students are doing: their efforts, results, products, process, diversity, and standards (Tierney, Carter, and Desal 49).

Contents of Portfolios

Portfolios contain (a) a table of contents, (a) the selections of writings, (c) a rationale for the selections, and (d) their future goals, all written and selected by students. Student involvement in their own evaluation is the most important reason for using portfolios. Evaluations should matter first to the students and secondarily to parents and teachers. To achieve this, students must be involved in creating the portfolios right from the start.

TABLE OF CONTENTS.   A list of the contents gives the teacher an overview of what the portfolio contains and provides the context for the selections. Selections are listed in order by date so progress is more apparent.

SELECTIONS.   To begin, students choose what goes into the portfolios by going through their writing folders and other work they have accumulated and selecting what they believe best represents their effort, progress, and achievement. The selections vary depending on the teacher and level of the class, but basically they are a collection of work assigned by the teacher. However, students may want to include writing done on their own. Students are also encouraged to add assignments from other classes (e.g., a paper written for history or science). In addition to student-selected work, some teachers designate assignments they want included in the portfolio. Teachers can specify a minimum number of pieces that students select and then add one or two teacher-selected pieces, such as an assignment everyone has in common (e.g., a short story, a poem, or a report). Teachers may have general input in this choice by requiring a certain number of level 2 writings, assignments based on particular readings, and types of activities; however, each student selects the actual piece to include. For example, one teacher requested that the following writings be included in her students' portfolios (Maxwell 146):

1. A level 3 writing, including all of the discovery activities, drafts, revisions, and response sheets
2. An example of what you worked the hardest on
3. An example of what you learned the most from
4. The assignment you enjoyed the most
5. Anything of your choosing (explain why you are including it)

The selections do not have to be final copies; students may add a discovery activity they particularly like. Teachers need to encourage students to look at writing done at each stage of the writing process for two reasons: (a) In evaluating improvement, early drafts may give more information on fluency and thinking than those that go through all of the steps of revising; and (b) when early drafts are part of the material to be evaluated, students learn to value all of the writing they do.

Some teachers have students meet in groups to help each other decide what pieces to select. Whether students receive help from peers or select papers on their own, they write a rationale or explanation for the selections. Through this process of selecting and explaining their choices, students develop a sense of ownership in every step of the writing process.

RATIONALES. This is the reflective part of the portfolio. Students write a letter to the teacher explaining why they chose the pieces they did and what they believe the choices show.

A student, Christa Przytarski chose one piece because "it was a creative idea," another from her midterm because she "enjoyed the poetry," another because she "really had fun writing this story," and another because "it was a fun project to do, and I was very pleased with the way it turned out."

Thinking about their writing makes students begin to consider themselves as writers, and not just as students enrolled in a particular course. They could reflect about their learning, a novel experience for most secondary students; they are not often given that opportunity (Ballard 48).

Students in Mary Meiser's composition class reflected on the writing they did over a four-month period. Excerpts from their comments include the following:

"Just making a paper flow all together seems to be coming much easier. It is becoming more of a routine to check my sentences to see if they make sense and how they flow" (Krista Mickelson).

"It still is troublesome for me to get to the point I can say what I want to say in as few words as possible. I think the source of the problem is that I need more experience writing" (Angie Piper).

"At first I didn't write/include as many examples as I should have. My latest paper was on stereotyping. In this essay I did show concrete examples and let some of my feeling show, which resulted in a better paper" (Jessica Smith).

GOALS. Students look at all their accumulated work and write a reflection on their progress over a period of time. Based on this reflection, they write a number of goals for themselves; goals they plan on reaching during the next marking period. Alan Purves, Joseph Quattrini, and Christine Sullivan suggest that students ask themselves three things:

1. What do I want to know about?
2. What do I want to be able to do?
3. What habits and practices do I want to develop? (11)

A student, Laura, wrote the following goals: (Maxwell 147):

> First I would like to increase my vocabulary so that I am not always searching for words to use. I think my writing would be more effective if I had a broader range of vocabulary to choose from. And second, I would like to expand my creativity. I am much better at writing accounts of something that has already happened. I lack in the area of coming up with my own story.

Purves et al. urge students to take charge of their own writing. Directing their remarks to student writers, they write that students need to "focus on three facets of you as a writer: what you know, what you can do if you are really put to the test, and what you can do on your own" (10). They suggest looking at portfolios as a self-portrait, showing the world the variety of things you know.

Each time students work on their portfolios, they read the goals from the last one. Part of their reflection, then, is to think about how well they met those goals. If teachers realize the student's goals are unrealistic, the teacher and student need to have a conference. Occasionally students write lofty goals that are impossible to achieve, and their expectations for themselves need to be more sensible. On the other hand, some students need to be encouraged to stretch themselves to achieve more difficult goals. When teachers evaluate the portfolios, they can specifically check to see if goals and student abilities are a good match.

Evaluating Portfolios

Because portfolios are designed to show progress, teachers, as a rule, do not include ungraded work. Every piece needs to include the date it was written and, if appropriate, the dates of revision. The writing level of each piece is included as well. If students place the papers in the portfolio in order by date, the teacher can evaluate progress more easily. A variation of an analytical scale helps the teacher during evaluation and helps the student to understand the evaluation. Figure 11–7 shows an example of a scale.

Teachers often assign a certain number of points as a grade for the portfolio; others record a pass/fail grade. The benefits come not from a specific grade, but from what both students and teachers learn in the process. An analytical response lets stu-

1. The goals are specific enough to be helpful.

   Comments:

2. The goals are a realistic reflection of your past work.

   Comments:

3. The goals are realistic considering the period of time you have to achieve them.

   Comments:

4. Your reflection is a thoughtful response to your work.

   Comments:

5. The reasons for your selections are clear and thoughtful.

   Comments:

6. I think your effort and progress is:

   Comments:

7. Suggestions I want to make:

   Comments:

Your total points for the portfolio are _____.

FIGURE 11–7
An analytical scale used for portfolio evaluation.

dents know if a teacher's goals fit with what they see as their personal goals. Selecting and evaluating portfolios takes time, but it is the most successful way of involving students in evaluation.

TEACHERS' EXPERIENCES

Margie Krest, a high school teacher, has used portfolios for several years to document her students' growth and risk-taking (29). Her students keep all of their writing, "including drafts, revisions, prewriting material, and final papers" (29). Students date the papers so they can keep track of their own progress. Because not every piece of writing is graded, students are more willing to experiment and to take more risks. Krest devised a method for evaluating that rewards multiple drafting, revising, and practice, all elements of the writing process. In addition to the graded work the students select for their portfolio, she includes an ungraded final draft. She gives two grades on the portfolio; one for all of the writing and one for a paper grade on one final product. She weights the two grades according to what she wants to emphasize.

For instance, if fluency is more important than creating an error-free paper, then the portfolio grade might be 75 percent and the paper grade 25 percent. The reverse situation might be appropriate for seniors. By adjusting the percentages, Krest finds portfolios adaptable to different grade levels and student abilities (31).

High school teacher Roberta J. Herter uses portfolio evaluation because she wanted a "fuller picture of a writer's growth over time" (90). She found portfolios helped students assume responsibility for their writing.

> Portfolios involve students in assessing the development of their writing skills by inviting self-reflection and encouraging students to assume control over their writing. Accumulating a body of work to return to, to reject, revise, or simply revisit calls on students to become responsible for the content and quality of their portfolio, and ultimately to confront their personal writing inventories and investments in activities of the class. (90)

Other teachers who have used portfolios echo this same belief. One teacher reports, "The first thing that struck me was their insight into their own strengths and weaknesses and their willingness to be honest about their efforts" (Ballard 46). Students also realize the benefits of revision—substantive revision, not just editing changes (47).

Parents and Evaluation

Parents can also become involved in evaluation through portfolios. Teacher Ruth Mitchell has her students take the portfolios home and includes a questionnaire for parents asking them what they think of their child's work. Mitchell reports that parents, for the most part, have a positive response. They know what is happening at school and feel more involved in the school-home relationship (110–14).

Portfolios also help with the parent connection at parent-teacher conferences. They provide a concrete illustration of each child's work, which is more helpful than discussing evaluation in abstract terms. Parents can more easily see evidence of growth and process (or lack of it), something a test grade does not tell them.

THE FUTURE OF ASSESSMENT

In a recent article, Arthur Applebee makes a strong case that we need to make assessment decisions based on curricular grounds. He lists five principles that language arts assessment should reflect:

1. Assessment should be based on a wide range of situations where students read and write—the same situations we create in our classrooms.
2. The contexts of assessment must involve students in "higher literacy" activities that are "thought-provoking and that give students time and space to develop their own interpretations and defend their own points of view."

3. Assessment must include time for "reflection and revision" to allow students to use their abilities and return to a task over time.

4. Assessment must "provide room to discuss and make explicit the basis of judgments about quality." Reports on student performance at district, state, or national levels must include sufficient samples of student work.

5. Assessment must be classroom-based and in the context of a rich and varied curriculum. (45–46).

For assessment to be authentic it must reflect an ongoing process of learning where varieties of activities provide the most favorable opportunities for a diverse group of students to learn.

CASE 11–1

Evaluating a Student Paper

Teacher Pat Stellick shares an assignment she gives to her 10th graders. The assignment is part of a unit on biographies. The following is her explanation to the students:

In "Open Letter to a Young Negro," "Hitler's Games Tarnished Gold," and *The Jesse Owens Story* video, we were given a variety of views of Jesse Owens. By referring to specific examples from our biographical selections (try to use all three sources), explain in a well-developed essay what you think are the most outstanding characteristics of Jesse Owens.

Assume the role of a teacher and develop an analytical scale to use for evaluating the student paper that follows. The paper is worth 50 points, is a level 3, and the class is 10th grade. Once you develop the scale, evaluate student Elizabeth Ehlert's paper using your scale.

JESSE OWENS

Jesse Owens was an incredible, well-rounded person who influenced the entire world, using his life to benefit others. I think one of Jesse Owens most outstanding characteristics was his selflessness. He respected everyone and was never too busy to take the time to help someone. In *The Jesse Owens Story* video, he went out in the middle of the night to get a young negro out of jail and talk to him. He also volunteered his time to help young black athletes succeed. During the 1936 Olympics, Jesse helped a broad jumper from Mexico to improve his jumping, even though this person was one of his competitors. In the article "Hitlers's Games Tarnished Gold," Jesse showed his unselfishness. When the Jewish runners were taken out of the relay race, Jesse was put in their place. He stood up for them saying they deserved to run, as he had already won three gold medals and was exhausted. These things took a lot of courage.

Another outstanding characteristic of Jesse Owens was his positive attitude and outlook throughout life. This was evident in the video. While his life was being picked apart by the investigator, Jesse was positive and very honest. He kept a glimmer of hope and responded positively towards the investigator. In "Open Letter to a Young Negro" he tells people that we can get along without violence. He tries to impress upon us that people are people. It doesn't matter what color their skin is, what their religion or beliefs are, or anything else. Jesse Owens used his life and well-known name to help others. He was very honest and was often treated unfairly, but he fought through those tough times. Jesse Owens made a great contribution to the world, and I feel we should all learn from him.

After you have evaluated Elizabeth's paper, meet in small groups and consider the following points:

1. What did each of you write in your comments that would help Elizabeth with her next writing assignment?
2. What specific positive comments did you make?
3. Where you disagreed on scores or evaluations, what were the reasons for the discrepancies?
4. What mini-lessons, if any, could you use with this 10th-grade class to better prepare them for writing their essays?
5. What follow-up writing assignment could you ask students to do to build on the skills they learned from the activity?

REFERENCES

Abbott, Jim. "Changing the Perception of Assessment." *Center X Quarterly* Spring 1995: 11.

Applebee, Arthur N. "English Language Arts Assessment: Lessons from the Past." *English Journal* Apr. 1994: 40–46.

Ballard, Leslie. "Portfolios and Self-Assessment." *English Journal* Feb. 1992: 46–48

Davis, Barbara Gross, Michael Scriven, and Susan Thomas. *The Evaluation of Composition Instruction.* New York: Teachers College Press, 1987.

Diederich, Paul B. *Measuring Growth in English.* Urbana: NCTE, 1974.

Elbow, Peter. *Embracing Contraries.* New York: Oxford UP, 1986.

Elbow, Peter. *What Is English?* New York: Modern Language Association, 1990.

Everly, Pamela. *Teaching Teenagers and Living to Tell about It* Englewood, CO: Teachers Ideas Press, 1992.

Herter, Roberta J. "Writing Portfolios: Alternatives to Testing." *English Journal* Jan. 1991: 90–92.

Johnson, Martha. *Portfolio News* Spring 1991: 2.

Krest, Margie. "Adapting the Portfolio to Meet Student Needs." *English Journal* Feb. 1990: 29–34.

Johannessen, Larry R. "Enhancing Response to Literature: A Matter of Changing Old Habits." *English Journal* Nov. 1994: 66–70.

Maxwell, Rhoda J. *Writing Across the Curriculum in Middle & High Schools.* Needham Heights, MA: Allyn & Bacon, 1996.

Mitchell, Ruth. *Testing for Learning.* New York: Free Press, 1992.

Murphy, Sandra. "Writing Portfolios in K–12 Schools": Implications for Linguistically Diverse Students." *New Directions in Portfolio Assessment.* Eds. Laurel Black et al. Portsmouth: Boynton/Cook, 1994: 140–56.

Parsons, Les. *Response Journals.* Portsmouth: Pembroke Publishers, 1989.

Purves, Alan C. *Testing Literature: The Current State of Affairs.* Bloomington: ERIC Clearinghouse, 1990.

Purves, Alan C., Joseph A. Quattrini, and Christine I. Sullivan. "Using Portfolios to Take Charge of Your Writing: Advice to Students." *Portfolio News* Fall 1994: 10–12.

Schuman, Baird R. "Assessing Student Achievement in the Study of Literature." *English Journal* Dec. 1994: 55–58.

Smede, Shelly D. "Flyfishing, Portfolios, and Authentic Writing." *English Journal* Feb. 1995: 92–94.

Tierney, Robert, Mark A. Carter, and Laura E. Desal. *Portfolio Assessment in the Reading-Writing Classroom.* Norwood, MA: Christopher-Gordon, 1991.

12

The Nature of Language

Language is not only the principal medium that human beings use to communicate with each other but also the bond that links people together and binds them to their culture. To understand our humanity, therefore, we must understand the language that makes us human. (1)

Clark et al.

THE IMPORTANCE OF LANGUAGE STUDY

Although most teacher education programs include the study of language, we don't always grasp the significance of language principles on the first exposure. Nor do we necessarily make the cognitive leap from principle to practice, that is, to teaching adolescents, when we are not yet involved in designing and implementing lessons in listening, speaking, reading, and writing. Similarly, our understanding of language diversity may remain academic until we must consider diversity in our own classroom. For this reason, we address basic language principles before we discuss language activities for middle and secondary level students.

LANGUAGE CHARACTERISTICS

Wherever you find humans, you find language. It binds us into communities of shared meanings, where our thoughts reach across time and space and connect us to those who have been and those who will be. In some cultures, oral language is the sole means of communication; in others, both oral and written language form the base of communication. No language is any less complex than any other. It is a mistake to believe that the language of an African tribe, for example, is "primitive" simply because the culture is less technological than our own. Every language is equally complex and complete as a system of communication. That is, no language or dialect is inherently superior or more satisfactory as a means of communication, a fact that has implications for teaching students with dialects or limited English proficiency.

Commonalities Among Languages and Learning

All languages share certain characteristics. One of the most obvious is the arbitrary relationship between the sounds and the meanings of spoken language or, in the case of languages for the deaf, between the signs and the meanings. That is, there is no connection between an object and what a language group has chosen to call it. Sometimes, people get confused with this notion, mainly because we attach so much importance to our own language. We tend to believe that it alone has the "right" names for things in the world; of course, millions of other people all over the globe are equally certain their language has got it "right" too. All languages use a finite set of discrete sounds (or gestures in sign language) that combine to form an infinite number of words and sentences.

What makes a language different from others is the discrete set of sounds chosen. As we listen to French or Arabic or Russian, we are instantly aware of this phenomenon. Similarly, all languages have distinct rules for forming words and sentences. When we learned our native language, mainly between birth and age 5, we learned these language patterns. No one taught us; we simply absorbed them from the language around us. Native speakers, then, come to school with considerable intuitive knowledge. We can use this knowledge when we work with students, especially in writing skills.

Any normal child is capable of learning any language to which he or she is exposed. Nationality or race has nothing to do with the acquisition of language per se: It is the sustained language environment that provides the child with a native language. Children all over the world acquire their native languages in remarkably similar ways. Without instruction, they grasp the rules of the language—the basic sounds, how sounds are arranged to form words, and how words are arranged to form sentences. In the process, children also learn social behavior, that is, how to use their language appropriately in their cultural community. Because this knowledge does not always transfer easily to classroom culture, we have to help students adjust to school language and to ways of knowing and doing within the mainstream culture. At the same time, we must value their home language and approach the acquisition of standard American English as another variant needed for versatility and succeeding in the world at large.

Language Variation

Each language has variations in sounds, words, and more rarely, in grammar. In the United States, regional, social, and ethnic differences provide our language with a rich diversity known as American dialects. Generally, American dialects are intelligible; that is, we can understand a speaker from any dialect region, despite differences in pronunciation, vocabulary, or grammar. Everyone speaks a dialect, although usually one dialect rises to a position of prestige. This position has nothing to do with that dialect being superior, but its speakers have achieved social prestige and power. Value judgments about dialects are common, however. When John F. Kennedy was president, people sometimes referred to his Boston dialect as "aristocratic," mainly because it had traces of British English; although some of our southern dialects also bear traces of British English, they may be dismissed as "hillbilly." Language judgments, then, are very much linked to social prestige.

Other variations allow us to adjust our language to social situations. With some people we speak very informally, with others very formally. We use certain vocabulary with one group but not with another. We know what is appropriate to the situation and the audience. These language adjustments are learned as part of our native language, and they explain one of the most difficult aspects of learning a second language as an adult. We can learn the sounds, words, and sentences, but that is only half the knowledge. We also have to learn the appropriate contexts for them. There is, then, an intimate connection between our culture and our native language. In the classroom, we have to be continually aware of both the social and cultural implications of language as we work with students from cultures different from our own. We also need to acknowledge the time involved in learning not only form but also function, especially in academic settings. Expecting too much too quickly only sets a stage for frustration and, ultimately, high potential for failure.

COMPETENCE VERSUS PERFORMANCE

Students whose native language is English come to the classroom with considerable, although largely unconscious, knowledge of how the language works. Textbooks often fail to consider this fact and approach students as though they had to learn English as a second language. Teachers can use many strategies to take advantage of native speaker knowledge or "competence." We address these in the chapter on grammar.

There is, however, a difference between "competence"—what every native speaker carries as a linguistic system—and "performance"—how we use that knowledge in actual behavior. Every normal child is competent in his or her native language, but every child differs in performance. Unfortunately, judgments of performance are linked to deviation from what is termed "standard American English." This is a social issue rather than a linguistic one. There is no such thing as linguistic superiority; every grammar is equally complex and equally capable of expressing whatever thoughts the speaker intends.

The rules of our grammar may differ from someone else's, but neither set of rules is better—only different. Thus grammar as we discuss it here includes everything speakers know about their native language: the sound system, the system of meanings, the rules of word order and sentence formation, and a dictionary of words. The amazing thing is that we know this complex system unconsciously and intuitively and that we learned most of it between birth and the time we started school.

WHAT NATIVE SPEAKERS CAN DO

"And how are you?" said Winnie-the-Pooh
Eyore shook his head from side to side.
"Not very how," he said. "I don't seem to
have felt at all how for a long time."

                                                        A. A. Milne

The delight we experience at Eyore's answer comes from our awareness of our native language and its social context. There are days when we would *all* like to respond "not very how" and explain just "unhow" we are. Turning the language on its ear now and then is part of the fun, at least for the native speaker. It is only one of the many capabilities we have.

Recognition of Grammatical Sentences

As native speakers of a language, we know which strings of words form acceptable arrangements and which do not, and other speakers of the language agree with us; native speakers know the grammar of their language. "Grammar" in this instance refers to what we know intuitively about our language, specifically, its structure.

> Alex hit the red ball into the street.
> It was a red ball that Alex hit into the street.
> *That was it red ball hit into the street Alex.
> *It was street that red ball hit Alex into the.

These are extreme examples of either grammatical or ungrammatical sentences. However, there is an in-between area where native speakers still recognize English sentences that deviate from their normal expectations. Eyore's response to Winnie-the-Pooh, for example, violates our normal expectations but nonetheless carries meaning in a most interesting and captivating way. Authors and poets know that native speakers will not only understand these "violations" but also appreciate them. As native speakers, our ability to judge sentences for both sense and nonsense comes from our knowledge of the possibilities of meaning. When we work with students who have syntax problems, it is important to remember that this native ability does not come from studying formal grammar, diagramming sentences, or labeling parts of speech.

Recognizing Relations Within Sentences

One of the key principles in language is that of the relationships among parts. We know that acceptable sentences are not randomly ordered groups of words. The conversation between Alice, the March Hare, and the Hatter makes the point:

"Then you should say what you mean," the March Hare went on.

"I do," Alice hastily replied; "at least—at least I mean what I say—that's the same thing, you know."

"Not the same thing a bit," said the Hatter. "Why, you might just as well say that 'I see what I eat' is the same thing as 'I eat what I see'!" (Lewis Carroll)

In English, word order does make a difference in meaning:

The angry teacher scolded the naughty boy.
The naughty boy scolded the angry teacher.
The angry boy scolded the naughty teacher.
Scolded the angry teacher the boy naughty.

Who does what to whom is altered considerably by the arrangement of words. Deciphering a sentence with nonsense words is another way to test the importance of word order in English:

The tirly lapets linged silsily on the waping pob.

Even without any meanings for basic words, we can answer a number of questions about who is doing what to whom. Word order helps us. We know that subjects normally come before verbs, that adjectives normally come before nouns, and that adverbs normally settle around verbs. We receive more help than word order, however. The word endings, suffixes, provided important clues: the plural *-s* as a noun marker; *-ed* as a verb marker, and *-ly* as an adverb marker. The structure words (e.g., *the* and *on*) also helped us identify the function of various words and word groups. If we ask who did what, a native speaker would give a quick response of "lapets linged." If we asked how the lapets linged, we would be told "silsily," and if we asked where, we would learn "on the waping pod." Word order and endings, then, are important clues for native speakers of English. Conversely, they represent a body of knowledge to be acquired by the non-native speaker.

In a basic English sentence, we can also determine where to break word groups into units. Look, for example, at this sentence:

The angry teacher was chewing on her pen.

We would probably make a major break between *teacher* and *was* and between *chewing* and *on*. No native speaker would see *the angry* as a major unit. It is also very unlikely that anyone would note *teacher was chewing* without also noting what was being chewed. The intuitive sense of "incomplete" would take over. If we take a longer, more complex sentence, we would still able to break it into units. For example, the sentence "The old man raised his voice when he saw the mayor coming onto the platform" can be broken into these units:

- the old man
- raised his voice
- when he saw the mayor
- (the mayor was) coming onto the platform.

Even without analysis, native speakers know how the units form a larger unit. This ability has little or nothing to do with the exercise and drill often associated with secondary English classes. If we recall drawing one line under the subject and two under the predicate or diagramming sentence parts, we may be thinking that is the reason we could easily pick out the units in the examples above. It isn't. The reason is that we have unconscious knowledge of how words cluster together and function as units. Although sensitivity to our native language probably allowed us to do the labeling, it is unlikely that the act of labeling caused us to know the division between subjects and predicates. Again, we need to consider this linguistic reality when we ask students to revise sentences. They know a great deal about their language. With our help, they can use that knowledge to construct and manipulate sentences.

Recognizing Relationships Among Sentences

As native speakers, we are able to move beyond the parts of a single sentence. We also recognize when sentences are stylistic variants, that is, saying the same thing in different ways, as in the following example:

Alice's mother fed the cat at midnight.
The female parent of Alice provided food for the feline at the bewitching hour.

We can also recognize when sentences are not variants but are, nonetheless, related to each other:

Alice's mother fed the cat at midnight.
Alice's mother dislikes the cat.
The cat knows Alice's mother dislikes him.
The cat refused to eat.
Alice's mother didn't care.

Recognizing Ambiguities

Another language ability of native speakers is knowing when a sentence can be understood in more than one way. For example:

The shooting of the hunters was terrible.
They are eating apples.
Visiting relatives can be boring.

In each of these sentences, the reader could come to two different conclusions about meaning. As native speakers of English, we know the possibilities. That does not mean that every student will recognize all of them; the ability to recognize and deal with ambiguity varies with individuals.

Creating Novel Sentences

Perhaps the most remarkable ability of native speakers is the ability to create and understand sentences never before uttered. If we keep track of our utterances for a few hours, we will no doubt be astonished at the number of novel sentences. Aside from some stock sentences or phrases (e.g., see you around, how are you doing, nice to see you), we are constantly creating and listening to new sentences. The human mind creates rather than stores. This ability has led some linguists, notably Noam Chomsky, to believe that we come "wired" for language, which is now one of the leading theories of language acquisition. English language arts teachers need to know something of the acquisition process because it affects how we approach writing instruction.

ACQUIRING OUR NATIVE LANGUAGE

Although you have probably studied language acquisition in other areas of your pre-service program, it bears repeating here. A knowledge of the acquisition process can help teachers understand the importance of providing an appropriate classroom environment and using authentic oral and written language activities. And it is essential knowledge for developing and fostering writing processes among novices.

Knowledge of language acquisition is a critical base when planning lessons and units; it may also be extremely useful in explaining certain classroom practices questioned by parents, administrators, or colleagues. Because you planned on being a secondary teacher, you might not have considered how young children's learning to speak is connected to the talkative adolescents who will fill your classrooms. For this reason, we will refresh your memory a bit.

THEORIES OF LANGUAGE ACQUISITION

Despite considerable research, we do not have complete knowledge of the language acquisition process; nonetheless, we do know some of the things that children do in acquiring a native language. Understanding this knowledge is critical to teachers in the English language arts, for it allows us to intervene successfully in the learning process. This knowledge can provide us with answers when we are frustrated by what appears to be a lack of progress. It can also help us tap into students' intuitive knowledge of language. The following are some of the most basic principles of acquisition:

- Children do not learn a language by storing words and sentences in a giant mental dictionary. Although the number of words in a language is finite, the number of sentences that children can construct is infinite.
- Children learn to put sentences together, the vast majority of which they have never heard before, without direct instruction.
- Children understand sentences they have never heard before, again without instruction.
- To utter or understand sentences never spoken or heard before, children must learn "rules" that allow them to use their native language creatively.
- No one teaches children the "rules." Parents or caregivers are no more aware of the various rules than the children are. Children internalize these rules, the grammar of their native language, through language experience.

It appears, then, that normal children acquire their native language rather effortlessly, at least with regard to the complex rules of grammar. They must, however, also learn how to use this language appropriately, adapting to various audiences and situations. How children manage this complex undertaking has been a central research question in linguistics and psychology. Over the years, a variety of theories arose, some of which have been recently discarded. We'll briefly look at some of the most prevalent theories and their limitations.

Imitation

Various theories have been offered to explain how children acquire their native language. One of these is *imitation,* the belief that children merely imitate what they hear. There are times, of course, when children imitate adult language. However, if we consider the thousands of words and sentences children produce, many of them in forms no adult would utter, we have to conclude that the imitation theory is inadequate. For example, children say things like "It got two foots," "I helded the bunny," and "Hitted me boy." They have never heard these forms from an adult. Even when children are deliberate in imitating, they simply cannot produce sentences that cannot be produced by their own internal grammar (i.e., their own set of developing rules), as the following example shows:

Child: My teacher holded the baby rabbits and we patted them.
Adult: Did you say your teachers held the baby rabbits?
Child: Yes.
Adult: What did you say she did?
Child: She holded the baby rabbits and we patted them.
Adult: Did you say she held them tightly?
Child: No, she holded them loosely. (qtd. in Cazden 92)

Until this child is mature enough to understand and produce *held* on her own, no amount of coaching or prodding will help. We also know that children who cannot speak because of a speech impairment learn the language spoken to them. When the speech impairment is corrected, these children immediately use this language in speaking. If acquisition were merely imitation, such use would be impossible.

Reinforcement

Another theory of acquisition suggests that children learn to produce correct sentences through reinforcement. They are positively reinforced for getting a sentence right and negatively reinforced when they get it wrong. If we accept this view, then we must believe that children are being constantly corrected for using "bad" grammar. One has to wonder if proponents of this theory spent any time at all around children and adults. If children are corrected at all, it is usually for the truthfulness of what they say—the content, not the form. If, for example, a child says "I helded the bunny," an attentive parent is more likely to correct with " You held a guinea pig, not a bunny." No parent or caregiver lapses into a lecture on the correct form of the verb.

Further, any attempt to correct the child would fail, as shown in the following example:

Child: Nobody don't like me.
Mother: No, say "Nobody likes me."
Child: Nobody don't like me.
(dialogue repeated 8 times)
Mother: Now, listen carefully, say "Nobody likes me."
Child: Oh, nobody don't likes me. (example from Roger Brown)

Children's language development proceeds on its own timetable, so they will not understand why something is right or wrong even when it is pointed out to them. Such a conversation would be a rarity, in any case. Parents, caregivers, and older siblings are usually too involved in their own matters to correct children's speech. Further, most families are too pleased with a child's effort to talk to squash it through correction. The "errors," if noted at all, are often recorded in the baby book as a cherished bit of language development.

Creativity

Both the reinforcement and imitation theories fail because they cannot account for the fact that children construct their own language rules. We have different rules for constructing sentences. For example, we can make sentences negative, use questions, and tell about something in the past. A child will at first use a simple construction and gradually move on to the more complex, adult forms. To make a sentence negative, for instance, the child will at first just tack on a *no* or *not,* as in "No go out" or "No want coat."

It is understandable to anyone that the child doesn't want to go out or doesn't want a coat. Since the child never heard such "sentences," we can conclude that she figured out how to transform *go out* to *not go out.* Later, she will produce more fully formed sentences: "I no want coat" and "I don't want coat," again without instruction. The same process occurs with questions. At first, she uses pitch to indicate the question, as in "Teddy?" Later she will add a question word, as in "Where teddy?" These sentences are not mistakes; they merely reflect a child's grammar at a certain stage of development.

Children seem to form the simplest and most general rule possible from the language data received. We are probably most aware of this when we hear children extend the rule, creating an invalid form, as in "I helded the bunny." The child learned the past tense form, *-ed,* and applied it whenever she wanted to speak about a past event. When a child says "two foots" or "mouses," she is applying a rule, even when it shouldn't be. This phenomenon should convince people that children acquiring language are not imitating adults.

What's the Right Theory?

Although we can discard some theories, linguists still don't have a definitive answer for us. There are basically two schools of thought: nativism and empiricism. Nativism is the theory that language is, for the most part, biologically determined. In other words, we are born "wired" for language. The only requirement for language acquisition is exposure to human language. In this way, language is both biologically and culturally determined. The mechanisms for language are present at birth, but the child's interaction with a specific language environment sets the acquisition process in motion.

The empiricist (sometimes called behaviorist) position, by contrast, holds that culture is the more dominant factor in the acquisition of language. Empiricists believe that stimuli in the environment cause us to speak. Although both nativists and empiricists disagree on how much structure the human mind has for language, they do agree that there must be some innate structure allowing humans to acquire language. The difference in their positions lies in whether that structure is the determining factor.

Keep in mind that we have simplified these positions here and that the extreme of either view is untenable. There are probably dozens of positions along a continuum between these two theories. Because empiricism has been largely discredited within linguistics, the nativist theory is currently dominant. Because of the work of Noam Chomsky, the nativist theory is the most clearly articulated and, for many people, the most convincing theory currently available. However, this theory is not universally accepted, and controversy over the details continues, especially among linguists convinced that social interaction plays a much larger and critical role in the acquisition process.

ORAL AND WRITTEN LANGUAGE ACQUISITION:
IMPLICATIONS FOR TEACHING

Although theories of language acquisition are compelling, for classroom purposes, teachers need to focus only on general principles of acquisition. Their relevance to classroom environment and instructional methods are readily accepted among English educators.

We learned to speak in a language-rich environment. We were surrounded by people who spoke to us and encouraged us to take part in listening and speaking activities. We were rewarded for our efforts, and no one penalized us for our errors. We concentrated on being understood, on meaningful content, before we concentrated on being correct. And because others assumed we would get things right eventually, we grew in confidence and, ultimately, in competence. We were motivated to speak because we had things to say; language was purposeful and contextual. Language was at the core of our social selves.

The acquisition and development of writing skills depend on similar experiences. Consequently, teachers who maintain a perspective of "this takes time" are far less likely to become frustrated with the "forward and backward" movement of students learning to write. Similarly, these teachers sustain an environment that conveys to students "you can do it." Our expectations of students are a powerful factor in their academic well-being—and expectations in oral and written language must be tied to realities of maturation and individuality.

Teachers who consider the following principles of language acquisition in their planning will foster language competency in young writers.

- We need a language-rich environment in which comprehensible language provides the data from which we draw our knowledge of how the language works. Reading, therefore, is an important corollary to writing; the more students read, the more opportunities they have to absorb knowledge of grammar, syntax, and mechanics—without even knowing the "lessons" underway.
- We participate actively in the learning process and analyze (although unconsciously) language in use.
- We test our hypotheses of how language works. We try out various forms on our listeners and readers and make adjustments from feedback and continued self-analysis of language in use.
- We receive positive feedback when we use language, regardless of the errors.
- We enjoy a tolerance for error and the expectation that we will get things right eventually.
- We need sufficient time for practice.
- We concentrate on meaning first, developing fluency and clarity before correctness.
- We are acknowledged to be individuals, with our own maturation schedule and variable rates of development and competence.

- We are presumed to be growing in competency and proficiency, although at times we appear to be uneven or even regressing in certain areas.
- We develop confidence from sustained experience and positive reinforcement for our linguistic efforts.
- We learn about audience, appropriate language forms, and context through authentic uses of language.

Although oral acquisition of our native language is natural (that is, unschooled), the process is enhanced when the environment and pedagogy foster writing development. The process approach to composition draws on very similar principles of language and human development. Teachers who involve students in meaningful oral language activities are necessarily structuring their classroom and lessons on these basic principles of language growth and development.

Most young students find language fascinating, but after years of language as textbook exercises, they associate language with drudgery rather than discovery and pleasure. Language becomes a mine field of errors rather than a treasure trove of meaning and expression. As English language arts teachers, we have the opportunity to bring students back to the joy of language. Language activities that allow students to discover and play with sounds, words, and sentences—rather than mimic or manipulate through text exercises—foster an understanding of their native language and reinforce their confidence to use this language well.

LEARNING ABOUT LANGUAGE: ACTIVITIES FOR ADOLESCENTS

As English teachers, we can never make our students care about a semicolon if they do not care about language. (17)

G. Lynn Nelson

Movement from elementary to middle school and junior high school often signals the end of playfulness with language. In senior high school, curriculum and instruction seem to move even further from language play. As a result, students at all levels miss rich opportunities, not only for play and pleasure but also for learning about the nature of language itself. Teachers who consider the basic principles of language as they create lessons and units find that they can include language lessons throughout the English language arts curriculum. Literature and young adult fiction, nonfiction, print and electronic media, and oral language units are rich resources for teaching language concepts. Occasional lessons or units concentrated entirely on language concepts are also a good idea. What is important is including language study as an integral part of the curriculum at every level.

Origins and Relationships

One of the most basic principles of language is its arbitrariness. People all over the world use different sets of sounds and symbols to represent the same object or phenomenon. Although the impulse to label our world is universal, the result is specific to our cultures. Most Americans, for example, have no need to define and label eight varieties of rice. But some people do need such definition within their culture. We can introduce students to the principle of language as both universal and culturally specific through activities in naming.

Naming People

Naming is a basic human impulse and a lesson easily introduced through an old friend of many American students, Dr. Seuss. The correlation between naming and physical description is easily seen in such characters as the Star-Bellied Sneetch and the bug named Von Fleck. Illustrations from various Seuss books allow students to make other connections very quickly. Once provided with a representative list of American surnames, students can work deductively to discover other basic characteristics of naming: derivation from physical characteristics, occupation, place of dwelling, character traits, from parent (e.g., -son, mac). With the vast influx of names from diverse cultures, students have a rich field of inquiry. Once students have discovered the ways in which we name, they might enjoy researching their own names. I recall seventh graders, even the "toughest" of them, diligently going through their baby books, asking parents and caretakers about the processes of naming in their family, and calling relatives to learn more about family history. They were surprised and very interested to learn that their given and surnames had meaning. Their personal quest and discovery, culminating in oral discussion, were appropriate research for middle level students.

Although given names are fairly easy to research, surnames require teacher assistance. For this project, bringing public library books into the classroom is a good idea. Students from Asian or Native American cultures may have to rely on family information rather than texts for their research. For senior high school students, name research offers an easy introduction to formal research methods and requirements. It also offers an excellent way to combine library and people sources, since most students will talk with parents and relatives in the process of gathering data. Middle school students might enjoy developing a family coat of arms or a personal crest with information they gather, or they might keep a discovery journal, an informal record of how they proceeded and what they learned. Because linguistic and cognitive maturation is a factor in *formal* research writing, most young students should not be asked to produce it.

Elizabeth Radin Simons offers an intriguing unit on the folklore of naming in *Student Worlds, Student Words: Teaching Writing Through Folklore*. She includes learning log entries, interviewing, reading a chapter in Alex Haley's *Roots*, role playing, and expository writing as part of this unit; in brief, all the language arts. She has used this unit with junior and senior high students from inner city to suburbia and found that it works well, especially since it goes to the heart of cultural diversity, family, and society.

Naming Places

Investigating place names is another worthwhile activity. Students can use any level (e.g., city, street) or geographic site (e.g., river, mountain) to explore how and why these places received their names and if there is any relationship between the name and the site. Many states have a rich cultural heritage in place names, so students of Hispanic or Native American cultures may become important informants. City malls also offer an interesting view of naming places, which in some cases is linked to Madison Avenue advertising rather than to regional logic. For example, in our city, one of the malls is called "London Square" even though the city has a French name, no British ancestry or ties whatsoever, and a predominantly Scandinavian heritage. The mall also offers firsthand research into the naming of businesses and restaurants. A telephone book, of course, could also be a resource for such investigation. Library resources are available for searching for place names, many of them appropriate for middle level as well as senior high students.

The Naming Game

Most students enjoy the naming process itself. Alastair Reid's delightful admonition that "it is most important to be a good namer, since it falls to all of us at some time or other to name anything from a canary to a castle," offers endless possibilities (qtd. in Littell and Fletcher *Language of Man 1*) Thinking about naming elephants and whales, for example, can show students how we name. Reid also suggests creating new names for numbers from words not ordinarily associated with them: ounce, dice, trice, quartz, quince, sago, serpent, oxygen, nitrogen, denium; instant, distant, tryst, catalyst, quest, sycamore, sophomore, oculist, novelist, dentist; acreage, brokerage, cribbage, carthage, care, sink, sentiment, ointment, nutmeg, doom (Littell and Fletcher *Language of Man 1*). The interplay with sound and syllable, the search for the "right" combination, offers a valuable lesson in what makes a language unique. Vocabulary may be enhanced as students search for unusual words. Middle level students might also work a bit backwards in the naming process. Armed with maps, they could choose a real place name that appeals to them and then develop an oral or written history for that name.

Naming and Culture

A lesson on the arbitrariness of naming "things" within a culture naturally emerges. Projects that present language as both a universal and culturally derived phenomenon help students see that what is needed and thus named in one culture may be superfluous in another. Students can discover this principle through a bit of field research in a subculture. One way is to group students by activities in which they participate, such as music and sports. Together they would develop a list of vocabulary words they need to participate in this group. A group of skiers, for example, would differentiate snow into "corn snow," "powder snow," and so forth, something of no interest or importance to people who merely shovel it or never see it. People outside of music would have no use for the term *pianissimo* or *allegro*. Students who are whiz kids with computer programming could easily exclude everyone else with a specialized vocabulary. Using the subculture of "teen," both middle level and senior high students could devise a vocabulary relatively unknown to most adults. This vocabulary could be used in a multitude of oral or written tasks demonstrating the principle of language and cultural relativity.

Students from diverse cultures could draw on their native languages to develop informative oral presentations, informal classroom drama, or miniature written dictionaries for their classmates. Considering naming and culture from another perspective, students could demonstrate how things in mainstream culture have very different names and connotations if one is African American, Native American, Asian American, or Hispanic. Another way for students to showcase language that is culturally based is to examine "rap," a variant of English that has both the power to exclude and include (witness the popularity of rap with white students) at the same time.

Sounds, Rhythms, Rhymes

Students need to understand that although humans are physically capable of making many sounds, we chose and use a finite set for English. Again, this is a basic language concept that many students are surprised to learn. Unless they are bilingual or have studied foreign languages, they tend to assume that all people, regardless of their native language, hear and represent real-world sounds in the same way. Literature, of course, has wonderful examples of the onomatopoeic features of English, as well as its rhythms and rhymes.

Dr. Seuss again provides an easy and playful way to demonstrate how our native language works, as shown in this excerpt from *Horton Hears a Who*:

> On the fifteenth of May, in the Jungle of Nool,
> In the heat of the day, in the cool of the pool,
> He was splashing . . . enjoying the jungle's great joys . . .
> When Horton the Elephant heard a small noise. (1)

The sounds, rhymes, and rhythms are English and would not translate well because the very elements that delight English listeners would be lost. Similarly, the rhythm and alliteration of Maurice Sendak's *Where The Wild Things Are* are built on English sounds and syllables:

> The wild things roared their terrible roars and gnashed their terrible teeth and rolled their terrible eyes and showed their terrible claws . . .
>   . . . and he (Max) sailed off through night and day and in and out of weeks and almost over a year.

The onomatopoeic features of English are illustrated in many ways in children's literature. Aardema tells the African folktale *Why Mosquitoes Buzz in People's Ears,* in which the representation of various animals is tied to the sounds of English and how we interpret the sound as English speakers and listeners:

King Lion called the python, who came slithering, wasawusu, wasawusu, past the other animals.

The iguana did not answer but lumbered on, bobbing his head, badamin, badamin.

When the rabbit saw the big snake coming into her burrow, she was terrified. She scurried out through the back way and bounded, krik, krik, krik . . .

KPAO! (a hand slapping a pesky mosquito)

The presentation of sound, imitative of animal or action, has been formulated from English sounds. The original African sounds would be very different, as would those of any other language. Many libraries have an audio version of this folktale, which emphasizes the sounds, rhythms, and rhymes even more effectively.

One of the easiest lessons in the arbitrariness of language lies in common animal sounds, which Mario Pei investigated worldwide. In many languages, for example, the name for the rooster's crow retains the initial *k* sound but little else: *Cock-a-doo-dle-do* becomes *cocorico* in French, *quiquirque* in Spanish, *Ko-ko* or *qee-qee* in Arabic, and *kokokkoko* in Japanese. Similarly, our favorite pooch may say *bow wow* or *woof woof* to us, but *oua-oua* (wah wah) in French, *vas-vas* in Russian, and *wan wan* in Japanese (*What's in a Word* 23, 25). Students can work in pairs or small groups to discover contrasts; at the same time, they will learn how various language groups distinguish sounds. Foreign language dictionaries, pronunciation guides, foreign language textbooks at the appropriate level, and library resources will assist the students. If access can be provided, students might enjoy talking with natives of other countries to learn firsthand how we hear sounds, interpret sounds, and rearrange them according to our culture.

Translating

Not only are sounds and rhythm intimately tied to English, but concepts and shared meanings are as well. For this reason, translating from one language to another is not an easy task; straight, literal translations don't always work, especially in literary works. Students whose native language is not English could provide examples for the class. At the same time, native speakers can work with a piece of translated material.

If Words Imitated Meaning

Just as onomatopoeic words try to sound like they mean, some words try to look like they mean—when forced by people who like to play with language. For example:

Born 13

Poetry uses this principle as well:

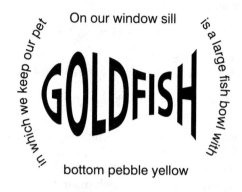

Dunning et al. 63

If students work with form and meaning in these enjoyable ways, they will come up with remarkable examples of relationships. Sometimes teachers think that such "experimentation" is a waste of time, perhaps because it appears to be frivolous. But students actually learn a great deal about words and meanings as they create their own forms. These language tasks also provide freedom for students with varied ability. Right or wrong is not an issue; only individual perception and personal interest matter.

More Than Just Fun

Relationships among language, thought, and culture are important concepts in their own right. But they should have a place in the English language arts curriculum for another reason: They lay the foundation for later considerations of dialect and latent prejudice. Discussion of the complexity and integrity of all languages, of their usefulness as communication systems, and of the tendency to make value judgments about those different from our own must have a place in the classroom.

Discovering Relationships

Relationships among various languages is another area of study well within the reach of middle and senior level students. With foreign language dictionaries, students can examine words across language families. Teachers can designate a corner of the room for gathering and recording data and provide a supply of foreign language dictionaries—not just Germanic and Romance languages but also Asian and Middle Eastern. If the class has students from various language groups, these students can be resources as well. Students should look up words that are certain to be part of every language group (e.g., family members, numbers, and geographical terms). They can record their findings on a large chart and later analyze the information to draw conclusions about language families.

Word Searching

We most often take words for granted; they're simply there. Students can begin to develop awareness of words by first hypothesizing about the origins of common idioms and both literal and figurative expressions. Once they have made some educated guesses, they can search for origins. The library will have resources for this inquiry.

Students can also trace the origin of various American English words; most are surprised at the extent of global borrowing in our language. Students could work in small groups or pairs to search particular categories, such as food, holidays, music, crime, art, science, and mathematics. Students could also take a particular category and try to discover how many words come from a single foreign language. For example, much of our vocabulary for such diverse categories as art, crime, and the military come from Italian; place names from Spanish; mathematics and science from Arabic. Aligning this work with social studies, mathematics, literature, and music makes sense. Again, Mario Pei's books are good resources for middle and senior level students.

Students might also be assigned to discover what George Bernard Shaw meant by this quotation: "England and America are two countries separated by a common language." If British newspapers or magazines are available, students can research vocabulary and spelling differences. The advertisements alone offer possibilities. If British publications are unavailable, library resources will do. Mario Pei's *Talking Your Way Around the World* is a good one. Common foods are one area students enjoy looking up (e.g., American *potato chips* = British *crisps;* British *chips* = American *French fries).* Pronunciation differences are another enjoyable area (e.g., the British pronounce *clerk* as *clark* and *schedule* as *shedule),* as are spelling differences (They write a *cheque* to purchase some *petrol* or to replace a *tyre).* Working with oral language, the many varieties of English, is a natural companion here. Videos from any PBS series set in Great Britain, as well as any series on language (e.g., *The Story of English),* or recordings of modern British English could introduce the lesson.

Searching for Meaning

Words can be real chameleons, changing right in front of our eyes. We need to understand the context before we can use and respond to words appropriately. We also need to understand the difference between literal and figurative language. A humorous way to remind students of this reality lies in the *Amelia Bedelia* books, tales of the loveable maid who takes directions and idioms literally. When told to change the towels, Amelia takes a scissors to them. "Putting out the lights" finds her hanging all the bulbs on the clothesline, and when she dusts, the furniture is covered with bath powder (Parrish). At every level of the curriculum, literature provides us with ways to explore both literal and figurative language. Although we most often think of poetry as a source of figurative language, we need to think of all genres of written and oral expression as a sources of figurative language.

Another way for students to discover shades of meaning in our language is through advertisements. The word *body,* for example, has various meanings, depending on whether shampoo or diets are being sold. Middle level students can gather and analyze the data themselves; they can then formulate language principles from their own conclusions. Similarly, older students can examine the language of politics and discover just how many ways words can be turned around, blurred, and generally misused. NCTE's Doublespeak Awards are good sources of such language in action. Older students should also study euphemisms, which can be approached from two directions: words that soften realities (e.g., *passed on* or *putting the cat to sleep* for *death;*) or words that cover up, deceive, and hide harsh truths (e.g., *final solution* for *killing Jews* in World War II; *soft targets* for *killing humans* in the 1991 Gulf War). Cultural values also come into play. NCTE's 1991 Doublespeak Award went to the U.S. Department of Defense for its use of language during the Persian Gulf War. Because Saudi Arabia has significantly different views of women, our female military personnel became "males with female features." Studying these aspects of language with civics, social problems, or history is an excellent way to help students see how "meaning" permeates and directs our lives.

Word Magic

As Lawana Trout points out:

> For primitive people, words were alive before all else. Words were here before the sun, the earth, the dawn, and even man. Words had special power. If you lived in a tribal society, words could make things happen for you. You could sing songs to cure the sick, to scare enemies, to fight danger and fear, or to make someone love you. (46)

Modern people may be more sophisticated, but the power of words nonetheless affects them. Unfortunately, students often fail to see how language influences and shapes how we think about ourselves and others.

For this reason, they may not understand our concerns about sexist language in their essays, why it makes any difference whether we use *he* or *she*. We can address the power of language through a discussion of labels. Senior high students can quite easily come up with lists of labels applied to males and females throughout their school years; with some nudging, they might classify labels by reference to animals and plants (e.g., old hen, bat, fox, pansy, peach). Although we have to caution them about language that is too offensive for class, that in itself is a lesson in language as a social phenomenon. Also, we must make clear our point: We are influenced by labels. Referring to women as *girls* or *chicks* or *broads* demeans them, just as references to black males as *boy* is demeaning. Writings by Alleen Pace Nilson, Robin Lakoff, Casey Miller, and Kate Swift are good sources of information both for teachers and upper division senior high students.

Younger students could work with "sticks and stones may break my bones but words will never hurt me," a modern incantation. Most students could supply personal examples to disprove the old taunt; however, it might be more challenging to work through appropriate literature, where characters rather than students are the focus of discussion. Young adult fiction offers powerful material for exploring the effect of language in everyday life. The important thing is to get students to recognize just how language does influence us.

Chants Old and New
Middle and junior high school students might enjoy learning about word magic through songs of the North American Indians and African tribes. Trout suggests the following activity:

> heya heya heya-a-yo-ho- yaha hahe-ya-an
> ha-yahe- ha-wena
> yo-ho-yo-ho yaha hahe-ya-an
> ha-yahe- ha-wena
> he-yo-wena hahe-yahan
> he he he he-yo
> he-you-wena hahe-yahan
> he he he he-yo
> he-yo-howo heyo
> wana heya heya (46–47)
>
> *Navaho*

Students would need to experiment with this song, first dealing with the repetition that creates such a strong rhythm and feeling. By varying the tempo and beat, students can create different moods in the chant (e.g., angry, warlike; lonely, mournful; or happy). Students could create their own song, first delineating the mood and for whom it is to be sung (46–47). Students might also search out modern examples, such as those found at sporting events throughout the world. For example, the New Zealand Haka, a chant performed before every rugby match, has a definite rhythm, a feeling of power and triumph.

Another creative activity suggested by Trout focuses on words as weapons. Trout notes that "songs always had a purpose for people living uncertain lives. They grew out of the important forces to be dealt with: fear, food, love, sickness, or war" (48). Students can easily relate to chants needed for support and for courage. They can experiment with writing their own chants, perhaps presenting them orally through masks, puppets, or shadow puppets if they appear a bit hesitant about going public.

This work can be aligned with social studies and cultural geography, where students have the opportunity to see how necessary and powerful language is, no matter how primitive or sophisticated the society. They will also see how peoples of different cultures and of different times used language for similar needs. One teacher we know described the powerful memories she had of hearing a sixteenth-century ritual "calcio" match (soccer) in Florence, Italy. Each team had a haunting, beautiful chant reflecting

400 years of tradition. Even with no idea of what the words meant, she was deeply affected by the chant's rhythm and emotion.

Although most students have daily auditory experiences, they seldom talk about their effects. Nor do they often travel beyond their immediate culture unless we structure ways for them to do so, such as through audiotapes. Students might, for example, discern what the chants or songs tell us about ancient peoples and what was important in their society. They could also investigate what modern songs might tell people in the year 2500 about us.

Students of all ages can examine modern "chants" found in advertisements. Coke and Pepsi have both developed several, each with a distinctive tag line (e.g., "It's the real thing"). Using both print and voice media, students can classify the various ads by the intended audience. Then, using only electronic media, they can analyze the words and music. They'll need to note differences between television and radio ads: What happens when vision is added to sound? Which "chants" stay with them? Why?

Another easy source of modern chants is the athletic field or court. And yet another is the playground, especially if children are skipping rope. Asking an older adult about chants associated with outdoor games would be another way to create awareness and, at the same, involve students in oral language activities such as interviewing. Most students like working with media and popular culture, welcoming the oral language activities they so easily promote. Writing activities are also easily included, everything from notetaking in a learning log or journal to development of ads in print.

A wonderful example of the power of words is found in Martin Luther King, Jr.'s "I Have a Dream" speech. The rhythm and repetition provide strength to the ideas Dr. King presented. The text of this speech is easily accessed, but a tape recording would be more effective. Students have to hear the cadence and feel the rhythm to understand its effect. Similarly, older students who have studied World War II might profit from seeing a film of Hitler at Nuremburg.

The Symbolic Nature of Language

A good way to introduce students to the symbolic nature of language is through logos. Students can easily collect logos by examining the yellow pages of phone books. Once they have a good sample, they can analyze the logos to determine what the symbol represents. Younger students might like to design a personal logo, a symbolic representation of themselves.

Ancient writing systems are another good way to introduce symbols. American Indian pictographs and Egyptian hieroglyphics are two interesting places to start. The first is from the "Interpretation of Red Horse Owner's Winter Count" (Wagner):

1783–1784 "Soldier froze to death." A man with his knees drawn up and his arms clasped around him is shown. A Dakota warrior (soldier here means "warrior") froze to death in the winter; the drawing indicates his futile attempt to keep warm.

1861 They stole a big herd of horses.

1789 First time they rode horseback against the enemy.

The second example is from the Delaware Indians' creation story (Trout 6–7):

At first, forever, lost in space, everywhere, the great Manito was.

He made the extended land and the sky.

He made the sun, the moon, the stars.

He made them all to move evenly.

After students have read and discussed pictographs, they might read a creation story and draw pictographs in the margins. Or they might create both the story and the pictographs. Students would need a good sense of myth and how ancient peoples wanted to explain the universe and its creatures before doing this task.

Egyptian hieroglyphics are no doubt familiar to students from their cultural geography classes or movies. However, they may not have studied them from the viewpoint of a symbolic language system. With limited examples, such as those that follow, they could figure out passages, as well as create some.

Less familiar are Aztec symbols, as shown in the following figure. Children's literature provides wonderful access to symbols and their connections with culture. Debo-

bull   beer jug   cobra   knife

leg   legs walking   hoe   house

jaguar   feathered serpent   blanket

eagle   stars   coyote

reed boat   rattlesnake   bee

chicken

potted cedar trees

sun

rah Nourse Lattimore's *The Flame of Peace* contains authentic illustrations, vibrantly presented. Students can examine the endpapers, where Lattimore has provided an additional key to the illustrations, and then explore the symbols in the text itself. The mythic tale echoes those of many cultures, so students might pursue comparisons of cultures and symbols.

Viking *runes,* as shown in the following figure, are yet another example of an early writing system. Our writing system represents sounds we make, but runes are symbols both for things and ideas. The Vikings came to believe in the magic of the runes. An *X,* for example, offered protection against a poisoned cup; an arrow pointing upward would ensure victory in battle; a figure somewhat like our letter *p* was a safeguard against giants (Born 2, 9). The runes, left on thousands of stones, are part of Norse mythology, as well as an authentic writing system. Students could link history and mythology and try writing with runes. With all writing activity, students should have a purpose in mind, associating purpose with their mythical audience and setting. The fact that ancient peoples developed various writing systems should make clear to students the power of words and the basic human need to communicate across time and distance.

f u þ a r k g w

USING YOUNG ADULT LITERATURE TO TEACH LANGUAGE CONCEPTS

Noticing Language

Young adult literature is a powerful vehicle for getting students to notice and discuss language. In *Using Young Adult Literature in the English Classroom,* John H. Bushman and Kay Parks Bushman provide teachers with a wealth of resources. They note, for example, how author Chris Crutcher is bound to catch kids' attention through his vivid descriptions:

> In *Chinese Handcuffs,* Crutcher uses the language most effectively. He describes Mrs. Crummet's cat as a "three legged alley Tom with a face like a dried-up creek bed and the temperament of a freeway sniper." (Crutcher 9; qtd. in Bushman and Bushman 103)

In another example, Bushman and Bushman discuss Katherine Paterson's *The Great Gilly Hopkins:*

> [This novel] provides students with an interesting use of language. Questions about Trotter often surface due to the language that she uses. Most realize that, although Trotter speaks less-than-perfect English, she is a truly admirable human being. A

study of Trotter's language patterns could be productive. For example, such a study should determine whether Trotter's English actually enhances her powerful use of language and her image. In addition, students should explore the effects of Mr. Randolph's old-fashioned, flowery, highly literate style of speaking. What effect does this language style have on the reader's image of Randolph? (105)

Bushman and Bushman also point out that Robert Newton Peck and S. E. Hinton, authors much admired by young readers, offer similar language explorations.

A Matter of Style

Just as young adult literature provides teens with opportunities to see the descriptive power of language, it similarly allows them to discuss language as a stylistic device important to authors: Is the language used by a character appropriate for his or her age, educational level, and social background? How does a character's language reveal his or her identity to a certain degree? How does dialogue enhance our understanding of that character? (Bushman and Bushman *Using Young Adult Literature* 31–32). Teens would be quick to notice characters not "acting their age," perhaps being too adult for the situation at hand. Extending to language, a discussion focused on "kids don't talk that way" could lead to increased appreciation of language's role in readers' acceptance or rejection of a character. S. E. Hinton was a teenager herself when she wrote *The Outsiders,* a text that has remained a favorite for at least two generations of students. Zindel's *The Pigman* has similar staying power. These novels might be a good place to start an investigation of language as integral to appropriate characterization.

Arthea J. S. Reed, in discussing young adult novels as a way of modernizing *Romeo and Juliet,* points to Cormier's *The Chocolate War* as a good bridge to understanding Shakespeare's use of language in character development. She suggests comparing the language of the villain, Archie, with that of the hero, Jerry: How does language convey their personalities, identify their social class, and help readers predict outcomes? From their experience with this contemporary model, students might more easily approach the more challenging language of *Romeo and Juliet* (103–04).

Another discussion might focus on language, character, and context, especially in novels where profanity is used. Bushman and Bushman argue that in the context of particular situations, along with a specific character developed by the author, *not* to use profanity would be ridiculous. They note Cormier's novels and Meyer's Vietnam War novel, *Fallen Angels,* as examples of profanity appropriate to events and characters (*Using Young Adult Literature* 31).

American Dialects

America is home to many varieties of English, and young adult literature can help students both understand and appreciate these variations. In addition to three major geographical dialects (Northern, Southern, Midland), we have many social dialects. The most prominent of these are, arguably, Black English Vernacular and southern.

Nonetheless, other social dialects are also important (Appalachian English, Alaskan English, Hawaiian nonstandard English, New York nonstandard English, and Spanish-influenced). To interest students in dialect, teachers could use *To Kill a Mockingbird,* where attitudes about language are revealed in the dialogue between Jem and Calpurnia, a speaker of black dialect (Bushman and Bushman *Using Young Adult Literature* 107).

Bushman and Bushman point out that young adult literature can be used to showcase the standard features of black dialect, like omitting the *be* form of the verb. Good pieces for such study include Tate's *Secret of Gumbo Grove,* Meyer's *Scorpions,* Childress' *Rainbow Jordan,* Irwin's *I Be Somebody,* and Taylor's *Let the Circle Be Unbroken.* In Reaver's *Mote,* black dialect itself is discussed by two characters. Interestingly, in some novels with black characters, like Hamilton's *M. C. Higgins, The Great,* no black dialect is used. This "omission" could lead to interesting speculation about why some authors choose not to use it (*Using Young Adult Literature* 109–10).

A Window on History

American English has been influenced by many languages, both those brought by settlers and those already here, the rich languages of Native Americans. Speare's novels, whose settings take us back to colonial America, introduce young readers to words commonly used earlier in our history but not in use now. Borland's *When the Legends Die* uses words borrowed both from Native Americans and Spanish. George's novel *Julie of the Wolves,* a favorite among young readers, provides a fascinating look a language, culture, and identity. In accepting or rejecting English, Julie reinforces cultural links embedded in one's native language. An added language feature lies in the wolves, who have their own "language" but nonetheless communicate with Julie (Bushman and Bushman *Using Young Adult Literature* 114–15).

A medieval English setting for *Catherine, Called Birdy* by Cushman, introduces students to vocabulary and an occasional phrasing that might pave the way for later enjoyment of Chaucer. Additionally, Birdy plays with language for its shock value and comments on her experimentation with it. The characterization of Birdy rests heavily on her language and offers another chance to explore the role of language in developing our knowledge of characters and predicting their fates.

Language as Manipulation

Young adult fiction provides many examples of the manipulative aspects of language and, when paired with classic novels, serves as a bridge to more sophisticated language devices. Bushman and Bushman suggest pairing *1984* and *The Chocolate War* to investigate both motivations for and the effects of abusive language ("Dealing" 221). Additionally, *The Chocolate War* is a rich resource for exploring the language devices characters uses to get others to act and think in a certain way. Blume's *Tiger Eyes* and Sleator's *Singularity* are other books suggested by Bushman and Bushman (*Using Young Adult Literature* 113–14).

WORD AND SENTENCE GAMES

Word and sentence games are both fun and valuable for students of all ages. James Moffett and Betty Jane Wagner warn, however, that student choice is essential here: "Far too many exercises and drills have been imposed on learners under the phony guise of games. Unless a person chooses to play a game, she's not really playing" (265). Their point is well taken. Forcing students to play word or sentence games not only diminishes their enjoyment but also fails to achieve an important goal: an understanding of the more technical side of language.

Chanting and Cheering

Teachers and curriculum planners sometimes associate chants and cheers only with elementary-age children. But these verbal playthings can be used successfully with students of all ages. In fact, chanting and cheering are found in every middle and senior high school during athletic events. Extending the use of chants and cheers to the classroom can be fun and instructive. Students could invent new cheers and chants, not just for athletics but for other events.

As suggested earlier, students need only turn to popular culture and the media for modern chants. Radio and television ads depend them. Collecting some on audio- or videotape can lead to a provocative discussion of modern chants and incantations. Students could also develop their own for various products or for some product they themselves devise and market.

Tripping Up the Tongue

Books of tongue twisters help students not only to exercise their physical articulation of words but also enhance critical auditory and visual discrimination of similar words. Moffett and Wagner illustrate the process:

Same sound, different spelling—*which, witch*
Same spelling, different sound—*plain plums on plaid plastic*
Same letter, different combinations—*freshly fried flying fish*
Same ending, different beginning—*youth's tooth was underneath*
Same beginning, different ending—*Tom threw Tim three thumbtacks* (265–266)

Moffett and Wagner suggest students make recordings and compare their readings, do choral readings, and make up new tongue twisters to share with one another (266).

Puns and Conundrums

Puns are found throughout classic literature and in collections by authors like Ogden Nash. Not only are they fun, but they require students to closely read the text, a valuable skill. Conundrums are an elaborated form of punning:

What's the difference between a cat and a sentence?
A cat has claws at the end of its paws, and a sentence has a pause at the end of its clause. (Moffett and Wagner 267)

Ready to Buy

Popular commercial games that require close attention to words and spelling are handy "fillers" for extra class time or chaotic days. Probe, Anagrams, Scrabble, Password, and Wheel of Fortune are just a few typical board games—some of which may also be found on computer software. Students could also make up their own board games, using the commercial versions as models.

Mad Libs

Students like this game, despite its association with grammar and parts of speech. Although we don't advocate teaching parts of speech for their own sake, this game won't do any harm. And it may actually improve some students' understanding of how English words and sentences work. One student reads a story that lacks certain parts of speech; listeners supply the missing sentence elements named by the reader. For example:

Yesterday [noun] went to the [noun] where [noun] were sitting [adverb] in the sun. The [adjective] postman [adverb] walked by and asked [noun] what was going on.

When completed and read back, the story is grammatically correct but totally nonsensical. Students may need sample sentences marked for the major parts of speech before they start the game.

Found Poems

As pointed out in the composition chapter, found poems are another favorite student activity. Students will need print resources (e.g., magazines, catalogues, phone books, newspapers, and ads) in their search for phrases or excerpts that form the basis of their "found poem." By isolating or shifting segments, students create a poem.

Telegraphic Messages

Moffett and Wagner suggest situations for players to make up a message that would have to be worded economically: just before the final beep on an answering machine; a 2-inch square paper being sent by carrier pigeon; a TV program needing a written message to flash on screen. Terse Verse, poems expressing actions or ideas in two or three words that rhyme, fit here nicely as well:

WARNING TO FELLOW CIA AGENT
Fly,
Spy

Through this game, young writers explore both the merits and dangers of sentence reduction (280–81).

Moffett and Wagner's *Student-Centered Language Arts K–12, 4th ed.,* from which these suggestions for word and sentence games are taken, is a wonderful resource for teachers. It is filled with activities that celebrate language play and engage students in both verbal and nonverbal expression. Moreover, its integrated language arts approach ensures that students use oral and written language in many forms and for many purposes. We recommend it as a useful addition to your professional library.

Your school and public libraries can also provide you with many resources for language play. Books devoted entirely to chants, puns, rhymes, and limericks, for example, are readily available. Audio recordings are also part of most library collections. Ask your professional librarians for their advice and assistance in collecting language resources for your grade level.

Adolescents and Language Activities

Whether they are 12 or 17, adolescents are inherently interested in language. Jokes, the Magic Ring Decoder in the cereal box, board games, music lyrics, cryptic notes, love notes, cheers, jeers, and even taunts are examples of their experience with language. However, language is often transparent to them, something they see right through and use but seldom examine. We can make it opaque. We can bring language into focus for them through varied activities that ask them to discover for themselves the power of language.

Developing units that focus primarily on language is one way to do it. Another is to examine every unit for its potential to focus on language itself. With an integrated English language arts curriculum, that potential is virtually unlimited. The activities presented here are only a small sample or what is available. Observing students and asking them questions about language and their related language interests provides many ideas for working with language at any curricular level.

CASE 12–1

Exploring an Instructional Unit

As you evaluate Amy Henquinet's unit, "What's in a Name?" we'd like you to review important curricular concepts once more:

1. What is Amy's philosophy of teaching and learning? How do you know? Use specific examples to support your response.
2. What are Amy's goals and desired student outcomes for this unit? What does she want her students to understand or be able to do better as a result of this unit?
3. How does Amy's selection of materials and activities reflect her understanding of the English language arts as cognitive and linguistic processes? How does it reflect her understanding of young adolescents?

4. In her planning, has Amy considered potentially varied ability levels among her students? Multicultural differences? Gender differences?

5. Consider Amy's structure for this unit. Why do you think she chose parallelism with this topic? Note the movement through each section. Why do you think she included both realism and fantasy?

6. In her introduction to this unit, Amy tells us she chose the topic of names because "names are important, personal, and an everyday part of life." Naming is one of the basic language concepts. Are there others in her unit? Could there be?

WHAT'S IN A NAME?

GRADE LEVEL: MIDDLE SCHOOL/GRADE 6 OR 7

Introduction: This portion of the unit is the largest and consumes at least a week and a half. The introduction of names and naming begins with lyrics, comics, and television shows.

Teacher Activity: Bring examples for students to explore. Examples of song titles include these:

"Cecilia" by Simon and Garfunkel
"Bobby" by Reba McIntire
"Layla" by Eric Clapton
"Jack and Diane" by John Cougar Mellencamp
"Help Me, Rhonda" by The Beach Boys
"Oh Donna" by Richie Valens
"Billy Jean" by Michael Jackson
"Prince Ali" *Aladdin* soundtrack

Examples of comics include:

"Doonesbury"
"Hagar the Horrible"
"Cathy"
"Ernie"
"Andy Capp"

Examples of television shows (film clips if possible) include:

Blossom	*Cybill*
Seinfeld	*Murphy Brown*
Martin	*Frasier*

Student Activity: Throughout the week, students bring their own examples from popular culture/media for 5 to 10 minutes of daily sharing.

SEGMENT 1: PEOPLE

Class Arrangement: Desks in circle.

WEEK ONE

Mini-Lesson: Researching personal names through resource books and interviews. Teacher provides resources from public library (e.g., dictionaries of first and last names, various easy-reading texts on first and surnames, texts featuring ethnic names).

Student Activity: Use texts and family resources to investigate the meaning and origin of their names. Ongoing, week-long activity.

Mini-Lesson: Preparation for story *Tikki Tikki Tembo,* a Chinese naming story; relevant aspects of Chinese culture.

Whole-Class Activity: Read together the children's story, *Tikki Tikki Tembo* (retold by Arlene Mosel).

Mini-Lesson: Creating "self" poems: examples of five-liners, diamond-shaped, and name poems.

Student Activity: Write poems and share in large-group discussion. Use of thesaurus for increasing descriptive vocabulary.

Student Activity: Reporting research about personal names through poster-making.

Student Activity: Brief research "report" on personal names. Poster and "report" will be placed around the room.

WEEK TWO

Teacher Activity: Read *The Lorax* by Dr. Seuss.

Student Activity: Small-group discussion followed by whole-class discussion.

Student Activity: 10- to 15-minute listing of names or nicknames they like for themselves, friends, and pets. With a partner, students share lists and choose a new name for self or pet and then find out its meaning. Students will have time to walk around and introduce themselves (or pet) with their new names.

Teacher Activity: Introduce creation of book titles and authors' names that fit titles (e.g., *A Dog's Life* by Ken L. Keeper).

Student Activity: Make up five examples of book titles/author names.

Whole-Class Activity: Share examples.

Small-Group Activity: Work with stories from *Strange, But True Sports Stories* by Howard Liss (stories allow students to create names or rename the sport's team or players). Within small group, students will have roles (e.g., recorder, facilitator, presenter). Choice of assignment: Design and make a book cover with author's name matching title of book or write sports story, playing with names of player, team, or sport. All group members must be part of presentation to class.

Small-Group Activity: Presentation to whole class.

SEGMENT 2: PLACES

Student Activity: Choose one state to research origin of its name (teacher provides resources). Each student will "teach" classmates about his or her state.

Teacher Activity: Provide "beats" in local community for each student to research (e.g., name of town, river, mall, park, civic building). Provide some resources and help, but general expectation for students to investigate their "beat."

Whole-Class Activity: Following research, create a history of community.

Teacher Activity: Read *Oh The Places You'll Go* by Dr. Seuss.

Student Activity: Trace foot or hand on sheet of paper. Make imaginary map using hand or foot as an island. Invent places such as Arch Town, Toe Jam Valley, Finger Mountain, adding any features and map symbols desired and a key to symbols. Share maps with classmates.

SEGMENT 3: THINGS

Because the term *thing* is too large and vague, this segment will focus on animals.

Mini-Lesson: Introduce Native American cultural and spiritual beliefs about creation and naming of animals. Tell story of animal creation based on *Ojibway Heritage* by Basil Johnson (includes animal symbols).

Student Activity: Read two creation stories from *Keepers of the Animals* (e.g., "How Butterflies Came to Be" or "How Grandmother Spider Named the Clans").

Small-Group Activity: Discuss differences between Native American and American storytelling. Discuss naming.

Teacher Activity: On transparency, show examples from Edward Lear's "Nonsense Botany" (drawings/fanciful names to match).

Student Activity: In pairs, create drawings similar to Lear's. Place drawings around room. Circulate, trying to guess at intended names for them. A prize goes to the student getting the most "correct" answers.

Whole-Class Activity: Brainstorm names for animals and discuss how different names reflect the appearance of the animals (e.g., from *Language of Man Book I*).

Whole-Class Activity: Read *If I Ran the Zoo* by Dr. Seuss.

Teacher Activity: [Taken from *Activities for an Interactive Classroom* by Jeff Golub]. Provide class with tall tales "starters" and examples done by other students. Present final project for unit; give students a choice among options or, with teacher approval, they can create their own "option."

1. Create a tall tale by inventing a person, place, or thing.

2. Create an ad for a new product (describe and illustrate the product, tell how to get it, etc.)
3. Write letter to a court official explaining why you want to change your name.
4. Research how to change one's name and describe the required legal process.
5. Write a "Dr. Seuss"-type story about a person, place, or thing.

EVALUATION FOR UNIT

Oral work:	Group and individual presentations
Group work:	Participation and cooperation
Portfolio:	Collection of written work; the pieces to be formally evaluated are chosen by the student; a reflective piece (student self-evaluation) should be included.

FOR DISCUSSION OF AMY'S UNIT

1.   In her reflection on this unit, Amy asks herself some important questions. One of them centers on student discussion: "I fear that the lack of direction in some of the discussions may lead to no discussion at all. Do sixth graders need more guidance than I gave them?" Quickly review the places where students are working in small groups. Do you think Amy should be concerned? And if so, what could she do to ensure more purposeful and productive discussion? Does Amy need to worry about paired work too? Or is that arrangement significantly different in terms of discussion and roles?

2.   Another of Amy's questions involves classroom structure and time management: "I am not only afraid of not enough structure, but also of too much structure. I am an extreme planner and fear that this unit may be too 'busy' . . . It is hard for me to plan how long an activity will take, and thus, feel I may have overdone this unit. I don't want my students bored, but at the same time, too busy. I'm having a hard time finding a happy medium." What do you think? Has Amy overplanned? Or is it better to have "too much" rather than "too little"? How do teachers arrive at a happy medium in their unit planning?

3.   We've given you only a sketch of Amy's evaluation plans. How do you think she will actually implement them? How will she know the level of student performance in each category? Imagine that a parent questions Amy about his son's grade of D for this unit. What must Amy be able to tell this parent? Or for that matter, the student? Do you think Amy would expect *any* student to do poorly in this unit? Why? Now imagine that a parent questions Amy about his daughter's grade of B, a low grade for this student. Would Amy say the same thing to both parents? How do teachers justify their assessment of their students when explaining grades to parents or caregivers? How do you ensure that both D students and B students are treated equitably?

SUGGESTED ACTIVITIES

ORAL AND WRITTEN LANGUAGE ACQUISITION

1. Examine at least one composition/language text-book used in middle school and senior high school. Does the text take advantage of what we intuitively know about our native language, or does it approach English as though students were learning it in a foreign country? Give specific examples to support your opinion.

2. Examine the questions and activities in a literature anthology for senior high students. What are the teaching implications of these questions and activities given the fact that students are creative rather than imitative language users? Which questions and activities would you eliminate and why?

LEARNING ABOUT LANGUAGE: FOCUSING ON LANGUAGE CONCEPTS THROUGH LITERATURE

1. Select a piece of children's literature that illustrates one or more of the basic language concepts. If you are uncertain which books would be best, ask a children's librarian for assistance. Consider these concepts: meaning and context, symbolism, figurative and literal language, and English sounds and rhythms. Also consider opportunities to use texts that introduce various cultures and extraordinary art and design. For students who are primarily visual learners, these texts offer unique opportunities. Similarly, for students who are auditory learners, much children's literature will have audiotapes available.

   Note your rationale for selecting this piece of literature: What does it offer as an instructional tool? What thinking, reading, and writing skills might it enhance? How might it contribute to students' language appreciation? What curricular level are you using it with? Why?

2. How would you introduce children's literature to a group of high school juniors? Would you anticipate some resistance, such as "This is baby stuff"? Or do you believe that children's literature is appealing across all age levels? How would you plan for success here?

3. Young adult literature is a wonderful resource for exploring language concepts—everything from dialect to symbolism, manipulative power to character development. In this chapter, we provided a limited number of titles and authors. With the help of a children's librarian or annotated book lists, explore young adult novels with potential for teaching about language.

4. Explore classic pieces of fiction as vehicles for teaching language concepts. You might want to use a typical senior high anthology for this exercise.

POPULAR CULTURE

1. Watch television shows that you know are popular with middle or senior level students. Devise an assignment based on one or more of these shows that would lead to a better understanding of the power of language. Be certain you choose shows that parents and caregivers would not find objectionable.

2. Choose magazines popular with teenagers (e.g., those about sports, cars and motorcycles, fashion, dating, and music). Devise an assignment that draws student attention to the power of language.

WORLD OF WORK

1. Call a local business that generally employs teenagers (e.g., fast food restaurants, service stations, nursing homes, or grocery stores). Ask if they have written guidelines or instructions as they train new employees and, if so, if you might have a copy. Explain that you are interested in how businesses approach communication and sensitivity to language, and that you would like to incorporate useful lessons about "on the job" language into your English language arts class. With samples in hand, devise a single lesson for senior high students, one emphasizing the importance and power of language in dealing with customers.

2. Collect samples of business correspondence, as broadly based as possible, and evaluate its use for classroom lessons on language (e.g., jargon, context, and audience).

WORD GAMES

1. Go to one or more bookstores and toy departments and examine materials useful for developing language skills and knowledge. Also check computer resources. Prepare a list of these materials and annotate their educational value for your English language arts classroom. How could you convince the district's curriculum coordinator to purchase them for your classroom?
2. Prepare one collection of riddles, puzzles, and other "nonsense" word games appropriate for middle school students and another collection

appropriate for senior high students. There will be some overlap, especially as you consider the range of interests and abilities across those levels. Your library and bookstores can provide you with many resources. How would you incorporate these into your classroom? Would they be used as part of larger units or as "fillers" on days when regular lessons would be suspended due to school programs, testing, etc.? What value are these various activities and games? How would you defend their use to a colleague or parent who believes you are just wasting time?

REFERENCES

ORAL AND WRITTEN LANGUAGE ACQUISITION

Cazden, Courtney B. *Child Language and Education.* New York: Holt, 1981.

Clark, Virginia et al., eds. *Language: Introductory Readings.* 5th ed. New York: St. Martin's, 1994.

LEARNING ABOUT LANGUAGE

Aardema, Verna. *Why Mosquitos Buzz in People's Ears.* New York: Dial, 1975.

Born, Thomas. *Understanding Language 1: The Magic of Words.* Columbus, OH: American Education Publications, 1969.

—. *Understanding Language 2: How Words Use You.* Columbus, OH: American Education Publications, 1969.

—. *Understanding Language 3: The Impact of Words.* Columbus, OH: American Education Publications, 1969.

—. *Understanding Language 4: The Levels of Meaning.* Columbus, OH: American Education Publications, 1969.

Bushman, John H., and Kay Parks Bushman. *Using Young Adult Literature in the English Classroom.* Columbus: Merrill, 1993.

—. "Dealing with the Abuse of Power in *1984* and *The Chocolate War.*" *Adolescent Literature as a Complement to the Classics.* Vol. 1. Ed. Joan F. Kaywell. Norwood, MA: Christopher-Gordon, 1993.

Dunning, Stephen, Andrew Carrigan, and Ruth Clay. *Poetry: Voices, Language, Forms.* New York: Scholastic, 1970.

Henquinet, Amy. "What's in a Name." English 406. University of Wisconsin-Eau Claire, Spring 1995.

Lattimore, Deborah Nourse. *The Flame of Peace.* New York: Harper, 1987.

Littell, Joy, and Joseph Fletcher Littell, eds. *The Language of Man 1.* Evanston: McDougal Littell, 1972.

MacNeil, Robert. "Listening to Our Language." *English Journal* Oct. 88: 16–21.

Moffett, James, and Betty Jane Wagner. *Student-Centered Language Arts K–12.* 4th ed. Portsmouth: Boynton/Cook, 1992.

Parrish, Peggy. *Amelia Bedelia.* New York: Harper, 1963.

—. *Thank You, Amelia Bedelia.* New York: Harper, 1964.

Pei, Mario. *Talking Your Way Around the World.* 2nd ed. New York: Harper, 1967.

—. *What's in a Word?* New York: Hawthorn, 1968.

Reed, Arthea J. S. "Using Young Adult Literature to Modernize the Teaching of *Romeo and Juliet.*" *Adolescent Literature as a Complement to the Classics.* Vol. 1. Ed. Joan F. Kaywell. Columbus: Merrill, 1993.

Sendak, Maurice. *Where The Wild Things Are.* New York: Harper, 1967.

Seuss, Dr. (pseud.) *Horton Hears a Who*. New York: Random House, 1954.

Simons, Elizabeth Radin. "My Name is Carlos." *Student Worlds, Student Words: Teaching Writing Through Folklore*. Portsmouth: Boynton/Cook Heinemann, 1990.

Tollefson, Stephen K., and Kimberly S. Davis. *Reading and Writing About Language*. Belmont, CA: Wadsworth, 1980. 120–21.

Trout, Lawana. *Myth: Student Log*. New York: Scholastic, 1975.

Wagner, Betty Jane. *Chronicle 1*. Boston: Houghton Mifflin, 1973.

13

Varieties of American English

[It took me] years to understand that my words weren't bad—they were just the words of the working class. For too long, I felt inferior when I spoke. I knew the voice of my childhood didn't belong to the group who made the rules. I was the outsider, a foreigner in this world. (40)

Linda Christensen, high school English teacher

UNDERSTANDING LINGUISTIC DIVERSITY

Diversity is the foremost characteristic of oral language in America. Everyone in America speaks a dialect that marks each of us as belonging to a certain race, gender, social class, and geographic region. With the exception of speech related to age or profession, most people retain their original dialect throughout their lives. Only when speakers change their status or role do they find it necessary to acquire a second dialect; many speakers, therefore, have little need to learn a new American dialect. There is, however, a dialect marked as "standard American English," which is the form taught in U.S. schools and to non-native speakers. This dialect is useful because it facilitates communication in many situations. At the same time, we must also be aware of its dangers.

Because teachers value so highly the role of language and the its standard forms, we may easily fall into linguistic chauvinism: We assume that our own dialect, standard American, is the most appropriate way of speaking. Further, we may assume, as Jean Berko Gleason points out, that "differing dialects are . . . degenerate, illogical, or 'simpler' versions of our own" (334–35). Nothing could be further from the truth. And nothing could be more damaging in the classroom than an assumption that students with nonstandard dialects are less than competent—linguistically or cognitively. Standard American English may be the dialect of status, but it is not intrinsically better or any more complete as a means of communication than any other English dialect. Further, actual differences between standard dialect and its variants are few. Understanding that variance is just that, variance should be regarded as part of the rich linguistic life of America and should be the foundation for teaching and learning the standard dialect (Meiser "Note" 6).

DIVERSITY IN THE SCHOOLS

Linguistic diversity is a fact of life in American schools. Students bring to school a wide range of backgrounds that is reflected in their language. Marcia Farr and Harvey Daniels point out that although "all students have a highly developed linguistic competency, a set of underlying rules that enables them to use their language, they do not share exactly the *same* set of rules." They further note that most language rules are shared by all English-speaking students; nonetheless, those systematic differences in the rules result in English dialects, a regional variety of language that usually differs in vocabulary and pronunciation (13). In American English, with rare exception, speakers of one dialect can comprehend speakers of another, although perhaps imperfectly at first. American English dialects also borrow words from one another, just as we use words from hundreds of other languages.

Even within a dialect, speakers do not share exactly the same set of rules. For example, in Black English Vernacular, there is considerable variation in its speakers' use of the dialect. This variation may be related to gender, age, social class, or the context in which the speaker finds self. Speakers of standard American English demonstrate the same variations, but they are not usually perceived as linguistically undeveloped or inadequate. Educators have consistently valued "standard dialect" more highly than American English dialects such as black, Appalachian, and Puerto Rican (Farr and Daniel 24). The low prestige attached to these dialects is a serious matter, for dialect differences do act as social class barriers (Schwartz 49).

Some educators cannot understand why students entering school with nonstandard dialects leave school 12 years later with the same nonstandard dialect. These educators forget a basic principle of language: Our ways of using and understanding language are deeply ingrained in our internal language system and are therefore not easily changed through direct teaching (Farr and Daniels 24). Thus, the failure to learn may be the result of cultural differences in U.S. society and the subculture of our classrooms, where we reflect mainstream (usually white, middle-class) culture. Shirley Brice Heath's *Ways With Words,* a study of home and school cultures, illustrates this phenomenon. Children, she found, are socialized into ways of using language, both oral and written, and are thus bound up in the patterns of their own culture. When they enter school, they generally enter the mainstream culture. It is no wonder, then, that complex differences between a student's home culture and school culture contribute to frustration and failure. Farr and Daniels argue that "cultural differences in language practices that are part of very different ways of viewing and operating in the world must be taken seriously" (32).

WRITING AND DIALECTS

Teaching writing to students with different dialects can be a challenge, mainly because it is difficult to use conscious strategies to change a largely unconscious process. This difficulty also explains why the direct teaching of grammar fails, no matter which dialect students speak. Many educators believe that standard dialect patterns are learned through meaningful and sustained interactions with speakers of standard dialect—not by exposure to school or television (Farr and Daniels 35). Mina Shaughnessy's powerful study of writing, *Errors and Expectations,* adds another view and a warning. Teachers should not be mislead by errors in writing. The problem has less to do with dialect than it does with lack of exposure to written English. The problem is one of making sense on paper, in an academic setting; the problem is not the home dialect per se (5).

Because fundamental language processes work the same for all students, there is no reason to believe that the process of learning to write is different for nonstandard dialect students. We are not suggesting that instruction is identical or that we don't need to make some adaptations for nonstandard dialect speakers. We do make such adaptations in both oral and written work, but on the whole, we teach writing—not writing to various subgroups within our classrooms.

THE SUPPORTIVE CLASSROOM

Speakers of nonstandard American dialects need abundant opportunities for using language in the classroom. This means committing time to the development of listening skills, oral comprehension, and production through (a) natural interaction among peers; (b) oral language built into all content area experiences; and (c) teacher anticipation of error and a positive procedure for reinforcing standard usage and syntax. In such a classroom, teachers and students not only use a great deal of oral and written language, but they also talk about language itself. The lessons are natural: What is a dialect? What features do our dialects share? What features of pronunciation and syntax are different? Which vocabulary words are different? How does vocabulary reflect our culture? How does rhythm differ? These lessons can be taught by the students. We need only lead them into critical listening and thinking, to keen observation of themselves and others as users of language, and then into discussion. Such discussions provide both awareness of language and respect for the diverse cultures represented.

DIALECT AND IDENTITY

Because dialects are closely tied to culture, family, and identity, they are an integral part of self-concept. Educators know that self-concept is perhaps the most powerful factor in academic success; therefore, we must not only understand these basic principles of language but also apply them in our curriculum, methodology, and classroom environment. To ignore them is to place students at risk. Students who feel deficient and devalued because of their language will most certainly fail, thus continuing a cycle of illiteracy and poverty. We also know that attitude is a critical factor in a student's acquisition of a second dialect or language; thus, teachers themselves may become the critical difference. Moreover, teachers whose classrooms focus on linguistic and cultural diversity enrich all students, not just those who are acquiring standard American English.

Research has demonstrated that a nonstandard dialect, in and of itself, is not a barrier to learning. All dialects are highly structured, logical, and complete. Standard English is no more expressive or logical and no more capable of communication than nonstandard dialects. Judgments about the superiority of one dialect are social, not linguistic. Teachers who understand this will not underestimate the language abilities of students with nonstandard dialects, nor will they fail to build the self-esteem critical to academic success. Our knowledge, our attitude, and our willingness to acquire specific dialect knowledge will make a difference.

DIALECTS OF AMERICAN ENGLISH

Philip Dale notes that "typically, [variation] is not a black problem but prejudice arising from inability of the larger society to accept linguistic diversity—the Chicano, the Puerto Rican, the Appalachian, the Native American" (282). To these, we can add Southeast Asian, Haitian, and Cuban immigrants. It is important to remember that within the categories of Hispanic, Native American, and Asian reside many distinct cultures and languages; for example, *Hispanic* may mean Mexican, Cuban, Central American, or Puerto Rican. The values, customs, and ways of speaking are different, despite Spanish being the native language. Similarly, *Native American* refers to hundreds of distinct languages and Indian nations with differing cultures. *Asian* also covers distinct language groups with distinct cultures.

As students acquire standard dialect, it is critical for us to understand that bidialectism or bilingualism is a complex situation—a matter of degree rather than all or nothing. A student possesses different levels of fluency in speaking, reading, and writing, all at the same time. The same student may vary in listening comprehension or in the capability to understand. We cannot expect students to be equally capable in all areas or acquire communicative competency evenly. Native speakers are similarly uneven, a fact that is often overlooked in the English language arts curriculum.

Language "problems" arising out of dialect or second language are not problems of intelligence or educational ability but, rather, the consequence of certain differences between the language of home, certain ways of knowing and doing, and the language of school.

Black English

Black English is perhaps the most widely discussed dialect of English; it may also be the most misunderstood. Too often people believe that black English is simply sloppy talk. Pronunciations such as *jus* for *just* cause some teachers to label black Americans as careless or lazy, despite the fact that white speakers of southern variants demonstrate similar pronunciations. There isn't one correct way of speaking, only variations that are appropriate to the situation. Attempts to erase black dialect differences by correcting "errors" are ineffective, as well as insulting. Our goal should be to increase communicative competence: the student's ability to use language effectively in a variety of settings for many purposes.

Our job, then, is not to change a student's language but to expand the potential. Accepting black dialect, recognizing it as different, not defective, is the first step in the process. We also need to understand that the label itself, black English, is misleading. It equates ethnic identification with a genetic characteristic, being black. Many African Americans never speak black English, whereas people of other ethnic groups do. Moreover, certain standard dialects share some of the features of black English. Black dialect is important; many students speak it. Both for establishing a respect for the culture it represents and as a base for teaching, we need to respond by learning something of this American dialect.

Understanding Black English

This dialect has the same number of sounds as standard dialect but a different pattern of distribution; the real distinction is in rhythm, inflection, and tone. Anyone who has listened to the public speech of Martin Luther King, Jr., or Jesse Jackson, who keep the cadence of black dialect even when using standard dialect, has no doubt been struck by these elements.

As with any dialect, notable variations in pronunciation, (e.g., substitutions and deletions of certain sounds) are standardized and predictable. Teachers familiar with black dialect are thus able to recognize the difference between an error and a mere substitution of sounds. For example, a student who reads *with* as *wif* is not making an error; in black dialect, the final /th/ is pronounced /f/. Similarly, a student who reads *sore* as *saw* and *star* as *stah* is following a regular rule of black dialect that deletes both the middle and final /r/. Most final consonants or consonant clusters are also deleted. A student who asks about her *tes* grade demonstrates a regular feature of her home language—not an error.

After an initial period of adjustment, most people readily understand the pronunciation differences. Some southern dialects have similar characteristics, and few people have real difficulty understanding a speaker from Georgia or Texas—if they want to. As Geneva Smitherman, a noted African American scholar, reminds us: "Southern Black speech sounds pretty much the same as Southern White speech . . . when you talk about pronunciation, there is no national standard even among white speakers" ("It Bees" 522).

Grammar is the most rigid part of our language system and is the least likely to change over time. Therefore, differences in grammar are fewer than those in pronunciation, but at the same time, they carry a greater stigma. Most people, regardless of dialect, find grammar differences irritating and unacceptable. Teachers are no exception. Despite their knowledge of the integrity of every dialect, many English language arts teachers respond negatively not only to black dialect but to any variance in grammar. For some reason, knowing that certain verbs (e.g., *be*) pattern themselves in well-defined ways or that plural and possessive markers are often absent does little or nothing to alleviate a negative response. Teachers who work with speakers of black dialect must not only overcome such a response but also learn the distinctive features of the dialect.

As teachers, we need to remember that not all African Americans speak this dialect, and that many features of black English are present in other southern dialects. Differences between black English and standard English are not great. Many non-African Americans react to the rhythm and rhetorical style and respond emotionally, thereby exaggerating the differences. It is most often the attitude of school personnel toward the dialect, rather than the dialect itself, that contributes to poor scholastic performance. No one assumes a speaker of Boston dialect who says *idear* cannot learn to write *idea*. Yet, many African American students are victims of an assumption that says their dialect is a barrier to learning.

NATIVE AMERICAN LANGUAGES

There is no such thing as an "Indian culture" or talking "Indian." The approximately 300 different tribal groups in the United States are each divided to some degree by language, culture, and tradition (Knop 24). It is not surprising, then, that linguists believe there are approximately 14 language groups and, within each, many dialects. Within the state of Wisconsin, for example, six nations and three language groups are represented. Within one of these language groups, the Algonquian family, Chippewa, Menominee, and Potowatomi are all dialects.

> Contrary to beliefs, the vast majority of languages are still spoken today. Many Indian children grow up in families hearing language spoken around them but not to them. Unfortunately, the adults have been led to believe that speaking the native language to some children is detrimental to their growth. One of the consequences of this way of thinking is that the children do not have a grasp of either one of the languages, English or the native. (Knop 25)

If we keep in mind that cultural and language patterns are set in childhood, we recognize that through school some Native American children are learning a new language that may be of no use at home and, in very serious ways, may be unrelated to the world and environment in which these students live. Further, the organization of classroom talk—such as the interactions between students and teacher and between students, and the regulation of getting and holding the floor—is designed to fit the white, middle-class student. This means that language in school neither fits with nor builds on interactional skills held by Native American students. Dialect differences no doubt cause some misunderstanding, not only because there are different rules of discourse but also because little world knowledge is shared.

Susan Philips' study of the Warm Springs Indian Reservation, *The Invisible Culture,* illustrates how Indian children's verbal and nonverbal communication patterns conflict with those of the mainstream school. Philips argues that this conflict means that speaking is less easily integrated into the normal sequences and structure of classroom talk. This, in turn, leads to more instances in which Native American students suffer the consequences of teacher judgments of inappropriate listening and speaking behaviors. Philips also points out that even well-intentioned teachers often find minority students' efforts to communicate incomprehensible. Unfortunately, because many U.S. classrooms are built around the teacher as authority, the students end up being defined as those responsible for breakdowns in communication (128).

Bridging the Difference

Teachers aware of language as a cultural phenomenon will want to learn something of language and interaction patterns in the native culture. We must neither praise nor scold Native American students publicly. Praise may embarrass the student because doing the "right" thing is expected. Private consultation is more appropriate for correction. Our questions may also pose a danger because, in many Indian cultures, questions are a form of trial. Native American youngsters more often observe, try things out on their own privately, and perform when ready. Privacy is important; therefore, we cannot expect students to talk or write freely about themselves. We also need to be aware of nonverbal language patterns. Eye contact, for example, is viewed differently. Lowered eyes and head show respect for a teacher, not lack of interest. One-on-one dialogue between teacher and student often doesn't work, nor does placing a Native American student before the class, which runs counter to cultural training in cooperation and sharing of leadership and responsibilities among the group.

The attributes of Native American pedagogy are good for all students. Discovery and activity are basic to learning. Cooperative learning groups have become part of many mainstream classrooms. According to Johnson et al., in cooperative learning groups, all students share leadership action and a responsibility to ensure that all group members are learning; students are expected to help and encourage their group members. Further, students are taught the social skills necessary for collaborative work; they are not assumed to have them (n.p.). The fundamental difference between competitive and individual learning, which is basic to Native American philosophy, is addressed in cooperative learning groups. As with all students, opportunities to use language, rather than to hear about language, are critical in developing oral and written language skills.

HISPANIC ENGLISH

Hispanic English is a dialect spoken by students whose native language is Spanish. Although Spanish is the native language of students of Mexican, Cuban, Puerto Rican, and Central American descent, each of these cultures has its own ways of knowing and doing. The dialect is found mostly among bilingual speakers; in areas of the United States that border Mexico, the Spanish influence reinforces and maintains Hispanic English. As with all dialects, there are systematic differences in pronunciation, stress, and syntax (Fromkin and Rodman 270). Hispanic English, nonetheless, is comprehensible to speakers of other American dialects. Ricardo Garcia tells us that "while speaking his *colo,* or dialect of English, the Chicano thinks little of borrowing or mixing of Spanish and English," whether it be sound, vocabulary, or grammar (540). We can therefore expect Hispanic students to substitute Spanish sounds for English ones, as well as to make literal translations.

Roseann Duenas Gonzales notes that Chicano English (a dialect spoken by Mexican Americans) serves an oral communication purpose. In written form, however, it is "distinguished by characteristics such as incorrect or incomplete verb formations (no *ed*, no *s*, no *ed* on past participle), inappropriate prepositions (such as *in* for *on*), inappropriately used vocabulary and syntactic patterns that differ from those acceptable in edited American English" (21). She adds that the lexicon of this dialect is limited both in breadth and precision. Consequently, these students need not only to understand the differences between oral and written English but also to acquire an expanded and enriched vocabulary (21). Because Mexican American students generally come from highly structured families, Gonzales believes writing instruction that is structured (e.g., formal invention strategies, organizational patterns, and sentence combining) will be more successful (20). Similarly, these students' orientation to communal family and neighborhood lives produces a learning style that thrives in small groups and cooperative activities; they are also less competitively oriented. Furthermore, in observing Mexican American students, Gonzales concluded that the majority were interested in how to improve their writing rather than in grades. If mainstream teachers are to unlock the academic potential of these students, they must first understand and then capitalize on different cultural characteristics.

Because Hispanic English derives from Spanish, these students may be placed in programs or classes for non-native speakers. However, appropriate placement or instruction is complicated. According to Gonzales, "Understanding Mexican American students demands familiarity with their complex, yet simply perceived, linguistic situation" (20). She explains that too often people assume that all Chicanos are bilingual, whereas "their linguistic situation reflects a complex spectrum of bilingualism" (21). In reality, students may be Spanish dominant with limited oral and written English skills or English dominant with limited Spanish language ability or somewhere along a language continuum.

Box 13–1

PROBLEM-SOLVING ACTIVITY FOR CLASSROOM DIVERSITY: VARIETIES OF AMERICAN ENGLISH

Problem 1:

The Setting: Rainy Lake Senior High School. The high school is fed by three small, rural communities and a Native American reservation. The Native American students have attended school on their reservation through eighth grade; now they comprise about 30 percent of the student.

The Class: English 10, with a total of 25 students: 16 whites (10 male, 6 female) and 9 Native Americans (4 males and 5 females).

The Teacher: You are a first-year teacher in an unfamiliar school district. You know from conversations in the teachers' lounge that the potential for racial conflict cannot be ignored. You quickly learn that tension between white and Indian students has increased, resulting in name-calling on both sides. You also notice, uneasily, that a few teachers appear to be racist, making remarks about Indian students' lack of class participation and inability to achieve even mediocre grades. However, you conclude that indifference is perhaps the greatest problem in this district.

The Problem: What can you do to create a "peaceable" classroom and motivate both Native American and white students to do their best work. Think in terms of classroom environment, teaching materials, and instructional strategies.

Problem 2:

The Setting: Forrest Gump Middle School. The middle school setting serves the urban poor in a racially mixed neighborhood.

The Class: English 7 with 23 students: 12 Hispanics, 7 blacks, and 4 whites. The students' home languages offer a rich linguistic environment; however, standard American English is seldom heard or used in the home or immediate community. Inclusion is district policy, so you have a wide range of abilities and talents within this class.

The Teacher: You are in your first teaching assignment, and although you know the city quite well, this neighborhood is unfamiliar. Your principal is black, as are a majority of teachers, all of whom welcome you warmly. You are immediately drawn to the school environment: a "comfort zone" for kids but one with high expectations for academic success, as well as clear guidelines for appropriate behavior. But you also learn from your experienced colleagues that some students come to school hungry, abused, or neglected; most are street-smart beyond their years.

The Problem: How will you meet the challenge of teaching 23 students with diverse cultural backgrounds and home dialects, varied abilities, and low socioeconomic status?

STUDENTS WITH LIMITED ENGLISH PROFICIENCY

The Importance of Bilingualism

Given the continuing numbers of immigrants to the United States today, most English language arts teachers can expect to have some ESL students, that is, those for whom English is a second language. Districts with significant numbers of ESL speakers may have a bilingual program. Because bilingual programs are often criticized,

English language arts teachers should understand the role and significance of bilingual education. Although appearing to be counterintuitive, programs that provide limited English students with significant content instruction in their native language result in more English acquisition than do programs in which all instruction is in English. The students' native language helps them develop expressive skills and conceptual under-standing that then build a strong conceptual base for the acquisition of English.

Thus, students in a bilingual program not only acquire English more quickly and thoroughly but also become truly bilingual. Loss of the native language also means loss in English competency. Research suggests that the level of proficiency in English depends partly on the degree of native language proficiency at the time when intensive exposure to English occurs. For many students with limited English proficiency, this exposure coincides with their entry into U.S. schools. Development of the native language and English are then interdependent to a certain degree; their interaction influences the success of the student with limited English profi-ciency (Bilingual Education Dept.).

The loss of native language is detrimental from two perspectives: The develop-ment of the second language, in this case English, may be slowed, and the student may feel in psychological limbo. The native language has been the linguistic system associ-ated with the development of basic concepts. If students are forced to drop it alto-gether, the loss affects both conceptual development and identity. In extreme cases, stu-dents can end up with neither the native language nor English as a useful tool. The ideal program for the limited English student would be one that provides comprehen-sible and meaningful "input" in English and, at the same time, content area instruction in both languages. Content knowledge instruction is critical to cognitive development and to helping students make sense out of learning activities conducted in English.

The language limbo extends beyond the classroom; students who lose their native language lose important family ties as well. Listen to the following voices of high school Hmong students, refugees from Laos. Youa, at age 15, reveals a very personal and poignant side of language loss:

> Even though I love my mother very much I hardly talk to her. We do not sit down and discuss things like most American girls do with their mother. I do not talk to her much because my vocabulary in Hmong is very limited and she has no English vocabulary.

She goes on to explain other difficulties:

> Once when we went to the cities [Minneapolis/St. Paul] for a visit, a relative of ours thought that I was deaf because I did not answer him.

And as 16-year-old Ye tells us, the loss of a native language becomes a source of ten-sion within the family:

> As a result of the lack of communication, many of the Hmong generation have lost their language and their culture. The lack of communication and culture causes a big deal of anger between the parents and the young generation. (Meiser *Teaching* 1–2)

Bilingualism, then, is critically important in maintaining family relationships, tradition, and culture. For Southeast Asian students like Youa and Ye, there was no bilingual program available. Having to make a choice between English and their native Hmong, they chose English, a pragmatic decision—but one with a high price tag in terms of family and culture. As David E. Freeman and Yvonne S. Freeman explain:

> Some students are unable to move successfully between worlds because they never fully enter the mainstream school community. They are marginalized by the instruction they receive and the attitudes they encounter. Eventually, many of them drop out or are pushed out of school. Unfortunately, these students are often not able to succeed in school or return to their home community. They may be in a state of cultural ambivalence, not really accepted at school or at home. When this happens, increasing numbers of students turn to alternate communities, such as gangs. Rather than experiencing the best of both worlds, they cannot participate fully in either one.
>
> Other students succeed in school, but in the process become alienated from their home community. These are students who enter school as monolingual Spanish or Korean speakers and leave school as monolingual English speakers. They are unable to communicate with family and friends in the home community. These students may reject their heritage language and culture to become part of the mainstream. Rather than experiencing the best of both worlds, they simply trade one world for another. (*Between Worlds* 3)

Bilingual education is, and will no doubt continue to be, controversial. Unfortunately, it is an issue of politics and emotions and seldom viewed from an educational perspective. People have strong feelings about English and only English in America; further, they believe students become fluent in English only by being taught in English. To many people, first language support for English learners appears to be a complete waste of time, effort, and taxpayers' money. The idea that continued development of a native language leads to faster acquisition of English is, unfortunately, counterintuitive and therefore preposterous to most people. However, research findings support bilingual education, as do teachers watching the progress of individual ESL students.

ACADEMIC ENGLISH

The difficulty of the limited English student in a mainstream classroom stems from the differences between conversational and academic English. When non-native speakers become reasonably fluent in English, it is easy to forget the level of difficulty they must confront in academic language, both spoken and written. Research reminds us that immigrant students may reach proficiency in basic oral communication in two to three years; however, the level of proficiency needed in school requires five to seven years (Chamot and O'Malley 109). The language of school is both unique and complex, although as teachers we don't often consider this fact. The higher the curricular level, the more abstract we become, moving even farther away from experiential and contextual learning. For the second language student, this situation can be a formula for failure.

At greatest risk are students arriving in U.S. schools at age 12 or older. The heavy cognitive demands and level of academic language used in secondary schools make it very difficult to catch up. Consequently, students need content area instruction in their native language rather than only intensive English language instruction (Chamot and O'Malley 110). Moreover, secondary students can't afford to lose two to three years of academic instruction while mastering English if they expect to go on to post-secondary institutions (Collier 520). English language arts teachers can help by including materials and concepts from various content areas in their classrooms.

We must remember, however, that the student may or may not have developed academic language skills in the native language, thus affecting whether the student must learn to transfer these skills to English or learn them for the first time. Teachers need to make English comprehensible, fully contextual, and rich in nonverbal cues. The higher the grade level, the more decontextualized the language and instruction. Language no longer refers to the concrete, the here and now, but to ideas and events far removed from the student. Immigrant students also lack a historical and cultural context for these ideas and events, which compounds the level of difficulty.

A student's progress through the stages of language acquisition is both personal and uneven. The amount of time each learner spends in each stage and the consistency of performance depend on several variables. One is the individual development of the student, another is willingness to learn the second language, and yet another is the quality of instructional planning and language environment in the classroom. Self-esteem, the ability to take risks, and good learning strategies are critical to the process. Age may also be a factor (Raimes "Working") However, assumptions that young children are faster and more efficient in acquiring a second language have been disputed by research (Collier 510). At the same time, research has not provided information of an optimal age. What is not disputed is that age cannot be separated from other key variables in language acquisition, such as cognitive development and proficiency in native language.

Concerning students' acquisition of a second language, Ann Raimes ("Working") notes some agreement among researchers on the following points:

- Acquisition is complex, gradual, non-linear and dynamic.
- Acquisition of certain structures follows a definite order.
- Students acquire competency gradually; some learners remain stuck at one stage of competency.
- Learners develop an interlanguage midway between the native language and the target language, a system that approximates the target language but is neither the native nor the target language.
- Learners transfer cognitive strategies, which may be positive or negative for learning in the second language.
- Learners rely on native language when the target language is not adequate for their communicative needs.
- Fewer errors can be attributed to the native language, to interference, than previously thought.

Because of the nature of language processes themselves, some obvious parallels exist between native and second language acquisition. As with native language, a sustained and comprehensible second language environment fosters students' progress in both listening comprehension and oral production. And in both native and second language learning, grammatical and pronunciation errors are normal, indicating important developments in learning. Purposeful language, that is, authentic communication, is also central to both native and second language learning.

Despite some striking similarities, there are also profound differences between native and second language learning. One of these is time. Students learning a second language cannot return to infancy and enjoy a similar time frame for growth and the unconditional tolerance for error it provided. A necessary variable for the second language learner is to provide as much comprehensible language (i.e., that they can understand) as possible in whatever time is available. A great deal of talking, reading, and writing is basic to acquisition; looking at language, analyzing it, and writing things down all assist the students. One inventive second language learner discovered toll-free telephone numbers and used them extensively to hear English and to learn new vocabulary; the same student also listened to an all-news radio station by day and watched eight hours of television at night (Raimes "Working"). Suggesting ways for students to access spoken and written English, however strange-sounding to the native speaker, provides them with options.

Unfortunately, many ESL students must hurry into literacy, attempting to gain reading and writing skills while their oral language base is still being formed. Although development of oral and written skills may occur simultaneously, time may be a significant problem for the secondary student. Like other young adults, second language students are faced with many demands. Another problem with acquiring literacy is the effect of the native language because rhetorical patterns are culturally based. For example, in Japanese texts, writers do not provide full explication, relying more on nuance, hints, and other devices; the reader is responsible for "filling in the gaps." In most English texts, the writer is responsible for clarity, delineating everything for the reader. The concept of the topic sentence, for instance, is very American. How students link sentences is also culturally based. In Arabic, the written language is linked to the Koran, resulting in rhythmic coordination and balance. Arabic students writing in English thus rely heavily on *and* and *so* rather than on subordination. An ESL student, then, must learn an entirely new rhetorical system (Raimes "Working").

With our native language, we also acquire, gradually and naturally, its social uses and applications. Since expectations of speakers and writers vary from culture to culture, students cannot simply transfer this knowledge to English. Similarly, academic expectations vary considerably from culture to culture. Some students may be from a culture that venerates the written word and thus may have great difficulty with the expectation that students challenge it. Others may be from a culture where rote learning is the accepted method of instruction; self-discovery would be very alien to them. Cultural differences also affect motivation for learning the second language. If students have negative feelings about U.S. culture, they may resist its language. In any case, students acquiring a second language are finding and processing a new identity, an American one (Raimes "Working"). Mainstream teachers should not underestimate the emotional and social complexity of this undertaking.

The School Environment

Whole Language for Bilingual Learners

Freeman and Freeman argue that "for students whose first language is not English, whole language is not only good teaching but is essential. Whole language may be the only road to success for bilingual learners" (*Whole* 5). Why do Freeman and Freeman make such a strong case for whole language? Mainly because traditional methods have not worked well for bilingual students. High school dropout rates are very high for this population, with the rate for Hispanic students edging toward 50 percent. "To reverse this trend of school failure," say Freeman and Freeman, "a new approach is required, and for many teachers, whole language seems to be the answer" (*Whole* 6).

We discussed whole language in Chapter 1, where we noted that whole language is a philosophy, a way of viewing teaching and learning. And like Freeman and Freeman, we also believe that whole language translates into a powerful methodology for working with students—all students, regardless of their language ability. Because whole language for bilingual students is such an important concept, we'll briefly review its major principles here.

1. Learning proceeds from whole to part. Students develop concepts by beginning with general ideas and then filling in the details—not from taking small parts and building into a whole.
2. Lessons should be learner-centered. Because learning involves constructing (rather than being given) knowledge, teachers create contexts in which students can construct knowledge.
3. Lessons should have meaning and purpose now. Students have choices, reflect on what they learn, and apply learning both in and out of school. Students see connections between school and the "real world."
4. Lessons should engage groups of students in interaction. Sharing ideas fosters both individual growth and the important life skill of collaboration.
5. Lessons should develop both oral and written language. Literacy need not be delayed. Oral and written language can and should be developed simultaneously.
6. Lessons that show a belief in the learners' potential expand that potential. (adapted from Freeman and Freeman *Whole* 7–8)

Whole language is not a cure-all. It will not solve all the challenges and problems faced by bilingual students and their teachers. And as we pointed out earlier, whole language is not an easy way to teach; it requires excellent planning and monitoring. It also requires commitment. Teachers may face resistance as they implement new ways of structuring their classrooms and lessons. Nonetheless, we believe whole language classrooms are worth the effort. And for second language students, it may be, as Freeman and Freeman argue, the only reasonable hope for achieving educational goals.

Building the Oral Base

When we learned our native language, we had substantial time to develop oral language—to easily absorb the sounds of our language with no contrasting influences and to build strong receptive skills. We had many language models and many varied opportunities to use the language, interacting constantly in varied ways. ESL students must, therefore, have a good program in oral language, not only for its own sake but also as a base for literacy.

Because new sounds are being substituted for sounds and structures of the native language, students may experience some difficulty. Teachers need to learn major differences between the sounds and structures of the native language and English and teach *as needed* those that contrast with the native language. It's important to note, however, that language acquired in informal school activities is likely to be more important than any direct instruction (Holdzkom et al. 1).

Teachers also need to maintain a reasonable perspective on pronunciation. Flawless English is not the goal; comprehensible English is. The older the students, the more difficult it is for them to position tongue, teeth, facial muscles for the new language. Because most teenagers find it quite difficult to master sounds, they are easily intimidated by the process. Teachers have to assure them that no one expects them to sound like native speakers; syntactic control, the ability to control structure, is more important than pronunciation (Holdzkom et al. 4–5).

Listening skills are key to acquiring the second language and often are very limited. In some families, English is spoken little or not at all. Immigrant students may also cluster in national groups for out-of-school activities. Students thus have limited exposure to English, which results in limited receptive skills. The classroom therefore needs a structure to promote listening, conversation, and interaction. Interaction is vital; learners need meaningful language and practice, not exercises and drills. Teachers cannot assume that, because students are in an English-speaking environment, they will develop competency. As second language learners, they need organized, directed, and purposeful communication. They also need varied contexts for this communication. Teacher planning, then, is critical in developing the oral base.

Concepts and Context

In learning a native language, we develop and understand a concept and then associate a word with that concept. A student learning English will have to do one of two things: either match concepts already learned in the native language to English words or learn both the concept and the word simultaneously in English. For this reason, teachers need to ensure that the student understands the concept before teaching the word that represents it. Acquisition of native language takes place in a natural setting, with language exposure occurring every waking hour. For a second language, the number of hours of learning are limited, and the language activities are structured and contrived and the setting more formal. Classrooms that simulate everyday life and varied language use assist ESL learners.

Culture and Reinforcement

Language is an integral part of culture and vice versa. In learning our native language, we are part of that culture, understanding it in important ways. With a second language, the learner often has little or no knowledge of the culture, making it far more difficult to relate words and ideas. In teaching language, then, we need to include activities that teach about culture at the same time. In the native language, the learner is given wide latitude for error and for producing imperfect language because people recognize language acquisition as a developmental process. When working with ESL students, we need to give students the same latitude, attending more to meaning-making and less to form. If we concentrate on the speaker's communication effort and provide the correct model without being too explicit about it, the student will probably respond well and continue efforts to communicate.

The native language develops linguistically, socially, and cognitively; the second language is often overconcentrated linguistically, providing less time for content knowledge development and social interaction. If no bilingual program is present to develop content knowledge, teachers can ask for native language tutors. As native speakers, we received tremendous support and reinforcement for learning our language; people were pleased with our efforts, rewarded us, and tolerated error. An ESL student may encounter negative attitudes and settings, and reinforcement may be given for errors but not for accomplishments. The classroom should be a place where cultural and linguistic acceptance and appreciation are commonplace.

Acquiring Oral Language

As we consider language development, it is important to remember that each student's progress varies. Designating "stage" boundaries, therefore, is merely a guide to general progress, not an absolute. The Bilingual Education Department in the San Francisco School District developed the following categories to help its mainstream teachers.

- In the preverbal stage, the student has no comprehension of English; a response may be based on guessing, using either context or another student's response as the basis. We should continue to surround the student with meaningful English, answer our own questions as a natural model of response, and demonstrate with concrete items and experiential learning as often as possible.
- In the next stage, the student comprehends English but is still be unable to respond in English; he or she may respond appropriately in the native language, however. Acceptance of student response in the native language is important. We should continue to provide opportunities where the student can imitate or speak, but not force a response. Through learning experiences, we can draw the student into speaking.

- Next, the student may try out English through spontaneously imitating teachers and other students. We need to encourage the student, inviting him or her to imitate a response after we have given it and, if necessary, correct in a positive way. Providing natural models through regular classroom interactions is important. From here, the student moves into simple spontaneous verbalizations which may not be grammatically correct. Again we need to encourage speaking and play down the correcting of grammar. The more peer interaction, the better.
- Finally, the student moves into intermediate fluency, controlling many basic English structures. The student may be quite fluent in conversation and social situations, but lack comprehension and production related to academic language. At this point, we monitor both meaning and form and keep track of persistent grammar errors. Although we may use more complex structures in clear contexts, we still need to check that the student really understands us. (n.p.)

Acquiring Written Language

Often, mainstream teachers believe that they have no knowledge of how to work with ESL students. However, teachers who understand the underlying concepts of native language acquisition and its relevance for teaching composition do have a good base for working with ESL writers. Similarly, teachers who approach writing instruction holistically, emphasizing process skills before turning to product evaluation, are already using beneficial strategies. Teachers who have integrated the language arts—weaving reading, writing, speaking, and listening into all instructional activities—also have a sound basis for working with second language learners. Nonetheless, it is important that mainstream teachers treat ESL writers neither exactly the same nor completely different from native speakers (Chan 85).

STRATEGIES FOR TEACHING WRITING

One of the most important strategies is actually an attitude: Let students write, regardless of how limited their English vocabulary is. Based on her research and extensive experience with ESL writers, Ann Raimes believes "the acquisition of adequate vocabulary does not necessarily have to precede writing. If ESL students are given enough time, shown ways to explore topics, and given enough feedback, they will discover and uncover the English words they need as they write" ("What Unskilled" 248).

Raimes goes on to note that ESL writers need more of everything: talking, listening, reading, writing; instruction and practice in generating, organizing, and revising ideas; attention to rhetorical options; and an emphasis on editing for linguistic form and style (250).

A second strategy involves reading—lots of it. Because ESL writers do not have native intuitiveness to guide them in revision, they need to read a great deal of well-written English prose (Chan 84). Providing a wealth of reading resources, along with sustained time for reading, helps students see how the language functions. Asking students to keep a journal for reflection, both on what they read and on their own writing processes, is another useful strategy. A double-entry notebook is another strategy that asks students to reflect on their own learning. In it, they can record their errors, enter a corrected version, and an explanation of what went wrong or why they made the language choice they did. Their responses provide an invaluable resource for understanding them and focusing instruction.

Group work and teacher conferences are needed strategies; students benefit most from response to work in progress. Further, as Raimes reminds us, we have to take into account the anxiety that accompanies writing in a new language; sharing with peers or the teacher may alleviate some anxiety or frustration. Oral rehearsal, composing out loud, and other interactive activities work well for second language writers ("Language" 461). Providing written questions for revision and editing also helps, as do specific proofreading strategies.

UNDERSTANDING STUDENTS' ERRORS

Traditionally, teachers focused almost entirely on anticipated interference from a student's native language. Although teachers must, of course, be aware of the major differences between English and the student's native language, recent studies have demonstrated that second language learners often make errors that have less to do with interference from their native language and more to do with their developing competency in English. Another major consideration is the uniqueness of each student. The type of errors that occur in one student's work may be very different from those of another student sharing the same native language. Errors generally fall into patterns, which makes it easier for teachers to analyze the source and devise instruction. Errors also provide evidence of systematic decision making, providing a key to the student's language development and understanding of English.

ESL students make errors for some of the same reasons that native speakers do. One is simply performance—making a mistake despite underlying competency. Another is lack of exposure to the correct form or lack of correction, often in an oral pattern that the student simply transfers to paper. However, ESL writers also make mistakes due to transfer from the native language or applying an idiosyncratic set of rules in an effort to approximate English.

RECOGNIZING AND WORKING WITH "SMART ERRORS"

For mainstream teachers working with ESL writers, a useful perspective is one of "smart errors." Many written language errors provide evidence that the ESL student is gaining insight into how English works and that his or her errors are logical. For example, a student may have learned the plural rule and has overextended its use to an irregular plural. Applying the rule, however wrong in this case, is evidence of growth. Similarly, a student who writes "it made me cried" or "it was very complicated for me to learned" is making connections about English verbs and tense, despite the obvious problem with infinitives. Further, when we consider the sophistication of the syntax used, we realize just how much progress the ESL writer has made. Seeing the logic in ESL errors is important, not just to guide the student's development but also to save both teacher and student from unnecessary frustration.

Examples from high school Hmong students, whose native language is from the Indochinese family, provide striking evidence of "smart errors" (Meiser adapted from *Teaching*):

> Our parents complain that our generations are losing our own language and culture.

> I have been losing my Hmong's big vocabularies.

This student has an amazing control of English syntax. She also understands plurals well enough, lacking instead specific word knowledge; in the context she has used them, *vocabulary* and *generation* remain singular.

The same student might use the word *everythings* in a sentence. Although grammatically singular, *everything* is psychologically plural, and again, the student writer has applied the plural rule logically. Most ESL students demonstrate inconsistency with plurals—omitting when needed and adding when not needed. An additional confounding element for ESL writers lies in the English system of using -s to indicate plural on a noun and singular on a verb. And in some instances, the error may relate to semantic constraints on the word itself, such as the word *vocabulary*. Learning these constraints takes a great deal of time. For this reason, sustained reading experience is critical. The more often ESL students see how English words function in full discourse, the better. Similarly, sustained oral interaction with native speakers promotes an "ear" for the correct forms. Sustained writing experience—not drills on plurals but full discourse—is the appropriate response.

Should you point out the errors? Yes, but only if you are going to discuss them with the student. Annotating papers does little to foster the kind of internal grammatical knowledge ESL writers need to acquire. Individual conferences or small-group mini-lessons on a specific problem will help. As with native speaker writing instruction, you should use examples from the students' text and limit your instruction to one or two concepts at the very most. If you provide students with samples of similar, correct text, they can often draw conclusions about the appropriate forms. One advantage of working with secondary students lies in their higher level of cognitive development. They do understand language as an object to be worked with.

Pronouns often cause trouble. The choice of subject or object forms, for example, can be confusing, as can demonstratives:

> Those delicious food . . .

If you talked with this student about "those delicious food," you would probably learn the logic of her construction. The word *food* covers both a single apple and a table filled with 15 desserts. Before determining whether to teach pronoun forms once more, check the consistency of the error. If you do decide that a review of forms is warranted, don't present them all at once. Also, group them (i.e., work with subjects only). And keep in mind that when you work with demonstrative pronouns, such as *this, that, these,* and *those,* you are also working with agreement. The student has to understand the concepts of singular and plural before agreement makes any sense. One pronoun error, the bane of every English teacher, has little or nothing to do with logic or ESL:

> . . . because me and Blia have to go to the store.

This error is common among native speakers, probably because of students' oral language patterns. Unfortunately, ESL speakers make the same kind of transfer.

One of the characters in *Alice in Wonderland* notes that English verbs have a temper. ESL students would no doubt agree. For many, the system of verbs and tenses is the most challenging and frustrating part of the learning process.

> Many people get marry.
>
> I haven't master . . .

Using the base form of the verb is a reasonable thing to do because the meaning is clear even if the form is incorrect.

> We can laugh, giggling, teasing, and all kinds of things.
>
> We were arguing for a while and then she sort of accept . . .
>
> We came back to my house for a drink and get relax.

The inconsistency in verb forms in these sentences can be viewed positively because, again, they show normal development. Also, before we worry about a single error, we need to consider just how sophisticated the student's syntax is—and celebrate with that student.

Note how Hmong student Youa changes her use of verb forms from draft to draft in the following example:

Draft 1	Some of the kids that *was born* in this country could speak Hmong anymore.
Draft 2	Many Hmong kids that *were born* in this country could speak Hmong anymore.
Draft 3	Many Hmong kids that *born* in this country can not speak Hmong very well.

ESL writers, just like novice writers in their native language, are limited in their ability to focus on multiple problem areas. As Youa corrects the verb form in the subordinate clause in Draft 2, she ignores the main clause. When she turns her attention to the main clause, she reverts to an incorrect verb form in the subordinate clause. This is not cause for despair, only an indication of normal cognition at work. And Youa needs to know that. Similarly, Blia needs support for her sophisticated expression:

> As long as life goes well, my dream could always be *accomplish* any time. Whenever I feel I could handle my life, that's when it will be *accomplish*.

As teachers, our attention quickly focuses on the incorrect verb form. What is far more significant, however, is this student's sophisticated intent. Blia is using a combination of tenses to convey abstract ideas. We can best help her by focusing first on her intended meaning and working with tense as appropriate to that meaning before turning to the incorrect verb form. Because most high school students use increasingly complex structures, mere notations in the margins don't work well. Talking with Blia would be far more effective.

When we work with errors of tense, we must necessarily work with full discourse. Notice how our understanding changes when we look beyond a single sentence:

> My family and I usually stayed home for we *have not learned* to *survived* the jungle of America. We *spend* most of our time sitting in the living room.

Without additional information, we cannot know the time sequences Xiong intended or which tense is appropriate. It's always tempting to focus immediately, and usually solely, on the obvious errors, but we need to keep a different perspective. Xiong is writing fairly complex sentences, showing remarkable progress with English. His intended meaning should be the first priority.

Subject-verb agreement is another problematic area for ESL students, but one in which we often see "smart errors":

> Children thinks . . .

> . . . they feels . . .

This student is no doubt thinking of -*s* as the plural marker, and therefore, making a logical use of it. However, some errors result from sheer sentence complexity and are typical of native speakers as well:

> The kinds of hardship encounter *varies* greatly with different people.

Instead of giving students a rule or assigning work in the grammar text, give them examples of interrupted subject-verb agreement and ask them to draw conclusions about the appropriate form. You'll be teaching them to be critical readers and conscious observers of how English functions.

Subordination is a late-developing skill. These sentences, with no identification of ESL writers, would easily serve as examples of many high school students' writing:

The reason why I do not talk to her is because my vocabulary is limited.

Not having many friends also leads me to not wanting to join any school activities.

Other sentence errors occur because spoken English is a powerful influence, and in speech we are often redundant:

. . . so Ka and I, we invited them to our picnic.

The part where E.T. was about to die, it made me cried.

And, similar to other novice writers, ESL students make punctuation errors that are very logical, often related to oral language:

Once when we went to the cities for a visit; a relative of ours thought I was deaf because I did not answer him. So when he asked our neighbor about me; she told him that I spoke mostly English and very little Hmong.

Youa doesn't need a drill on semicolons and commas—only an explanation based on her own text and continued encouragement to use both marks. A few conventions aside, punctuation must be learned as part of syntax. ESL students need to learn the punctuation marks when they are constructing sentences that need them. When students need the marks to make clear *their* intended meaning, motivation remains high.

Your view of error will be a powerful factor in how you approach and work with ESL writers. Substantial and creditable research in language and learning processes tells us that errors are a normal part of language learning. Moreover, as we have just demonstrated with high school Hmong students, most errors are "smart" errors that illustrate increasing competency with English. Students who understand that their errors are "smart" will take risks in learning a second language (Meiser adapted from *Teaching* 26–32).

TEACHER STRATEGIES

Monitoring Classroom Language

Teachers can begin by monitoring their own language for clarity, pacing, and word choice; use of natural rhythms and pronunciation, normal tone, and gestures. Although we may slow down a bit, we shouldn't do so to the point where English is unnatural, an alien form that students may not be able to relate to outside of our class. We should use complete sentences and be continually aware of the importance of giving examples and paraphrasing. As we present information, we should provide as much context as possible, such as concrete objects, pictures, manipulatives, and demonstrations. Similarly, the chalkboard or overhead projector can serve as visual background, providing key words or other graphic representations.

Teachers need to be aware of the language in textbooks, which are generally dense with information and specialized vocabulary. Textbooks assume native language competency. At the same time, we should beware of workbooks that deprive students of the rich context of "real books." ESL learners should use trade books that support their language development. Vocabulary lists do not promote acquisition, simply because there is no context and the words are thus easily forgotten. Contextualized vocabulary, both oral and written, relates to meaning and is therefore more easily retained. The emphasis must be on meaning first. Because reading aloud has a significant effect on both literacy acquisition and language development, we should provide many opportunities for this activity.

Keeping Language Meaningful

The principles of authentic language (i.e, purposeful, not drills) that apply to native language acquisition and development are the same for a second language. Students without a rudimentary knowledge of natural, spoken language should not be given formal training in grammar. Nor should they be doing exercises. Exercise sheets have a real weakness: The student who is asked to choose between correct and incorrect answers may end up confused and ultimately adopt the wrong usage. Fill-in-the-blank or forced-choice exercises do not demonstrate whether a student can speak or write a complete sentence correctly. We need to make good judgments, then, about when and why we use worksheets or text exercises.

Teachers also need to be aware of nonverbal language in the native culture. For example, how does the culture define space between speakers? Americans generally become somewhat uncomfortable when people stand too close to them; in other cultures, such distance would be viewed as insulting. What are the rules for eye contact? In our schools, we expect students to look straight at us when they respond; such eye contact in other cultures would indicate disrespect for the teacher. How does taking turns during conversation occur in the native culture? Americans tend to dislike "sound gaps" and fill them, allowing very little time for response. Other cultures use "sound gaps" as part of the conversation, signaling respect for what the speaker has just said. What gestures may have double meanings? Not finding out could have disastrous consequences. When students enter the classroom, they are entering a culture within a culture. We need to keep in mind that many "rules" are unknown to non-native speakers.

Structuring the Supportive Classroom

Pat Riggs and Virginia Allen provide some general principles to support acquisition of second language:

Grouping Students
Students with limited English proficiency (LEP) need to be with native speakers. Being in a language-rich environment with real interaction and students their own age

is critical to language development. It is a mistake to view LEP students as though "speaking a language other than English were a terrible form of retardation that prevented communication and play" with native speakers (xi). The teacher should organize lessons so that small groups of LEP and native speakers work together on meaningful tasks. If a task involves particularly difficult information, the teacher may want to keep LEP students together and provide them with extra help. For the most part, however, groups should be a mix of LEP and native speakers.

Using "Real" Language

LEP students need many and varied opportunities to use language; the impetus for learning is tied to achieving communication with other speakers of the language. Thus, students should not be concentrating on the forms of language, forms to use someday in some possible situation. Producing rows of correct forms is not the goal and certainly not the desired pedagogy.

Learning Holistically

A second language, like the native one, develops very gradually and not linearly. That is, "language is not learned as a jigsaw of tiny bits of mastered skills, each fitting into a pattern, but rather as an entire picture, that is at first blurred, only gradually coming into focus" (xi). The classroom implication is clear: Teachers should not waste students' time with worksheets, word lists, or pronunciation drills. Students need to be actively engaged in real activities, have a context for language, and hear and participate in conversations.

Achieving Literacy

Literacy is part of the LEP students' language development. "Writing, speaking, listening and reading all nourish one another; we don't wait for mastery of one before encouraging development of the other three" (xiii). Given this, teachers should encourage reading and writing and not wait until the LEP student is a fluent speaker of English. Teachers must choose comprehensible reading materials and, as noted earlier, stay away from workbooks that fragment language. Writing should be authentic, that is, not for purposes of answering text questions or evaluation. Dialogue journals provide an important place for student writing and teacher comment—not on form, only on content.

A Nurturing Environment

Teachers also need continual awareness of the affective variables that influence learning English. Self-esteem and self-confidence are linked to acquisition, especially at the secondary school level. To achieve competence in English, LEP students need strong motivation to learn, to withstand the errors that are inevitable and to take the risks critical to growth. A supportive classroom environment is key to this. Second language learners need to feel socially part of a group before they are willing to experiment with the new language.

Holdzkom et al. advocate the use of peer tutors to help students with limited English proficiency in the mainstream classroom. With peer tutors, LEP students would be less likely to develop self-segregating behaviors that limit their linguistic and social development (3). At the same time, native speakers would learn far more about language and about another culture. Since peer groups and peer response are integral features of the integrated English language arts curriculum, such pairing is both natural and desirable.

Box 13–2

PROBLEM-SOLVING ACTIVITY FOR ESL

Every now and then, teachers are asked to explain why they use certain materials or instructional methods: to administrators, colleagues, parents, or members of the community. Knowledge of research in human development, the English language arts, and classroom practice must support such explanations.

Choose one of the following situations. In a brief one-page paper, write a response. Consider your audience carefully, and be aware of the critical differences in education, background knowledge, and motivation.

1. You are teaching in a Midwest community of roughly 70,000 people. Although diversity is quite limited, you have a small population of immigrant students from Southeast Asia, Haiti, and Central America. Eight are in one of your classes, and you find that their English skills vary considerably. You have adjusted teaching materials and methods, and you believe that your English class is doing well. However, some majority parents are complaining that their kids are being slighted in English 6, especially in composition instruction. The principal has brought the parental complaints to you and asks that you write a letter to the parents to explain the following concerns: what you are doing and why you are doing it; how all students benefit from this instruction or materials; how ESL students enrich English 6.

2. You are teaching in an urban community with a large immigrant population, some of whom are in this country illegally from Mexico and Central America. The community is already divided on racial issues linked to the economy, and the school is a "lightning rod" for criticism among the community at large. They argue the ESL classes are expensive and worthless and that these kids can learn English on the street, the way every immigrant in the United States learned it. The ESL teachers are upset, as is the bilingual aide in your 10th-grade classroom. As an English educator, you decide you must speak out and that you will do so in a Voice of the People column that is less likely to be edited than a regular letter to the editor.

3. You are teaching in a small southern community that just had an influx of Hispanic students with limited English proficiency. There is no ESL program or teacher available for these students, and regular classroom teachers are concerned. Since the middle school and senior high are in adjacent buildings, the administration is thinking of putting all 15 students (ranging in age from 12 to 17)

into one classroom for English; one "regular" English teacher would then be given this assignment. As the newest teacher, the most recently trained, and least senior staff member, you know that you are a likely candidate.

Choose one of the following scenarios and respond in an informal letter to your superintendent.

> If you decline such an assignment, how would you explain your rationale? What would you suggest be done to accommodate these new students?
>
> If you accept the challenge, what would you ask for and why?

Whatever task you choose, remember to evaluate your audience carefully. Think of ways to make your position relevant to their best interests, not their fears. And above all, keep the well-being of students at the center of your remarks. Your job is to keep kids out of harm's way, to represent the school and yourself in a professional manner, and to be a good liaison with the community.

TEACHING ACTIVITIES FOR ESL

1. Identify the problem areas in each of the following groups of phrases and sentences from ESL writers. Then, note how you would work with each writer. How would you explain the problem, not only in "kid" language but in language totally comprehensible to an ESL student?
   a. Certain American do show . . .
   b. Some student really invited me . . .
   c. Some of the problem for him was . . .
   d. . . . . that really made me felt helpless.
   e. I came to realized . . .
   f. We do not sit down and discussed things.
   g. Many people got sick and some of them had died.
   h. The reason our clocks was disturbed and stop by the absences of electricity last night, so it didn't went off as usual.

2. Read the following essay by Blia, a student mentioned earlier in this chapter. What would be your first priority in helping her revise and edit? Sketch out a plan for working with her on this essay.

   One time, I had to go with my dad to the court because the police accused my dad of selling drugs, such as opium. He didn't know any English so I had to help him with the translation. I was so nervous and had a tough time translating Hmong to English and English to Hmong. When my dad spoke, I could translate it to English without much hassle. However, I have been losing my Hmong's big vocabularies so as the police and judge spoke, I was stuck. My dad had a hard time understanding me because I used my hands to help out a lot. This moment, I realized that I should've listend to my parents for wanting us to learn our language. I have never been so helpless in my life.

3. In some cultures, students are accustomed to memorization rather than self-expression in a school setting. If this is the case, you will need to provide the ESL student with English works that illustrate expressive writing. What would you choose as a representative work for an ESL student in 7th grade? For an 11th grader? How would you bridge the gap between what was appropriate in the home culture classroom and what is expected in your American composition class?

4. Read Xiong's paragraph and decide how you would help him revise and edit it. Your analysis should include the following: Xiong's intent (i.e., what does he want to communicate?); sentence problems that derail the reader; and recurring errors or patterns. Keeping in mind that a

novice or ESL writer can attend to a very limited number of problems at one time, note what you would address first, second, and so on. Provide a rationale for your decision.

Struggling my ways through school was the only way to helped my family survived in the community. One of my most important is going with my parents to the grovery store. While in the store I helped my parents to find their ways around. I also helped them locate certain food and how much they cost. Sometimes I got really mad at myself for being unable to interprets for my parents. This happened because I have troubling with both languages. I don't know enough English and my own native language.

REFERENCES

Bilingual Education Department. San Francisco Unified School District. *Excellence in Leadership and Implementation: Programs for Limited English Proficient Students.* San Francisco: Unified School District, 1985.

Chamot, Anna Uhl, and J. Michael O'Malley. "The Cognitive Academic Learning Approach." Ed. Pat Riggs and Virginia G. Allen. *When They Don't All Speak English: Integrating the ESL Student into the Regular Classroom.* Urbana: National Council of Teachers of English, 1989. 108–25.

Chan, Michele M. "What We Already Know About Teaching ESL Writers. *English Journal* Oct. 88: 84–85.

Christensen, Linda. "Teaching Standard English: Whose Standard?" *English Journal* Feb. 90: 36–40.

Collier, Virginia P. "How Long? A Synthesis of Research on Academic Achievement in a Second Language." *TESOL Quarterly* 23 (1989): 509–31.

Farr, Marcia, and Harvey Daniels. *Language Diversity and Writing Instruction.* Urbana: National Council of Teachers of English (ERIC), 1986.

Freeman, David E., and Yvonne S. Freeman. *Between Worlds: Access to Second Language Acquisition.* Portsmouth: Heinemann, 1994.

Freeman, Yvonne S., and David E. Freeman. *Whole Language for Second Language Learners.* Portsmouth: Heinemann, 1992.

Garcia, Ricardo L. "Linguistic Interference and the Chicano." Ed. Virginia P. Clark et al. *Language: Introductory Readings.* New York: St. Martin's, 1981. 539–45.

Gonzales, Roseann Duenas. "Teaching Mexican Americans Students to Write: Capitalizing on the Culture." *English Journal* Nov. 1982: 20–24.

Heath, Shirley Brice. *Ways With Words.* Cambridge: Cambridge UP, 1983.

Holdzkom, David, et al. "What Teachers Can Do With Non-English Speaking Children in the Classroom." *Research Within Reach: Oral and Written Communication.* Washington D.C.: National Institute of Education, n.d.

Johnson, David, et al. "Circles of Learning." Association of Supervisors and Curriculum Directors, 1984.

Knop, Constance K. *Limited English Proficiency Students in Wisconsin: Cultural Background and Educational Needs.* Part III. Madison: Department of Public Instruction, 1982.

Meiser, Mary Jordan. *Teaching Writing: A Guide for Teachers of Hmong and Other ESL Students.* Wisconsin Council of Teachers of English, 1992.

—. "A Note on Diversity." *Classroom Activities in Speaking and Listening.* Madison: Wisconsin Department of Public Instruction, 1991. 6.

Peterson, Betty. "Why They Talk That Talk: Language in Appalachian Studies." *English Journal* Oct. 82: 53–55.

Philips, Susan Urmstorm. *The Invisible Culture.* New York: Longman, 1983.

Raimes, Ann. Lecture. "Working with International Students and Immigrants." CCCC Winter Workshop on Teaching Composition to Undergraduates. Clearwater Beach, 6 Jan. 1992.

—. "Language Proficiency, Writing Ability, and Composing Strategies: A Study of ESL College Student Writers." *Language Learning* Sept. 1987: 439–68.

—. "What Unskilled ESL Students Do As They Write: A Classroom Study Of Composing." *TESOL Quarterly* June 1985: 229–58.

Riggs, Pat, and Virginia G. Allen. *When They All Don't Speak English: Integrating the ESL Student Into the Regular Classroom.* Urbana: National Council of Teachers of English, 1989.

Schwartz, Judith. ed. *Teaching the Linguistically Diverse.* New York: State English Council, 1980.

Smitherman, Geneva. " 'It Bees Dat Way Some-times:' Sounds and Structures of Present-Day Black English." Ed. Virginia Clark et al. *Language: Introductory Readings.* New York: St. Martin's, 1981. 521–38.

14

Developing Thematic Units

The use of thematic units permits a broadening of pedagogical concerns in English studies beyond those of genres, periods, and particular authors and works. The thematic approach reflects a concern with the personal growth of the reader/writer versus an emphasis on specific literary works as objects worthy of study for their own sake. (72)

Robert C. Goldbort

INTERACTIVE TEACHING

Throughout this text, the different aspects of teaching English are presented in individual chapters, but only as a way of discussing each one. Language, composition, literature, speaking, and listening are all part of English instruction. The interaction among the parts is the foundation for planning the curriculum. For instance, a unit on listening is a poor way to teach the skills of listening. When listening is incorporated *throughout* the curriculum, teachers have a better chance of achieving their goal of improving students' listening habits.

The same is true for speaking. The most effective way to provide opportunities for both listening and speaking is to use small groups, which shifts the class from being teacher-centered to being student-centered. Students listen to each other and contribute to the discussion. When groups become part of an instructional plan, the balance among reading, writing, listening, and speaking more closely approximates our use of these skills in the world outside the classroom. In real life we speak and listen far more than we read and write. Creative dramatics also provides opportunities for interactions among the four components. One way to include a variety of activities that promote an ongoing interaction among all the components is through thematic units. The theme serves as an umbrella for a whole host of activities involving all strands of the language arts.

ORGANIZING AROUND A THEME

Thematic units are designed with many different focuses: art, music, history, literature, and language, although literature is the most common focus. One reason, of course, is that literature is a major part of an English class; more importantly, using a thematic approach is a more effective way to teach literature than using a single author or chronological organization.

In *Novels of Initiation* David Peck agrees that the best way to teach literature is by theme. "Somehow our secondary literature curriculum has gotten locked into historical and genre approaches that have lost much of whatever usefulness they once had" (xxi). He explains that when students read thematically related works they are able to connect the ideas and characters to their own lives and to other works as well. As an example he writes, "Why is tolerance such an important idea in Harper Lee's *To Kill a Mockingbird*? How different is its treatment in Mildred D. Taylor's *Roll of Thunder, Hear My Cry*? What relevance does it have to our own lives? And what relationship does it have to the idea of self-respect that we find in both novels?" (xxi) To read with a focus, as in Peck's example of the theme of tolerance, helps students clarify their own ideas and values about things that matter in their lives. Such units allow students to pursue topics that concern and interest them while learning the course content mandated by the curriculum (Maxwell 152).

When literature is taught chronologically, the teacher must play the major role of one who knows the answers. George Hillocks explains, "Since the knowledge gained about one writer is unlikely to be applicable to the next, students are almost necessarily forced into the role of passive recipient of knowledge about individual writers and works" (149). Chronological organization doesn't help students make connections from one text to another or to connect the literature with their own life experiences.

A high school teacher, David T. Anderson, uses thematic units because a "problem with chronological sequencing is that it goes against a basic principle of education: Begin with simple experiences on which to base learning and move to complex understandings" (62). He explained to his students that the next novel they would be reading was easier than the one they just finished. "Upon saying this, one of my students raised her hand and asked, 'Then why didn't we read it first?' Even a junior in high school realized when this basic rule was compromised" (62). When novels for young adults are included in the units, students can read these easier works first and then be better able to understand the more difficult selections. Because the concepts are the same, the easier texts help students comprehend the ideas in the more difficult reading.

BEGINNING TO PLAN

Developing a unit that encompasses many components might seem overwhelming to a new teacher. The best way to begin is to choose literature selections on a common theme. Every student in each class must be capable of reading at least one of the selections, and each unit must have at least three reading levels. Many other titles should also be available for students who want to read several books or for those who find the original choices too difficult. Every poem, short story, drama, essay, or article included in the unit must be on the common theme.

Every unit will not have every genre of literature represented, but as much as possible, a variety of readings should be included. One type of text enhances another. For instance, Faulkner's "Rose for Emily," *To Kill a Mockingbird* by Harper Lee, poems by Dickinson, and current newspaper and magazine articles all contribute to students' wider understanding of the theme of societal values. Organizing a unit around a theme provides opportunities to include poetry, nonfiction, short stories, drama, and novels. A unit ties all of the literature together in a unified approach to teaching.

Teaching and Learning in Groups

Once the literature selections are made, the next step is to devise ways to discuss the literature and write about it. The listening and speaking strands of English are most naturally incorporated through small- and large-group discussion, although projects can also be designed to include oral presentations. Traditionally, teachers talked and students listened. But for students to improve their skills in listening and speaking, the focus must shift from the teacher to the students. Teachers do occasionally need to give information and explanation through a lecture format, but students need opportunities to talk among themselves. James Moffett describes discussion as "a process of amending, appending, diverging, converging, elaborating, summarizing, and many things" (46). He is referring to small-group discussion, not a whole-class discussion in which the teacher dominates the talk and only a few students join in. In a whole-class group, a teacher is often looking for specific answers to questions, but even if the questions are intended to draw out students' opinions, they succeed with only a few.

For an interchange of ideas, feelings, and opinions, four to six in a group works best, particularly if students are discussing literature or responding to each other's writing. Directions to the groups need to be clearly understood and have a well-defined purpose. To keep students on task, teachers may limit the length of time for the group work to be accomplished and then have each group present the results of their discussion orally to the whole class. Middle school students may need further structure, and a teacher might require that written notes be handed in following the discussion. Also, if a teacher walks around the room listening to one group and then another, students are more likely to stay on task. Group work should be part of every unit and should be a planned activity, not left to chance or used as a fill-in for extra time.

Including Writing Activities

A unit includes many opportunities for writing. All three levels of writing described in Chapter 6 are appropriate throughout the unit. A level 3 writing is usually the final project, whereas level 1 activities occur almost daily, and level 2 activities occur two or three times a week. Also, a unit provides many opportunities for different types and purposes of writing: poetry, factual, autobiographical, analytical, summaries, responses, and informational.

Developing a thematic unit that includes all of the elements mentioned takes a great deal of time, but a beginning teacher can start slowly and keep adding to the unit. Teaching units may never be "finished." Even if the unit is repeated for several years, it should be revised each year, especially if the teacher uses current news stories on a regular basis. Once teachers decide on the units and begin to develop them, material is not difficult to find. Files full of poems, articles, clippings, notes, and suggestions are continually added to. Longer units often grow into two files, providing many choices so that a unit isn't the same from one year to the next. All this takes time, but if new teachers enter the classroom with one well-thought-out thematic unit, they will have a head start in their planning and be well prepared for the beginning of the year.

COMPONENTS OF A UNIT

Perhaps the easiest way to begin planning a unit is to choose a literature selection. The curriculum may specify that *Romeo and Juliet* is to be taught at 9th grade or *Great Expectations* at 10th grade. That is the place to start. Because many high school students are going to have difficulty with either of these selections, the first task is to choose additional literature on the same theme that is easier to read. Literature as complex as *Romeo and Juliet* or *Great Expectations* has several themes, and teachers decide what seems the most appropriate for their students. Young adult literature can be added fairly easily because many reference books are available with annotated bibliographies that are grouped thematically. Short stories are more difficult to find, but anthologies available in the schools help. Choosing poetry for a particular theme is even more difficult and requires reading poetry from a variety of sources. Literature chosen for units must represent a variety of authors and include both minorities and women. Once teachers make a few literature selections, they can add writing activities, group activities, language play, and creative dramatics.

The sequence described above varies. For example, sometimes a teacher selects a theme before deciding on any literature. But, in general, the steps in planning a unit might follow these steps:

- Select a theme.
- Choose literature at two or three reading levels.
- Decide on writing activities at levels 1 and 2.
- Add short stories, poetry, drama, and nonfiction selections appropriate to the theme.
- Look at the connections among the literature selections, and between the literature and the students' lives. Include group activities that strengthen the connections and allow listening and speaking to be major activities.
- Add creative activities such as drama, drawing, and music.
- Looking at the unit as a whole, create several choices for a level 3 writing assignment or some other type of final project or presentation.

Planning a Unit

To illustrate how one experienced teacher goes about planning a unit, Jackie Pickett shares a unit she is developing for her high school class (see Case 14–1).

Family and Peer Conflict

I decided to make a unit on family, peer, and relationship conflicts because these are the conflicts teens most commonly face. Therefore, I think kids will easily identify with characters facing some of the same conflicts. After some free writing about conflicts, the kids have a chance to share. Then I will introduce the first reading, "Through the Tunnel" by Doris Lessing. I'll mention that as they read they should note the relationship between Jerry and his mother and think about how that relationship affects his actions with peers. Students in my class are used to doing response writing, so I'll assign that for the next day. Then we share the responses in class.

Following the same basic format, the students read and/or view the following stories, poems, movies, and a novel: "The Sleeper," a poem by Edward Field; the movie *Bernice Bobs Her Hair* from the story by the same name by F. Scott Fitzgerald; the short story "Sucker" by Carson McCullers; the short story "Sixteen" by Maureen Daly; the short story "A Visit to Grandmother" by William Melvin Kelley; the short story "Forgiveness in Families" by Alice Munro; the poem "Lineage" by Margaret Walker; the poem "Mother" by Nagase Kiyoko; the movie *The Three Warriors;* and the novel *The Contender* by Robert Lipsyte. [*Note:* The movie *The Three Warriors* is about Native Americans and played by Native Americans—a fine film for junior and senior high.]

There will, of course, be breaks from the routine of reading and responding. Here are some of the ideas I'll use.

1. Choose a character from the story. Become this character for a short time and write how you feel about "your" portrayal in the story. Were you presented accurately and fairly? Is there more to you than we saw?
2. Again, choose a character from a story. Become this character and write a letter to Ann Landers or Dear Abby, describing a problem you have. Then, exchange your letter with another person. This person is Ann or Abby and will answer your letter and give advice while you do the same for him or her.
3. (This is one of my ideas) Because some of the reading selections in this unit are rather dated (e.g., the stories such as "Sucker" and "Sixteen" and movies like *Bernice Bobs Her Hair*), rewrite a portion of one of them. Bring it up to date, including modern slang, descriptions of what is stylish or attractive now.
4. (Another one of my ideas) As a post-script to *Bernice Bobs Her Hair,* write a story or play of what happened when Majorie woke up the next day to discover that her hair was bobbed. Or write what happened when Bernice returned to Eau Claire.

I usually have students write open-book essay tests after our units, and I expect I will do so with this unit, too. They work well and get the kids to write in a different format, which gives some balance to the writing they do.

I'll do the novel last because I want to spend the most time on it. I think kids are more confident of themselves after successfully dealing with shorter writings and are then ready to go on to novels. As a prereading activity, I'll have the kids do a variety of things: write journal entries, answer personal experience questions, or conduct a survey. Another idea is to have them complete the Literary Characters' Values Profile (found in Kahn, Calhoun, and Johannessen's *Writing about Literature*). I would like to incorporate some type of formal speaking activity in the unit, but at this time my mind is blank.

Jackie worked on this the year before she planned to implement it. She began with the literature choices and filled in activities she read about or developed on her own.

Developing Questions for One Novel

To begin, a teacher inexperienced in planning might select one piece of literature and design only the writing activities. Dale Clark, an English education student, wrote this kind of unit for *The Catcher in the Rye* by J. D. Salinger (see Case 14–2). Examples from students in the English methods class include a rationale for teaching the unit. Teachers are not required to do this, but we believe that knowing what one wants to accomplish in a unit and why the particular selections were made help when talking to parents and administrators. Teachers need to always know why they are teaching a particular topic or selection.

CASE 14–2

Literature Unit: *The Catcher in the Rye*

CENTRAL PURPOSE OF THIS UNIT

The writing assignments in this unit are designed to give the students an opportunity to gain a better understanding of Holden Caulfield. The assignments center around Holden's progression in the story through his relationships and experiences, his reactions and feelings toward life. The basic question is "Why?" Why does Holden feel the way he does or do what he does?

The following assignments are designed for in-class work where students meet in groups and discuss their responses. Much of the writing can be done collaboratively. When the teacher prefers individual writing, the group work remains a vital part of the writing process.

ASSIGNMENTS FOR STUDENTS

1. Write an initial reaction to the introduction of the story in Chapter 1. Explain how you feel about Holden and what you think might happen to him (level 1).

2. Holden said, "I got the ax. They give guys the ax quite frequently at Pencey. It has a very good academic rating, Pencey." Compare Pencey to our school. In what ways do you think they are the same? Different? (level 1)

3. Write a letter from Holden to his brother, D. B., in Hollywood explaining why Pencey is a lousy school and why he flunked all of his classes except English (level 2).

4. The fencing team ostracized Holden for leaving equipment on the subway. Explain a similar situation that happened to you. How did you feel? Or explain how Holden felt. (Level 1)

5. Write a phone conversation between Holden and Jane Gallagher. (Level 2)

6. Have you ever had a special possession that someone else may not consider special, such as Alice's glove is to Holden? Write a description of that special item and explain why it is special to you. (Level 1)

7. "I'm not too tough. I'm a pacifist, if you want to know the truth," said Holden. Is Holden a pacifist because he isn't very tough or because he doesn't believe in violence? Explain what you believe to be true and why. (Level 1)

8. Write a plea from Holden to a TV audience asking them to not act phoney. Have Holden explain why they should not act phoney. (Level 2)

9. After Holden gets in the fight with Stadlater, he goes to talk with Ackley. Holden thinks to himself, "I felt so lonesome, all of a sudden. I almost wished I was dead."

   • Write a letter from Holden to Ann Landers describing how he feels at this time and asking her for advice.

   or

   • Write a reply from Ann Landers explaining to Holden what he should do about his depression. (Level 2)

10. Rewrite part of Chapter 8 when Holden is on the bus with Mrs. Morrow. Have Holden tell her the truth about Pencey and her son, Ernest. You may write it as a script. (Level 2)

11. Write a reaction from the prostitute's point of view explaining why she believes Holden won't sleep with her. (Level 1)

12. Holden accidently blows smoke in the two nuns' faces and is terribly embarrassed. Describe a situation where you have done something that you didn't mean to do that was embarrassing and you regretted afterward. (Level 2)

13. Sally accepts Holden's proposal to go and live in the mountains. Rewrite the end of the story explaining what happens. (Level 2)

14. James Castle jumped out of the window instead of taking back what he said about Phil Stabile. From James' point of view, explain why he jumped. Describe his emotional state. (Level 1)

15. Phoebe asks Holden to name something he really likes, but he can't. Write a short paper from Holden's point of view about why he feels this way. (Level 2)

16. Mr. Antolini describes a "fall" he believes Holden is heading for. Explain what he means and describe what you think is going to happen to Holden. (Level 1)

17. Write a level 3 paper on one of the following two subjects, or you may select another subject, but discuss with me first.

   a. Explain Holden's emotional progression through the story and explain what you think his future will be.

   or

   b. Write a comparison between Holden's depression and similar experiences you or someone you know have had. Explain how you feel Holden should deal with his depression.

Clark included a variety of purposes and modes for writing, as well as connecting the literature to students' lives. His next step is to add other reading selections on a common theme. Then, he would add activities and opportunities for creative dramatics, art, music, speaking, and listening.

Maureen McManus, the teacher who wrote the following unit, and Dale Clark use writing activities to connect the literature to students' lives (see Case 14–3). By making these connections, they help students understand the characters in the novel and gain a deeper knowledge of the literature. Maureen developed writing activities for *To Kill a Mockingbird* by Harper Lee. She explains that the journal and in-class writing are assigned daily and used for class or group discussions. The activities labeled "writings" are all level 2 and are not daily activities, but can also be the basis for class or group discussions. Although McManus wrote writing activities and discussion questions for every chapter, only a few are included here as examples of how a teacher might begin planning for a literature unit.

CASE 14–3

Writing Activities for *To Kill a Mockingbird*

CHAPTER 1
Journal Options

1. Describe a person, place, event, or TV show that frightened you when you were young, but now that you are older you realize you let your imagination get the best of you.

2. Discuss your family traditions or community customs. Are they important to you? Do they seem outdated?

Writings

Write a character sketch of Boo Radley. Describe his appearance, mannerisms, how he talks, and what he does.

CHAPTERS 2 AND 3

Journal Options

1. Reflect on how you felt about your experiences in kindergarten or first grade. How did you feel about school? Offer some examples.
2. What are some of Scout's innocent mistakes? How are ideas of good and bad, right versus wrong, manners, and politeness expressed so far in the story?

Writings

Write about a time when you didn't mean to be bad, but did something because you didn't know better and people were angry with you.

CHAPTER 11

Journal Options

1. How are Scout and Jem changing their attitudes about Atticus? What are some reasons for this new outlook?
2. What are the various evidences of prejudice, not only racial, but ways in which Scout notices a great difference between other characters and herself? Do some of these prejudices exist today?

Writings

Prepare a dialogue between Boo and Mrs. Dubose concerning Jem and Scout.

CHAPTERS 13 AND 14

Journal Options

1. What are the differences between the town's acceptance of Aunt Alexandra and that of Jem and Scout?
2. What are some evidences of Jem's growing maturity? How does this change his friendship with Dill? How does it affect the relationship between Scout and Dill?

Writings

Write a character sketch of Dill including his personality and physical attributes. Describe his family life and how it has affected him.

CHAPTER 16

Journal Options

1. In what ways are Aunt Alexandra's views even narrower than those of the children?

2. How are Scout and Jem finally beginning to realize the differences and similarities between blacks and whites? What are some questions they discuss about this?

Writings

Describe the atmosphere of the courthouse lawn and the moods of the various groups scattered about.

Chapters 18 and 19

Journal Options

1. Throughout the story what are the various ways Scout describes blacks? Name both physical and personality attributes. Is her particular association with the person a factor in her opinion?
2. Atticus once told Scout that she can never really understand a person unless she "wears his shoes." How is Scout's understanding of this statement becoming more apparent throughout the novel?

Writings

Write an account of the trial as it might appear in the Maycomb newspaper from Mr. Underwood's point of view.

Chapters 22 and 23

Journal Options

1. Jem gives serious thought to the trial and its outcome. What are various aspects of the trial that he questions? What people help Jem draw his conclusions?
2. What were the various reactions of different people when Bob Ewell spit in Atticus' face? How does this reflect their character?

Writings

Show how Scout's thought process changes, especially about prejudice, after the trial. Compare her to other characters in how they changed or failed to change. In what ways has Scout learned to question what others say rather than simply accept it? Who does she question now and in what ways? Create dialogue or cite actual passages in the book.

Chapters 29 and 30

Journal Options

1. In what ways are both Boo and Tom Robinson like mockingbirds? How is the way they are treated like killing a mockingbird?
2. How are the lives of Tom Robinson and Boo similar or different? How do Scout and Jem change their attitudes about both Boo and Tom as the story progresses? What brings about this change?

Writings

Scout tells this story in retrospect. Describe her as she writes this book. How old is she? What is her occupation and education? Where does she live? What are her contributions to society?

Writings

Level 3 Writing Options [to be completed after students finish reading the novel].

1. Choose one character from the book and describe one wish the character would choose and explain why. Who else is affected by the wish? What does this say about the character? How would the wish change certain aspects of the story?
2. If Atticus was the guest speaker at a high school graduation, what messages, warnings, and encouragements might he offer the graduates? How would he prepare them for the real world? Write his speech or take the standpoint of a graduate listening to him.
3. Write a series of letters between Scout and Dill. What would they share in a letter?
4. Choose a character from the book who keeps a journal or is a closet poet. Make a series of journal entries or prepare a collection of poetry by this character.
5. Write a collection of Letters to the Editor or journal entries from several different characters showing their various opinions of the trial.
6. Compile a list of guidelines for raising children. How might parents and teachers promote open-mindedness or instill values/morals in children?

A third example of writing activities based on one work of literature comes from English education student, Cassie Scharber (see Case 14–4). Cassie chose a young adult novel, *Finding My Voice* by Marie G. Lee.

CASE 14–4

Writing Activities for *Finding My Voice*

SUMMARY

It is Ellen Sung's last year of high school. She is a typical teenager who is preoccupied with good grades, fun, varsity letters, college, and boyfriends; however, one thing makes her different from her classmates—she is Asian American. This leads to big problems for Ellen: name-calling, fist-fights, and so on. This novel is about Ellen's year of decisions and discrimination, the year in which she finally "finds her voice" and stands up for what she believes in.

ACTIVITIES

1. (Level 2) This activity introduces the novel. Because Lee's book deals extensively with the issues of prejudice and discrimination, students need to understand the words before they begin reading. The teacher asks students to come up with their own definition for being prejudiced. The definition should include the following information about what prejudice is, who it affects, why it occurs, and some examples of prejudice. Writing the definition is a homework assignment so that students can really think about the word and what it means.

   The next day the class is divided into groups of 4 or 5 students. Each group member reads his or her definition of prejudice to the group. The group discusses the definitions and develops one that the whole group agrees on. Each group then reports to the whole class, and the class develops a common definition of prejudice. The teacher discusses the difference between prejudice and discrimination (a belief or feeling and acting out of these beliefs).

2. (Level 1) Now that the class understands what prejudice and discrimination are, Cassie has the students observe behavior in the school and communities to understand how common and widespread prejudice is—prejudice against age, sex, intelligence, religion, opinions, appearance, wealth, athletic skills, and so on. Students keep a journal for one week and record every act of discrimination they see, hear, or experience. They respond to their feelings and those of others. She hopes by keeping the journal the students come to realize how common and how unnecessary discrimination is. The activity helps students to identify with the character, Ellen.

3. (Level 1) After the week of journal writing, students write about a time when they were discriminated against, focusing on their feelings and reactions. Through discussion, the students compare their reactions to those of Ellen's.
   - Was their reaction similar to Ellen's?
   - Why did Ellen react the way she did to the taunts and jeers of her classmates?
   - How do you think she felt?
   - How did you feel when you read about it?

4. (Level 3) Discussion continues throughout the reading of the book. When students have completed the reading, the final writing activity centers on the title "finding my voice." Examples of discussion questions include the following:
   - What does the title mean?
   - When does Ellen "find" her voice?
   - How did she use it?
   - Did she use her "voice" when Marsha broke the bottle over her head?
   - Does silence have a "voice"?

The assignment for students is to write a paper about a time when they found their voice; the paper may be an essay or story. The following questions help guide their writing:

- When did you discover your "voice"?
- Who or what helped you discover your voice?
- How did you feel before you used your "voice"?
- What were the advantages and disadvantages of using your "voice"?

Students follow the writing process to produce a high quality level 3 paper.

The discussion and writing questions described for *Catcher in the Rye, To Kill a Mockingbird,* and *Finding My Voice* are only the beginning of an unit. The next step is to find other novels, poetry, drama, and nonfiction on the same theme.

Developing Writing Activities for More Than One Novel

A four-week unit written by teacher, Gail Servoss, for the ninth grade, illustrates how a teacher begins planning activities for a unit using more than one novel (see Case 14–5).

CASE 14–5

Four-Week Literature Unit

Four novels are used in this unit. Students are required to read two of them, but can read all four if they wish. The novels are paired so that students have a choice during the first two weeks of reading *A Day No Pigs Would Die* by Robert Newton Peck or *The Bloodroot Flower* by Kathy Callaway. For the next two weeks, they choose from *Where the Red Fern Grows* by Wilson Rawls or *A Killing Season* by Barbara Brenner.

STUDENT GUIDE

WEEK ONE

Read the first two chapters in the novel you chose. Write reading responses in your journal (level 1). Meet in groups to discuss your responses and to compile a list of adjectives that describe the main character in the novel you are reading (level 1).

Read the next two chapters and write responses (level 1). The first four chapters in both novels give us information about the parents. In class, begin to write a short paper on what you think Peck's father and Carrie's father are like. What does the story say about each of them? Give examples from the story that support your own view. For example, look at their personalities: Are they strict, lenient, happy, sullen, friendly, mean, or understanding? The paper is due the next day. Before handing them in, meet in groups to read aloud and discuss (level 2).

Read the next three chapters and write responses (level 1).

Week Two

Share responses in groups from the last chapters read. Hand in the response journals for the teacher's comments. Working in small groups discuss the characters' values. Find phrases or paragraphs that represent the values.

Continue reading and responding. In small groups discuss the feeling the text evokes through word choice and details about the weather, actions, and character behavior. Choose one scene and write descriptive words about it. Write a poem using the descriptive words (level 2). Work on the poems in class, sharing in small groups. Finish up reading by the next week.

Week Three

Read the first two chapters in a novel you chose and write responses in journal (level 1). In small groups discuss what effect the setting has on the characters. Collaboratively, write a description of what would change in the book if the setting were urban (level 1). Continue reading and writing responses.

Choose one of the characters from a novel and write a dialogue this person might have with someone else in any situation. Be sure to keep the character true to his or her personality. Do not tell anyone which character you chose. Other students will try to guess your character by listening to the dialogue you write. Be prepared to tell each other why you chose the words you did for the character. Base your reasons from examples in the novel (level 1).

The following day share your dialogues in small groups. Discuss the influences of dialogue on developing characterization and in moving plot along. Each group then reports to the whole class. Working in pairs, draw a map on a large sheet of paper showing all the places described in the novel. Trace the action with short descriptions from the book and use X's to denote important areas (level 2).

Week Four

Continue writing responses. When you are through reading the novel, review the responses in your journal. In groups of four or five students who have the same book, discuss your feelings and thoughts about the book. Answer the following questions in writing:

- How did this book make me feel?
- Was the book believable?
- What do I think about the characters?
- What other places or situations does the book make me think of?
- What are the major differences or similarities between the main character and me?

Discuss all the answers in the small group.

The final activity is to write a level 3 paper using one of the novels. Possible topic choices include:

	Possible points 30	Your points
Introduction explaining what paper is about	3	___
Main points clear and related to each other	4	___
Examples to support your ideas	7	___
Conclusion states what you discovered	2	___
Word choice: descriptive, appropriate, correct forms	4	___
Mechanics: correct spelling, punctuation, capitalization	5	___
Original, creative, interesting	5	___
Comments:	Total points	___

FIGURE 14–1
The scoring guide for the level 3 paper.

1. The connection between nature or setting in the plot or/and characterization
2. The relationship between a character and an animal
3. The trials some people have to go through in their life and how these trials change them
4. What a character might be like in 10 years from the conclusion of the story

You are free to choose any topic you wish. You will meet in groups to talk over possible choices. With any topic you develop, be sure to include examples from the book to back up what you write. In addition, you may use personal examples to help develop your ideas.

A Literature Unit With a Variety of Literature

Literature units need to include a variety of genres, as well as literature with different reading levels. This example of a literature unit is based on the theme "Families in Literature" written for ninth graders by Barbara Dressler, a high school teacher (see Case 14–6). Barbara's unit begins with a rationale explaining why she chose this particular theme.

CASE 14–6

Families in Literature

This literature unit for ninth graders centers on families in different eras and different cultures. The unit is designed for approximately four weeks. Selections were chosen to show the wide variety of combinations of people held together by a bond that we call family. Male and female characters and authors from minority groups, including African Americans, Asian Americans, Shakers, and Native Americans, are included. Special emphasis is given to relationships between teenagers and other family members because these relationships trouble most teens. I hope reading and thinking about characters in situations similar to their own will help students discover that they can achieve their individual identities and still appreciate and enjoy their families.

The problems encountered by today's teenagers in understanding and communicating with other members of their families are certainly not new. Through the years, young adults in literature experienced difficulty in getting along with adults, especially parents. The rejection of "old ways and ideas," and even alienation from the rest of the family, is a common conflict. A goal of this unit is to allow students to experience vicariously the problems and resolutions that characters find. They will realize that they are not unique in having problems in their families and may find ideas for solving or living with the problems through reading the literature.

INTRODUCTION

The introductory activity for the unit starts with a short brainstorming period for students to write words and ideas they associate with the word *family*. After sharing the lists, commenting and questioning, students write a paragraph defining family (level 1).

PART 1

- "Blues Ain't No Mockin' Bird," a short story by Toni Cade Bambara
- "Brother Carlyle," a short story by William Melville Kelley
- "To My Father," a poem by Wing Tek Lum
- "The Funeral," a poem by Gordon Parks
- "Believing It Will Rain Soon," a poem by Simon J. Ortiz

The first reading assignment is "Brother Carlyle," a short story that centers on the behavior of one of two black brothers and the disagreement between their parents about whether the boy's treatment of his younger brother is appropriate. Students write a response to the story when they finish reading. They share their responses in a group and discuss them with the large group. The issue of parents giving different treatment to children based on birth order will probably be part of the discussion. I chose this short story to begin the unit because students often feel that their parents treat them differently from their siblings. Students enjoy talking about the advantages and disadvantages of being the first born, a middle child, or the youngest.

The second reading is "Blues Ain't No Mockin' Bird." I chose this story because it shows a loosely structured, nontraditional family with grandparents and distant cousins living together. The theme concerns the need for pride and dignity regardless of family income. After the reading, students respond in writing and then choose specific details used for the development of one of the characters. With emphasis on significant details, student write a character description of someone they know well (level 2).

PART 2

The poems are read aloud during class. The first, "The Funeral," tells of the great admiration and respect a young man feels for his father. Many things in the poet's childhood seemed enormous to him, but as an adult, only his father remains larger than life. Students select lines that show how the poet's perspective changed as he matured. Many examples of hyperbole are used. As a group activity, student write their own descriptive sentences using hyperbole (level 1).

"To My Father" tells of the rebellion of the Chinese against the emperor. The speaker, whose grandfather was involved in the rebellion, knows his way of life changed because of the revolt. In a group, students discuss ways their lives are affected by actions of their grandparents or other ancestors.

"Believing It Will Rain Soon" expresses a faith that is passed from one generation to another as shown through the description of the promise of rain over the mountains. Students discuss how they learn their beliefs and values, including prejudices, through the family. Students write a letter to a future son or daughter expressing an important belief about the world (level 2).

PART 3: INDIVIDUAL NOVEL READING

Students chose one novel from the list, which contains books at different reading levels. All feature different types of families.

* *To Kill a Mockingbird* by Harper Lee
* *Growing Season* by Alden R. Carter
* *Permanent Connections* by Sue Ellen Bridgers
* *A Day No Pigs Would Die* by Robert Newton Peck
* *What About Grandma?* by Hadley Irwin
* *A Figure of Speech* by Norma Fox Mazer
* *Kim, Kimi* by Hadley Irwin

Students keep a response journal while reading the novel. After writing responses, students meet in small groups based on the book they read. They choose a character from the book that they would like to interview and answer interview questions as they believe their character would. Possible interview questions include the following

1. Did the author describe you accurately? What would you like to change in the description?
2. How did you feel about your family early in the story?
3. How did your feelings change before the end?

4. What was the happiest time for you in the book?
5. What would you like to say to a member of your family that you didn't get a chance to in the book?
6. If you could change anything in the story, what would it be? (level 1)

When the time for the novel reading is about half over, students write a want ad in search of a good mother, father, teenage son, or teenage daughter. Ads are shared in groups (level 1).

After reading and discussing the novels, students choose from the following level 3 writing assignments:

1. Write an obituary for the family member who dies during the course of the book.
2. As a friend of the main character, write a letter of condolence after the death of the family member.
3. Imagine you are a good friend of the main character. How would you have tried to help at any point in the story?
4. As one character, write a letter to another explaining your actions during the book.
5. Write a campaign speech that the main character could use to run for student council president at your school.
6. Write a summary of the story's events from the point of view of the main character after 10 years have passed.
7. Write your description of a good parent. Include your evaluations of the parents in the book.

By including novels of different reading levels, Barbara allowed students to find the one they were comfortable with without embarrassing them. Some students choose books that are too difficult but later ask to switch to another book. Or they may find they don't care for the book they started. Students need the flexibility to change their minds about a self-selected book. A person may check out four books from the library but read only two because the others didn't hold his or her interest. We must make sure we apply the same commonsense rules to our students that we use in our own lives.

Students who read well may decide to read all four books. Having a selection of books avoids the problem of what to do when students come to the teacher two days after the unit begins and say they have finished the assigned book. The readings provided for these students are on the same general theme as the current unit. What they read then is part of what is going on in class, and they can share their reading with others.

Because of the policy of mainstreaming, students with special learning problems are now included in the regular classroom rather than taught in a separate class. For these students to feel a part of the class, their work, however adapted for their needs, must be a part of the same thematic unit that the rest of the class is involved in. That's why including texts on a variety of reading levels is critical.

The same is true for gifted students. Too often, these students are sent to the library to work on their own. Perhaps even more than the average student, the gifted ones need to interact with peers and feel part of a group. Social skills are vitally important and need to be part of the learning environment. Every student in a class is responsible for getting along with the other students and respecting their rights. Working in groups that are all working on the same theme enhances a sense of community effort.

Selecting a variety of reading texts is a the first step in providing for all the students in a class. In addition, optional activities create a wide range of activities. One way to incorporate the activities into the current thematic unit is to tape the suggestions on the inside of file folders. The folders can then be placed in an open box available to students when they want additional projects. To accommodate all students in a class, the ideas need to vary greatly in difficulty: puzzles, reports, interviews, word searches, articles, essays, and poems. Also, they should cover a wide range of interests, such as reading nonfiction, writing movie reviews, writing based on art or music, drawing, creating music, and reading and performing drama. Each unit has an accompanying box of activities, such as one on courage, growing up, choosing careers, or environmental issues. Finding additional materials is difficult for inexperienced teachers, but one starts with only a few ideas and gradually adds to the number and variety of the activities.

All of the activities include a way to bring the work back to the class as a whole. Artwork is displayed on the walls, reports are available for others to read or are orally presented to the class, skits are acted out, videos shown, music played, and puzzles distributed. Students may work in the library on their own or do the work outside of school, but the result is enriching the learning for everyone in the class.

COMPREHENSIVE THEMATIC UNITS

Units need to include a list of other readings on the same theme. Cathy Steffen, a former English education student, wrote a unit on heroes (see Case 14–7). An abbreviated version of Cathy's unit shows how she includes listening, speaking, reading, and writing.

CASE 14–7

Unit on Heroes

My primary objective in teaching a unit on heroes is to introduce students to alternatives to the traditional hero and to offer new perspectives on the idea of heroes. The activities in this unit include music, all levels of composition, language study, listening, and speaking. Both fiction and nonfiction are included.

PART 1: INTRODUCTION TO THE UNIT

Propose the following questions to the class and write responses on the board. First, explain that the term *heroes* refers to both genders.

1. What are some examples of heroes?
2. What qualities are found in heroes?
3. What does someone have to do to be considered a hero?
4. Which of these people do you consider heroes? (Suggest people whom students know through the media.)
5. Do you know any "quiet heroes?" Read a recent newspaper or magazine article to the students about a quiet hero.
6. Who do you know who fits the description of a quiet hero?

Students search for articles on people (or animals) who acted heroically. They write a short paragraph describing some action they consider heroic (level 1).

PART 2: READING

Students read *A Hero Ain't Nothing but a Sandwich* by Alice Childress, *Roll of Thunder, Hear My Cry* by Mildred Taylor, or *The Chocolate War* by Robert Cormier. Students must read one of the novels, but may read all three if they wish. Students keep response notebooks as they read (level 1).

In class students write a description of one of the main characters based on these questions: What is she or he like? What do you like or dislike the most about the character? Students meet in small groups to share what they wrote. The group members then discuss how the character would react to the following situation:

Your character is in charge of a public place where students and adults can come to read books and listen to music. He or she tries hard to give quality materials to the people who come in, but some have started to complain that the books and music are trashy. Your character is told to get rid of the books and records or else lose the job. What will your character do?

Then in one large group, the smaller groups report, and discussion follows of the possible consequences of the characters' actions.

PART 3: LANGUAGE

Give the class examples of different ways that a sentence can be spoken. Point out that an author can establish the emotional tone of the speaker by using certain words. Such clues help readers understand how a character feels.

Students work in pairs for this activity. Give each pair a slip of paper with an expressive word written on it. Explain that all the words come from the novels they are reading. Students look up the meaning of the word in a dictionary and then discuss when the word might be used. Each pair writes the word on the board, pronounces it for the class, and gives an example of a sentence containing the word. A few examples of the words used are *consolingly, taunting, tentatively, abstractedly,* and *resignedly.*

PART 4: MUSIC

Be sure the classroom has available several headphones, tape players, and tapes. All of the songs should suggest something about heroes. The following songs might be appropriate:

- "Wild West Hero" by ELO
- "Along the Road" and "Face the Fire" by Dan Fogelberg
- "Roy Roger" and "The Ballad of Danny Bailey" by Elton John
- "Holding Out for a Hero" by Bonnie Tyler
- "Never" by Moving Pictures

After listening to several songs, students discuss the themes and descriptions of the heroes. Each student writes a paragraph about one of the songs, exploring the concept of hero.

PART 5: A FINAL WRITING ASSIGNMENT (LEVEL 3)

Students write a two- or three-page paper on some aspect of a hero. Suggestions could include the following:

- Describe a hero from your own family history.
- Compare any two of the heros we talked about in class—from music, the newspaper, novels, or any other genre used.
- Create a fictional story about a hero.
- Write a poem about a hero—real or fictional.

Also, students are free to select any topic, as long as it deals with heroes.

Another Unit on Heroes

The concept of hero can be the basis for many thematic units. Teachers design units representing their own interests and try to capture their students' interests and imaginations through literature choices and selected activities. The next unit written by Connie Flug, a former English education student, is also on heroes and illustrates the wealth of materials available (see Case 14–8). Only a small part of the total unit is presented here. Connie begins with her rationale for choosing the theme of heroism.

Heroism

The theme of heroism has been present in all times and places. Mom and Dad are probably the earliest heroes in most youngsters lives; however, other figures, both real and fictional, through media, soon become an integral part of a child's life and development.

This unit is intended for students in 9th or 10th grades and examines heroes in literature, art, film, music, and, most importantly, through the students' own lives. The unit is planned for seven to eight weeks because of the amount of material available. Tall tales, western folklore, and many other stories and poems have much to offer but are not included in the unit. Two novels for young adults (taught simultaneously), ancient and modern poetry, a 30-year-old film, and a modern version of *Cyrano de Bergerac* are the "meat" of this unit. Bridges from past to present are important; teachers will want to emphasize the idea that heroism was "then" and is "now."

Connie begins the unit by sharing a quote with students.

Heroes have within themselves the resonance that comes from imagination supplanting despair. These heroes can recognize the possibilities inherent in living a human life to win and lose, perhaps, but also to discover and use our own voices yet in a common tongue; to use and be used by our passion and intellect; to deal with complexity and ambivalence; to be proud, to err, to be humbled, to grieve, and to grow. To live in such a manner is noble and heroic (Sandra A. Engle, "Of Jocks and Heroes," *English Journal* Dec. 1984: 32–33).

The materials selected for the unit include the following:

Literature

- *Close Enough to Touch* by Richard Peck
- *Chartbreaker* by Gillian Cross
- *The Miracle Worker* by William Gibson
- *Class Dismissed* by Mel Glenn
- *Collected Poems* by Robert Hayden
- *Strings: A Gathering of Family Poems* by Janeczko
- "Negro Hero" by Gwendolyn Brooks
- "Ex-Basketball Player" by John Updike
- "To an Athlete Dying Young" by A. E. Housman
- "The Lady Pitcher" by Cynthia Macdonald
- "That Stranger on the Lawn" by Ray Bradbury
- "Fist Fight" by Doug Cockrell
- "Ulysses" by Alfred L. Tennyson
- "Flowers for Algernon" by Daniel Keyes

Films

- *Helen Keller*
- *Man as Hero Tragic and Comic*
- *The Miracle Worker*
- *Roxanne*

Music

- "West Side Story"
- "Free to Be"
- "Great American Hero"
- "You Won't Believe in If Anymore"
- "Wind Beneath My Wings"
- "Big Dad John"
- "Oh, Mine Papa"

Although the entire unit is not included here, the beginning of the unit is explained because introducing units is an important part of creating student interest and sets the tone for the next several days.

DAY 1

The bulletin board contains many pictures, poems, lyrics, and paintings with room for student additions during the next several weeks. The day begins with student responses to an opinionnaire on heroes (see Figure 14–2).

Directions: Write *agree* or *disagree* beside each statement.

1. A hero does better than just about anyone else.

2. Heroes are forever.

3. The values of heroes are old-fashioned.

4. If you say something often enough, it becomes true.

5. If you hear something often enough, you come to believe it.

6. Heroes never have to say "I'm sorry."

7. To become a hero one must be lucky.

8. TV has helped destroy today's heroes.

9. A real-life hero fills a need for all of us.

10. Anyone can be a hero.

FIGURE 14–2
Opinionnaire on heroes.

Students agree or disagree with the items, and discussion follows. Students brainstorm on the meaning of heroism. Responses are listed on the board. The following questions might be used to lead into the session:

1. What do you think a heroic quality is?
2. What are some qualities in real-life heroes?
3. What makes a hero? Is it more deeds or personality?
4. Consider heroes of different ages, nationalities, centuries, and interests. Do they bring to mind any other characteristics?

The next day's assignment is to bring in examples of today's heroes using newspapers, magazines, TV, record jackets, and comics as resources. Every Monday for the rest of the unit, students are asked to bring in information on heroes of the week.

Day 2

Students share their examples of today's heroes. Discussion in small groups gives students an opportunity to explore aspects of heroes. Then, students watch the slide/tape presentation, *Man as Hero: Tragic and Comic*. Discussion follows. Students write in their journals and choose from the following suggestions:

1. I was a hero once . . .
2. My hero at school is . . .
3. A local hero from this town is . . .
4. If I were a hero I think I would feel like . . .

Day 3

Students share their journal responses in small groups. The teacher writes a mystery formula poem on the board. For example:

> Chunky, rumpful
> Leaping, agile, extraordinary
> Smiling, friendly, moon-faced, sincere
> Hero

The students try to guess the name that goes on the first line, which in this case is Kirby Puckett, a major league baseball player. The class as a whole writes a similar poem using one of the heroes from the bulletin board. The formula for the poem is to write the person's name on the first line. Then:

- Write two adjectives that describe the person.
- Write three verbs that tell what the person does.
- Write a thought or four words about the person.
- Write another noun for the person or repeat the same name.

The assignment for the following day is for students to write their own poem, leaving off the name in line one.

DAY 4

Students share their poems and others try to guess who they are about.

Two other sections of Connie's unit are included here. One is her list of suggested end-of-the-unit activities for the students. The other is a partial list of additional readings.

SUGGESTIONS FOR END-OF-THE-UNIT ACTIVITIES

1. Write your own song about heroes.
2. Create a comic strip featuring a hero.
3. Write a folktale about a hero.
4. Interview a local hero and write a news article.
5. Review the comic section of the Sunday paper and evaluate the images of heroes. Write a report of your findings.
6. Write a modern fairy tale.
7. Make a class scrapbook of all the heroes in the news over the duration of this unit.
8. Put together a slide presentation on heroes.
9. Write a poem about a personal hero.
10. Invite a local hero to class for a presentation. Write a follow-up report.

What follows is a comprehensive list of readings students choose from as the unit progresses. The list demonstrates the wealth of readings available to teachers as they design units. Because Connie wrote annotations, the list is helpful to those looking at resources for units on heroes, survival, and self esteem.

READING LIST

- Aldrich, Bess Streeter. *A Lantern in Her Hand:* Abbie MacKenzie, a talented singer and aspiring artist, is 19 when she marries Will Deal in 1865. Homesteading in Nebraska, Abbie and Will face droughts, dust storms, blizzards, and locust infestations. Abbie's courage and her love for her husband and children lead her to sacrifice her dreams for theirs.
- Barrett, William E. *The Lilies of the Field:* Homer Smith, a young black man recently discharged from the army, comes upon a group of immigrant nuns who are trying to build a chapel in the desert. This is a delightful story about Smith's role in this undertaking.
- Brancato, Robin. *Uneasy Money:* Mike Bronti loses track of values after winning money in a lottery. Spending the money quickly, he finds himself losing family and friends.
- Chester, William L. *Kioga of the Wilderness:* This is the tale of Kioga, or Snow Hawk, who rises to the position of war chieftain in the wild region north of Siberia.

- Ching, Lucy. *One of the Lucky Ones:* An autobiography of a blind Chinese girl's fight for education and a future. Her nanny helps Lucy find a productive life that results in her helping other blind Chinese.
- Collier, James L., and Christopher Collier. *The Winter Hero:* After the Revolutionary War, Justin is caught up in the Shay's Rebellion. Through his experiences, he learns the truth about heroism, cowardice, and war.
- Crutcher, Chris. *Running Loose:* For Louie Banks, living by what is right is more important than being popular. When instructed to "play dirty," Louie walks off the playing field. This turns out to be the most important decision of his life.
- Easwaran, Eknath. *Gandhi the Man:* Gandhi's own words and an array of photos accompany this biography. A string of failures leads the young Gandhi to a job in South Africa where he begins his life of service to others.
- Froehlich, Margaret. *Reasons to Stay:* Babe's determination to piece together her past leads to hard discoveries, but she becomes a strong memorable hero.
- George, Jean Craighead. *The Talking Earth:* Billie Wind, a young Seminole, survives on her own in the Florida Everglades. Her courage finds a link between an ancient and modern culture.
- Haskins, James. *Sugar Ray Leonard:* This biography follows Sugar Ray from the beginning of his boxing career at age 14 to his turning pro.
- Hughes, Monica. *Hunter in the Dark:* Mike Rankin, star basketball player, is dying of leukemia. He goes to the Canadian wilderness to escape overprotective parents. Through his experiences he comes to understand that death is not always the enemy.
- Magill, Kathleen. *Megan:* An independent woman struggles for freedom and a sense of self. She runs away to a boomtown where she discovers the truth about herself.
- Mazer, Harry. *The Island Keeper:* Cleo runs away from her family pressures and the death of her sister. She proves herself as she struggles to survive on a deserted island.
- McKinley, Robin. *The Hero and the Crown:* Aerin, with the help of a wizard and the blue sword, battles the Black Dragon. She wins her birthright as the daughter of the Damarian king and alters the history of Damar.
- Myers, Walter Dean. *Hoops:* Lonnie is at a key point in his life. If his team does well in a city-wide tournament, he may have a professional career. Integrity becomes as important as talent.
- Portis, Charles. *True Grit:* Mattie Ross and Rooster Cogburn, an old federal lawman, set out on an incredible journey to avenge her father's death.
- Rosa, Joseph G. *They Called Him Wild Bill: The Life and Adventures of James Butler Hickok:* Hickok led an eventful life, working as a U.S. marshall, an army scout, and a wild west performer. This biography describes the man beyond the legend.
- Roth, Arthur. *The Castaway:* This novel is based on a true story of a young man who is the lone survivor after a shipwreck. He survives alone for five years on a rocky reef.

- Savage, Deborah. *A Rumour of Otters:* This wilderness survival story takes place in New Zealand where 14-year-old Alexa sets off on her own to prove she is as heroic as her brother.
- Townsend, Peter. *The Girl in the White Ship:* Tran Hue, a 13-year-old, and her family must flee Vietnam in 1978. She battles to survive and escape.
- Valens, E. G. *The Other Side of the Mountain:* This is the true story of Jill Kinmont, who became paralyzed while training for the Olympic ski team. Jill's determination to lead a meaningful life is inspiring.
- Voigt, Cynthia. *The Runner:* A dedicated runner distances himself from other people. His experience in coaching his teammates helps him to change.
- Wheeler, Robert W. *Jim Thorpe: World's Greatest Athlete:* Thorpe is probably best known for winning both the decathlon and pentathlon in the 1923 Olympics, only to be disqualified later. His early life on the reservation, Indian school, football triumphs, and Olympic feats are recounted.

INTERDISCIPLINARY UNITS

The units previously described are not interdisciplinary units. Although they encompass a wide range of topics and interests, they are designed by English language arts teachers and taught during their classes. When teachers of other subjects join together to plan units that include topics and activities related to several disciplines, they create interdisciplinary units. Interest in planning curriculum around such units is increasing because of the recognition that teaching across subject lines more closely resembles "real life." Consequently, student motivation increases because the subject matter appeals to a wider range of learning styles, abilities, and interests. Students have questions about their world and wonder about the environment, human rights, race issues, and justice. Heidi Hayes Jacobs, an authority on designing interdisciplinary curriculum, writes that the "idea is to bring together discipline perspectives and focus them on the investigation of a target, theme, issue, or problem" (54). Units that are organized around a range of topics and approaches help learners understand the variety of perspectives and the complexity of issues involved.

An example of a unit that connects the "real" world with school learning is one on an environmental issue designed for middle school by Jackie Williams and Terry Deal Reynolds. In the area of science, activities centered on wastewater discharge and water pollution. The social studies activities were based on the political, economic, and social implications. English language arts focused on current readings, interviews, vocabulary, notetaking, and oral presentations. Students learned there are many sides to an issue; in this case, jobs and livelihoods had to be balanced with concerns for the environment and natural resources (14). Students learn that there are no simplistic solutions.

A unit on an environmental issue might include some literature, but the major focus is current media information and community involvement. A unit on aging would include community work, trips to nursing homes, and interviews, as well as literature. Language provides the focus for many different units, such as politics, advertising, history, and cultures. In the following unit on advertising, developed for middle school, the theme is the power of language to persuade and its effect on middle schoolers who are becoming critical consumers of goods (see Case 14–9).

Advertising Unit

The first purpose for teaching the unit is to help middle school students become better informed as consumers and more aware of the role of advertising in their lives. Because of the age of the students, literature isn't included, although there are many essays and articles appropriate for older students. The second purpose for teaching the unit is to give students opportunities to draw, sing, compose music, and act—in general, to be creative. This is a long unit—four to six weeks—and because of the amount of independent and unstructured work, it is best to include in the curriculum later in the year. The teacher needs to know students well enough to know who could work on their own and who needs supervision. The unit is divided into sections, not weeks, because the amount of time needed for each part depends on the student's interests and could be quite different from one year to the next.

SECTION 1: ANALYZING ADVERTISEMENTS

The first activity is to ask students what their favorite advertisements are. They talk about TV ads exclusively. Actually, they do more than talk; they sing the songs, repeat dialogue, act out the scenes, and interrupt and correct each other. After a time, the teacher asks what their least favorite ads are. Although less enthusiastic, they report several, with some saying one's most disliked was their favorite. Then the conversation shifts to why they liked or disliked certain ads, which leads to a discussion of audience. Most of the ads they dislike are not meant for teenagers. From this point we move to the purposes of ads and discuss how advertising companies conduct market research. Next, we look more closely at the ads, examining the particular approach used to entice consumers. Together we put the responses into categories. The responses are not the same from one year to the next, but they fall roughly into the same categories: popularity with the opposite sex, you owe it to yourself, everyone has one, having fun, being healthy, staying young and beautiful, loving one's family, and owning the best. The assignment that follows is to collect printed ads that represent each of the categories, put them in booklet form, and label each one. Although students considered the activity fun, they were improving a critical skill of classifying.

SECTION 2: DESIGNING A PRODUCT

Next students design a new and unknown product that later is advertised for sale. The design is on paper only and they do not actually construct it. The following questions help get them started: What new product would make your life easier? Can you think of a product that might become a new fad? What item might be improved if you made major changes in the design? The assignment was to describe the product and draw it if they desired. They have to keep their product a secret since they do not own a patent on the design. Descriptive language is vital for an activity later in the unit, so we spent time on choosing specific words and using comparisons. Because of the secret nature of the project, they cannot ask other students if the descriptions are clear, so the teacher acts as the editor. Students turned in the designs for the teacher's safe keeping. Students think of a variety of products: a watch-radio-telephone, edible dishes, a walkie-talkie am-fm radio pen, computerized pencil, convertible shoes, a shoe phone, and instant moat mix (in case you have a dry moat—it comes with creatures and muck).

SECTION 3: ADVERTISING MEDIA

This is a short section where the class members explore all the places ads might appear. People who work in ad agencies are invited to speak to the class. Also, people who design ads for newspapers or billboards talk to the class. The students write interview questions before the visitors speak to the class. Students need to prepare for a class visitor by planning ahead. Asking appropriate questions is not easy, and they meet in groups to brainstorm questions. Following the visits, students—again working in small groups—write letters thanking the presenters.

SECTION 4: MEDIA GROUPS

Students become part of a media group. The types of groups are newspapers, magazines, billboards, radio, and television. Students write their top two choices on a card and hand it in to the teacher, who then forms the groups. Each media group first selects a name for itself, then researches the cost of advertisements placed in their media. Next they design an ad for advertising space, trying to make their company the most attractive for people who want to advertise, but the rates have to be realistic. Each group makes one poster to try to entice customers.

At this point, each student receives five copies of the product description he or she wrote earlier. Individually they decide on where to place ads for the products. They all have a set amount of money to use on advertising so it is impossible for anyone to buy the top advertising five times. If they decide on a back page ad and a one minute TV commercial, they will be out of money. However, if they use the money sparingly, they can afford five ads in a variety of media. To maintain secrecy, the teacher is the only one who knows who designed each product and serves as the broker. When students decide on the type of ad, they write the specific information on the back of each card, such as, "1/2 page on an inside sheet of Wonder Magazine." The teacher, then, delivers the card to the Wonder Magazine group. This procedure is repeated until all the students have selected the advertising they want for their product, and each group has received all the advertising jobs.

Before the ad production goes into full swing, we review techniques we discussed before: use of statistics, well-known personalities, humor, music, color, drawings, logos, animals, and children.

Section 5: Production

Each media group designs the ads it received orders for. Except for the billboard group, the ads are placed in a larger context. The newspaper group produces a newspaper with local news, pictures, human interest stories, announcements, and sports. The television group produces a show: a situation comedy, soap opera, mystery, or talk show. The radio group usually uses music as the content. If the billboard company has extra time, the members draw a public service ad.

At the conclusion of the unit the students display their work for other students, teachers, and parents. The last assignment is to write a one- to two-page paper explaining what they learned.

Units planned across disciplines are advantageous for a number of reasons. They provide a model for students who erroneously believe writing and reading fiction belong only in the English language arts classrooms. Also, breaking down the walls among disciplines creates more true-to-life experiences for students and, consequently, often heightens interest. Teachers of a variety of subjects can plan the objectives and activities together. Depending on the school's organization, teachers may team-teach the units, but even if the classes have to remain separate, the students and teachers benefit from the shared planning. A word of caution is in order here. By working with other teachers, we do not mean that the English teachers only grade a social studies paper for mechanical errors, but rather that planning and carrying out the ideas is a joint effort.

A unit designed by Becky Olien, a teacher, demonstrates how English, social studies, art, and music are woven together to create a rich tapestry of experiences for young people (see Case 14–10). Becky is particularly fortunate because her classroom is multicultural. The unit can be used for a variety of age levels.

Case 14–10

Tracing One's Roots

Becky begins the unit with a discussion about students' ancestors. She might ask what it means to say one has ancestors or an ethnic background. After students have an opportunity to talk about ancestors, ask questions, and listen to others, she gives them a survey on ethnic background to be filled out in class. The survey includes questions about where their ancestors came from, how long ago they came, whether they were married, whether they had jobs, and whether they came with friends or traveled alone. By filling out the survey, students become aware of what they know and don't know about their family history. They take the survey home and ask parents and grandparents to help complete the information.

Once the surveys are completed as much as possible—and this may take a while—the discussion continues and students share their information with each other. Students then choose a person who is knowledgeable about their family to interview. Usually this is a relative, but not always. A Native American, for example, may interview a tribal leader; another student may talk to a family friend who knows a great deal about a particular immigrant group. Before the interview takes place, students develop the questions, meeting in groups for ideas and feedback. Once the interviews are completed—and again this may take a few days—the students write a report based on the information from the survey, interview, and additional sources as needed. Because many students are a mixture of ethnic backgrounds, they choose which one they want to work on.

Over the period of time the students are working on these activities, they also are reading historical fiction. The literature is discussed in class, and they consider what makes historical fiction interesting. When the reports are finished and the novels and short stories are read, the next activity is to write a fiction story based on their reports. Most of the stories are patterned after historical fiction, but students may wish to make the work more contemporary. [This is especially true of the Hmong and Native American students in Rebecca's class.]

The culminating activity is a cultural week in which students work in groups to present their culture to the class. Students select the cultural group they want to work in; usually it is the one they wrote the report on. They may focus on any aspect they wish, but music, crafts, dance, and food are usually part of the presentations. Students bring maps, flags, or any artifact that helps explain the family background. Many teach the other students a few words of the language their ancestors spoke. Some dress in native costumes [particularly the Hmong girls]. Everyone learns from listening, talking, and sharing.

Units are a way to organize reading, writing, speaking, and listening to ensure continuity among the activities. They give purpose to classroom activities and actually are a much easier way to teach than using disjointed lesson plans because their flow carries students along. Often students themselves will think of activities to do and, therefore, can play a major role in planning curriculum. Once a theme is decided on, students can suggest stories, poems, music, films, and activities that complement the unit. The more students are involved, the more ownership and responsibility they accept, and that is the beginning of a learning/teaching partnership between student and teacher.

We include one last unit here to help you as a beginning teacher to see how comprehensive thematic units can be (see Case 14–11). The unit is written by Don Heil for a 10th-grade class.

Literature of Conflict—Societal and Personal

RATIONALE FOR SELECTING THIS THEME FOR THIS AGE GROUP

We are all exposed, directly or indirectly, to various forms of conflict. There is possibly no greater time of turmoil and conflict in a person's life than adolescence into young adulthood. At this time in our lives we find out that the world is bigger than the limited scope of our experiences. We discover that the conflicts in which we have been embroiled as adolescents are just a part of the bigger conflicts that go on in the world every day. As 10th graders, these kids have begun to understand the greater implications of many kinds of conflicts and are at a crossroads in their lives. They are no longer children, but they are not yet adults. They are no longer as naive about the world as they once were, but they have not yet made the connection between themselves and the wider world. Because of this, I feel that presenting a unit on conflict in literature at this point in their lives provides an insight into what they have experienced already and what is yet to come. By further dividing the topic into two parts, societal and personal conflicts, they are exposed to types of conflict that affect them immediately and directly, as well as conflict of a farther reaching and longer lasting quality. It is my hope that by seeing conflict on both a personal and societal level they will be able to make the connection between the two levels of conflict and that they understand that there is more in the world than their own problems—that they are part of something much bigger than themselves.

UNIT OBJECTIVES

I want my students to gain or further develop:

- An awareness of the various forms of conflict around them on a personal and societal level
- An understanding of how literature portrays conflict and how it is a means of recording, discussing, and resolving conflict
- An understanding of how conflicts are best resolved and, if unresolvable, how they are best dealt with
- The ability to read literature critically to extract its meaning and value
- The ability to express their own thoughts and talents through writing and other means of expression
- An awareness of the wider world outside of their personal lives and their connection to that world
- A love of literature and, more generally, a love of reading

OVERVIEW

The first part of the unit covers conflict on a societal level, touching on subthemes of race, religion, economics, politics, and war. The second part is conflict on a personal level and includes family, peer, and internal conflict. The third part is reading a novel students choose from a selection of three, which represent three levels of difficulty in reading. The shorter readings and writings are in the first two parts to provide background information and make the novel and final writing more meaningful.

INTRODUCTION TO THE STUDENTS

Students first do free writing in their journals on the topic of conflict, responding to these questions:

- What is conflict?
- What do you think of when you hear the word *conflict*?

Students write for 10 to 15 minutes and then share their ideas. The teacher lists their responses on the board, demonstrating the possible perceptions and variety of conflict. The students and teacher then group the conflicts under the headings of societal and personal conflicts. The following class period the teacher provides students with a copy of the list that students keep in their writing folders. Students also create bulletin boards to further define the theme of the unit.

PART 1
Activity 1

To begin, the teacher shows clips from the PBS television series "The 60s: A Decade of Conflict" to show various kinds of societal conflict and how they were manifested in the turmoil of that time. Also, the clips give a historical perspective on much of the literature the students will read for the unit. After viewing the clips, students write in their journals describing what they think societal conflict is.

Activity 2

The students then read and discuss Chapter 27 from *I Know Why the Caged Bird Sings*. They respond in their journals; they may respond to the following guide questions:

- What main themes do you see in this passage? What is going on?
- What has happened to the Japanese in San Francisco? Why are they disappearing and being replaced?
- What reasons did the woman on the streetcar give for refusing to sit with the black man? Are these valid reasons?

Activity 3

The class reads and discusses "Ruby's Drawings," "Self-Portrait," and "The Sign," all from the Robert Coles anthology, *A Festering Sweetness*. These poems emphasize conflict caused by racial differences. Students also read a selection of poems focusing on conflict caused by war from *Class Dismissed* by Mel Glenn.

Activity 4

The students read and discuss the short story "The Other Foot" by Ray Bradbury. The story focuses on conflict caused by both racial differences and warfare.

Activity 5

Students watch an episode from the television series *M*A*S*H,* which focuses on the effects of war on various people at a fictitious field hospital. The students are asked to bring in newspapers, magazine clippings, songs, and examples from TV shows as further examples of war-related conflict and its effect on individuals.

PART 2: PERSONAL CONFLICT

Activity 1

Students write in their journals about various conflicts they may have experienced at home, school, or other places. They compare their list to the one the whole class generated at the beginning of the unit in order to reflect on their own experiences.

Activity 2

Students view the film *The Three Warriors,* which deals with contemporary Native American culture and their efforts to survive in the modern world. Students write a paper from the perspective of one of the film's characters.

Activity 3

The students read and discuss "Everyday Use" by Alice Walker.

Activity 4

The teacher plays songs expressing a conflict from his or her adolescence. The class then listens to a short selection of songs with historical significance. The students are encouraged to bring in songs they believe are examples of conflict. Discussion and journal writing follows.

Activity 5

The students form groups and each group is given a scenario that includes a conflict. They finish the story by resolving the conflict or at least getting the parties involved in a process of resolution. Each group acts out the scene for the class.

PART 3: INDIVIDUAL NOVELS

Activity 1

The three literature selections chosen for this unit are *The Chocolate War* by Robert Cormier, *All Quiet on the Western Front* by Erich Maria Remarque, and *Romeo and Juliet* by William Shakespeare. Each student must complete one selection but are encouraged to read more if appropriate. After students choose which one they will read, they write a journal entry about why they made their choice, what they think it is about, and what kinds of conflicts they think are presented in the book.

Activity 2

The activities for this part of the unit are of two types: whole-class and novel-specific. The whole-class activities include activities and questions that pertain to all three of the readings because they are of a general nature on the theme of conflict. The novel-specific activities are done in conjunction with part 4 of the unit. When one group meets to discuss one selection, others may work on their final projects. Some students prefer more reading and discussions, whereas others will want more time for the individual work. Students are free to move in and out of the activities that appeal to them and best meet their needs. The students are required to write a response journal entry every day after completing the reading. Discussion groups are held throughout the time the students are reading.

PART 4

In this part of the unit students complete a major project related to a thematic literature unit. The following are choices for the project:

- Write a research paper with the theme of conflict as your focus.
- Write at least two poems with the theme of conflict as your focus.
- Write a song on the theme of conflict or collect at least five such songs on a tape. You must include a short description of how each song includes conflict.
- Write a short story on the theme of personal conflict.
- Write a one-act play on the theme of conflict.
- Suggest your own final project. This must be approved by the teacher and submitted in writing.

All of these options are level 3 writing projects and involve the writing process.

In summary, units are as varied as the teachers who teach them. The major advantage of units is that the teacher has great flexibility in planning and choosing activities that meet a wider range of student abilities and interests. Units are rich sources of material so all students can find literature selections, activities, and topics that appeal to them. Students who wish to explore a topic in depth can do so. Others who prefer a wide spectrum of readings and activities can use this approach. No students are left out or made to feel that they do not fit in. Although units may be more work for teachers initially, they are much more interesting to teach than the "one book at a time with no continuity" approach.

CASE 14–12

Developing Your Own Instructional Unit

Throughout this chapter, we have shown several examples of how teachers plan for thematic units. Now, work through a unit of your own following these suggested guidelines.

1. In small groups, brainstorm ideas for unit themes. Decide on one that the group can work on. Now brainstorm ideas for readings that fit the theme. Share with the rest of the class.
2. Individually choose a theme you are personally interested in. Decide what grade level you would like to develop it for. Choose one or two pieces of literature that would be appropriate for this grade level. In small groups, share your ideas and help each other think of additional literature. Write a rationale for teaching the theme you have chosen and explain why it is appropriate for the grade level you selected. What do you want the students to learn from the unit?
3. Choose literature for young adults on the same theme to include in your unit.
4. Select poems that are appropriate.
5. Add film and music selections. Remember to add a variety of readings (for example, nonfiction, drama, journals, articles, and so on). Selections may be found in local newspapers, television, magazines, and a wide variety of anthologies. Don't limit yourself to what you were taught in school.
6. Plan activities that include listening and speaking (for example, creative dramatics and small-group activities).
7. Plan writing activities throughout the entire unit and specify what levels they are. Remember to have many level 1 activities, several level 2, and only one level 3. Develop a grading scale for your level 3 assignment.

How will you encourage students' interest in the unit? How will you focus on the theme? How will you accommodate the different ability levels and interests you will have in your classroom?

Developing this unit will help you in two ways: You have a teachable unit all set to go when you enter the classroom, and it is a wonderful example of your abilities to add to your portfolio when you are interviewed for a teaching position.

REFERENCES

Anderson, David T. "An Apology for Teaching American Literature Thematically." *Wisconsin English Journal* Fall 1989: 58–66.

Clark, Dale. "Literature Unit: *The Catcher in the Rye*." English 406/606. University of Wisconsin-Eau Claire, 1995.

Dressler, Barbara. "Unit on Families in Literature." English 705. University of Wisconsin-Eau Claire, 1989.

Flug, Connie. "Heroism." English 406/606. University of Wisconsin-Eau Claire, 1992.

Goldbort, Robert C. "Science in Literature Materials for a Thematic Teaching Approach." *English Journal* Mar. 1991: 69–73.

Heil, Don. "Literature of Conflict—Societal and Personal." Unpublished paper, 1995.

Hillocks, George, Jr. "Literary Texts in Classrooms." *Socrates to Software: The Teacher as Text and the Text as Teacher.* Eds. Philip W. Jackson and Sophie Haroutunian-Gordan. Chicago UP, 1989. 135–58.

Jacobs, Heidi Hayes., ed. *Interdisciplinary Curriculum Design & Implementation.* Alexandria: Association for Supervision & Curriculum Development, 1989.

Kahn, Elizabeth A., Carolyn Calhoun, and Larry R. Johannessen. *Writing About Literature.* Urbana: NCTE, 1984.

Maxwell, Rhoda J. *Writing Across the Curriculum in Middle and High Schools.* Boston: Allyn & Bacon, 1996.

McManus, Maureen. "Writing Activities for *To Kill a Mockingbird.*" English 404. University of Wisconsin-Eau Claire, 1993.

Moffett, James. *A Student-Centered Language Arts Curriculum.* Boston: Houghton Mifflin, 1973.

Olien, Rebecca. "Tracing One's Roots." Unpublished paper, 1994.

Peck, David. *Novels of Initiation: A Guidebook for Teaching Literature to Adolescents.* Teachers College, Columbia University, 1989.

Pickett, Jackie. "Family and Peer Conflict." English 705. University of Wisconsin-Eau Claire, 1989.

Scharber, Cassie. "Writing Activities for *Finding My Voice.*" English 404. University of Wisconsin-Eau Claire, 1995.

Servoss, Gail. "Four-Week Literature Unit." English 402. University of Wisconsin-Eau Claire, 1988.

Steffen, Cathy. "Unit on Heroes." English 404. University of Wisconsin-Eau Claire, 1994.

Williams, Jackie, and Terry Deal Reynolds. "Courting Controversy How to Build Interdisciplinary Units." *Educational Leadership* Apr. 1993: 13–15.

15

Becoming a Teacher

As you read through this chapter, you'll be asked many questions about becoming and being a teacher. Thus, we'd like you to keep a response journal—a dialogue with yourself that will extend to your classmates and instructor. Self-reflection is at the core of effective teaching, of being and becoming the kind of teacher we know you wish to be. Like learning itself, teaching is a journey of discovery. We ask you to begin that journey now, using your journal as a reflecting pool along that path.

WHY ARE YOU HERE?

Choosing a profession is one of the most profound acts of our lives, a commitment to our future. It's important, then, to know just why you chose teaching. It's not an easy career: Students live in an uneasy and complex world; funding and resources go in cycles of "feast and famine"; and parental and community expectations, demands, and criticism are very public. Preparing, teaching, and evaluating go well beyond a 40-hour week, and at times, dealing with so many students can be stressful. However, working with students can also be rewarding, and teachers have a tangible opportunity to make a difference in some students' lives. We suspect you're here because you want to make that difference. Nonetheless, it's important to explore the question (see Box 15–1).

We asked some of our methods students why they wanted to teach English language arts, and Aimee Peterson's first response surprised her: "The idea of answering the question of what attracted me to teaching and more specifically teaching English *scared* me." She went on to explain that there were many answers she could give and that having to pinpoint her motivation was scary. We noted that delving into self and motivation can be unsettling, but it's also a positive act. Another student, Mike Le Bouton, had no hesitation at all: "I have never doubted that I would teach—I was raised by teachers." Complimenting his parents in his remarks, Mike explored growing up with what seemed a normal and effortless gravitation to teaching English.

Several students noted that they too had role models, though not so close at hand. Jason Hedrington told us: "The catalyst of [my] decision was a high school English teacher that opened my eyes into myself and showed me the wonderful world of English." For Mary Beth Koehler, it was a college teacher who asked the critical questions. As Mary Beth explained it, she started off as a broadcast journalism major with no interest in teaching English. In her junior year, however, she ended up in an 8 A.M. creative writing class—because it was the only class open. Because she was running around "chasing ambulances and writing up stories" for the campus station, her work in creative writing was perpetually late. Finally the teacher called her in and got her to blurt out her unhappiness with her major and her desire to be like the creative writing teacher in front of her. The professor convinced Mary Beth that not knowing the difference between a noun and a verb—Mary Beth's reason for not considering teaching English—could be dealt with. She could learn all about nouns and verbs through tutoring in the peer composition lab. As Mary Beth noted, "That's what I did. My life has been pretty great, exciting, and fulfilling ever since." And we hope those adjectives remain active throughout her career—and yours.

Box 15–1

A TEACHER? WHY?

In your journal, explore your reasons for wanting to teach English language arts. Like Mike, have you always known that teaching was meant for you? Or like Mary Beth, did someone jolt you into recognizing it? If you come up with several reasons, consider which is most important to you and why. There's a difference between explaining what drew you to teaching and what you want to accomplish as a teacher. Here, concentrate on what drew you to teaching English.

AS A TEACHER, I WANT TO . . .

As you thought about why you were drawn to teaching, you no doubt also thought about what you wish to accomplish as a teacher. The first thing that comes to mind is probably a broad goal: I want to make a difference in kids' lives; I want kids to love literature and reading; or I want kids to learn the power of language. And that's an important start. But just as we have to take broad curricular goals and turn them into specific student outcomes, we need to go a step further here. For example, if you want to make a difference in kids' lives, how will you do that? You'll need to think about curricular materials and instructional methods that will help you achieve your goal (see Box 15–2). How does "making a difference" translate into cognitive or affective effects? Or into new or improved skills?

Box 15–2

As a Teacher, I Will . . .

In your journal, list at least three things you wish to do or accomplish as an English teacher. If you know you want to teach middle school or high school, you might want to consider the age level as you frame your response. First think about your broad goals as an English language arts teacher and then turn the goals into more specific student outcomes. It's okay if things seem a little fuzzy at first. We just want you to get a sense of your personal stake in your profession.

SCHOOLHOUSE MEMORIES

Many of our methods students came to the teaching profession because of their teachers, men and women whose knowledge, care, and dedication inspired them. But they also were keen observers of unhappy teachers. Brian Quade believed that "many of them feel trapped. A couple that I had, I am sure were trapped in a job they did not enjoy. I think one of my English teachers was a teacher because he wanted to coach; unfortunately, by the time I got to high school, I don't think he liked coaching either. I think he simply didn't like teenagers—which makes secondary education a rather uncomfortable place to be." As Brian speculated on reasons why teaching doesn't work out for some people, he concluded:

> Some teachers get swamped by the apathy of their students, the apathy of the administration, the apathy of the community, or an interesting combination of the above. Some get hired by districts that do not have the resources they had hoped for and simply fall into the rut of using the same materials that have always been available. Others just do not know what is available. Some have become disillusioned by the students or the system. In other cases, teachers are forced into teaching situations that they are unprepared for or do not want and find themselves with few options other than using the curriculum established before they got there. It can be difficult to change an established curriculum when you don't know what to choose from, have no passion for the material, or simply don't know how.

Brian brings up an important point, one that we have made throughout this book, that curriculum and instruction are inextricably bound together. Moreover, teachers must have some freedom, or their creativity and motivation fade.

The most memorable teachers, however, were those who "lit a fire" in our students. Kendra wrote of her senior English teacher: "He changed my life, the way I thought, the way I looked at the whole world." Jason Hedrington had similar memories: "He really opened my eyes in general. He made me see that I could really be anything that I wanted to be. 'When the dream dies, you die,' he often told me." Jason went on to note that this teacher "made us feel important, and he showed that he really cared about each and every one of us." The words *care* and *respect* came up often when our methods students reflected on their secondary teachers. Kris Westphal echoed Jason: "What it comes down to is his [teacher's] respect for his students. That was what made everything else fall into place." Later, we will share with you the remarks from current high schoolers from Green Bay, Wisconsin—remarkably similar to these college students' views. In fact, when we ask almost any generation of students to reflect on memorable teachers, the positive and negative attributes remain constant. What does this tell us?

I REMEMBER YOU

In your journal once more, reflect on your most memorable teacher from middle school or high school. Don't hesitate to use *memorable* as a negative if that is your strongest memory. We can learn from both positive and negative role models. Try to be specific about words or actions that led you to choose the person you did.

IF YOU HAD A TEACHING "FAIRY GODMOTHER"

If there were such a thing as a "perfect" English language arts teacher, what qualities do you think this person would possess? Make a list. Then, rearrange the list into characteristics that are related to one's personality (aspects that would not be easy to change) and characteristics that one acquires through experience or development (aspects that can be added to or erased). Then rank them in importance.

We asked middle and high schoolers to tell us what characteristics they believe are important. In fact, we asked them what would they say if they could talk to a college class where students are studying to become English teachers. Here are their responses, from South Middle School in Eau Claire, Wisconsin, and due east hundreds of miles in Bay Port High School, Green Bay, Wisconsin:

respects kids	flexible	openminded
knows material	fair/evenhanded	sense of humor
listens	knows kids' interests	gives choices
thinks kids' opinions are worthwhile	shares	
knows when kids need help	adjusts to student's level	
keeps things interesting	can control class	
makes kids feel wanted and smart	energetic	
creative		

Now try to rank their responses. What do you think these students considered the most important characteristics of good teachers? Before we tell you, let's listen to some of their voices from Bay Port High School:

Senior Summer Delvoye said, "It is important that a teacher acts like a human being." Think about that for a moment. What does she mean "act like a human being"? When wouldn't a teacher "act like a human being"?—at least from the perspective of a high school senior.

Tara Beth Boerner, a junior, cautions: "Be yourself—don't put up a fake front because you're a teacher." What's a "fake front"? And what does it have to do with being a teacher? What is Tara talking about here? And why would Jason Hundt, a senior, say something so similar: "Be yourself. Don't try to put on a false front for the students because they may end up taking advantage of you later." What do you think may have happened to cause these students to talk about "fake and false"?

Another senior, Dave Vander Leest, had a different perspective: "Try not to be a popular teacher. Some teachers don't give homework and try to be everyone's friend instead of teaching like they are supposed to." What negative effects would a "popular" teacher have on students?

Junior Tami Gialdini believed, "English teachers should be first of all comfortable with themselves." Do you know people who aren't "comfortable with themselves"? How do you know? What would make you uncomfortable with yourself as a teacher? Why has Tami hit on something critical to the teaching environment?

Sue Johnson, also a junior, advised, "If you love what you do, then show it." How do we show a love of teaching English language arts? Is there a danger here? Consider what another junior, Jill Witthuhn, says, "Many teachers are stuck on their pedistle [sic] of superiority." How could you meet Sue's criterion without climbing up Jill's "pedistle"?

Brooke Johnson echoes Jill with rather strong words: "We're not stupid; we can pick up on negativity, and it stays with us a long time. As does anything that is said or done in class." What would you consider "negativity" in an English class? Have you ever experienced it? Since no teacher would begin his or her career with negativity, how do you think it develops?

The characteristic "stupid" came up again when Stacy Lewis talked about a memorable teacher who "always listened to both sides and never once made anyone feel as if they were totally wrong or stupid." What kind of words or actions convey to students that their opinions do count? Knowing that teens are often hypersensitive to criticism, real or perceived, how would you deal with responses that are off the mark?

"Command respect, but don't *demand* it" was the advice of Paul Sheedy. What does Paul mean? How does a new teacher command respect? Did you have any high school teachers you didn't respect? If yes, what caused you to lose it? Could that teacher have gained it back? Why or why not? Why caused you to develop respect for a teacher?

Alisa Frederici's best advice to someone who wants to become a good English teacher is to remember "that teenagers try to be tricky and malicious, but it's only a flagrant attempt for attention." What would you consider "tricky" or "malicious" behavior? One of our methods students, Aimee Peterson, told us about a high school class in which she and her classmates walked across the desktops and made the teacher cry. Is this malicious behavior? Or is it simply a "looney tunes" kid response to a teacher with no discipline in place? Alisa's point, that teenagers want attention, is a good one. Despite their bravado, many of them don't receive all that much of it, at least in constructive ways. What can English teachers do other than say things like "pay attention now"? How does construction of the curriculum and care in instructional methods translate in "attention"?

Box 15–5

How Students Rate the Teachers
Let's look at how both middle schoolers and senior high students ranked teacher qualities:

Middle School
listens
gives choices
values our opinions
fair

Senior High School
listens
fair
values our opinions
gives choices

Also mentioned often were humor, sharing, understanding the level of students and adjusting to it, and knowing student interests.

How did your ranking compare to that of the students? If there were significant differences, why do you think that was so?

If you had a fairy godmother who could grant your "I want to be this kind of teacher" wish, what would you tell her? As you consider the wish list, you need to be realistic about who you are and what kind of teacher you would like to be in the classroom (see Box 15–6). As a couple of the high school students pointed out, being yourself is critical. What are your strengths? What are potential problem areas when you picture yourself in the classroom? Having some "butterflies" is normal, but you want to anticipate areas where better planning and specific classroom procedures will help you start out well. If, for example, you tend to procrastinate, or if you aren't particularly well organized, you know that about yourself. You no doubt also realize that you can't procrastinate or be disorganized when over 100 students depend on you to frame and facilitate their work. That's why it's important that you reflect on potential problem areas as well as on your strengths. We know the strengths are there, recognized by others as good "teacher traits"—or you wouldn't be this far along in becoming a teacher.

Box 15–6

THE BEST OF ME

List what you consider your best personality traits—and don't be modest! Then from this list, choose three that you believe will help you as a teacher. Next to each trait, indicate how it will play a role in your classroom.

NO FAIRY GODMOTHER NEEDED

Although there are studies and tests of personality traits suited to the teaching profession, we don't need such measures to tell us the basic qualities of effective teachers. What's more, people with remarkably different personalities are considered good teachers by both their students and professional peers. We suspect part of the reason lies in the different personalities and learning styles found among us all. We need and benefit from different kinds of teachers throughout our academic career. But an underlying thread links most successful teachers; they share certain qualities.

Realism

As we have already noted, successful teachers know something about students, both from what research tells them and from what students themselves say. Successful teachers also know things about themselves. For example, our upbringing, culture, and social class do influence us. Many English teachers come from middle-class backgrounds that may conflict with those of some students. Further, we aren't facing a classroom full of prospective English teachers for whom English is easy and pleasurable. Being knowledgeable and realistic about ourselves and our students is an important base for teaching.

Openness

Being honest with both ourselves and our students is an important characteristic. If we don't know something, we should say so. We can tell the students that we will find out, or better yet, we can find out together. We can also share some experiences with students, not divulging sensitive or highly personal incidents, but certainly recounting experiences that meant something to us. We also need to do what we expect students to do: read, write, and share ideas. A certain hypocrisy is involved when English teachers require students to read and to write, but fail to do so themselves.

Positive Expectations

We need to see students as individuals, not as the fifth-hour class or the slow group. Developing or strengthening the attitude that every student has a right to learn is an essential part of teaching. Believing that every student brings to the classroom knowledge that enriches others in the learning community is equally essential. Similarly, effective teachers believe that their students *can* learn. These attitudes foster both individual growth and class cohesiveness. Students who know their ideas are taken seriously and their efforts valued are far more likely to participate in the learning process.

Responsiveness

Our attitude is always the baseline of what happens. The time we spend initially getting to know students and allowing them to know one another and us is time well spent. Similarly, being honest, genuine, and responsive sets the tone for productive work. We are not advocating being "the friend" and throwing discipline and structure aside. Students need us to take charge, orchestrate, and lead; neither we nor they can function in an environment that lacks structure, planning, and leadership. At the same time, we can do this in ways that incorporate students rather than dominate them. Being a good listener is another important form of responsiveness; in fact, it is listed as number one among our student respondents. Listening, not just hearing, *will* make a difference.

Flexibility

Planning well is part of teaching well. However, plans are carried out among individuals who hear, respond, and think in unique ways. Every classroom experience is full of surprises, and while teachers need carefully thought-out plans, they also need to be ready to change those plans on a moment's notice. We cannot remove the equivocal nature of teaching, nor would we want to when we consider that our focus is teaching people, not subject matter.

Sense of Humor

Laughter is important to our well-being. Our classrooms should be places of shared laughter, the light-hearted and playful moments that tell us we are connected and connecting with one another. What might pass for humor among peers—biting humor, sarcasm, and mockery—however, could quickly disconnect us and dissolve any sense of community. Keeping these harsher elements outside the classroom and operating instead from a gentle humor within helps build a classroom climate in which students feel safe to be themselves.

Evenhandedness

Few things bother teenagers more than the sense that a teacher is "unfair." And when we think about it, we realize that we adults react pretty strongly to real or perceived unfair treatment, too. No one likes it. For this reason, teachers need classroom procedures that are evenhanded and fair to all students. Students need to know these procedures on day one and to see consistent application throughout the school year. Favoritism is quickly noted and resented, as is changing rules in midstream. Even when teachers are thought to be "tough," if they are also considered "fair," they receive high marks from their students.

Intellectual Curiosity

Effective teachers like to map the territory, to try out new paths, discover new places, and venture into "foreign" lands. In brief, they have a strong desire to be perpetual learners. Intellectual curiosity is a critical trait. Without it, teachers depend on the same materials and methods, and as one high school student pointed out, they bore themselves and us. Moreover, with these approaches, student thinking will never be engaged, pushed, or fostered—the very core of teaching and learning. The best teachers we know continue to be students 20 years into their careers by reading professional journals, participating at conferences, and attending graduate courses in summer or night school.

Drawing Conclusions

In 1986, Richard Lloyd-Jones, then president of the National Council of Teachers of English, outlined qualifications for future teachers of English language arts. He listed many of those we have just discussed and, like us, believed insatiable curiosity and a strong will to discover and try out new ideas were critical (3). It is not enough, however, just to try out new ideas; we must reflect on them. The habit of reflection, of thoughtful analysis of what we do and observe in our classrooms, is a critical part of teaching well. Mitch Cox, a high school teacher, describes the connections among planning, teaching, and reflection.

> Planning is the prewriting stage where attention must be given to the connections among the teacher/writer, students/audience, and the needs and goals of the two. It is also recursive, involving revision not only after an initial delivery of a lesson but also during the act of teaching itself. In fact, planning for the present always requires looking back to the previous year and being ready to adjust ideas to past experience. (33)

Looking back requires a written response to teaching activities: how one feels about the day, what could have gone better, and what went right, too. Given this, teachers' most valuable tool in assessing their teaching is a reflective journal. With a journal, patterns of problems and successes are easier to see and to understand. Too often, students are blamed for the failure of plans or activities that didn't work. When we transfer blame for poor results to students, we close the door to considering how and what we ourselves might change to achieve better results. To be effective teachers, we must continue to be learners as well.

REALITIES FOR THE BEGINNING TEACHER

Although we have already talked about important attributes of effective teachers, we want to go one step further to translate these attributes into classroom practice. You will thus hear some echoes of attributes here, but we believe that we need to mull them over from different perspectives.

Beginning teachers may find themselves running a more structured classroom than they imagined or would like, not only in their academic planning but also procedurally. Middle school and senior high students have had years to develop certain expectations of what teachers and school are all about. Teachers who depart radically from those expectations may be in for some shocks, simply because students, regardless of what they may say, like security and predictability. They also like to test their teachers. This is not perverse, just kid behavior. And for some students, school is simply another "way station" in an unhappy world. They may come to school hungry, lacking sleep, and lacking a nurturing and supportive environment at home; for these students, school holds little relevance. As the principal at a southern California middle school noted, "We can't fix the world" ("Good Morning, John Adams"). This perspective, however tragic, is reality. The principal also noted that in the United States, we try to educate everyone who comes through our doors, whether that is children of poverty and drug abuse or of traditional families. Sometimes, teachers simply cannot reach students, no matter how often they try.

What can beginning teachers do? Above all, be consistent and fair with students. Few things rankle adolescents as much as the sense that they are being treated like yo-yos or unfairly— differently depending on who they are. Middle school students in particular may react (or overreact) to a sense of inconsistency, largely because they themselves are in the midst of tremendous emotional and physical changes. When we tell students what we expect—in behavior, in work habits, in classroom procedures— we need to stick to it. If we need to make changes, we should tell students what we are doing and why, involving them in their own classroom. We are the adults, and there is no question that we need to set and maintain guidelines. However, the more we involve students in decision making and the more we talk with them rather than at them, the better.

Following what they themselves have experienced, beginning teachers may talk too much and fail to listen to their students. Heather Berry, a ninth-grade student, said this in a letter to the editor of a local paper:

> Everyone says that in high school you are getting prepared for the rest of your life. Then maybe people should start treating us like adults instead of little kids. Even though I am "only a freshman," I feel very strongly in this matter and feel it shouldn't be taken lightly. Everyone has a right to be heard, even young people.

Berry was responding to being ignored so that a parent could speak at a local school board meeting. She and a number of friends were there to defend a teacher. Her point that young people deserve to be heard is a legitimate one, in the classroom and in the

Board room. In taking young people seriously, we build their self-esteem, teach them important communication skills, and learn important lessons for instructional planning.

Keeping one's sense of humor, especially in middle school, should be a priority. As noted earlier, things can and do go wrong, no matter how well we plan and prepare. We all tend to take ourselves a bit too seriously when we are new to the job, are very conscious of our limited experience, and want to do the best job we can with our students. A sense of humor goes a long way in helping us not only get through an occasional bad day but also in enjoying the eccentricity of kids and teaching.

If students are truly disruptive, however, teachers need to have their own procedures for handling the situation, as well as know school or district procedures. Berating a student in front of peers, for example, is the worst response possible. Ridicule is also an inappropriate response. Sometimes moving a student or talking to the student outside the classroom will work. Talking to experienced teachers who seem to have good rapport and classroom control is one of the best ways to learn about what may work in a particular school. Teachers also need to know just what is considered serious enough to send a student out of the classroom and to whom that student should be sent.

The bottom line in classroom discipline is consistency. Teachers and students need to know the guidelines of acceptable behavior. Rather than drawing up a set of rules, it is better to establish the parameters: for instance, a strong guiding principle that no one has the right to interfere with anyone's opportunity to learn in your classroom. Such a guide might include talking if talking is disruptive to the learning environment; at other times, talking would be appropriate and encouraged. Cruel remarks directed at other students are always wrong because such comments harm the intended victim's self-esteem, and that affects learning. Two or three comments at the beginning of a course set the stage for well-defined rules of behavior.

PERSONAL DILEMMAS

Regardless of where they teach, teachers may face the dilemma of whom they must please: themselves? the school? the community? Teachers who abide by the standards, values, and beliefs of the school or community and ignore their own may find themselves frustrated and angry much of the time. However, teachers who completely ignore the norms and mores of school or community may find themselves out of a job. Often, teachers have strong ideas about freedom of speech and other rights guaranteed by our Constitution. However, no matter what they believe personally, they will find themselves in trouble if they attempt to use a controversial, censored book as a class project. Similarly, teachers who convey their personal convictions about controversial subjects such as abortion within the structure of their class lessons may find themselves in trouble. For this reason, teachers who have exceptionally strong religious or social beliefs may choose to teach in schools that match their own beliefs and values and operate independently of state support.

Failing to follow the district's curriculum in individual planning and implementation is another area with serious consequences for teachers. If the district says traditional grammar is to be taught and a teacher refuses to do so, the teacher has violated district expectations. Being "right" is not much consolation when one is out of a job. What does a teacher do in this kind of situation, where the curriculum clearly is out of sync with learners and research? Work with the district and the community; educate people, despite the delicacy of the task. Craig Hitchens, a district supervisor of curriculum and instruction, believes that well-informed teachers need to assist in curricular change. John Fortier, another district coordinator of English language arts K–12, agrees, noting that unless teachers get involved, they are stuck with what they get. Concerning the issue of teaching grammar, for example, teachers have been known to teach only enough traditional grammar to ensure that students are not at risk when they move to the next curricular level. For the most part, they teach grammar contextually in ways that are congruent with young language learners. Whatever the situation, what is critical is that teachers do work on district issues of curriculum and instruction, despite the personal freedoms they enjoy in individual lesson and unit planning.

THOUGHTS, SUPPORT, AND ADVICE FROM THE VETS

The February 1995 *English Journal* turned its full attention on the newest members of the teaching profession: students like you and first-year teachers. In her editorial, Leila Christenbury writes:

> Those of us in the school want the universities to send us perfectly polished teachers; those of us in the universities want the schools to finish what we haven't already done. While there are notable exceptions, many in the schools often want beginning teachers to fit neatly into the system; many in the universities often expect beginning teachers to revolutionize that system. What, it appears, all of us veterans expect is, perhaps, the most impossible of all: We not only want the best from our new teachers, we want them, in essence, to be better, from the very beginning, than we ever were. (13)

Although Christenbury confronts us with a dilemma, her recognition that veteran teachers want you to be better than they were, right from the beginning, is also a positive force: We believe in you. What needs to be done, however, is support for that belief in the form of tangible, in-the-schoolyard strategies.

Mark Franek, from Montgomery Academy in Alabama, talks about his passage and offers some strategies in "The Rookie Year: First-Year Advice from a Second-Year Teacher." In his opening remarks, Franek notes:

> Rookie teachers have the hardest first year of any profession. Take baseball's major leagues: Most rookies have played ball since they could walk. Even rookie lawyers have three years of graduate study and a few well-paid summer internships before they make it to the Firm. (120)

Franek goes on to tell us that he has just completed his first two years of teaching and:

I feel a bit like Huck Finn, who said at the end of his long adventure: "If I'd'a'knowed what a trouble it was . . . I wouldn't'a' tackled it." But I did, and now the hard part is over, and I'm looking forward with confidence and excitement to my third year. (120)

What does Franek advise first-year teachers to do? First of all, he recommends one of the things that we also advised you to do: Keep a journal. In it, he says, record what did and didn't work and why—and do it right away. Franek warns: "If you wait until the end of the day, too much will have happened, and you'll often be too tired to write or think clearly. (Or you'll be too busy running to the gym for that sport you claimed you could coach on your resume)" (120).

Franek offered this example from his first-year journal:

During an introductory discussion of Lee and Lawrence's play, *Inherit the Wind,* (about the Scopes Monkey Trial), only a few students knew the details of the creation story as told in the Bible, and these students were very defensive and adamant about their beliefs. The rest of the students were only vaguely familiar with *Genesis,* and none of the students knew anything about the scores of creation stories around the world. The students were fascinated when I shared with them a few creation stories from North and South American Indians. (120)

Franek then explained that his students now study *Genesis* and creation stories from around the world as well write their own creation stories as part of their study of this play. "Without my journal notes, it might have taken me years to develop an engaging and successful approach to the play," he concludes. Franek believes that the journal is the critical difference in building for the next year, "so you don't have to start again from scratch." He also notes that you don't have to be particularly articulate or complete in the journal: "The journal serves as your treasure map, and like most maps, it's okay if it's approximate and not drawn to scale" (120).

We liked some of the other advice Franek offered to first-year teachers: Meet and observe other teachers and ask "dumb" questions. He correctly observed that you will be burdened with excessive preparations and extracurricular activities during that first year, right when you would most benefit from a reduced load. Since a reduced load is not in the realm of reality, Franek suggests finding other beginning teachers and meeting with them regularly as a way to reduce some of the first-year anxiety. Although the informal meetings may seem like "thinly disguised group therapy sessions," Franek believes they "help immensely in grounding you in the classroom (you're not the only one with problems) as well as in the community." Observing other teachers is another way of reducing anxiety. As Franek put it, you will realize that "teaching well takes many years of hard work and reflection, and no one expects you to be a master your first year." He also believes that you'll learn you are better than you thought—some "old timers" make fundamental mistakes and struggle with the same problems. From the truly impressive teachers, he says, "steal." When you observe a strategy or technique that works and appears to match your style well, try it in your classroom (121).

Franek also advises new teachers to never shy away from dumb questions, like when you get paid and where the teachers' bathroom is. He also suggests that you learn how to use (and unjam) the copy machine before the first day of classes. Other practical suggestions for starting the year: Figure out your grading scale and stick to it; try planning in one-week blocks at first, since you won't have a good idea of the shape and direction of the entire course yet; don't sink yourself in paper work, give reasonable assignments and don't collect or grade them all on the same day, and "as soon as you can, figure out what portfolios are and start implementing them in your classroom" (121).

Starting your professional life as a professional, says Franek, is critical: "Whenever and as often as you can, seek out and attend teacher conferences and seminars—and ask your school to defray the costs." With budget crunches, we're not sure the school will pay your way, but regardless, you should go. As Franek points out: "Professional meetings do at least two things: They give you new teaching ideas and materials, and they reinforce what somebody at your own school should be telling you— you're already doing a lot of things right." Another professional necessity: "Get a subscription and start reading *English Journal*" (121). Even if you don't have much time during the week, your journal can be a nice place to browse. On the weekend or during a break, you can go back and pull out promising teaching ideas and materials. Keeping up with the profession is a vital habit. How would you feel if your physician or dentist seldom read his or her professional literature? We suspect you would quickly find someone who did keep up, who did have alternatives available, and who could explain to you the reasons behind a decision or practice. As teachers, we have to be similarly professional, especially since students are entrusted to our care—and have few options in seeking other professionals.

We also encourage you to join your state English language arts affiliate and other professional education organizations on the local, regional, and state levels. In addition to journals and newsletters, you will receive reduced fees at conferences and seminars. When you attend, you will find yourself engaged in wonderful conversations with others doing what you do, loving what you do, and facing some of the same frustrations and questions.

A veteran teacher from Tulsa, Oklahoma, Eileen Simmons wrote that she is still becoming a teacher: "Twenty-five years of experience have taught me that teaching and teachers are always 'in process,' never completed" (73). From that perspective, she offered "some advice on beginning the process." Her first recommendation is one that we have touched on as well: Teach without a textbook if you can, and if you can't, then at least ignore the teacher's guides and other prepared, supplemental materials. Simmons shares how she arrived at this conclusion:

> One of my students taught me this lesson. She was using the teacher's edition of the literature book and asked. "Why do you have to go to college to teach this? The book gives all the answers and directions." (73)

Another of Simmons' conclusions came from students as well: Trust your students and yourself to explore the subject area together:

> No teacher's guide taught me the connection between Shakespeare's play *The Tempest* and Ray Bradbury's novel *Fahrenheit 451*. But a high school sophomore saw that

Prospero and Beatty were both into "mind control." A junior English literature student spotted the similarity between King Arthur's Court and modern society: Gang members are controlled by a code as rigid as that of any medieval knight. (73)

Simmons is right: Students are wonderful teachers, smart and insightful, if only we give them the sense of a shared journey and the importance of their responses. And they are ever so much more fun that a teacher's guide.

One piece of advice we hadn't thought of is a very useful one: Enroll yourself in a class in something where you're not proficient. Simmons relates that she became a "back row aerobics student" who takes two weeks to master a new routine and when faced with a new step is puzzled again. What Simmons gains (in addition to stress relief through intense physical activity) is an invaluable reminder:

> My instructor is patient. She never singles me out; she lets me learn at my own rate; she encourages any kind of progress—the very model of what a writing teacher should be with students for whom writing is as challenging as aerobics is for me. I know how my students feel . . . (74)

Just as Mark Franek, the rookie teacher, advised, Simmons also encourages you to keep a journal: "Set aside some time during the school day to write and reflect on your teaching and your students." For her, it is the quiet time when school is out, when she can reflect on that day, the frustrations, the bright spots, think about lesson plans, "and generally bring order to the chaos of a normal teaching day." The journal is a place where perspective can be gained. As Simmons put it: "Mastery teaching is reflective teaching—a journal is essential for reflection" (74).

Simmons provides a good ending: Expect great rewards:

> From the perspective of twenty-five years, I can tell you that the rewards will be greater than you ever expect. They may not be immediate, nor will they be readily apparent, but when one of your former students says—five or ten or twenty years later—"You know, you taught me so much. You're a great teacher"—you'll be ready to do it again for another five, or ten, or twenty years. (74)

Like Eileen Simmons, we've been teaching for a long time and we too know the rewards. You are about to discover them. As Mark Franek says, "Good luck, Rookie! See you in class . . . "

REFERENCES

Berry, Heather M. Letter. *Leader-Telegram.* (Eau Claire, WI) 10 Dec. 1991.

Christenbury, Leila. "From the Editor." *English Journal* Feb. 1995: 13.

Cox, Mitch. "Bards and Beatles: Connecting Spontaneity to Structure in Lesson Plans." *English Journal* Mar. 1991: 33–41.

Fortier, John. Personal Interview. 10 October 1991.

Franek, Mark. "The Rookie Year: First-Year Advice from a Second Year Teacher." *English Journal* Feb. 1995: 120–21.

"Good Morning, John Adams." Narr. Anne McDermott. CNN. Atlanta. 29 Nov. 1991.

Hitchens, Craig. Personal Interview. 14 April 1991.

Lloyd-Jones, Richard. "What English Teachers Need to Know—and to Be." News Release. Urbana: National Council of Teachers of English., 1986. N. Pag.

Meiser, Mary. "Teaching Kids, Not English." Afterwords in *Wisconsin Dialogue*. Eau Claire: University of Wisconsin, Spring, 1989.

Simmons, Eileen. "A Quarter of a Century and Not Finished Yet." *English Journal* Feb. 1995: 73–74.

Index

A Raisin in the Sun, 217
Abbott, Jim, 315
Academic English, 388–391
Acquisition of a second language, 389–391
  strategies for teaching writing, 394
  teacher strategies, 399–400
  teaching activities, 403–404
  working with errors, 395–399
Adolescent traits, 2, 16
Affective curriculum, 63
African American literature, 237
Alienation, 21
  gender, 21
  immigrants, 21
  learning disabilities, 22
  minority, 21
All Together Now, 195, 196–197
American Library Association, 247
Analysis charts, 269
Analytical scales, 327–330
  examples, 327, 328, 337
Anderson, David T., 407
Anderson, Philip M., and Gregory Rubano, 193
Anson, Chris, 224
Applebee, Arthur N., 213, 236, 338
Asian American literature, 238
Assessment, 2, 34–35, 317–318
  models, 10
Atwell, Nancie, 84, 269–270
Average kids, 23

Back to basics, 35
Barnes, Douglas, 96
Beach, Richard and James Marshall, 204, 207
Bennett, William, 223
Black English, 381–383
Blake, Robert and Anna Lunn, 203
Bloom's taxonomy, 6
Bonney, Karen, 86

Boyer, Ernest, 61
Britton, James, 83, 155
Bruner, Jerome, 41, 56
Burress, Lee, 246–248
Burton, Dwight, 27, 83
Bury My Heart at Wounded Knee, 217
Bushman, John H. and Kay Parks Bushman, 124, 206, 365

Calkins, Lucy, 83
Cameron, Jack, 123
Canterbury Tales, 194, 238
Capitalization, 287–288
Carlsen, G. Robert, 221
Carrier, Warren and Kenneth Oliver, 232
Carter, Candy, 26, 194
Catcher in the Rye , 411
Cazden, Courtney, 98
Censorship, 246–251
  strategies for action, 249–251
Characteristics of good teachers, 447–451
Characterizing English language arts, 3
Checkpoint scales, 330
Chomsky, Noam, 304, 351
Christenbury, Leila, 77, 79, 454
Clark, Dale, 411
Classroom climate, 84–85, 179
Cleland, Janell, 9
Cognitive process, 4, 7
Cole, Pam B., 116
Collaborative writing, 173–174
Comenius, John Amos, 5, 7
Composition and the world of work, 174–176
Constructing tests, 321
Cooke, Karin, 198
Cooperative learning groups, 384
Cox, Mitch, 174, 451
Crime and Punishment , 197
Cry, The Beloved Country, 233

Curriculum goals, 41
  K–12 perspective, 69

Dabydeen, David, 233
Daily oral language, 263, 268
Dale, Helen, 173
Dale, Philip, 381
Dartmouth Conference, 138
Delpit, Lisa, 99
Developing questions, 319, 411
Developmental stages, 17
Dewey, John, 5, 7
Dialects, 380–383
Diederich, Paul, 327
Discipline, 452–453
Discussion, 108–114
  about literature, 115–117
  reader response, 114–115
Diversity, 2
Dixon, John, 138
Dressler, Barbara, 198, 420
Duff, Ogle, and Helen Tongchinsub, 238

Editing guide, 148, 149
Ehlert, Elizabeth, 339
Elbow, Peter, 224, 333
Elliott, Anne, 153, 201, 251
Emig, Janet, 27, 140
Enders, Linda, 293
Engle, Sandra A., 427
Essay exams, 320
Evaluating oral language activities, 126–127,
  331–333
Evaluating software, 53–54
Evaluation by levels, 322–325
Everly, Pamela, 321
Exploring an instructional unit
  A Look into the Future, 70–73
  Families in Literature, 228, 420
  Family and Peer Conflict, 410
  Generation X, 89–93
  Family Pressures, 179–182
  Friendships, 11–13
  Heroic values, 28–29
  Mexican Culture, 225–226
  Pourquoi, 132–133
  Root of Aggressive Behavior, 251–254
  Simple Pleasures, 254–258

The Trickster, 127–131
What's in a Name?, 370–374
The American Dream, 213–218

Fagin, Larry, 164
Farnam, Nancy and Patricia Kelly, 194
Farr, Marcia and Harvey Daniels, 379
Fehlman, Richard, 123
Firpo, Christine, 174
Flug, Connie, 426
Formal analyses, 193–194
Fortier, John, 96, 282, 454
Franek, Mark, 454
Freeman, David E. and Yvonne S. Freeman, 388
Friedmann, Thomas, 285
Furlong, A. D. and V. J. Edwards, 97, 98
Fyre, Northrop, 222, 223

Gallo, Don, 197
Garcia, Ricardo, 385
Gardner, Howard, 37
George, Paul, 62
Gifted adolescents, 22
Gilbride, Amy, 10
Gonzalez, Roseann Duenas, 99, 235, 385
Goodlad, John, 27, 61, 315
Grammar
  definition, 294–296
  structural, 301–304
  traditional , 298–301
  transformational, 303–306
Graves, M. F., Palmer, R. J., and Furniss, D. W., 194
Gray, James, 298
Great Expectations, 409
Group work, 103–106, 198, 408
Grubgeld, Elizabeth, 289
Gunner, Elizabeth, 233

Hamlet, 209
Hartwell, Patrick, 296
Hartzell, Jennifer, 168
Harvey, Amanda, 87
Heath, Shirley Brice, 108, 379
Hedrington, Jason, 444, 445
Heil, Don, 436
Hellman, Sally, 178
Henquinet, Amy, 70, 370
Herter, Roberta J., 338

High school students, 18
Hillocks, George, 407
Hirsch Jr., E.D., 223
Hirsch, Tim, 172
Hispanic English, 384–385
Hispanic literature, 237
Historical criticism, 184–185
Hitchens, Craig, 47, 454
Hodges, Richard, 288, 290, 291
Hoffman, Joy, 28
Hoffman, Marvin, 175
Holistic education, 5, 7, 8, 81
Holistic grading, 326
Huevel, Mindy Vanden, 86
Hughes, Langston, 216
Hymes, Dell, 152, 156

I Know Why the Caged Bird Sings, 252, 438
Impression grading, 325–326
Improving usage
    using literature, 266
    using music, 267
    using video, 266
Informal classroom drama, 124–126
    drama activities, 125
        mask making, 126
        puppets, 126
        readers' theater, 125
Integrated curriculum, 3, 65–66
Interactive process, 3
Interactive teaching, 406
Interdisciplinary teaching
    oral language activities, 117
    units, 432–436
        Advertising, 433–435
        Tracing One's Roots, 435
Iser, Wolfgang, 186
I-search paper, 171

Jacobs, Heidi Hayes, 432
Janowski, Sebastian, 87
Johannessen, Larry, 80, 82, 316
Johnson, Martha, 333
Johnson, Robert, 22
Johnson, Terry and Daphne Louis, 116–117
Journal writing, 157–160
    project journals, 159
    response journals, 158–159

language journals, 159
writers' journals, 160
Joy Luck Club, 206

Kean, John, 251
Kell Jr., John T., 204
King, Nancy, 120–122
Kirby, Dan and Tom Liner, 262, 265
Knight, Lester, 47
Koch, Kenneth, 163
Koehler, Mary Beth, 127–131, 241, 444
Koehler, Nancy, 89–93, 132–133
Kohn, Alfie, 64
Krest, Margie, 337
Krogness, Mary Mercer, 23

Langer, Judith, 189
Language
    activities, 375–376
    games, 368–370
    in literature study, 208–209, 366–367
        metaphor, 208–209
        tone, 208
    limited proficiency, 386–388
Language acquisition, 348–351
    activities, 353–362
    implications for teaching, 352–353
Language diversity, 378–381
Language variation, 343–344
Lattimore, Deborah Nourse, 365
Learner outcomes, 41–45
Learning environment, 1
    for bilingual learners, 391–394
    for acquisition of second language, 400–402
Learning logs, 160
Learning styles, 24
LeBouton, Mike, 443
Levels of writing, 153–155
    in a unit, 154–155
    in assignments, 412
Lightfoot, Nik, 97
Lightfoot, Sara Lawrence, 15
Lindemann, Erika, 274
Listening, 99–106
    attributes, 102
    strategies, 102
    goals, 99
    group work, 101

Literature selection for units, 242–244
    Coming of Age, 242
    Courage, 243
    Family Relationships, 242
    Women studies, 234
Lloyd-Jones, Richard, 451
Lord of the Flies, 194
Lothe, Kurt, 197
Lundsteen, Sara, 101

MacArthur, Mary Ellen, 117
Martin, Medway, Smith, D'Arcy, 153
Maturation, 4
Mauger, Marilyn Lee, 112
McCarthy, Renee, 201, 205
McDonald, Joseph, 75
McElmeel, Sharon, 238–239
McManus, Maureen, 413
McNeil, John D., 38
Meadows, Darcy, 87
Meisner, Mark, 179
Mexican American literature, 201, 205
Meyer, Emily and Louise Z. Smith, 262
Middle school students, 16
Miller, Bruce, 184
Miller, Jr., James E., 137
Mini-lessons, 268–269
Minority literature, 235
    recommended books, 239–241
Mitchell, Ruth, 338
Models of teaching and learning, 6
Moelter, Jean, 208
Moffett, James and B. J. Wagner, 56, 61, 67, 124
Moffett, James, 14, 36, 156, 408,
Morris, Barbra, 122
Mortensen, Cheryl, 167
Murphy, Sandra, 316, 333

Nagy, William E., 290
Native American languages, 383–384
Native American literature, 236–237
Native speaker abilities, 345–348
Nature of language
    symbolic, 362–365
NCTE English Coalition, 38–39
Nelms, Ben, 23
Nesbit, Stan, 213
Neuman, Susan B., 249

New criticism, 185, 186
Noguchi, Rei, 272, 280–281, 295, 297
Noll, Elizabeth, 248–249
Non-native speakers, 270
Normality of errors, 264–265
Novice teachers, 452–457
    realities facing, 452–454
    advice for, 454–457

O'Keefe, Virginia, 101, 104–106, 108, 115
Olds, Alan, 232
Olien, Becky, 165, 435
Olien, Jessa, 165
Olmen, Leslie, 176
Olson, Vicki, 197
On-line services, 54–55
Our Town, 254, 257–258

Parsons, Les, 331
Peck, David, 407
Peer tutoring, 109
Perrin, Robert, 172
Peters, Nicole, 86
Peterson, Aimee M., 179, 443
Pickett, Jackie, 420
Planning, 86–89, 407, 409, 441
    variables, 76–79
    steps in, 409
Poetry activities, 202–206
    formula, 429
Pope, Carol, 175
Porter, Carol, 9
Portfolios, 9, 333–337
Postman, Neil and Charles Weingartner, 83
Probst, Robert E., 187
Professional knowledge base, 2
Publishing student writing, 150–152
Punctuation, 283–287
Purves, Alan C. and Dianne Monson, 225
Purves, Alan C., 184, 318, 336

Quade, Brian, 445

Raimes, Ann, 389
Reader Response theory, 186–187
Reader response, 114–115
    implementing, 187–188
        dialogue among students, 190

dialogue between students and teacher, 191
   in written work, 191
   response questions, 188–189
      discussions, 190
   writing responses, 188–189
Reading levels, 228–229, 408, 423,
Realities of students' lives, 25
Reed, Arthea J. S., 366
Rehrauer, Liz, 227
Reports and research papers, 169–172
Resch, Jodi, 225
Research on writing, 137–138
Response sheet, 146, 147
Revising sentences, 273–279
Revision memo, 145
Reynolds, Terry Deal, 432
Richards, I.A., 155
Rief, Linda, 18
Riggs, Pat, and Virginia Allen, 400
Rohman, D. Gordon, 140
Roll of Thunder Hear my Cry, 407, 425
Romano, Tom, 261
Romeo and Juliet, 194, 198–200, 409, 439
Rosenblatt, Louise, 186, 187
Rubin, Donald, 152

Sample curriculum units, 37, 39, 40, 43, 57–61,
   66–67, 68
Sasse, Mary, 235
Schafer, John C., 283
Schaffer, Jane, 108
Scharber, Cassie, 254, 416
Schuman, R. Baird, 275, 318
Scope and sequence, 55–56
Scoring guide, 329, 420
Self-editing, 264
Self-esteem, 63–64
Self-help, 264
Servoss, Gail, 165, 418
Shanahan, Timothy, 47
Sharing books, 211–213
Shaughnessy, Mina, 273, 288, 307, 309, 311,
   380
Shaw, Ella, 205–207
Simmons, Eileen, 456
Simmons, John S. and H. Edward Deluzain, 193
Sizer, Ted, 63, 66, 94
Smagorinsky, Peter and Steven Gevinson, 189

Smith, Frank, 192, 222
Social criticism, 185
Socioeconomic status, 2
Sontag, Susan, 186
Sorenson, Marge, 112
Sowder Jr., Wilbur H., 110
Speaking, 106–108
   functions, 106
   goals, 106
Special needs students, 80–82
Speech levels, 152
Spelling, 288–291
Spiral curriculum, 56–61
Standard dialect, 295, 378
Steffen, Cathy, 424
Stellick, Pat, 339
Storytelling, 119–120
Strickland, Kathleen, 5, 81
Structuralism, 185
Stubbs, Michael, 98
Student needs and interests, 67
Students at risk, 20
Study sheets, 192
Summer of my German Soldier, 241
Sutton, Jan, 195
Swartz, Larry, 119
Syntax, 273

Tchudi, (Judy) Stephen, 15, 36
Teaching English, 443–458
   choosing English teaching, 443–445
   memorable teachers, 445–446
   student responses to teachers, 446–448
Teacher help, 149–150
Teacher's role, 262
Teaching literature objectives, 221
Teaching philosophy, 1
Television, 122, 244–245, 267
Textbooks, 45
   selection, 46, 49
   examples, 49–52
The Blue Hotel (film), 217
The Cay, 197
The Great Gatsby, 218, 232
The Revolt of Mother (film), 246
The Three Warriors, 410
The Wizard of Oz, 246
Their Eyes Are Watching God, 237

Thematic units, 49
  organizing, 226–228
  Heroes, 424–432
  Literature of Conflict, 437
  lists of literature, 427, 430–432
Thomas, Sharon, 23
Thompson, Chandra, 86
To Kill a Mockingbird, 194, 407, 408, 422
Toffler, Alvin, 26
Tollefson, Stephen, 270
Tracking, 21, 61–63
Tucker, Gene, 25

Understanding student errors, 307–312
Using film, 123, 244
Using slides, 123

Van Horne, Geneva T., 249–251
Verbal folklore and American dialects, 118
Videos, 245–246, 266
Vocabulary, 209–211

Wagner, Betty Jane, 14, 125
Walden, 256
Wall, Linda, 204
Weaver, Connie, 300, 303
Whitt, Anne Genevieve, 207
Whole language, 207
  for bilingual learners, 391–392
Willert, Lisa, 167

Williams, Jackie, 432
Williams, Lynda, 119
Willis, Terry, 111
Wisconsin Department of Instruction, 124
Wisconsin's Curriculum Planning in English
      Language Arts, 41
World literature, 231–233
  China, 232
  list of resources, 233
  South African, 233
Writing categories, 155–157
Writing poetry, 163–169
  pattern poems, 165–167
Writing process, 139–149
  discovery stage, 140–141
    free writing, 141
    mapping, 142
    outlining, 142
    creative dramatics, 142–144
    drawing, 141
  drafting stage, 144–145
  revising stage, 145–147
  editing stage, 148–149
Writing short stories, 160–163

Young adult literature, 229–231
  language, 365–366
  outcomes, 230

Ziegler, Alan, 177